P9-CCI-419

MOON HANDBOOKS®
YUCATÁN PENINSULA

EIGHTH EDITION

LIZA PRADO CHANDLER & GARY PRADO CHANDLER

AVALON TRAVEL

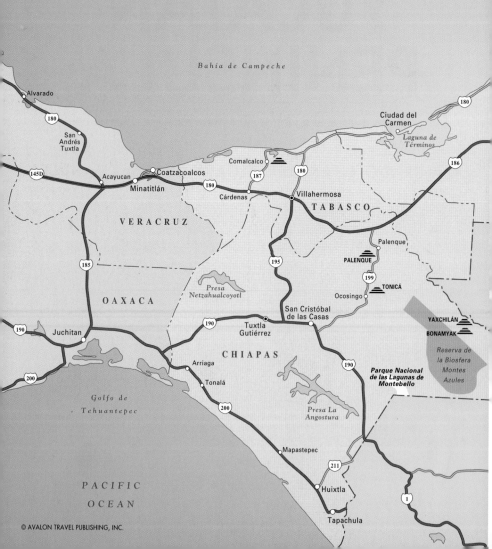

YUCATÁN PENINSULA, TABASCO, AND CHIAPAS

GULF OF

MEXICO

Bahía de Campeche

Alvarado

180

San
Andrés
Tuxtla

Ciudad del
Carmen

Laguna de
Términos

180

145D

Acayucan

Comalcalco

180

186

Coatzacoalcos

187

Minatitlán

180

Cárdenas

Villahermosa

TABASCO

VERACRUZ

Palenque

185

195

PALENQUE

199

TONICÁ

Presa
Netzahualcoyotl

Ocosingo

OAXACA

San Cristóbal
de las Casas

YAXCHILÁN

190

Juchitan

190

Tuxtla
Gutiérrez

BONAMYAK

Reserva de
la Biosfera
Montes
Azules

CHIAPAS

200

Arriaga

190

Parque Nacional
de las Lagunas de
Montebello

Tonalá

Golfo de
Tehuantepec

200

Presa La
Angostura

Mapastepec

PACIFIC

211

OCEAN

Huixtla

1

© AVALON TRAVEL PUBLISHING, INC.

Tapachula

CONTENTS

Discover the Yucatán Peninsula

Explore the Yucatán Peninsula

Know the Yucatán Peninsula

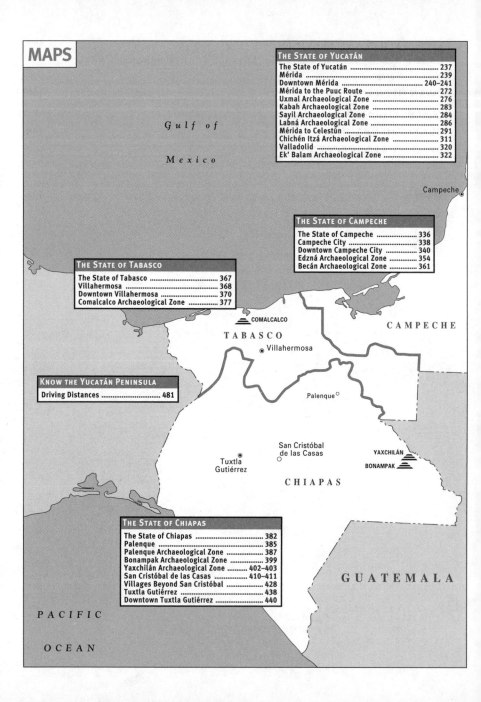

MAPS

Gulf of

Mexico

Campeche

CAMPECHE

▲ COMALCALCO

TABASCO

◉ Villahermosa

Palenque ○

San Cristóbal
de las Casas
○

Tuxtla ◉
Gutiérrez

YAXCHILÁN

BONAMPAK ▲

CHIAPAS

GUATEMALA

PACIFIC

OCEAN

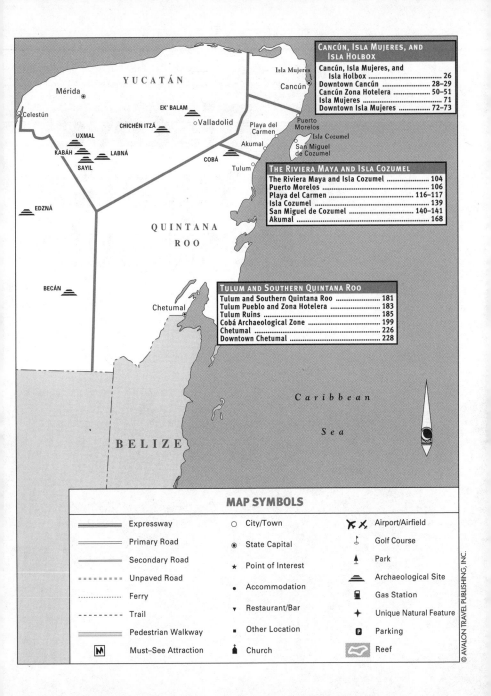

MAP SYMBOLS

═══	Expressway	○	City/Town	✈ ✗	Airport/Airfield
───	Primary Road	◉	State Capital	⚲	Golf Course
───	Secondary Road	★	Point of Interest	▲	Park
-----	Unpaved Road	•	Accommodation	≧	Archaeological Site
....	Ferry	▼	Restaurant/Bar	⛽	Gas Station
- - - -	Trail	■	Other Location	✚	Unique Natural Feature
═══	Pedestrian Walkway	⚓	Church	Ⓟ	Parking
Ⓜ	Must–See Attraction			〰	Reef

© AVALON TRAVEL PUBLISHING, INC.

Discover
the Yucatán
Peninsula

© LIZA PRADO CHANDLER

On the northern coast of the Yucatán Peninsula is a place called Uaymitún, where swampy coastal wetlands reach almost to the ocean. A thin strip of land is just big enough for a two-lane highway and a few houses. On the inland side of the road stands a high platform with a set of stairs winding up the center. From the top, you can see that the swamp—unappealing from below—is actually filled with tens of thousands of flamingos, their bright pink feathers a stark contrast to the gray-green surroundings.

Behind you is the Gulf of Mexico. To the east is a small Mayan ruin called Xcambó—the coastal wetlands were a major salt production area for ancient Mayans and they remain so today, more than 1,000 years later. Some 40 kilometers (25 miles) south is the great colonial city of Mérida, known as the "White City" for the traditional white cotton dresses and suits its residents used to wear. And just down the road from Uaymitún is the quiet town of Chicxilub, where 65 million years ago a meteor 10 kilometers (6.2 miles) wide smashed into the earth. The meteor gouged a hole 200 kilometers (124.3 miles) wide and 2.5 kilometers (1.6 miles) deep, known today as the

Chicxilub Crater. The impact and its subsequent effects wiped out the dinosaurs and ushered in the age of humankind, making this, in a sense, the spot where the world as we know it began.

Uaymitún is not a major tourist destination—were it not for the flamingos it probably wouldn't rate a mention. But in a way that's what makes it all the more amazing. The Yucatán Peninsula has so much history, culture, wildlife, natural wonders, and outdoors opportunities that even a dusty roadside town seems rich with stories and possibilities.

For travelers, the Mayan ruins may be the biggest draw—from the stunning size and scope of sites such as Chichén Itzá and Uxmal to the incredible artistry of Ek' Balam, Chicanná, and others. Cities such as Mérida and San Cristóbal show off the region's rich colonial history with distinctive architecture, broad plazas, and soaring churches. If you are a snorkeler or diver, Isla Cozumel is internationally known for its visibility and pristine coral reefs, while the mainland hides the longest underground river system in the world, filled with crystalline water and spectacular cave formations. The Yucatán is also a world-class bird-watching area, and the northern wetlands from Celestún clear around to Isla Holbox teem with flamingos, herons, egrets, cormorants, spoonbills, pelicans, and more. If you love beaches…well, you know that you've come to the right place. Cancún and the Riviera Maya are as famous for their white sand beaches and clear, turquoise waters as they are for their vibrant nightlife.

The Yucatán is also a place of many stories, and it has been for millennia. The monuments and platforms at Mayan temples are inscribed with hieroglyphics that tell complicated tales of kings and succession, war and conquest, gods and rituals. When the Spanish arrived, the letters and journals of early sailor-explorers describe the beautiful seas, the thick forests, and the native peoples' reaction to their arrival, from friendly to ferocious. Yucatán was a favorite haunt of pirates and buccaneers, whose exploits are still the subject of fairy tales and feature films. The Yucatán's colonial era was rife with boom and bust, following the rise and fall of products such as Campeche wood, henequen, and chicle. The same tales include (or should include) the misery and exploitation of indigenous workers, and of the Caste War, in which Mayans rose against the colonialists and nearly succeeded in driving them off the peninsula for good. More recently is the remarkable story of Cancún, which only 30 years ago was a mosquito-infested sandbar in an isolated corner of Mexico and is now one the world's top vacation destinations.

The Yucatán Peninsula is one of those places everyone ought to visit sometime in his or her life. It is a place of beauty and mystery, and it has witnessed events of global—even globe-shattering—importance. It's also a fun place to visit and home to a diverse and gracious population. For us, the authors of this book, it has been a joy to explore the region, and it is our sincere hope that the Yucatán not only meets your expectations, but reveals, as it has to us again and again, places and people and stories beyond your imagination.

WHEN TO GO

The best time to visit the Yucatán Peninsula is October, November, and the first part of December. This is at the end of the rainy season (April to October) but before the peak tourist season (mid-December to March). October is at the end of the hurricane season, but you can always visit places inland if one happens to hit while you're on the coast. May and June are the hottest months and can be the muggiest, especially if the rains are starting. Yucatán in general, and Mérida in particular, are infamous for being brutally hot during the summer. While not as bad as many make it out to be—daily rains help cool things off—some days can really boil and travelers should take the proper precautions against dehydration and heat exhaustion. September can bring considerable rain and clouds.

The busiest times of the year are July and August (with national tourists and Europeans), mid-December to mid-January (especially Christmas to New Year, when prices can double or triple), and during *Semana Santa* (Holy Week; the week before Easter) which usually coincides with spring break for most American universities. These can be interesting and rewarding times to be in Mexico—religious ceremonies during Semana Santa can be especially memorable—but expect certain tourist destinations to be packed.

© GARY PRADO CHANDLER

the Temple of Five Stories in Campeche's Edzná Archaeological Zone

The Yucatán's flamingos are the largest and pinkest in the world.

HOW LONG TO STAY

This is a tough question to answer because, in truth, there are more than enough attractions and activities in the Yucatán Peninsula to fill weeks or months of your time. Distances are not short, so you have to account for travel time as well. Yucatán state, Quintana Roo, and Chiapas are where most travelers spend their time; Campeche has some interesting sights that can be visited relatively quickly; Tabasco is well down the priority list. To see a little of everything—beaches, ruins, cities, nature—you will need at least two weeks, more if you include Chiapas. With a week or less, you should stick to one or two main things—beaches and ruins, say—and start planning your next visit.

WHAT TO TAKE

Take what you would take on any vacation or trip. Mexico has modern stores, supermarkets, and malls in case you forget anything. Consider taking extra sunscreen—you'll probably use more than you think and it is very expensive in Mexico, especially along the coast. The same is true for film, if you aren't using a digital camera. If you plan to visit ruins, a good pair of shoes—sandals with a heel strap at the very least—and a hat are vital. An extra set of contacts or glasses is handy if the ones you have get washed away while swimming or snorkeling. Take enough of any prescription medication you need. Birth control pills, condoms, and feminine products are available in Mexico, of course, but not always in the brand you may prefer. A travel clock also is useful, as many hotels don't have reliable wake-up call systems.

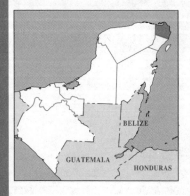

CANCÚN, ISLA MUJERES, AND ISLA HOLBOX

Cancún is the center of the action—if you want to be in the thick of everything, this is the place to go. Granted, it is the most commercialized and "artificial" spot along the Quintana Roo coast, but it also has the biggest beaches, best hotels, and by far the wildest nightlife. Few people who book a week at an all-inclusive in the Zona Hotelera (Hotel Zone) are expecting a deep cultural experience, and sure enough, they don't get one. What they do get is an easy, fun Caribbean vacation, where no one blames you for sitting on the beach all day and dancing yourself dizzy all night.

That said, Cancún does have a surprisingly rich—and totally overlooked—cultural scene. Those who pooh-pooh Cancún as a tourist trap are shocked to discover its jazz bars, bohemian cafés and live music venues, its leafy streets and peaceful parks. All of this is downtown, just a few kilometers—and a world apart—from the glitz and glare of the Zona Hotelera.

Isla Mujeres is a long thin island a short distance from Cancún, and it has long offered a change of scene—and pace—from the mainland. Though increasingly busy, Isla Mujeres still offers beautiful white-sand beaches and glassy blue water in a small-town atmosphere.

For a really small-town experience, Isla Holbox is one of the last outposts of deserted Caribbean beach. The streets are sand, and there are no cars or buildings higher than three stories. The water isn't as crystalline as in Cancún or Isla Mujeres, nor are beaches as wide or manicured, but the tranquility and sense of isolation more than make up for it.

THE RIVIERA MAYA AND ISLA COZUMEL

The Riviera Maya, the coastal area of Quintana Roo between Cancún and Tulum, is dotted with small towns and developments that have grown up around numerous bays and inlets. Most towns feature a collection of hotels and condos, a few private homes, a restaurant or two, and services such as Internet cafés and mini-marts. Most have good beaches and one or more dive and snorkel operations—**Akumal, Aventuras Akumal,** and **Tankah Tres** all have excellent snorkeling sites.

Many travelers, especially Europeans, prefer **Playa del Carmen** to Cancún for its smaller size and slower pace. Playa del Carmen is still a lively place—and gets more so every year—but the hubbub of Cancún's busy main drag is replaced here with a long and colorful pedestrian walkway. The southern end of the walkway is a major tourist trap, but the northern end has a distinctly European ambience, including great food, hip bars, and funky shops. **Playa Tukán** is the best beach between Cancún and Tulum.

Isla Cozumel is a diving and snorkeling wonderland, with a pristine coral reef and crystal-clear water. The island has about 100 dive shops, and underwater enthusiasts flock here from around the world. The island was an important religious pilgrimage site for the ancient Mayans, and it's fun to rent a convertible VW bug and explore the ruins and the island's rough and mostly undeveloped windward side.

TULUM AND SOUTHERN QUINTANA ROO

At the southern end of the Riviera Maya, the **Tulum archaeological site** is one of the most widely recognized (and most photographed) Mayan ruins. It's perched on a bluff overlooking powdery beaches and aqua-blue water; whoever built these ruins knew how to pick a spot. The structures themselves don't rate all that high as ruins go, but the views alone are worth the time and ticket price. The **town of Tulum** is a short distance south, and it has improved considerably from the dusty tourist trap it once was. Tulum's famously beautiful beaches and cabana-type hotels are a few kilometers east.

Southern Quintana Roo is the least developed stretch on Mexico's Caribbean coast. The Sian Ka'an Biosphere Reserve is a huge nature reserve encompassing the beautiful and untamed Ascension Bay. The shallow water and tangled mangrove islands are ideal for fly-fishing. Punta Allen (also known as Rojo Gómez) is the area's only real town and is little more than a scattering of simple homes occupied by subsistence fishermen and their families. Farther south, the isolated area known as the Costa Maya encompasses a few small towns. Those traveling to Belize will want to visit Laguna Bacalar, a lovely freshwater lagoon, and will pass through the border town of Chetumal, which is Quintana Roo's capital city.

THE STATE OF YUCATÁN

If Quintana Roo is the place to go for beaches, Yucatán is the place to go for Mayan ruins and colonial charm. The state capital, Mérida, is a cultural powerhouse. Every day of the week the city hosts a free public performance, usually traditional music and dance, which is well attended by locals and travelers alike. Mérida also has excellent museums and many beautiful colonial homes and buildings. Other colonial cities in the state include Izamal and Valladolid, both with distinctive ex-convents.

But Yucatán's Mayan ruins are what draw most visitors. Chichén Itzá is a spectacular site and one of the most widely recognized (and heavily touristed) ancient ruins in the world. Uxmal archaeological zone is in some ways even more impressive than Chichén Itzá and it is surrounded by four smaller, but no less intriguing, sites that make up the so-called Puuc Route. Other important and easily visited archaeological sites include Ek' Balam, Mayapán, Oxkintok, and Dzibilchaltún.

On top of its colonial cities and Mayan ruins, Yucatán also happens to have world-class bird-watching. Among hundreds of other species that nest in the state's extensive coastal wetlands, the biggest colony of the largest and pinkest species of flamingos calls Yucatán home. Río Lagartos and Celestún are popular places to take boat tours to see these distinctive creatures.

THE STATE OF CAMPECHE

Campeche sees many fewer tourists than its peninsular brethren Yucatán and Quintana Roo. But it is a state coming into its own tourism-wise, and many travelers are surprised by the richness of its Mayan ruins and the appeal of its colonial capital.

Campeche's archaeological sites are as impressive as they are little known and little visited. In southern Campeche, Calakmul is home to the tallest known Mayan structure and is now thought to have been one of the largest of all Mayan cities. It is ensconced in a protected forest reserve, and it is not uncommon to see parrots and howler monkeys in the trees here, and jaguars and pumas are occasionally spotted. In the same region, at least a half-dozen smaller but equally intriguing sites display what is known as the Río Bec architectural style, with high steep spires, extremely precise masonry, and macabre stone facades.

The capital, Campeche City, was recently designated a UNESCO World Heritage site, and the buildings in its historic center gleam with new paint and restored facades. While Campeche has yet to fully embrace tourism and tourists—many locals seem ambivalent about all the attention—it certainly has the potential to be another Mérida (or at least a Valladolid). Once the primary shipping port for the entire peninsula, Campeche suffered innumerable attacks by pirates and buccaneers for almost two centuries. Spain eventually built a massive wall with bastions around the city, which today have been cleverly converted into a series of historic museums. The archaeological museum at the San Miguel bastion is one of the best in the region and a highlight of any visit to Campeche.

THE STATE OF TABASCO

Tabasco probably wouldn't qualify for a guide to the Yucatán but for its role in the region's earliest organized inhabitation; it was in Tabasco that the Olmecs, Mesoamerica's first major civilization, emerged and prospered. At an outdoor museum in the state capital, Villahermosa, you can marvel at the immense carved stone heads left by this intriguing and little-understood culture. Tabasco boasts another unique ancient site, the Mayan ruins of Comalcalco, which are notable for being made of adobe-like brick instead of stone. (There is very little stone in Tabasco, in fact, which makes the Olmec stone heads all the more peculiar.)

The town of Comalcalco is also famous for its chocolate. Cacao has been cultivated here for centuries—and it was here that Columbus first tasted it. It would have been extremely bitter, in keeping with the traditional Mayan preparation, but Columbus thought enough of the drink to bring some back to Europe, who added milked sugar to create the chocolate we know today. Visitors here can take tours of area farms to learn how cacao is grown and processed.

THE STATE OF CHIAPAS

No tour of the Mayan world is complete without a visit to Palenque archaeological site, arguably the most beautiful of all the Mayan ruins (so beautiful, in fact, we put it on the cover of this book). Palenque's detailed and well-preserved inscriptions were vital to deciphering Mayan hieroglyphic writing. Chiapas is home to several other important archaeological sites, such as Yaxchilán, Bonampak, and Toniná—a great Classic city and today the location of an excellent Mayan museum.

Chiapas is vital to a complete appreciation of contemporary Mayans, as well. (In case you thought the Mayans had disappeared, there are more than five million people who speak a Mayan language.) Chiapas was where peasant rebels belonging to the Zapatista Liberation Army grabbed the world's attention with a New Year's Day armed occupation of government offices in four cities in 1994. The incident—and the sometimes-vexed peace process that followed it—drew attention to the plight of indigenous farmers in rural Chiapas and throughout Mexico, including the Yucatán.

Chiapas's cultural and tourist center is San Cristóbal, a truly glorious colonial city. Travelers often find themselves postponing their departure there, having fallen in love with San Cristóbal's colorfully painted streets, mild climate, and bohemian atmosphere. The city has a strong indigenous influence. Visitors can forge deeper contact with and appreciation for indigenous Chiapanecans in a number of ways, including tours of nearby villages, film and lecture programs, and programs offered by local Spanish schools and human rights organizations.

This is the biggie—see and do a little of everything in the Yucatán Peninsula in just two weeks. There are beaches to enjoy, ruins to explore, museums to visit, cenotes to snorkel in, and cities to discover—this is a trip for travelers with plenty of energy and a hankering to see it all. Renting a car for all or part of this trip will give you added speed and flexibility and ensure you have time to enjoy every stop. But if a rental car isn't in your budget, Mexico has a great public transportation system and you should still be able to complete just about everything. (A good compromise is to rent a car for a few key days—we've mentioned where you should do this.) Here goes:

DAY 1

Arrive in Cancún and check into your hotel. If you're in the Zona Hotelera, head to the beach—the afternoon sun is great. If you're in downtown, either hop on a bus to the beach or stroll through Parque Las Palapas if you prefer.

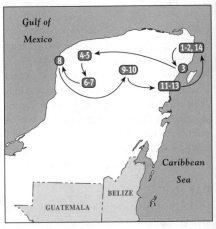

DAY 2

Spend the day on the beach. Consider visiting Playa Delfines, which has a bus stop in front and a Mayan ruin just across the boulevard. Stop at the La Casa de Arte Popular Méxicano on the way back.

DAY 3

Explore the Riviera Maya. Go snorkeling at Puerto Morelos or Hidden Worlds, both reachable by bus or van. Stop for dinner in Playa del Carmen or Puerto Morelos.

DAY 4

Catch an early bus to Mérida. Settle in and rest up, but definitely go exploring by mid- to late afternoon. Go to the anthropology or modern art museum, the market, or just visit the church, murals in the government buildings, and the plaza. Plan to go to the nightly cultural performance.

DAY 5

More sightseeing in Mérida. If you like cenotes, head out to Cuzamá, and finish up Mérida in the afternoon. If possible, rent a car for the next two days.

DAY 6

With a rental car, get an early start to be able to see as much as possible. Visit Uxmal first (be sure not to leave your bags in view in the car). After Uxmal, check into a hotel in Santa Elena or Ticul on your way to the Puuc Route. Visit as many ruins as you have the time and energy for. Go to the sound and light show in Uxmal at night. If you don't have a rental, take the ATS Puuc Route tour from Mérida.

DAY 7

Spend this day checking out the less-visited

places in the Puuc region (or any of the main ones you didn't get to yesterday). Some of these can be visited on your way back to Mérida, so it pays to plan a schedule in the morning. Good options include the Loltún caves, Hacienda Tabi, Calcehtok caves, Oxkintok ruins, and Mayapán ruins.

DAY 8

Take a morning bus to Celestún for a flamingo tour. There's not much else to see or do, so it is best to take the bus back. It's a long day, but doable.

DAY 9

Do any sightseeing in Mérida that you didn't get to do before, and then take an afternoon bus to Pisté. Check in to your hotel, relax, and check your email. At night, go to the sound and light show at Chichén Itzá. Be sure to explain you are planning to visit the ruins tomorrow, but that you want to use the show part tonight (if you don't, you'll be sold a separate show-only ticket and you'll still have to pay full price tomorrow).

DAY 10

Get to Chichén Itzá at or before opening time. Visit El Castillo and the ball court first thing because before long they will both be swarmed with day-trippers from Cancún. By the time that happens, you'll be exploring the outer areas. Catch the afternoon bus to Tulum.

DAY 11

Spend the day relaxing at the southern beaches of Tulum's Zona Hotelera.

© LIZA PRADO CHANDLER

Yucatecan handicrafts are considered among the finest in Mexico.

DAY 12

Go early to the Tulum ruins to avoid the crowds. Wear your swimsuit if you want to hang out on the beach there. Or plan to go snorkeling in one or more of the cenotes on the road to Cobá. Return to Tulum for the evening.

DAY 13

Your last full day: From Tulum, take a tour of Sian Ka'an Biosphere Reserve, visit the Cobá ruins, or hit another snorkel spot on the Riviera Maya—or just spend it lounging on the beach.

DAY 14

Fly home.

Lazing on a beach or contemplating museum displays is all right, but some travelers crave a little more action. The Yucatán has plenty to offer active, outdoorsy travelers, including sports such as scuba diving and kiteboarding, and activities such as bird-watching and snorkeling with whale sharks. This tour is a workout for the eyes, too, taking you to some of the peninsula's most stunning (and little-visited) natural areas, from deserted windswept shores to tangled mangrove forests to limestone caverns filled with the clearest, bluest water you've ever seen.

DAY 1

Arrive in Cancún and pick up your rental car. Then check into your hotel in the Zona Hotelera and head straight to the beach—the afternoon sun is great.

DAY 2

Drive to Río Lagartos, with an optional stop at Ek' Balam ruins along the way. Once you've checked into your hotel, reserve a spot in a flamingo tour for the next day.

DAY 3

Take a flamingo tour in morning. Afterward, drive to Chiquilá to catch the ferry to Isla Holbox. Leave your car in one of the guarded lots. Check into your hotel in Holbox and arrange for a tour to go snorkeling with whale sharks the next morning.

DAY 4

Go snorkeling with whale sharks in the morning and spend the afternoon on the beach. Or sign up for a day of kiteboarding or sailboarding classes.

DAY 5

Return to Chiquilá by ferry and drive to Playa del Carmen. Time permitting, stop in Puerto Morelos for snorkeling and an early dinner.

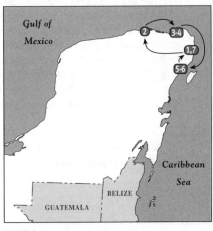

DAY 6

Spend a day exploring the Riviera Maya. Visit Hidden Worlds, Laguna Yal-Ku, or Cenote Tankah (Tankah Tres). For more action, go kiteboarding or even skydiving. Have dinner in Playa del Carmen or Puerto Morelos.

DAY 7

Fly home.

Mayan Archaeology and Culture

Many people come to the Yucatán Pensinsula with one thing in mind: Mayan ruins. Who can blame them? The massive pyramids and sprawling palaces are awe-inspiring, even spellbinding. It is impossible not to be impressed by the astronomical and mathematical genius of the Mayans, who could predict lunar and solar eclipses, whose calendar accounted for leap years, and whose timing of the orbit of Venus was within seconds of modern-day, telescope-aided measurements. This tour will take budding Mayanists to a wide range of sites, from the must-sees to the oft-overlooked. Along the way, you will explore caves and sinkholes, which were also important features of the Mayan landscape. You will see firsthand that Mayan people continue to live and thrive in communities and cities across the Yucatán Peninsula, deftly blending ancient traditions with modern mores. This itinerary starts in Mérida—if possible, fly directly there. If you arrive in Cancún, it's easy enough to catch a bus to Mérida and then begin the tour. Also, while this itinerary is best done by rental car, you can also do it by bus—budget a few extra days to complete the whole tour.

DAY 1

Fly into Mérida and settle into your hotel. Attend that evening's cultural performance.

DAY 2

Arrange a rental car. Spend the day exploring Mérida: Go on a free walking tour of downtown (offered daily by the City Tourist Office), visit the anthropology museum, the market, the cathedral, and the government buildings (with murals inside). Plan to go to the nightly cultural performance.

DAY 3

Drive to Santa Elena or Ticul, stopping at a few sights along the way. Good options include Mayapán ruins, Calcetok caves, and Oxkintok ruins.

DAY 4

Visit Uxmal and the Puuc Route. There's a lot to see, so start early. Throw in Loltún caves or Hacienda Tabi if you've got the time and energy. Return to Uxmal for the sound and light show.

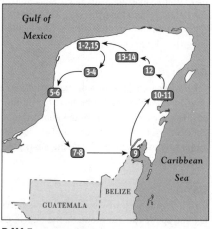

DAY 5

Drive to Campeche City with a stop at Edzná or Santa Rosa Xtampak on the way. If you start early it's possible to visit both, but be ready for a long day.

DAY 6

Spend the day sightseeing around Campeche. Don't miss Fuerte de San Miguel's Archaeological Museum.

DAY 7

Drive to Xpujil and check into a hotel. Visit Becán or Chicanná in the afternoon.

DAY 8

Visit Calakmul and Balamkú ruins.

DAY 9

Drive toward Chetumal. Stop in Kohunlich archaeological zone—and if you're up for the bumpy ride—Dzibanché archaeological zone. Arrive in Chetumal and relax.

DAY 10

Go to the Museo de la Cultura Maya first thing in the morning. Drive to Tulum, with a stop at the Muyil ruins. Check into your hotel in Tulum's Zona Hotelera and relax on the beach.

the observatory at Mayapán archaeological zone

DAY 11

Go early to the Tulum ruins to avoid the crowds. Wear your swimsuit if you want to hang out on the beach there. Go snorkeling in the cenotes, either at Hidden Worlds or at one or more of the cenotes on the road to Cobá. Or just relax on the beach. Stay another night in Tulum.

DAY 12

Drive to Cobá and arrive at opening time to see toucans, green parrots, spider monkeys, and other wildlife (and have the place to yourself too!). Head to Valladolid or onwards to nearby Ek' Balam. Check into a hotel—Valladolid is a small city while Ek' Balam is a tiny village. Explore Ek' Balam village or the churches and cenotes in Valladolid.

DAY 13

After visiting Ek' Balam archaeological site in the morning, drive to Pisté and settle into your hotel. At night, go to the sound and light show at Chichén Itzá. Be sure to explain you are planning to visit the ruins tomorrow, but want to use the show part tonight (if you don't, you'll be sold a separate show-only ticket and you'll still have to pay full price tomorrow).

DAY 14

Get to Chichén Itzá at or before opening time. Visit El Castillo and the ball court first thing because before long they will both be swarmed with day-trippers from Cancún. By the time that happens, you'll be exploring the outer areas. Drive back to Mérida and check into a hotel. Return the rental car.

DAY 15

Fly home, exhausted but happy.

© LIZA PRADO CHANDLER

For all its terrestrial wonders, the Yucatán Peninsula's underwater treasures are no less compelling, including the world's longest underground river system, the second-longest coral reef, and the Western Hemisphere's largest coral atoll. Isla Cozumel, fringed by pristine coral reefs and remarkably clear water, is one of the world's top diving and snorkeling destinations, while Isla Holbox is a favorite feeding ground of manta rays and huge (but harmless) whale sharks. But you need not leave the mainland to appreciate the Yucatán's underwater realm—eerily beautiful cenotes and healthy coral reefs all along the Caribbean coast offer fantastic views and unforgettable experiences and can be enjoyed either on an organized tour or on your own.

DAY 1

Arrive in Cancún's International Airport and zoom down the coast to Playa del Carmen. Spend the afternoon at Playa Tukán—the white sand and turquoise water will be a welcome sight after hours on a plane. If you don't have your own snorkeling equipment, arrange an extended rental (at a discount) at any of the dive shops in town. Have dinner at one of the eateries along Quinta Avenida.

DAY 2

Explore the Riviera Maya—there's great snorkeling on the reefs at Puerto Morelos and in the lagoon at Akumal, and in the caverns at Hidden Worlds, all easy to reach by bus or *combi*. Divers can sign up for a cavern dive at Hidden Worlds, or at any of the shops in Tulum, where underground diving is the specialty.

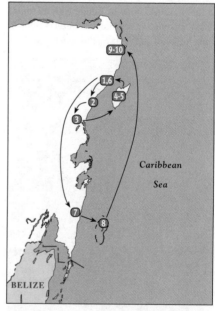

Caribbean Sea

BELIZE

DAY 3

Rent a car and go cenote-hopping. Great options for snorkelers and divers are Cenote Tankah in Tankah Tres, Cenote Azul and Cristalina (both on Highway 307 across from Xpu-Há), and the string of cenotes just west of Tulum on the road to Cobá, including Car Wash, Kolimba/Kin-Ha, Cenote Grande, and Calavera Cenote.

DAY 4

Take the ferry to Cozumel. Arrange a snorkeling trip or a set of dives for the next two days. Spend the rest of the day at a beach club south of town or check out the small town of San Miguel.

preparing to snorkel with whale sharks just off of Isla Holbox

DAY 5

Go on a snorkel or dive trip. Ask to take a break or stop for your surface interval at Playa Palancar.

DAY 6

Go on another snorkel or dive trip in the morning. Parque Nacional Chankanaab and Parque Ecológico Punta Sur both offer snorkeling. In the evening, take the ferry back to Playa del Carmen, return the snorkel equipment, and check out the nightlife on Quinta Avenida.

DAY 7

Head south to Mahahual or Xcalak, two small towns near the Belize border with fantastic snorkeling and diving right from the shore. Xcalak is the best jumping-off point for Chinchorro Bank, a spectacular coral atoll a two-hour boat ride away.

DAY 8

Spend this day snorkeling from the shore or taking a dive trip, either on the reef or at Chinchorro.

DAY 9

Head back to Cancún. Be sure to enjoy your last afternoon on one of its beautiful beaches.

DAY 10

Fly home.

The Yucatán Peninsula is a great place to take kids, whether youngsters or teenagers. The variety of activities and relative ease of transportation help keep everyone happy and engaged. Cancún and the Riviera Maya are especially family-friendly, with seven different ecoparks, miles of beaches, and (if all else fails) plenty of malls with movie theaters, arcades, bowling, miniature golf, aquariums, and more. Perhaps best of all, Mexico is a country where family is paramount and children are welcomed virtually everywhere.

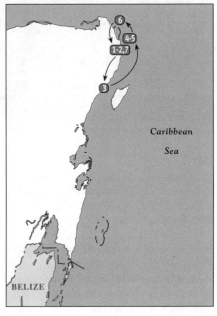

DAY 1

Arrive in Cancún and check into your hotel. If you're in the Zona Hotelera, you won't be able to resist the beach—the afternoon sun is great and the water is warm. If you're downtown, either hop on a bus to the beach or stroll through Parque Las Palapas. In the evenings, lots of local kids play games in the central plaza or ride the small ferris wheel and kiddy rides. Be sure to buy some *churros* filled with *cajeta* (similar to caramel syrup).

DAY 2

Spend the day on the beach. Head to Playa Chac-Mool, where you can rent boogie boards, parasail, or just build sand castles. Have lunch at the Rainforest Café in the Forum by the Sea Mall. After an afternoon break, go to Plaza La Isla, where you and the kids can choose between swimming with dolphins or sharks at the Interactive Aquarium, playing video games, or watching a movie. Book a tour to Xcaret or plan on taking a *combi* to the entrance.

DAY 3

Spend the day at Xcaret. Get there at opening to enjoy it to the hilt.

DAY 4

Head to Isla Mujeres and settle into a hotel. Spend the day on the beach, such as Playa Norte, where you can rent any number of beach toys. Playa Secreto also is a good option if you have small children.

DAY 5

Rent a golf cart and tour the island. Be sure to stop at the Tortugranja Turtle Farm and have lunch at Casa Tikinxik at Playa Lancheros. Afterward, head to Garrafón de Castilla Hotel and Beach Club, where you can snorkel on the reef that it shares with Parque Garrafón. If you're up for it, stop by the Mayan ruins and the sculpture garden at the southern tip of the island. Climb to the top of the renovated lighthouse.

Visit the Tortugranja Turtle Farm on Isla Mujeres.

DAY 6

Choose between taking a tour to Isla Contoy, spending the day at Dolphin Discovery, or taking a snorkeling trip down the coast. Head back to Cancún.

DAY 7

Spend your last hours on the beach. Fly home happy, tan, and rested.

10 Days in Chiapas and Tabasco

The previous itineraries don't include Chiapas or Tabasco, but that doesn't mean they aren't worth visiting. To the contrary, they are so full of things to do that it's impossible to combine Chiapas, Tabasco, *and* the Yucatán Peninsula proper into a brief itinerary. This tour takes you to the best of Chiapas and Tabasco, including the glorious Mayan site of Palenque and others like Ocosingo, Yaxchilán, Bonampak, and Comalcalco. You'll also spend time in San Cristóbal de las Casas, a one-of-a-kind colonial city, and the intriguing indigenous villages nearby. Big cities like Tuxtla Gutiérrez and Villahermosa have interesting sights as well, and are convenient transportation hubs. Chiapas and Tabasco are a wonderful addition to any tour of this part of Mexico—they can even be a whole trip unto themselves!

DAY 1

Fly into Tuxtla Gutiérrez. Settle into your hotel and then head to lovely Plaza Marimba to check out the dance scene. Better yet, get up and strut your stuff with the rest of the crowd.

DAY 2

Get up early and head to Chiapa de Corzo for a boat ride through Sumidero Canyon. In the afternoon, catch a bus to San Cristóbal de las Casas. After you've checked into your hotel, head out and explore the town. Be sure to visit the impressive Iglesia Santo Domingo and the huge outdoor market that surrounds it.

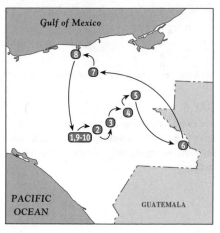

DAY 3

Join a morning tour of San Juan Chamula and other indigenous villages—Alex y Raul's tour is highly recommended. Upon your return, reserve a dinner spot at Na Bolom, a fascinating guest house, research center, and museum that hosts nightly family-style dinners. Continue exploring San Cristóbal—check out the myriad shops, museums, and cafés. Head to Na Bolom for dinner.

DAY 4

Take an early bus to Ocosingo. Store your bags at the bus station and take a cab to Toniná—a little-visited but impressive Mayan site and mu-

seum. Spend 1–2 hours there and then return to the bus station. Continue on to Palenque and check in to your hotel near the ruins.

DAY 5

Arrive at Palenque ruins at opening; you'll beat the heat and have this incredible Mayan site virtually to yourself. Be sure to stop in the museum before you leave. Take an afternoon break, then book a tour to Bonampak and Yaxchilán ruins for the next day. (Or you could stay closer to Palenque and book a tour to Misol Ha, Agua Clara, and Agua Azul if you'd prefer some outdoorsy fun.) In the evening, have dinner and

San Cristóbal de las Casas is one of the most beautiful colonial cities in Mexico.

enjoy the live music at Café Restaurante Don Mucho in El Panchan.

DAY 6

Go on your day-long tour, then return to your Palenque hotel.

DAY 7

Take an early bus to Villahermosa. After you've settled into your hotel, wander through the bustling Zona Remodelada. Spend the rest of the day exploring the Parque-Museo La Venta. If you're up for it, take in an Omnimax movie in the evening.

DAY 8

Take a *colectivo* to the town of Comalcalco. As soon as you arrive, take a cab or local bus to the unique Comalcalco ruins, which are made entirely of brick. Afterwards, head next door for an hour-long tour of Finca Cholula, a cacao-producing hacienda, which makes chocolate onsite. Return to Villahermosa.

DAY 9

Take a bus to Tuxtla. Spend the afternoon at ZOOMAT, regarded as one of Latin America's finest zoos. That evening, meander around the Plaza Cívica and San Marcos Cathedral.

DAY 10

Fly home.

Explore
the Yucatán
Peninsula

Cancún, Isla Mujeres, and Isla Holbox

Cancún is a world-class resort town. It has five-star hotels, high-end shopping, and beaches with impossibly fine white sand and clear blue waters. It's a place people come to party until dawn, to go to ecoparks such as Xcaret, and to visit one of the most impressive Mayan sites in the world—Chichén Itzá. Cancún is a working, breathing city too, with plazas, Internet shops, and a modern bus station that will get you anywhere you want to go in the country. You'll find great music here too—in jazz bars and bohemian cafés—and quesadilla stands that you wish you could resist.

Just 15 minutes away by ferry, you'll find the tiny island of Isla Mujeres, whose breathtaking blue waters will force you to sit back and take in the beauty. It's the place to come if you want to relax on a beach, to play in shallow waters, or to explore a healthy and varied reef on a snorkel or dive trip. The pace is slower here, businesses often close for a long lunch, tours leave a little later, and bars close *relatively* early. It's the type of place where people still smile at you when they pass and the type of place where you'll want to return.

To the north, where the Caribbean meets

Must-Sees

Look for **M** to find the sights and activities you can't miss and **M** for the best dining and lodging.

M **Zona Hotelera Beaches:** With expansive white sand and impossibly turquoise-blue waters, the beaches in Cancún's Hotel Zone are considered some of the most beautiful in the world. Playa Chac-Mool and Playa Delfines are especially breathtaking (page 30).

M **La Casa de Arte Popular Mexicano:** One of the best folk-art museums in the country, with a spectacular and varied collection of traditional handmade Mexican masks, pottery, figures, toys, and more (page 33).

M **Parque Las Palapas:** The "real" Mexico that naysayers claim Cancún lacks. A great family-friendly park in the heart of downtown Cancún, Parque Las Palapas has art exhibits, afternoon music performances, tasty street food, and several classy restaurants (page 34).

© LIZA PRADO CHANDLER

Cancún's spectacular beaches

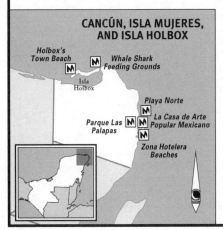

CANCÚN, ISLA MUJERES, AND ISLA HOLBOX

Holbox's Town Beach **M** — **M** Whale Shark Feeding Grounds

Isla Holbox

Playa Norte **M**

Parque Las Palapas **M** **M** **M** La Casa de Arte Popular Mexicano

Zona Hotelera Beaches

M **Playa Norte:** On this Isla Mujeres beach, walk 75 meters (246 feet) straight into the Caribbean before getting your Speedo wet. Or just soak up the sun on the peaceful white sand (page 72).

M **Whale Shark Feeding Grounds:** Snorkel alongside the world's biggest fish—up to 30 feet long, and weighing in at 10 tons—which congregate in feeding grounds off Isla Holbox between June and September (page 94).

M **Holbox's Town Beach:** On the island's north shore, this is the place to try the hot new sport of kiteboarding; beginners and experts alike will enjoy soaring above the emerald waters (page 94).

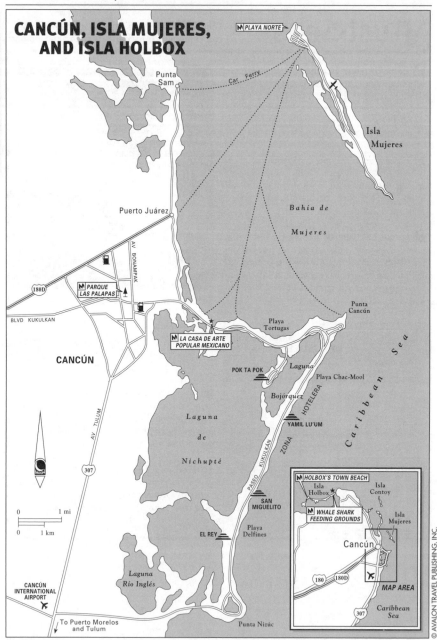

CANCÚN, ISLA MUJERES, AND ISLA HOLBOX

PLAYA NORTE

Punta Sam

Car Ferry

Isla Mujeres

Puerto Juárez

Bahía de Mujeres

AV BONAMPAK

180D

PARQUE LAS PALAPAS

BLVD KUKULKAN

Punta Cancún

Playa Tortugas

CANCÚN

LA CASA DE ARTE POPULAR MEXICANO

POK TA POK

Laguna

Playa Chac-Mool

Bojórquez

AV TULUM

Laguna

de

Nichupté

ZONA HOTELERA

YAMIL LU'UM

Caribbean Sea

307

PASEO KUKULKAN

HOLBOX'S TOWN BEACH

Isla Holbox

Isla Contoy

SAN MIGUELITO

WHALE SHARK FEEDING GROUNDS

Isla Mujeres

0   1 mi

0   1 km

EL REY

Playa Delfines

Cancún

Laguna Río Inglés

180   180D

MAP AREA

CANCÚN INTERNATIONAL AIRPORT

Caribbean Sea

To Puerto Morelos and Tulum

Punta Nizúc

307

© AVALON TRAVEL PUBLISHING, INC.

the Gulf of Mexico, is Isla Holbox. An island with sand streets, few cars, no banks, no post office— it's where to go if you *really* want to get away from it all. It remains relatively untouched, with miles of shell-strewn beaches, dolphins that swim alongside the ferry, and flamingos that make this one of their homes. Harmless whale sharks—the largest fish in the world—also troll these waters in the summertime; snorkel trips with them are thrilling. Here, you'll also find a growing number of hotels—most of them ecologically minded—that will cater to your every need, even if that's just lying in a hammock with a good book.

PLANNING YOUR TIME

Most people come to Cancún for a week and leave tan and satisfied. If your main goal is to relax in the sun and sand, then 5–7 days will give you lots of beach time while leaving room for a day trip or two, such as visiting an eco-park, one of the nearby Mayan ruins, or Isla Mujeres for a change of scenery and a chance to go diving. To really see the area and explore farther afield in the Riviera Maya, though, 10 days should be your minimum and two weeks the ideal. This leaves time for relaxing on the beach, exploring the region, and even spending a few days in the interior of Quintana Roo and nearby states.

Whatever the length, timing, and objective of your trip, you'll likely be based in Cancún. It's a logical choice, offering the widest range of hotels, restaurants, activities, and transportation options. The Zona Hotelera (Hotel Zone) is where the beaches, clubs, and high-rise hotels are, and it is best for maximum beach and party time. Just down the road, downtown hotels offer an insight into the rich culture of Quintana Roo as well as easier access to the bus station, which is convenient for do-it-yourself side trips, even just for the day.

We covered almost all the available tours and excursions in this area, from great to god-awful. The best ones (such as flamingo tours and snorkeling with whale sharks in Isla Holbox) were those that took a little extra effort to organize; we found these trips to be infinitely more interesting than one of the ubiquitous "jungle tours" sold throughout the hotel area. Likewise, getting to Chichén Itzá when the park opens requires renting a car and/or taking a bus there the night before, but it affords a much richer experience than joining a large organized tour; you'll be one of a handful of people exploring this ancient site. Definitely explore the possibilities—the region offers many incredible tours and excursions—just don't let a good sales pitch dictate your vacation.

Cancún

Cancún is one of those places that almost everyone has an idea or opinion about, even if he or she has never been there. For some, Cancún is the ultimate vacation destination, while others scoff at the gaudy commercialism of its malls and franchise restaurants. Others say Cancún has co-opted the region's rich Mayan history; at the same time, the city is rightly credited with having created thousands of jobs in an inhospitable and long-underdeveloped part of the world.

If you come to Cancún for the beaches, the nightlife, the top-end hotels and restaurants,

you will not be disappointed. But nor will you be disappointed if you are looking for interesting museums and fascinating ruins, or to sample authentic Mexican food and enjoy live music. Cancún and nearby destinations are the perfect places to sit by the pool and do nothing, but they also afford world-class diving and snorkeling, amazing caves and underwater rivers, and plentiful bird and marinelife.

Cancún is a new city in a new state. In the 1960s, the Mexican government set out to create the next Acapulco; in 1967 a data-crunching computer selected a small, swampy island

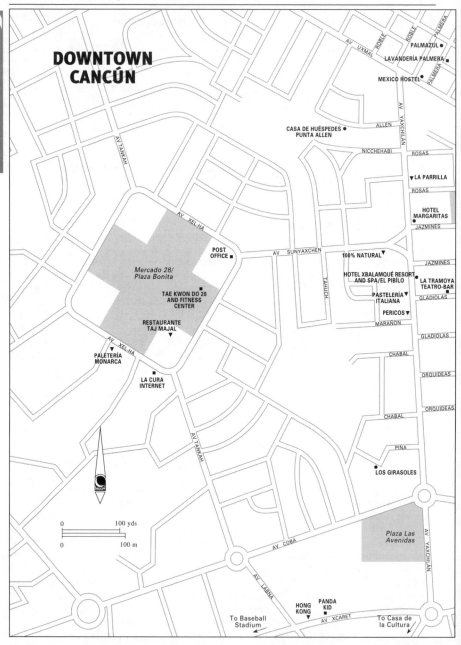

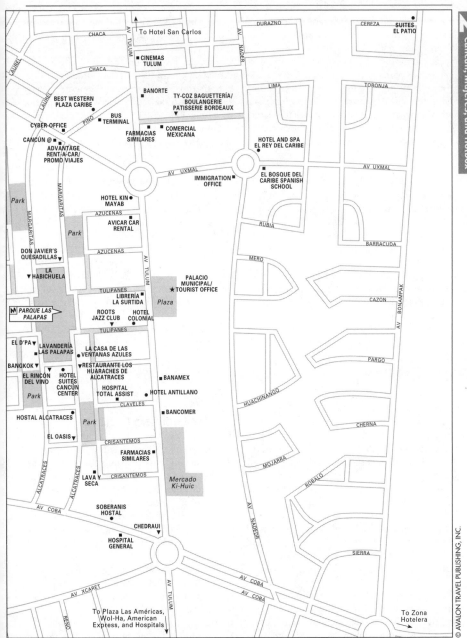

Cancún, Mujeres, and Holbox

ringed with sparkling white sand in an isolated part of the Mexican Caribbean as the country's most promising tourist town. The area was a backwater—not even a state yet. Nevertheless, thousands of mangroves were torn out to make room for an international beach destination, with new infrastructure, electrical plants, purified tap water, and paved avenues lined with trees. A small fishing village on the mainland was expanded to house workers for the new hotels—it is now downtown Cancún and serves much the same purpose. Cancún was officially "opened" in 1974, the same year the territory was elevated to statehood. (It was named after army general Andrés Quintana Roo, and is pronounced "keen-TA-nah Roh").

Today, hotels are filled with visitors from around the world, though Americans and Canadians make up the vast majority of visitors. Few people end up in Cancún by accident—if you're reading this you probably already have an idea of what you hope your trip to be like. But leave a little time and space to be surprised. No matter when or why you come, you may find a side of Cancún you weren't expecting.

ORIENTATION

Cancún's Zona Hotelera lies on a large narrow island in the shape of a number "7." The southern foot of the "7" is called Punta Nizúc—a few hotels and clubs are there, including Club Med. The bend or corner of the "7" is Punta Cancún—this is the heart of the Zona Hotelera and is crowded with hotels, restaurants, and most of the nightclubs and malls. Between Punta Nizúc and Punta Cancún is the island's long (13 km/eight miles) "leg," lined with high-end hotels and resorts on the ocean side, and restaurants, clubs, and some water-sport agencies on the other. (The latter overlook Laguna Nichupté, the lagoon formed between the island and the mainland.) Boulevard Kukulcán is the island's busy main drag—it runs the entire length and care should be taken whenever crossing it as cars and buses race by without seeming to notice the tourists in the crosswalks. Boulevard Kukulcán is

marked off by kilometer and most addresses in the Zona Hotelera include a kilometer number (e.g. Boulevard Kukulcán Km. 5.5). There are spectacular beaches up and down the island. Public buses run the length of Boulevard Kukulcán and into downtown Cancún all day and well into the night. Service is cheap and very frequent.

Downtown Cancún is on the mainland, near the northwestern tip of the "7." It is divided into various *super manzanas* (square blocks, not really great apples) and most addresses include the particular super manzana (e.g. S.M. 4) along with the street name and number. Avenida Tulum is downtown's main throughway. Boulevard Kukulcán intersects Avenida Tulum (and turns into Avenida Cobá) just south of the downtown center—look for a roundabout with huge shells and starfish stood on end. Cancún's bus terminal is a few blocks north of there, at the intersection of Avenida Tulum and Avenida Uxmal. West of Avenida Tulum is a large park (Parque Las Palapas) and beyond that Avenida Yaxchilán. Most of downtown Cancún's hotels, restaurants, and music venues are on or around Parque Las Palapas and Avenida Yaxchilán, primarily in Super Manzanas (S.M.) 22–25.

SIGHTS
Zona Hotelera Beaches

The beaches in Cancún are among the most spectacular in the world. You see postcards of them and you think they must be digitally enhanced—the sand could not be *so* white nor the sea *so* aquamarine. But a combination of clear Caribbean water, shallow sandy seafloor, and a high bright sun make for incredible colors. At high noon, even the postcards don't compare to the living picture show that is Cancún's coastline.

There is a notion that the high-rise hotels have monopolized Cancún's best beaches. This is only partly true. While most hotels *do* front prime real estate, all beach areas in Mexico are public (except those used by the military). Hotels cannot, by law, prohibit you or anyone from lying out on your towel and enjoying the

© LIZA PRADO CHANDLER

Cancún as seen from 20,000 feet

sun and water. Many high-end hotels subvert this by making it difficult or uncomfortable for non-guests to use their beaches: very few maintain exterior paths and others spread guest-only beach chairs over the best parts. (In the hotels' defense, they do a good job of keeping their areas clear of trash and seaweed, which can mar otherwise beautiful beaches.) If your hotel has a nice beach area, you're all set. If not, you can just walk through a hotel lobby to the beach—as a foreigner you are very unlikely to be stopped. (The real shame is that hotel employees seem much more apt to nab locals doing the same thing.) But even that is unnecessary if you don't mind a little extra walking. The city maintains several public access points, marked with large white signs along Boulevard Kukulcán. The area right around the access point is often crowded, but you can walk a hundred meters (328 feet) or so to less crowded areas. Also, some fantastic beaches (Playa Delfines, especially) are totally hotel-free and have a refreshing mix of both of Mexican and foreign beachgoers.

Be aware that the surf along the Zona Hotelera's long east-facing leg can be heavy. You

should pay attention to the colored flags on the beach: green is Safe, yellow is Caution, red is Closed. There are lifeguards near all public access points, but drownings (and near-drownings) do occur occasionally. The beaches along the short north-facing leg are much calmer. For really calm waters head to Isla Mujeres, where the water can be waist deep more than 75 meters (246 feet) from shore. The Laguna Nichupté is not recommended for swimming because of pollution and hungry crocodiles.

Playa Caracol (public access at Blvd. Kukulcán Km. 8.5, at "Xcaret Terminal") has a small stretch of beach right at the public access point, but it's not too pleasant and often very crowded with local families. The beach is much better just right (east) of there, in front of the Fiesta Americana Coral Beach. Getting there takes a bit of agility—either climbing up a slippery sandbag wall or walking down a concrete barrier. Otherwise try cutting through the hotel. The location is convenient to shops and restaurants and the beach is nice, though not as spacious as others.

Playa Chac-Mool (public access at Blvd. Kukulcán Km. 10, across from Señor Frog's) is the beach you see from Forum by the Sea mall. The beach and water are a bit rocky right at the access point, but wide and beautiful just a few hundred meters south, in front of the Hotel Sierra and Hyatt Cancún Caribe. There is parasailing here, and the hotels cast afternoon shadows on the beach, in case you forgot your umbrella. There is no food or water sold on the beach.

Playa Marlín (Blvd. Kukulcán Km. 12.5, at Plaza Kukulcán) is home to the **Beach Club Carisma** (tel. 998/885-1077, 10 A.M.–10 P.M. daily), an eclectic, slightly unkempt beach and sports facility. Playa Marlín itself is wide and clean, and the beach club has free beach chairs if you order something from the restaurant-bar (tacos, chicken nuggets, beers, etc.; US$4–10). You can rent a whirlpool tub on the beach (US$17 for up to four people) or swim in the pool (US$4.25 pp); both are valid all day. Above the beach are several glass-walled courts for playing "Carisma," a homegrown sport similar to racquetball. Rackets and balls are in buckets courtside; ask someone to explain the rules. There's a "sports show" at 4:30 P.M. and an air-conditioned spa area is expected to open by early 2006. The club often has loud music playing, but there's no obnoxious emcee like at many such places. It's a very informal place—we had a hard time finding an employee and when we did he gave us the prices, adding "but that's only if someone actually charges you." There is parking and Plaza Kukulcán, with a bowling alley and restaurants, is nearby.

Playa Ballenas (Blvd. Kukulcán Km. 14.5, by Cancún Palace Hotel) is yet another wide and gorgeous beach. A kiosk right at the entrance rents personal watercraft and boogie boards and offers parasailing and banana boats. As at other beaches, walk a little way in either direction to get away from the crowds. There is no food or drink service here, but the Cancún Palace has public miniature golf if you want a break from the beach. Parking is at the entrance.

Playa Delfines (Blvd. Kukulcán Km. 17.5, just past the Hilton) is our favorite, if we had to pick. The access path is on a bluff, affording a panoramic view of the beach and water unobstructed by hotels. There's a mix of tourists and local families, and you may see surfers. (The waves can be strong here—take care swimming.) The beach is also just across the road from Ruínas El Rey, which make a nice side-trip. There is no food or drink service here. Parking is at the entrance.

Archaeological Zones

Cancún has two archaeological sites, both in the Zona Hotelera. Both are minor compared to the big sites spread throughout the Yucatán Peninsula, but they are still worth visiting and can be easily combined with a day at the beach.

Ruínas El Rey (Blvd. Kukulcán Km. 17.5, across from Playa Delfines, 8 A.M.–5 P.M. daily, US$2.50, use of video camera US$2.50) consists of several platforms, two plazas, and a small temple and pyramid, all arranged along an ancient 500-meter (1,640-foot) roadway. The ruins got their name (Ruins of the King) from a skeleton found during excavation and believed to be that of a king. The ruins date from the late Postclassic period (A.D. 1200–1400); various plaques give explanations in English, Spanish, and Mayan. One curious note—the ruins are home to literally hundreds of iguanas, some quite beefy, which make a visit here all the more interesting.

Lodged between the Sheraton and the Park Royal Piramides, **Yamil Lu'um** (Blvd. Kukulcán Km. 12.5, free) consists of two small temples that were built between A.D. 1200 and 1550: the **Templo del Alacran** (Temple of the Scorpion), owing its name to the remains of a scorpion sculpture on one of its walls, and the **Templo de la Huella** (Temple of the Handprint), named so because of a handprint in the stucco. Unfortunately, neither the scorpion sculpture nor the handprint is visible these days. The ruins are well above the beach on Cancún's highest point, suggesting that the two small temples were used as watchtowers, lighthouses, and as navigational aids. To see the ruins, go to the concierge at either the Sheraton or the Park Royal Piramides and ask if you can walk through to the site. If you are refused, head to Playa Marlín—at the very least, you can see them from afar.

© GARY PRADO CHANDLER

view from the Mayan ruin of Yamil Lu'um in Cancún's Zona Hotelera

Two of the Yucatán Peninsula's most dramatic archaeological sites are within striking distance of Cancún. **Chichén Itzá,** two hours west of Cancún, is an enormous (and enormously impressive) site, with 18 excavated structures, including several pyramids and the largest ball court the Mayans ever built. Many consider this the best of all Mayan sites. **Tulum,** two hours south of Cancún, is much smaller, but it sits on a picturesque bluff overlooking the turquoise Caribbean waters. Enclosed by a wall, Tulum was once a part of a series of Mayan forts, watchtowers, towns, and shrines and is the largest fortified Mayan city in Quintana Roo. Both sites are well worth a visit. Hotels and travels agencies offer day tours, though doing it yourself is relatively easy and the only way to beat the crowds. (See the *Tulum and Southern Quintana Roo* chapter and *The State of Yucatán* chapter for details.)

La Casa de Arte Popular Mexicano

If you have any doubts about the genius of Mexican art, put them permanently to rest at La Casa de Arte Popular Mexicano (El Embar-cadero, Blvd. Kukulcán Km. 4, tel. 998/849-4332, 11 A.M.–7 P.M. daily, US$5). This small museum brims with folk art from around Mexico, including fantastic masks, intricate nativity scenes, and truly remarkable *arboles de vida* (trees of life)—large painted clay pieces that defy description. A free audio tour, available in English or Spanish, helps explain the techniques and stories behind much of the artwork. Surprisingly little known, even here in Cancún, this is one of the best displays of its kind in the country. Don't miss it.

Museo INAH

Named for the government agency that runs it (the National Institute of Archaeology and History, in English) the Museo INAH (Cancún Convention Center, Blvd. Kukulcán Km. 8.5, tel. 998/892-4789, 10 A.M.–2 P.M. and 4–9 P.M. Mon.–Fri., 10 A.M.–7 P.M. Sat., US$3) has a small but very fine collection of Mayan artifacts, mostly from the Postclassic period (A.D. 1200–1500). Clay urns, ceremonial masks, stones carved with Mayan script, and more are held in small glass cases. There was once a loose-leaf guide with English descriptions; it wasn't available when we came through but you may be luckier. Although no substitute for visiting the ruins and museums south and west of Cancún, a stop here is still worthwhile.

Scenic Views

La Torre Escénica (Scenic Tower, El Embarcadero, Blvd. Kukulcán Km. 4, tel. 998/849-7777, 9 A.M.–11 P.M. daily, US$9) is a tall tower with a rotating passenger cabin, affording a good 10-minute view of this part of the coastline. Audio is available in Spanish, English, German, and French; trips every 15–30 minutes.

M Parque Las Palapas

Parque Las Palapas is a classic Mexican plaza—complete with shade trees, quesadilla stands, and little girls running around in frilly dresses and sneakers a size too big. It's the place where locals come to take a break from the heat, to gossip with their friends, and to listen to the local teenagers playing their guitars. On weekends, artisans set up tables to sell their creations and the merry-go-round across the street lights up.

Parque Las Palapas also has two auxiliary miniparks—**Parque Los Artesanos** and **Jardín del Arte**—both kitty-corner to it. Parque Los Artesanos is a young bohemian hangout, with disaffected young artists who fill the small park with their bongo jam sessions, and on weekend evenings, with their beautiful handmade clothes, jewelry, and art. Jardín del Arte, diagonally across from its counterpart, is a space reserved for art expositions (artwork is displayed under a series of stationary white umbrellas) and concerts on its small stage. Some of downtown's best restaurants and hotels are situated here or on nearby Avenida Yaxchilán as well. Hands down, Parque Las Palapas—appendages and all—is one of our favorite places in all of Cancún.

Ecoparks

Visitors to Cancún have four major ecoparks to choose from: **Xcaret, Xel-Ha, Parque Garrafón** (all under the same ownership), and **Tres Rios.** Good for both kids and adults, all offer a combination of outdoor activities, including snorkeling, horseback riding, and kayaking, plus optional stuff such as dolphin-interaction programs and modified scuba diving. Admission is far from cheap, especially the all-inclusive packages that come with meals and extra activities and cost around US$80. Still, each park is unique and interesting in its own way, and many people list a visit as the highlight of their vacation.

Despite the deluge of advertising you'll see downtown and in the Zona Hotelera, none of the four parks is actually in Cancún. Parque Garrafón is the closest, situated on the southern tip of Isla Mujeres. The other three are 60–90 minutes south of Cancún, near Playa del Carmen and Tulum. You can buy tickets at the gates, though most people buy them at their hotels or in a travel agency in Cancún; discounted park tickets are also popular "gifts" for taking part in a time-share presentation. For Xcaret, Xel-Ha, and Parque Garrafón, get information and buy tickets at the **Terminal de Xcaret en Cancún** (Blvd. Kukulcán Km. 8.5, tel. 998/883-3143, www.xcaret.net, 7:30 A.M.–9 P.M. daily), under an immense palapa in front of the public access to Playa Caracol. Admission prices differ depending on the park and the level of pass you buy; senior citizens' and children's tickets are 50 percent off: Xcaret US$49–$80, Xel-Ha US$56–$75, and Garrafón US$29–59. This is also where many park buses pick up passengers, though you may have a different pickup location if you buy your tickets through a third party—be sure to double-check.

(For more detailed information about each park, see *The Riviera's Ecoparks* sidebar in the Playa del Carmen section.)

ENTERTAINMENT AND EVENTS

Cancún is justly famous for its nightlife, with a dozen or more world-class clubs throbbing with music of all sorts and filled with revelers of all ages and nationalities every single night of the week. The partying is especially manic during spring break, summer, and Christmas and New Year. But the city also offers a good mix of mellow dance spots; small venues for live jazz, folk, and instrumental music; pubs and sports bars; and theater and cinema. The downtown area is especially good for more low-key entertainment.

Live Music

For soft jazz, head to **Blue Bayou** (Hyatt Cancún, Blvd. Kukulcán Km. 10.5, tel. 998/884-7800, 6–11 P.M. daily) where every night artists serenade dinner guests with their instruments. When we were here, Alejandro Folgarolas, a sax musician who plays on Sundays and Mondays, was especially lauded. Music begins at 8 P.M.

As the name suggests, **Hard Rock Cafe** (Forum by the Sea mall, Blvd. Kukulcán Km. 9.5, tel. 998/881-2020, 11 A.M.–2 A.M. daily) is the place to go for live rock. Bands play at 10:30 P.M. every night except Monday, when the stage is dark.

A lively jazz and blues joint, **Roots Jazz Club** (Tulipanes 26, tel. 998/884-2437, open 6 P.M.–1 A.M. Tues.–Sat.) is arguably the best music venue in town. Get there early for a quality dinner and—almost more important—a seat near the small stage. Music starts at 10:30 P.M. every night and cover (US$3) is charged only on weekends.

El Pibilo (Av. Yaxchilán 31, inside Hotel Xbalamqué Resort and Spa, tel. 998/892-4553, 7 A.M.–midnight) is a small artsy café with great live music that changes nightly. Music featured includes *bohemia cubana,* fusion jazz, and flamenco. Shows start at 9 P.M. and are free. No music on Sunday.

Overlooking Parque Las Palapas, **El Rincón del Vino** (Alcatraces 29, tel. 998/865-4199, hile@CProdigy.net.mx, 5 P.M.–midnight daily) is a classy wine bar that carries labels from all over the world, including Mexico, Chile, and New Zealand. Tables are candlelit and are set either on the palapa-roofed terrace or indoors. Friendly staff provides recommendations if you'd like to try something new and wine tasting is also available. Live music, usually a guitar soloist, is featured Friday and Saturday nights.

For bongo drum jam sessions, wandering guitarists, and other street musicians, head to **Parque Las Palapas,** where every weekend you can catch one or all of these performers at their best.

Discos and Bars

Most of Cancún's biggest, most popular nightclubs are near the Forum by the Sea mall in the **Zona Hotelera,** with a few a bit farther afield. Each club has a different "on" night—Monday is Dady-O, Tuesday is Fat Tuesday, etc. These don't seem to change much, but definitely ask around before buying your tickets. Dress code is casual but don't wear flip-flops, Tevas, or bathing suits (unless, of course, it's Speedo Night).

Some hotels organize clubbing trips—this may seem cheesy, but it can mean priority admission, reserved tables inside, and a shuttle there (but typically not back). And the organizers head to the same nightly hotspots you're probably looking for anyway. Downtown venues are definitely on the quieter side, lacking the bells and whistles you'll find in the Zona Hotelera.

If you're looking to check out a few of these clubs and bars but your wallet is looking a little on the thin side, consider taking an organized barhopping tour (again—we know—this is veering toward the edge but it could save you a bundle). The most popular ones are: Gray Line's **VIP Party Tour** (office at Plaza Nautilaus, 2nd floor, across from Blue Bay Getaway, Blvd. Kukulcán Km. 3.5, tel. 998/849-4545, www.graylinecancun.com, 7 A.M.–9:30 P.M. daily; tour 10 P.M.–3 A.M., US$50), which takes you to Dady-O, The City, and Dady Rock for five hours of open bar and partying; and Best Day's **Señor Frog's Bar Leaping Tour** (Basement of the Riu Caribe, Blvd. Kukulcán Km. 4.5, tel. 998/881-7207, resdesk5@cancun.com, 7:30 P.M.–2:30 A.M., US$55) which starts off its seven-hour tour at Come and Eat Restaurant (presumably to fill your stomach before a night of heavy drinking), continues to Carlos'n Charlie's, moves to Señor Frog's, and finally ends at Coco Bongo. The price includes transportation between the bars, open bar, and all

PARTYING IN CANCÚN

Travelers flock to Cancún as much for its vibrant nightlife as for its white-sand beaches. Hands down, it's the hottest (and some say, wildest) scene on the Riviera.

Zona Hotelera

Dady-O (Blvd. Kukulcán Km 9.5, tel. 998/833-3333, www.dadyo.com.mx, 10 P.M.–6 A.M. nightly, US$15 admission, US$30 with open bar, US$33 entrance and open bar at Dady Rock and Dady-O) is the, well, daddy of Cancún's nightclubs, with seven different "environments," including CO_2 blasts, laser shows, and theme parties on several different levels. Hip-hop is the sound but on Fridays you can catch some '80s and '90s dance music. Monday and Thursday are especially crowded; ask about Ladies Night. Discounts available if you buy your ticket before 9 P.M.

Next door, **Dady Rock** (Blvd. Kukulcán Km 9.5, tel. 998/883-1626, 6 P.M.–4 A.M. nightly, US$12 with three free drinks, US$27 open bar, US$33 entrance and open bar at Dady Rock and Dady-O) is technically a restaurant and bar—there is no dance floor—but popular rock music has partiers dancing every place possible, including on the bar. DJ 9:30 P.M.–11 P.M., live band 11:30 P.M.–3 A.M. Dady Rock also has some, er, contests: "Hot Male" on Sundays, "Hot Legs" on Tuesdays, and "Wet Body" on Thursdays. (Gary was the runner-up in the "Hot Legs" contest.)

Bulldog Cafe (Blvd. Kukulcán Km 9.5, tel. 998/848-9850, www.bulldogcafe.com, 10 P.M.–6 A.M. daily, US$15 cover, US$28–35 open bar), features hip-hop, rock, and Latin dance music. Friday and Saturday are the big nights. Five enormous bars and a private VIP lounge with a whirlpool tub are the highlights.

The City (Blvd. Kukulcán Km 9.5, tel. 998/848-8380, www.thecitycancun.com, beach club US$5, 9 A.M.–5 P.M. daily, nightclub US$30 cover with open bar, women free on Sundays, 10 P.M.–3 A.M. daily) is a megaclub, having a total capacity of 15,000 people. During the day, you can hang out at the beach club, which has a wave pool and a restaurant. At night, you can party inside on its three floors, with your eyes on the cinema-sized screen, and under what's claimed to be the biggest disco ball in the world (it's pretty big). Be sure to break loose on the movable dance floor, which travels from the third floor to the center of the club below. Saturday is the big night.

CocoBongo (Blvd. Kukulcán Km. 9.5, tel. 998/883-5061, www.cocobongo.com.mx, US$35 cover, show and open bar until 3:30 A.M., open 10 P.M.–5 A.M. daily) is a spectacular show/club featuring live rock and salsa bands, flying acrobats, and rotating impersonator shows of Madonna, Michael Jackson, Beetle Juice, and Spiderman. Not only will you see them on stage, but you'll also find them on the bar and swinging in the air. Movie clips are also projected onto huge high-tech screens.

Six kilometers (3.7 miles) from the main clubbing action, **La Boom** (Blvd. Kukulcán Km. 3.5, tel. 998/849-7588, www.laboom.com.mx, 8 P.M.–3 A.M., US$28 cover, open bar) is an oldie but a very goodie—this place is always packed. Known for its live house (Eminem and Dr. Dre reportedly have performed here), underground dance and techno are also gaining play time. If you're into body-image contests, check out the "Male Hot Body" on Wednesdays and "Bikini Night" on Fridays. Look for the red London bus and old English telephone booth on Boulevard Kukulcán (or the line beside them) if you're lost.

Fat Tuesday (Playa Tortugas, Blvd. Kukulcán Km. 6.5, tel. 998/849-7199, www .fat-tuesday-cun.com, 8 A.M.–3 A.M. daily, US$5 cover on Tues. only, no open bar) has a grubby low-ceilinged bar and dance area that spill onto a patio and beachfront. Catering to an 18- to 25-year-old crowd, it's infamous for its partying excesses, especially on Tuesdays. Fridays were reggae night when we came through—check for the latest.

Old standbys **Carlos'n Charlie's** (Blvd. Kukulcán Km. 5.5, tel. 998/849-4124) and **Señor Frog's** (Blvd. Kukulcán Km. 9.5, tel. 998/883-3454) both open at noon for meals and stay open until 2 A.M. for drinking, dancing, and general mayhem.

If you're looking for a sports bar, a popular one is **Champions** (Marriott Casa Magna, Blvd. Kukulcán Km. 14.5, tel. 998/881-2000, ext. 6341, noon–2 P.M. daily). It's got 40 screens, including a giant wide-screen TV, which play nonstop live sports. A few pool tables and a DJ also add to the mix.

Downtown Cancún

Urban hipsterish **XO Lounge** (Av. Yaxchilán 31, Mex cell tel. 044-998/704-4265, open 7 P.M.–3 A.M. daily) next to the Hotel Xbalamqué is a great place to meet for drinks if you're looking to relax, talk, and check out the clientele. Happy hour runs 7–10 P.M. and a varying two-for-one drink special is featured nightly. It gets busier on weekdays after 11 P.M.

Across the street and toward Uxmal, **La Taberna Yaxchilán** (Av. Yaxchilán 23, tel. 998/887-5433, noon–6 A.M. daily) has daily two-for-one drink specials, pool tables, darts, dominoes, cards, backgammon, chess, Jenga—you name it, it's got the game. Across the street, **Los Arcos** (Av. Yaxchilán 57, tel. 998/887-6673, 10 A.M.–3 A.M. daily) doesn't do much business as a restaurant—La Parilla a few doors down is better—but it gets packed at night with a young mix of locals and tourists. National beers are two-for-one all day and night.

Following a Mexican discotheque trend by being within a mall (no joke!), **Mambo Café** (Plaza Las Américas, Av. Tulum at Av. Sayil, tel. 998/887-7891, open 10 P.M.– 4 A.M. daily, cover US$4 for women, US$5 for men, no cover on Wednesday or Sunday) is one of the hot spots in the downtown Cancún scene. Any night of the week you'll be assured of spinning to the sounds of salsa, *cumbia,* merengue, and *danzón.* Live music is featured daily midnight–2 A.M. While the clientele varies greatly in age, Friday and Saturday nights tend to bring in a younger crowd.

cover charges. You also can book either tour online (and before you even arrive) at www .cancuncare.com/nightlife/partytours.

For a complete listing of the bars and discos in Cancún, see the *Partying in Cancún* sidebar.

Music, Dance, and Theater Performances

Teatro Cancún (El Embarcadero, Blvd. Kukulcán Km. 4, tel. 998/849-4848, ticket office on ground level open 9:30 A.M.–7 P.M. daily, cash only) stages shows by a variety of performers, from dance schools to professional musicians, several times per year. The theater is large and has some interesting murals, though overall it's a bit auditorium-like. Ticket prices vary depending on the event, but range US$10–25.

For *ballet folklórico* (traditional dances from around Mexico) head to **La Joya** restaurant at the Fiesta Americana Coral Beach (Blvd. Kukulcán Km. 9.5, tel. 998/881-3200, ext. 4200). At 7:30 P.M. every Tuesday, Friday, and Saturday a colorful live performance is given; US$5 cover charge.

With couches, candlelit tables, and a full-service bar, **La Tramoya Teatro-Bar** (Gladiolas 8, cell tel. 044-998/105-5670, shows at 8 P.M. and 10 P.M. Tues.–Sat., free–US$9) offers an ever-changing array of music, dance, and theater performances in a bohemian setting. Call or check listings on the front doors to see what's scheduled for the week.

Casa de la Cultura de Cancún (Av. Yaxchilán s/n, S.M. 21, tel. 998/884-8364 or tel. 998/884-8258, casaculturacancun@prodigy.net.mx, www.casaculturacancun.gob.mx) is a state-funded institute, which offers an incredible gamut of artistic workshops, performances, and expositions (most free–US$3.50). While the institute has an ever-changing schedule, which often includes dance, dramatic, and visual art presentations, some events are fixed: 8 P.M. Mondays is movie night, with films falling into a monthly theme; 8 P.M. Tuesdays is open-mike night, when artists are invited to share their poetic, musical, and story-telling talents; 8:30 P.M. Thursdays a live concert—varying from folk to classical—is presented;

and Saturday mornings are dedicated to children in what is called "Sábados de Minicultura" with offerings including puppet shows, educational movies, and theater. Be sure to call for weekly listings, as the calendar is packed with programming.

Cancún Jazz Festival

Organized by the Cancún Hotel Association, the Cancún Jazz Festival (tel. 998/884-7083) is a weeklong event held in late May, drawing top jazz musicians from around the world. This is a huge crowd-drawing event so be sure to reserve tickets early. Prices and venues vary—ask your hotel concierge for details.

Cinema

Cancun has a few major movie theaters, all offering the latest American and Mexican releases. Make sure you see *subtitulada* after the listed titles unless, of course, you want to hear Arnold Schwarzenegger dubbed. Also, if you can, go on a Wednesday, when most movies theaters throughout the country feature discounted ticket prices.

Cinemark (Plaza La Isla, 2nd floor, Blvd. Kukulcán Km. 12.5, tel. 998/883-5604, for reservations at no cost tel. 998/883-5603, US$4 all day) has five screens showing fairly recent Hollywood films, plus a Mexican or Latin American option now and again.

Cinemas Tulum (tel. 998/884-3451, US$4, matinees US$3) is on Avenida Tulum a couple of doors down from the Comercial Mexicana and half a block from the bus station.

In Plaza Las Américas, **Cinépolis** (Av. Tulum at Av. Sayil, 1st floor, tel. 998/884-0403, for reservations at no cost tel. 998/892-3030, US$4, matinees US$3–3.50) is a popular choice among locals.

Upstairs, treat yourself to a first-class movie experience at **Cinépolis VIP** (Plaza Las Américas, Av. Tulum at Av. Sayil, 2nd floor, tel. 998/884-1410, for reservations at no cost tel. 998/892-2103, US$5, matinees US$3.50–4). Inside you'll find overstuffed leather seats with extra leg room, side tables for your munchies, and waiters who will bring you sushi, crepes, gourmet baguettes, cappuccinos, cocktails and—oh, yeah—popcorn, soda, and candy.

SHOPPING

With five major malls, several smaller ones, and hundreds of independent shops, you can buy just about anything in Cancún. The malls are large, modern, and busy, with name-brand clothes, jewelry and watches, movies, arcades, bowling, aquariums, and a full range of restaurants. The malls also have T-shirts, souvenirs, and handicrafts, but you may find better prices at **Flea Market Coral Negro** (Zona Hotelera, across from Forum by the Sea, 8 A.M.–midnight daily) or **Mercado Ki-Huic** (downtown, Av. Tulum at Av. Cobá, 9 A.M.–9 P.M. daily), both easy to reach by bus or foot. There are many more shops north of Ki-Huic on Avenida Tulum (the other side of the street is best) and a couple of open-air markets are nearby. Most mall and independent shops accept credit cards, but plan on paying in pesos at the markets.

Open-Air Markets

Mercado 28 (Av. Sunyaxchen at Av. Xel-Ha, 9 A.M.– 9 P.M. daily) is a large open-air market featuring a wide variety of Mexican handicrafts: ceramics from Tonalá, silver from Taxco, hammocks from Mérida. You'll also find a fair share of T-shirts, key chains, and women offering to braid your hair. If you're hungry, head toward the center of the complex, where a handful of restaurants offer traditional Mexican fare.

On weekend evenings, **Parque Las Palapas** is a great place to pick up local handicrafts and Chiapanecan clothing. Next to it, **Parque Los Artesanos** also has bohemian clothing, jewelry, and art on the same nights as its neighbor.

Art and Handicraft Boutiques

Next to Mercado 28, wander into **Plaza Bonita** (Av. Sunyaxchen at Av. Xel-Ha, 9 A.M.– 9 P.M. daily), a multileveled shopping center built to look like a colonial village—bright courtyards, greenery, and all. You'll find similar items as in Mercado 28 at slightly more expensive prices

but the quality is often better. You also won't leave looking like Bo Derek in *10*.

Definitely worth a look, **AJ Artesanías** (Plaza Las Avenidas, Av. Cobá at Av. Yaxchilán, tel. 998/883-9624, 10:30 A.M.–7:30 P.M. Mon.–Fri., 10 A.M.–6 P.M. Sat.) is a small shop offering high-end furniture and decor from Mérida. Most items are made from pine and *caoba* wood.

In the Zona Hotelera, the gift shop at **La Casa de Arte Popular Mexicano** (El Embarcadero, Blvd. Kukulcán Km. 4, tel. 998/849-4332, 11 A.M.–7 P.M. daily) has a large selection of excellent authentic Mexican folk art from around the country. Prices are high, but so is the quality. The real challenge is getting the stuff home in one piece! (And visit the museum while you're there—it's superb.)

Malls

Plaza Caracol (Blvd. Kukulcán Km. 8.5, tel. 998/883-1088, www.caracolplaza.com, 8 A.M.–10 P.M. daily) is a modern mall with narrow, winding corridors and mostly midrange clothing and souvenir shops. The main food court fails to inspire, but an open-air café and pastry shop near the escalators is surprisingly pleasant, with sofas, newspapers, and live piano music most days. The U.S. and Canadian consulates are on the third floor.

Forum by the Sea Mall (Blvd. Kukulcán Km. 9, tel. 998/883-4425, www.forumbythesea.com.mx, 10 A.M.–11:30 P.M. daily) is a doughnut-shaped building with all three of its floors opening onto the airy main lobby. The stores offer mid- to high-end goods varying from nice T-shirts to expensive jewelry. The main reason people come to this mall is either the Hard Rock Cafe or the Rainforest Cafe (see *Food* for details). The best reason to come, however, is the view from the third-floor balcony. Once used by clients of the now diminished food court, this balcony offers a few chairs and tables with an unbelievable view of the Caribbean. It's so good, it'll make you wonder what you're doing in a mall.

Plaza La Isla (Blvd. Kukulcán Km. 12.5, tel. 998/883-5025, www.laislacancun.com.mx,

9 A.M.–7:30 P.M. daily) is the most pleasant of the Zona Hotelera malls, and the only one set outdoors. Arranged around an artificial river, it has wide airy passageways and plenty of genuinely good shops and restaurants. There are also the popular Interactive Aquarium and a five-screen movie theater.

Plaza Kukulcán (Blvd. Kukulcán Km. 12.5, just past La Destilería, tel. 998/885-2200, www.kukulcanplaza.com, 9 A.M.–10 P.M. daily) was once Cancún's chic shopping center, and though you can still buy Cartier watches or Gucci glasses here, it has been surpassed by larger, better-situated malls at Punta Cancún. It was undergoing a major renovation when we came through (estimated to be completed in the fall of 2005), which we hope will bring better shops and more people.

You don't have to go to the Zona Hotelera for your mall fix. **Plaza Las Américas** (Av. Tulum at Av. Sayil, tel. 998/887-4939, 9 A.M.–midnight daily) stretches almost a block and includes dozens of mid- to upscale shops, a disco, and two movie theaters (including Cancún's only full-service Cinépolis VIP). Unlike in the Zona Hotelera, here you'll be among mostly Mexican shoppers. Note this is not to be confused with Plaza América, a smaller commercial plaza on Avenida Cobá.

SPORTS AND RECREATION

While relaxing by the pool or on the beach is more than enough sports and recreation for many of Cancún's visitors—and who can blame them?—there *are* a number of options for those looking for a bit more action. From golf and fishing to scuba diving and kiteboarding (and a whole bunch of things in between), Cancún has something for everyone.

Parasailing, Personal Watercraft, and Banana Boats

Parasailing (called *paracaídas* in Spanish) is that classic beach thrill-ride in which you don a parachute and are pulled behind a boat to a dizzying height. If you do it only once, do it in Cancún for views of the endless white beaches and

parasailing in Cancún

© LIZA PRADO CHANDLER

impossibly turquoise sea. You can choose a traditional one-person ride (with takeoff from the shore) or a newer two-person ride, in which you sit in a small raft and take off from the boat or the water. Price and duration are fairly uniform: US$40–45 per person for a 10–12-minute ride. Look for independent operators at most public beaches, especially **Playa Ballenas** (Blvd. Kukulcán Km. 14.5, Cancún Palace Hotel), **Playa Chac-Mool** (Blvd. Kukulcán Km. 10, near the Hotel Sierra), and **Playa Delfines** (Blvd. Kukulcán Km. 17.5, near the Hilton) roughly 10 A.M.–6 P.M. daily. Or sign up at friendly **Solo Buceo** (Dreams Cancún Hotel, formerly Camino Real, Blvd. Kukulkán Km. 9.5, tel. 998/883-3979, www.solobuceo.com, 9 A.M.–6 P.M. daily) and **Aqua World** (Blvd. Kukulcán Km. 15.2, tel. 998/848-8300, www.aquaworld.com.mx), which both offer many other activities as well.

Personal watercraft (aka wave runners) are rented at various places along the beach, including all the same places that offer parasailing. Prices are US$50 for a half hour or US$90 per hour; one or two people can ride at a time. **Banana boats** (those big yellow rafts pulled behind a motorboat) are somewhat less common but are definitely available at Playa Ballenas. The cost there is US$20 per person for a 20-minute ride.

Windsurfing, Kiteboarding, and Sailing

Escuela Tabla Vela (Blvd. Kukulcán Km. 3, next to Villas Juveniles, cell tel. 044-998/842-9072, 9 A.M.–6 P.M. daily) is a casual two-man operation that offers sailboarding, sailing, and kiteboarding classes and rental. Windsurfing instruction is US$40 for a two-hour session, or US$104 for a series of eight hour-long classes. Sailing, using small Hobie Cat catamarans, runs US$130 for four hour-long classes. Kiteboarding costs US$60 for a two-hour class or US$130 for eight hour-long sessions. Students can rent equipment, most very new, for US$25–35 per day; for nonstudents it's US$25–35 per hour. The best wind and water conditions are from November to April.

If you just want to go sailing, **Solo Buceo** (Dreams Cancún Hotel, formerly Camino Real, Blvd. Kukulkán Km. 9.5, tel. 998/883-3979, www.solobuceo.com, 9 A.M.–6 P.M. daily) offers one-hour Hobie Cat sailboat trips for US$50 (up to three people).

The **Asociación de Surf de Quintana Roo** (Quintana Roo Surf Association, Blvd. Kukulcán Km. 13, tel. 998/847-7006 or cell tel. 044-998/810-0724, surfcancunmex@hotmail.com) offers surf classes and rentals and hosts occasional surf competitions. The group has a kiosk on Playa Delfines, which is generally the best surf beach.

Waterskiing

Waterski Cancún (Shrimp Bucket, Blvd. Kukulkán Km. 4.5, cell tel. 044-998/841-5242, www.waterskicancun.com, feryjoe@prodigy.net.mx, 8 A.M.–5 P.M. daily, US$40/half-hour) has waterskiing and wave-boarding trips in the lagoon.

Snorkeling and Scuba Diving

For experienced snorkelers and divers, Cancún proper is less interesting than Isla Mujeres and doesn't even compare to Cozumel, one of the best dive spots in the world. Cancún's sandy seafloor simply doesn't have the coral and rock formations that make for great underwater excursions. Where there are large reefs, as at Punta Nizúc, neglect and heavy boat traffic have left much of the coral dead. If you're aching for a fix, there are a few good sites, including a ship intentionally sunk 24 meters (80 feet) down. Most local shops also offer diving and snorkeling trips to Cozumel and the cenotes—inland freshwater sinkholes south of Cancún offering superb cavern and cave diving.

For the best **snorkeling,** talk to a scuba diving shop. All those listed below offer guided snorkeling trips, usually accompanying a dive outing (i.e., you go to decent reefs). Manta Divers seems to have the best program, offering one- and two-reef snorkel trips with 45–60 minutes in the water at each.

One of our favorite snorkel trips is to the cenotes. The water is unbelievably clear and swimming through and among the cave formations is otherworldly. You can definitely do it as a day trip from Cancún, even by bus (ask a local dive shop or see the *Tulum* section in the *Tulum and Southern Quintana Roo* chapter to do it yourself). Either way, make sure your tour includes a wetsuit, as the water can be quite cold.

The snorkeling excursions offered as part of the ubiquitous "jungle trips," are not worth the time or money. Most of the trip is spent getting to the site, which will be described as a national marine park but is in fact a dead coral reef; once there, you spend 30–45 minutes in the water with dozens of other snorkelers but few fish. Even beginners will have more fun with a professional shop.

For **diving,** the shops in Cozumel and Isla Mujeres have easier access to better sites. That said, if your hotel is in Cancún, a local dive shop can get you to a good site for about the same cost (and less hassle) than you'd spend on a day trip to either of the islands. There are cavern diving trips open to PADI open-water divers; true cave diving requires advanced training.

Solo Buceo (tel. 998/883-3979, www.solo buceo.com, 9 A.M.–6 P.M. daily) is a friendly shop at the Dreams Cancún hotel (formerly the Camino Real) with a strong reputation for service and professionalism. English, Spanish, German, and Japanese are all spoken, and most dives are led by instructors rather than dive masters. Choose among one-tank dives (US$55), two-tank dives (US$66), one-tank twilight dives (US$88), two-tank Cozumel or cenote/cavern dives (US$135, including full lunch); all prices include full equipment except wetsuit (US$10). Beginners can try the one-day resort course (US$88) or complete an open-water (US$370, 2–4 days) or advanced diver (US$350, 2–4 days) certification course. Two-tank Cozumel or cavern/cave dives can be arranged (US$135) and include transportation and a box lunch. Despite its name, Solo Buceo offers more than "only diving," including snorkeling (US$25, two spots on the same reef), parasailing (US$40), and Hobie Cat rides (US$50/hour).

Run by down-to-earth Dallas transplants Mimi and John Dykes, **Manta Divers** (Playa Tortugas, next to Fat Tuesday, Blvd. Kukulcán Km. 6.5, tel. 998/849-4050, www.mantadivers.com) offers daily one-tank dives (US$50), two-tank dives (US$60.50), one-tank night dives (US$60.50), two-tank Cozumel or cenote/cavern dives (US$141, including full lunch); all prices include full equipment. Most PADI and NAUI certifications are also available, including open water and advanced diver (US$350, 2–4 days) and cave diver (US$400, two days). Guided snorkeling trips can also be arranged (US$39 for two reefs, US$29 for one, including equipment). All instructors and guides speak English.

Scuba Cancún (Playa Langosta, Blvd. Kukulcán Km. 4.5) tel. 998/849-4736, scuba cancun@prodigy.net.mx, www.scubacancun.com.mx, 7 A.M.–8 P.M. daily) is one of Cancún's oldest dive shops, founded in 1980 and still run by the same family. It offers the standard selection of dives, including one-tank (US$50), two-tank (US$64), night (US$54), and two-tank cavern and Cozumel dives (US$135, including lunch); all prices include equipment.

Snorkel trips are offered in Cancún (US$27), Cozumel (US$88), and the caverns (US$76). This is a popular shop and dives can sometimes get crowded—ask ahead.

Aqua World (Blvd. Kukulcán Km. 15.2, tel. 998/848-8300, www.aquaworld.com.mx) is Cancún's biggest, most commercialized water sports outfit, of which scuba diving is only a small part. Come here if you are looking for activities for the whole family, divers and non-divers alike, all in one spot. Otherwise, head to smaller shops for more personal attention.

Other shops in Cancún include **Planet Scuba** (Blvd. Kukulcán Km. 10.3, next to Pizza Hut, tel. 998/885-1141, www.cancundives.com) and **Marina Punta del Este** (Blvd. Kukulcán Km. 10.3, in front of the Hyatt, tel. 998/883-1210, www.mpuntaeste.com).

Swimming with Dolphins

Swimming with dolphins is a popular, albeit pricey, activity. The best value is at Dolphin Discovery, with more interaction and large pools built in natural seaside habitats. (It also has programs with sea lions and manatees, and snorkeling with sharks and manta rays.) The Interactive Aquarium at Plaza La Isla is popular, though perhaps more for its location than quality. The program is fine, but the pools are small and not very naturelike, needless to say. The shark program there is fairly interesting. Xcaret has a good dolphin facility and program, but the fee is in addition to the already steep park admission.

Dolphin Discovery (Playa Langosta, Blvd. Kukulcán Km. 4.5, tel. 998/849-4748 or toll-free Mex. tel. 800/713-8862, www.dolphindiscovery.com) has three different *delfinarios* (dolphin corrals) with a variety of programs offering varying levels of interaction. From Cancún, the easiest site to visit is in Isla Mujeres, which also has manta ray and shark pens (see the *Isla Mujeres* section for details). You can go directly, but most people sign up at their hotels, online, or at the office at Playa Langosta, where there's a direct ferry for US$5. You can also sign up for the Golden Cruise, an all-day excursion to Isla Mujeres that can be combined with dolphin interaction packages (see *Day Trips to Isla Mujeres* for details). Dolphin Discovery's other sites are in Cozumel and Puerto Aventuras, and they have additional programs such as sea lion and manatee interactions (US$59–179) and scuba diving with dolphins (US$165–195) (see those sections for details).

The **Interactive Aquarium** (Plaza La Isla, Blvd. Kukulcán Km. 12.5, tel. 998/883-0411, toll-free Mex. tel. 800/812-0856, 9 A.M.– 7 P.M. daily, adults US$13, children US$10) has disappointingly small display of fish and invertebrates, but its main raison d'être are the interactive dolphin and shark exhibits. To swim with the dolphins, choose between the "educational swim" (US$55; 30 minutes, including 10 minutes' instruction and 20 minutes' petting and watching the dolphin; 1 P.M. only), "advanced swim" (US$115; 50 minutes, including the educational swim program plus 20 minutes' swimming with dolphins; 10 A.M., 11 A.M., noon, 3 P.M., and 4 P.M.), or "trainer for a day" (US$200; all day; various activities and interactions). In all cases, you must reserve a spot two days in advance. The aquari-

um's shark tank has a huge glass wall and up to eight bull, brown, and nurse sharks, plus groupers and other fish. To get even closer, you can climb into a clear acrylic cage, which is lowered into the tank. The lower part of the cage fills with water, and you feed the sharks from small slots (US$65 one person, US$100 two, US$120 three; 30 minutes, including 15 minutes' instruction and 15 minutes in the cage; every half hour 10 A.M.–6 P.M. daily). It's interesting to watch, even if you don't do it. A fun, 20-minute dolphin show is held daily at 6 and 7 P.M. (free with admission) and makes a visit here more worthwhile.

Jungle Tours

It sure *looks* as if it would be fun: driving your own personal watercraft or two-person speedboat across the lagoon and through the mangroves to a national marine park where you snorkel with the fishes before returning home. Unfortunately the rules—Stay in line! Don't go too fast! Don't pass!—keep the boat part pretty predictable and you see very few birds in the mangroves. The snorkeling is also disappointing, with dozens of

© LIZA PRADO CHANDLER

speed boating on Laguna Nichupté

tourists swarming a dead coral reef that is home to few fish. We don't recommend this sort of trip, but dozens of agencies will gladly take your money (US$50 pp, 1.5–2 hours).

Fishing

More than a dozen species of sport fish ply the waters off Cancún, including blue and white marlin, sailfish, tuna, barracuda, *dorado* (mahi mahi), and grouper. **Fishing Charters Cancún** (tel. 998/849-4766, fishingcharters@yahoo.com.mx, www.fishingcharters.com.mx, Bluewater Adventures Marina, Blvd. Kukulcán Km. 6.5 across from Fat Tuesday, 6 A.M.–9 P.M. daily) operates 10 custom fishing boats in Cancún, ranging 30–38 feet. Expert anglers can reserve the type and size boat they like and request particular captains. The boats hold 4–8 people and go out for 4–8 hours; prices range US$450–795. Individual fishermen can sign up for "shared" trips; prices range US$99–115 for a 4–6-hour trip. All trips include captain, mates, gear, bait, tackle, drinks, and in some cases, lunch. Note that this company is distinct from Bluewater Adventures—it just uses the same pier. The company guarantees you'll catch something or it'll take you again. Reservations required.

Fly-fishing for bonefish, tarpon, snook, and permit is also good in this part of the world. **Hotel El Manglar** (Blvd. Kukulcán Km. 19.8, tel. 998/885-1808, www.villasmanglar.com) organizes trips to the shallow waters surrounding Isla Blanca, about 40 minutes away. The trip costs US$375 for two and runs 5:30 A.M.–4 P.M. The trip includes equipment, box lunch, and drinks. The hotel will also provide free door-to-door service.

Golf

The **Pok Ta Pok Club de Golf** (Blvd. Kukulcán Km. 7.5, tel. 998/883-1230, poktapok@sybcom.com, www.cancungolfclub.com) is an 18-hole championship golf course designed by Robert Trent Jones. The course runs along the Caribbean and the Laguna Nichupté and features its own Mayan ruin near the 12th hole, discovered when the course was built. Green fees are US$125 and drop to US$87 after 2 P.M. Rates include a half golf-cart rental and equipment can be rented at the pro shop.

Another fine golf course is at the **Hilton Cancún Beach and Golf Resort** (Retorno Lacandones Km. 17, tel. 998/881-8016, www.hilton.com.mx). This par-72 course hugs Laguna Nichupté and is surrounded by small Mayan ruins. Alligators are also rumored to be in one of the water hazards so consider leaving those water-bound balls behind. Green fees are US$175; after 2:30 P.M. they are US$125. Both rates include a shared golf cart. Equipment rental is also available.

Fifteen minutes west of the Zona Hotelera, you'll find the **Golf Club at Moon Palace** (Carretera Cancún-Chetumal Km. 340, tel. 998/881-6088, www.palaceresorts.com/moongolf). This 7,201-yard course was designed by Jack Nicklaus and is laid out among mangroves. Green fees are US$250 and include a golf cart, snacks, drinks, and a round-trip transfer from the Moon Palace's hotel lobby. The clubhouse also features a spa.

There are also par-3 courses in front of the **Melia Cancún** (Blvd. Kukulcán Km. 16.5, tel. 998/881-1100, 7 A.M.–2:30 P.M., US$28 green fees, US$5 club rental) and the **Oasis Cancún** (Blvd. Kukulcán Km. 16, tel. 998/885-0867, ext. 6277, 8 A.M.–4 P.M., last tee time 2:30 P.M., US$20 green fees, US$15 club rental).

Tennis

Many of the hotels in the Zona Hotelera have their own tennis courts. Most are lit for night play and many are open to non-guests for a fee. Good choices include the **Fiesta Americana Coral Beach** (Blvd. Kukulcán Km. 9.5, tel. 998/881-3200, US$25/hour indoor clay courts), **Sheraton Cancún Resort and Towers** (Blvd. Kukulcán Km. 12.5, tel. 998/981-4400, US$12/hour, US$24/hour after 6 P.M.), and the **Hilton Cancún Beach and Golf Resort** (Retornos Lacandones Km. 17, tel. 998/881-8000, US$10/hour, US$20/hour after 6 P.M.).

Horseback Riding

Rancho Loma Bonita (Carretera Cancún-Chetumal, four km/2.5 miles south of Puerto Morelos, tel. 998/887-1708, www.lomaboni-tamex.com, US$57 adults, US$53 children) is the place to go to ride horses. Tours last two hours and include horseback riding along the beach or into the jungle. Drinks and lunch are included in the rate. There's also free pickup and drop-off from Okay Maguey restaurant (Plaza Kukulcán, Blvd. Kukulcán Km. 12.5) at 8:30 A.M., 10:30 A.M. and 1:30 P.M.—reservations required.

Exercise

Ever wanted to train with an Olympic gold medalist? Next to Mercado 28, **Tae Kwon Do 28 and Fitness Center** (Av. Xel-Ha 5, tel. 998/884-6765, 6 A.M.–10 P.M. Mon.–Fri.) offers just that in its boxing course with Profesor Ricardo Delgado. If boxing isn't your thing, this modern gym also offers a wide variety of classes, including yoga, spinning, Pilates, kick boxing, and *capoeira*. Classes cost US$3 per session but if you're staying longer than a couple of weeks, ask about the monthly rates.

Scenic Flights

In case you got stuck with the aisle seat on your flight here, **Magic Sky Tours** (El Embarcadero, Blvd. Kukulcán Km. 4, tel. 998/848-5311, 9 A.M.–6 P.M. daily) offers full-day scenic airplane tours to Isla Holbox, Chichén Itzá, and Havana, Cuba (overnight). Prices range US$250–500 per person and include extras such as guided tours, snorkeling, full meals, and so on. Helicopter and overnight trips are also available.

Sky Tour (tel. 984/803-3718, US$99 one person, US$149 two people) is a small operation offering scenic flights from the Playa del Carmen airport using a modern ultralight aircraft. Flights last 25 minutes and include free pickup and drop-off from Playa del Carmen. Available 8 A.M.–6 P.M. any day—recommended times are morning, when there is very little turbulence, or sunset, which is beautiful but more bouncy. Each plane fits only one passenger (plus the pilot), but a couple can go up together in separate planes with radio communication. Discounts available for larger groups.

Day Trips to Isla Mujeres

A number of outfits in Cancún offer the familiar "booze cruise," a classic tourist trap and the most common gift for going to a time-share presentation (you should hold out for something better, by the way). The best of the bunch is probably the **Golden Cruise** tour to Isla Mujeres, including breakfast and lunch, all-day open bar, use of a private beach club, and bike, kayak, and downtown shopping tours. It's operated by Dolphin Discovery (see *Swimming with Dolphins*) and can be taken alone (US$59 adult, US$29.50 child, 10 A.M.–6:30 P.M.) or in combination with any of the company's dolphin programs for an overall savings of about US$10. All cruise guests get free entry to Dolphin Discovery's stingray and shark snorkeling areas.

Bullfighting

Curious about bullfights? Head to Cancún's **Plaza de Toros** (Av. Bonampak at Sayíl, tel. 998/884-8372, US$35, children free) where at 3:30 P.M. every Wednesday you can get a glimpse of what makes this sport so popular in Latin America. Cancún's bullfights differ from traditional *corridas* (runnings) in that only one bull is fought and it is preceded by a mini-*charrería* (rodeo) and a *ballet folklórico* performance. (Typically five to six bulls are "run" and no other performances are held). Because of this, you won't see bullfight aficionados here—which changes the experience dramatically—but it's a good sampler of traditional Mexican pastimes. Tickets are available at the box office or through most tour operators.

Professional Baseball

Baseball is huge in Mexico, particularly in the north, where you'll see as many baseball diamonds as you will soccer fields. While still not having the pull in the Yucatán as it does elsewhere, it is a sport on the rise. The local team **Los Langosteros** (The Lobstermen) are one

© LIZA PRADO CHANDLER

Bullfighting is a popular sport throughout Mexico.

of the 18 teams that make up Mexico's professional baseball league, the Liga Mexicana de Beisbol. You can catch a game from the beginning of March through the end of June at the **Estadio Beto Avilá** on Avenida Xcaret, behind Wal-Mart. Seats go for US$2–7.

Miniature Golf and Bowling

The first two listings are easy walking distance from public beach access points in the Zona Hotelera and may be a good way to split up a long day in the sun and sand, especially for kids.

Golfito (Cancún Palace Hotel, Blvd. Kukulcán Km. 14.5, tel. 998/881-3699, ext. 6655, open 10 A.M.–10 P.M. daily) is open to the public—don't be deterred by the gated hotel driveway. Two 18-hole courses don't have the fiery volcanoes and giant mechanical zoo animals common to miniature golf courses in the States, but they are still fun and relatively challenging. Course fees for 18 holes are US$6 adults, US$5 children under 12 or for 36 holes, US$9 adults, US$7 children under 12.

Bol Kukulcán (Plaza Kukulcán, Blvd. Kukulcán Km. 12.5, tel. 998/885-3425, open 10 A.M.–12:30 A.M. daily) is almost never full,

with a dozen or so lanes on the second floor of the Kukulcán mall. Prices are US$3.50 per person per game, plus US$1 for shoes, and there's a small snack stand. Near Playa Marlín and Beach Club Carisma.

Across from Plaza Las Américas, **Wol-Ha** (Av. Tulum at Av. Sayil, tel. 998/887-2616, noon–midnight daily, US$3/game before 5 P.M., US$3.50/game after 5 P.M., US$1.50/shoe rental) is a decent place to bowl, especially 2–7 P.M. on Monday afternoons, when there is a two-for-one special on games.

Activities for the Kids

If you're tired of the hotel pool, check out **Parque Nizúc** (Blvd. Kukulcán Km. 25, tel. 998/881-3000, www.parquenizuc.com, US$29 adults, US$22.50 children, 10 A.M.–5:30 P.M. daily), a Wet 'n Wild theme park. As the name suggests, it's a water park complete with such classics as twisting slippery slides, high-speed water toboggans, and family-sized inner tubing—a great way to cool off. The park also has a dolphin interaction program (US$115 including park admission, 30 minutes' orientation, 30 minutes in the water). To get there, take a southbound red R-1 bus that has "Parque Nizuc" printed on front (not all R-1s go there).

Across from Cinemark in Plaza La Isla, **El Dilema** (tel. 998/883-0285, noon–11:30 P.M. Mon.–Thurs., 10:30 A.M.–2 A.M. Fri.–Sat.) is a large arcade with video games, air hockey, and so on.

Above the food court in Plaza Las Américas, **Recórcholis!** (Av. Tulum at Av. Sayil, 11 A.M.–11 P.M. daily) offers a fully loaded kids' zone, with video games, air hockey, skeet ball, and other carnival games. There is also an area reserved for children ages 4–10 that has—among other things—jungle gyms, playhouses, and an arts and crafts section. For US$5, children are supervised by employees while parents enjoy the mall on their own.

Wol-Ha (across from Plaza Las Américas, Av. Tulum at Av. Sayil, tel. 998/887-2616, noon–9 P.M. Mon.–Thurs. and noon–midnight Fri.–Sun., US$4) offers a modern indoor playground, housing a brightly colored (and gigantic) jungle gym with ramps, tubes, slides, and other fun obstacles.

ACCOMMODATIONS

Cancún has scores of hotels, varying from backpacker hostels to ultra-high-end resorts. Price usually dictates where people stay, but definitely consider the type of experience you want, too. The most important decision is whether to stay in the Zona Hotelera or downtown. The Zona Hotelera has spectacular views, easy access to glorious beaches, excellent familiar foods, but not much "authentic" interaction with local people. Expect to pay U.S. prices or higher. Downtown Cancún is culturally rich—offering good hotels, varied culinary treats, bohemian music venues, and a great central park. It's less expensive in almost every way from the Zona Hotelera (hotels, restaurants, telephone, Internet) but staying here means taking a bus to the beach and not having access to hotel pools and beach clubs. Many locals live and shop in this area, and Mexicans generally outnumber tourists.

We prefer staying downtown. We go to the Zona Hotelera for the beach, a fancy dinner, or a night at the clubs, but we love returning to downtown's shady parks and small eateries where Spanish is the dominant language. We also spent almost two months here—if you have only a week, staying in the Zona Hotelera might be just the thing for maximum rest and relaxation. Either way, don't let anyone guilt or pressure you into an experience you're not looking for. And it's easy to have it both ways—no matter where you stay, buses run late into the night and cabs are relatively affordable.

Hotel rates are lowest in late spring and early fall; they rise in July and August when Mexicans and Europeans typically take long vacations, and from November to January when many Americans travel. Prices can double between Christmas and New Year's Day, and the week before Easter (Semana Santa). The Internet is the best place to find a bargain, especially in the Zona Hotelera—there are some amazing deals in the off-season. Package deals are worth investigating too, but be aware of pseudoperks such as welcome cocktails or "free"

a high-rise view of Cancún's beaches

© LIZA PRADO CHANDLER

excursions. Most of that stuff you can arrange when you arrive for a fraction the cost. On the other hand, car rentals, airport pickup, or a free meal or two can be handy. Keep in mind that most prices you'll be quoted do not include the 12 percent room tax and unless otherwise noted, all listings have air-conditioning.

Zona Hotelera

Under US$50: Villas Juveniles (Blvd. Kukulcán Km. 3.2, tel. 998/849-4361, US$5 pp tent, US$10 pp dorms with fan, US$44 cabanas with a/c) is the Zona Hotelera's answer to a youth hostel. It's a good thing, then, that there is only one of them. The lobby smells like a gorilla house, there are holes in the floors, broken glass for windows, dark and dirty bathrooms (with no doors on the stalls), and the beach is sad-looking. So why bother? The private villas. They're decent, stand-alone buildings, with three bunk beds apiece, a bathroom (with a door), and a view of the ocean. Camping's not bad either.

US$50–100: Barceló Club Las Perlas (Blvd. Kukulcán Km. 2.5, tel. 998/848-9100, bookings@clublasperlas.com, www.barcelo .com, US$65 s/d, US$66 pp all-inclusive program) is a basic resort hotel for those on a limited budget. Seven kilometers (4.3 miles) south of the action in the Zona Hotelera, this hotel makes its own party with rowdy daily activities, a poolside bar, a small beach in front, and theme nights that keeps interested guests busy. Snorkels, kayaks, and pedal boats also are offered free of charge.

Well-situated for club-hopping, **Hotel Girasol** (Blvd. Kukulcán Km. 9.5, tel. 998/883-5045, giracun@hotmail.com, US$99 s/d) offers dated rooms with views of the ocean or lagoon. The hotel boasts a spectacular beach, an early-model infinity pool, and a tennis court. Rooms are slowly being redecorated in traditional Mexican decor and silent air conditioners. Be sure to ask for a remodeled room when you arrive.

US$100–150: Next door to Hotel Girasol, **Condominios Carisa y Palma** (Blvd. Kukulcán Km. 9.5, tel. 998/883-0287 or U.S./Canada tel.

866/521-1787, www.carisaypalma.com, US$130 s/d) has rooms with fully equipped kitchenettes. Accommodations are sparse but clean and all have magnificent views of the ocean or the lagoon. Strangely, some rooms feature kitchenettes within a few inches of the bed so make sure you look at your room before moving in. Breakfast is included in the rate. A small gym, sauna, tennis court, and pool also are on-site. Be sure to ask for a 15 percent discount if you are a student, teacher, or a senior citizen.

A great place for families, **Miramar Misión Cancún** (Blvd. Kukulcán Km. 9.5, tel. 998/883-1755, reservascancun@prodigy .mx, www.hotelesmision.com, US$144 s/d) offers 300 rooms and suites with balconies, many with views of the ocean or lagoon. A lovely pool runs between the two buildings of the hotel and is the focal point for most of the hotel's activities. If you want something a little quieter, a large rooftop whirlpool tub is a great place to relax. The Miramar also has two ocean-view restaurants, a club, and a bar on-site. A breakfast buffet is included in the daily rate.

On the lagoon side of the road, the quiet **Hotel El Manglar** (Blvd. Kukulcán Km. 19.8, tel. 998/885-1808, www.villasmanglar. com, US$100 s/d) has eight spacious and nicely appointed rooms. Each one has a king-sized bed and two couches that can double as twin beds—perfect for a family with children. There is a pool on-site and a free continental breakfast is served under a palapa. If you're interested in fly-fishing, ask at the front desk about booking a trip.

US$150–250: Resort and Suites Costa Real (Blvd. Kukulcán Km. 5.5, tel. 998/881-7340, www.realresorts.com.mx, US$140 s, US$200 d, US$150 s/d, all-inclusive package) is a Mediterranean-style resort where, while there is a party feel to it with pumping music and ongoing pool and beach games, people of all ages are in the mix. Offering 342 cool and airy rooms, a seemingly endless number of balconies, and a good-sized beach, this is a solid choice. Be sure to ask for a 30 percent discount if you are a senior citizen.

The **M Westin Regina Resort** (Blvd. Kukulcán Km. 20, tel. 998/848-7400, www.wes-tin.com, US$219 ocean view, US$199 lagoon view) is a study in modern Mexican architecture with clean lines, square windows, and lots of white paint with an occasional *rosa méxicana* (fucshia) wall. It's breathtaking. Situated at the southernmost end of the Zona Hotelera, the Westin also is in a prime photo location—with a beach on the Caribbean, and another on Laguna Nichupté, both lined with palapas. There are three impressive pools, two infinity ones oceanside, one "normal" pool lagoon-side. Service is impeccable. A full-service spa and two tennis courts are on-site as well.

Constructed in 1975, **Presidente Inter-Continental** (Blvd. Kukulcán Km. 7.5, tel. 998/848-8700, www.intercontinental.com, room only: US$220–280 s/d depending on the view; all inclusive, add US$48–86 pp) boasts one of the most ample beaches in the Zona Hotelera. Service is top-notch, rooms are recently renovated, and palapas sprinkle the white sand expanse overlooking the turquoise waters to Isla Mujeres. The hotel provides free use of inner tubes, kayaks, and snorkel gear to all of its guests. Before moving into a room, ask to take a look at the lagoon-side rooms—the view is impressive. Discounts apply if you are a senior citizen or a AAA member.

Over US$250: The **Hilton Cancún Beach and Golf Resort** (Retornos Lacandones Km. 17, tel. 998/881-8000, www.hilton.com.mx, US$269–289 s/d standard, US$329–349 s/d villa) is a classy resort spread luxuriously on 250 acres of land. Water is a theme, as cascades encircle the grounds, pools upon pools stretch to the ocean, and seemingly endless windows look out onto the Caribbean and the Laguna Nichupté. As expected, the rooms are nicely appointed and many have glorious views. The Hilton also has two tennis courts and an 18-hole golf course (one of two in the Zona Hotelera). At the full spa, opened at the end of 2004, guests and non-guests alike can get massages (50/80 min. US$110/160) and facials (US$110), and use the sauna and hot tub (US$15 per person, or free with paid treatment).

Considered the epitome of luxury, **The Ritz-Carlton** (Retorno del Rey 36, tel. 998/881-0808, www.ritzcarleton.com, US$370 s/d), is unparalleled in its elegance. Fine art, chandeliers, and marble floors greet you the moment a white-gloved porter opens the door for you. The staff is friendly and strives to make you feel at home—although, frankly, you'll feel more like you've entered a very conservative country club. All 365 rooms have ocean views and balconies and while tastefully appointed, lack the presence that the lobby evokes—it feels like just another hotel room. The pool area also is somewhat lacking—there are two nice but unremarkable ones on-site—but the beach is beautiful and the beach chairs inviting. The gym is definitely a highlight as is the intimate spa. The Italian restaurant on-site—Fantino's—is also a must (see *Food*).

M Fiesta Americana Grand Coral Beach (Blvd. Kukulcán Km. 9.5, tel. 998/881-3200, res2facb@posadas.com, www.fiestamericana.com/grand-coralbeach-cancun, US$541 s/d) is an elegant hotel offering 602 spacious suites all with ocean-view balconies. It features a spectacular series of infinity pools, lush and manicured gardens, and views that will leave you breathless. It's set on one of the calmest beaches of the Zona Hotelera, and guests can lounge under one of the many palapas, wade into the impossibly clear turquoise water, and enjoy service at one of its five restaurants. Indoor tennis courts and free use of a par-72 golf course also is available. Catering to families and older couples, this hotel feels calm and soothing in a sea of rowdy hotels.

All-Inclusive Resorts: The current trend is toward all-inclusive packages, which often include all meals, drinks, activities, taxes, and tips. The deal is a great one if you plan on spending most of your time at your hotel but if you stay for more than a few days, it can get tiresome.

Self-described as being "sexy," the adults-only **Blue Bay Getaway and Spa** (Blvd. Kukulcán 3.5, tel. 998/848-7900, www.bluebayscancun.com, US$120 pp) is a perfect place for 20- and 30-somethings looking to be in a racy atmosphere. Along with five restaurants

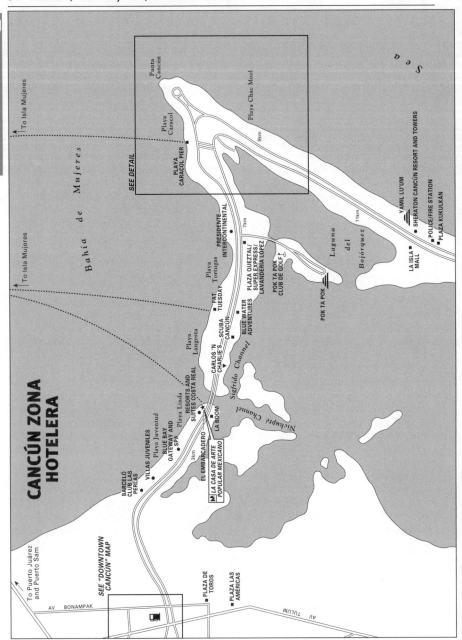

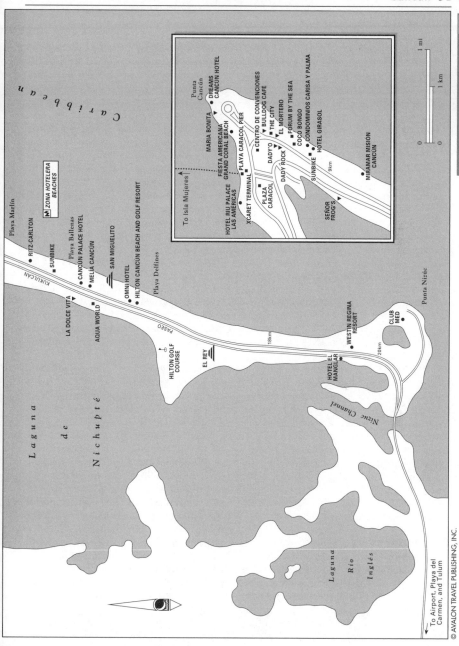

© AVALON TRAVEL PUBLISHING, INC.

to choose from, three pools to play in, and a discotheque and spa on-site, Blue Bay also offers daily games in which losers have to give up their clothes (and find them in the buff), kissing games in which the most outrageous kiss wins, and inventive sexual position games (with swimsuits on, of course). Toplessness is also invited.

Opened in early 2004, **M Hotel Riu Palace Las Americas** (Blvd. Kukulcán Km. 8.5, tel. 998/891-4300, www.riu.com, US$180 pp) is the most elegant of the three Riu hotels in the Zona Hotelera. As soon as you walk into this starkly white complex, you'll feel as if you've been transported to a Victorian-age hotel: crystal chandeliers, gilt-framed mirrors, mahogany detailing, bronze statutes, and an enormous stained-glass ceiling all combine to create a spectacular introduction to the hotel. Boasting 368 junior suites, six restaurants, five bars, two infinity pools, endless water activities, a wide stretch of calm Caribbean beach, and nightly variety shows, the cost is well worth it.

Club Med (Blvd. Kukulcán Km. 20.5, tel. 998/881-8200, toll-free U.S. tel. 800/258-2633, US$146 s, US$200 d, club membership required, US$55/year) was one of the first hotels built in Cancún, occupying the southernmost tip of the Zona Hotelera's long ocean-facing leg. It's an adults-only resort with snorkeling, sailboarding, kayaking, and other activities, plus instruction if you need it, all included. Two restaurants and a bar are on-site. There are also a nightly show and disco. All-inclusive day passes are US$40 10 A.M.–6:30 P.M.; US$40 6:30 P.M.–3 A.M. including dinner, show, and disco; or US$61 for day and night.

Downtown Hotels

Under US$25: If you don't mind dorm rooms and sharing a bathroom, **Mexico Hostel** (Palmera 30, tel. 998/887-0191, www.mexicohostels.com, US$10 with propeller-sized fans, US$12 with a/c) is a fantastic budget option. In a palapa-roofed building, the hostel offers clean—though somewhat cramped—single-sex and mixed rooms. All guests sleep in bunk beds

and have access to a fully equipped kitchen, lockers, self-service laundry, Internet, book exchange, board games, and cable TV. Continental breakfast is included.

Popular with backpackers, **M Hostal Alcatraces** (Alcatraces 49, tel. 998/884-8967, www.hostalalcatraces.com, US$10 dorm with fan, US$12 dorm with a/c, US$23 s/d with a/c) is a remodeled one-story house, offering 24 beds in single-sex and mixed dorms as well as one private room. If you can swing it, the dorms with air-conditioning are worth the extra two bucks—they're more private and (obviously) cooler. The hostel offers a huge and well-equipped kitchen, cable TV, Internet access, board games, self-service laundry, lockers, and parking. The shady front lawn is a great place to relax.

If you want your own bathroom but have a limited budget, try **Hotel San Carlos** (Cedro 28, tel. 998/884-0602, tuffo84@hotmail.com, www.hotelsancarloscancun.com, US$16 s/d—one bed—with fan, US$24 d with fan, US$30 d with a/c), which offers bare-bones accommodations in a central location. Rooms vary in size and cleanliness—definitely check out a few before deciding. The air-conditioned rooms aren't worth the price.

Great for a couple looking for a kitchen and privacy, **M PalmaZul** (Palmera 41, tel. 998/884-8861 or tel. 998/884-7716, palmazul23@hotmail.com, US$22 s/d, US$209 s/d monthly) is your best bet. Hidden a few blocks from the bus station, this converted home offers four *tiny* and spotless one-bedroom apartments. All have been recently refurbished, have full kitchens, and TV. All utilities except electricity are included in the rate.

US$25–50: On a quiet street just half a block from lively bars and restaurants, **Casa de Huéspedes Punta Allen** (Punta Allen 8, tel. 998/884-0225, punta_allen@yahoo.com, www.puntaallen.da.ru, US$31 s/d) is a good option. Friendly service, hanging plants, and continental breakfast complement the clean accommodations. Rooms in front are larger and have small balconies, which let in lots of light.

A great little hotel on a quiet street, ℕ **Los Girasoles** (Piña 20, tel. 998/887-3990, losgirasolescancun@hotmail.com, www.los-girasoles-cancun.web.com, US$31 s/d with kitchenette) offers 18 spotless and colorful rooms with new furniture. If you want one without a kitchenette, try for a discount.

Opening onto a lively pedestrian walkway lined with shops and restaurants, **Hotel Colonial** (Tulipanes 22, tel. 998/884-1535, hotelcolonialcancun@hotmail.com, www.hotelcolonial.com, US$31 s/d with fan, US$35 s/d with a/c) offers ample rooms with bright bedspreads that light up the somewhat dark rooms.

Next to the Chedraui supermarket, **Soberanis Hostal** (Av. Cobá 5, www.soberanis.com.mx, US$39 s/d, US$12 dorms) offers urban chic–type rooms with minimalist wood furnishings and tile floors. All private rooms have lockboxes and cable TV. Four single-sex dorms have two bunk beds apiece, lockers, and bathrooms attached. All rooms have been recently renovated and although clean, some are musty. Continental breakfast is free for all guests. Be sure to ask for a 20 percent discount if you have an ISIC card.

Suites El Patio (Av. Bonampak 51, tel. 998/884-3500 or tel. 998/884-2401, www.cancun-suites.com, US$39 s/d) is a charming colonial hotel with clean, airy rooms decorated with Mexican tiles and hand-carved wardrobes. Although it's seemingly in the middle of nowhere, the bus headed directly to the Zona Hotelera stops a few blocks from its front door and downtown Cancún is only minutes away by foot. Continental breakfast is served in the lush outdoor patio or in the common room, which has board games, books, and several decks of cards.

US$50–100: Owned by the same French expat who operates D'Pa crepery across the park, ℕ **La Casa de Las Ventanas Azules** (Parque Las Palapas s/n, tel. 998/884-7615 at D'Pa, dpa@cancun.com.mx, US$60–90) has just eight rooms, all attractively decorated according to a different international theme—an India room, a Mexico room, a France room, and so on. Rooms have comfortable beds, cozy

bathrooms, air-conditioning, TVs on request, and great blue European-style shuttered windows. (The name means House of the Blue Windows, which everyone shortens to Casazul.) Six rooms have small sitting areas with sofas and great views of the park, and rates include continental breakfast of croissants, coffee, and fruit, served in a sunny guest-only patio dining area. The hotel has a clean tiny swimming pool and a good first-floor restaurant specializing in Provençal cuisine from the south of France.

Kitty-corner to the bus station, **Hotel Kin Mayab** (Av. Tulum 75, tel. 998/884-2999, kinmayab@prodigy.net.mx, www.hotelkinmayab.com, US$44 s/d with fan, US$57 s/d with a/c) has rooms in two buildings. The main building has clean rooms with air-conditioning and cable TV. While the rooms are a decent size, the bathrooms are tiny (one person barely fits!). Ask for a room in back, as those facing Avenida Tulum are pretty loud. If you are able to handle no air-conditioning or TV, the adjacent building has rooms with fans that are well worth the sacrifice in sweat. These ample accommodations are beautifully decorated with traditional Mexican tile work and open onto the hotel's pool and palapa. If you are a senior citizen, be sure to ask for the 50 percent discount on accommodations in either building.

Bougainvillea and a gurgling fountain welcome you to the excellent ℕ **Hotel y Spa El Rey del Caribe** (Av. Uxmal at Nader, tel. 998/884-2028, www.reycaribe.com, US$58 s/d with kitchenette), an environmentally friendly hotel two blocks east of the bus terminal. While rooms here are comfortable and spotless, it is the tropical garden with hammocks, whirlpool tub, and pool that make this a memorable place—you'll feel you've left the city! The hotel employs solar heating, rainwater recovery, organic waste composting, and even asks guests to take off their shoes when entering the outdoor dining area (and even a few rooms) to protect the tropical hardwood floor. Be sure to ask about the milk-and-honey massage offered poolside.

In the heart of the downtown tourist district, **Hotel Antillano** (Claveles at Av. Tulum, tel. 998/884-1532 or tel. 998/884-1132, www .hotelantillano.com, US$54 s, US$62 d) offers friendly service, 48 well-appointed rooms, and daily continental breakfast. Rooms facing the interior courtyard are small but quiet. Be sure to check out the mosaic dolphin decorating the center of the pool. There is a 25 percent discount if you can prove you are a teacher, a government employee, in the military, or a senior citizen.

Hotel Suites Cancún Center (Alcatraces 32, tel. 998/884-2301 or tel. 998/884-7270, scancun@prodigy.net.mx, www.suitescancun .com.mx, US$57 s/d, US$70 s/d with kitchenette) opens onto the tree-lined Parque Las Palapas, where quesadilla stands, corn carts, and running children liven the night air (but not too late!). Rooms are ample, colorful, and clean. An 8-shaped pool in back provides a nice break from the heat.

As soon as you step into the **Hotel Xbalamqué Resort and Spa** (Av. Yaxchilán 31, tel. 998/884-9690 or tel. 998/887-3055, www.xbalmque.com, US$65 s/d) you'll know you're in the heart of the Mayan world. Imposing replicas of Mayan statues and steles decorate the hotel and complement the impressive mural in the main lobby. Cozy rooms are decorated in traditional Mexican decor and floors are lined in pebbles and colorful tiles. Be sure to set aside some time to relax by the lush pool, which features a beautiful cascade. Xbalamqué also is home to a naturalist center offering a variety of massages, facials, traditional Mayan saunas, reiki, yoga, and tai chi. A bohemianesque coffeehouse is also on the premises, offering nightly live music.

In the middle of the Yaxchilán strip, **Hotel Margaritas** (Av. Yaxchilán 41, tel. 998/884-9333, ventashic@sybcom.com, www.margaritas.com, US$74 s/d) is a comfortable option. Rooms, though somewhat sterile, are ample and feature marble floors. The hotel also has a pool, a kiddy pool, an open-air restaurant, and a daily shuttle to the beaches. A 20 percent discount applies if you are a senior citizen.

Best Western Plaza Caribe (Av. Tulum at Av. Uxmal, tel. 998/884-1377, www.hotel-plazacaribe.com, US$86 s/d) is a solid choice. Conveniently situated across the street from the bus terminal, this hotel offers smallish yet nice rooms, some of which open onto two lush courtyards—one with a pool, the other with a playground. Continental breakfast is included and served under a palapa with resident macaws that whistle at you as you walk by. A 30 percent discount applies if you have an ISIC card or are a senior citizen.

FOOD

Cancún has dozens of excellent restaurants. Seafood is the area specialty, especially lobster and shrimp, but you'll find a full range of options, from Cajun to Japanese, and vegetarian to big juicy steaks. The finest restaurants are in the Zona Hotelera, mostly along the west side of Boulevard Kukulcán or in the high-end hotels. You'll also find several very good restaurants in the malls, believe it or not. Eating out in the Zona Hotelera is not cheap, though— live lobster fetches U.S. prices or higher. The malls have some cheap(ish) eats, mostly fast food such as Subway, McDonald's, and Burger King, and we've included a few budget restaurants as well. The largest selection of good, affordable sit-down restaurants is definitely downtown, just a short bus ride away. While there are some great upscale restaurants too, downtown is especially good for tasty eateries that won't blow your budget. In each category below, we have listed the Zona Hotelera restaurants first, followed by downtown options.

Mexican

This is the category where you will find the widest price range, from upscale restaurants to good cheap eateries.

With great views of the lagoon, especially at sunset, **La Destilería** (Blvd. Kukulcán Km. 12.5, tel. 998/885-1086, 12:30 P.M.–midnight daily, US$11–25) serves inventive Mexican food, including cilantro fish fillet, tenderloin medallions in chipotle sauce, and shrimp cooked with tequila and lime. Speaking of tequila, the restaurant has more than 150 types of the agave-derived drink and even offers a guided "tequila tour" (5:30 P.M. Mon., Wed., Fri., US$3–4), with descriptions of tequila brewing (the restaurant itself is a replica distillery) and a tasting at the end. Dinner, appetizers, and drinks can add up to a hefty outlay here, but it's worth the expense. Reservations recommended.

El Mortero (Blvd. Kukulcán KM. 9.5, next to Bulldog Café, tel. 998/848-9800, ext. 777, www.elmorterocancun.com, 6:30–11 P.M. daily, US$15–35, Visa, MC, AmEx) is an authentic replica of an 18th-century hacienda, complete with a fountain on the patio. Grilled dishes are the specialty, from huge steaks for two to *camaron al pastor*—literally "shepherd's shrimp," a tasty recipe using red adobo chili. This is an adaptation of *tacos al pastor,* a perennial favorite at roadside taco stands and made from beef or pork grilled on large vertical spits. Served, as it should be, with pineapple slices.

Tucked behind the Fiesta Americana Coral Beach, **Ⅵ María Bonita** (Punta Cancún, tel. 998/848-7082, 6 P.M.–midnight daily, brunch noon–4 P.M. Sunday, US$13–35, Visa only) is a real find, serving creative quality Mexican dishes in a pleasant dining room overlooking Playa Caracol. Try the quail in rose-petal sauce or pork loin wrapped in banana leaf and seasoned with *achiote* seed, a spice used by the Mayans. There are also a dozen different types of homemade *mole,* a classic Mexican sauce originally made from chocolate and served over chicken, pork, or beef. The restaurant has live music, usually mariachi or marimba, 6:45–10:30 P.M. daily.

Next to María Bonita restaurant, a **no-name market and deli** (Punta Cancún, Blvd. Kukulcán Km. 9.5, tel. 998/883-3818, 7 A.M.–11 P.M. daily, US$4–10) serves basic, affordable meals, from sandwiches and fries to fajitas and seafood. A small outdoor eating area usually has a soccer game on the TV, and there's a full bar. The market has premade sandwiches, plus chips, soda, water, sunscreen, and so on. Nothing too memorable, but it's one of few genuinely cheap places to eat in the Zona Hotelera.

Nearby, **Mocambo** (Blvd. Kukulcán Km. 9.5, tel. 998/883-0398, noon–midnight daily, US$8–22, Visa, MC, AmEx) is sandwiched between the towering Fiesta Americana Coral Beach and Riu hotels. It's a low-key, affordable restaurant specializing in Yucatán-style seafood, such as shrimp in a coconut and mango sauce. There's an outdoor patio overlooking the busy public section of Playa Caracol, and a seafood buffet on Wednesday and Thursday (US$12, drinks included).

Downtown, in the southeast corner of Parque Las Palapas, **Restaurante Los Huaraches de Alcatraces** (Alcatraces 31, tel. 998/884-3918 or tel. 998/884-2528, 7:30 A.M.–6:30 P.M. Tues.–Sun., entrées US$3–5) is a nice place for lunch or early dinner. Served cafeteria-style, traditional Mexican dishes, such as garlic-baked fish or chicken in homemade mole, come with a choice of two sides, such as veggies or beans. There are some pre-Hispanic options, too, such as quesadillas made with blue-corn tortillas. Simple, friendly, popular with locals.

If Disneyland ever created a Mexican Revolution ride, it would surely look like **Pericos** (Av. Yaxchilán 61, tel. 998/884-3152, open 1 P.M.–midnight daily, US$13–34), one of downtown Cancún's most well-known restaurants. In a huge eating area bedecked in Revolution-era photos and classic Mexican artwork, *bandito* waiters sport headbands and criss-crossed ammo belts, the bar has saddles instead of stools, there are not one but two gift shops, and kids may get a rubber chicken on their plates as a joke. Low-key it is not, but Pericos has a solid reputation for serving good grilled meats, seafood, and fish in a boisterous, family-friendly atmosphere. Daily live music includes marimba 7:30–10:30 P.M. and a roving mariachi band 10:30 P.M.–1 A.M.

El Oasis (Alcatraces 57, no phone, 7 A.M.–9 P.M. Mon.–Sat.) is a very simple friendly downtown place operated in the front yard of the cook's home, next to the family bodega. *Tortas,* hamburgers, and sandwiches are all US$1–1.30, main dishes with chicken or pork are US$3. A pleasant little park is in front. Your heart won't be pleased, but your belly sure will be at **N Don Javier's Quesadillas** (Alcatraces at Jazmines, no phone, 8:30 A.M.–midnight Mon.–Sat.), a staple at Parque Las Palapas. Day or night you can get Yucatecan *antojitos* (snacks) such as *sopes, panuchos, salbutes,* tostadas, and—of course—quesadillas. All items come with your choice of a dozen stuffings, including *nopales* (cactus), *rajas* (sautéed *poblano chile*), mushrooms, and potatoes. All items cost US$1 each. Two items will satisfy a small appetite, four might push you over the edge.

Caribbean

The owners of **The Plantation House** (Blvd. Kukulcán Km. 10.5, tel. 998/883-1433, www.plantationhouse.com.mx, noon–midnight daily, US$16–33, Visa, MC, AmEx) could have picked a more sensitive name, but they could hardly do better with the island-style seafood and ambience. The house specialty is the seafood *sable* (sabre), lobster or shrimp grilled on a small sword, kaboblike. As if that weren't enough, the grill is in a kiosk in the lagoon—live fish or lobster are rowed over in a little boat, and rowed back to your table when cooked. The breezy dining area gets great sunsets, and live music keeps the mood light. Lorenzillo's, a slightly more upscale sister restaurant, is next door.

One of downtown's finest restaurants, **La Habichuela** (Calle Margaritas 25 at Parque Las Palapas, tel. 998/884-3158, www.lahabichuela.com, noon–midnight daily) has been serving excellent Caribbean and Mexican dishes since 1977. The seafood here is especially good—try the giant shrimp in tamarind sauce or *cocobichuela,* the house specialty, with lobster and shrimp in a sweet Caribbean curry. Dishes range US$13–27.

Seafood

Almost every restaurant in Cancún serves seafood, regardless of the particular genre. The following are ones that specialize in seafood, especially lobster.

Across from the Omni Hotel, **Captain's Cove** (Blvd. Kukulcán Km. 16.5, tel. 988/885-0016,

7 A.M.–11 P.M., US$12–40) is a large breezy seafood restaurant with an informal feel and a good view of the lagoon. Buffet specials are popular here—the dinner buffet (US$26, US$32 with lobster, 5–9:30 P.M. Tues. and Fri. only) is large and varied, if somewhat ordinary; kids ages 6–12 pay half price. The breakfast buffet (7–11:30 A.M. daily, US$9) is a better deal.

At **Lorenzillo's** (Blvd. Kukulcán Km. 10.5, tel. 998/883-1254, www.lorenzillos.com.mx, noon–midnight daily, US$18–45, Visa, MC, AmEx), live lobster is kept in an adapted rowboat at the entrance—select the one you want, weigh it on an old-time scale and before long, dinner is served. A bit more elegant than its Caribbean sister restaurant next door (The Plantation House), Lorenzillo's has classic seafood dishes and a tasteful airy dining area. Smaller tables line the narrow patio overlooking the lagoon and have small bowls with pellets to throw to the blue trumpet fish schooling below you.

Faros (Blvd. Kukulcán Km. 14, tel. 988/885-1107, 2–11 P.M. daily, US$15–33) is a small, elegant seafood restaurant with glass walls and attractive settings, including huge wine goblets. Dishes include seared ahi tuna, a mixed seafood platter, and Xtabentun Shrimp, an in-house creation made of shrimp marinated in *xtabentun* flowers and roasted red tomatoes. All dishes come with wine suggestions. Faros is adjoined to its sister restaurant, Mango Tango, which has a nightly Caribbean dance and acrobatics show and fixed-price dinners that include open bar (see *Dinner Shows* for details).

Italian

An award-winning Italian restaurant and Cancún institution, **La Dolce Vita** (Blvd. Kukulcán Km. 14.6 across from the Marriott Hotel, tel. 998/885-0161 or tel. 998/885-0150, dolcevita@sybcom.com, noon–11:30 P.M., US$10.50–26) has excellent service and inventive dishes, including lobster ravioli and *boquinete Dolce Vita:* white snapper stuffed with shrimp and mushrooms and baked in light golden pastry. The atmosphere is casual but elegant, and there's live jazz nightly except Sunday. It can get busy, so reservations are recommended. La Dolce Vita Centro, a downtown location (Av. Cobá at Av. Nader, tel. 998/884-3393, 1 P.M.–midnight), has similar prices and dishes.

Fantino's, at the Ritz Carlton Hotel (Retorno del Rey 36, tel. 988/881-0808, 7 A.M.–11 P.M. Mon.–Sat., US$30–60), is a very fine Italian restaurant—one of the best in Cancún, in fact. It is one of few places with strict dress codes: slacks, collared shirt, and dress shoes for men. The intimate room—it has only 16 tables—is the epitome of elegance with plush chairs, gilt mirrors, heavy curtains, and a spectacular ocean view (get here before the sunset to see it!). Choose a main dish (such as Chilean sea bass in caramelized onions, or lamb with basil risotto) or order a four-, six-, or nine-course tasting menu. The nine-course menu with wines runs a cool US$208. Downstairs, a sister restaurant, The Grill Club, open daily except Monday, serves a more international menu and has music, dancing, and a cigar lounge. The dress code still applies, but the atmosphere is less formal.

La Madonna (Plaza La Isla, Blvd. Kukulcán Km. 12.5, tel. 998/883-4837, www.lamadonna.com.mx, noon–midnight, US$10–18, specials US$28–42) is one of Cancún's "Are we really in a mall?" restaurants. A huge modern replica of the Mona Lisa peers over a classy dining room with fine fixtures and settings. The Swiss and Italian menu includes veal, shrimp fettuccini and risotto, plus specials such as live lobster and New Zealand lamb. Doubling as a martini bar, this is also a nice place to stop for a mid-mall drink.

Downtown, **Rolandi's** (Av. Cobá 12, tel. 988/884-4047, noon–midnight) is a Cancún institution, with sister pizzerias in Plaza Caracol in the Zona Hotelera and Isla Mujeres village, plus an excellent boutique hotel and restaurant on Isla Mujeres's southwestern shore. The food at the downtown restaurant—and all of them—is consistently good; choose among thin-crust pizzas, calzones, and great homemade pastas. The atmosphere is casual and the prices reasonable.

Asian

At the Marriott Casa Magna, **Mikado** (Blvd. Kukulcán Km. 14.5, tel. 988/881-2000, 5:30–11 P.M. daily, US$12–17, Visa, MC) serves authentic Japanese and Thai food in a simple eating area with glass tables and Asian art on the walls. Main dishes vary from teriyaki shrimp brochettes to yellow curry chicken, or try sushi, *nigiri,* sashimi, or combination platters.

Looking onto downtown's Jardín de Arte, **Bangkok** (Margaritas 16, tel. 988/887-7269, noon–midnight daily, US$6–16) transports you across the world the moment you step onto the foyer. In a two-story open-air structure, colorful fabrics, objets d'art, and Thai table settings surround you. The food is toned down, but what it lacks in authenticity, it makes up for in interesting flavors and beautiful presentation. Consider eating in the lounge upstairs, which feels like someone's plush home. There are great views of the park on both floors.

Across from Mercado 28, **Restaurante Taj Majal** (Andador 8, 2nd floor, tel. 998/887-6758, noon–10 P.M. daily, entrées US$7–16) has a good sampling of dishes from around India. While connoisseurs of Indian fare won't be blown away, the selection is tasty and especially ample for vegetarians.

A bit off the beaten path, but the only Chinese restaurant around, **Hong Kong** (Plaza Hong Kong, Av. Labná at Av. Xcaret, tel. 998/892-3456, noon–11 P.M. daily, US$4–11) is a casual place with a large and standard selection of entrées. And if the kids don't feel like eating, drop them off next door at **Panda Kid** (tel. 998/892-4654, 8 A.M.–11 P.M.), an affiliated baby-sitting service that offers free supervision if you're dining after 7 P.M. or at reasonable prices any other time of the day (see *Services* for more information).

Meat Lovers

M Puerto Madero (Blvd. Kukulcán Km. 14, tel. 998/885-2829, www.puertomaderocancun.com, 1 P.M.–3 A.M. daily, US$15–45, Visa, MC, AmEx) is cool, classy place serving extremely fresh and carefully prepared meats in huge Argentinean-style portions. The dining rooms have dark bricks and exposed iron beams, reminiscent of a shipyard warehouse (in a good way), and there's an elegant half-moon patio. The menu includes salads, pastas, and grilled fish, in addition to the many cuts of beef, some of which serve two.

Cambalanche (Forum by the Sea, 2nd floor, Blvd. Kukulcán Km. 9.5, tel. 998/883-0902, www.grupocambalanche.com.mx, 1 P.M.–1 A.M. daily, US$20–45, Visa, MC, AmEx) is also known as Argentinean Big Steak House, which pretty much describes the menu. Huge cuts serve two or more; the rib eye and top sirloin will leave you panting. The subdued ambience, frosted glass, and tuxedoed waiters help you forget the fact that, yes, you're in a mall.

Ruth's Chris Steak House (Plaza Kukulcán, Blvd. Kukulcán Km. 12.5, tel. 988/885-0500, 1:30–11:30 P.M. daily, US$24–26) will already be familiar to steak aficionados, serving its signature USDA corn-fed Midwestern beef. The atmosphere is casual—no one should mind if you loosen your belt a notch or two before tucking into a 40-ounce porterhouse. (Your arteries may object, however.) The blackened tuna steak is also recommended.

Downtown, **La Parrilla** (Av. Yaxchilán 51, tel. 998/287-8118, 12:30 P.M.–2 A.M. daily, US$8.50–25) is one of the most popular of the restaurant-bars on this busy street, grilling a variety of delicious beef fillets, plus shrimp and lobster brochettes, chicken, fajitas, and tacos—the fiery spit in front is for *taquitos al pastor,* a Mexican classic. The breezy streetside eating area is comfortable and casual—good for families.

Oddly situated between the downtown Comercial Mexicana supermarket and a pharmacy, **Ty-Coz Baguettería** (Av. Tulum at Av. Uxmal, tel. 998/884-6060, 9 A.M.–11 P.M. Mon.–Sat.) is nonetheless a small, very agreeable shop serving French- and German-inspired baguette sandwiches and *cuernos* (horns)—large stuffed croissants. All but two sandwiches have ham, salami, or chicken and range US$3–5.

Vegetarian

With locations in the Zona Hotelera and town, **100% Natural** (Av. Sunyaxchén at Av. Yaxchilán, tel. 998/884-3617, 7 A.M.–11 P.M. daily, entrées US$3–6.50) is known for its fruit salads, veggie sandwiches, and freshly squeezed juices and makes a great option for those seeking vegetarian meals. All bread and pastries are also made on the premises. Be sure to ask for a 10 percent discount if you are a senior citizen or student. There's another branch in the Zona Hotelera (Blvd. Kukulcán just north of Plaza Caracol, tel. 998/883-1180, 7 A.M.–11 P.M. daily).

Eclectic

Classy and unassuming, **Ⲙ Laguna Grill** (Blvd. Kukulcán Km. 15.6, tel. 998/885-0267, www.lagunagrill.com.mx, 2 P.M.–midnight, bar area 6 P.M.–1:30 A.M., US$15–30) has an excellent lagoon-side patio with tables set wide apart, diminishing the bustle found at other Zona Hotelera restaurants. The tables themselves are made of varnished tree trunks, with iron chairs and attractive glass candleholders. Contemporary gourmet offerings include sesame blackened ahi tuna with asparagus, and grilled lamb chops with pasta, grapes, and goat cheese. The bar has old-time armchairs and sofas set on a breezy deck.

Blue Bayou (Hyatt Cancún, Blvd. Kukulcán Km. 10.5, tel. 998/884-7800, 6–11 P.M. daily, US$10–25, Visa, MC, AmEx) is a prize-winning Cajun restaurant, with dishes such as blackened grouper and "sailfish Mississippi"—grilled sailfish with mushroom-sauce risotto and vegetables. Chicken and meat dishes are also available. The space has dozens of hanging plants, and tables are set along a circular slow-sloping ramp, allowing maximum intimacy in the relatively small space. Enjoy great live jazz starting at 8 P.M. nightly; reservations recommended.

Hard Rock Cafe (Forum by the Sea mall, Blvd. Kukulcán Km. 9.5, tel. 998/881-2020, 11 A.M.–2 A.M. daily, US$8–15, Visa, MC) has a dress code, which is that you must wear shirt *and* shoes after 10 P.M. Otherwise, the place is pretty casual. Burgers, big sandwiches, and chicken-fried-chicken are popular, served with fries in a two-level circular eating area. Most tables have a view of the stage, where live rock bands play nightly except Monday, starting at 10:30 P.M. During the day, there's an outdoor area overlooking the beach.

Downtown, **M Roots Jazz Club** (Tulipanes 26, tel. 998/884-2437, 6 P.M.–1 A.M. Tues.–Sat., US$6–15) has friendly service and a good varied menu, varying from Thai vegetables to squid stuffed with cheese and served in a tomato and mango sauce. But the best reason to come is the great live jazz played from a small intimate stage, starting at 10:30 P.M. every night (cover US$3 Fri. and Sat.).

In nearby Parque Las Palapas, **El D'Pa** (Margaritas at Gladiolas, tel. 998/884-7615, 4 P.M.–1 A.M. Mon.–Sat., 4–11 P.M. Sun., entrées US$3–7) is an eclectic French-inspired restaurant offering creative crepes, baguettes, quiches, and salads. While the outdoor seating is great for people-watching, the charming interior is worth a look—turn-of-the-20th-century prints, antiques, lamps with feathers, and even a pink sofa might just lure you in.

For the Kids

On the second floor of the Forum by the Sea mall, **Rainforest Cafe** (Blvd. Kukulcán Km. 9, tel. 998/881-8130, 7 A.M.–2 A.M. daily, US$8–19) is a fantastic place to take your kids. Trumpeting elephants, giant flapping butterflies, and life-sized gorillas set in a—you got it—rainforest-themed room will have your children giggling with delight. Be sure to keep an eye out for the clown, who makes the rounds every few minutes to entertain the young clientele.

Sweets and Coffeehouses

Part of the Hotel Xbalamqué downtown, **M El Pibilo** (Av. Yaxchilán 31, tel. 998/892-4553, 7 A.M.–midnight, US$3.50–5.50) describes itself as a *cafebrería,* a classy but unassuming combination café, bookstore, and art gallery. Indeed, you can get excellent coffee and light meals here, and enjoy rotating exhibits and books in various languages, many for sale. Better still, every night but Sunday starting at 9 P.M., you're treated to a great live music, a different genre each night from *bohemia cubana* to fusion jazz and flamenco.

Pastelería Italiana (Av. Yaxchilán 67, tel. 998/884-0796, 8:30 A.M.–10:30 P.M. Mon.–Sat., 1–8 P.M. Sun.) offers good coffee and a large selection of fresh cakes—US$2 per slice, US$13–17 whole cake—served at comfortable outdoor tables. Yaxchilán is a busy avenue, but a long awning and tall plants help block out the noise.

Boulangerie Patisserie Bordeaux (Av. Tulum at Av. Uxmal, behind Comercial Mexicana, tel. 998/887 6219, 7 A.M.–9 P.M. Mon.–Sat., 8 A.M.–4 P.M. Sun.) offers fresh baked danishes, pastries, cakes, and homemade chocolates, most for around US$.50 apiece. There are no tables, so you have to take it to go. It's also a bit hidden—take the narrow street past Ty-Coz sandwich shop.

For a taste treat, head to **Paletería Monarca** (across from the Super San Francisco, Av. Xel-Ha 75, 9 A.M.–10 P.M., US$.50–1), which offers *paletas* and *nieves* (popsicles and ice cream) homemade with watermelon, tamarind, and pistachio—just to name a few.

Dinner Cruises

Operated by Dolphin Discovery, the **Columbus Lobster Dinner Cruise** (tel. 998/849-4748, US$69 surf-and-turf, US$74 two lobster tails, open bar, no children under 12 years, departures 5:30 P.M. and 8:30 P.M. nightly) is dubbed "Cancún's most romantic evening." Couples enjoy lobster or steak dinners aboard a 62-foot galleon while cruising the lagoon at sunset or under a starry night sky, accompanied by soft jazz saxophone. Dress is casual, but reservations are necessary. Departures are from the pier in front of Hotel Omni (Blvd. Kukulcán Km. 17.5).

Operating from the same marina, the **Galleon of Captain Hook** (Playa Langosta, Blvd. Kukulcán Km. 4.5, tel. 998/849-4451, US$60 steak, US$70 lobster or surf-and-turf, children ages 6–12 half price, under six free, 7–10:30 P.M. nightly) has a larger, more boisterous trip, including costumed crew members and a pitched pirate "battle" while cruising the bay.

Operated by AquaWorld, the ***Cancún Queen***

(Blvd. Kukulcán Km. 15.5, tel. 998/848-8300, www.aquaworld.com, US$49.50 fish or chicken, US$71.50 lobster, open bar, children half-price, 6–9 P.M. nightly) is the only dinner cruise aboard a paddle steamer. Meals are served in an air-conditioned dining-room, and there's live music and dancing on the deck, all while the old-time river boat makes a three-hour tour of Laguna Nichupté. Reservations recommended.

Dinner Shows

Under a huge palapa roof, **Mango Tango** (Blvd. Kukulcán Km. 14, tel. 988/885-0303, www .mangotango.com.mx, 5:30 P.M.–1 A.M., show starts at 8:30 P.M., dinners US$42–55) is the lively sister restaurant to Faros, an upscale sea-food restaurant next door. Enjoy multicourse dinner packages varying from pasta and chicken to steak and live lobster, plus three hours of free drinks. The show is an *espectáculo Caribeño* (Caribbean extravaganza) and includes island-style music, dance, and acrobatics, all with plenty of audience participation. Afterward, guests climb on the stage for more music and dancing. There's also a play area for kids.

Groceries

If you just want to stock up for a picnic on the beach, there are numerous small markets along Boulevard Kukulcán in the Zona Hotelera where you can get basics such as chips, water, film, and sunscreen. For a more complete grocery, head to **Super Express** (Plaza Quetzal, 100 m/328 feet west of Hotel Presidente-Intercontinental, Blvd. Kukulcán Km. 8, tel. 998/883-3654, 8 A.M.–11 P.M. daily), which has canned food, meats, fruit and veggies, bread, chips, drinks, and more. There's also an HSBC ATM inside.

For mega-supermarkets with everything from in-house bakeries to snorkel gear, head to the downtown locales of **Chedraui** (Blvd. Kukulcán at Av. Tulum, 8 A.M.–11 P.M. daily) and **Comercial Mexicana** (Av. Tulum at Uxmal, 7 A.M.–midnight daily). Both supermarkets have ATMs just inside their doors.

Just a couple of blocks from the bus station, **Mercado 23** (Calles Ciricote and Cedro, three blocks north of Av. Uxmal via Calle Palmeras) is the place to go if you're looking for fresh fruits and vegetables. The selection is somewhat limited but the produce is the freshest around. Most shops are open 6 A.M. to 6 P.M. daily.

INFORMATION
Tourist Information

Downtown, the **Dirección de Turismo** (Palacio Municipal, Av. Tulum 5, tel. 998/887-4329, turismo@cancun.gob.mx, www.cancun .gob.mx, 9 A.M.–8 P.M. Mon.–Fri.) is a busy municipal tourist office with people who happily answer questions and provide information on city and regional sights. A kiosk just outside of the office has brochures and maps. English and Italian spoken. In the Zona Hotelera, try your luck with the **Secretaría Estatal de Turismo** (State Tourism Department, tel. 988/881-9000, www.sedetur.qroo.gob.mx, 9 A.M.–5 P.M. Mon.–Fri., 9 A.M.–3 P.M. Sat.) on the second floor of the Centro de Convenciones. It's tough to get useful information but occasionally it comes through, and it has good tourist maps and magazines.

There are also several excellent publications that are worth picking up to supplement the information in this book: *Cancún Tips* is a free tourist information booklet available in many hotels and shops; *Restaurante Menu Mapa* is one of several ubiquitous brochures put out by Cancún Travel (www.cancuntravel.com); this one has maps, restaurant menus, and reviews and discount coupons; *Map@migo* also has maps and coupons; *Entérate* (tel. 998/886-9876, www.enteratecancun.com) is a great two-page monthly pamphlet with day-by-day listings of all the music, dance, theater, literary, educational, and sports activities going on in Cancún. It can be hard to find, but ask at the tourist office or at the **Casa de la Cultura** (Av. Yaxchilán s/n, S.M. 21, tel. 998/884-8364). Another monthly cultural calendar is the *Agenda Cultural* issued by **Instituto Quintanarroense de la Cultura** (Quintana Roo Cultural Institute, www.iqc.gob.mx). It also can be hard to find—ask at the Casa de la Cultura.

GETTING MARRIED IN CANCÚN

We were married in Guadalajara in November 2003, including a civil wedding before a Mexican judge. For most Mexicans, the civil wedding is a formality and very much secondary to the "true" wedding held in the church. (Legally, the opposite is true.) We found the process fun, a bit frustrating, and in the end, surprisingly moving, having trooped down to our local *registro civil* (civil registry office) with a gaggle of friends and family the day before our main ceremony. If you are thinking of getting married in Cancún—congratulations! And here are a few things to plan for:

Go to a Registro Civil office (Calle Margaritas at Parque Las Palapas, tel. 998/884-9522, 9 A.M.–4 P.M. Mon.–Fri.) and request a list of the documents you will both need to submit. In Cancún, as in most cities, these include:

- Copies of your passport and valid visa (tourist visa is okay).

- Copies of the passports and valid visas (if not Mexican citizens) of two witnesses who will attend the service.

- A recently issued copy (six months or less) of your birth certificate plus an *apostille*, an internationally recognized certification. You typically obtain new birth certificates from the city you were born in, and then send it to a state office for the *apostille*. Ask about ordering them together, especially if you're doing this from Mexico. Both must be translated into Spanish by an official translator; the Registro Civil will give you a list of its approved translators. Bring the originals and

one copy of each. (Note: There are a few special rules if either of you is divorced, widowed, or a Mexican citizen. Be sure to ask the Registro Civil for details.)

- Certified blood test, which checks for reproductive compatibility and several infectious diseases, including HIV/AIDS. The Registro Civil has a list of clinics that perform prenuptial exams, which must be done no more than 15 days before the ceremony.

The Registro Civil needs at least three days to process your documents once they are all in order. Then make an appointment for the civil service. You can get married at the office (US$262, 9 A.M.–2 P.M. Mon.–Fri. only) or have the judge come to your hotel or ceremony site (US$276, Mon.–Sat.). Hold off on the champagne—neither you nor the witnesses are allowed to have consumed alcohol before the ceremony (and you cannot change witnesses once the forms are submitted). The ceremony takes around 30 minutes and consists mostly of the judge making declarations, and you, your witnesses, and your parents (if present) signing numerous forms, even taking fingerprints.

Once you're married, there's just one last hoop to jump through. After your ceremony, stop at the Registro Civil and order a few copies of your marriage certificate. Be sure to ask about getting *apostilles*—you'll need them back home to prove your marriage was genuine.

Cheers!

Booths with tourist information signs abound along Avenida Tulum and Boulevard Kukulcán, but they are virtually all operated by hotel and condo companies offering free tours and meals in exchange for your presence at a time-share presentation. Unless you are willing to spend a morning or afternoon in a hard-line sales pitch, stay clear of these kiosks.

Tours and Travel Agencies

There are literally scores of travel agencies in Can-

cún. Prices at most are pretty uniform, both for area trips (such as Chichén Itzá excursions) and national and international flights. In the Zona Hotelera, most large hotels have reliable in-house travel agencies. Downtown, there are numerous agencies on Avenida Tulum and Avenida Uxmal, including **American Express** (Av. Tulum 208 at Calle Agua, tel. 998/881-4000, 9 A.M.–6 P.M. Mon.–Fri., 9 A.M.–1 P.M. Sat.) and **PromoViajes** (Av. Uxmal 26, tel. 998/884-3128, www.promoviajesmexico.com, 9 A.M.–7 P.M., Mon.–Sat.).

Nómadas Travel Agency (Hostal Soberanis, Av. Cobá No. 5, S.M. 22, tel. 998/892-2320) specializes in youth travel services, including international hostel cards and student air tickets, but it is still a full-service travel agency with professional service and good fares for all travelers.

Medical Assistance

The Zona Hotelera does not have a hospital, though many hotels have a clinician on duty. Downtown, there are three recommended private hospitals within a few blocks of each other near Plaza Las Américas south of the center. All have emergency rooms and English-speaking doctors: **Amerimed** (Av. Tulum 260, just past Plaza Las Américas, tel. 998/881-3434), **Hospiten** (Av. Bonampak Lote 7, tel. 998/881-3700), and **Hospital Americano** (Retorno Viento 14, tel. 998/884-6133). A smaller private hospital in the downtown center is **Hospital Total Assist** (Clavales 5, tel. 998/884-8017 or tel. 998/884-8082, totalassist@prodigy.net.mex), which also has a hyperbaric chamber. **Hiperbárica Cancún** (Alcatraces 44, tel. 998/892-7680 or cell tel. 044-998/105-7791, hiperbarica@prodigy.net .mx, www.hiperbarica-cancun.com) also has a hyperbaric chamber and specializes in diving-related ailments. English, French, and German are spoken and someone is on call 24 hours a day; cash only.

Hospital General (Av. Cobá at Av. Tulum, tel. 998/884-1963) is the downtown public hospital—emergency visits and consultations are free, but expect long lines and medical standards lower than those you're probably used to.

Pharmacies

Farmacia Bazar (Retorno Viento 14, tel. 998/892-1159) is attached to the Hospital Americano in the downtown area and open 24 hours. The pharmacy at Amerimed hospital is open 24 hours Monday through Saturday, and from 7 A.M. to 10 P.M. on Sunday. **Farmacias Similares** is a national chain offering discounted generic medications—there are two locations on Avenida Tulum downtown, one next to the Comercial Mexicana supermarket

(tel. 998/887-4883, 8 A.M.–9 P.M. Mon.–Sat., until 8 P.M. Sun.), and another at Calle Crisantemos (tel. 998/898-0190, open 24 hours). In the Zona Hotelera, there are numerous small pharmacies along Boulevard Kukulcán and near the malls. **Farmacia Express** (Centro Comercial El Parian, tel. 998/883-0923 or cell tel. 044-998/874-2393) is in an annex of the Centro de Convenciones on the southbound section of Boulevard Kukulcán and has 24-hour delivery service of both brand-name and generic medications.

Police and Emergencies

For 24-hour emergency assistance (police, ambulance, fire) anywhere in Cancún, dial **060** or **066** from any pay phone to reach the tourist or state police. It is a free call. For the Red Cross (ambulance only) dial 065 or tel. 998/884-1616; for the fire department dial 116. In the Zona Hotelera, the tourist police, ambulance, and fire station are all at the same station on Boulevard Kukulcán Km. 12.5, next to Plaza Kukulcán and across from La Destilería restaurant. Downtown, the police station is on Avenida Xcaret at Avenida Kabah, in front of the Carrefour supermarket; dial 060, 066, or tel. 998/884-1913.

Newspapers

Novedades de Quintana Roo is the local daily paper and costs US$.75. The Cancún version of the *Miami Herald Tribune* (US$1), is a good English-language alternative. Both can be found at newsstands along Avenida Tulum as well as the bookstore listed below.

Bookstores

Librería La Surtida (Av. Tulum directly across from Palacio Municipal, tel. 998/887-1428, 9 A.M.–10 P.M. daily) has a very small selection of English-language guidebooks to Cancún, the Yucatán Peninsula, and often Mexico, Cuba, and Central America, plus a number of maps and Spanish phrasebooks. It's just one shelf—and the markup is steep—but the store does a decent job of stocking at least one copy of most relevant titles. You'll also find some mysteries and romance novels in English and usually the *New York Times* ($2.50) and *Miami Herald Cancún Edition* (US$1), in addition to a huge selection of Spanish magazines and newspapers.

The pharmacy next door, **Farma-kun** (Av. Tulum, tel. 998/884-3419, 9 A.M.–10 P.M. daily), also has a large selection of maps.

SERVICES
Money

In a town as popular as Cancún, you will have no problem getting access to or exchanging your money—banks, ATMs, and *casas de cambio* (exchange houses) are everywhere tourists are. In the Zona Hotelera, shopping centers are the easiest place to find them. Downtown, you'll find all the money services you'll need lining Avenida Tulum and, to a lesser extent, Avenida Uxmal. Often, hotels will exchange your money, too (at pitiful rates, however).

For the best *casa de cambio* rates, head to the full-service **American Express** (Av. Tulum 208 at Calle Agua, tel. 998/881-4000, 9 A.M.–6 P.M. Mon.–Fri., 9 A.M.–1 P.M. Sat.). American Express also has a small outpost in the Plaza La Isla that is open 9 A.M.–3 P.M., 4–6 P.M., and 7–10 P.M. daily.

If you prefer a bank, the most convenient ones in the Zona Hotelera are: **Bancomer** (Plaza El Parían, Blvd. Kukulcán Km. 8.5, tel. 998/883-0834, 8:30 A.M.–4 P.M. daily) and **Banamex** (Terremar Plaza, Blvd. Kukulcán Km. 8.5, tel. 998/883-3100, 9 A.M.–4 P.M. daily); both have ATMs.

Downtown, the best-located banks are on Avenida Tulum between Boulevard Kukulcán and Uxmal: **Bancomer** (Av. Tulum 20, tel. 998/881-6210, 8:30 A.M.–4 P.M. Mon.–Fri.), **Banamex** (Av. Tulum 19, tel. 998/881-6403, 9 A.M.–4 P.M. Mon.–Fri., 10 A.M.–2 P.M. Sat.), and across from the bus terminal, **Banorte** (Av. Tulum s/n, tel. 998/887-6815, 9 A.M.–4 P.M. Mon.–Fri., 10 A.M.–2 P.M. Sat.). All of these banks have 24-hour ATMs.

Post Office

The downtown post office is in front of Mercado 28 (Av. Sunyaxchen at Av. Xel-Ha, tel. 998/834-1418, 9 A.M.–6 P.M. Mon.–Fri., 9 A.M.–1 P.M. Sat.—stamps only). There is no post office in the Zona Hotelera, but your hotel may be able to send mail for you. Letters and postcards to the United States cost US$.75; to Europe the cost is US$.90.

Internet and Fax

Downtown Internet cafés charge around US$1–1.50 per hour, while those in the Zona Hotelera charge 5–10 times as much. Downtown, look for cafés on Avenida Uxmal near the bus terminal; most offer reasonable national and international phone and fax service as well. In the Zona Hotelera, all the malls have at least one place to check your email. Most of the cafés listed below can also download digital photos and burn them onto CDs (bring your own cables).

Cancún @ (Av. Uxmal 22-D, tel. 998/892-3484, 8 A.M.–midnight daily) is a quiet, friendly downtown shop with fast Internet for under US$1 per hour; CD-burning US$1, plus computer time. Across the street, **Cyber-Office** (Av. Uxmal at Calle Pino, tel. 998/892-3854, 8 A.M.–3 A.M. daily) has reliable Internet and cheap international phone service—under US$.25/minute to the United States and Canada. CD-burning US$1, plus computer time; bring your own CD. Across from Super San Francisco de Asis at Mercado 28, **La Cura Internet** (Av. Xel-Ha 83, tel. 998/884-4610, 9 A.M.–10:30 P.M. Mon.–Sat., 5–9 P.M. Sun., US$1/hour) offers a fast connection in a cool, quiet space.

In the Zona Hotelera, the best rates we could find were in Plaza La Isla at **Hippo's Café and Bar** (tel. 998/883-5518, 11 A.M.–midnight daily), where an hour of Internet costs US$3.50 and burning a CD is US$2.50 plus computer time. There are **Internet kiosks** at Plaza Caracol (10 A.M.–10 P.M. daily, US$5.25/hour), Plaza Kukulcán (10 A.M.–10 P.M. daily, US$10.50/hour), and Forum by the Sea (10 A.M.–10:30 P.M. daily, US$6/hour). In the commercial center just west of the Hotel

CANCÚN CONSULATES

Cancún's consulates include:

Belgium: Plaza Protical, Av. Tulum 192, Local 59, S.M. 4, tel. 998/892-2512, 10 A.M.–2 P.M. Monday–Friday.

Belize: Av. Nader 34, S.M. 2-A, tel. 998/887-8417, 9 A.M.–1 P.M. Monday–Friday.

Canada: Plaza Caracol, Blvd. Kukulcán Km. 8.5, Local 330, tel. 998/883-3360, 9 A.M.–5 P.M. Monday–Friday. In case of an emergency, call the embassy in Mexico City at toll-free Mex. tel. 800/706-2900.

Cuba: Pecari 17, S.M. 20, tel. 998/884-3423, 8 A.M.–1 P.M. Monday–Friday.

France: Av. Bonampak 239, Suite 8, S.M. 4, tel. 998/887-8141, 9 A.M.–1 P.M. Monday–Friday.

Germany: Punta Conoco 36, S.M. 24, tel. 998/884-1898, 9 A.M.–noon Monday–Friday.

Great Britain: Royal Sands Resort, Blvd. Kukulcán Km. 13.5, tel. 998/881-0100, ext. 65898, 9 A.M.–2:30 P.M. Monday–Friday.

Guatemala: Av. Nader 148, S.M. 3, tel. 998/884-8286, 9 A.M.–1:30 P.M. and 5 P.M.–8 P.M. Monday–Friday.

Italy: Parque Las Palapas, Alcatraces 39, Retorno 5, S.M. 22, tel. 998/884-1261, 9 A.M.–2 P.M. Monday–Friday.

Netherlands: the International Airport, by Mexicana's offices, tel. 998/886-0070, 10 A.M.–2 P.M. Monday–Friday. Closed July and August.

Spain: Oasis Cooperativo, Blvd. Kukulcán Km. 6.5, tel. 998/848-9900, 10 A.M.–1 P.M. Monday–Friday.

Switzerland: above Rolandi's restaurant, Av. Cobá 12, Local 214, tel. 998/884-8446, 9 A.M.–1 P.M. Monday–Friday.

United States: Plaza Caracol, Blvd. Kukulcán Km. 8.5, Local 323, tel. 998/883-0272 9 A.M.–1 P.M. Monday–Friday, and for emergencies after regular business hours call Mex. cell tel. 044-998/845-4364 or tel. 998/947-2285. The U.S. consulate should be contacted after regular business hours only in emergencies involving an American citizen, including death, arrest, hospitalization, serious crimes (such as assault, rape, or murder), or accidents or disputes likely to involve litigation. The consulate does not offer assistance of any kind in nonemergencies outside of its regular business hours.

Presidente InterContinental, **Hip-Hop Internet** (tel. 998/883-3880, 10:30 A.M.–8 P.M. daily) charges US$4.75 per hour for Internet and US$2.50 plus computer time.

Photo-Net, the photo and Internet shop at Gran Puerto in Puerto Juárez (tel. 998/843-2386, 9:30 A.M.–7 P.M. daily), has Internet for US$2.50 an hour and burns CDs for US$7.

Telephone

Downtown Internet cafés offer the best international telephone rates. Public phones aren't terribly expensive either and can be used for local, domestic, or international calls. They operate with prepaid cards, which you can buy at just about any small market in denominations of 30, 50, and 100 pesos (be sure you get one for a *teléfono público*, with a little memory chip on one end, not for a cell phone). Rates and dialing instructions are inside the phone cabin; note that calls to cell phones cost double the normal rate. Beware of phones offering "free" collect or credit card calls; far from being free, their rates are outrageous.

Laundry

Downtown, **Lava y Seca** (Retorno Crisantemos 22, tel. 998/892-4789, 10 A.M.–2 P.M. and 4–9 P.M. Mon.–Fri., 10 A.M.–7 P.M. Sat.) charges US$4 for a three-kilo (6.6-pound) load of laundry but will usually knock off 10 percent. You can pick up the same day, often within two hours. **Lavandería Las Palapas** (Parque Las Palapas, tel. 998/884-3664, 7 A.M.–9 P.M. Mon.–Sat., 8 A.M.–3 P.M. Sun.) is one of a couple of laundry places facing the park. It'll wash a three-kilo load for you for US$4 (same-day service), or you can do it yourself for around US$2.25. **Lavandería La Palmera** (Calle Palmera 44, tel. 998/887-2779, 8 A.M.–8 P.M. Mon.–Sat.) charges US$1.25 per kilo (2.2 pounds) and is one of the few launderettes that doesn't have a three-kilo minimum, except on bargain Wednesdays when a kilo is only US$1.

In the Zona Hotelera, **Lavandería López** (Plaza Quetzal, 100 m/328 feet west of Hotel Presidente InterContinental, tel. 998/705-9677, rpcancun@prodigy.net.mx, 8 A.M.–7 P.M. Mon.–Sat., until 6 P.M. Sun.) is about your only option. A load up to four kilos is US$4.25 self-service (soap provided) or US$6 drop-off. Pickup and delivery is an extra US$4.25 for next-day service or US$6 same-day. Ironing and repairs start at about US$1 apiece. You can also rent an iron or cell phone here; call for details.

Storage

On the second floor of the bus station, **Guarda Volumen** (tel. 998/884-4352, ext. 2851, 7 A.M.–9:30 P.M. daily) is the only place to store your belongings. Charging US$.35–1 per hour (a medium-sized backpack costs US$.45/hour), it's convenient for the day but not much longer.

Consulates

For a complete listing of the consulates in town, see the *Cancún Consulates* sidebar.

Immigration

The little white card you received at the airport or border is your tourist visa. Do not lose it as you need to turn it in when you leave. The visa is good for the length of time written in the lower right-hand corner—typically 30 to 90 days, but you can request the maximum permitted—180 days—when you enter. To extend your stay, head to the **immigration office** (Av. Nader 1 at Av. Uxmal, tel. 998/884-1404, 8 A.M.–1 P.M. Mon.–Fri.) *before* your current one expires. You'll fill in several forms (available in Spanish and English), then go to the nearest bank to pay the US$18.25 fee, and then return to the office to get the extension. For every extra 30 days, you'll have to prove you have US$1,000 available, either in cash, travelers checks, or by simply showing a current credit card. Be sure to bring your passport and current visa; the process can be completed the same day if you arrive early.

Baby-Sitting

Need a little down time? While some Zona Hotelera resorts offer help, many don't. If you need a sure thing, try **Panda Kid** (Plaza Hong Kong, Av. Labná at Av. Xcaret, tel. 998/892-4654, 8 A.M.–11 P.M.), which offers baby-sitting services in a large room with a jungle gym, computers, games, movies, toys, paints—all the things a child could want. Four baby-sitters are on staff to care for the children, who must be between ages 1–10 and smaller than 1.3 meters (4.25 feet) tall. Prices vary between age groups but begin at US$2 per hour. Packages of 20 hours can also be purchased for a discount.

Spanish Schools

Classes at **El Bosque del Caribe** (Av. Nader 52, tel. 998/884-1065, www.cancun-language.com.mx) never have more than six students (and often just one or two). All levels are available, and cooking classes and salsa lessons can be arranged as well (US$5/hour). Weekly rates are US$135 for 15 hours of instruction, US$187 for 25 hours; private lessons US$20/hour. A US$100 registration fee includes airport pickup and beginner books, but you can avoid it by going directly to the office instead of signing up on the Internet (beginners will still need to buy the books, about US$40). **La Casa del Escritor** (Pulpo 5,

FLYING TO CANCÚN

The following airlines service Cancún International Airport (CUN):

Aerocaribe (Plaza América, Av. Cobá 5, tel. 998/884-2000 or tel. 998/287-1827 at the airport)

Aerocosta (Av. Tulum 29 at Av. Uxmal, tel. 998/884-0383)

Aeromexico (Av. Cobá 80 at Av. Bonampák, tel. 998/287-1860 or tel. 998/287-1827 at the airport, toll-free Mex. tel. 800/021-4000)

Alaska Airlines (airport only, tel. 998/886-0803, toll-free Mex. tel. 800/426-0333)

ATA (airport only, tel. 998/886-0782)

Aviacsa (Av. Cobá 37, tel. 998/887-4211 or tel. 998/886-0093 at the airport)

Cubana (Av. Tulum 232, tel. 998/887-7017 or tel. 998/886-0355 at the airport)

Delta (airport only, tel. 998/886-0367)

Grupo TACA (airport only, tel. 998/886-0156)

Iberia (airport only, tel. 998/886-0234)

LanChile (airport only, tel. 998/886-0360)

Lineas Aereas Azteca (Plaza América, Av. Cobá 5, tel. 998/892-3126 or tel. 998/886-0831 at the airport)

Magnicharter (Av. Nader 94, tel. 998/886-0373 or tel. 998/886-0836 at the airport)

Mexicana (Av. Tulum 269 past Plaza Las Americas, tel. 998/886-0068 or tel. 998/886-0068 at the airport, toll-free Mex. tel. 800/502-2000)

Spirit Airlines (Retorno Jazmines at Av. Yaxchilán, tel. 998/886-0708 or tel. 998/887-1862 at the airport)

US Airways (airport only, tel. 998/886-0373)

S.M. 27, tel. 998/887-6360, tropoalauna@yahoo.com) offers two- to five-week writing tutorials, including *ortografía* (using accents) and *redacción* (punctuation, paragraph organization, and so on). These are not Spanish classes, per se, but for native or advanced speakers looking to improve their writing. Poetry and fiction courses also available; courses meet 6–10 hours per week and cost US$15–20 per week.

GETTING THERE

Plane

The Cancún International Airport (CUN) is 20 kilometers (12 miles) south of Cancún. Most flights arrive and depart from the airport's Terminal 2 (tel. 998/848-7200, ext. 107), which also has the airline, taxi, bus, and car rental desks, and ATMs. Charter flights, including Spirit Airlines, use Terminal 1 (tel. 998/886-0341); a free shuttle van ferries between the two.

Taxis from the airport officially cost US$35, but you can sometimes haggle it down to around US$30; a taxi from downtown to the airport costs around US$10.50, and from the Zona Hotelera it's US$15. ADO/Riviera has frequent comfortable airport bus service to/from the downtown bus station (US$1.25, 25 minutes, every 30 minutes) and to/from Playa del Carmen (US$6, 50 minutes, hourly; 9:30 A.M.–10:30 P.M. to Playa del Carmen, 8:30 A.M.–6:15 P.M. to the airport). There are also shuttle vans outside both terminals whose drivers jockey for passengers and charge US$8, stopping at hotels in the Zona Hotelera and then downtown.

Bus

Buses leave Cancún's clean and modern bus terminal (on the corner of Av. Tulum and Uxmal)

CANCÚN BUS SCHEDULES

Departures from Cancún's **bus station** (Av. Tulum and Uxmal, tel. 998/887-4728) include:

Destination	Price	Duration	Schedule
Chetumal	US$15.50	5.5 hrs	12:30 A.M., 5 A.M., 6 A.M., 8 A.M., 9:30 A.M., 10:30 A.M., noon, 1:15 P.M., 3:15 P.M., 4:15 P.M., 6:15 P.M., 8 P.M., and 11 P.M.
Chiquilá	US$5	3 hrs	8 A.M. and 12:40 P.M.
Mérida	US$16	4 hrs	1 A.M., 2 A.M., and every hour on the hour 5 A.M.–4 P.M., 4:30 P.M., 5:30 P.M., 6:30 P.M., 8 P.M., 10 P.M., and midnight
Mexico City (Norte)	US$74.50	24 hrs	7:45 A.M.
Mexico City (TAPO)	US$74.50	24 hrs	6:15 A.M., 10 A.M.*, 11 A.M., 1 P.M.*, 6 P.M., and 8 P.M.
Palenque	US$40.50	12 hrs	5:45 P.M.*
Pisté	US$7.25	4 hrs	every hour on the hour 5 A.M.–9 P.M., 11 P.M., and 11:45 P.M.
Playa del Carmen	US$2.75	70 min.	every 15 min. 4:30 A.M.–midnight
Puebla	US$72.75	23 hrs	10 A.M.*, 1 P.M.*, and 5 P.M.
Puerto Morelos	US$1.25	30 min.	every 15 min. 4:30 A.M.–midnight
Río Lagartos (Tizimín)	US$6.50	3 hrs	3:30 A.M., 10 A.M., 5:30 P.M., and 6:30 P.M.; connect to a local bus from Tizimín
San Cristóbal de las Casas	US$52.50	18 hrs	5:45 P.M.*
Tulum	US$5	2 hrs	8 A.M., 9:15 A.M., 9:30 A.M., 10:15 A.M., 10:30 A.M., 11 A.M., 12:45 P.M., 1:15 P.M., 4:15 P.M., and 7 P.M.
Tuxtla Gutiérrez	US$57	22 hrs	5:45 P.M.*
Valladolid	US$7.50	2 hrs	5 A.M., 8 A.M., 9 A.M., 11:30 A.M., and 2 P.M.; plus 5:30 P.M. Friday and Saturday only.
Veracruz	US$74.50	15 hrs	10 A.M.* and 1 P.M.*
Villahermosa	US$48	12 hrs	10 A.M.* and 1 P.M.*

*Denotes ADO-GL deluxe service; fares are 10–30 percent higher, and travel time may be slightly faster.

for destinations in the Yucatán Peninsula and throughout the interior of Mexico. **ADO** (tel. 998/884-5542, ext. 2404) and its deluxe-service line **ADO GL** (tel. 998/884-1365, ext. 2803) will get you just about anywhere. Fares and departure times change somewhat regularly, so it's best to call ahead.

Car

It's a long drive from the nearest U.S. border—1,450 miles—but it's bound to be an adventure. Make sure to get Mexican automobile insurance when you cross the border and remember that your vehicle is allowed in the country only for as long as you are, 180 days per year. (If you prefer to skip the drive but still want your car, check out the *Ferry* section.)

Ferry

Normally operating from November to April, the **Yucatan Express** (toll-free Mex. tel. 800/514-5832, U.S. tel. 866/670-3939, www.yucatanexpress.com, US$120–750 r/t pp, depending on the room) offers one-way and round-trip cruise ferry service from Tampa, Florida, to Progreso, on the Gulf Coast northwest of Cancún. It's a two-day trip on a cruise ship with everything from economy cabins to suites, five-star dining, casinos, and live entertainment. You also can bring your car, van, SUV, and truck over on it (US$298 r/t)—Yucatan Express agents also will help you get temporary Mexican auto insurance. Packages with seven-, 11-, and 14-day stays in the Yucatán and Florida are also offered. However, service had been halted indefinitely when we were in the area; call ahead for the latest. The agency was hoping to recommence service in November 2005.

Neighboring Countries

Cancún is an important international hub, not only for tourists from North America and Europe, but for regional flights to Central America and the Caribbean. Guatemala, Belize, and Cuba are especially popular destinations. Any of the numerous travel agencies in town can book a tour for you, or you can get there yourself by plane or bus. Travelers of most nation-

DRIVING DISTANCES FROM CANCÚN	
Location	**Distance**
Airport	20 km (12.5 miles)
Akumal	105 km (65 miles)
Bacalar	320 km (199 miles)
Campeche	487 km (302.5 miles)
Chetumal	382 km (237.5 miles)
Chichén Itzá	178 km (110.5 miles)
Cobá	173 km (107.5 miles)
Mahahual	351 km (218 miles)
Mérida	320 km (199 miles)
Paamul	82 km (51 miles)
Playa del Carmen	68 km (42.5 miles)
Puerto Aventuras	87 km (54 miles)
Puerto Juárez	5 km (3 miles)
Puerto Morelos	36 km (22.5 miles)
Tulum	130 km (81 miles)
Valladolid	158 km (98 miles)
Xcalak	411 km (255.5 miles)
Xcaret	74 km (46 miles)
Xel-Há	122 km (76 miles)
Xpujil	501 km (311 miles)

alities do not need prearranged visas to enter either Belize or Guatemala, but they may have to pay an entrance fee at the airport or border. Call the respective consulates (or your own) for additional information.

Note: The U.S. government prohibits most ordinary travel to Cuba by U.S. citizens—technically, Americans without permits are not allowed to spend money in Cuba, and the Bush administration has recently increased enforcement against Americans traveling there, typically fines. That said, tens of thousands of

Americans travel to Cuba every year, a large share of them via Cancún. Most Cancún travel agencies sell air tickets to Cuba; you'll be issued a separate paper visa that Cuban officials stamp (instead of your passport) upon arrival. Needless to say, most travelers manage to lose that paper before getting onto a plane back to the States. Remember you won't be able to use any U.S.-based credit cards, debit cards, or travelers checks in Cuba—take plenty of cash as Cuba can be shockingly expensive. Don't count on any help from the U.S. State Department if you have problems.

GETTING AROUND

Bus

Frequent buses (US$.50) run between downtown Cancún and the Zona Hotelera—you'll rarely have to wait more than five minutes for one to pass. These buses are red, new, and have "R-1," "Hoteles," or "Zona Hotelera" printed on the front—you can't miss them. There are 105 stops on the line that drop you off in front of or near major points of interest, including hotels, beaches, the bus station, and ferries to Isla Mujeres. If you are downtown and want to take a bus anywhere but the Zona Hotelera, you can jump on a city bus (US$.35), which are often older, painted white, and have a handwritten list of their destinations on their windshields. If you're in doubt, ask any driver or waiting passenger, *¿Cual camión va a _____?* (Which bus goes to_____?); bus drivers are typically very helpful.

Taxi

You'll have no trouble finding a taxi around town or in the Zona Hotelera—these white and green cars are everywhere tourists are. Before getting into one, however, make sure to agree upon a price—meters are often not used and drivers occasionally abuse their customers. When we were here, rates around downtown were US$1.15, from downtown to Isla Mujeres ferries were US$1.40, and from downtown to the Zona Hotelera were US$4–16, depending on the destination. Rates within the

Zona Hotelera jump dramatically. The minimum we paid was US$4, while the maximum was US$12.

Rental Car

Renting a car is a great way to see the inland archaeological sites without being part of a huge tour group. It is cheaper to rent in Mérida, but if you plan to go only as far as the nearest sites (Tulum, Cobá, and Chichén Itzá), getting a car for a day or two from Cancún makes sense. A rental also makes exploring the Riviera Maya a little easier, though buses cover that route fairly well. Driving in the Cancún area is relatively pain-free—unexpected speed bumps and impatient bus drivers are your biggest concern. It takes four hours to cover the 320 kilometers (198.8 miles) to Mérida on the old highway, a scenic drive that passes through many small villages; Pisté and the Chichén Itzá ruins are about halfway. The new highway cuts 30–60 minutes off the total drive, but the tolls are quite steep (US$20 to Chichén Itzá and US$25 to Mérida). For now there are no tolls to Tulum (about two hours), but a new highway is being built piece by piece and may be a toll road when completed.

Car rentals are available at the airport, many, hotels and small agencies downtown on Avenida Tulum and Avenida Uxmal, and scattered along Boulevard Kukulcán in the Zona Hotelera. Most rent all sorts and sizes of cars, from SUVs to Volkswagen bugs (optimistically dubbed VW "sedans"); prices with insurance and taxes start at around US$50/day. The best rates are usually with online reservations, though some of the small agencies offer great deals when business is slow. You also can get discounted rates if you can handle spending half a day in a time-share presentation. Car-rental agencies include: **Advantage** (Av. Uxmal 20, tel. 998/884-9931, www.advantagecancun.com, advantagecancun@hotmail .com); **Alamo** (Condominios Salbia, tel. 998/883-3621, Blvd. Kukulcán Km. 9.5 or tel. 998/886-0168 at airport, www.alamocancun.com); **Avicar** (Azucenas 1, tel. 998/884-9635, www.avicar.com); **Budget** (Av. Tulum

231 at Av. Labná, tel. 998/884-6955 or tel. 998/886-0417 at airport, www.budgetcancun .com); **Europcar** (Blvd. Kukulcán Km. 13.5, tel. 998/885-0483 or tel. 998/886-0902 at the airport); **National** (airport only, tel. 998/886-0152); **Thrifty** (Sheraton Hotel in Zona Hotelera, tel. 998/891-4400 or tel. 998/886-0333 at the airport); **VIP Rent-A-Car** (airport only, tel. 998/886-2391, www.viprentacar.com); **Zipp Rent-A-Car** (Blvd. Kukulcán Km. 4 across from El Elbarcadero, tel. 998/849-4193,

or Avalon Grand Hotel, Blvd. Kukulcán Km. 11.5, tel. 998/848-9350, www.zipp.com.mx).

Moped

Under small white tents in front of the Carisa and Marriott hotels, **SunBike** (Blvd. Kukulcán Km. 9.5 and 14.5 respectively, tel. 998/885-3909, ext. 113, 9 A.M.–7 P.M. daily) rents scooters at prices ranging from US$15 per hour to US$60 per 24 hours. Helmets are included but gas isn't. Test a couple before you choose one.

Isla Mujeres

Just 15 minutes away by ferry from the hustle of Cancún is the island of Isla Mujeres. Small in size—eight kilometers (five miles) long and 400 meters (1,312 feet) at its widest point—it has shallow turquoise waters and fine white sand beaches that you can lounge on for hours. Isla Mujeres also is on a healthy reef—the second longest in the world—which makes for good diving and snorkeling opportunities. It's an island in slow transition, though: Once a fishing village, it became a backpackers' haven a decade ago and is now moving toward higher-end travelers. While this has certainly increased the price of accommodations (as well as the number of T-shirt shops, golf carts, and tour operators), it has yet to rock the core of this tropical island. It's still a mellow place. Locals will greet you as they pass, people stroll in the middle of streets, and many businesses close for long lunches. Stay a few days and you'll find it'll be hard to leave; the pace gets into your bones. And you'll see that as soon as you step onto the ferry, you'll start thinking of ways to come back again.

HISTORY

The history behind the name Isla Mujeres (Island of Women) varies depending on whom you ask or what book you happen to open. One version is that pirates who trolled these waters kept their female captives here while they ransacked boats on the high seas. The other story is that

when the Spaniards—ransackers of a different ilk—arrived they found a large number of female-shaped clay idols and named the island after them. The latter is the more likely story, and the one to which most archaeologists subscribe. It is thought that the idols were left behind by the Mayans using the island as a stopover on their pilgrimages to Cozumel to worship Ix Chel, the female goddess of fertility.

SIGHTS

The town of Isla Mujeres (known as the *centro* or center) is at the far northwestern tip of the island, and at just eight blocks long and five blocks deep, it's very walkable. This is where most of the hotels, restaurants, shops, and services are. There is no real "main" street, though Avenida Matamoros is notable for its bohemian shops and atmosphere, while Avenida Hidalgo has a busy pedestrian-only section and intersects with the town *zócalo* (main plaza) and city hall. Avenida Rueda Medina is a busy street that runs along the south side of the *centro*—most ferries dock at one of three piers here—and continues all the way to the island's other end, becoming Carretera Punta Sur at Parque Garrafón (for that reason it is also known as Carretera Garrafón). If you are staying in town and traveling light, you should be able to walk to your hotel; otherwise taxis queue up along Avenida Rueda Medina close to the piers. A ride in town costs around US$1,

ISLA MUJERES

SEE "DOWNTOWN
ISLA MUJERES" MAP

PLAYA
NORTE

Caribbean

Sea

NAVY DOCK

Car ferry to
Cancún
(Punta Sam)

CAR
FERRY
PIER

LIGHTHOUSE

Bahia

de Isla

Passenger ferries
to Cancún (Puerto
Juárez and the
Zona Hotelera)

Mujeres

Islote
Tiburon

*Salina
Chico*

DOLPHIN DISCOVERY
HOTEL VILLA ROLANDI

ZAMA

*Laguna
Makax*

VILLAS HI NA HA

Salina

Grande

Playa México

TORTUGRANJA
TURTLE FARM

HACIENDA MUNDACA

Playa Paraiso

Playa Lancheros

AV. GUSTAVO RUEDA MEDINA

CASA TIKINIXIK

INDIOS

Playa Indios

CASA O'S

CASA DE LOS SUEÑOS RESORT

GARRAFÓN DE CASTILLA
HOTEL AND BEACH CLUB

PARQUE
GARRAFÓN

LIGHTHOUSE

IX CHEL

0		1 mi

0		1 km

to spots down-island it's US$2–4, depending on how far south you go.

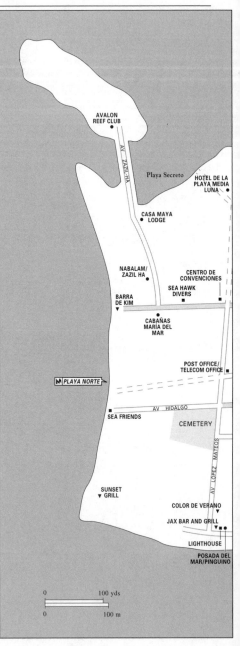 Playa Norte

The closest downtown beach—and arguably the most beautiful on the island—is Playa Norte. It runs the width of the island on the northernmost edge of town. Here you'll find people sunning themselves on colorful beach towels, sipping margaritas at beachside restaurants, and relaxing under huge umbrellas. You'll also find plenty of people playing in the calm turquoise sea that is so shallow you can wade 35 meters (115 feet) and still be only waist deep. If you are in the mood for some activity, head to the middle of the beach where a small white structure housing **Water Sports Playa Norte** (end of Av. Guerrero at Playa Norte, 9 A.M.–5 P.M. daily) begrudgingly rents the following beach toys: snorkel gear (US$9/day), paddleboats (US$13/half hour), huge beach tricycle (US$13/half hour), windsurfs (US$17/hour), Hobie Cats (US$35/hour), and personal watercraft (US$48/half hour). Windsurfing lessons are offered as well—ask about prices if you're interested. Farther west along Playa Norte, **Sea Friends** also rents personal watercraft (US$50/half hour), kayaks (US$12/half hour), paddleboats (US$12/half hour), and beach chairs and umbrellas (US$6.50/day for set).

Other Beaches

Around the northeastern bend of Playa Norte in front of the Casa Maya bungalows, **Playa Secreto** is a great place for young children. It is a small beach with calm and shallow waters and no boats. While there are no amenities on the beach, Playa Norte's services are steps away.

At the south end of the island, on the main road heading out of the *centro,* **Playa Lancheros** awaits you. A rustic beach, it affords incredible views over the Caribbean to Cancún. The fantastic restaurant **Casa Tikinxik** (11 A.M.–6 P.M. daily, US$5–8) is the only amenity on-site, which allows the beach to retain a sense of what it once was: a serene hideaway for giant sea turtles. Today, Playa Lancheros can get rowdy, especially on weekends when Cancúnenses and foreign tourists come over for the day, but it's

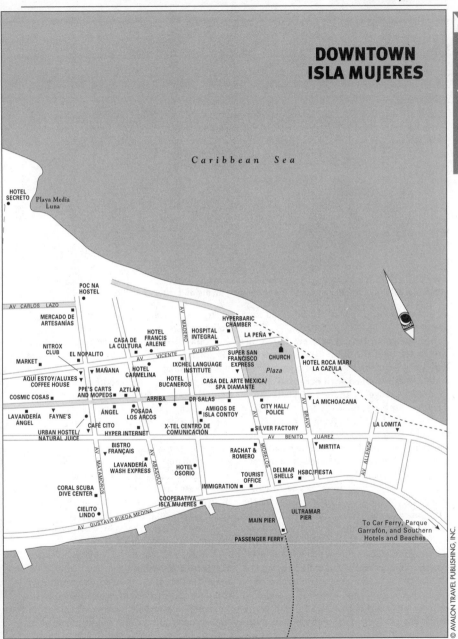

DOWNTOWN ISLA MUJERES

Caribbean Sea

HOTEL SECRETO

Playa Media Luna

POC NA HOSTEL

AV CARLOS LAZO

MERCADO DE ARTESANÍAS

NITROX CLUB

EL NOPALITO

CASA DE LA CULTURA

HOTEL FRANCIS ARLENE

HOSPITAL INTEGRAL

HYPERBARIC CHAMBER

LA PEÑA

AV MADERO

MARKET

AQUÍ ESTOY/ALUXES COFFEE HOUSE

MAÑANA

HOTEL CARMELINA

AV VICENTE

GUERRERO

IXCHEL LANGUAGE INSTITUTE

SUPER SAN FRANCISCO EXPRESS

CHURCH

HOTEL ROCA MAR/ LA CAZULA

Plaza

COSMIC COSAS

PPE'S CARTS AND MOPEDS

AZTLÁN

HOTEL BUCANEROS

ARRIBA

DR SALAS

CASA DEL ARTE MEXICA/ SPA DIAMANTE

LAVANDERÍA ÁNGEL

FAYNE'S

ÁNGEL

POSADA LOS ARCOS

AMIGOS DE ISLA CONTOY

CITY HALL/ POLICE

LA MICHOACANA

URBAN HOSTEL/ NATURAL JUICE

CAFÉ CITO

HYPER INTERNET

X-TEL CENTRO DE COMUNICACIÓN

SILVER FACTORY

AV BRAVO

LA LOMITA

AV BENITO JUAREZ

BISTRO FRANÇAIS

LAVANDERÍA WASH EXPRESS

AV ABASOLO

HOTEL OSORIO

RACHAT & ROMERO

MORELOS

MIRTITA

AV ALLENDE

CORAL SCUBA DIVE CENTER

AV MATAMOROS

TOURIST OFFICE

DELMAR SHELLS

HSBC/FIESTA

IMMIGRATION

CIELITO LINDO

COOPERATIVA ISLA MUJERES

AV GUSTAVO RUEDA MEDINA

ULTRAMAR PIER

To Car Ferry, Parque Garrafón, and Southern Hotels and Beaches

MAIN PIER

PASSENGER FERRY

© LIZA PRADO CHANDLER

Isla Mujeres' Playa Norte is a popular spot among locals and travelers alike.

well worth a visit if you're on the island for a few days.

Just south, **Indio's** (Carretera Punta Sur Km. 5, tel. 998/877-0699, 10 A.M.–3:30 P.M. daily) is a beach club on—you got it—Playa Indios. It is equipped with oceanside chairs, hammocks, kayaks, and a volleyball court. Travelers are free to use the facilities as long as they order food or beverages from the restaurant (US$5–8). There is also a captive (and somewhat depressed-looking) nurse shark that guests are free to swim with for 10 minutes at a time. Like all nurse sharks, it's harmless. Note: Aqua World uses the facilities as a base for day-trippers from Cancún, which can render the club somewhat of a scene.

A kilometer (0.6 mile) farther south, **Garrafón de Castilla Hotel and Beach Club** (Carretera Punta Sur Km. 6, tel. 998/877-0107, hotelgarrafondecastilla@hotmail.com, 9 A.M.–5 P.M. daily, US$3) offers a small beach, comfy chairs to lounge on, and the ocean to swim in. In fact, rent snorkel gear (US$5) and you're free to explore the reef in front of it too, which it happens to share with its hyped neighbor, Parque Garrafón. Showers, changing rooms,

lockers, towels, and a restaurant are also available to guests.

Zama (Carretera Sac Bajo, near Hotel Villas Rolandi, tel. 998/877-0739, 10 A.M.–6 P.M. daily) is a small, very pleasant beach club and spa on the island's calm southwest shore. You can relax in a comfy beach-bed on the large clean beach, or in a hammock in the shady garden. The water here has a fair amount of seagrass, but you can always swim from the pier or in one of the two midsized pools—there's even an infinity whirlpool tub. And it's all free, amazingly enough, if you eat at the small outdoor restaurant (US$5–12, drinks US$1.50–3). An on-site spa offers massage (US$80/90 regular/deep, 50 min.) and facials (US$70, 50 min.); call or ask at the bar at least one hour in advance for an appointment.

Hacienda Mundaca

In the middle of the 19th century, a wealthy former slave trader named Mundaca arrived on Isla Mujeres and promptly fell in love with a local young woman. He set out to build a castle for his queen: a hacienda with gardens, stone pathways, and even a couple of cannons. The girl did not return his affection—in fact she married another islander before the hacienda was completed—leaving Mundaca despondent and, increasingly, a bit crazy. Before he died he was known as being combative and reclusive, often leaving his crops and animals to wither and die rather than allowing the locals to make use of them. The hacienda fell into deep decay, which is basically the state you'll find it in now. There is a sad little "zoo" and some reasonably pleasant paths (bring bug repellent), along with the unimpressive main residence. To get there, take a cab (US$2) or catch the bus; you can also bike there fairly easily. (You'll find it at Av. Rueda Medina at Carretera Sac Bajo, 9 A.M.–4 P.M. daily, US$1.)

Tortugranja Turtle Farm

The **Instituto Nacional de la Pesca** (Carretera Sac Bajo Km. 5, tel. 998/877-0595, 10 A.M.–5 P.M. daily, US$2) houses a low-key, no-frills sea turtle sanctuary on the beach just south of the Hotel Villa Rolandi. During the nesting season, one section of sand is fenced off as the hatchery, where the turtles dig their nests and lay their eggs. Eggs are collected from their nests and put into protected incubation pens. After they hatch, the baby turtles are placed in three large pools to live in until they are at least a year old and can be safely released into the sea. A holding area in the sea is netted to keep adult turtles close by and within easy reach of the hatchery beach for the summer. This ensures they will come to *this* shore to lay their eggs under the watchful eye of marine biologists. Once the laying season is over, the adult turtles are released back to the open sea. Rickety walkways have been built around these holding areas, so that visitors can look at the turtles swimming in the ocean. On the grounds you'll find restrooms and a gift shop (proceeds from sales and admissions go toward the care of the turtles). There is also a modest aquarium (renovated in 2005) where visitors can touch and handle sea creatures native to the area.

Dolphin Discovery

Dolphin Discovery (Carretera Sac Bajo, just past Hotel Villas Rolandi, Isla Mujeres tel. 998/877-0875, Cancún tel. 998/849-4748, toll-free Mex. tel. 800/713-8862, www.dolphindiscovery.com) offers the area's best dolphin experience. The Royal Swim program (US$125; 30-minute orientation, 30 minutes in water) is the most interactive, with two dolphins per group of eight people doing a "dorsal tow," "footpush," and "kiss," plus some free swim time. Other options are the Swim Adventure (US$99 adult/child) and Dolphin Encounter (US$69/64). You can also snorkel in a pool of manta rays and on the outside of see-through shark cage (US$15; one-hour total), and the site has a shop, eatery, and lockers. Most people come from Cancún, either on Dolphin Discovery's private ferry or on an all-day cruise/dolphin package—(see the *Cancún* section for details). Oddly, there is no Dolphin Discovery kiosk in Isla Mujeres *centro,* but most hotels can arrange your visit or you can just go yourself. Taxi fare is US$6; call ahead for reservations and to be sure what time the program you want is starting. Dolphin Discovery also has locations in Cozumel (tel. 800/627-3503) and Puerta Aventuras (tel. 984/873-5078), which have additional interactive programs with sea lions and manatees US$59–179, plus scuba diving with dolphins (US$165 certified divers, US$195 noncertified divers; 35 minutes); see those sections for details.

Parque Garrafón

Promoted as one of the best water activities parks in the Riviera, Parque Garrafón (Carretera Punta Sur Km. 6, tel. 998/849-4950, 9 A.M.–5 P.M. daily, US$29 adults, US$14.50 children; entrance plus one meal US$49 adults, US$24.50 children; all-inclusive US$59 adults, US$29.50 children) falls short. While visitors do have a variety of activities to choose from—snorkeling, kayaking, snubaing, or just hanging out by the pool—it's hard to mask the damaged reef. (For more details, see *The Riviera's Ecoparks* in the *Playa del Carmen* section.)

Ix Chel Ruins and Sculpture Garden

At the southern tip of the island, a crumbling ancient Mayan temple stands guard on a cliff overlooking the sea. Thought to be dedicated to the goddess Ix Chel, who was sacred to Mayan women as the goddess of the moon, fertility, weaving, and childbirth, the ruins were likely a pilgrimage site but may have also doubled as an observation post (for invading people or storms) or as an astronomical observatory. In any case, they were long since abandoned by 1517, when Francisco Hernández de Córdoba became the first European to report their existence. By themselves, the ruins aren't too exciting—hurricanes have all but destroyed them—but a visit here also includes stopping in a tiny museum, climbing a renovated lighthouse, and enjoying the sculpture garden—a dozen or so multicolored metal sculptures lining the path to the ruins. Just past the ruins, the trail continues to the very tip of the island— the easternmost point of Mexico actually—before looping back along the craggy waterfront to the entrance. A decent side trip, especially if you have a golf cart at your disposal.

Admission to the site is included in the ticket price to Parque Garrafón; all others must pay US$2.50 (open 7 A.M.–8 P.M. daily). There is also a kitschy Caribbean "village" with shops and a restaurant. No buses go there, unfortunately. By moped or golf cart, continue south on the main road past Parque Garrafón. The road bends and you'll see the lighthouse down a small dead-end road.

Scenic Views

Like the one in Cancún, **La Torre Escénica** (Carretera Punta Sur Km. 6, 9 A.M.–5 P.M. daily, US$9 adults, US$4.50 children 12 and under) is a tall tower with a rotating passenger cabin, affording a spectacular view of Isla Mujeres and Cancún's coastline. It's just a pity the tower itself is such an eyesore.

Two **lighthouses** also afford decent views: The one on the north end of Avenida Rueda Medina (near Jax restaurant and bar) is easy to get to, while the one at the southern end of the island (at the Mayan Ruins and Sculpture Garden) has a better view. Both are free.

Isla Contoy

Bird and nature lovers especially will enjoy a trip to Isla Contoy, a national bird sanctuary

sculpture garden on the southern tip of Isla Mujeres

© LIZA PRADO CHANDLER

24 kilometers (14 miles) north of Isla Mujeres. Surrounded by crystal-clear water, Contoy's saltwater lagoons, mangrove trees, and coconut palms make this a perfect home to more than 100 species of birds: herons, brown pelicans, frigates, and cormorants are among those most seen. In the summertime, you might also catch a glimpse of a sea turtle or two, when many come to lay their eggs. The island's only structures are a three-story viewing tower and a visitors center, which houses a small museum. The rest of the island is lush tropical jungle that is accessible by hiking trails and the beach. Visitors to the sanctuary, recently reopened to the public, are limited to 200 per day to protect the local ecology.

Isla Mujeres has lots of tour operators that offer the same basic trip to Isla Contoy for approximately US$40: continental breakfast at the office between 8:30 and 9 A.M., a departure shortly thereafter with beer and nonalcoholic drinks served on the boat trip, snorkeling on a reef a few minutes before arriving at Contoy, a tour of the island on foot, including a trip to the museum and observation tower while lunch is prepared on the beach, barbecued chicken and (freshly caught) fish, rice, salad, guacamole, and (more) beer and nonalcoholic drinks are served in the early afternoon. Afterward sunbathing, swimming, snorkeling, and general exploring are encouraged before the return boat trip at approximately 4 P.M. What typically distinguishes one trip from another are the size of the boat, the number of tourists taken on each tour, the knowledge of the guide who takes you, the quality of the food, and whether there is an open bar. That's all good—but how do you choose the best outfit for you? Easy! Check out the following agencies that have been set up specifically to help you decide:

Amigos de Isla Contoy (Madero 8, 10 A.M.–3 P.M. daily) works with two groups of tour operators: the Isla Mujeres and Isla Bonita cooperatives. It has the specific details on each operator that it is affiliated with and can direct you to the best tour for you. Captain Tony García, a one-man operation and member of the Isla Mujeres Cooperative, is a popular choice because of his 20 years' experience and his sta-

tus as the local photo-historian. Amigos de Contoy also doles out information on snorkeling and fishing trips.

Isla Travel (Hidalgo 15, tel. 998/877-0845, islatravel@hotmail.com, 9 A.M.– 2 P.M. and 4–7 P.M. Mon.–Fri., 9 A.M.– 4 P.M. Sat.) is a good option too—agents are familiar with all the outfits that go to Isla Contoy. Stop by and let them know what you are looking for and they should be able to book one that you will like.

ENTERTAINMENT
Bars
On the main plaza, **La Peña** (Av. Guerrero at Av. Bravo, tel. 998/845-7384, iguanadel@yahoo .com, 7 P.M.–3 A.M. daily, drinks US$2–3) is a hipster beach bar without the attitude, featuring unique and mammoth *roble* (a tropical wood) chairs imported from Thailand. Like the furniture, it's a huge and fascinating place that you can get lost in. The back deck offers swings that overlook the ocean while the front room has shutters that transform into tables. It's a must-see. The place gets going after 12:30 A.M.

Om (Matamoros 30, 7 P.M.–1:30 A.M. Mon.–Sat., drinks US$1–3) is a bohemian-urbanesque bar with cool tunes, dim lighting, and seating mostly on the floor and a single couch. Three low tables feature beer taps: Customers request the type of beer they want hooked up and the bar measures the keg for consumption at the end of the night. Try the house specialty—*la viuda express*—which includes a shot of espresso, tequila, Baileys, Kahlua, and a little sugar to kick the night off.

Overlooking Playa Norte, **Barra de Kim** (Av. Carlos Lazo at Playa Norte, 9 A.M.–1 A.M. daily, drinks US$2–3) is a fun beach bar, with swings surrounding the bar, shells and buoys serving as decor, and hammocks well within reach. Happy hour runs 2–5 P.M. daily and features two-for-one beers and cocktails.

Live Music
The Texan-owned **Jax Bar and Grill** (Av. Lopez Mateos at Av. Rueda Medina, tel. 998/877-1218, thomcorp@hotmail.com, 10 A.M.–2 A.M.

daily, drinks US$1–3) is known as a yacht crew hangout. Nightly live music—mostly country and blues—fills the air 9–11 P.M. and partying continues until late into the night. Check out the T-shirts that line the walls from the crews that have stopped in. Breakfast and great burgers (US$4–7) are also served until 9:30 P.M.

Fayne's (Hidalgo 12, tel. 998/877-0528, adelitafaynes@isla.com, www.adelitafaynes. tourguide.net, 5 P.M.–midnight daily, no cover, drinks US$1.50–3.50, food US$7–13) is a popular spot to listen to live music 9 P.M.–midnight daily. Music featured includes rock, salsa, and reggae. Food is also served and includes seafood, chicken, and pasta dishes.

Discotheques

Nitrox Club (Guerrero 11, 10 P.M.–4 A.M. Tues.–Sun., no cover) is the only dance club downtown and features mostly techno, although sometimes reggae and Latin dance music are played. Unfortunately, it has a tiny dance floor and, in places, smells like vomit. If you're desperate to dance and don't want to go over the bridge to Avalon's club, this is your best bet.

Cast Away (Avalon Reef, Calle Zahil Ha s/n, tel. 998/999-2050, 9 P.M.–2 A.M. daily) is a small bar and dance club just across the bridge to the Avalon resort, open to guests and nonguests alike. There is no cover; nonguests pay for consumption.

SHOPPING

As soon as you step off of the ferry, you will be bombarded with visions of kitschy souvenirs, flimsy postcards, and cheap T-shirts. Don't be discouraged! Isla Mujeres has a burgeoning market of specialty stores, most of which showcase the talents of local and nationwide artists alike. Below are the main trailblazers:

A jewel hidden in a street of T-shirt shops, **Aztlán** (Hidalgo at Abasolo, tel. 998/887-0419, aztlancaribe@hotmail.com, 10 A.M.–9 P.M. Mon.–Sat.; credit cards accepted) specializes in Mexican masks brought from every corner of the country. The owners, Ana Lidia and Juan

© LIZA PRADO CHANDLER

Aztlán, a shop on Isla Mujeres, has an incredible variety of masks from around Mexico.

Carlos, also make interesting religious items that fill one corner of the small shop.

Across the street, **Ángel** (Av. Hidalgo at Av. Abasolo, 1–10 P.M. Mon.–Sat., credit cards accepted) offers high-end handicrafts from throughout the country—woodwork, textiles, pottery, and jewelry are among the amazing works you'll find in this store.

Casa del Arte Mexica (Hidalgo 6, tel. 998/877-1432, 10 A.M.–8 P.M. daily) specializes in indigenous art from Chiapas and Oaxaca. It also sells incredible batik work made by islanders.

Rachat and Romero (Av. Juárez at Av. Morelos, tel. 998/877-0331, vcaimu@prodigy.net. mx, 9:30 A.M.–5:30 P.M. Mon.–Sat., 12:30–5 P.M. Sun., credit cards accepted) is an elegant jewelry store featuring certified gold works of art. If you're interested in silver, go across the street to its affiliate, **The Silver Factory,** which sells jewelry by the gram.

Delmar Shells (Av. Morelos at Av. Rueda Medina, tel. 998/887-0114, 10 A.M.–6 P.M. daily, credit cards accepted) specializes in pearls, coral, and other jewelry from the sea. It also sells unique and beautiful shells from Mexico and the Philippines.

In the market for decent diving, snorkeling, or fishing gear? Try **Bahía Dive Shop** (Av. Rueda Medina 166, tel. 998/877-0340, bahiaislamujeres@hotmail.com, 9 A.M.–8 P.M. Mon.–Sat., 9 A.M.–2 P.M. Sun.), which has a wide—if somewhat pricey—range of equipment, including flippers, masks, spear guns, and tackle. Visa and MasterCard are accepted.

Located in Mañana café, **Cosmic Cosas** (Av. Matamoros at Av. Guerrero, 998/877-1501, 9 A.M.–6 P.M. Tues.–Sat.) has long been one of the best English-language bookstores in the area (Cancún included). You can buy, sell, and trade a wide variety of books, from trashy romance novels to Mayan history books (and a few guidebooks thrown in for good measure). It changed location in 2004 only to be nearly destroyed by a fire, which began in a nearby bar. Its new location is smaller than before, but the selection is still excellent.

SPORTS AND RECREATION
Snorkeling and Scuba Diving
There is something for everyone who wants to explore Isla Mujeres underwater. It is on a healthy reef with lots of shallow (7–10 meters/23–32.8 feet), calm areas on its western side, making it good for snorkelers and beginner divers. Its eastern side has deeper (up to 40 meters/131.2 feet), faster waters (with a couple of shipwrecks to boot!), which is fun for more advanced divers. Snorkelers will soon find that tours hit the same sites: **Lighthouse** (by the ferry piers) and **Manchones** (off the southern end of the island). Despite the popularity of the sites, the fish and coral are still in good shape—you're sure to get an eyeful. You can also go to **Garrafón** or **Garrafón de Castilla** (see *Beaches*), which share a reef that is somewhat damaged but still good for spotting some fish.

Divers have a bunch of sites to choose from—30, in fact. Popular ones include **La Bandera** (a reef dive), **La Media Luna** (a drift dive), **Ultrafreeze** (a shipwreck), and the famous **Sleeping Shark Cave**—a deep cave that once teemed with sharks in a strangely lethargic and non-aggressive state. The reason behind this phenomenon varies by the teller: salinity of the water, low carbon dioxide, or the flow of the water. Unfortunately, today there is only a 30–50 percent chance of seeing these sharks—they were disturbed too often and also fished out. Some dive instructors say the chances of seeing the sharks increase in September, but you'll always find someone to disagree with that.

There are a handful of dive operations on the island. The ones listed below are recommended and cater to both snorkelers and divers. Snorkelers can also sign up for a trip with the same operators that go to Isla Contoy—snorkel trips typically cost US$25 and last 2–3 hours.

At the end of Avenida Hidalgo on Playa Norte, **Sea Friends** (Playa Norte, tel. 998/860-1589, seafriendsisla@yahoo.com.mx, 8 A.M.–5 P.M. daily) is a professional and welcoming shop that has been in operation since 1974. It offers small groups—six or fewer—and most dives are led by instructors rather than dive masters. Its instructors are certified by PADI, MDEA, NAVI, and SSI. Divers can choose one-tank reef dives (US$45), sleeping shark cave dives (US$59), wreck dives (US$98), twilight dives ($59), and night dives (US$45). Add US$10 for equipment rental. Ask about four-, six-, and eight-dive packages. Sea Friends also offers training: Beginners can take resort courses (US$65) or an open-water certification course (US$340) and certified divers can take an advanced open-water course (US$250). Referrals (US$175) are also available for those travelers who want to complete their training on the island. Travelers checks and cash only.

Sea Hawk Divers (Av. Carlos Lazo at Av. Lopez Mateos, tel. 998/877-1233, seahawkdivers@hotmail.com, www.sea-hawk-divers.islamujeres.info, 9 A.M.–10 P.M. daily) is a highly recommended dive shop owned and run by Ariel Barandica, a PADI-certified instructor. Service is friendly, professional, and geared toward groups of six or fewer. Divers can choose from the wide variety of dive sites around Isla Mujeres: A one-tank dive costs US$35 and two-tank dives run US$50. Add US$10 for equipment rental in either case. The sleeping shark cave and deep dives run a little higher—be sure to ask about current rates. A resort course including theory, confined water exercises, and a shallow dive also is offered for US$85.

Employing three instructors and owning four boats, **Coral Scuba Dive Center** (Matamoros 13-A, tel. 998/877-0763, www.coralscubadivecenter.com, 9 A.M.–10 P.M. daily) is recognized as the biggest dive operation on the island. While this PADI resort is certainly bigger, it isn't necessarily better: Boats typically carry 12–14 divers at a time and dive masters, instead of instructors, often guide dives of six to seven divers each. While diving with Coral can take on a party feel, the success of the dive shop is testimony to happy customers. Equipment is in top condition, prices are lower, and a variety of options are offered: one-tank reef dives (US$29), two-tank reef dives (US$39), three types of adventure dives (US$59), and twilight dives (US$59). Add US$10 for equipment rental. Dive packages of four (US$74), six (US$115), and eight (US$150) are also offered. Add a one-time fee of US$15 for equipment per package. PADI courses, including discovery, open-water certification, and specialty courses also are offered.

Sportfishing

Two fishermen's cooperatives, Cooperativa Isla Bonita (at UltraMar pier) and Cooperativa Isla Mujeres (at Av. Madero pier) offer sport fishing, or *pesca deportiva*. Boats carry up to six people for the same price, and up to three sorts of trip are usually available, depending on the season: Pesca Mediana (US$175, 4–5 hours) focuses on midsized fish, including snapper, grouper, and barracuda; Pesca Mayor (US$350, eight hours) goes after large catch such as marlin and sailfish; and Pesca Nocturna (US$350, 5–7 hours) is a night-fishing trip in search of deep-sea and bottom fish, including shark

and grouper. Trips with the cooperatives usually do not include food or drink; you can reserve directly at the pier. Alternatively, many dive shops, including Sea Hawk Divers and Sea Friends, offer more all-inclusive trips for slightly higher prices.

Yoga

Yoga classes are offered at **Hotel Nabalam** (Calle Zazil-Ha #118, tel. 998/877-0279) at 9 A.M. every day except Wednesday and Friday, when relaxation classes are held at the same hour. All classes cost US$9 per session. Ask about monthly rates if you plan to stay awhile. They are also offered at **Casa de los Sueños** (Carretera Punta Sur 9, tel. 998/877-0651) by appointment only, US$40 per hour.

Art Classes

The **Casa de la Cultura** (Av. Guerrero at Av. Abasolo, tel. 998/877-0639, 9 A.M.–4 P.M. Mon.–Fri.) is a publicly funded organization that offers artistic workshops that are open to tourists and locals alike. Geared toward children and adolescents, classes include dance, painting, ceramics, and singing and are free.

Massage and Spa Services

In a space renovated in 2004, **Spa Diamante** (Hidalgo 6, tel. 998/877-1432, como estatussalud@hotmail.com, 9 A.M.–10 P.M. daily, cash only) is the only spa in downtown Isla Mujeres. Three certified professionals offer body treatments beginning at US$40, massages ranging US$60–70 per hour, and facial treatments starting at US$65 per hour. The spa also offers haircuts, manicures, pedicures, and waxing. Treat yourself to the natural moor mud antistress body wrap to ease yourself into the island's laid-back rhythm.

Casa de los Sueños (Carretera Punta Sur 9, tel. 998/877-0651, www.casadelossuenosresort.com, 10 A.M.–5 P.M. daily) offers its Feng Shui–inspired Almar Lounge for eight different body relaxations, from a 50-minute back and neck massage (US$99) to an 80-minute hot-stone massage (US$165). Reiki—an emotional energy flow through the hands and body—is also offered for US$110. Facials start at US$105.

ACCOMMODATIONS

Isla Mujeres has a surprising number of places to stay, varying from youth hostels to upscale boutique hotels. Most are concentrated in the *centro,* though a few high-end resorts dot the island's long, southwest-facing shore. In the *centro* you can walk almost everywhere, while staying out of town means renting a golf cart or taking taxis (or else never leaving the hotel grounds, which may be just what you're looking for!).

Under US$50

High-end hotels and Cancún day-trippers aside, Isla Mujeres is still a backpacker's haven, the heart of which is the **Poc Na Hostel** (Av. Matamoros 15, tel. 998/877-0090, www .pocna.com, US$5.50 pp camping, US$7.75–11 pp dorms, US$21–30 s/d, all with continental breakfast). In this large, labyrinthine hostel, dorms (including one for women only) have 4–10 comfy bunks and a small bathroom, while private rooms are simple and roomy—prices vary according to amenities such as fan, air-conditioning, TV, or fridge. The airy common area has food service and Internet, there's a pool table and Foosball room, and there are daily organized activities, from volleyball and chess tournaments to trips to Isla Contoy. The island's best beach is a three-minute walk away. Visa, MC, and AmEx accepted; ask about Spanish and salsa classes.

Just down the street, **Urban Hostel** (Av. Matamoros at Calle Hidalgo, 2nd floor, tel. 984/879-9342, urbanhostel@yahoo.com, dorms US$8 per person, private rooms with shared bath US$17.50–21.50, all with full breakfast) is a smaller, mellower alternative to Poc Na. Two dorm rooms with 6–10 bunks apiece share a bathroom and air conditioner; smallish private rooms are brightly painted cubes with a mattress on the floor. Bathrooms are very clean, and there's a fully equipped kitchen, which Poc Na does not have. The

common area and balcony are nice for people-watching with a cool beer.

If you've outgrown hostels but your wallet hasn't, **Hotel Carmelina** (Av. Guerrero 4, tel. 998/877-0006, US$15.50–17.50 s/d with fan, US$24 s with a/c, US$30 d with a/c) is a good budget choice. The exterior is rather run-down and there's a slight weekly-motel feel (the managers live in a few ground-floor rooms and another room houses a manicure shop), but the rooms are large, clean, and get decent light from the wide breezy corridor.

Posada Isla Mujeres (Av. Juárez 20 at Av. Abasolo, no phone, US$17.50 s/d, US$30 s/d with a/c and TV) is another good deal and less of a scene. Clean, simple rooms are arranged on two narrow corridors—air-conditioned rooms are downstairs and a bit dim, but they have been recently renovated.

Hotel Osorio (Av. Madero at Calle Juárez, tel. 998/877-0294, US$17.50 s/d) has spartan but clean rooms in a good location. Service is rather reluctant and rooms have ceiling fans only (no air-conditioning), but those upstairs open onto an outdoor corridor with decent light and some breezes.

Across from the Hotel Carmelina and a step up in quality, the **Hotel Francis Arlene** (Av. Guerrero 7, tel. 998/877-0310, hfrancis@prodigy.net.mx, www.francisarlene.com, US$35 s/d with fan, US$45 s/d with a/c) has 26 simple, old-fashioned, but immaculately clean rooms, with tile bathrooms and comfy beds. Some have cable TV, refrigerator, coffeemaker, and stove; all open onto a peaceful plant-filled courtyard. Larger, top-floor rooms have ocean views and cost US$60.

US$50–100

Ⓜ Suites Los Arcos (Av. Hidalgo 58, tel. 998/877-1343, suiteslosarcos@hotmail.com, www.suiteslosarcos.com, US$65–70 s/d) is a great deal in this range, offering large, very comfortable rooms with modern bathrooms and wood furniture, and either a king-sized bed or two queens. Better yet, all rooms have a small fridge and microwave for snacks and leftovers. Visa and MC accepted; summer rates are a third lower.

Another option is **Hotel Bucaneros** (Calle Hidalgo 11, tel. 998/877-1222 or toll-free Mex. tel. 800/712-3510, www.bucaneros.com, doubles US$40–55 s/d, with kitchen US$65–72 s/d), with comfortable, well-appointed rooms decorated in earth tones, all with modern bathrooms and air-conditioning. Basic rooms can be a bit stuffy, but the larger rooms, with kitchen, balcony, and a separate dining area, are a decent deal.

In operation since 1958, **Hotel Roca Mar** (Av. Nicolás Bravo at the main plaza, tel. 998/877-0101, rocamar@mjmnet.net, US$75 s/d with fan) is a favorite among returning vacationers. Just a few feet from the Caribbean, it has spectacular ocean views that make up for the somewhat bare rooms. A constant and cool breeze off of the Caribbean also makes air-conditioning unnecessary—just open the windows a little wider if it's too warm inside. A small pool with an adjacent hammock and sunning area gives the place a homey feel. The price, which is high for the goods, reflects the view; three rooms without a view are US$45 s/d. Prices drop by a third in the summer.

Posada del Mar (Av. Rueda Medina 15-A, tel. 998/877-0770, www.posadadelmar.com, US$67–77 s/d) is a friendly, long-time favorite. Spacious, modern rooms have spotless bathrooms, balcony, air-conditioning, and cable TV. Bungalows cost less but are a bit worn. The pool is decent, fed by an attractive stone aqueduct; try a Mayan Sacrifice cocktail at the adjoining bar. The advantage here is the location, across from a pleasant, active beach, where hotel guests have free use of the beach chairs, umbrellas, and kayaks. Pets okay; Visa, MC, and AmEx accepted; summer rates are a third lower.

Casa Maya Lodge (Calle Zazil-Ha 129, tel. 998/877-0045, casyamayalodge@hotmail.com, www.kasamaya.com.mx, US$50–120 s/d) offers wooden, thatch-roof bungalows, varying from simple fan-cooled rooms to "honeymoon" suites with king-sized bed, air-conditioning, and ocean views. There are two fully equipped kitchens, and kid-friendly Playa Secreto and beautiful Playa Norte are both just steps away. The rooms are pretty rustic for the price, but recovering backpackers may find them more appealing than a standard hotel.

For a very homey place, **M Cielito Lindo** (Av. Rueda Medina at Av. Matamoros, tel. 998/877-0585, joyw@prodigy.net.mx, US$70–80 s/d) is a great option. There are just two studio apartments, both charmingly decorated with Mexican bedspreads and artwork, tile floors, shelves of used books, and small kitchens (only one has a stove). Both have air-conditioning and share a balcony overlooking a busy street. The owner, New York transplant Joy Williams Jones, has lived on the island since 1987. Three-day minimum and adults-only preferred. Prices drop US$20 or more in the low season; reservations recommended.

US$100–300

The best hotel in the *centro* is **M Hotel Secreto** (Sección Rocas 11, tel. 998/877-1039, www.hotelsecreto.com, US$165–220 s/d), an angular glass and stucco hotel exuding discreet, understated class. Modern rooms have stone floors, CD players, thick mattresses, and private balconies with excellent ocean views. A curvy infinity pool is surrounded by comfortable deck chairs and overlooks the attractive (though often very rough) Playa Media Luna.

Next door, **Hotel la Playa de Media Luna** (Sección Rocas 9-10, tel. 998/877 0759, www.playamedialuna.com, US$110–200 s/d) offers clean, classic rooms, many with the same excellent ocean view as the Hotel Secreto. Though not as cool as its neighbor—some facilities and decorations are aging a bit—the Media Luna is still one of the *centro*'s top hotels; suites have a large balcony and whirlpool tub, and go for US$150 in the low season.

Right on Playa Norte, **Nabalam** (Calle Zazil-Ha 118, tel. 998/877-0279, www.nabalam.com, US$162–270) used to be one of Isla Mujeres's top hotels and is still one of the most popular. The restaurant and beach area are excellent—worth visiting even if you don't stay here—and there are daily meditation, yoga, and relaxation sessions for guests.

© LIZA PRADO CHANDLER

view from a balcony at Villa Rolandi

(The hotel receives many yoga tour groups.) But the rooms leave something to be desired, especially the garden rooms, which are dreary and not worth the price. Most of those facing the water, especially the suites, have attractive whitewashed walls, stone floors, recessed lights, and (some) private whirlpool tubs. But they need some touching up—what some in Mexico call *una manita de gato,* literally "a little cat's paw." Bare light bulbs, exposed power breakers, and scum in the whirlpool tub aren't the end of the world, but not what you expect for US$200 a night. The good news is the hotel is renovating its units a few at a time.

A half block away, **Cabañas María del Mar** (Av. Carlos Lazo 1 on Playa Norte, tel. 987/877-0179, US$99–121) is also steps from Playa Norte. The hotel has three types of rooms: The cheapest ones are pretty dated and have small bathrooms—there are better options in this range elsewhere. Middle-priced rooms, near the hotel's garden swimming pool, are larger and more comfortable with tile bathrooms and some patio space. The priciest rooms are smallish, but sleek and modern with king-sized beds and good ocean views.

Outside of town, **Villas Hi Na Ha** (Carretera Sac-Bajo No. 55-56, tel. 998/877-0615, villasenisla@prodigy.net.mx, www.villashinaha.com, US$110–$220 plus 12 percent tax) offers seven ample apartments varying from one to two bedrooms, one to three bathrooms, and one to three floors. Each condo has a full kitchen, dining room, and living room and is decorated with traditional Mexican furniture and art. While most of the kitchens are due for an overhaul, the other rooms are in top shape. A pool overlooking the Caribbean and a small beach make up for the somewhat unkempt grounds. Breakfast is included in the rate and is served under a beachside palapa. All-inclusive plans are available upon request.

Over US$300

Ⓜ Hotel Villa Rolandi (Carretera Sac-Bajo No. 15-16, tel. 998/877-0500, www.villarolandi.com, US$290–420 s/d) is one of two gorgeous boutique hotels on Isla Mujeres's calm, southwestern shore. Here, each of 20 suites has a private terrace with whirlpool tub, deep comfortable beds, two-person shower and steam bath, plus robes, slippers, and breakfast and one meal at the hotel's excellent oceanfront restaurant. An attractive infinity pool overlooks a small beach with umbrellas and beach chairs. The hotel can arrange personalized snorkel, scuba, and other activities, and delivers guests to/from Cancún in a private yacht. Visa, MC, and AmEx accepted; no children under 14. A taxi from town costs around US$4.

Casa de los Sueños Resort (Carretera Punta Sur 9, tel. 998/877-0651, www.casadelossuenosresort.com, US$300–550 s/d plus 12 percent tax, depending on season) is even more intimate and isolated. All eight rooms (with names such as "Abundance" and "Harmony") are individually decorated with breathtaking Mexican and international artwork and furniture, and have marble baths, large terraces, and Feng Shui touches such as small gurgling fountains. The hotel has a full spa, with outdoor and private massage areas and a meditation room. A small restaurant serving Mexican-Asian fusion is for guests only—breakfast and one dinner are included. The hotel's only drawback is the somewhat small infinity pool and no beach,

though you can swim from the yacht pier. Visa, MC, and AmEx accepted; adults only.

All-Inclusive

The island's only all-inclusive resort is **Avalon Reef Club** (Calle Zahil Ha s/n, tel. 998/999-2050 or toll-free U.S. tel. 800/261-5014, www.avalonvacations.com, US$225 s standard, US$300 d standard, US$330 s villa, US$440 villa, US$380–508 suites, all meals and drinks included). Perched on a small gusty island off the main island's northwest tip and connected by a wooden bridge, the resort looks nice but is not worth the price. Standard rooms in the main building are very plain; the villas are newer, larger, and better appointed but still nothing to write home about. The pool appears to have been an afterthought, and the beach on the mainland is better. The famous "Baño del Rey" (King's Bath) is an almost perfectly round natural tide pool where you can relax in the water shielded from the waves by high rocks, but it is hardly reason to blow 440 bucks a night.

For weekly rentals, try the apartments at **Color de Verano** (Av. López Ma-

poolside at Casa de los Sueños

teos at Rueda Medina, tel. 998/877-1264, colordeverano@prodigy.net.mx, www.colordeverano.com, one bedroom US$670–750/week, studio penthouse US$800/week). Over a classy boutique café, the apartments are attractive and fully furnished, with full-sized kitchens and large modern bathrooms. All three have air-conditioning and large patios; two have outdoor whirlpool tubs. The studio penthouse is smaller than the one bedrooms (queen bed instead of king) but has a larger terrace and a view of the ocean. Guests also get maid service and have free use of a washer/dryer, bicycles (two per apartment), and the café's Internet terminals.

FOOD

As in Cancún, seafood is the specialty here, much of it caught just offshore and delivered fresh to restaurants daily. The island's popularity among backpackers, especially Europeans, means you'll find a number of modest artsy, bistrolike places—look on Avenida Matamoros especially. You'll also find plenty of reliable mid-priced restaurants serving mostly grilled meat and fish, plus pasta and pizza, and a few high-end places at the top hotels.

Breakfast Places
With tables overlooking the Caribbean, **La Cazuela** (Av. Bravo at Av. Guerrero, 7 A.M.–3 P.M. Tues.–Sun., US$3–6) has one of the best views on the island. Combine that with a hearty breakfast and this is definitely a winner. Daily breakfast specials include Mexican-style eggs, fresh fruit with granola and yogurt, and freshly squeezed OJ.

Café Cito (Matamoros 42, tel. 998/888-0351, cafecito_mexico@yahoo.com, 7 A.M.–2 P.M. Mon.–Sat., 8 A.M.–2 P.M. Sun., US$2–6) is reminiscent of a classic Cape Cod eatery with its breezy blue and white decor and shell-encrusted tables. It's a great breakfast place, offering tasty crepes, waffles, and coffee drinks.

A small eclectic café, **M El Nopalito** (Guerrero 70, tel. 998/877-0555, 8 A.M.–1 P.M. Thurs.–Tues., US$2.50–4) offers tasty breakfasts, featuring homemade bread, granola, muesli, yogurt, and marmalade. Good sandwiches and interesting crepes are also worth a stop. The restaurant and attached folk-art store are owned and run by Anneliese Warren, who speaks English, German, and Spanish and has lived on the island since 1986.

Mexican Seafood
On Playa Lancheros, **M Casa Tikinxik** (11 A.M.–6 P.M. daily, US$5–8) is a classic Mexican beach restaurant, with metal tables, cold beer, and finger-licking portions that make the long wait worth it. Be sure to try the specialty—*pescado tikinxik*—grilled fish with a spicy red sauce, which is prepared in the parking lot by a trio of men.

La Lomita (Av. Juárez Sur 25-B, tel. 998/826-6335, 9 A.M.–11 P.M. Mon.–Sat., US$3.50–4.50), a restaurant frequented by locals, offers standard, solid Mexican fare. *Comida corrida*—a two-course meal with drink—is offered daily for US$3.50 and often includes *chiles rellenos,* tacos, and stews. Ceviche, grilled whole fish, and other seafood meals are also featured at reasonable prices.

With a view of the ocean, Posada Del Mar's **Pinguino** (Rueda Medina 15-A, tel. 998/877-0044, 7 A.M.–11 P.M. daily, US$4–11) is a relaxing place to get a bite to eat. It offers three meals a day: Breakfasts are huge and the chef prepares fabulous lobster and seafood dishes for lunch and dinner. This is an especially good place to watch the sunset.

Italian
M Casa Rolandi at Hotel Villa Rolandi (Carretera Sac-Bajo No. 15-16, tel. 998/877-0500, noon–11 P.M. daily, US$10–20) is one of the best restaurants on the island, even the whole area. With candlelit tables overlooking the calm southwest-facing shore, the restaurant has impeccable service and a creative Italian-Swiss menu. We can vouch for the black fettuccini and pumpkin-stuffed ravioli, and there are plenty of additional pasta, meat, and fish dishes to choose from. The wine and drink selection is large—try a *mojito*, a classic Caribbean drink

Cancún, Mujeres, and Holbox

On laid-back Isla Mujeres, pedestrians take over the streets.

© UZA PRADO CHANDLER

made of rum, lime, sugar, and fresh mint. Rolandi's also has a popular pizzeria in town (Av. Hidalgo between Avs. Abasolo and Madero) and two in Cancún.

Aqui Estoy (Av. Matamoros at Av. Hidalgo, cell tel. 044-998/734-0036, noon–10 P.M. Mon.–Sat., US$1–2.50) is a small pizzeria, offering slices and personal pizzas. Cheese, veggie, and Hawaiian pizzas are typical. Try the specialty—spinach and goat cheese pizza—for a taste treat. Takeout and standing-room only.

French

The preppy café boutique **Color de Verano** (Av. Lopez Mateos at Rueda Medina, tel. 998/877-1264, colordeverano@prodigy.net .mx, www.colordeverano.com, 3–11 P.M. Tues.–Sun., US$4–7) is definitely worth a visit for a light meal, a glass of wine, or a homemade dessert. Specialties include quiche, pâté, and *huitlacoche* crepes. A three-course dinner special is offered nightly for US$11. Three fully furnished apartments also are on the premises for long- and short-term rental.

Ⓜ Bistro Français (Matamoros 29, 8 A.M.–noon and 6–10:30 P.M. daily, breakfast US$2.50–3.50, dinner US$5–15) offers fantastic food in a quirky turquoise room decorated with bright bubble writing, cartoonish drawings, and Mexican hand-painted tiles. French toast is a must for breakfast and *coq au vin* is the specialty in the evening. If vegetables are your thing, the veggie kabob is top-notch and features an unforgettable portabella mushroom.

Vegetarian

Somewhat hidden on a second-story landing, **Arriba** (Hidalgo 12, 2nd floor, tel. 998/877-1333, 3–11 P.M. daily, US$4–15) is a great option for vegetarians and travelers on a tight budget; veggie kabobs, salads, and vegetable tempura are excellent and tasty seafood and chicken meals are all served at reasonable prices. All entrées include a choice of a salad (coleslaw or chef salad) and a starch (sautéed potatoes or Caribbean rice).

Specializing in salads and baguettes, **Mañana** (Av. Matamoros at Av. Guerrero, tel. 998/877-1501, 9 A.M.–6 P.M. Tues.–Sat., US$2–3) is a hip café with outdoor seating, couches inside, and smooth music throughout. Be sure to try its mammoth papaya-banana-strawberry smoothies—they are well worth the US$2.

On the first floor of the Urban Hostel, **Natural Juice** (Av. Matamoros at Av. Hidalgo, 8 A.M.–8 P.M. daily, US$1.50–2.50) is exactly what its name states: a place to buy juices and smoothies made from fruits and veggies such as mango, papaya, melon, kiwi, beets, and carrots. You can also get a great fruit salad to go.

Eclectic

One street below Casa de los Sueños, **Casa O's** (Carretera Garrafón 9, tel. 998/888-0170, www.casaos.com, 1–10 P.M. daily, US$9–20, credit cards accepted) is a romantic palapa restaurant, with tables overlooking the turquoise waters all the way to Cancún. The menu is varied and features some of the finest catches and cuts on the island.

The **Zazil Ha** restaurant, part of the Nabalam hotel, (Calle Zazil-Ha 118, tel. 998/877-0279, 7 A.M.–11 P.M. daily, US$8–14) has great patio eating areas, especially good for watching the sunset. Below, a covered area has a sand floor and low wood tables, which are dressed up in the evening with candles and simple off-white tablecloths. The menu is more than reliable for lunch or dinner, from excellent mixed ceviche and fish tacos to rib-eye steak and tofu-and-veggie skewers, all in generous portions. Get here from along the beach or from Avenida Zazil-Ha.

On Playa Norte, **Sunset Grill** (Av. Rueda Medina, tel. 998/877-0785, sunsetgrill1@prodigy.net.mx, 8:30 A.M.–10 P.M. daily, US$4–12, credit cards accepted) offers a great view with cool music on one of the best beaches on the island. Beachside chairs and umbrellas are also available for the day if you order from the menu. Food is standard—grilled fish, ceviche, and hamburgers—but good. The location is the main reason to come here.

Sweets and Coffeehouses

Frequented mostly by locals, **La Michoacana** (Av. Bravo at Av. Hidalgo, 9 A.M.–10 P.M. daily, US$.60–1.50) offers homemade *aguas, paletas,* and *helados* (juices, popsicles, and ice cream). Choose from seasonal fruits including passion fruit, watermelon, pineapple, and mamey. You can get chocolate- and vanilla-flavored treats too.

Aluxes Coffee House (Matamoros at Hidalgo, 7 A.M.–2 P.M. and 4–10 P.M. daily US$1–2.50) is a great place to hang out with jazz playing in the background, comfy chairs, and simple but beautiful decor. Have a cup of caffeine, nibble on homemade brownies, muffins, and cheesecake, and catch up on your postcards. Milk shakes, ice cream sundaes, and smoothies are also offered.

Groceries

If you want a snack or prefer to cook your own meals, you can find basic foodstuffs in the corner stores that are sprinkled throughout downtown. For a wider selection, however, try the following:

Mirtita (Av. Juárez 14, tel. 998/887-0157, 6 A.M.–9 P.M. Mon.–Sat., 7 A.M.–5 P.M. Sun.) is a grocery store that has been run by the Familia Magaña since 1965. It carries a little bit of everything: fresh meats, dairy products, cereal, canned goods, toiletries, and Tupperware. It also carries some items you might miss from home such as brownie mix, mac and cheese, and even (gasp!) pretzels.

On the northwest side of the main plaza, **Super San Francisco Express** (Av. Morelos, 7 A.M.–10 P.M. Mon.–Sat., 7 A.M.–9 P.M. Sun., Visa and MasterCard accepted) is a chain supermarket offering all the usual suspects: fruits, vegetables, canned goods, toiletries, and so on. Just inside the front door, you'll also find a small pharmacy and an HSBC ATM.

The **Mercado Municipal** (Av. Carlos Lazo at Av. Matamoros, 6 A.M.–4 P.M. daily) is the place to go if you're looking for the freshest fruits and vegetables on the island. There are also a handful of restaurants outside that serve cheap eats.

INFORMATION AND SERVICES
Traveler Assistance

Across from the ferry docks, the **Oficina de Turismo** (Av. Rueda Medina 130, tel.

FERRIES TO ISLA MUJERES

Various passenger ferries and one car ferry to Isla Mujeres leave from Cancún every day. There are myriad boats to choose from—just pick the one that suits your needs best.

Zona Hotelera Passenger Ferries

Barcos Mexicanos (El Embarcadero, Blvd. Kukulcán Km. 4, tel. 998/849-7515, US$15 round-trip, 30 minutes each way). Departure: 9:30 A.M., 11 A.M., 12:30 P.M., and 1:30 P.M. Return: noon, 3:30 P.M. and 5 P.M.

Bluewater Adventures (Playa Tortugas, Blvd. Kukulcán Km. 6.5, tel. 998/849-4444, US$15 round-trip, 20 minutes) drops off passengers at the Avalon Reef Resort. It's farther from the center of town and you may get diverted into an Avalon time-share presentation, but it's closer to the best beach on the island. Departure: 9:45 A.M. and 11:45 A.M. Return: 10:30 A.M. and 5 P.M.

Playa Caracol Ferry (Blvd. Kukulcán Km. 8.5, no phone, US$15 round-trip, 30 minutes each way). Departure: 9 A.M., 11 A.M., and 1 P.M. Return: noon and 5 P.M.

Playa Tortugas Ferry (Blvd. Kukulcán Km. 6.5, tel. 998/849-5015, US$15 round-trip, 30 minutes). Departure: 9:15 A.M., 9:45 A.M., 10:45 A.M., 11:15 A.M., noon, 12:45 P.M., 1:15 P.M., and 1:45 P.M. Return: 10:15 A.M., 11:30 A.M., 2:30 P.M., 3:30 P.M., 5 P.M., and 7 P.M.

Puerto Juárez/Gran Puerto Passenger Ferries

Ferries operating from this pier are faster, more frequent, and cost half as much as in the Zona Hotelera. To get to Puerto Juárez, take the red R-1 bus on Boulevard Kukulcán or on Avenida Tulum in downtown Cancún (US$.50, 20 minutes from downtown). Look for Gran Puerto's tall observation tower; the older pier is a few hundred meters farther. Note: Gran Puerto has a gleaming outdoor waiting area, fast-food operators,

998/877-0307, infoisla@prodigy.net.mx, 8 A.M.– 8 P.M. Mon.–Fri.) offers general information on the island, including hotel, restaurant, and tour information. It also has free brochures, maps, and copies of *Islander,* a twice-yearly magazine with boat schedules, tips, and advertisements.

Isla Travel (Hidalgo 15, tel. 998/877-0845, islatravel@hotmail.com, 9 A.M.– 2 P.M. and 4– 7 P.M. Mon.–Fri., 9 A.M.– 4 P.M. Sat.) is run by islanders who know all the different operators on the island. They can help you organize your vacation by booking any tours you'd like to take on and off Isla Mujeres. Tours booked include snorkeling, diving, and Isla Contoy trips as well as land tours of the island. They can also book trips to Chichén Itzá, Xcaret, and Cuba. Isla Travel is also the only travel agency on the island that sells ADO bus tickets.

An Iowa couple named Laura and Perry produce a fantastic user-friendly **map** of Isla Mu-

jeres. It is extremely detailed, including several professional-quality color maps; annotated listings and reviews of almost every restaurant, hotel, and point of interest on the island; and photos, ferry schedules, and other tips. It may be more than the average visitor needs, but is worth getting if you plan to stay any length of time. It costs US$7 and is available at many restaurants and hotels—we got one at Jax bar. The couple also produces maps of other Riviera Maya areas; get more info at Laura's website, www.mapchick.com.

Medical Services

The only English-speaking doctor on the island, **Dr. Antonio E. Salas** (Hidalgo 18-D, tel. 998/877-0021, 24 hours tel. 998/877-0477, cell tel. 044-998/845-2370, drsalas@prodigy .net.mx, 9 A.M.–9 P.M. daily) is highly recommended by islanders. Dr. Salas is a family-practice physician, works directly with the

a convenience store, and a gift shop. Lockers big enough to store a large backpack also are available (US$4/24 hours) and there's a small money-exchange booth and an Internet/photo shop (tel. 998/843-2386, 9:30 A.M.–7 P.M. daily, Internet US$2.50/hour, CD-burning US$7).

Transportes Marítimos Magaña (Puerto Juárez, tel. 998/884-5479, US$3.50 each way, 15 minutes). Departure: every 30 minutes 6:30 A.M.–11:30 P.M. daily. Return: every 30 minutes 6:30 A.M.–8:30 P.M. daily.

UltraMar (Gran Puerto pier, tel. 998/843-2011, www.granpuerto.com.mx, US$3.50 each way, 15 minutes) boats feature comfy seats in an air-conditioned cabin, an open-air deck, and televisions playing a short promotional program on Isla Mujeres. Departure: every 30 minutes 5:30 A.M.–12:30 A.M. Return: every 30 minutes 6 A.M.–1 A.M.

Punta Sam Vehicle Ferry

This lumbering vehicle ferry takes 45–60 minutes to cross between Punta Sam, on the mainland, and Isla Mujeres. Rates are according to your vehicle: US$16 for cars, $19.50 for SUVs, US$6 motorcycles, and US$5 for bicycles. Rates include the driver only—passengers (including walk-ons) are US$1.25 each way. On Isla Mujeres, the car ferry pier is a few hundred meters south of the passenger piers, past the naval dock. To get to Punta Sam, drive north on Avenida Tulum, turn right on López Portillo and follow it to the pier, about five kilometers (3.1 miles) past Gran Puerto. The red R-1 bus also goes there (US$.50, 30 minutes from downtown). Arrive an hour before your departure to get in line; tickets go on sale 30 minutes prior. Departure: 6:30 A.M., 9:30 A.M., 12:45 P.M., 4:15 P.M., and 7:15 P.M. plus 11:15 A.M. and 4:15 P.M. in high season. Return: 8 A.M., 11 A.M., 2:45 P.M., 5:30 P.M., and 8:30 P.M., plus 1 P.M. and 7 P.M. in high season.

Centro de Salud in town, and has connections at most of Cancún's hospitals. He also speaks basic German.

Hospital Integral Isla Mujeres (Guerrero 7, tel. 998/877-0117, 24 hours daily) is equipped to handle walk-in consultations, simple surgeries, and basic emergencies. In case of a serious injury or illness, patients are taken to a Cancún hospital by boat. Some English is spoken and cash only is accepted.

Isla Mujeres has two **hyberbaric chambers** (*unidades de terapia hiberbárica*) for treating decompression sickness. One is at the naval base, but a more accessible one is on the pedestrian-only extension of Avenida Morelos, just north of the *zócalo* (Dr. Martín Tito Avila Frías, tel. 998/877-0819, 9 A.M.–4 P.M.). Mostly used to treat bent lobster fishermen, who pay monthly dues for the unit's operation and upkeep, the chamber is available to visitors as well for US$130 per 90-minute treatment.

Pharmacies

Farmacia La Mejor (Madero 16, tel. 998/877-0116, 9 A.M.–10:30 P.M. Mon.–Sat., 9 A.M.–3:30 P.M. Sun.) has a fully stocked pharmacy. It also carries film, toiletries, sunscreen, and other personal items. English is spoken.

Farmacia Similares (Juárez 9, tel. 998/877-1245, 9 A.M.–10 P.M. Mon.–Sat., 9 A.M.–9 P.M. Sun.) is a simple pharmacy that is open late on Sunday.

Money

Immediately in front of the ferry docks, **HSBC Bank** (Av. Rueda Medina between Av. Madero and Av. Morelos, tel. 998/877-0005, 8 A.M.–7 P.M. Mon.–Sat.) provides currency-exchange services and has two ATMs that are available 24 hours a day. Another of its ATMs is inside the Super San Francisco Express, which is on the main plaza.

Banamex also services one 24-hour ATM

on the island, in front of the Silver Factory (Av. Juárez at Av. Morelos).

If you need to receive or wire money quickly, **Western Union** has an outpost in the Telecomm/Telegrafos office (Av. Madero, between Av. Guerrero and Av. Hidalgo, tel. 998/877-1368, 8 A.M.–10 P.M. daily).

Post Office

The post office (Av. Guerrero at Av. Lopez Mateos, tel. 998/877-0085) is open 9 A.M.–4 P.M. Mon.–Fri. Cash only.

Telephone and Fax

X-Tel Centro de Comunicación (Av. Madero, between Av. Guerrero and Av. Hidalgo, tel. 998/877-1368, 8 A.M.–10 P.M. daily) offers telephone and fax service. Calling or sending faxes to the United States and Canada costs US$.70 per minute, to Europe US$1.40 per minute, and within Mexico US$.26 per minute. Receiving faxes from any location costs US$.44 per page. Cash only.

Next to the post office, **Telcomm/Telegrafos** (Av. Guerrero at Av. Lopez Mateos, tel. 998/877-0113, 8 A.M.–7:30 P.M. Mon.–Fri., 9 A.M.–12:30 P.M. Sat.) is the official Mexican fax service. Sending to or receiving faxes from the United States and Canada costs US$1.50 per page, to/from Europe US$2.40 per page, and within Mexico US$1.45 per page.

Internet

A smattering of Internet places have popped up around the *centro,* which has helped to bring down the once-exorbitant prices. A couple of reliable and air-conditioned places are listed below but if you see a better price at a comparable place, take it!

IslaMujeres.com (Madero 17, 8 A.M.–10 P.M. daily, US$1.30/hour) offers fast connections and a break from the heat in its small shop.

Hyper Internet (Av. Abasolo, between Av. Hidalgo and Av. Juárez, 9 A.M.–10:15 P.M. Mon.–Sat., 9 A.M.–8:30 P.M. Sun., US$1.60/hour) has reliable connections in a quiet environment. You also can plug in your own laptop, which is especially helpful when you have digi-

tal photos from your tropical vacation that you want to email home.

Laundry

Tucked into Plaza Isla Mujeres, **Lavandería Ángel** (Av. Juárez, Local A3, 8 A.M.–8 P.M. Mon.–Sat., 9 A.M.–noon Sun., cash only) offers the friendliest and cheapest laundry services in town: US$2.60 for four kilos (8.8 pounds) of clothes, US$.90 each additional kilo (2.2 pounds). The price makes the place popular, so be sure to get your clothes in early if you want them back the same day.

Lavandería Wash Express (Abasolo 13, tel. 998/887-0944, 7 A.M.–9 P.M. Mon.–Sat., 7 A.M.–2 P.M. Sun., cash only) offers same-day service, with a three-hour minimum wait. Prices begin at US$3.50 for four kilos (8.8 pounds) of clothes with additional kilos charged in four-kilo increments, regardless if your clothes weigh less. Hammocks (US$3.50), backpacks (US$3.50), sneakers (US$4.40), and sleeping bags (US$6) are also accepted.

Immigration

The immigration office (tel. 998/877-0189, 9 A.M.–3 P.M. Mon.–Fri., 9 A.M.–noon Sat.–Sun.) issues tourist cards to those arriving by boat from another country, but you have to go to Cancún for all other matters, including extending your visa.

Spanish School

Isla Mujeres can be enchanting with its turquoise waters, its laid-back atmosphere, and its welcoming inhabitants. For these reasons, many people—Mexican and foreign alike—choose to extend their stays, sometimes indefinitely. Whether you want to stay for a month or a lifetime, here's an activity that might help you fill the days.

Opened in 2001, **Ixchel Language Institute** (western corner of Av. Madero and Av. Guerrero, cell tel. 044-998/939-5508 or 044-998/939-1218, ixchelinstitute@hotmail.com, www.stormpages.com/ixchel, 11 A.M.–2 P.M. and 5–8 P.M. Mon.–Fri.) is the only Spanish-language school on Isla Mujeres. It is run by two friendly women—one Mexican, the other American—who have more than five years' experience teaching Spanish. The school prides itself on its small class size: one-on-one instruction is typical, although occasionally a class will grow to the maximum of six students. Courses offered include survival Spanish to learn basic phrases and vocabulary for traveling as well as beginning, intermediate, and advanced conversation classes. Costs are reasonable—US$10.50 per hour—and negotiable if you sign up as a couple or with a group. Cash only.

GETTING THERE

Isla Mujeres has a small airstrip but almost everyone takes the ferry—a cheap, fast scenic ride through the gorgeous turquoise Bahía de Mujeres (Bay of Women).

Passenger Ferries

Passenger-only ferries leave for Isla Mujeres from several spots in the Zona Hotelera and from Puerto Juárez, about three kilometers (1.9 miles) north of downtown Cancún. If you are just going for the day, reconfirm the return times and remember the late-night ferries go to Puerto Juárez, not the Zona Hotelera.

Car Ferries

A vehicle ferry operates from Punta Sam, about five kilometers (3.1 miles) north of Puerto Juárez.

GETTING AROUND

Isla Mujeres is a small and mostly flat island. In town you can easily walk everywhere. You could conceivably walk the length of the island, but it's a long, hot walk with no sidewalks. Consider taking the bus or a taxi or—better yet—rent a bike, moped, or golf cart for a little bit more adventure.

Public Bus

The bus is the cheapest way to get around Isla Mujeres—US$.25 a ride. Unfortunately, it runs only between downtown and Playa Lancheros, about halfway down the island. Theoretically it runs every 30 minutes, but be prepared to

© LIZA PRADO CHANDLER

a ferry and catamaran docked at an Isla Mujeres pier

wait from 45 minutes to forever (gas on the island is limited and sometimes runs out—ask at your hotel about the current situation). Bus stops are every couple of blocks on Rueda Medina and Avenida Martínez Ross and are well marked with big blue and white signs—they're hard to miss.

Taxi

Isla Mujeres has many more taxis than seem necessary—in town, you may be more likely to get hit by a cab than have trouble hailing one. They are especially numerous near the piers. Out of town, you shouldn't have to wait too long for a taxi to pass; otherwise, make your way to Garrafón, Dolphin Discovery, or Playa Lancheros, which all have taxi queues. From downtown, rates are US$1.15 to Playa Norte and within the *centro,* US$2 to Playa Lancheros and to the Tortugranja, and US$4 to Parque Garrafón and Punta Sur. You can also get a private driving tour of the island for US$13 per hour.

Bicycle, Golf Cart, and Moped

Most rental operations on the island have fixed rates: golf carts—US$13 per hour, US$39 per day (store hours), and US$48 per 24 hours; mopeds with 50cc/100cc engines—US$7/9 per hour, US$18/22 per day, US$26/30 per 24 hours; and bicycles—US$1.75 per hour, US$7 per day. If you rent for more than three days, try to negotiate a better price; otherwise, these rates are non-negotiable. Some words of warning: Some of the agencies right in front of the docks charge more than those just a few blocks away; also, there are many road accidents, some very serious, involving both tourists and locals driving mopeds—use caution.

Try these: **Cárdenas Motos y Carritos** (Guerrero 105, tel. 998/877-0079, 9 A.M.–5 P.M.daily); **Ppe's Carts and Mopeds** (Hidalgo 19, tel. 998/877-0019, 9 A.M.–5 P.M. daily); and **Fiesta** (Av. Rueda Media 3, next to HSBC, no phone, 8 A.M.–5 P.M. daily).

Isla Holbox

Lying completely within the Yum Balam national reserve, Isla Holbox (ohl-BOASH or hole-BOASH) is one of the last obscure islands in the Yucatán Peninsula, lying off the northeastern tip of Quintana Roo where the Caribbean Sea mingles with the Gulf of Mexico. The town of Holbox is a fishing village (pop. 2,000) with sand roads, golf carts instead of cars, no ATMs, no cell phone service, no hospital, and no post office. Instead you'll find brightly painted homes, palapa-roofed hotels, and a handful of Italian expats. The beaches here are loaded with shells of all sorts but don't have the thick sand and reliably crystalline waters that Cancún has (though they are still awfully nice). In the summer mosquitoes, sand flies, and horseflies can be vicious (come prepared!). Still, Holbox offers a peace and tranquility that are increasingly hard to find in the Yucatán and the feeling of a place as yet untouched by big business. Holbox also offers great opportunities for sportfishing and bird-

watching and from June to September you can snorkel with whale sharks. Whale-shark tours are monitored by the government and environmental groups to protect these creatures from harm. Sea turtles nest on Holbox as well, but tours to see them have been suspended.

HISTORY

Mayans definitely inhabited Holbox but appear to have abandoned the island more than 300 years before the first European arrived. The name of the island and town, long a secret redoubt for wayward pirates, is a matter of some dispute. "Holbox" is reportedly a Mayan term meaning "black water" and one story is that the town's founders settled beside a spring whose water appeared to run black. A more popular story is that a pirate named Francisco de Molas buried a treasure on the island and cut off the head of his African bodyguard to watch over the spot for eternity. De Molas was promptly killed by a snakebite, but the disembodied head of his bodyguard appears occasionally to island residents, evidently trying to divulge the treasure's location but succeeding only in scaring everyone away. By this account, the island was originally called "Pool-box," meaning "black head," and the name was bastardized by subsequent Dutch arrivals.

This much is certain—the original town, located farther west, was destroyed by a hurricane and was rebuilt in the current location about 150 years ago. Storms are serious business on this low, flat island, which is buffeted by tropical storms with some regularity; the most recent hurricane to strike was Isadora in 2002. *Nortes* (Northerns) are fall and winter storms that sweep down the Gulf coast bringing rain and turbid seas. *Maja' che* is the Mayan name for sudden winds that can knock over trees; they are most common in April and May. In major storms, the whole island is evacuated.

Storms, however, have not managed to destroy Holbox's oldest house—a red wooden building with a palapa roof on the north (beach) side of the park. It belongs to Doña Trini, whose father bought it from the original owner almost a century ago. Doña Trini is a well-known hammock weaver; you can knock on the door to see her work or buy one of the finished products (Igualdad in front of the park, tel. 984/875-2262). Most of the town lives by fishing, though, and Holbox has almost 400 fishing boats and several fishing cooperatives. The town holds a land-and-sea parade on April 14 in honor of Saint Thelmo, patron saint of fishermen. Other festivals include Environmental Week (July 1–5), when a group of local residents leads activities and presentations at local schools. Tourists can join the kids in one of the week's biggest events: picking up trash from the beach.

SIGHTS

Island Tours

An island tour is essentially a bird-watching tour with additional stops at Isla de la Pasión (a deserted island just 50 meters/164 feet across) and Yalahau Spring, an *ojo de agua* (literally an "eye of water," meaning a

LIZA PRADO CHANDLER

snorkeling with whale sharks off of Isla Holbox

SEA TURTLES

At one time sea turtles were plentiful and an important supplement to the Mayan diet. Turtles were (and continue to be) easy prey: They were captured and killed as they clambered onto shore to lay eggs. After the hunt, the turtle meat was sun-dried so that it could be eaten over time and the fat saved for soups and stews. The eggs—gathered from the nest or cut from the turtle—were eaten or saved for medicinal purposes.

Today, all species of sea turtles are on the endangered species list. Four of these eight species—hawksbill, Kemp's ridley, green, and loggerhead—nest on the shores of the Yucatán Peninsula. Various environmental protection organizations in the Yucatán have joined forces with the Mexican government to save these ancient creatures; they have developed breeding programs and maintain strict surveillance of known nesting beaches to stop poaching.

It is strictly prohibited to capture and trade sea turtles or their products in Mexico. Do not buy their eggs, meat, or products such as leather, oils, or tortoise-shell combs. By not participating in the trade of turtle products, you will help to promote the protection of these noble sea creatures.

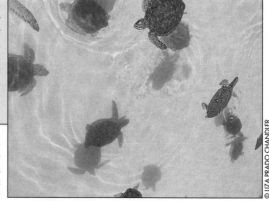
© LIZA PRADO CHANDLER

Various organizations protect sea turtles.

natural spring) on the mainland that was once used by pirates to fill their water barrels but is now a picturesque swimming hole. This tour typically runs around US$20 and lasts three hours.

Whale Shark Feeding Grounds

Whale sharks congregate in shallow waters about 10 miles east of the village from June to September. Snorkeling with whale sharks is a unique and (to some) nerve-wracking experience. The sharks themselves are harmless—like baleen whales, they eat plankton, krill, and other tiny organisms. But they are big—at 20–25 feet and more than 10 tons, they're the biggest fish in the world. The captain pulls the boat alongside a shark (at Holbox they tend to feed on the surface) and two guests and a guide slip into the water with life jacket, mask, snorkel, and fins. The water tends to be murky—it's all the sea life in the water that attracts the sharks in the first place—and the sharks are surprisingly fast. Still, you get a good view of these enormous, gentle animals, with their tiny eyes, bizarre shovel-mouths, and dark spotted skin. It's best to be on a small tour—since you go in two by two, you'll get more time in the water. Tours cost US$80 and typically include snorkel gear, a life preserver, a box lunch, and nonalcoholic beverages. If there is time at the end of the tour, ask to stop off Cabo Catoche for a little snorkeling (see *Snorkeling and Diving*).

Town Beach

The town's main beach, on the island's north shore, has no name but you can't miss it. People kiteboard right off the beach since Holbox's steady winds and shallow, waveless shore make it ideal for wind sports. The strongest winds are September to March, while July and August tend

© LIZA PRADO CHANDLER

a windswept beach on Isla Holbox

with beautifully polished samples from all over the world. The owner—Maestro Lalo—lives below the shop so if you'd like to see his goods, ring the doorbell, and he'll open up.

If you're interested in buying a hammock or just seeing how they're made, wander over to **Doña Trini's** house (Igualdad in front of the park, tel. 984/875-2262). There, Doña Trini makes hammocks in endless colors and varying sizes. She also welcomes onlookers—whether they buy or not—and enjoys talking about her trade and her island. It takes Doña Trini about a month to complete a hammock so she often is steadily working away at one of her creations; if you want to be sure to see her at work, however, give her a call the night before to let her know when you'll be stopping by. Hammocks cost US$44–78, depending on the size and material, and can be custom-ordered.

to have lighter, novice-friendly breezes. Watching the kiteboarders fly high above and come soaring down to the emerald waters is a sight to behold. To try it yourself, see *Sports and Recreation* for information on classes and rentals.

SHOPPING

Arco Iris (Igualdad at Av. Morelos, beso mirosy@hotmail.com, tel. 984/875-2420, 6–10 P.M. Mon.–Sat.) is an artsy shop run by a friendly Swiss expat named Rosy. Most of the items sold are handmade by locals or artists passing through town. Silver jewelry, bohemian clothes, handbags, and coconut objets d'art decorate this tiny shop.

A similarly artsy shop, **Pirulin y Tulipan** (Palomino between Porfirio Díaz and Escobedo, 9 A.M.–10 P.M. Thurs.–Sun.) is coincidentally run by another Swiss expat. It sells locally made candles, hand-painted pillowcases, knitted bags, and original paintings—the two shops are different enough to complement each other.

Lalo.com (Abasolo 139, tel. 984/875-2118) is the place to go if you're into shells—it's filled

SPORTS AND RECREATION

There is a lot to do on Holbox, and lying in a hammock is one of the most popular activities. If you want to stretch your legs, hotels can arrange various tours, and there are a number of independent tour operators looking for your business. Either way, be clear on what you're getting before you sign up. Ask how many people will be on the tour, how long you will spend at the various sites (as opposed to getting there and back), whether any meals are included, whether the boat has shade from the sun, and whether the guide speaks your language (remembering that the person selling you the trip may not be the guide). You can also see about combining activities, such as going snorkeling before or after bird-watching or visiting the whale sharks. Although there are a handful of tour operators (and more certainly on the way), try these established and highly recommended ones first: Carmelo at **Posada Mawimbi** (Av. Igualdad on the beach, tel. 998/875-2003, mawimbi@prodigy.net.mx, www.mawimbi .net) and Alberto at **Banana Tours** (Av. Igualdad between Avs. Palomino and Bravo, tel. 984/875-2082, nicebanana@hotmail.com, 9 A.M.–10 P.M. daily).

Snorkeling and Diving

Cabo Catoche, a coral reef in about 2–4 meters (6.6–13.1 feet) of water at the far eastern end of Isla Holbox, is the go-to spot for snorkeling. The water isn't as clear as in Isla Mujeres or Cancún, but the reef and animal life here are more pristine. We snorkeled in two spots and saw stingrays, moray eels, nurse sharks, sea stars, conch, and myriad fish and soft coral. Posada Mawimbi (Av. Igualdad on the beach, tel. 998/875-2003) offers snorkeling trips to Cabo Catoche for US$220 for up to five people, or to nearer sites for much less (US$9 pp). But because it is so far from town, Mawimbi and other operators usually prefer to combine it with another outing, such as an island tour or visiting the whale sharks.

There are two dive shops on the island—Posada Mawimbi (Av. Igualdad on the beach, tel. 998/875-2003, two-tank US$80, four-person maximum) and Banana Tours (one-/two-tank US$80/130, four-person minimum, reserve 10 days in advance). Prices are somewhat high because the dive site is an hour boat

ride from town. As with snorkeling, diving from Holbox usually involves so-so visibility but a high concentration of marine life; April to August is the best time of year. Trips include lunch and all equipment.

Kiteboarding

Take Off (www.takeoff.nl/html-nieuw/mexico/index-mexico.htm) offers one-on-one kiteboarding courses for around US$290 for three sessions, all equipment included. If you want to improve your jumps, back loops, or just want a refresher, you can take a private two-hour lesson for US$135. Once you get the hang of it, you can rent equipment from Mike for US$65 per three hours or US$90 per day. There were no formal windsurfing or sailing classes or tours when we passed through, but they were reportedly in the works—try asking at the Faro Viejo hotel, which caters to wind-sport enthusiasts. Take Off is a one-man operation with no fixed office, so the best way to arrange a course is to reserve via the website; otherwise, ask at Faro Viejo for more information.

kiteboarding on the emerald waters of the Gulf of Mexico

© LIZA PRADO CHANDLER

Fishing

Holbox is a good spot for sportfishing and still not very well known. A deep-sea fishing tour costs US$250–400, depending on how long you go out. A "family fishing" tour, which goes for small and more plentiful catch, lasts 4–5 hours and costs US$130. If you know how to fly-fish, a seven-hour tour in search of tarpon runs US$220. Most hotels can arrange trips, including Faro Viejo and Posada Mawimbi.

Bird-Watching

Holbox has more than 30 species of birds, including herons, white and brown pelicans, double-crested cormorants, roseate spoonbills, and greater flamingos (the brightest pink of the five flamingo species). A bird-watching tour (US$20–40 pp, 3–4 hours) generally includes taking a boat through the mangroves, to Isla Pájaros (Bird Island), and finally, to the flamingo nesting grounds. Most hotels can arrange a standard trip—**Xaloc Resort** (Calle Chacchí s/n, Playa Norte, tel. 984/875-2160) has an island tour for US$25 per person that is usually guided by a working biologist—a nice addition. Posada Mawimbi (Av. Igualdad on the beach, tel. 998/875-2003) has kayak tours—you visit only the mangroves but typically succeed in seeing more birds since there is no motor to scare them off. More specialized bird-watchers may want to contact Juan Rico Santana (tel. 984/875-2207 or tel. 984/875-2021)—he leads many of the hotel trips, but he can arrange separate, more focused trips that are tailored to your interests.

Baseball

Holbox has an amateur baseball team, known simply as *Selección Holbox* (Team Holbox). The season lasts all summer, and games against visiting teams are held most Sundays at noon at the baseball "stadium" on Avenida Benito Juárez a few blocks from the pier. It's a popular outing for island families, who typically bring tostadas and huge bowls of fresh homemade ceviche to go with the cold beer and soda on sale in the stands. Games are free; bring a hat as there is little shade.

Horseback Riding

Cueva del Pirata (Av. Benito Juárez at Porfirio Díaz, tel. 984/875-2183) offers daily tours of the island on horseback. Typical outings include visits to the mangroves, flamingo sanctuaries, and crocodile hideaways. Costs range from US$18 (one hour) to US$44 (three hours) and include a guide.

Massage

If you want to unwind (even more!), give the island's resident masseuse, **Selene Chablé,** a call at tel. 984/875-2062. She is highly recommended, comes to your hotel, and is very reasonably priced at US$26 per hour.

ACCOMMODATIONS

Room prices and availability vary considerably by season. The rates listed here are for the summer—July and August—which is a relatively busy season. Rates tend to drop 10–15 percent in May and June and September and October, and climb a bit November to April. The highest rates are around Christmas and New Year (and Semana Santa, the week ending in Easter), when reservations with a deposit are highly recommended.

Under US$25

It is usually possible to camp on the beach, but **Ida y Vuelta** (tel. 984/875-2344, Calle Plutarco Elias Calles s/n, idayvueltacamping@yahoo. com, www.camping-mexico.com, US$5.25 pp hammock, US$7 pp tent) is a much better option. About 200 meters (656 feet) from the beach, the "campground" has several large simple palapas with mosquito screens, in which you can hang hammocks or pitch a tent—the Italian brother-sister owners will lend you either one (plus a pad and sheet) if you don't have them. There's a clean common bath and a full kitchen was being built when we passed through.

Posada Los Arcos (Av. Benito Juárez at the park, tel. 984/875-2043, US$21 s with a/c, US$26 d with a/c, US$35 s/d with a/c and kitchenette) has long been a cheap, reliable option for budget travelers. The place is definitely starting to show its age in peeling paint, saggy mattresses, and so on. Rooms upstairs are better, brighter, and have a patio overlooking an interior garden. Good location and a friendly owner.

A few blocks from the park, **M Posada Anhelyng** (Av. Porfirio Díaz s/n, kitty-corner from the soccer field, tel. 998/875-2006, US$26 s/d) is a better deal, but call ahead because there are only five units. Rooms have air-conditioning, two beds, and are clean and spacious enough to make up for the somewhat sterile decor. Some rooms have a separate kitchen/eating area with a fridge—if you're staying a while, see if the owners will set up a small stove and lend you some dishes. Reception is at the family's blue house on Avenida Porfirio Díaz a block from the park—look for the sign.

US$25–50

Rooms at **Posada D'Ingrid** (Av. Morelos at Av. Pedro Joaquín Coldwell, tel. 984/875-2070, US$30–39 s/d) are clean and comfortable, though a bit small. Cheaper rooms have a queen and twin bed, instead of two queens; six have air-conditioning. The prices are a bit high, but there are a full common kitchen and palapa-covered eating area in the courtyard. Friendly owner.

Hotel La Palapa (Av. Morelos 231 on the beach, tel. 984/875-2121, l.pompeo@libero.it, www.hotelpalapa.com, 2–6 people US$39–70) is owned and operated by an Italian family that's been on the island since 1989. (The hotel, which is built alongside their home, opened in 1999.). Rooms vary in size and quality—some are a bit dim, but the double with kitchen for US$50 is a decent deal. The hotel has a nice garden and small beach area, which the owners keep clean and free of boats (though boats pull up on shore on either side).

M Posada Mawimbi (Av. Igualdad on the beach, tel. 998/875-2003, mawimbi@prodigy.net.mx, www.mawimbi.net, US$43–61 s/d, US$52–78 s/d with kitchenette) is a classic palapa-roofed posada with eight attractive, comfortable rooms and nice touches such as

Guatemalan bedspreads and decorative stone and tile work. There's a small garden with hammocks and chairs, and the beach is steps away. Italian owners Onny and Carmelo maintain a low-key friendly atmosphere, and offer recommended excursions, including whale-shark tours, snorkeling, and scuba diving.

The three cabanas and two apartments at **Villas Los Mapaches** (Av. Pedro Joaquín Coldwell s/n, tel. 984/875-2090, holboxmapaches@hotmail.com, www.losmapaches.com, US$35 s/d, US$50–90 s/d with kitchenette) aren't as flashy as elsewhere, but you may find yourself feeling very much at home there. Each unit is different, but most have solid wood construction, large bedrooms and bathrooms, a loft with a queen-sized bed, and a small kitchen and/or patio. The cabins are scattered in a large palm-shaded garden which fronts an okay beach. It's about five blocks into town and a bit farther to the best swimming and beach areas.

Over US$50

Faro Viejo (Av. Benito Juárez at the beach, tel. 984/875-2186, faroviejo@prodigy.net.mx, www.faroviejo.com.mx, US$52–63 s/d, US$105–155 suites with kitchen) has medium-sized, clean, and comfortable rooms, all with patio and air-conditioning. The hotel is a bit underwhelming, especially for the price, but it's a good option if you just want a regular, affordable hotel room with air-conditioning and an ocean view. The suites—with either three bedrooms or two bedrooms and a kitchen—are a better deal. You can pay with credit card here, which is a bonus. Ask here about wind sports, such as sailboarding, kiteboarding, and sailing.

Xaloc Resort (Calle Chacchí s/n, Playa Norte, tel. 984/875-2160, www.holbox-xaloc-resort.com, US$90–150 s/d, including a full breakfast) is a classy, understated resort (pronounced "sha-LOKE") about a 15-minute walk from town. Cabanas have thick beds, red-tile floors, and modern furnishings, including a telephone and coffeemaker. Service is excellent and there are a reading room and good restaurant. For the price, however, the grounds are a bit crowded and the pool and beach-chair areas somewhat uninviting. Also, the beach-front units—definitely the nicest—get noise from the sand street in front. A working biologist usually accompanies the hotel's island, whale-shark, and turtle tours, which is nice. (But you don't have to be a guest to sign up for a tour.)

For price, quality, amenities, and location, **M Villas Los Delfines** (beachfront east of town, tel. 984/875-2196, www.holbox.com, US$150–180) gets our vote. Deluxe beach-front cabanas are spacious and attractive, with wood floors, two comfortable queen-sized beds, fridge, coffeemaker, and a large patio perfect for morning coffee. The pool and beach areas are better maintained here than else-where, and the restaurant serves good, standard meals. About a 25-minute walk from town, the beach is large and boat-free, and there is less golf cart and moped traffic. Delfines is also an ecofriendly hotel, with waterless composting toilets (nicer than they sound!), solar power, and fans only—an admirable feature consid-ering the island's limited resources. Garden units are smaller, have concrete floors, and are missing the details that make the beachfront cabanas special—they aren't worth the price. Rates are 35–50 percent lower in low season.

FOOD

There are only a handful of restaurants on Isla Holbox, and most are on or near the main park. A few more are at hotels on the beach. If you stay for more than a day or two (most people do) you will probably eat at every restaurant.

Restaurants
M El General Taquitos (at the park on Igual-dad, 8 P.M.–midnight daily, US$4–10) is a classic Mexican taco joint, with metal tables, fluorescent lighting, and taco fillings desig-nated by animal parts. Great for local food and ambience.

Antojitos Los Chivos (Av. Benito Juárez at Av. Igualdad, no phone, 8 P.M.–midnight daily) is another classic snack-shack serving good cheap Mexican food at plastic tables set up on the street. Everything is US$.50, includ-ing Quintana Roo staples such as *salbutes* and *panuchos,* variations of tostadas.

La Isla del Colibrí (at the park on the cor-ner of Benito Juárez and Av. Porfirio Díaz, tel. 984/875-2162, 7:30 A.M.–1 P.M. and 6–11 P.M. daily, US$3.50–8) is especially good for break-fast, with big juices and *licuados* (milk- or water-based fruit shakes). The fish dishes in the evening aren't bad. A sister restaurant just down the street is a bit fancier and quite good, but it is open only in the high season.

Pizzería Edelín (on the park at Av. Palomino and Porfirio Díaz, tel. 984/875-2024, 11 A.M.–midnight daily, US$3.50–10) has decent thin-crust pizza—try the lobster or olive-and-caper toppings. Other options include fish, pasta, cev-iche, and Mexican finger food. This is one of the island's more popular restaurants—the ta-bles outside are much cooler.

Enjoy the breeze on the veranda of **Viva Zapata!** (Igualdad at Av. Benito Juárez, tel. 984/875-2330, 6 P.M.–midnight daily, US$4–10). Specializing in grilled meat and seafood, this is a popular place with travelers. Be sure to check out the homage to Latin American revo-lutionary leaders inside.

Overlooking the park, **M Cueva del Pi-rata** (Av. Benito Juárez at Porfirio Díaz, tel. 984/875-2183, 6 P.M.–midnight daily, US$5–16) is considered the classiest place in town. Soft jazz fills the room and spills out to the candlelit tables on the front porch. Offering a handful of homemade pastas, a dozen sauces to choose from, and imported wine—this is the place to go all-out. Try the lobster marinara sauce—it's worth the premium price. Meat, poultry, and seafood dishes are also offered.

Baked Goods and Ice Cream
The only bakery on the island, **Panadería La Conchita** (Av. Palomino at López Mateos, tel. 984/875-2319, 7 A.M.–10:30 P.M. Mon.–Sat., 6 A.M.–noon and 5–10 P.M. Sun.) makes bread, cookies, cakes, and other baked goods for the en-tire island's population. Even if you don't buy di-rectly from the store, you're sure to eat some of its products in the town's restaurants and hotels.

Cool off with a homemade treat from **Palatería Ancona** (Morelos between Díaz and Igualdad, tel. 984/875-2095, 8 A.M.–10 P.M. daily), which makes juices (US$.85), popsicles (US$.45), and ice cream (US$.60–.85). Choose from such varied flavors as coconut, peanut, tamarind, rice, and corn.

Groceries

The town of Holbox has a smattering of corner stores. Since they are stocked only periodically, you might have to go to a few before you find what you're looking for. Don't worry, it's a small town—you should hit at least three stores within five minutes. A couple of the bigger and more reliably stocked stores include:

Super Monkey's (half a block south of the park on Av. Benito Juárez, 6:30 A.M.–11 P.M. Mon.–Sat.) has canned and packaged food, bug repellent, sunscreen, and toiletries.

Abarrotes Holbox (behind Pizzeria Edelín on Porfirio Díaz, tel. 984/875-2327, 7:30 A.M.–10 P.M. Mon.–Sat., 7:30 A.M.–2 P.M. and 6–10 P.M. Sun.) has an arsenal of basic foodstuffs and also offers fresh eggs.

Frutas y Verduras (in front of Super Monkey's on Av. Benito Juárez, tel. 984/875-2287, 7 A.M.–3 P.M. daily) has the best selection of fruits and vegetables on the island. You'll also find beans, pastas, and spices. In case it's closed, try **Frutería Ruby** (Av. Palomino at López Mateos, tel. 984/875-2320, 7 A.M.–9 P.M. daily), which has a small selection of fruits and veggies and is open late.

INFORMATION AND SERVICES

Holbox has no bank, no ATM, and no post office. Few hotels, restaurants, or tour operators take credit cards, so definitely bring enough cash for your trip and in case you decide to stay an extra day or two. (In a pinch, try buying your tours through the top-end hotels, where credit cards are accepted.) Hours of operation on the island are decidedly flexible—"open all day" usually means "closed for a couple of hours in the middle of the day for lunch."

Medical Services

If you can help it, don't get sick, become injured, or need surgery of any kind when you're on Holbox. The only health center on the island, **Centro de Salud** (Av. Benito Juárez between Oceano Atlántico and Adolfo López Mateos, 8 A.M.–2 P.M. and 5–7 P.M. Mon.–Sat., 9 A.M.–1 P.M. Sun.) has no phone and often no medicine. There are two physicians on staff—one who speaks English, the other Italian—but they are equipped to handle only minor injuries, basic illnesses, and walk-in consultations. If you need more advanced medical attention, there is a fisherman on call who can take you on his boat to Chiquilá, where you can take a taxi to the nearest hospital. You can also charter a small plane to get you to Cancún or Mérida.

Pharmacy

Farmacia Pepe's (next to Super Monkey's on Av. Benito Juárez, tel. 998/875-2084, 8 A.M.–2 P.M. and 5–11 P.M. daily) is the only pharmacy on Holbox.

Internet, Fax, and Telephone

Internet El Parque (Av. Benito Juárez at the park, tel. 998/875-2107, 9 A.M.–midnight daily) was the only Internet café in town when we passed though, charging US$1.75 per hour for reasonably fast Internet, and US$.60 per minute for calls to the United States and Canada and US$1.40 per minute for calls to Europe (the prior is cheaper at a payphone).

Telecomm/Telegrafos (Porfirio Díaz at Av. Benito Juárez, tel. 984/875-2029, 9 A.M.–3 P.M. Mon.–Fri.) is a national fax and telegraph office. It offers friendly but pricey fax service: US$1.50 per page to/from the United States and Canada, US$2.40 per page to Europe and US$1.45 per page within Mexico.

Laundry

The shiny new **Lavandería Holbox** (Av. Benito Juárez between Avs. López Mateos and Lázaro Cárdenas, 9 A.M.–2 P.M. and 4–8 P.M. Mon.–Sat.) has self-service machines: Washers and dryers are each US$1 per three kilos (6.6 lb) and US$3 per 18 kilos (40 lb). Same-day laundry service is also begrudgingly offered at incredible prices: US$1 per three kilos and US$2 per 18 kilos. Detergent, bleach, softener, and dryer sheets are not included in either case but are offered at reasonable prices.

GETTING THERE

To get to Holbox, you need to first get to the small coastal village of Chiquilá. There are direct buses from Cancún and Mérida (see those sections for fares and schedules). If you're driving, take old Highway 180 (not the *autopista*) to El Ideal, about 100 kilometers (62 miles) west of Cancún. Turn north onto Highway 5 and follow that about 140 kilometers (87 miles) to Chiquilá, passing though the town of Kantunilkín. (There are shortcuts from both Mérida and Cancún, but they follow smaller, less-maintained roads). You'll have to leave your car in Chiquilá. A few families run small overnight parking operations—**Don Patricio's** (turn right when you hit the dock parking area) is the only one with a gate, and charges US$2.50 per day or fraction.

Passenger boats (US$3.50; 25 minutes) to Isla Holbox leave Chiquilá daily at 6 A.M., 8 A.M., 10 A.M., noon, 2 P.M., 4 P.M., 5 P.M. and 7 P.M. Returning boats leave Holbox at 5 A.M., 7 A.M., 9 A.M., 11 A.M., 1 P.M., 3 P.M., 4 P.M. and 6 P.M. Going to Holbox, it's a good idea to get to the dock a half hour early as the boat occasionally leaves ahead of schedule. Private boatmen make the trip in either direction for US$17.50 for up to six people; ask at the dock.

Back in Chiquilá, second-class buses to Cancún (US$5.50) leave the dock parking area at 5:30 A.M., 7:30 A.M., and 1:30 P.M.; all wait for the boat arriving from Holbox. There's usually an additional 4:30 P.M. departure during high season—ask ahead. To Mérida, there's just one bus at 5:30 A.M.—ouch.

If you get stuck in Chiquilá, the **Hotel Puerta del Sol** (tel. 984/875-0121, Av. Delfins s/n, US$13 s/d with fan, US$21.75 with a/c) is your only option. A few dozen meters back down the main road from the dock, rooms here are very simple, all with TV and private bath. Fan rooms are old and fairly dumpy, but those with air-conditioning are newer and nicer. There are several basic restaurants facing the dock parking area.

GETTING AROUND

Holbox is very easy to get around on foot. Even the farthest hotels are no more than a half hour's walk from town, and it's very safe day or night. Though you can rent golf carts the only time you really need one is getting between the pier and your hotel with your bags. Golf carts serve as the island's taxis (some are even painted in yellow and black checkers). A ride from the pier into town is US$.90 or US$2.50 to the hotels farther down the beach. There are always taxis parked around the plaza, or your hotel can call one.

Note that taxi drivers on Holbox (as elsewhere) earn/charge significant commissions from hotels for bringing new guests—in some cases US$10 per person per night or more. Some midrange hotels refuse to pay the fee (which would wipe out their own earnings) and taxi drivers retaliate by convincing incoming tourists that those hotels are closed, roach-infested, burned down, destroyed by hurricane, whatever—and then taking them to more "cooperative" hotels instead. Don't fall for it. You may have to be firm, but insist the driver take you to the hotel you want. The best thing is to call ahead for reservations, which are recommended and also serve to confirm the place is open. At worst, you'll have to pay an extra dollar to be taken to another hotel.

Golf Cart Rental

It's hard to imagine really needing a golf cart, but if you find a reason there are numerous *rentadoras* (rental shops), including **Rentadora Glendy** (Av. Porfirio Díaz at Av. Morelos, tel. 998/875-2093, 7 A.M.–11 P.M.). and **Rentadora El Brother** (Av. Benito Juárez at Av. Igualdad, tel. 998/875-2018, 7 A.M.–11 P.M.). All charge the same: US$7 per hour, US$30 half day, US$39 for 24 hours.

The Riviera Maya and Isla Cozumel

While Cancún is the name everyone knows, Isla Cozumel and the coastal towns south of Cancún of it draw as many or more tourists every year. The coastal area known as the Riviera Maya stretches from Cancún to Tulum, a distance of about 131 kilometers (81 miles). (We've placed Tulum in the next chapter, *Tulum and Southern Quintana Roo*, though many people consider it part of the Riviera Maya.) Cozumel lies 19 kilometers (11.8 miles) offshore and directly east of Playa del Carmen.

The Riviera Maya has an incredible array of tourist options: all-inclusive resorts and modest trailer parks, the world's longest underground river and the world's second-longest coral reef, beaches packed with sun-lovers and beaches strewn with driftwood, ancient Mayan ruins and modern nightclubs and movie theaters. It's amazing to think that as late as the 1970s, this area was mainly dotted with isolated communities, all but unknown to mainstream Mexico and the world.

Playa del Carmen and Playacar are the most popular towns in the Riviera Maya, with rapid development attracting mass tourism (though

© LIZA PRADO CHANDLER

Must-Sees

Look for **M** to find the sights and activities you can't miss and **Ṁ** for the best dining and lodging.

M **Puerto Morelos Coral Reef:** Skip the tourist-trap snorkeling trips in Cancún and Playa del Carmen and go snorkel where the reef is still healthy, the water is uncrowded, and the price unbeatable (page 105).

M **Playa Tukán:** One of the best beaches on the Riviera Maya, this beach in Playa del Carmen is a favorite spot for the exhilarating new sport of kiteboarding (page 114).

M **Isla Cozumel Coral Reefs:** Pristine coral reefs, crystal-clear water, vibrant sealife, and a slew of challenging wall and drift dives make Cozumel one of the world's best places to dive (page 143).

M **San Gervasio:** Thought to be dedicated to Ix Chel, the goddess of fertility, this is Cozumel's best Mayan ruin (page 145).

M **Laguna Yal-Ku:** A huge lagoon/estuary

THE RIVIERA MAYA
AND ISLA COZUMEL

Puerto Morelos
Coral Reef

Playa Tukán

San
Gervasio

Laguna Yal-Ku

Isla Cozumel
Coral Reefs

Riviera Maya and Cozumel

at the northern end of Akumal's Half Moon Bay. Beautiful underwater plant and fish life, and even a sea turtle or two if you get lucky (page 167).

© GARY PRADO CHANDLER

enjoying Cozumel's clear water

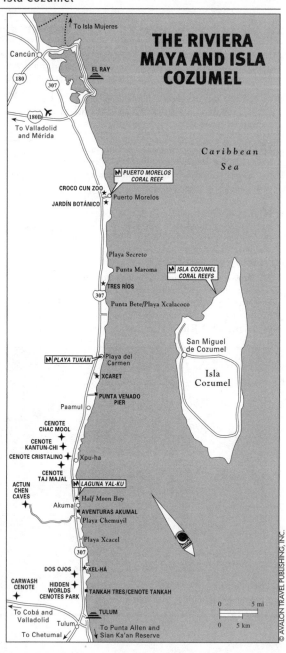

with fewer high-rise hotels and high-tech nightclubs than Cancún). A few towns, such as Puerto Morelos, still preserve their small, fishing village ways and charm, despite receiving more and more foreign visitors yearly.

Isla Cozumel, with its spectacular diving and snorkeling, is also growing but its awesome underwater beauty is still undeniable.

Highway 307 runs parallel to the ocean and is intersected by access roads to various towns, resorts, ecoreserves, and other destinations along the coast. Public buses and vans zip up and down the highway in great numbers and at great speed, and most points of interest are easy to reach on public transport. That said, having a car can make life a lot easier—some of the access roads are more than a kilometer (0.6 mile) long and it's easy to miss your stop on the bus.

PLANNING YOUR TIME

You can sample the Riviera Maya in four days, but as always, you won't have any trouble filling a week here. Playa del Carmen, 64 kilometers (40 miles) south of Cancún, is the Riviera Maya's main city and the gateway to Isla Cozumel. It is also the most logical base for exploring the area, with a wide variety of accommodations, excellent restaurants, and a beautiful beach that's popular for sailboarding and kiteboarding. From Playa del Carmen, take a ferry to Isla Cozumel for a day or two—it's one of the world's top snorkeling and diving destinations and a fun place to explore by car or scooter. You'll want another two days for the mainland—you can snorkel at the coral reefs in Puerto Morelos (32 kilometers/20 miles north of Playa), in a mixed salt-/freshwater lagoon at Akumal (36 kilometers/22.5 miles south of Playa), and in cenotes (limestone sinkholes) at several points along the coast. The Riviera Maya also has three ecoparks, which are themselves full-day excursions. Between activities, definitely squeeze in some quality beach time: Playa del Carmen, Xpu-Há (26 kilometers/16 miles south of Playa del Carmen), and Playa Tankah (44 kilometers/27 miles south of Playa del Carmen) are the area's best. Public buses and vans ply the coastal highway and make getting to and from many places easy and cheap; however, a few spots have long access roads and are better reached by taxi or rental car.

Puerto Morelos

Somehow this little beach town has escaped the megadevelopment that has transformed other coastal fishing villages—namely Playa del Carmen—into the tourist meccas they are. Though it can fill up with foreign tourists in the high season, Puerto Morelos (17 km/10.6 miles south of Cancún) is still at its heart a tranquil sleepy town where dogs and kids romp in the streets and life revolves around the central plaza. The beach isn't great, but most people here come for one of two different things: yoga and snorkeling. Puerto Morelos is a popular destination for yoga groups (as well as meditation, channeling, spas, rebirthing, and more) and a number of hotels and resorts cater to that growing market. And Puerto Morelos has long been considered one of the best snorkeling spots on the coast. Local residents fought tirelessly (and successfully) to have the reef designated a national reserve and a town cooperative runs well-recommended tours to the reef, as do dive shops and some hotels. Note that the low season here is *very* low and many businesses close in May, September, and the first part of October.

SIGHTS
Beach
The beach here is disappointing—rocky in many places and strewn with seaweed that has washed ashore. The best spot is at the Ojo de Agua hotel, where even a small purchase at the restaurant lets you use the beach chairs, umbrellas, and the pool. You can arrange snorkel and ATV tours here, as well.

ⓜ Coral Reef
Puerto Morelos's most spectacular attraction is snorkeling on the reef. Directly in front of the village, around 500 meters (0.3 mile) offshore, the reef here takes on gargantuan dimensions—between 20 and 30 meters (65.6 and 98.4 feet) wide. Winding passages and large caverns alive with fish and sea flora make for great exploring. And since it's a marine reserve and fishing and motor traffic is limited, the reef is more pristine here than almost any place along the Riviera. (See *Snorkeling* under *Sports and Recreation* for information on guided tours of the reef.)

The Plaza
The little plaza has restaurants and shops on three sides, and the water and a kelp-strewn beach on the fourth. On Sundays a small *tianguis* (flea market) is held here, and you can have fun browsing through someone else's old treasures. Otherwise, expect it to be quiet and unoccupied, save for a few people chatting on shaded benches.

Croco Cun Zoo
Five kilometers (3.1 miles) north of the Puerto Morelos turnoff is Croco Cun Zoo (Carretera Cancún-Chetumal Km. 31, tel. 998/850-3719, crococun@hotmail.com, 9 A.M.–6 P.M. daily, US$14/8.50 adults/kids under 12). A 90-minute guided tour (English or Spanish) through

this charming little crocodile farm and tropical zoo brings visitors up close to all sorts of crocodiles, from small juveniles to mongo adults. You can even touch, hold, or feed baby crocodiles—and a number of other creatures such as iguanas, snakes, and deer—depending on the season and their development.

Botanical Garden

A half kilometer (one-third mile) south of the Puerto Moreles turnoff is the **Jardín Botánico Dr. Alfredo Barrera Marín** (8 A.M.–4 P.M. daily Nov.–Apr., 9 A.M.–5 P.M. Mon.–Sat. May–Oct., US$6 adults, free under 11), a peaceful botanical garden, study center, and tree nursery spread over 60 hectares (150 acres). Three kilometers (1.9 miles) of trails wind through a wild natural atmosphere under a canopy of trees and past specimens (labeled in English, Spanish, and Latin) of the peninsula's plants and flowers. Habitats vary from semi-evergreen tropical forest to mangrove swamp. Look for the epiphyte area, with a variety of orchids, tillandsias, and bromeliads. As you wander around you'll also find a re-creation of a Mayan *chiclero* camp (showing how chicle was harvested to be used in chewing gum), some small ruins from the Postclassic period, and a contemporary Mayan hut illustrating day-to-day life—from cooking facilities to hammocks. One annoyance can be the mosquitoes, which are always around but come out in force in the morning, late afternoon, and after a good rain. If possible, wear long shirt and pants, closed shoes, and bring bug repellent.

SHOPPING

Shopping is definitely not a highlight of this town. What you'll mostly see are a handful of kitschy stores selling T-shirts, silver jewelry, and key chains. Don't distress—if shop you must, there are a few stores that manage to distinguish themselves from the (small) pack.

The artisans' market of **Hunab Kú** (1.5 blocks south of the plaza, 9 A.M.–10 P.M. daily) may be your best bet for finding nice handicrafts. Here, you'll find a bunch of stands with

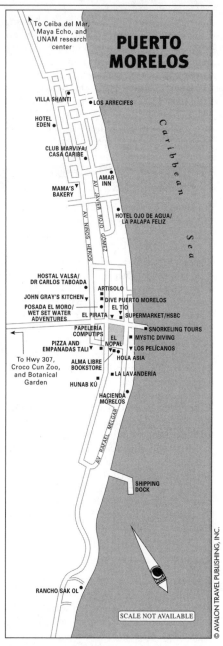

PUERTO MORELOS

To Ceiba del Mar, Maya Echo, and UNAM research center

Caribbean Sea

VILLA SHANTI
LOS ARRECIFES
HOTEL EDEN
CLUB MARVIYA/ CASA CARIBE
AMAR INN
MAMA'S BAKERY
HOTEL OJO DE AGUA/ LA PALAPA FELIZ
AV. JAVIER ROJO GOMEZ
AV. NIÑOS HEROS
HOSTAL VALSA/ DR CARLOS TABOADA
ARTISOLO
JOHN GRAY'S KITCHEN
DIVE PUERTO MORELOS
POSADA EL MORO/ WET SET WATER ADVENTURES
EL PIRATA
EL TÍO
SUPERMARKET/HSBC
PAPELERÍA COMPUTIPS
SNORKELING TOURS
MYSTIC DIVING
EL NOPAL
PIZZA AND EMPANADAS TALI
LOS PELÍCANOS
HOLA ASIA
To Hwy 307, Croco Cun Zoo, and Botanical Garden
ALMA LIBRE BOOKSTORE
LA LAVANDERÍA
HUNAB KÚ
HACIENDA MORELOS
AV. RAFAEL MELGAR
SHIPPING DOCK
RANCHO SAK OL
SCALE NOT AVAILABLE

© AVALON TRAVEL PUBLISHING, INC.

QUEEN CONCH

Tasty, easy to catch, beautifully packaged—the queen conch (pronounced CONK) is a commercial fisherman's dream. Every part is sold: meat is exported to the United States and shells are bought as souvenirs by tourists. An easy way to make money—yes—but it's disappearing. Smaller conchs are being sold and fishermen are being forced to go farther afield to collect profitable catches.

It takes 3–5 years for this sea snail to grow from larva to market size. It also takes about that long for planktonic conch larvae, carried into fished-out areas by the currents, to replenish themselves. What's worse, the conch is easy to catch—large (up to 39 centimeters/15.4 inches) and heavy (about three kilograms/6.6 pounds), the mollusk moves slowly and lives in shallow, crystalline water where it's easy to spot.

Biologists are working with various governments to impose restrictions on the fishing of queen conch, including closed seasons, minimum size of capture, limits on the total numbers taken, and the cessation of exportation. Along with these proposed legal restrictions, technology is lending a hand. Several mariculture centers, including one in Puerto Morelos, are experimenting with the queen conch, raising animals in a protected environment until they're large enough to be released into the wild. Unfortunately, this is not always successful. One group in 10 will survive, as conch have to contend not only with humans but also with its other predators: lobsters, crabs, sharks, turtles, and rays.

While not on the endangered species list yet, the queen conch must be protected so that the risk of its complete demise does not become a reality.

colorful blankets, ceramics, hammocks, masks, jipi hats, shell art … pretty much anything you'll see sold up and down the coast.

Artisolo (Av. Javier Rojo Gómez, tel. 998/871-0394, 10 A.M.–2 P.M. and 6–10 P.M. Mon.–Sat.) is another decent place to shop; it sells locally made arts and crafts as well as items brought from around Mexico.

Possibly the best English-language bookstore on the peninsula, **Alma Libre Bookstore** (main plaza, tel. 998/871-0713, www.almalibrebooks .com, 10 A.M.–3 P.M. and 6–9 P.M. Tues.–Sat., 4–9 P.M. Sun.) has a whopping 20,000 titles varying "from beach trash to Plato," in the words of the friendly Canadian couple who own and operate the store. Mayan culture, Mexican cooking, learning Spanish, bird-watching, snorkeling guides, classics, philosophy, mysteries, fiction, nonfiction, and not just in English but Spanish, French, German, Dutch, Italian, Norwegian, and more—your taste in books would have to be extremely narrow to not find something worthwhile here. The store also has a wide selection of guidebooks and maps, and

the owners will download your digital pictures and burn them to a CD for US$9 (US$7 with a book purchase). Books are both new and used, and trades are possible.

SPORTS AND RECREATION
Snorkeling

Snorkeling tours (US$20 pp, two hours, including equipment and life jacket) are conducted by members of the local fisherman/boatman cooperative and have fixed prices and terms. Trips visit two locations on the reef, spending 45 minutes at each one. Boats carry up to 10 snorkelers, and you may have to wait up to a half hour (but no more, according to the cooperative rules) for additional passengers to come. You can arrange a tour at the kiosk at the northeast corner of the plaza, or down on the pier itself 8 A.M.–3 P.M.; late morning is best as the sun is high but the afternoon winds haven't started. The price includes a US$2 park fee.

The **dive shops** in town (see *Diving*) also offer snorkeling tours for around US$20–25 pp for a two-hour trip visiting two different sites. Prices include snorkel gear. Trips with Wet Set dive shop leave at 11:30 A.M.; ask at other shops for current schedule. **La Palapa Feliz** (8 A.M.– 7 P.M. daily) is the beach club at Hotel Ojo de Agua on Avenida Javier Rojo Gómez and has 1.5–2-hour snorkel tours for US$27 pp.

Note: *Do not swim to the reef* from anywhere along the beach. Although it's close enough for strong swimmers to reach, boats use the channel between the reef and the shore. Tourists have been struck and killed in the past. If you can't countenance a tour, ask at the pier about arranging private boat service with one of the *lanchistas* (boatmen).

Diving

Divers have three shops to choose from in town. All offer one- and two-tank dives, night and specialty dives, cenote dives, and a range of certification courses. Prices are fairly uniform, and all the dive shops are within a few blocks of each other. (Wet Set and Dive Puerto Morelos are neighbors.) Reservations are strongly recommended in the high season. **Wet Set Water Adventures** (Posada el Moro, tel. 998/871-0198, www.wetset.com, 9 A.M.–noon and 4–8 P.M. Tues.–Sat.) is run by long-time diver and guide Paul Hensley. One-/two-tank dives (US$45/65) leave at 9 A.M.; price includes all rentals. No credit cards.

Next door, **Dive Puerto Morelos** (Av. Javier Rojo Gómez 14, tel. 998/206-9084, www.divepuertomorelos.com, 8 A.M.–6 P.M. Mon.–Sat., 8 A.M.–noon Sun.) is the newest shop in town and has similar prices. Run by an Australian transplant, the shop also has night snorkeling (US$37 pp) and six-dive packages (US$165).

On the main plaza near the beach, **Mystic Diving** (Av. Rafael Melgar No. 2, tel. 998/871-0634, www.mysticdiving.com, 8 A.M.–5 P.M.) is locally owned and operated and offers one-/two-tank dives for US$34/50, including weights, mask, fins, and tank. Buoyancy control device (BCD), regulator, and wetsuit rental is US$6/day. Most trips have no more than six divers per dive master.

Fishing

Wet Set Water Adventures (Posada el Moro, tel. 998/871-0198, www.wetset.com, 9 A.M.–noon and 4–8 P.M. Tues.–Sat.) guarantees you will catch fish on its tour, or the trip is free. Sportfishing tours (US$175 for two anglers, 5.5 hours) reel in wahoo, mackerel, bonito, and barracuda year-round, plus marlin and sailfish in the late spring and summer. Bottom-fishing tours (US$55/hour for two, two-hour minimum) bring home grouper, snapper, and other tasty fish—the crew will even prepare the fish for your hotel restaurant to cook.

Jungle Tours

Dive Puerto Morelos (Av. Javier Rojo Gómez No. 14, tel. 998/206-9084, www.divepuerto-morelos.com, 8 A.M.–6 P.M. Mon.–Sat., 8 A.M.–noon Sun.) runs a half-day jungle and cenote tour (US$45 pp) that includes a short truck ride and walk, swimming and snorkeling in three cenotes, and a stop for picnic lunch.

La Palapa Feliz (Hotel Ojo de Agua, 8 A.M.–7 P.M. daily) offers a four-hour ATV tour (US$48 s, US$58 d) that weaves through sand dunes and coastal forest with stops at two cenotes (freshwater sinkholes) to cool off. One cenote has a zip line for a bit of a rush.

Massage

If your vacation has left you aching, contact **Mauro Jaramillo** (deep tissue and sports massage, tel. 998/871-0062, mjpowerof touch@yahoo.com) or visit the spa at the Ceiba del Mar hotel (1.5 km/0.9 mile north of town, tel. 998/872-8060).

ACCOMMODATIONS

Under US$50

On a quiet street two blocks from the beach, **Hotel Eden** (Av. Andrés Quintana Roo No. 788, tel. 998/871-0450, US$25 s/d with fan) is a good budget option. While having no decorative frills, it offers spacious studios with small kitchenettes and private bathrooms. Rooms are very clean and service is especially friendly. Serious discounts for stays of two weeks or more.

Hostel Valsa (Av. Niños Héroes, half block north of plaza, tel. 998/871-0233, hostelvalsa@hotmail.com, US$40/220/475 day/week/month) has eight homey studio apartments connected by sunny outdoor corridors, and just a couple of blocks from the plaza. The units aren't big, but all have a nook by the door with refrigerator, sink, and burners, and some have a terrace looking onto the street. Ground-floor offices and a number of long-term residents mean there are kids, pets, and other traffic—and the "Do Not Pee in the Stairwell" sign is somewhat disconcerting—but the general ambience is calm and friendly.

Half a block from the main plaza, **Ⓜ Posada El Moro** (Av. Javier Rojo Goméz, tel. 998/871-0159, morelos01@sbcglobal.net, www.posada-elmoro.com, US$45–60 s/d with a/c) is a pleasant hotel offering standard hotel rooms (US$45), larger suites with balconies (US$60), and studios with kitchenettes (US$50). The bright units have cable TV and air-conditioning and are very well kept. There were plans to add a pool. Breakfast—fruit, yogurt, and cereal—is included.

In front of the Caribbean, **Amar Inn** (Av. Javier Rojo Goméz at Av. Lazaro Cardenas, tel. 998/871-0026, amar_inn@hotmail.com, US$40–65 s/d with fan) is a hurricane-battered inn run by the Aguilar family. The eight rooms vary from cramped garden cabanas with lofts to spacious ocean view rooms in the main house. All are reasonably clean and come with fans and refrigerators. Breakfast also is included.

US$50–100

Just beyond Villas Latinas, **Hotel Ojo de Agua** (Av. Javier Rojo Gómez, two blocks north of plaza, tel. 998/871-0027, www.ojo-de-agua .com, US$52–72 s/d) offers 36 basic rooms overlooking a pretty beach. Rooms are clean and comfortable, if lacking in character—the flowered bedspreads and tile floors are classic hotel-room. All rooms come with cable TV and air-conditioning; standards feel a bit cramped, deluxes are bigger, and studios have a refrigerator, stove, and sink. Other features include a decent restaurant (8 A.M.–10 P.M. daily; try

the paella), family-friendly pool area, and a tour operator on the beach who rents snorkel gear and kayaks and organizes ATV and snorkel tours.

On a little side street two kilometers (1.25 miles) north of the center, **Maya Echo** (Calle Las Palapas, tel. 998/871-0136, www.maya echo.com, US$50 s/d, US$125–135 condos) is a small bed-and-breakfast run by an amiable American couple from Ohio, who also manage four large condos across the street. One of the three bed-and-breakfast rooms has a private bath and a small terrace with garden view, the other rooms share a bath, and one has air-conditioning. All three are smallish but homey, and the decor is charming even as it shows its age. Rates include a hearty breakfast, served in the family dining room on the first floor. Across the street are four spacious condos, each with two bedrooms, two baths, large and fully equipped kitchen, maid service 2–3 times weekly, a small swimming pool, and direct beach access. A good deal for two couples looking for a place of their own, though you'll probably want a car or bikes to get back and forth from town. Take Avenida Niños Héroes north past Ceiba del Mar Hotel and the UNAM research center and look for signs on your right.

One block south of the plaza, **Hacienda Morelos** (Av. Rafael Melgar, tel. 998/871-0015, US$70 s/d with a/c) has spacious—though somewhat dated—rooms on the beach. Units have *tiny* kitchenettes, white furniture, and spectacular views of the Caribbean. A concrete sunbathing patio with a small pool separates the hotel from the beach. A decent restaurant also is on-site.

Formerly known as Rancho Libertad, **Ⓜ Rancho Sak Ol** (one km/0.6 mile south of the main plaza, tel. 998/871-0181, www .ranchosakol.com, US$69 s with fan, US$79 d with fan, US$79 s/d with a/c) is a palapa hideaway on a broad beach. Most rooms in the two-story cabanas have hanging beds and all have private baths and a pair of hammocks on their individual terraces or balconies. Guests have access to a fully equipped kitchen, which is in a huge beachside lounge. Use of snorkel equipment and bicycles is included in the rate as is a tasty breakfast. Adults only, except during the low season when children over the age of 10 are welcome.

On a windswept stretch of beach, **Los Arrecifes** (just off Av. Rojo Gómez, two blocks north of Club Marviya/Casa Caribe, tel. 998/871-0488, zeppelinmario@yahoo.com, US$50 apartment with fan, US$89 apartment with a/c) has 12 recently remodeled one-bedroom apartments. All face the ocean and have airy living rooms and kitchens. Bedrooms, unfortunately, are nowhere near as nice—with two queen beds and a tiny window, you'll feel as if you're sleeping in a large closet. For longer stays, ask about weekly or monthly rates.

The bright red **Club Marviya/Casa Caribe** (Av. Rojo Gómez s/n, three blocks north of the main plaza, tel. 998/890-1866, www.marviya .com) is a small hotel with five rooms just a few steps from the beach. On the brink of opening when we stopped by, this Quebecois-run business looks as if it'll be a charming spot. Call for rates.

Over US$100

A block from the beach, the yoga-friendly **Villas Shanti** (Av. Niños Héroes s/n, tel. 998/871-0040, vshanti@ncia.net, www.villasshanti .com, US$100 s/d with a/c) is a comfortable eight-apartment villa complete with a clover-shaped pool, barbecue area, and a large palapa strung with hammocks. Each one-bedroom unit has a modern bathroom, fully equipped kitchenette, and private patio. Yoga instruction is offered twice a week here (7–8:30 A.M. Tues. and Thurs., US$6/class) as are weeklong yoga retreats in the high season. Classes are offered in a bright indoor studio or a large palapa in the garden. Villas Shanti also is used by private groups for yoga, rebirthing, channeling, and healing retreats. Call for more information on upcoming events.

If you're looking for luxury, head straight to **M Ceiba Del Mar** (1.5 km/0.9 mile north of town, tel. 998/872-8060, U.S. tel. 877/545-6221, www.ceibadelmar.com). A high-end re-

sort, it has 120 rooms and junior suites—all with at least a partial view of the Caribbean—in eight three-story stucco buildings. Each building has a sunroof whirlpool tub and concierge services that cater to your every need. The rooms themselves are nicely appointed and have modern amenities, including plush robes, cable TV with VCR, CD player, minibar, and daily newspaper delivery. Continental breakfast is included and is served in your room through a butler box—you won't even have to throw on your robe to open the door. In addition, the resort boasts three glorious pools, a full-service spa, three restaurants (international, Mexican gourmet, and seafood with an Asian flair), a dive shop, and a tennis court with night lights. Use of bicycles, snorkel gear, and kayaks is included. Rates start at US$335; be sure to ask about half/full-board rates, spa packages, and weekly prices. Ceiba Del Mar also offers a day pass (9 A.M.– 5 P.M., US$49), which entitles guests to use the facilities; it includes breakfast, lunch, and all the soft drinks you can handle.

FOOD

International

M John Gray's Kitchen (Av. Niños Héroes, half block north of plaza, tel. 998/871-0665, 6–10 P.M. Mon.–Sat., US$10–25) is a reincarnation of the now-closed but famously good Johnny Cairo Restaurant. It is without question the finest restaurant in Puerto Morelos (as was its predecessor), featuring an inventive menu that changes every other day. When we passed by, the specials included various fine cuts of beef and pasta with almonds and chorizo. Occupying a boxy building two blocks from the plaza, the dining room is elegant and understated and the service excellent. Cash only.

Giving John Gray's Kitchen a run for its culinary money is **M Hola Asia** (main plaza, tel. 998/871-0679, 5–11 P.M. Mon. and Wed.–Sat, 3–11 P.M. Sun., closed Tues., US$5–12) a small, popular restaurant serving a great pan-Asian menu of mostly Thai and Chinese inspiration. The simple one-room dining area can get crammed with diners, many who've come from Cancún or Playa del Carmen to eat here. For sweet and sour try General Tso's Chicken, for spicy go with Indian Yellow Curry. Closed in September.

A half block from the plaza, **M Pizza and Empanadas Tali** (Calle Tulum, tel. 998/871-0475, 10:30 A.M.–11 P.M. daily except Tues., 7–11 P.M. Tues., US$1–5) serves good pizzas and authentic—and delicious—Argentinean empanadas: puffy, crispy fried dough filled with cheese or other goodies. A plate of five or six empanadas and a couple of sodas makes a great snack for two. Take them to go or eat at one of a few small tables on the sidewalk.

Mexican and Seafood
Facing the main plaza, **El Nopal** (tel. 998/100-2742, 8 A.M.–6 P.M. daily except Wed., US$3–5) offers an excellent *comida corrida* (lunch special) that includes a full plate of rice, beans, and choice of main dish (veggie options always available) and a refillable glass of cool fruit juice for US$4.50. Closed September and October. The same owners run **Porto Bello** (tel. 998/871-0039, 3–11 P.M. Tues.–Sun., US$6–15), a more upscale restaurant also just a few doors away.

El Pirata (main plaza, tel. 998/871-0489, 8 A.M.–11 P.M. Mon.–Thurs., until 2 A.M. Fri.–Sun., US$5–15) has a good location on the main plaza just up from the pier where you take snorkeling tours. Choose from a large selection of hamburgers, fish burgers, *tortas,* tacos, and full entrées such as roast chicken or grilled beef, all served in a simple open-air dining area just off the street. Like many businesses here, El Pirata cuts back its hours in the low season, closing Mondays and the entire month of May.

Around the northeast corner of the plaza, tiny **El Tío** restaurant (no phone, 6:30 A.M.–11 P.M. daily) cooks up wonderfully *casera* (homemade) meals and service. Lunch specials change most days, but typically include soup and main dish. A popular lunch spot for local workers, the tables fill up quickly—all three of them.

Los Pelícanos (main plaza, tel. 998/871-0014, 8 A.M.–10:30 P.M. daily, US$5–16) has

a wraparound patio overlooking the plaza and the ocean—perfect for an afternoon beer or margarita. Food here can be a bit uneven, but with so many fishermen it's hard to go wrong with shrimp, octopus, or fish, all served fresh in a half-dozen different ways.

Bakery and Sandwiches
Perhaps Puertos Morelos's most charming eatery, **M Mama's Bakery** (Av. Niños Héroes at Calle Lázaro Cárdenas, Mex. cell tel. 044-998/845-6810, 8 A.M.–4 P.M. Tues.–Sat., 8:30 A.M.–1 P.M. Sun., US$3–5.50) is run by a friendly expat and baker extraordinaire—don't leave town without trying the sticky buns or carrot cake. Mama's is also a great place to come for fresh, healthy meals—mainly ready-made breakfast burritos in the morning and sandwiches made with homemade bread for lunch. Two blocks north of the plaza; closed most of September, and open Tuesday–Saturday only in May and October.

Groceries
The **supermarket** (north side of the main plaza, 6 A.M.–10 P.M. daily) has a fairly large selection of canned foods, pastas, snacks, and drinks, and has a small produce section near the back.

INFORMATION AND SERVICES
Although this town sees a fair number of tourists, the services are somewhat sparse. As this handbook goes to print the offerings included:

Medical Services
Dr. Carlos Taboada (Av. Niños Héroes, adjacent to Hostal Valma, cell tel. 044-998/894-0832, 9 A.M.–1 P.M., 5–8 P.M. Mon.–Fri., 9 A.M.–1 P.M. Sat.) comes well-recommended by local residents and expats living in town. There is a **pharmacy** facing the main plaza and two on the highway near the Puerto Morelos turnoff.

Money
There is no bank in Puerto Morelos. However, you can get cash from the HSBC ATM, which

is just outside the supermarket on the plaza's north side.

Internet

At the southwest corner of the main plaza are two places to check your email—**Papelería Computips** (tel. 998/871-0361, 9 A.M.–10 P.M. Mon.–Sat., 2–10 P.M. Sun.) charges US$1.40 per hour for Internet access, edging out **Marand Travel** (tel. 998/871-0332, 8:30 A.M.–8:30 P.M. Mon.–Sat.) which charges US$1.75 per hour.

Laundry

A block south of the plaza, the aptly named **La Lavandería** (Av. Javier Rojo Gómez s/n, no phone, 8 A.M.–8 P.M. Mon.–Fri. and 9 A.M.– 5 P.M. Sat.) charges US$1/kilo (mininum three kilos—6.6 pounds) for full service or US$1.25 per wash or dry if you do it yourself. Another launderette appeared to be opening when we passed through—look for it on Avenida Javier Rojo Gómez near Posada El Moro.

GETTING THERE

Bus

Buses pass the Puerto Morelos turnoff on Highway 307—they do not enter town. The northbound stop (with a small ticket kiosk, tel. 998/871-0759, 6 A.M.–10 P.M. daily) is right at the turnoff, while the southbound stop is across the street and south about 100 meters (328 feet). There is no shortage of public transportation on this highway. For Cancún (US$1.50, 30 minutes) and Playa del Carmen (US$1– 1.50, 20 minutes), second-class buses, white *colectivos* (shared vans), and **Playa Express** minibus all pass roughly every 10 minutes 6– 12:30 A.M. daily, with van service continuing as late as 1–2 A.M. Many but not all buses and vans that pass continue to Tulum (US$3.50– 5.25, 1.5 hours), but be sure to ask before get-

ting on. For the **airport** (US$3, 25 minutes), special Riviera/ADO airport buses stop at the Puerto Morelos turnoff every hour on the half hour 8:30 A.M.–6:45 P.M. daily.

The only long-distance service from here is to Mérida (US$17, four hours), with daily departures at 8:45 A.M., 3:45 P.M., and 5:45 P.M. For all others (and more to Mérida) go to Cancún or Playa del Carmen.

Ferry

The car ferry here no longer offers regular passenger service. For Cozumel, the car ferry is at Punta Venado, just south of Xcaret (see the *Playa del Carmen* section). For Isla Mujeres, head to Punta Sam, north of Cancún.

GETTING AROUND

Unless you're staying at Ceiba del Mar, Maya Echo, or Rancho Sak Ol, you'll have little need for a car. The town is compact—you can walk it from end to end in about 20 minutes—and the beach runs the length of it and beyond.

Taxis

Taxis line up day and night at the taxi stand on the northwest corner of the plaza. Current prices are prominently displayed on a painted signboard—at last pass a ride to the highway cost US$2, and to Ceiba del Mar hotel was US$2.25.

Car Rental

You can arrange **Thrifty** car rentals at Mama's Bakery (Av. Niños Héroes at Calle Lázaro Cárdenas, cell tel. 044-998/845-6810, 8 A.M.–4 P.M. Tues.–Sat., 8:30 A.M.–1 P.M. Sun.). **Autorent Car Rental** (tel. 998/872-8060 or cell tel. 044-998/937-0165, autorent_gerencia@prodigy.net.mx) has a representative at Ceiba del Mar hotel.

Punta Bete/Playa Xcalacoco

Continuing south on the highway you'll soon arrive at a turnoff for Punta Bete and its beach, Playa Xcalacoco. Here, you'll find a mellow beach scene with a few hotels where locals and travelers alike lose themselves in the swaying palms and gentle blue waves; you'll see more people beachcombing or reading books than playing volleyball. The snorkeling also is reasonably good here.

ACCOMMODATIONS

Under US$50

On the beach, **Los Pinos** (tel. 998/873-1506, US$35 s/d with fan) offers simple rooms, each with two queen beds, private bathroom, and a fan. Rooms could be cleaner but are adequate. Ironically, while the beach is at the doorstep, none of the rooms has ocean views. There's a popular restaurant on-site.

Camping is the best option at **Juanitos** (on the beach south of Ikal del Mar, tel. 984/806-8058, camping US$4 pp, rooms US$30–40) as the private rooms are musty and unpleasant, especially for the price. You can set up tents on the sand, or under small open-air palapas for a bit more. Showers and bathroom are grimy but acceptable. Snorkel gear rents for US$7/day.

US$50–100

Two kilometers (1.25 miles) from the highway at the end of the sand road, **Coco's Cabañas** (tel. 998/874-7056, reservations@travel-center.com, US$35 s/d hotel room with a/c, US$50–55 s/d bungalows) has five very private bungalows and one hotel room set 30 meters (98.4 feet) back from the beach in a lush garden setting. The accommodations are charmingly decorated, enjoy 24-hour electricity, and have spotlessly clean bathrooms. The palapa-roofed bungalows all also boast a private patio with hammocks to while away the day. Check out the heart-shaped pool as you walk in.

Over US$100

Some say the **Ikal de Mar** (on the beach, tel. 984/877-3002, toll-free Mex. tel. 800/012-3569, U.S. tel. 888/230-7330, Europe tel. 800/525-48-000, www.ikaldelmar.com, US$640, including breakfast) is the Riviera Maya's finest boutique hotel-resort. The reviewer for the *New York Times* certainly seemed to enjoy herself, judging from the glowing review the hotel got in the paper's February 8, 2004, travel section. Guests stay in spacious individual villas—there are 30, but you'd never know it as they are hidden down curved paths and behind thick tropical foliage. The villas have a cool, understated elegance, from the wood and marble floors to the wispy mosquito net hanging over the bed from the high palapa roof. Each has a private pool—yes, a whole pool—and a patio where meals can be served. Otherwise, guests eat by candlelight in the poolside restaurant. Poolside is a nice way to spend the day here too, as the beach (rocky and narrow) leaves something to be desired. The hotel also offers an astounding array of massages, body and face treatments, and natural healing sessions. Service is impeccable.

FOOD

The eateries on this part of the coast are almost all exclusively family-run and operated out of simple palapas.

Right on the beach, **Los Pinos** (tel. 998/873-1506, 7 A.M.–10 P.M., US$4–18) is a popular place for seafood. The food is a little pricey considering the simple surroundings, but it is definitely tasty.

GETTING THERE AND AROUND

The tiny sand access road is easy to miss from the highway. Look for it just south of the big Cristal water plant. Once you're there, Punta Bete is all beach—walking is really the best way to get around its small cluster of hotels and restaurants. If you want to head farther out by foot, turn right (south) at the ocean, and 1.5–2 hours later you should be in Playa del Carmen.

Taxis

There is no taxi stand in this tiny community.

Ikal del Mar offers free daily van service to Playa del Carmen; otherwise your hotel can call you a taxi from Playa del Carmen or Puerto Morelos. A ride to the airport will cost you US$30, to Playa del Carmen around US$7.

Playa del Carmen

Not all that many years ago, your stroll through Playa del Carmen would have been escorted by children, dogs, little black pigs, and incredibly ugly turkeys; you might even have seen the milkman delivering milk from large cans strapped to his donkey's back. No more. With its population increasing nearly 20 percent annually, Playa del Carmen is the fastest-growing city in Quintana Roo.

Playa is not Cancún, however. It's smaller, for one thing, and has almost none of the glitzy high-rises and all-night dance clubs. Playacar, a planned community south of town, does have many high-end resorts but is also largely residential and does not have the "strip" atmosphere that Cancún's Zona Hotelera does. Playa is still very much a walking town. The area around the pier and local bus terminal can be kitschy and intrusive (and unfortunately it is the first area most people see) but the northern section has a more low-key atmosphere with some excellent restaurants, cool bars, and offbeat shops. And while Cancún caters to Americans, Playa attracts Europeans, and even has a nascent "Italian quarter."

Playa del Carmen has some pretty beaches (if you know where to go) and good snorkeling, diving, Mayan ruins, cenotes, golf, and more are all nearby. It is a convenient base from which to explore and sample everything the Riviera Maya has to offer.

SIGHTS

Quinta Avenida

Playa's main pedestrian and commercial drag is Quinta Avenida, or Fifth Avenue, which stretches almost 20 blocks from the ferry dock northward. Pronounced 'KEEN-ta av-en-EE-da,' you may see it written as 5 Avenida or 5a Avenida, which is akin to "5th" in English but refers to the same street. The first several blocks, especially around the ferry dock, are typical tourist traps, with souvenir shops and chain restaurants. Around Calle 10 or Calle 12, the atmosphere turns mellower, with bistros, jazz bars, and funky clothing stores. You'll probably walk the length of Quinta Avenida once or twice—the best beaches are in the northern part, the bus terminal and ferry dock in the southern—and everyone seems to find his or her favorite part.

Playa Tukán

By far the best beach in town is Playa Tukán (entrance at 1 Av. Norte at Calle 26), north of the center. There you'll find a broad swath of thick white sand and mild but not sedentary surf. It's a popular spot for **kiteboarding**—a hot new(ish) sport in which you strap on a modified surfboard and a huge parachute and tear across the water, sometimes soaring high over the water with the help of the wind. Playa Tukán, near the city's Italian area, is popular with European visitors and expats, and topless bathing is very common. (At the risk of sounding prudish, we can't help mentioning that topless bathing is *not* widely accepted among Mexicans, who also frequent Playa Tukán, especially on weekends.)

Two beach clubs—**Club Playa Tukán** (at the main beach access) and **Mamita's** (a few meters north, tel. 984/803-2867)—have beach chairs and umbrellas for rent, small swimming pools, showers, and full bar and restaurant. Between the two, Club Playa Tukán has a mellower ambience, while Mamita's caters to a younger, hipper crowd with a DJ, volleyball court, and occasional organized events. Prices are virtually identical at both: meals (US$4–12, including ceviche, pasta, hamburgers, and so on), drinks (US$2–5), beach chair and umbrella (US$1.75 each).

Other Beaches

Playa Principal is Playa's main beach, directly in front of the plaza just north of the ferry pier. The beach itself isn't bad, but all the activity around the pier and plaza, plus the ferries chugging in and out every half hour, are kind of a killjoy.

Coco Beach Club is just a short distance north of Shangri La Caribe. It has good food, beach umbrellas, and sun beds, plus changing rooms and showers. The snorkeling here is the best in the Playa area; you can rent gear here if you don't have your own.

You can also rent your own beach gear at **Playa Bike** (1 Av. Norte between Calles 10 and 12, cell tel. 044-984/745-1387, 8 A.M.–8 P.M. Mon.– Sat.) including umbrellas (US$2.20/ hour, US$6.50/day), snorkel equipment (US$6.50/day), and boogie boards and floating mats (US$4.50/day each).

Xaman Ha Bird Sanctuary

A short distance inside the Playacar entrance off 10 Avenida, **Aviario Xaman-Ha** (Av. Xaman Ha, cell tel. 044-984/106-8766, 9 A.M.–5 P.M. daily, US$13 adults, free under 12) has more than 60 species of tropical birds, including toucan, flamingo, cormorants, and various types of parrots, all native to southeastern Mexico. The birds are divided by habitat and held in a variety of enclosures along a winding path, and most people take a little less than an hour to see them all. Parking is just beyond the aviary's sign, on the same side. Bring some mosquito repellent, especially if you come in the morning or late afternoon.

Tres Rios

Tres Rios (Hwy. 307 between Puerto Morelos and Playa del Carmen, tel. 998/887-8077, www.tres-rios.com, adults US$35 entrance only, US$58 all-inclusive, US$80 grand all-inclusive, children half price) is an ecopark offering myriad activities—snorkeling, kayaking, speedboating, and horseback riding—in a nature preserve of cenotes, rivers, ocean, and

© LIZA PRADO CHANDLER

Travelers can ride horses in many places along the Riviera Maya.

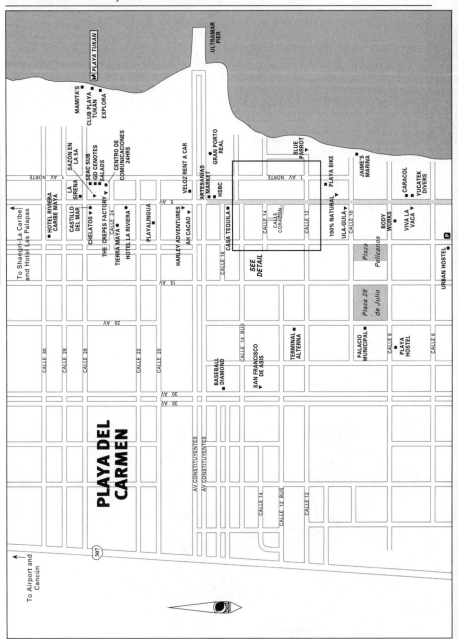

Riviera Maya and Cozumel

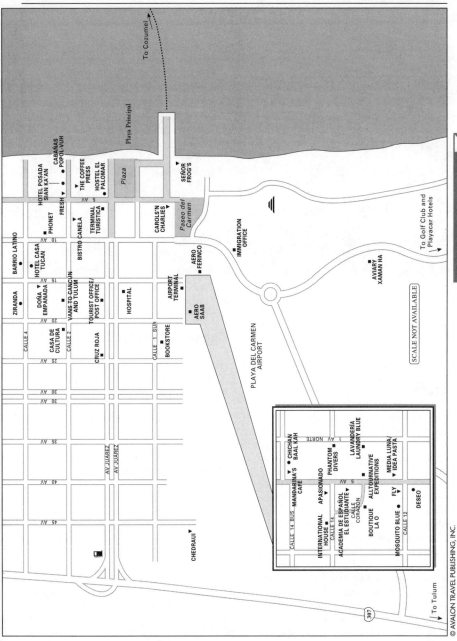

Riviera Maya and Cozumel

To Cozumel

Playa Principal

CABAÑAS POPOL-VUH
HOTEL POSADA SIAN KA AN
THE COFFEE PRESS
HOSTEL EL PALOMAR
Plaza
FRESH
AV 5
PHONET
AV 10
BISTRO CANELA
SEÑOR FROG'S
CAROL'S'N CHARLIES
Paseo del Carmen
TERMINAL TURISTICA
BARRIO LATINO
HOTEL CASA TUCAN
AV 15
AERO FERINCO
IMMIGRATION OFFICE
ZIRANDA
DOÑA EMPANADA
AV 20
VANS TO CANCUN AND TULUM
TOURIST OFFICE/ POST OFFICE
AIRPORT TERMINAL
CALLE 4
CASA DE CULTURA
AV 25
CALLE 2
CRUZ ROJA
HOSPITAL
CALLE 1 SUR
BOOKSTORE
AERO SAAB
AVIAR XAMAN HA
To Golf Club and Playacar Hotels
PLAYA DEL CARMEN AIRPORT
SCALE NOT AVAILABLE
AV 30
AV 30
AV 35
AV JUAREZ
AV JUAREZ
AV 40
AV 45
CHEDRAUI
To Tulum
307

CALLE 14 BUS
MANDARINA'S CAFE
CHICHAN BAAL KAH
AV 1 NORTE
APASIONADO
PHANTOM DIVERS
LAVANDERIA LAUNDRY BLUE
INTERNATIONAL HOUSE
CALLE 14
ACADEMIA DE ESPAÑOL EL ESTUDIANTE
AV 5
ALLTOURNATIVE EXPEDITIONS
MEDIA LUNA/ IDEA PASTA
CALLE CORAZON
BOUTIQUE LA O
FLY
MOSQUITO BLUE
CALLE 12
DESEO

© AVALON TRAVEL PUBLISHING, INC.

© LIZA PRADO CHANDLER

Mangroves, like this one near Playa del Carmen, are found throughout the Yucatán Peninsula.

beaches. Our visits have been somewhat disappointing lately, but a major renovation due to be completed in summer 2006 should give the park a much-needed new start. (For more information, see *The Riviera's Ecoparks* sidebar.)

Xcaret

Popular for good reason, Xcaret (Hwy. 307 between Playa del Carmen and Paamul, tel. 984/879-3077, www.xcaret.com.mx, 8:30 A.M.–10 P.M. daily, US$49/25 adult/child entrance only, US$75–89 adult all-inclusive with transport, US$38–45 child all-inclusive with transport) is a mega-ecopark offering water activities (such as snorkeling in underground rivers, swimming with dolphins, snubaing in reefs), educational areas focusing on regional flora and fauna (such as a wild bird aviary, a butterfly conservatory, a jaguar island, and an orchid greenhouse), as well as spectacular shows (including a Mayan ballgame, regional dance and music performances). If you're into organized activities, this is definitely a worthwhile stop. (For more information, see the sidebar, *The Riviera's Ecoparks*.)

ENTERTAINMENT AND EVENTS

Cinema and Arcade

Cines Hollywood (Plaza Pelícanos, 2nd floor, tel. 984/803-1417, 15 Av. between Calles 8 and 10) has three screens showing fairly recent Hollywood movies. Shows start around 5 P.M. daily; tickets US$4, US$2.60 on Wednesdays. Next to the movie theater, **Recórcholis** (tel. 984/803-1419, 10 A.M.–10 P.M. Mon.–Thurs., 10 A.M.–11 P.M. Fri.–Sun.) is a large, loud arcade.

Clubs, Bars, and Live Music

Cool and classy, **Fly** (corner of 5 Av. and Calle 12, tel. 984/803-1150, 1 A.M.–2 P.M. daily) tries hard to be a New York hangout on the streets of Playa del Carmen. Lots of outdoor seating makes for prime people-watching as you sip your martini. Meals here are good though a bit pricey, and service can be a bit uppity. Then again, that's kind of the point.

Considered one of the hottest spots in town, **Blue Parrot** (Calle 12 at the beach, tel. 984/873-0083, www.blueparrot.com, 11 A.M.–4 A.M. daily) is a beachside bar complete with hanging chairs, a small dance floor, and a party feel—day

© LIZA PRADO CHANDLER

Riviera Maya and Cozumel

lagoons and palapas in Xcaret

or night. Service can be a bit brusque but seems to improve as your bikini (or Speedo) shrinks.

Apasionado (5 Av. at Calle 14, 4 P.M.–midnight daily) features live jazz on Friday and Saturday nights in its breezy, second-floor dining area overlooking 5 Avenida. The music starts around 8 P.M.

And of course you can always find a party at **Señor Frog's** and **Carlos'n Charlie's,** both near the ferry dock. Open all day every day, these beach-town fixtures serve overpriced but familiar dishes, including steak and hamburgers, and offer a variety of drink specials and special events.

SHOPPING

One of the most popular destinations on the Riviera Maya, Playa del Carmen offers some of the best shopping around and 5 Avenida is where it's at. Here, you'll find high-end clothing boutiques, Cuban cigar shops, tequila specialty stores, spectacular *artesanía* shops, jewelry shops specializing in silver and amber, T-shirt and postcard stands. You name it, Playa del Carmen probably has it.

Handicrafts

Newcomer **La Sirena** (5 Av. at Calle 26, tel. 984/803-3422, 9 A.M.–9 P.M. Mon.–Sat.) is a small shop selling exceptional art from around Mexico. Italian shop owner Patrizia personally selects the myriad of beauties that she sells in her charming shop—think whimsical skeleton art, colonial statuettes of Virgen de Guadalupe, tin-framed mirrors, funky portrait art, bright shawls. You're sure to find something you can't resist.

A popular place, **La Calaca** (5 Av. between Calles 12 and 14, tel. 984/873-0174, la_calaca_playa@hotmail.com, 9 A.M.–midnight daily) sells Mexican masks, colorful *alebrijes* (fantastical wooden creatures), and quirky skeleton art. The quality is just alright but the variety is impressive. For higher-end collection pieces, check out its branch in Paseo del Carmen.

Clothing

Caracol (5 Av. No. 173 between Calles 6 and 8, tel. 984/803-1504, 9:30 A.M.–11 P.M. daily) is a great place to stop, if even just to admire the spectacular fabrics—tablecloths, bedding, and decorative art—that the German owner

THE RIVIERA'S ECOPARKS

The Riviera Maya plays host to a variety of ecoparks—as soon as you step off the plane or bus, you'll be bombarded with advertising, each promising something just a little different (and better) than the other. Some travelers swear by them; others can't stand the idea. Here's what to expect:

Riviera Maya

Tres Rios: Less grandiose than the other ecoparks on the coast, Tres Rios (Hwy. 307 between Puerto Morelos and Playa del Carmen, tel. 998/887-8077, www.tres-rios.com, adults US$35 entrance only, US$58 all-inclusive, US$80 grand all-inclusive, children half price) offers a little of every outdoorsy activity in the region: snorkeling in the Caribbean, swimming in cenotes, kayaking in mangroves, driving a miniature speed boat up and down the coast, horseback riding on the beach … even just relaxing in a hammock. Unfortunately, the reef isn't very healthy and has few fish, and the horseback and speedboat tours are dull. The highlights are definitely the namesake *tres rios* (three rivers), especially the one reserved for snorkeling. There, a beautiful, crystal clear cenote feeds into a deep channel that winds down to the ocean (you can snorkel or float in it from beginning to the end). The other two rivers are for kayaking; one winds through the mangroves, a common but little-explored landscape, and the other leads to a lagoon for bird-watching. Tres Rios recently underwent a major renovation, scheduled to be complete in summer 2006. The park is expanding, improving its facilities, and revamping the way guests visit and experience it—with any luck, it will chuck its use of activities coordinators, a system that was meant to save time but never really

worked. Most people visit on an organized trip from Cancun or Playa del Carmen; as always, going with a tour is convenient, but you get less of a bang for your buck. It's easy enough to get here independently, and you'll spend less time waiting around.

Xcaret: The mother of all of the Riviera's ecoparks, Xcaret (Hwy. 307 between Playa del Carmen and Paamul, tel. 984/879-3077, www.xcaret.com.mx, US$49 adult, US$25 child entrance only; US$75–89 adult, US$38–45 child all-inclusive with transport) is an immense park set on lush grounds and along a brilliant network of lagoons. Here, you'll truly find a taste of everything that the Yucatán Peninsula has to offer: snorkeling in underground rivers and Caribbean reefs, horseback riding on white sand beaches, a spectacular aquarium, dolphin and manatee swims (be sure to reserve in advance), bat caves, a Mayan village, butterfly pavilions, jaguar and puma islands, a flamingo reserve, mushroom farms, even a spectacular show highlighting ancient Mayan ceremonies (complete with a live ballgame). Beyond this, the park also is dedicated to protecting the flora and fauna of the region; programs include scarlet macaw- and turtle-breeding areas, protection of the endemic stingerless bee, and an orchid greenhouse—all with educational exhibits for visitors. It may be a little too commercialized for some, but hands down, Xcaret blows away its competition.

Xel-Há: One of the most popular ecoparks on the coast, Xel-Há (9 km/5.6 miles north of Tulum, www.xelha.com, 9 A.M.–sunset daily, US$29 adults and US$15 ages 5–12 Mon.–Fri., US$22 adults and US$11 ages 5–12 Sat.–Sun.) is promoted as a snorkeler's paradise. Here, you'll have your choice of lagoons, mangrove, river, or ocean to explore with a mask, snorkel, and fins (or on inner tubes, if you prefer to keep your head above water). While beginners will probably enjoy themselves, experienced snorkelers may find the waters overpopulated with tourists—and as a result—somewhat underpopulated by fish. Dolphin swims, snuba discovery, and cenote trails also are offered.

Isla Mujeres

Parque Garrafón: Built on a sloping bluff at the far south end of Isla Mujeres, Parque Garrafón (Carretera Punta Sur Km. 6, tel. 998/849-4950, 9 A.M.–5 P.M. daily, US$29 adults, US$14.50 children; entrance plus one meal US$49 adults, US$24.50 children; all-inclusive US$59 adults, US$29.50 children) is smaller than its sister ecoparks. You can snorkel, go up the observation tower, ride a zip line, paddle around in kayaks, or float in inner tubes. There's also a long curving infinity pool, plus hammocks, lockers, restaurant, and snack bars. For an extra fee, try snubaing (like scuba diving, but with a long tube instead of an air tank) or Sea Trek (a short underwater walking tour using a Martian-like helmet and breathing device). The snorkeling here is just okay: a fair amount of fish on a heavily damaged reef. Families, especially those with young kids, seem to enjoy themselves but the park typically receives lukewarm reviews.

Isla Cozumel

Parque Ecológico Punta Sur: Declared a national reserve in 1996, Parque Ecológico Punta Sur (Carr. Costera Sur Km. 27, tel. 987/878-8462, www.cozumelparks.com.mx, 9 A.M.–5 P.M. daily, US$10 before 2 P.M., US$6 after 2 P.M.) is less of a Disneyland experience and more of what you would expect from a park with "eco" in its name. Set on dunes, mangroves, and a lagoon, the park harbors more than 20 marine species, 30 types of seabirds (including roseate spoonbills and frigate birds) and a vast array of reptiles and amphibians (watch out for the crocodiles!). A viewing tower at Laguna Colombia helps visitors spot fauna. Guided tours—nighttime turtle-hatching expeditions or early morning flamingo tours—are offered seasonally at an additional cost. A colorful bus takes visitors through the park, or if you prefer, rent a bicycle or a golf cart and explore the park on your own. It's easy to spend an entire day here—not only bird-watching and animal-spotting but also swimming and snorkeling off the windswept beaches. Binoculars and snorkel gear can be rented for a small fee at the visitors center.

Parque Chankanaab: Parque Chankanaab (Carr. Costera Sur Km. 14, tel. 987/872-9723, www.cozumelparks.com.mx, 7 A.M.–6 P.M. daily, US$12, US$6 age eight and under) is a national park that is home to more than 60 species of marine life. Visitors come here to spend the day sunbathing, swimming in the ocean, and snorkeling or snubaing. **Dolphin Discovery** (toll-free Mex. tel. 800/713-8862, www.dolphindiscovery.com) operates a popular dolphin interaction program in the park (US$69–125 pp, 15–30 min.). Reserve your time slot as soon as you arrive, or better yet, call ahead or book online. There is also a fun sea lion program. Park facilities include two thatch-roofed restaurants, a few gift shops, and a fully equipped dive shop. Popular with families, it is a good place to spend the day if you have little ones in tow.

Riviera Maya and Cozumel

selects on her trips around southern Mexico. The store is also known for its especially good *bordado* (embroidery work) on clothing, which is locally made.

For funky, bohemian-style beachwear, head to **Boutique La O** (5 Av. No. 238 at Calle Corazón, tel. 984/803-3171, 9:30 A.M.–10:30 P.M. daily). You'll find tie-dye dresses, flowing linen pants, and cool cotton tops. Very comfortable and very Playa.

Tequila and Cigars

For one of the largest selections of tequila in town, check out **Casa Tequila** (5 Av. at Calle 16, tel. 984/803-2492, 9 A.M.–midnight daily). Here, you'll find an innumerable selection of labels ranging US$3–350 per bottle. The same store has another, larger outlet on 5 Avenida between Calles 4 and 6.

For the best in cigars, stop by **Havana Cigar Co.** (5 Av. between Calles 10 and 12, tel. 984/803-1047, 9 A.M.–11:30 P.M. daily). Cuban and Mexican *puros* are sold individually (US$5–10) or by the box (US$55–450).

Dive and Snorkel Equipment

The local **Seac Sub** shop (1 Av. Norte between Calles 24 and 26, tel. 984/803-1192, seacsub_mx@yahoo.com, 8 A.M.–9 P.M. Mon.–Sat.) has a large selection of masks, snorkels, fins, wetsuits, and other equipment, most decently priced. The shop has mostly Seac Sub products, of course, but carries other brands as well.

Bookstore

Near Chedraui supermarket, **Que Pequeño Es El Mundo** (Calle 1 Sur No. 189 between 20 and 25 Avs., tel. 984/879-3004, www.pequemundo.com.mx, 9 A.M.–8 P.M. Mon.–Sat.) is a small bookshop with a good selection of English language books—both new and used. You'll also find some excellent regional maps.

Shopping Centers

At the southern end of 5 Avenida, **Paseo del Carmen** (10 A.M.–10 P.M. daily) is a shady outdoor shopping center with high-end clothing boutiques, jewelry stores, art galleries, and restau-

rants. With a series of modern fountains, it makes for a pleasant place to window-shop—or enjoy an upscale lunch—after a day at the beach.

Plaza Pelícanos (10 Av. between Calles 8 and 10, 10 A.M.–11 P.M. daily) is a sad example of a mall with half-empty locales and a wilted food court. The only reason to come here is for the ATM, the movie theater, or the arcade (see *Entertainment and Events*).

For trinkets to take home, check out the **outdoor market** at the corner of 5 Avenida and Constituyentes (8 A.M.–10 P.M. daily). Here you'll find everything from Mayan pyramid key chains to silver jewelry from Taxco.

SPORTS AND RECREATION

Ecotours

Alltournative Expeditions (5 Av. between Calles 38 and 40, tel. 984/876-0616, www.alltournative.com) offers fun daily tours that include activities such as kayaking, rappelling, zip lines, off-road bicycling, caving, and snorkeling, plus (depending on the tour you choose) visits to a small Mayan village and Cobá archaeological zone. The agency has three principal tours to choose from (half- or full-day; US$67–89 pp adults and US$59–80 pp children under 12) and guides who speak English, Italian, French, German, Dutch, and Spanish.

Scuba Diving

Playa del Carmen has easy access to two of the most unusual diving experiences you may ever have: the awesome marine national park at Cozumel and the peninsula's famous cenotes, eerie freshwater caverns, caves, and underground rivers. There is also some fine open-water diving just offshore. Playa is perfect if you want a taste of both Cozumel and the cenotes, plus the convenience of being in town and near the airport. If diving is the main reason you came, it may make more sense to base yourself either at Cozumel itself or closer to the cenotes, such as at Akumal or Tulum. This will save you the time, money, and effort of going back and forth.

Prices in Playa del Carmen are pretty reasonable. When we passed through, ocean dives cost US$40–50 for one tank and US$50–60 for two tanks. Cozumel trips (always two tanks) cost US$80–100. Note that only one shop (Tank-Ha) sends a dive boat from Playa to Cozumel; with the rest, you take the ferry (US$16 round-trip, not included in dive price) and board your dive boat there. Cenote trips are always two tanks (and usually include lunch and drinks) and cost around US$90–100. These prices typically include full gear rental; divers with their own gear may get a small discount. Multidive packages are available at most shops, and earn you a 10–15 percent overall savings. Most shops also offer the full range of courses, from Discover Scuba and open-water certifications to nitrox and full cave diving courses.

It goes without saying that diving and snorkeling are potentially dangerous or even fatal activities. All the shops we list have proven safety records, but not every shop is right for every diver. A shop's "personality" is important, since safe diving means feeling comfortable with your guide and free to voice your questions or concerns. (Please see the *How to Choose a Dive Shop* sidebar in the *Cozumel* section for more tips.)

Tank-Ha Dive Center (5 Av. between Calles 8 and 10, tel. 984/873-0302, www.tankha.com, 8 A.M.–10 P.M. daily) is one of the longest-operating shops in Playa. Its prices are higher, but it's the only shop that takes divers to Cozumel by private boat instead of the ferry.

Dive Mike Caribbean Diving (Calle 8 between 5 Av. and the beach, tel. 984/803-1228, www.divemike.com, 8 A.M.–10 P.M. daily) is a very friendly, professional, reasonably priced shop. Check out its excellent and informative website for additional info and pictures.

Studio Blue (Calle 1 between 5 Av. and the beach, tel. 984/873-1088, www.cozumel-diving.net/studio-blue, 8 A.M.–10 P.M. daily) is a Cozumel-based shop (one of the oldest, in fact) but has a small storefront in Playa. It offers two-tank dives only, at reasonable prices.

Phantom Divers (formerly Yax-Ha Dive Shop, 1 Av. Norte between Calles 12 and 16, tel. 984/879-3988, www.phantomdivers.com,

8 A.M.–7 P.M. daily) is one of a handful of locally owned dive shops, offering friendly, casual service. No credit cards.

Yucatek Divers (5 Av. between Calles 6 and 8, tel. 984/803-1363, www.yucatek-divers.com, 9 A.M.–10 P.M. daily) uses an area hotel's pool for beginner certification training and all fun dives are led by instructors.

Go Cenotes (1 Av. Norte between Calles 24 and 26, tel. 984/803-3924, U.S. tel. 866/978-5086, www.gocenotes.com, 8 A.M.–8 P.M. daily) specializes in cave and cavern trips and courses for divers of all levels. Groups are always small (1–4 people) and the shop works hard to be sure you dive different cenotes every time.

Snorkeling

In Playa itself, you should take a tour since the snorkeling off the beach isn't too rewarding. The cenotes south of Playa also make for good, unique snorkeling (see those sections for more details).

Most of Playa's dive shops offer guided snorkeling tours to excellent sites. Ocean trips cost around US$25–30, while cenote trips are US$45–50, all gear included. Be sure to ask how many people will be on the trip, how long the trip will last, and how many reefs you'll be visiting (for ocean trips). For cenote trips, we strongly recommend a wetsuit, even if it means renting one for a few extra dollars. The water is chilly, there's no sun, and you'll be better protected against cuts and scrapes.

On Playa Tukán, **Explora** (tel. 984/879-7151, www.exploradive.com) offers daily guided snorkeling trips at 12:30 P.M. (US$25, 1.5 hours, including equipment).

Jaime's Marina (end of Calle 10, no phone, 9 A.M.–5 P.M. daily) is just a kiosk on the beach, but it offers friendly service and good snorkeling tours, among a number of water activities. Snorkel trips (US$30 pp) include sailing in small three-person sailboat to and from the reef (half hour each way) and an hour of snorkeling. If you come before 10 A.M., a 1.5-hour trip is only US$18. You can also rent snorkel gear (US$5/day) and a kayak (US$10/hour) and make your own snorkel trip—it's a long paddle but the best spot is in front of Coco Beach Club. Ask about a small anchor so your kayak doesn't float away.

Fishing

Playa de Carmen has excellent sport- and bottom fishing, with plentiful wahoo, *dorado*, mackerel, snapper, barracuda, and—especially April–June—sailfish and marlin. On average, trips for 1–5 people last 4–5 hours and cost US$200, including tackle and drinks. Most dive shops (including those listed in the *Diving* section) offer tours, or ask at **Jaime's Marina** (end of Calle 10, no phone, 9 A.M.–5 P.M. daily) on the beach.

Wind Sports

Kiteboarding, sailboarding, and sailing have grown in popularity along the Caribbean, a trickle-down effect from the world-famous wind-belt on the Gulf Coast northwest of here. You can catch at least some breeze almost any time of the year, but the strongest, most consistent winds blow November–March.

Ikarus (5 Av. at Calle 16, tel. 984/803-2068, 9 A.M.–10 P.M. Mon.–Sat.) is a retail shop that also arranges classes in kiteboarding. At the time of research, classes were being taught in Puerto Morelos (about 20 minutes north of Playa by frequent bus or van) and cost US$65/tel. 160/300 for one/three/six hours of private sessions, or US$55/tel. 105/275 in a group of three. The shop recommends 3–6 hours of instruction to learn the basics. A sister store is two blocks farther north at the corner of 5 Avenida and Calle 20 (tel. 984/803-3490).

Explora (Playa Tukán, tel. 984/879-7151, www.exploradive.com) is right on Playa's best beach, and offers kiteboarding courses (US$160 for a sixhour course) and rents sailboarding equipment (US$25/hour).

Fat Cat (tel. 984/876-3316, www.fatcatsail .com) is a spacious custom-designed catamaran used for daylong excursions that include sailing to secluded Xaac Cove, with a nice beach, good snorkeling, and a small Mayan ruin nearby. You can also try "boom netting," in which you are pulled through the water behind the boat on a thick boom net (US$70/42 adult/child standard, US$76/46 with transport to/from the marina).

Golf

The **Golf Club at Playacar** (Paseo Xaman-Há opposite Hotel Viva Azteca, tel. 984/873-0624 or toll-free Mex. tel. 800/672-5223, www.palace resorts.com, 6 A.M.–6 P.M. daily) is a sprawling, moderately challenging, 18-hole course in Playacar, the upscale hotel and residential development south of Playa del Carmen proper. Green fees are US$180/80 adult/under 17 or US$110 after 2 P.M., including cart, snacks, and drinks. Extra riders pay US$35/55 in low/high season and club rentals are US$30–50. Reserve at least a day in advance November–January.

Skydiving and Scenic Flights

Its gleaming white beaches and brilliant blue and turquoise seas make the Riviera Maya a spectacular place for skydiving. If you're up for it, **Sky Dive Playa** (Plaza Marina, tel. 984/873-0192, www.skydive.com.mx, 9 A.M.–6 P.M.) has been throwing travelers out of a plane at 10,000 feet since 1996. You cover 4,500 feet in about 45 seconds, followed by a 6–7-minute parachute to a soft landing on the beach. Tandem dives (you and an instructor; US$200) are offered every hour—reserve 1–2 days in advance in summer and high season.

If you enjoy the view but prefer to stay buckled in, several agencies at the airport and around town offer scenic flights and day trips. **Sky Tour** (tel. 984/803-3718) is a small operation offering scenic flights in a modern ultralight aircraft. Flights (25 minutes; US$99/149 one/two people) are available 8 A.M.–6 P.M. daily, but the best times are morning when there is very little turbulence, or sunset which is equally beautiful but a bit more bouncy. Each plane fits only one passenger (plus the pilot), but a couple can go up together in separate planes with radio communication. **Aero Saab** (Playa del Carmen airport, tel. 984/873-0804, 7 A.M.–7:30 P.M. daily) offers an all-day excursion that begins with a 45-minute flight inland to Chichén Itzá, a three-hour guided tour of the ruins, then lunch and swimming in a nearby cenote before flying back. (The price is US$230 pp, 2–5 people, entrance and guide fees included.) Ask about additional options, including trips to Palenque, Chiapas, or even Tikal, Guatemala.

Gym and Yoga

Playa's swankiest gym is **Area Body Zone** (Paseo del Carmen shopping center, south end of 10 Av., tel. 984/803-4048, www.areabody-zone.com, 6 A.M.–11 P.M. Mon.–Fri., 6 A.M.–10 P.M. Fri., 7 A.M.–5 P.M. Sat.–Sun.) with the latest exercise machines, a spacious free-weight and weight-machine areas, and regular sessions of aerobics, spinning, Pilates, and yoga. Day visits cost US$13, a 10-visit package US$90, and a month's membership US$110.

Body Works (Calle 8 between 5 and 10 Avs., 6 A.M.–10 P.M. Mon.–Fri., 9 A.M.–5 P.M. Sat.) is cheaper and more down to earth. The gym has a smallish free-weight and weight-machine area, and a large upstairs room for yoga, aerobics, and spinning. Day passes cost US$8.75, a 10-visit pass US$26, and a monthly membership US$61. Less expensive memberships or day passes also can be customized to your needs.

Across the street from the entrance to the Shangrí La Caríbe resort, **El Jardín de los Aluxes** (Calle 38 at Calle Flamingo, tel. 984/803-0391, jardinaluxes@hotmail.com) is an undeveloped jungle lot reserved for yoga instruction, tai chi classes, and spiritual growth seminars. Instruction is mostly held under a huge palapa in the middle of the grounds but students are free to wander (and practice) on the lush property. Regular yoga and tai chi classes are offered Monday, Wednesday, and Friday 10–11:30 A.M. and Tuesday and Thursday 8 A.M.–9:30 A.M. and 10 A.M.–noon. Classes cost US$5. Call for an updated events schedule.

Spas

Treat yourself to an afternoon of pampering at **Spa Itzá** (5 Av. at Calle Corazón, tel. 984/803-2588, www.spaitza.com, 10 A.M.–9 P.M. daily), a full-service spa in the heart of 5 Avenida. Massage therapies (US$35–85), Mayan healing baths (US$45–85), body wraps (US$45–75), and facials (US$45–85) are among the rejuvenating services offered every day.

A small operation, **Bella Spa-Tique** (5 Av. between Calles 26 and 28, tel. 984/803-3436, bellaspatique@aol.com, 10:30 A.M.–2 P.M. and 4–8 P.M. Mon.–Sat.) also offers massages (US$50), facials (US$31), and body treatments (US$22) in a peaceful environment.

ACCOMMODATIONS

Playa del Carmen has a huge selection and variety of accommodations, from youth hostels to swanky resorts. There is just one all-inclusive in Playa proper, but a great many in Playacar just south of town.

Under US$25

M Hostel Playa (Calle 8 s/n at 25 Av., tel. 984/803-3277, US$8 pp dorm, US$20 s/d with shared bath) is Playa del Carmen's best hostel, despite being somewhat removed from downtown and the beach. The dorm rooms—men's, women's, and mixed—are narrow but clean and have thick comfortable mattresses and individual fans. The simple, good-sized private rooms are also kept very clean, but light sleepers may be bothered by street noise. A very well-equipped kitchen has plenty of space to work your culinary magic and a good cubby system to prevent groceries from disappearing. And perhaps best of all is the hostel's enormous common area, with dining tables on one side and sofas, chairs, and cushions on the other that are perfect for playing cards, reading, watching TV, or whatever. Lockers and mosquito nets available; coffee and water provided (but not breakfast).

Urban Hostel (10 Av. between Calles 4 and 6, tel. 984/879-9342, urbanhostel@yahoo.com, US$9 pp dorm, US$17.50–22 s/d with shared bath) in Playa isn't as appealing as its sister hostel in Isla Mujeres. Where that one has plenty of open common space and a nice view from the bar-terrace, this one feels claustrophobic. The private rooms have low A-frame ceilings and a mattress on the floor. True, the dorms are in a huge, high-ceilinged room, but the artificial light and an overabundance of fabric hung up as decoration and room dividers reduce the space and give it a museum-closed-for-renovations feel. Other than that, the beds are comfortable, the bathrooms clean, and you're close to the bus station. You'll also have a full kitchen, TV room, free coffee, and purified water.

Hostel El Palomar (5 Av. between Av. Juárez and Calle 2, tel. 984/873-0144, US$9 pp dorm, US$26 s/d, including breakfast) has giant male- and female-only dorm rooms (a mixed area was planned) filled with row upon row of double bunks. The beds are comfortable enough but can feel pretty cramped—the management was thinking of removing a row or two, a good idea. Three smallish private rooms with clean, shared bathroom have a terrace with hammock and view of the ocean. On the rooftop—the only common area—the view is nice but the grubby open-air kitchen is not. Right across from bus terminal; continental breakfast and large lockers included.

Near the bus station and with private access to a nice stretch of beach, **M Cabañas Popol-Vuh** (Calle 2 between 5 Av. and the beach, tel. 984/803-2149, US$5.50 pp camping, US$16–17.50 s/d cabanas with shared bath, US$31 s/d with private bath) has a little of something for every budget traveler. As you walk through the gate, you'll take in the site in a glance: eight cozy cabanas and two hotellike rooms set up around a small shady lot where tents are pitched. The cabanas are simple wood-paneled constructions but they're comfortable, have good screens, and strong fans; they share exceptionally clean bathrooms with campers. The hotellike rooms are definitely a step up: cable TV, air-conditioning, and a private bathroom. In this town, these two units are a steal—and go fast! An excellent budget option.

US$25–50

A labyrinth of rooms, **Hotel Casa Tucan** (Calle 4 between 10 and 15 Avs., tel. 984/873-0283, casatucan@prodigy.net.mx, www.traveleasy-

mexico.com, US$22 s/d cabanas with shared bath, US$30–35 s/d rooms with private bath, and US$55 s/d apartment) offers basic accommodations in a social environment. Here, you'll find rustic cabanas with reasonably clean—though dark—shared bathrooms, simple hotellike rooms with fans (no frills here), and palapa-roofed studios with tiny kitchenettes (not really worth it). You'll also see what is likely the deepest pool on this coast—4.8 meters (15.7 feet). In fact, it's so deep that dive shops use it for open-water certification training! A nice rooftop lounge with a distant view of the ocean is a huge plus.

Just two blocks from the action, **Hotel La Ziranda** (Calle 4 between 15 and 20 Avs., tel. 984/873-3933, www.hotelziranda.com, US$31 s/d with fan, US$40 s/d with a/c) is a fine option. Sixteen sleek rooms—all with private balconies or terraces—are spread out between two modern buildings with a palapa-roofed lobby. Rooms are spacious, spotless, and have nice tile bathrooms. While all are upkept nicely, ask for a room on the second floor—they have high ceilings and the best cross breezes. Lots of ambivalent cats lounge about.

Set around a lush garden, **M Hotel Posada Sian Ka'an** (Calle 2 at 5 Av., tel. 984/873-0202, www.labnah.com, US$35–48 s/d with fan) offers 16 pleasant rooms just half a block from the Caribbean. All rooms have gleaming tile floors as well as balconies or terraces—some with partial views of the ocean, the rest overlooking the garden. Two units also have kitchenettes (US$48). Continental breakfast included.

US$50–100

Posada Barrio Latino (Calle 4 between 10 and 15 Avs., tel. 984/873-2384, US$40 s, US$50 d with fan, US$50 s, US$60 with a/c) offers charming well-kept rooms just two blocks from 5 Avenida. The 16 units are good-sized and have private terraces with hammocks. Continental breakfast (included in rates) is served in pleasant thatch-roofed breakfast area, which doubles as a lounge; guests can often be found writing postcards or playing cards there. Bicycles available free of charge.

Newcomer **Castillo del Mar** (5 Av. at Calle 26, tel. 984/803-2508, cdelmar2002@prodigy .net.mx, US$53 s/d with a/c) offers somewhat characterless rooms in a fantastic location. On 5 Avenida and a five-minute walk to the best beaches in town, rooms are spacious and have cable TV, phones, and *miniscule* kitchenettes. They also are remarkably clean. A good value.

On a peaceful section of busy 5 Avenida, the **Hotel La Riviera** (5 Av. No. 308 between Calles 22 and 24, tel. 984/873-3240, hotel_ lariviera@prodigy.net.mx, US$55 s with fan, US$65 d with fan, US$60 s with a/c, US$70 d with a/c) is a pleasant hotel. Recently renovated, the inviting rooms have sponge-painted walls, tile bathrooms, new televisions, and quiet air-conditioned units. Rooms in front also have balconies that overlook the avenue—a great people-watching spot. Continental breakfast included.

With its modern amenities and affiliation with a nearby beach club, **Hotel Riviera Caribe Maya** (10 Av. at Calle 30, tel. 984/873-1193, www.hotelrivieramaya.com, US$65–80 with a/c) is a good option. Rooms here come with cable TV, in-room phones, and minibars and are decorated with bright bedspreads and hand-carved Mexican furnishings. Most rooms also look out onto an inviting pool, which is tucked into the hotel's small courtyard. Internet access and continental breakfast are included in the rate.

Hotel Tierra Maya (Calle 24 No. 133 between 5 and 10 Avs., tel. 984/873-3960, www.hoteltierramaya.com, US$80 s with a/c, US$85 d with a/c) offers clean and ample rooms, decorated with appealing Mayan masks and fabrics. Amenities include the usual suspects in this range: in-room phone, cable TV, minibar, pool, and parking. Guests also can use the facilities free of charge at the two most popular beach clubs in town—Mamita's and Club Playa Tukán. With a hearty breakfast included, this is a favorite spot among travelers.

Over US$100

Chichan Baal Kah (Calle 16 between 5 Av. and the beach, toll-free U.S. tel. 800/538-6802, info@turqreef.com, www.mexicoholiday.com, US$120 s/d with a/c) is a charming little hotel on a shady street. Just half a block from the beach, this quiet hotel offers seven Mexican-style suites, each with one bedroom, a fully equipped kitchen, a living-dining room, and a patio. Each sleeps three. A small swimming pool and a sun deck with barbecue facilities also are available to guests. Ages 17 and over only.

The ultramodern **Mosquito Blue** (5 Av. between Calles 12 and 14, tel. 984/873-1335, www.mosquitoblue.com, US$149–189 s/d with a/c) is one of the classiest places to stay on the strip. Here, you'll find lush interior courtyards with two amoeba-shaped pools, an impressive palapa-roofed lounge with comfy couches and striking modern art, and a full-service spa with windows overlooking a peaceful jungle courtyard. Rooms—though somewhat cramped—are beautifully appointed and have the most modern in amenities: digital safes, wireless Internet (the hotel will even lend you a laptop!), plush bathrobes, minibar, and cable TV. Rooms with balconies are especially nice. Every afternoon, enjoy a free wine and appetizer hour with fellow guests or while you peruse one of the 2,000-plus titles (in five different languages!) in the library.

Take a Soho hipster hotel and combine it with a prime Caribbean location and you've got **Deseo** (5 Av. at Calle 12, tel. 984/879-3620, www.hoteldeseo.com, US$148–208 s/d with a/c). A sleek, urban-chic hotel, rooms here look as if they belong in a modern art museum. Really. Think bananas, flip-flops, and a bikini top hanging from the walls. Add minimalist furnishings, including a low-lying bed, streamlined fixtures, and photo-shoot lamps. Now, pump in some tunes—techno or some modern funk—and you've got your room. Outside your door, you'll find a pool with the words "Away from You" painted on the bottom, queen-sized cushions serving as beach chairs, and flowing white fabric strung high above your head to shade you from the sun. Finish off with free use of a hip beach club and what you've got is one of the hottest places to stay in town. Continental breakfast included.

Welcoming you to **Shangrí-La Caríbe** (5 Av. at Calle 38, tel. 984/873-0591, toll-free U.S./Can. tel. 800/538-6802, www.shangri-lacaribe.net, US$145–265 s/d with a/c) are 104 palapa-roofed bungalows and even more swaying palm trees. About 10 minutes from the hubbub on Avenida 5 but at the peak of the action on the beach, Shangrí-La is the epitome of a Caribbean resort. Bungalows here are strewn throughout lush gardens and along the beach. Each has tile floors, a *talavera* bathroom, and a balcony or terrace with hammocks. Sand paths connect the bungalows to the resort's facilities: two swimming pools, three restaurants, two bars, an Internet center, and a dive shop. It's definitely a party place but—no worries if you're looking to catch up on your romance novels—a quiet spot is never far away. Full breakfast and dinner are included in the rate.

Just south but significantly more low key is the lovely ◪ **Hotel Las Palapas** (Calle 34 between 5 Av. and the beach, tel. 984/873-0616, www.las-palapas.com, US$161–204 pp single, US$201–252 pp double). Set either in a lush garden brimming with native plants and trees or on a white sand beach with breathtaking views, the 75 thatch-roofed bungalows are truly idyllic. The peaceful units have comfortable beds, ample patios with hammocks, and radio access to an exceptional staff. No televisions or phones here. A stone-lined path also leads guests from their bungalows to an inviting freshwater pool, a clubhouse, a full-service spa, two restaurants, and—of course—beach chairs and umbrellas on the Caribbean. Be sure to climb the tall lookout platform for a spectacular bird's-eye view of Playa del Carmen (and Cozumel in the distance). Rates listed are per person and vary depending on the number of meals included (breakfast only or breakfast and dinner) and location of room.

All-Inclusives

There is only one all-inclusive in Playa del Carmen, the rest (and best) are in Playacar, an upscale hotel and residential development south of town. Playacar has dozens of all-inclusive options, many more than we're able to list here.

Rooms at the **Gran Porto Real** (Av. Constituyentes 1, at 1 Av. Norte, tel. 984/873-4000, reservations@realresorts.com.mx, US$140 s/d, US$130 pp for all-inclusive) have thick carved-wood doors, interior arches, and comfortable beds, plus the expected amenities such as air-conditioning and cable TV. Most rooms open onto wide, pleasant outdoor corridors; the suites (US$220, or US$170 pp all-inclusive) have ocean views. One drawback here is the beach, which is small and used by a constant stream of fisherman to haul up their boats. You may spot some huge fish being unloaded, but all in all we'd rather have the extra beach space. (Better beaches are a short walk away, however.) The pool area is pleasant though crowded, probably because none of the guests are on the sand.

Iberostar Tucan (Av. Xaman-Ha, tel. 984/877-2000, iberostar@playadelcarmen.com, www.iberostar.com, US$140–260 s, US$112–235 d, depending on season, all-inclusive only, US$50 extra for junior suite) has a spacious lobby-entryway and wide attractive beach with palm trees, beach chairs, and mild surf. Between the two is broad patch of healthy, well-maintained coastal forest, where you can spot monkeys, parrots, and other native birds and creatures in the treetops. Along the paths are signs identifying trees and flowers, plus a waterfall and natural-looking pool with a number of flamingos. After so many sterile and manicured resorts, this is a notable and welcome change of scenery. The pool is huge, and near the beach and two restaurants. Rooms are in large buildings along the property's edges, and are clean and comfortable if relatively nondescript. Standards look onto the leafy center, while junior suites have fine sea views.

Occidental Allegro Playacar (Av. Xaman-Ha, tel. 984/873-0340, www.occidental-hotels.com, US$112 pp d, US$172 pp s) is just a short walk from the golf club, which is nice for getting in an early-morning round. Two-story villas are scattered over the hotel's leafy tree-lined property. Inside, medium-sized rooms have tile floors, muted colors and decor, and modern bathrooms with distinctive stone sinks.

The beach here is thin but very attractive, and two large pools with a palapa-roof restaurant between them form a welcoming central area. Guests can make use of four tennis courts, five restaurants, and six bars, and the kids will enjoy the large outdoor playground.

Playacar Rental Properties

Playacar has scores of houses for rent of all different sizes and styles. Prices vary considerably, but expect to pay a premium for ocean views and during peak seasons. A number of property-management companies rent houses—some of the more prominent ones include **Playacar Vacation Rentals** (Calle 10 s/n, two blocks south of Av. Juárez near the Playacar entrance, tel. 984/843-0418, www.playacarvacationrentals. com), **Vacation Rentals** (tel. 984/873-2952, www.playabeachrentals.com), and **Playa del Carmen Vacation Homes** (www.playadelcarmenvacationhomes.com).

Paamul

How an unassuming trailer park and beach hotel scored such a nice stretch of private beach less than 20 kilometers (12.4 miles) south of Playa del Carmen is a real wonder. The large official-looking sign on the highway notwithstanding, there's only one establishment at the end of the 500-meter (1,640-foot) dirt access road. But then you could say **M Cabañas Paa Mul** (Carretera Cancún-Chetumal Km 85, between Xcaret and Puerto Aventuras, tel. 984/875-1053, www.paamul.com.mx, rooms and cabanas US$61, trailer US$20, camp US$10 pp) is a community all its own. The trailer park area has room for 60 units, and some of the guests—mostly American and Canadian retirees—have been here more than 15 years. Almost all the residents have built elaborate wood and palapa structures over and around their RVs, until the spaces look more chalet than mobile-home. The cabanas are popular with families staying a few days or a weekend. The simple but attractive freestanding wood constructions have two double beds, private bath, and a small patio. Some face the ocean and others a green garden area. A few

hotel rooms on the beach are the same size and price but are a bit musty and whipped by sticky surf wind. Tent campers set up nearby and use a shower and restroom on the beach. The on-site restaurant (8 A.M.–9 P.M. daily, US$5–15) serves basic Mexican meals, and a dive shop rents gear and offers snorkeling and diving tours. The beach is clean and pretty, and the water pleasant for swimming. The south end of the beach is mostly sandy, but the shallow water here harbors the prickly sea urchin—watch your step or wear water shoes.

At the Paamul turnoff is the very mini **Mini Super Paa Mul** (7 A.M.–7 P.M. Mon.–Sat., 8 A.M.–2 P.M. Sun.) and **Laundry Paa Mul** (8 A.M.–6 P.M. Mon.–Sat.) for when your clothes need a scrubbing.

FOOD

Attracting thousands from around the world, Playa del Carmen has scores of restaurants and eateries offering a variety of culinary delights. Walk a block or two down Quinta Avenida and you're sure to spot something that you like.

Mexican and Regional

If you're not going to make it to Oaxaca, **M Chelatos** (Calle 26 at 5 Av., no phone, 9 A.M.–5 P.M. Mon.–Fri., US$3–10) brings that state's unique, excellent cuisine to you. Here you can sample *tlayudas* (oversized corn tortillas filled with beans, cheese, and meat) or quesadillas with *nopales* (cactus). The truly adventurous should ask for quesadillas with *chapulines* (grasshoppers, typically sautéed in onion, garlic, and chili, a Oaxacan classic). Daily lunch specials are usually vegetarian, with hard-to-find options such as tofu or lentil soup, and are a steal at US$3. It's tiny—just a half-dozen tables set up along the sidewalk—but the ambience is comfortable and the service superb.

A few steps away, **Sazón en la 5a** (5 Av. between Calles 24 and 26, tel. 984/803-5881, 5–11 P.M. daily, US$6–10) also serves excellent Mexican fare in a low-key but distinctly refined atmosphere. The open-air dining room fronts the street and makes for pleasant people-watching.

La Palapa Hemingway (5 Av. between Calles 12 and 14, tel. 984/803-0003, 8 A.M.– midnight daily) has a good all-you-can-eat Mexican lunch buffet for under US$7. The menu has a varied selection of Mexican and Mayan favorites, including chicken mole, *chile en nogada,* and Yucatecan grilled fish, and there are a full bar and wine list. Sit inside for the air-conditioning or outside for the pleasant tile-covered tables right on the avenue.

Apasionado (5 Av. at Calle 14, 4 P.M.–mid-night daily, US$6–20) is a big lively restaurant and jazz bar overlooking 5 Avenida from a second-floor palapa-roofed patio, above all the hubbub. The menu has a bit of everything, from marinated seafood kabobs to ostrich burgers and grilled veggies. The drink menu is virtually endless, and there's live jazz Friday and Saturday, starting at around 8 P.M.

Vegetarian

Fresh (corner of Calle 2 and 5 Av., tel. 984/ 803-0233, 6 A.M.–1 A.M. daily, US$3–5) lives up to its name, serving good veggie omelets, crisp salads, and made-to-order baguettes in a bright, offbeat café-eatery. The smoothies and *licuados* taste great on a hot humid day, or as an early-morning snack on your way to the bus terminal.

Up the street, **Bistro Canela** (Calle 2 between 5 Av. and 10 Av., tel. 984/807-5530, 8 A.M.–11 P.M. daily, US$3–12) is a friendly, laid-back place where you can get simple breakfasts and good lunch specials (appetizer, main dish, and drink) for under US$5. *Canela* (cinnamon) figures into all the house specialties, though not obtrusively: mango chicken and pineapple shrimp have just a hint of the namesake spice. Many vegetarian options; service can be a bit uneven.

The Crepes Factory (Calle 24 at 5 Av., no phone, 8:30 A.M.–11:30 P.M. daily, US$3–5) is a simple semicovered sidewalk café that serves great smoothies and tasty crepes—you can oversee the production of both if you sit griddle-side at one of the counter stools, or have them delivered to the sunny table of your choice (there are only a half-dozen or so).

100% Natural (5 Av. between Calles 10 and 12, tel. 984/873-2242, 7 A.M.–11 P.M. daily, US$5–15) serves mostly vegetarian dishes and a large selection of fresh fruit blends. Service can be a bit inattentive here, but the food is fresh and well-prepared. Tables are scattered through a leafy garden area and covered patio.

For the perfect beach snack, swing by **M Doña Empanada** (15 Av. between Calles 2 and 4, 873-0655, www.donaempanada.com, 7 A.M.–11 P.M. daily) for some good greasy empanadas. They come in almost 20 different varieties, from spinach and cheese to strawberry and coconut, and cost about US$.50 apiece. There are all sorts of promotions: get 20 empanadas for US$7; 12 empanadas and a two-liter bottle of soda for US$6, or three for US$2 on Mondays and Wednesdays.

M Media Luna (5 Av. between Calles 12 and 14, tel. 984/873-0526, 1–11:30 P.M. daily, US$5–9) has an eclectic menu of creative and healthy dishes, many of them vegetarian and new ones constantly being invented, all in a quiet attractive dining area on Playa's main drag. Try potato zucchini pancakes for breakfast, a portabella mushroom, grilled pepper, and goat cheese sandwich for lunch, or farfalle in chipotle sauce for dinner. The fruit drinks are terrific.

International

Playa del Carmen has a sizable Italian community, and those craving Italian food won't go home disappointed. Next to Media Luna, **M Idea Pasta** (5 Av. between Calle 12 and 14, tel. 984/873-2173, noon–11:30 P.M. daily, US$5–15) combines excellent food with a comfortable, understated ambience. Favorite dishes include the lobster and shrimp fettuccini and the veggie cannelloni. The pasta and the gnocchi are made fresh and in-house (of course), but so are the pies and cakes, if you have any room for dessert. One interesting note: When Idea Pasta opened in 1998, it was the last restaurant on the strip. How things have changed....

Mandarina's Café (5 Av. at Calle 14 bis, tel. 984/803-1249, noon–1 A.M. daily, US$5–15) oozes cool, with low pulsing music, candles, and gleaming white tablecloths set in a semicovered patio dining area. The sign says "pizza and champagne," both of which come in a number of varieties. But the menu also has a long list of crepes, from egg and mushroom to asparagus and cheese, plus gnocchi, lasagna, and other pastas. Right on the avenue, this is fine place to see and be seen. Frequent two-for-one drink specials.

Viva la Vaca (5 Av. between Calles 6 and 8, noon–midnight daily, US$12–20) has to be the most disingenuous name for a Argentinean steak house—it means Long Live the Cow—but the all-you-can-eat steak special (US$16) has a way of fogging your critical faculties. Equally daunting is the two-person seafood platter, piled with shrimp, lobster, octopus, and grilled fish.

Seafood is the specialty at **M Ula-Gula** (corner of 5 Av. and Calle 10, 2nd floor, tel. 984/879-3727, 6 P.M.–midnight daily, US$8–15), a small appealing restaurant with an airy second-floor dining area overlooking the street corner. The Vietnamese-style sweet and sour fillet, served with caviar sauce and mashed sweet potatoes, is one of several recommended dishes. Or try one of several pasta, meat, or chicken plates.

M Babe's Noodles and Bar (Calle 10 between 5 Av. and 10 Av., tel. 984/804-1998, www.babesnoodlesandbar.com, noon–midnight Mon.–Sat., 5 P.M.–midnight Sun., closed Sun. in low season, US$5–10) is a Playa del Carmen institution, serving fantastic Thai and Asian-fusion meals in a hip, bistro setting. Dishes come in half and full orders; try the feta cheese noodles with olives, tomatoes, spinach, and chopped vegetables or Vietnamese shrimp salad with veggies and rice noodles in a Vietnamese dressing. There's a full bar, but definitely consider ordering the *limonmenta,* an awesome lime-mint slushie. It's not a huge place so you may have to wait for a table during high season, or order and eat right at the bar.

Coffee Shops
Chocolate-lovers will melt over **M Ah Cacao** (5 Av. at Constituyentes, tel. 984/803-5748, www.ahcacao.com, 7:30 A.M.–midnight daily, US$1.50–4), a chocolate café where every item on the menu—from coffees to cakes—is homemade from the sweetest of beans. Try a spicy Mayan Hot Chocolate for a true taste treat (US$3).

A half block from the beach, **The Coffee Press** (Calle 2 between 5 Av. and the beach, no phone, 7:30 A.M.–10 P.M. daily, US$3–5) is a modest café that's popular for breakfast. To really fill up, try the *huevos en su nido* (eggs in a nest)—poached eggs nestled in a big dollop of mashed potatoes. There's a two-for-one book exchange here too, but the selection is uninspiring.

News Café (Calle 13 between 5 Av. and 10 Av., tel. 984/803-5858, 8 A.M.–3 A.M. daily, US$3–6) has, as its name suggests, a stack of recent magazines and newspapers in Spanish, English, French, and Italian, from *Cosmo* to *The Economist.* Peruse the news while noshing on panini, baguettes, cake, and pie. Drinks vary from *licuados* and coffee to beer and cocktails. Open late for those après-disco munchies.

Groceries
Chedraui supermarket (Hwy. 307, 8 A.M.–10 P.M. daily) is Playa's biggest and best supermarket, on the highway two blocks south of Avenida Juárez. Chedraui supplanted **Super San Francisco de Asis** (30 Av. at Calle 12 bis, 8 A.M.–9 P.M. daily) as the main place in town to shop; its understocked shelves and run-down appearance may be signs it won't be around for long.

INFORMATION AND SERVICES
Tourist Information
The folks at the municipal tourist office (Av. Juárez at 15 Av., tel. 984/873-2804, 8:30 A.M.–8 P.M. Mon.–Fri., 9 A.M.–5 P.M. Sat.–Sun.) aren't terribly helpful, but the office has a large stock of tourist magazines, brochures, and fliers.

Playa del Carmen has a few free tourist magazines that are worth picking up, especially if you are here for more than a couple of days. *Dive 'n' Sports* (aka D'N'S) has good maps of

Playa, Puerto Morelos, Cozumel, Tulum, and Akumal, plus hotel and restaurant listings and short articles about kiteboarding, skydiving, and other activities. *Que Pasa? Playa Pocket Guide* is a small booklet with a somewhat confusing map but a good selection of ads and coupons, all organized into a convenient directory. *Sac-Be* and *Playa Maya News* are monthly magazines printed on newsprint and oriented toward the expat community. For tourists, they both usually offer a handful of useful articles, listings, and events calendars (and a dose of not-so-useful drivel, as well).

Medical Services

Centro de Salud (health center, Av. Juárez and 15 Av., tel. 984/873-0314) is a modest place with basic services and a 24-hour emergency room. Those with major ailments ought to go to Cancún. The **Cruz Roja** (Red Cross, Av. Juárez and 25 Av., tel. 984/873-1233) is two blocks away and also open 24 hours. It has ambulance service and responds to first-aid calls.

Pharmacies

Farmacia Yza has two 24-hour pharmacies—one on 10 Avenida between Calles 12 and 14, and the other on 30 Avenida between Calles 4 and 6.

Police

The tourist police (tel. 984/873-0291, tel. 984/877-3340, or 066 from any pay phone) have informational kiosks, theoretically manned 24 hours a day, at four locations around town—Avenida Juárez and 15 Avenida, 5 Avenida and Avenida Juárez, 5 Avenida and Calle 10, Calle 1 at Calle 26—and two locations on the highway, at the corners of Avenida Juárez and Avenida Constituyentes.

Money

Banks and free-standing ATMs are scattered around town. For ATMs or to change American dollars or AmEx travelers checks, try **Banamex** (corner of Calle 12 and 10 Av., 9 A.M.–4 P.M. Mon.–Fri., 10 A.M.–2 P.M. Sat.) and **Banorte**

(Plaza Pelícanos, 10 Av. between Calles 8 and 10, 9 A.M.–4 P.M. Mon.–Fri., 10 A.M.–2 P.M. Sat.). **HSBC** has freestanding ATM machines on 5 Avenida between Avenida Constituyentes and Calle 16, and at the Palacio Municipal.

Post Office

The post office (tel. 984/873-0300, 9 A.M.–5 P.M. Mon.–Fri., 9 A.M.–1 P.M. Sat.) is next to the tourist office at the corner of Avenida Juárez and 15 Avenida.

Internet and Telephone

Salads (1 Av. Norte between Calles 24 and 26, tel. 984/803-1111, 9 A.M.–11 P.M. daily Internet US$1/hour) was our office-away-from-the-office while researching Playa, with air-conditioning, a fast connection, and very friendly service. Though most people come for the Internet, it's also a good salad and sandwich shop (hence the name) and you can get coffee and pastries right at your computer. Tell Carlos we say hi!

Around the corner, **Centro de Comunicaciones 24 hours** (Calle 24 between 5 Av. and 1 Av. Norte, tel. 984/803-5778, Internet US$1/hour) has a fast connection and new flat-screen computers, and it is open all day and all night. You can also make international phone calls here, starting at US$.30/minute.

Closer to the center, **Cibernet** (Calle 8 between 5 Av. and the beach, tel. 984/873-3476, 8 A.M.–10 P.M. daily) is a huge Internet café that charges US$1.30 per hour for Internet, and US$2.60, plus computer time, to download pictures from your digital camera and burn them onto a CD (US$1.30 if you have your own blank CD).

Phonet Centro de Comunicaciones (10 Av. between Calles 2 and 4, 8 A.M.–11 P.M. daily) is a quiet place to make calls. Within Mexico calls cost US$.26 per minute, to the United States/Canada they rise to US$.65 per minute, and to Europe, it's a whopping US$1.05 per minute.

Laundry

Lavandería Laundry Blue (1 Av. Norte between Calles 12 and 16, tel. 984/873-1028, ext.

504, 7–1 A.M. daily) charges around US$1.25/kilo (2.2 pounds), less if you have a big load. You can check your email and wash your clothes at **Lavandería del Carmen** (Calle 2 between 10 Av. and 15 Av., no phone, 8 A.M.–10 P.M. Mon.–Sat., 8:30 A.M.–9 P.M. Sat.). Full service (wash, dry, and fold) is US$2.50 for 1–3 kilos and US$1/kilo thereafter. Self-service is US$1 per cycle (wash or dry) and US$.50 for the detergent. Internet costs US$.90 per hour.

Immigration

The immigration office (Instituto Nacional de Migración, 9 A.M.–1 P.M. Mon.–Fri.) is on the second floor of the Plaza Antigua mall, on Calle 10 just before the entrance to Playacar. Come here for a *prórroga* (visa extension), which entails filling out several forms, going to a bank to pay US$18 into a special account, and then returning to the office with your receipt to pick up the extension. It can be done in a day if you start early. You will have to show your passport, your current valid visa (the little white form you got at the airport), and your plane ticket out of Mexico. For every additional month you request, you usually have to show you have US$1,000 on hand—fortunately for your piggy bank, any valid credit card will do.

Spanish Schools

Playa del Carmen is becoming a popular place to study Spanish, with at least three recommendable schools, plenty of options for cultural and historical excursions, and of course good nightlife and easy access to the beach.

Playalingua del Caribe (Calle 20 between 5 Av. and 10 Av., tel. 984/873-3876, www.playalingua.com, 8 A.M.–8 P.M. daily) has simple, comfortable rooms in its large learning center, so you can roll out of bed and be conjugating verbs in a matter of minutes. The standard group course (US$160/week) has 3–6 students and meets weekday mornings for four hours/day, but private (US$20/hour) and two-person courses (US$14 pp/hour) can also be arranged. Students can stay with a local family (US$140/week including half-board); in a

room at the center (US$130–220 pp/week); or in a studio or apartment (US$50–100/day). One-time materials and inscription fees are about US$100; additional courses, from salsa to Mexican cooking, are held three evenings per week, and cost US$3–15 pp/class.

International House (Calle 14 Norte between 5 Av. and 10 Av., tel. 984/803-3388, www.ihriviera.com, 7:30 A.M.–9 P.M. Mon.–Fri., 7:30 A.M.–noon Sat.) occupies a pretty and peaceful colonial home, with a large classroom, garden, bar, and restaurant on-site. In this most polished of Playa's Spanish schools, all instructors are university graduates with training in teaching Spanish as a foreign language. Ten-week extended courses (US$260/term) begin four times yearly (typically January, April, July, and October) and include four hours of class per week. Intensive group classes (US$175/week, maximum eight students per class) include four hours of class per day and can be joined on any Monday. Private and Internet-based courses also available. Age 16-plus only for group classes; all materials and inscription fees included. Family stays are US$140–US$160/week; rooms and apartments—simple to deluxe, with or without meals—cost US$125–650/week.

Academia de Español El Estudiante (Restaurant Xlapak, 5 Av. between Calles 14 and 14 bis, cell tel. 044-984/876-0616, info@playaspanishschool.com, 8:30 A.M.–10 P.M. daily) is more low-key and backpacker-oriented, with a single open-air patio where groups of classes are conducted over small wooden tables. Group classes (US$7/hour, 2–4 people only) meet four hours every weekday morning; private classes (US$12/hour) can be conducted any time, including weekends. A one-time US$25 inscription fee covers books, copies, and other materials. The school helps organize outings, including guided tours to Cobá or Chichén Itzá or weekend excursions to Mérida, plus weekly cooking and salsa classes, volleyball games, snorkeling tours, and student-teacher dinners. Students can stay with a family (US$140/week, including breakfast) or in a guesthouse with private rooms, small kitchen, and a pool (US$140 s, US$190 d).

PLAYA DEL CARMEN BUS SCHEDULES

Terminal Turística (5 Av. and Av. Juárez, tel. 984/873-0109, ext. 2501) departures include:

Destination	Price	Duration	Schedule
Akumal	US$1.25	20 min.	take Tulum bus
Bacalar	US$9.50	4 hrs	take Chetumal bus
Cancún	US$2.75	1 hr	every 10 min., 5:45 A.M.– midnight
Chetumal*	US$13.75	4.5 hrs	5:15 A.M., 7:15 A.M., 8:15 A.M., 10:15 A.M., 12:15 P.M., 1:15 P.M., 3:15 P.M., 5:15 P.M., and 11:15 P.M.
Cobá	US$3.75	2 hrs	6 A.M., 8:45 A.M., and 10 A.M.
Dos Ojos	US$1.50	40 min.	take Tulum bus
Felipe Carrillo Puerto	US$5.50	2.5 hrs	take Chetumal bus
Hidden Worlds	US$1.50	40 min.	take Tulum bus
Limones	US$7.75	3.5 hrs	take Chetumal bus
Puerto Aventuras	US$.75	15 min.	take Tulum bus
Puerto Morelos	US$1.50	20 min.	every 10 min. 5:45 A.M.– midnight
Tulum	US$2.75	1 hr	9:20 A.M., 10:05 A.M., 10:50 A.M., 11:50 A.M. (first class) or every hour at the quarter hour 5:15 A.M.– 11:15 P.M. (second class)
Xcaret	US$2.25	15 min.	take Tulum bus
Xel-Ha	US$3.50	30 min.	take Tulum bus

*If your final destination is Chetumal, consider taking the first-class bus, as this one makes many intermediate stops.

Terminal Alterna (Calle 20 between Calles 12 and 12-Bis, tel. 984/803-0944, ext. 2501, toll-free Mex. tel. 800/702-8000) departures include:

Campeche	US$27	7 hrs	10:20 A.M.
Chetumal (Belize border)	US$13	4.5 hrs	6:15 A.M., 7:15 A.M., 9:15 A.M., 10:45 A.M., 11:45 A.M., 1:15 P.M., 2:30 P.M., 3:30 P.M., 4:30 P.M., 5 P.M., 5:30 P.M., 7:30 P.M., 9:15 P.M., 9:45 P.M., and 11:55 P.M.

Riviera Maya and Cozumel

Destination	Price	Duration	Schedule
Chichén Itzá	US$13	3.5 hrs	8 A.M.
Ciudad Cuauhtemoc (Guatemala border)	US$55	21 hrs	9:45 P.M.
Cobá	US$4.50	1.5 hrs	8 A.M.
Escárcega	US$25	8 hrs	12:15 A.M., 12:40 A.M., 7:30 A.M., 3:30 P.M., 5 P.M., 9:45 P.M.
Felipe Carrillo Puerto	US$7	2 hrs	6:15 A.M., 7:15 A.M., 10:45 A.M., 11:45 A.M., 1:15 P.M., 2 P.M., 5:30 P.M., 7:15 P.M., and 9:15 P.M.
Mérida	US$19	5 hrs	12:30 A.M., 6:30 A.M., 8:15 A.M., 10:15 A.M., 11:30 A.M., 1:30 P.M., 3:15 P.M., 5:15 P.M., 6:30 P.M., and midnight
Mexico City (TAPO)	US$72	24 hrs	7:30 A.M., 12:15 P.M., 9:15 P.M., and 9:10 P.M.
Ocosingo	US$39	17 hrs	3:30 P.M., 5 P.M., 7 P.M.*, and 9:45 P.M.
Palenque	US$34	12 hrs	3:30 P.M., 5 P.M., 7 P.M.*, and 9:45 P.M.
Puebla	US$74	23 hrs	6:15 P.M.
San Cristóbal de las Casas	US$42	19 hrs	3:30 P.M., 5 P.M., 7 P.M.*, and 9:45 P.M.
Tapachula (Guatemala border)	US$62	26 hrs	9:45 P.M.
Tuxtla Gutiérrez	US$46	20 hrs	3:30 P.M., 5 P.M., and 7 P.M.*
Valladolid	US$10	2.5 hrs	12:30 A.M., 8:15 A.M., 10:20 A.M., 11:30 A.M., and 6:30 P.M.
Veracruz	US$59	22 hrs	2 P.M. and 10:10 P.M.
Villahermosa	US$37	12 hrs	12:40 A.M., 12:15 P.M., 2 P.M.; 6:15 P.M., 7:15 P.M., 10:45 P.M., and 11:15 P.M.
Xpujil	US$19	5.5 hrs	12:15 P.M., 6:15 P.M., and 7:15 P.M.

*Denotes ADO-GL deluxe service; fares are 10–30 percent higher, and travel time may be slightly faster. There are many more ADO-GL departures from Cancún.

Riviera Maya and Cozumel

Other Classes

If you are staying for more than just a couple of weeks, consider taking a class or two at the **Casa de la Cultura** (Calle 2 at 20 Av., tel. 984/873-2654, fromero@solidaridad.com. mx, 9 A.M.–10 P.M. Mon.–Sat.). Instruction offered includes regional dance, guitar, painting, and singing. Three-month-long courses—which you can drop in on for a month at a time if there is space available—cost no more than US$20.

Travel Agencies

Mayaluum Travel Agency (corner of 10 Av. and Calle 2, tel. 984/873-2961, mayaluum@prodigy.net.mx, 9:30 A.M.–2 P.M. and 3:30–7:30 P.M. Mon.–Fri., 9:30 A.M.–2 P.M. Sat.) handles plane tickets, package tours, and other travel arrangements. Other options include **IMC Grupo Intermar** (Av. Juárez s/n at 25 Av., tel. 984/873-1436, www.travel2mexico. com, 8:30 A.M.–7:30 P.M. Mon.–Fri., 8:30 A.M.–4 P.M. Sat., 8:30 A.M.–2 P.M. Sun.) and **Cenote Azul Travel Agency** (Calle 12 Norte 128, tel. 984/803-2880, 9 A.M.–9 P.M. Mon.–Sat., 2–9 P.M. Sun.).

GETTING THERE

Bus

Playa del Carmen has two bus stations. **Terminal Turística** (aka. Terminal Riviera, 5 Av. and Av. Juárez, tel. 984/873-0109, ext. 2501) is in the center of town and has frequent second-class service to destinations along the coast, including Cancún, Tulum, and everything in between. The **Terminal Alterna** (Calle 20 between Calles 12 and 12 bis, tel. 984/803-0944, ext. 2501, or toll-free Mex. tel. 800/702-8000) has first-class and deluxe service to interior destinations such as Mérida, Campeche, and beyond. There is some overlap, and you can buy tickets for any destination at either station, so always double-check where your bus departs from when you buy a ticket. Also, departure times can vary by 15–30 minutes as most buses do not originate in Playa.

Combis

Taking a *combi* (public van) up or down the coast for a day trip is one of the easiest ways to get around. To head north of Playa del Carmen, take a *combi* at Calle 2 at 20 Avenida. *Combis* leave every 10 minutes, 24 hours a day, and cost US$2.60. You can be dropped off anywhere you ask along the highway—if you're going to Cancún go to the ADO bus terminal on Avenida Tulum (where you can catch another bus to the Zona Hotelera). If you're heading south catch a *combi* on Calle 2 between 15 and 20 Avenidas. Vans here leave every 10 minutes between 4 A.M.–midnight and cost US$2.25. They go as far as the ADO bus terminal on the south end of Tulum, passing the turnoffs for Akumal, Hidden Worlds, Tulum Ruins, and Tulum town among many others. To return to Playa del Carmen, simply flag down a *combi* anywhere along the highway.

Air

Playa del Carmen's airport does not receive regular commercial flights, though charters are available to and from locations around the peninsula and even Belize and Guatemala. (See *Sky Diving and Scenic Flights* in the *Sports and Recreation* section of this chapter for more information.)

Car

Driving to Playa del Carmen, look for the two main access roads to the beach—Avenida Constituyentes on the north end of town and Avenida Benito Juárez on the south. Playacar has its own entrance from the highway—most convenient—but can also be reached by turning south on Calle 10 off Avenida Juárez.

Ferry to Isla Cozumel

Ferries to Cozumel (US$8, 30 minutes) leave from the large pier at the end of Calle 1 Sur. Two companies (**UltraMar** and **Mexico Water Jets**) operate the boats and you will be harangued by competing ticket sellers in booths as you approach the pier. Their service and fares are identical, so you can really choose either one. The ticket seller will probably try to sell you a round-trip ticket, but it doesn't cost anything extra to buy *sencillas* (one-way tickets). Between the two companies, there are 1–2 ferries leaving every hour on the hour 8 A.M.– 9 P.M., plus an early and late departure at 6 A.M. and 11 P.M. daily.

UltraMar has built a second ferry pier in Playa del Carmen at the end of Avenida Constituyentes, 10 blocks north of the present pier. When service begins there—it hadn't yet as we went to press—you should be able to buy tickets and board a ferry at either location. If you plan to catch a bus right after returning from Cozumel, note that the new pier is closer to Terminal Alterna (for long-distance service) while the main pier is closer to Terminal Turística (for local service, including to Cancún and Tulum).

Just south of Xcaret is the **Punta Venado dock** (tel. 987/872-0916, mchanka@prodigy .net.mx, www.maritimachankanaab.es.mw, US$40 per car (including driver), US$2.60 pp). Once used by the Calica company to ship limestone products to the United States, today it is home to the only car ferry to and from Isla Cozumel. Monday through Saturday, ferries leave from Punta Venado at noon, 5 P.M., and 9 P.M. Sundays, it departs at 7 A.M., 1 P.M., 5 P.M., and 9 P.M. From Cozumel, the ferry leaves at the same time all week: 4:30 A.M., 9 A.M., 3 P.M., and 7 P.M. The trip takes about 1.5 hours. Be sure to arrive at least an hour before your departure time; travelers often compete with trucks carrying supplies to Cozumel for a spot on the ferry. Also, don't be surprised if you see throngs of day-trippers, the dock also is a popular resting place for cruise ships.

GETTING AROUND

Playa del Carmen is a walking town, though the steady northward expansion is challenging that description. The commercial part of 5 Avenida now stretches 15 blocks and is sure to get longer. You may want to catch a cab if you have bags or are going to the golf course or all-inclusives in Playacar. Frequent all-day bus service up and down Highway 307 makes it easy to reach many destinations beyond Playa, although a rental car will still save you time and is vital for visiting the less-accessible areas. Parking in Playa in the high season can be a challenge, especially south of Avenida Constituyentes—there's a 24-hour lot on 10 Avenida between Calle 6 and 8 (US$1/hour).

Bike Rental

A bike can make Playa's ever-extending commercial area more manageable—10 Avenida even has a dedicated bike lane—and you'll see plenty of expats and locals with wheels of their own. **Playa Bike** (1 Av. Norte between Calles 10 and 12, cell tel. 044-984/745-1387, 8 A.M.– 8 P.M. Mon.–Sat.) rents two-wheelers (US$3/ hour, US$9/day) plus snorkel equipment, umbrellas, and other beach gear.

Bike-Taxis

Triciclos (bike-taxis) line up on Avenida Juárez alongside the Terminal Turística. A ride costs US$1.25 and makes an interesting alternative to nonpedal cabs.

Taxis

Taxis around town cost US$1.25 (a bit more if you pick one up at an official taxi stand as opposed to flagging one down) but a lot of drivers will try charging much more than that. Prices do change every year or two, so ask at your hotel what the current rate is and be sure to agree on the fare with the driver before setting off.

Car and Motorcycle Rental

Playa has myriad car rental agencies—most offer the same vehicles and insurance plans, but prices can vary considerably. Definitely ask around and always negotiate the rate, especially in the low season or if you're renting for more than a day or two. Expect to pay US$45–60/day for a compact Chevy or VW, with tax and insurance included. Local agencies include **Hertz** (Corner of 5 Av. and Calle 10, tel. 984/873-1130, 7 A.M.– 8:30 P.M. daily); **Zipp Rent-A-Car** (Hotel Jungla Caribe, 5 Av. at Calle 8, tel. 998/849-4193, www.zipp.com.mx, 8 A.M.–6 P.M. daily); **Veloz Rent a Car** (Av. Constituyentes 111 between 5 Av. and 1 Av. Norte, tel. 984/803-2323, 8 A.M.–1 P.M. and 5 A.M.–8 P.M. daily); and **Wheels** (10 Av. between Calles 12 and 14, tel. 984/803-0230, wheels_rentacar@yahoo .com, 8 A.M.–8 P.M. daily).

For motorcycles or scooters, try **Harley Adventures** (Acá los Tacos restaurant, corner of 5 Av. and Av. Constituyentes, cell tel. 044-984/804-6532, www.harleyadventures.com) which rents Harley-Davidson Fatboys and 883 Sportsters for US$175 and US$75 per day; or **Moto Altavista/Eurobike** 10 Av. between Calles 12 and 14, tel. 984/803-1964) for Ducatis, Vespas, and more.

Isla Cozumel

The island of Cozumel has something of a split personality. The lee (west) side of the island faces a calm sea and while the beaches aren't spectacular, the water is—glittering a hundred shades of blue in the bright Caribbean sun. Beneath the low waves, Cozumel's coral reefs are among the most pristine in the world, making for spectacular diving and snorkeling. The west side also faces Playa del Carmen and the mainland and is the island's most developed area. San Miguel de Cozumel, the island's main town, has virtually all the offices, shops, banks, markets, hotels, and restaurants. The island's east coast is another world, relatively devoid of people but dotted with isolated coves and beaches—some with placid water, others with spectacular crashing surf. Between the coasts are Mayan ruins and a tangled, overgrown scrubscape. The island has a split personality when it comes to people too, between the modest easygoing local population and the loud crush of tourists, especially from cruise ships. In the middle are business owners and expats, who seem more inclined toward the local way of life but are deeply entwined in tourism here.

San Miguel de Cozumel (which most people just call Cozumel) is the island's main town and has a relaxed, unhurried atmosphere. But it is no longer the sleepy fishing village it once was. This is where cruise ships land—as many as 10 a day in the high season—disgorging thousands of tourists who form a human river along the Avenida Rafael Melgar, the town's main waterfront promenade. Jewelry shops, modern malls, and chain restaurants do fierce business to keep up with the sky-high rents they pay for their prime commercial property. The main plaza also sees heavy foot traffic when cruise ships arrive, as do few blocks of pedestrian walkways around the plaza, which are crammed with curio shops and scooter rental agencies.

But just a block or two beyond these areas, San Miguel de Cozumel remains a small friendly town where old folks sit in their windows and dogs sleep in the streets. In spring, masses of orange *framboyán* (poinciana) flowers bloom on shade trees in the plaza and in many a backyard, and festivals and religious celebrations are still widely attended. You can't avoid Avenida Rafael Melgar and the plaza completely (nor should you) but don't let the hubbub there turn you off from the town or island altogether. San Miguel has a good museum, a number of fine restaurants, and of course a slew of dive shops that will take you to the island's incredible coral reefs. Beyond town are classy hotels, good beach clubs, Mayan ruins, fun family parks, and the wild beaches and deserted coastline of Cozumel's eastern side.

ORIENTATION

The main passenger ferry pier (where you'll take the ferry to/from Playa del Carmen docks) is opposite the plaza at the foot of Avenida Benito Juárez. Avenida Juárez goes east through town before becoming the Cross-Island Highway, passing the turnoff to the San Gervasio ruins before intersecting with the coastal road and the ocean. North of the intersection, an unpaved road (which is not covered by most rental car insurance plans) rambles through the island's most deserted coastline to Punta Molas and an old lighthouse. South of the intersection

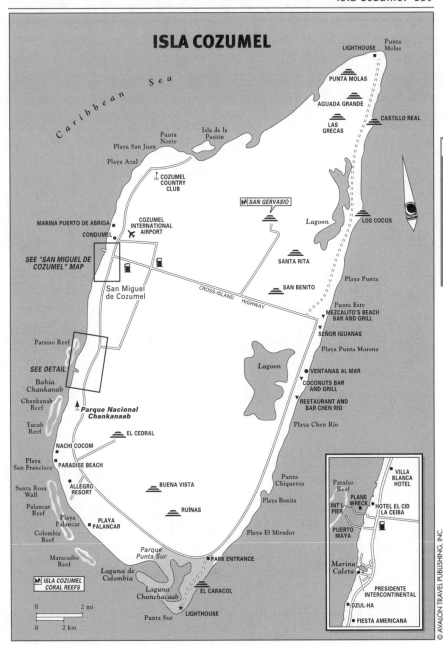

ISLA COZUMEL

LIGHTHOUSE Punta Molas

PUNTA MOLAS

AGUADA GRANDE

CASTILLO REAL

LAS GRECAS

Caribbean Sea

Punta Norte

Isla de la Pasión

Playa San Juan

Playa Azul

COZUMEL COUNTRY CLUB

SAN GERVASIO

Lagoon

LOS COCOS

MARINA PUERTO DE ABRIGA

CONDUMEL

COZUMEL INTERNATIONAL AIRPORT

SANTA RITA

SEE "SAN MIGUEL DE COZUMEL" MAP

San Miguel de Cozumel

CROSS-ISLAND HIGHWAY

SAN BENITO

Playa Punta

Punta Este
MEZCALITO'S BEACH BAR AND GRILL

SEÑOR IGUANAS

Paraiso Reef

Playa Punta Morena

SEE DETAIL

Bahía Chankanab

Lagoon

VENTANAS AL MAR

Chankanab Reef

COCONUTS BAR AND GRILL

Yucab Reef

Parque Nacional Chankanaab

RESTAURANT AND BAR CHEN RÍO

Playa Chen Río

EL CEDRAL

NACHI COCOM

Playa San Francisco

PARADISE BEACH

Santa Rosa Wall

ALLEGRO RESORT

BUENA VISTA

Punta Chiqueros

Playa Bonita

Palancar Reef

Playa Palancar

RUÍNAS

PLAYA PALANCAR

Colombia Reef

Playa El Mirador

Maracaibo Reef

Parque Punta Sur

PARK ENTRANCE

ISLA COZUMEL CORAL REEFS

Laguna de Colombia

Laguna Chunchacaab

EL CARACOL

0   2 mi

0   2 km

Punta Sur

LIGHTHOUSE

Inset (detail map, lower right)

Paraíso Reef

VILLA BLANCA HOTEL

INT'L PIER

PLANE WRECK

HOTEL EL CID LA CEIBA

PUERTO MAYA

Marina Caleta

PRESIDENTE INTERCONTINENTAL

DZUL-HA

FIESTA AMERICANA

Riviera Maya and Cozumel

SAN MIGUEL DE COZUMEL

Caribbean Sea

To Playa del Carmen

MAIN DOCK AND FERRY

Benito Juárez Park

To Hacienda San Miguel, Condumel, Airport, and Cozumel Country Club

To Cross-Island Highway

AV RAFAEL MELGAR

AV 5 NORTE

AV 10 NORTE

AV 15 NORTE

AV 20 NORTE

AV BENITO JUÁREZ

CALLE 10 NORTE

CALLE 8 NORTE

CALLE 6 NORTE

CALLE 4 NORTE

CALLE 2 NORTE

CALLE 1 SUR

PANCHO'S BACKYARD/ CINCO SOLES

GUIDO'S

HOTEL FLAMINGO

THE COFFEE PRESS

MUSEO COZUMEL/ MUSEO RESTAURANT

RACHAT & ROMERO

HARD ROCK CAFE

LAS PALMERAS

MANATÍ

SERVI-LAV LAVANDERIA

CLINICA SAN MIGUEL

BAKERY ZERMATT

RENTADORA ISIS

LA VERANDA

ALL SPORT

CAFÉ CHIAPAS

BANORTE

SOL Y MAR

TICKET BUS

TOURIST OFFICE

BANCOMER

TAMARINDO B&B

FARMACIA SANTA FÉ

LA MICHOACANA

RENTADORA COZUMEL

SAN MIGUEL CHURCH

SMART RENT A CAR

COZUMEL MINI GOLF

FARMACIA PORTALES

HSBC

CASA DENIS

AMBAR

HOTEL MARY CARMEN

LOS COCOS

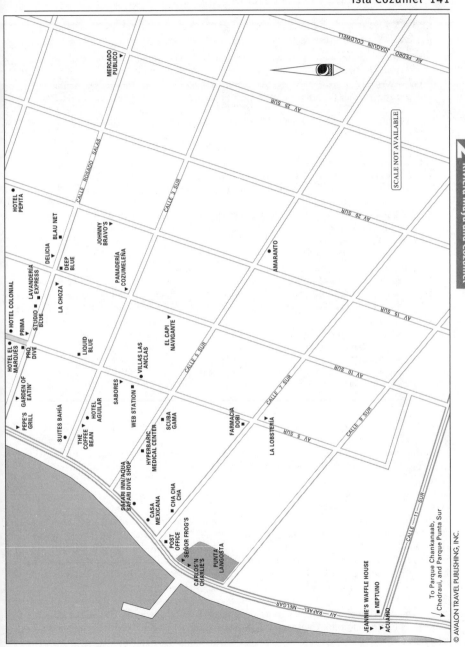

Riviera Maya and Cozumel

ISLA COZUMEL DIVE SITES

A diver's heaven, Cozumel's dive sites are among the best in the world. A few of the most popular include:

Plane Wreck: A 40-passenger Convair airliner—engines removed—lies belly up on the seabed, 100 meters (328 feet) off El Cid's hotel pier. Sunk in 1977 for the Mexican movie production of *Survive II*, the wreck is now home to myriads of fish, multicolored sponges, and coral heads. There is a 120-meter (393.7-foot) trail with underwater signs pointing out the various types of marine life on the reef. Average depth is 13 meters (42.7 feet).

Paraíso: About 200 meters (656 feet) off the beach just south of the International Dock and averaging a depth of 13 meters (42.7 feet), this is a site of impressive sea fans, star corals, and brain corals. The south end of the reef is teeming with life. Excellent for night dives.

Chankanaab: South of Laguna Chankanaab, the average depth here is 12 meters (39.4 feet). At the drop-off, stunning coral heads covered with gorgonian and sea fans are found. Striped grunt, mahogany snapper, basket starfish, octopi, and jail-striped morays are seen here. Good for beginners.

Tormentos: Innumerable coral heads are featured in this 8–12-meter/26.2–39.4-foot-deep site. The heads are decorated with fans, gorgonians, and sponges. Great numbers of invertebrates prowl the sandy bottom—look for flamingo tongue shell, arrow crab, black crinoid, coral shrimp, and sea cucumber. The farthest section of the reef drops to 21.5 meters (70.5 feet), where you'll see deep-sea fans, lobsters, and mammoth groupers. Excellent for photos.

Yucab: One kilometer (0.6 mile) south of Punta Tormentos, this reef is fairly close to shore, shallow, and alive with queen angelfish, star coral, brain coral, sponge, and sea whip. It is about 120 meters (393.7 feet) long with an average depth of nine meters (29.5 feet). Good for beginners.

is Cozumel's rustic eastern shore, which is dotted with a few beach clubs and isolated hotels. Rounding the southern tip are two not-too-charming restaurant-bars and the turnoff to Parque Punta Sur. The road eventually bends northward along the west shore, passing beach clubs, a few private homes, and high-rise hotels. Just offshore are most of Cozumel's best dive sites. The highway feeds onto Avenida Rafael Melgar, and you're back at the plaza. Continue north to reach the airport, country club, and more high-rise hotels.

The island is 47 kilometers (29.2 miles) long, 15 kilometers (9.3 miles) wide, and lies 19 kilometers (11.8 miles) offshore, across a channel nearly a kilometer (0.6 mile) deep. The island's high point measures a scant 14 meters (45.9 feet) above sea level. More than 50,000 people call Cozumel

home, but only 4 percent of the island has been developed. Temperatures are warm year-round. The rainy season runs from May to October, with daily (but short) showers in the summer.

HISTORY

Cozumel has been inhabited since as early as 300 B.C. and was one of three major Mayan pilgrimage sites in the region (the others were Chichén Itzá and Izamal in Yucatán state). The name is derived from the island's Mayan name *Cuzamil* (Land of Swallows). The height of its occupation was A.D. 1250 to 1500, when Putún people (also known as the Chontol or Itzás, the same group who built Chichén Itzá's most famous structures) dominated the region as seafaring merchants. Columbus reached the island in

Tunich: This 15–24-meter/49.2–78.7-foot-deep reef usually has a 1.5-knot current or more, which makes it a great drift dive site. The reef is loaded with intricately textured corals and the water activity attracts manta rays, jewfish, and barracuda. A good place to spot moray eels.

Santa Rosa Wall: With a sensational drop-off that begins at 22 meters (72.2 feet), tunnels, caves, and stony overhangs are hallmarks of this spectacular site. It's teeming with sea life; you'll see translucent sponges, gray angelfish, white triggerfish, and groupers. Strong currents make this a good drift dive. Best for experienced divers.

Paso del Cedral: This flat reef has a 22-meter (72.2-foot) depth. Sea life includes angelfish, lobster, and thick-lipped grouper.

Palancar: This five-kilometer (3.1-mile) series of spectacular coral formations is about 1.5 kilometers (0.9 mile) offshore. Some drop off dramatically into winding ravines, deep canyons, and passageways; others have become archways and tunnels with formations 15 meters (49.2 feet) tall. All are teeming with reef life. Maximum depth is 20 meters (65.6 feet).

Horseshoe: Considered one of the best dive sites in the Caribbean, this series of coral heads forms a horseshoe curve at the top of the drop-off. With a solid bronze, four-meter/13.1-foot-tall, submerged modernistic sculpture of Christ, this is a dramatic photo area. The statue, created especially for the dive site, was sunk on May 3, 1985.

Colombia: At this deep-dive site beginning at 25–30 meters (82–98.4 feet) depth, you'll encounter canyons and ravines. Sea turtles, groupers, and spotted eagle rays are commonly seen here. A drift dive, it is recommended for experienced divers.

Maracaibo: At the island's southern tip, this site has a depth of 23–37 meters (75.5–121.4 feet) and is known for its strong currents. Coral formations are immense.

Riviera Maya and Cozumel

1502, on his fourth voyage, marking the beginning of a slow painful dislocation of the native people by Spanish explorers and *conquistadores*. By the mid-1800s the island was virtually uninhabited. The henequen, chicle, and coconut oil booms attracted more and more people to the Quintana Roo territory (it didn't became a state until 1974) and Cozumel slowly rebounded, this time with a mostly Mexican mestizo population. With the establishment of Cancún in the 1970s, and the "discovery" of Cozumel's reefs by Jacques Cousteau, Cozumel's future as a tourist and diving destination was set.

SIGHTS

Coral Reefs

Whereas the coral off Cancún and elsewhere has suffered severe degradation, Cozumel's reef system was declared a national marine reserve more than two decades ago and has thrived under the park's strict protection. And in an area that can be frustratingly shallow, a 1,000-meter/3,281-foot-deep channel between Cozumel and the mainland provides for spectacular wall and drift dives. Combine all this with the Caribbean's famously crystalline waters—which are even clearer here—and you get a dive destination as good or better than any in the world. (See *Sports and Recreation* for information on dive shops and operators.)

The Plaza

In and around Cozumel's main park stand colonial and modern civic buildings, a boxy clock tower, and busts of the late Mexican president Benito Juárez and the general Andrés Quintana Roo. On Sunday evenings local citizens and tourists meet in the central plaza. Families—

sometimes three generations—gather around the white gazebo to hear Latin rhythms and tunes of the day played by local musicians. A few women still wear the lovely white *huipiles,* while men look crisp and cool in their traditional *guayaberas* and best white hats. Children, dressed as miniatures of their parents, run, play, and chatter in front of the band. It's hard to say who does the best business—the balloon man or the cotton-candy vendor. In short, a pleasant place to spend an evening.

Museo de la Isla de Cozumel

The town's small but very informative nonprofit museum (Av. Rafael Melgar at Calle 6, tel. 987/872-1434, 9 A.M.–5 P.M. daily, US$2.75) is on the waterfront north of the plaza in an old building that once housed a turn-of-the-20th-century hotel. Well-composed exhibits in English and Spanish explain island wildlife, coral reefs, and the fascinating and sometimes tortured history of human presence here, from Mayan pilgrims worshipping the fertility goddess to the devastating hurricanes of the mid-1900s. The museum also has a

bookstore, library, and a pleasant outdoor café overlooking the sea.

Archaeological Zones

Cozumel was one of the most important islands in the Mayan world—both as a port of trade as well as a pilgrimage site to worship the goddess of fertility, Ix Chel (She of the Rainbow). Today, 24 archaeological sites have been discovered—mostly on the northern, hard-to-reach part of the island—and date from A.D. 1. Whether you venture north or visit the more accessible ruins in the central and southern parts of Cozumel, you'll soon discover that most ruins on the island are of the "oratorio" type: small square buildings, low to the ground, with short doors. They're not as glorious as the ones found on the mainland, but interesting nonetheless to visit.

South of town and just beyond Playa San Francisco, a paved turnoff will lead you to **El Cedral** (8 A.M.–5 P.M. daily, free). Small and underwhelming, it is the oldest Mayan structure on the island. Amazingly, despite the passage of time—and its use as a jail in the 1800s—it still

one of the small temples of San Gervasio

© LIZA PRADO CHANDLER

bears a few traces of the paint and stucco applied by the original Mayan artist.

Inside Parque Ecológico Punta Sur, **El Caracol** is a small, conch-shaped structure that dates to A.D. 1200. It's believed to have been a lighthouse—Mayans used smoke and flames here to lead boats to safety. Small openings at the top of the structure also act as foghorns when hurricane-strength winds blow through them.

San Gervasio

The most accessible and rewarding of the ruins is San Gervasio (tel. 987/800-2215, 7 A.M.–5 P.M. daily, tickets sold until 4 P.M. only, US$5), which is just off the Cross-Island Highway. Three building groups are visible here and are connected by trails built along the old Mayan causeways. The structures are mainly small temples and shrines built on platforms. In the middle of one causeway is the Temple of Ix Chel, a small but well-preserved building that was probably a shrine, although the connection to the goddess is not certain. Archaeologists at San Gervasio have recently found a grave containing 50 skeletons as well as some Spanish beads, leading them to believe that these were victims of a European disease brought by the conquistadors. Guides are available at the entrance to lead you and up to five others around the ruins to explain the history and highlights of this fascinating place (US$17). English, German, and Italian spoken.

Parque Nacional Chankanaab

Nine kilometers (5.6 miles) south of town is Parque Chankanaab (Carr. Costera Sur Km. 14, tel. 987/872-9723, www.cozumelparks.com.mx, 7 A.M.–6 P.M. daily, US$12, US$6 age eight and under), a national park that doubles as a souped-up beach club. Among many water and beach activities offered, the dolphin swim is especially popular. (For more details, see *The Rivera's Ecoparks* in the *Playa del Carmen* section.)

Parque Ecológico Punta Sur

At the southern tip of Cozumel, you'll come upon a turnoff that meanders to the entrance of Parque Ecológico Punta Sur (Carr. Costera Sur Km. 27, tel. 987/878-8462, www.cozu-

melparks.com.mx, 9 A.M.–5 P.M. daily, US$10 before 2 P.M., US$6 after 2 P.M.). A national reserve, this park is the place to head to see wildlife in its natural habitat. The Mayan archaeological site of **El Caracol**—believed to be an ancient lighthouse—also is in the park. (For more details, see *The Rivera's Ecoparks* in the *Playa del Carmen* section.)

Beach Clubs

Cozumel isn't famous for its beaches, but they are still quite pretty and a good place to spend a free day. A series of beach clubs on the calmer west side are the best place to enjoy the sun and sand. They vary considerably in attitude and ambience—be sure to pick the one that has what you're looking for. Beaches on the east side are windy and picturesque, and the surf can be fierce. A few beach clubs have protected inlets, but still use caution when swimming here.

On the east side of the island right where the Cross-Island Highway hits the Caribbean, you'll find a wild and windswept beach with two low-key restaurants sitting alongside each other: **Mezcalito's Beach Bar and Grill** (tel. 987/872-1616, www.mezcalitos.com, 10 A.M.–6 P.M. daily) and **Señor Iguanas** (no phone, 8 A.M.–5 P.M. daily). Both have similar menus (ceviche, fried fish, hamburgers, US$5–14), drinks (beer, margaritas, and tequila shots, US$2.50–5), and services (beach side chairs, hammocks, and palapas, free if you buy something from the restaurant). If you're feeling brave and have experience in rough waters, rent a boogie board from Señor Iguanas (US$3, two hours)—a lot of fun if you can handle the surf.

About six kilometers (3.7 miles) south you'll come to **Coconuts Bar and Grill** (between Punta Morena and Chen Río beach clubs, tel. 987/100-6601, 10:30 A.M.–sunset daily, US$4–11). It's set on a magnificent bluff, and the view of the beach below is glorious. Tables are set and hammocks are strung along the cliff and as long as you have a drink or order some food, you're free to admire the view for as long as you want. Meals are classic beach fare: nachos, ceviche,

© LIZA PRADO CHANDLER

Mezcalito's beach club on the east side of Isla Cozumel

tacos—finger foods that go great with a cold beer. A broad beautiful beach called Playa Tortugas is just on the other side of the Ventanas al Mar hotel. Usually too rough for swimming, it's popular with surfers and is a good place to watch the wild and crashing waves.

The best place to swim on the east side of the island is **Chen Río Beach** (one km/0.6 mile south of Coconuts Bar and Grill) fronting a wide protected bay and clear calm seas. It's popular with families, and lifeguards are on hand in case of any problems. Here you'll also find **Restaurant and Bar Chen Río** (11 A.M.– 6 P.M. daily, US$12–24). It's a pricey restaurant with tables under small palapas—your time (and money) is better spent playing at the beach and eating up the road. If you forget your snorkel gear, the closest place to rent it is at Playa Punta Morena, just north of Chen Río.

On the west side of the island with calm turquoise waters, a small beach, and lots of coconut trees, **Playa Palancar** (Km. 19.5, no phone, 9:30 A.M.–4 P.M. daily) is a mellow club catering to those visitors who want to spend a day lounging in a hammock or snorkeling in the nearby Palancar reef. A palapa-roofed restaurant serves classic Mexican seafood and a wide range of drinks (US$9–12). If you're interested in snorkeling or diving in Palancar, trips leave as soon as there is a critical mass of people (snorkel US$30, 1.5 hrs, scuba US$80, two tanks). Snorkel gear also can be rented (US$10) but with no reef within an easy striking distance, there's not much point in spending your cash on it.

A glorious stretch of white sand beach and endless turquoise waters is what you'll find at **Playa San Francisco.** That, and two of the busiest beach clubs on Cozumel: **Nachi-Cocom** (Carr. Costera Sur Km. 16.5, tel. 987/872-1811, www.cozumelnachicocom.net, 9 A.M.–5 P.M. daily) and **Paradise Beach** (Carr. Costera Sur Km. 14.5, tel. 987/871-9010, www.paradise-beach-cozumel.net, 9 A.M.– sunset Mon.–Sat., 11 A.M.–6 P.M. Sun.). Both clubs have huge open-air restaurants serving lots of finger foods and seafood (US$8–14), water toys (wave runners, banana boats, kayaks), snorkel trips (US$27, 1.5 hrs.), and a countless number of beach chairs and umbrellas. Both cater to the cruise-shipper scene and charge US$5 (Nachi-Cocom waives it if you order something from the restaurant or bar). So how are they different? The ambience. Nachi Cocom is a hard-core party zone: You'll see lots of tequila being shot, music blaring, and the whirlpool tub teeming with minimally clad visitors. Paradise Beach, while certainly a lively place, is geared toward families with children or people looking to catch up on their backlogged *New Yorker* subscriptions. Either way, San Francisco Beach is glorious. Stop in and check it out. If you don't like either club, you can always drive up the road a bit.

North of the Cross-Island Highway

Windswept and wild beaches see little traffic on the northeastern side of the island. That's because the 24.5-kilometer (15.2-mile) sand road is basically impossible to ride without a four-wheel drive vehicle. Visitors to this part of the island pay a premium to rent a jeep (make sure the four-wheel drive hasn't been disengaged) or simply hike in, camping gear and all. It's adventure for sure, and a beautiful one at that. The first beaches you'll hit are good beachcombing spots, and make for good places

to pitch a tent. From here, you can follow the trails west, and you're guaranteed to run into little-known Mayan sites, abandoned cenotes, and caves. Continuing north 22 kilometers (13.7 miles), you'll see the Mayan site of **Castillo Real** and farther on the **Punta Molas Lighthouse** at the northeasternmost tip of the island. Whether you come on wheels or by foot, don't come unprepared—there are absolutely no facilities out here. Take plenty of water, food, a hat, sunscreen, bug repellent, a flashlight, extra batteries, and a mosquito net if you plan to camp—you'll need it.

ENTERTAINMENT AND EVENTS
Carnaval

Cozumel is one of the few places in Mexico where Carnaval is celebrated with vigor, though the island's one-night celebration is still pretty mellow compared to the weeks or months of partying that mark the holiday elsewhere in the Caribbean and in South America. Held in February, Carnaval in Cozumel centers around a parade of floats and

© GARY PRADO CHANDLER

Carnaval in Cozumel is celebrated with parades and dancing in the streets.

dance troupes, all decked out in Caribbean style, with colorful dresses, masks, and glitter. Entire families come out together to participate and watch. Spectators dance and cheer in the streets as the floats go by, and many join the moving dance party that follows the floats with the largest speakers. Eventually the party ends up in the center of town, where more music, dancing, and revelry continue late into the night.

Nightclubs, Lounges, and Bars

The urban chic **Ambar** (Av. 5 No. 141 Sur between Calles 1 and Rosado Salas, tel. 987/869-1955, ambarlounge@terra.com.mx, 5:30 P.M.–3 A.M. Tues.–Fri., 6:30 P.M.–3 A.M. Sat.–Sun.) is *the* lounge to go to on Friday and Saturday nights. Billowing white fabrics, dim lighting, modern white furniture and a DJ spinning jazz, funk, and house make this one of the hottest spots in town. A full martini bar gives it just that much more edge. You also can enjoy the balmy weather in a great outdoor area with lounge chairs, umbrellas, and piped in (well, out) music—perfect if you want to enjoy the ambience but still have a conversation. A small restaurant in front serves homemade pastas until 11 P.M. (US$8–14).

More a bar than a restaurant—and very laid-back at that—**Viva México** (Calle Rosado Salas at Av. Rafael Melgar, tel. 987/872-0799, 10 A.M.–2 A.M. daily) has colorful tables and a good view of the water. There's live music some nights during the high season but mostly you'll find a DJ spinning a good variety of vinyls.

If you're looking for a more local party scene, **Neptuno** (Av. Rafael Melgar at Calle 11, www .neptunodisco.com) is a good place to check out. Things at this nightclub, popular among islanders, don't really get going until after midnight.

Dying to catch the big game and your hotel doesn't carry ESPN? Head to **Caliente/ All Sports Bar** (Calle 2 at Av. 5 Norte, tel. 987/869-2246, 9 A.M.–11 P.M. daily). With 22 TVs and beer on tap, you're sure to feel right at home. And if you're feeling lucky, there are off-track-betting booths on-site.

If shopping at the mall has left you bushed,

head to **Carlos'n Charlie's** (Punta Langosta, tel. 987/869-1648, 10 A.M.–1:30 A.M. Mon.–Fri., 11 A.M.–1:30 A.M. Sat., 5 P.M.–1:30 A.M. Sun.) and **Señor Frog's** (Punta Langosta, tel. 987/869-1650, 11 A.M.–2 A.M. Mon.–Sat., 7 P.M.–2 A.M. Sun., live rock, reggae and other music Tues.–Fri.) for food, drink specials, and lively music in a spring break atmosphere that lasts all year long.

Buggies

Once a way for islanders to get around town, *calesas* (horse and buggies) are now mainly used by tourists to see San Miguel. For US$20 you can hire a buggy to take you and three of your closest friends on a 40-minute tour of the town—from the waterfront to the interior. Look for the horses on Avenida Rafael Melgar by Calle 1.

Cinema and Arcade

Catch a relatively recent movie at **Cinépolis** (Av. Rafael Melgar between Calles 15 and 17, tel. 987/869-0799, tickets US$3.50 3–6 P.M., US$2.25 before 3 P.M. and all day Wed.) in the Chedraui supermarket complex. Shows noon–10:30 P.M. daily. **Aventuras** (10 A.M.–10 P.M. daily) is an arcade in the same complex.

SHOPPING

Most of the shops here are aimed 100 percent at cruise chip passengers—packed along Avenida Rafael Melgar, they even put out welcome signs with the names of the boats in dock that day. Jewelry is definitely the item of choice followed by T-shirts and little knick-knacks, most overpriced. That said, there are a few stores worth checking out if you're in the mood.

Though a little pricey, **Pro Dive Cozumel** (Calle Rosado Salas No. 198 at Av. 5, tel. 987/872-4123, prodivecozumel@prodigy.com .mx, www.prodivecozumel.com, 8 A.M.–10 P.M. Mon.–Sat., 9 A.M.–10 P.M. Sun.) has a great selection of snorkel and dive equipment—perfect if you've forgotten your mask or have lost a fin.

For a phenomenal display of Mexican folk art, check out **Los Cinco Soles** (Av. Rafael Melgar No. 27 at Calle 8, tel. 987/872-0132,

© GARY PRADO CHANDLER

a beach break between dives

www.loscincosoles.com, 9 A.M.–8 P.M. Mon.–Sat., 10 A.M.–5 P.M. Sun.). Here, you'll find room upon room of some of the best examples of the country's artisanry—from pre-Colombian replicas and *barro negro* (literally, black clay) pottery to colorful *rebosos* (shawls) and hand-carved furniture. Definitely worth a stop, if even just to admire the art.

For one of the best jewelry shops on the strip, head to **Rachat and Romero** (Av. Rafael Melgar No. 101 at Calle 2, tel. 987/872-0571, 9 A.M.–8:30 P.M. Mon.–Fri., 9 A.M.–4 P.M. Sat.). Popular with cruise shippers.

Punta Langosta (Av. Rafael Melgar between Calles 7 and 11, 9 A.M.–8 P.M. daily) is the island's most posh shopping center. In this open-air mall, you'll find high-end boutiques, air-conditioned jewelry stores, and even fancy T-shirt shops.

SPORTS AND RECREATION
Scuba Diving
Without a doubt, diving is the best reason to come to Cozumel. It should be no surprise then that Cozumel has a profusion of dive shops

and operators—around 150 at last count. Rates are relatively uniform across the island: Expect to pay US$65–80 for a two-tank dive (plus US$10–20 for equipment rental) and US$325–400 for a three- or four-day PADI open-water certification course. Most shops also conduct more advanced courses and offer discounts on multidive packages. Note that posted prices often do not include equipment rental, the US$2 park entrance fee, or a US$1/day surcharge to support the SSS (*Servicios de Seguridad Sub-Acuática,* Underwater Safety Services), which helps maintain Cozumel's hyperbaric chambers (see *Medical Services*), marine ambulance, and trained personnel.

Cozumel's diver safety record is good, and there are many more responsible, competent outfits in town than those listed here. Consider this list your base, to be augmented by the recommendations of fellow divers, travelers, locals, and expats—whose judgment you trust, of course. (See the *How to Choose a Dive Shop* sidebar for tips and advice on picking a shop.) Most important, go with a shop you feel comfortable with, not just the cheapest, the cheeriest, or the most convenient.

HOW TO CHOOSE A DIVE SHOP

There are around 100 dive shops on Isla Cozumel alone, scores more at Isla Mujeres, Tulum, and elsewhere on the Riviera Maya. Narrowing them down to just one—and then placing all your underwater faith and dreams into its hands—is, well, not easy.

Safety should be your number one concern in choosing a shop. Fortunately, the standards in Cozumel and the Riviera Maya are almost universally first-rate. Accidents here are rare, and very few can be blamed on the dive shop. But that is not a reason to be complacent. For example, do not dive with a shop that doesn't ask to see your certification card or logbook—if it doesn't ask you, that means it probably didn't ask anyone, and an inexperienced or ill-trained diver is as much a danger to other divers as he is to himself.

Equipment is of course a crucial issue. Dive equipment is remarkably resilient, but it can and does wear out, especially with the amount of use it gets at a dive shop. You should ask to inspect the shop's equipment, and the dive shop should be quick to comply. Although most beginners and even many advanced divers aren't trained to spot problems, a good dive shop will appreciate your concern and be happy to put you at ease. If the staff are reluctant to show you their gear, either they aren't too proud of it or don't see clients as equal partners in dive safety. Go elsewhere.

Of course, the most important gear is not what's on the rack but what you actually use. Get to the shop early so you have time to **double-check your gear.** Again, you don't have to be an expert to do this. Old gear is not necessarily bad gear, but you should ask for a different buoyancy control device (BCD), wetsuit, or regulator hose if the one set out for you makes you nervous. Ask the dive master if he checked the O-ring (the small rubber ring that forms the seal between the tank and the regulator) on your tank. Once the regulator is attached, open the tank and listen for any hissing between the regulator and the tank, and in the primary and backup mouthpieces. If you hear any, ask the dive master to check it and, if need be, change equipment. There are truly *no stupid questions.*

In fact, feeling comfortable and free to ask questions or raise concerns (of any sort at any time) is a crucial factor in safe diving. That's where a dive shop's **personality** comes in. Every dive shop has its own culture or ambience, and different divers will feel better in different shops. (This is especially important if you are taking a certification course.) Spend some time talking to people at a couple of different dive shops before signing up. Try to meet the person who will be leading your particular dive—you may have to come in in the afternoon when that day's trip returns. Chances ar e one of the shops or dive masters will "click" with you.

Finally, there are some specific questions you should ask about a shop's practices. How many people will be going on your dive? How advanced are they? How many dive masters or instructors will there be? Is there a fixed bottom time—that is, does the dive master surface after 45 minutes regardless of your air? If it depends on air, does the whole group surface together once one person is low on air, or can the other divers continue diving? If you like a couple of shops equally, go with the one with fewer divers or the one that allows the longest bottom time. And, of course, have fun!

Dimi Divers (Calle 3 between Av. Rafael Melgar and 5 Av., tel. 987/872-2915, www.dimiscubatours.com) offers very reasonable rates and comes highly recommended.

ScubaTony (www.scubatony.com, tel. 987/876-1171 or tel. 044/872-2248) is one of a growing number of scuba operations run without an actual storefront—lower overhead typically means lower prices. American Tony Anschutz leads all his own

dives and courses and offers excellent service before, during, and after your trip.

Deep Blue (Calle Rosado Salas No. 200 at Av. 10 Sur, tel. 987/872-5653, U.S. tel. 214/343-3034, deepblue@cozumel.com.mx, www.deepbluecozumel.com, 7 A.M.–9 P.M. daily) is a long-standing shop with a reputation and track-record that keep it busy even through the low season.

Liquid Blue (5 Av. between Calle Rosado Salas and Calle 3, 987-869-2812, www.liquidbluedivers.com) has somewhat higher rates than most shops, but it offers small groups and attentive, personalized service.

Careyitos Advanced Divers (Caleta harbor, near Hotel Presidente InterContinental, tel. 987/872-0111, U.S. tel. 301/948-8366, www.advanceddivers.com) caters to advanced divers and is known for offering top-notch service. Good multidive packages available.

Blue Note (Calle 2 Norte between Av. 40 and Av. 45, tel. 987/872-0312, www.bluenotescuba.com) is a bit removed from the center, but that may be a good thing. Popular with European divers, this shop has been recommended for its professionalism and service.

Scuba Gamma (Calle 5 No. 400 at Av. 5 Sur, tel. 987/878-4257 or Mex. cell tel. 044-987/878-5437, scubagamma@hotmail.com, www.scubagamma.com, 9 A.M.–7 P.M. daily) is a mom-and-pop shop (literally) run by an amiable French family.

Snorkeling

If you don't have the time, money, or inclination to take up diving—and it's not for everyone—don't let that stop you from enjoying Cozumel's pristine coral reefs. In fact, many divers are also avid snorkelers, if for no other reason than plunking down US$100 a day for two 45-minute dives adds up really fast.

Most dive shops offer guided snorkeling tours, visiting 2–3 sites and spending a half hour at each one (US$30–40 pp). You will probably go out with a group of divers, and either snorkel in the same general location or go to a nearby one while the divers are under. While this can mean some extra downtime as divers get in and out of the water, you typically go to better, less crowded sites and have fewer people in your group. Be sure to agree beforehand on the number of sites you'll visit and for how long.

A number of shops and agencies sell snorkel tours from booths on the main passenger pier. Though they are less personalized, you may prefer this if your time is short, as they have several trips per day and can be booked right as you debark from the ferry. **Cha Cha Cha Dive Shop** (Calle 7 No. 9 between Avs. Rafael Melgar and 5 Sur, tel. 987/872-2331, www.chachachadiveshop.com, booth opens at 8 A.M.) has a booth at the pier and offers 2–2.5-hour snorkeling trips on its glass-bottom boat for US$20–30 pp, including equipment). You'll snorkel for 30 minutes at each of three different sites.

There are several terrific snorkeling spots right off the shore and not far from town where you don't need a guide at all. Some of these are established snorkeling areas, others are recommended by locals and expats. Cozumel's boat drivers are careful about steering clear of snorkelers, but even so do not swim too far from shore, look up and around frequently, and stay out of obvious boat lanes. If you plan to do a lot of snorkeling, especially outside of established snorkeling areas, consider buying an inflatable personal buoy at a dive shop in town. Designed for snorkelers, they are brightly colored with a string you attach to your ankle or to a small anchor weight, alerting boat drivers of your presence. Also, be aware of the current, which typically runs south to north and can be quite strong.

The best place for snorkeling from the shore may be **Dzul-Ha** (9 A.M.–5 P.M. daily, free, gear rental US$10), a modest beach club just south of the Presidente InterContinental hotel. The coral reef is close to the surface and supports a beautiful array of tropical fish and colorful sea plants, and steps make getting in and out of the water easy. Small tour groups sometimes stop here, but even so it rarely feels crowded; a small restaurant serves basic meals and drinks. On the other side of the Presidente Intercontinental (and the marina) is a **no name beach** where you'll find no services and even fewer people—just a beautiful underwater reef system teeming with sealife.

Closer to town, in front of El Cid La Ceiba hotel, you can snorkel to an **underwater plane wreck** that was deliberately sunk as part of a movie production. From the hotel dive dock (you can just walk through the lobby) swim toward the end of the large cruise ship pier in front. The plane is six meters (19.7 feet) down, about a quarter of the way there. Other recommended spots for snorkeling are **Playa Villa Blanca** (near the Villa Blanca Hotel, about a half mile north of El Cid), **Parque Chankanaab,** and **Parque Punta Sur.**

Fishing

Cozumel boasts good deep-sea fishing year-round. Red snapper, tuna, barracuda, dolphin, wahoo, bonito, king mackerel, and tarpon are especially plentiful March–July, which is also the high season for marlin and sailfish. The Hernández brothers of **3 Hermanos** (tel. 987/872-6417, oscarhernandez68@prodigy .net.mx) have years of experience and an English-speaking staff, and are one of various fishing outfits on the island. Trips (half day US$350, 6:30–11:30 A.M., full day US$400, 6:30 A.M.–2:30 P.M.) include all equipment and beer and soda on board. Many of the dive shops also offer fishing trips for similar prices.

A **billfish tournament** is held every year in May, bringing fishing enthusiasts from all over—especially boaters from the United States who cross the Gulf of Mexico to take part in the popular event.

Golf

Jack Nicklaus designed the beautiful par-72 championship course at **Cozumel Country Club** (tel. 987/872-9570, www.cozumelcountryclub.com.mx, 6 A.M.–6 P.M. daily) at the far end of the northern hotel zone. Green fees are US$89/149 for 9/18 holes 6:30 A.M.–1:30 P.M. and US$60/99 1:30–6 P.M. (7 P.M. in the summer), and US$12/23 for nonplayers accompanying those playing 9/18 holes. Club rentals are US$17/29 for 9-/18-hole games. Men must wear polo shirts and a golf cart is required (US$23/cart). In addition to the slightly rolling, moderately challenging course (the only one on the island), the club has a driving range, putting and chipping areas, overnight bag storage, restaurant, retail shop, and available golf pro.

For something a little more laid-back, try **Cozumel Mini Golf** (Calle 1 at Av. 15 Sur,

tel. 987/872-6570, www.cozumelminigolf .com, 10 A.M.–11 P.M. Mon.–Sat., 5–11 P.M. Sun., US$7 adults, US$5 children under 11). Set among 300 banana trees and a waterfall or two, the tropical 18-hole course is challenging and a lot of fun. And don't forget to ask for your walkie-talkie when you're selecting a putter; with it, you can order drinks—soft or hard—to be delivered along the way.

Racquet Sports

A rarity in this part of the world is **Squash Time Cozumel** (Av. 75 No. 100 Norte at Calle 2, tel. 987/872-7445, 7 A.M.–10 P.M. daily, US$13/hour), a brand-new club dedicated exclusively to this lightning-fast indoor sport. Reservations are recommended as it has only two courts.

Horseback Riding

Rancho Palmitas (inland side of highway between Nachi Cocom beach club and Occidental Allegro hotel) offers two horseback tours. A 2.5-hour tour (US$37 pp) includes stops at a cenote and a few unexcavated Mayan ruins. A shorter, 1.5-hour tour (US$27 pp) visits the cenote only. Departures for either tour are at 8 A.M., 10 A.M., noon, 2 P.M., and 4 P.M. daily. A few additional ranches along this stretch of highway offer similar tours and prices.

Buggy Tours

On the east side of the island, **Wild Tours** (tel. 987/872-5876 or toll-free Mex. tel. 800/202-4990, www.wild-tours.com) offers two ATV excursions to Mayan ruins and deserted beaches along the island's undeveloped northeast shore. The most common tour includes driving to one Mayan ruin and stopping for kayaking and snorkeling (US$94 s, US$160 d, four hours, 9 A.M., 11 A.M., and 1 P.M., including box lunch, water, and soda). A shorter tour does not make stops for kayaking and snorkeling but visits two ruins, including El Castillo, 22 kilometers (13.7 miles) each way (US$80 s, US$140 d, 3 P.M. only, including water and soda). Tours leave from a staging area next to Mezcalito's restaurant on the east side of the island, where

© LIZA PRADO CHANDLER

Dune buggy tours on the east side of Isla Cozumel are popular excursions.

the cross-island highway meets the coastal highway. Buses pick up guests at two locations in town (in front of the Occidental Allegro hotel and at the Burger King in Punta Langosta) a half-hour before the tour and return them afterward. Reservation required. Most people sign up for this tour at their hotels—typically the high-rises and all-inclusives—but you can also call or sign up online.

Gym and Spa

Gym Club (Av. Benito Juárez between Calle 2 and Av. Pedro Joaquín Coldwell, tel. 987/872-7432, 6 A.M.–11 P.M. Mon.–Fri., 8 A.M.–7 P.M. Sat.) has free weights and weight machines in a smallish two-level exercise area. Hour-long aerobics classes are held at 8 A.M., 5 P.M., and 8 P.M. Mon.–Fri. One-time passes are US$4.50/day or US$10/week. Monthly memberships are US$24/52 for weights/weights-and-aerobics, plus a US$17 inscription fee.

Acqua Spa (Av. 10 Norte at Calle 10, tel. 987/872-1421, www.acquaspa.com.mx) is an upscale spa and gym that offers the latest in cardiovascular machines, weights, and classes. After you've worked out your body, you also

can give it a treat with any number of spa treatments—massage (US$45–100), facial (US$40–80), hydrotherapy (US$35)—in one of four luxurious palapa-roofed rooms. Open Monday to Saturday: women only 8 A.M.–3 P.M., men welcome 3–9 P.M. Day passes US$7, monthly membership US$50.

ACCOMMODATIONS

Room prices can rise considerably during high season (mid-December–mid-April). Those listed here are high season (but not Christmas and New Year rates, which are even higher)—if you visit at another time rates may be 10–40 percent lower.

Under US$50

Tamarindo Bed and Breakfast (Calle 4 No. 421 between Avs. 20 and 25 Norte, tel. 987/872-3614, www.tamarindoamaranto.com, US$44 s/d with fan, US$52 s/d with a/c) is a pleasant bed-and-breakfast just a few blocks from the center of town, but comfortably removed from the hubbub there. Run by a friendly French/Mexican family (who live on-site), the hotel has five rooms bordering a large garden. Each room is different, from a midsized palapa-roofed unit near the entrance to two small boxy but comfortable apartments farther back. All have cable TV and guests are free to use the family kitchen. A library and reading nook were being built. A good full breakfast is included (high season only; US$3 in low season) and served on a sunny second-floor terrace. A tamarindo tree in the garden inspired the hotel's name and lends shade to the property. The owners also run the Amaranto Villas and Suites.

A third-floor sundeck at the **Hotel Flamingo** (Calle 6 No. 81 between Avs. Rafael Melgar and 5 Norte, tel. 987/872-1264 or toll-free U.S. tel. 800/806-1601, www.hotelflamingo.com, US$49 s/d) has a nice view of the channel between Cozumel and the mainland and is a highlight of this welcoming hotel three blocks north of the plaza. All 20 rooms here have air-conditioning, cable TV, and plenty of space (though some of the beds are saggy). A good laid-back restaurant on the ground floor is open 7 A.M.–10 P.M. daily. Families and small groups should ask about the three-bedroom "penthouse" (US$130); the hotel sometimes closes for part of the low season.

N Hotel Pepita (Av. 15 Sur No. 120 between Calles 1 and Rosado Salas, tel. 987/872-0098, US$26 s/d, extra person US$4.50) is a modest but well-located and surprisingly comfortable hotel—a good value. The friendly owners keep the rooms very clean and were repainting and installing new toilets and bathroom tiles when we visited. All rooms have air-conditioning and ceiling fan, cable TV, and two double beds, and the hotel provides a common refrigerator and fresh coffee in the morning. Same rates year-round.

Hotel Mary Carmen (5 Av. Sur between Calles 1 and Rosado Salas, tel. 987/872-0581, US$30 s/d without TV, US$33 with TV) is another simple but unexpectedly pleasant hotel, right in the center of town. Smallish rooms have new air-conditioners and clean bathrooms. Though not luxury, it's a good value for those with a limited budget who'd rather

spend their money on diving than on a fancy hotel. Friendly service; some rooms may get noise from the street in front.

Just down the street, rooms at the **Hotel El Marqués** (Av. 5 Sur between Calles 1 and Rosado Salas, tel. 987/872-0677, US$30 s, US$34 d) have eclectic furnishings, air-conditioning, and small in-room refrigerators; the third-floor rooms have good views. Some rooms have saggy beds, others are a bit dim—ask to see a few before deciding.

US$50–100

Sister hotel to the Tamarindo Bed and Breakfast, **N Amaranto Villas and Suites** (Calle 5 between Avs. 15 and 20 Sur, tel. 987/872-3614, amarantotamarindo@prodigy.com.mx, www .tamarindoamaranto.com, US$47–57 s/d) also offers seclusion and privacy, while still within easy walking distance from the center. The free-standing bungalows are fairly large and very clean, with modern bathrooms and attractive decor. But the two suites are what make Amaranto special. Occupying a three-story circular tower, both are spacious, with king-sized beds, a separate sitting area, and nearly 360-degree windows, plus amenities such as cable TV, microwave, and toaster oven. The lower suite has a high ceiling and more modern feel, while the upper unit looks up into the palapa roof, where a small lookout affords great town and ocean views. A large kitchen and dining room on the first floor has a TV and VCR and is open to all guests. The Amaranto doesn't have a full-time attendant, so walk-ins should go to the Tamarindo Bed and Breakfast if no one answers the bell. Better yet, call ahead.

A lush courtyard and gurgling fountain greet you at the **Hacienda San Miguel** (Calle 10 No. 1500 between Avs. Rafael Melgar and 5 Norte, tel. 987/872-1986, U.S. tel. 866/712-6387, www.haciendasanmiguel.com, US$79–129 s/d with a/c), a colonial-style hotel on the edge of town. Rooms, while needing a little sprucing up (new paint, a little extra scrubbing in the showers) are comfortable nonetheless with air-conditioning, cable TV, and fully equipped kitchenettes. A decent choice, especially if you like having the option of cooking a meal or two.

In town, Cozumel's most modern hotel is **Casa Mexicana** (Av. Rafael Melgar No. 457 between Calles 5 and 7, tel. 987/872-9090, toll-free Mex. tel. 800/227-2639, U.S. tel. 877/228-6747, www.casamexicana.com, US$100 s/d city view, US$120 s/d ocean view) with its small infinity pool in its spacious lobby area and a view over the road to the big blue ocean beyond. The view is even better from the private patio of the 20 oceanside rooms—notwithstanding the docked cruise ships and a large McDonald's sign. The other 70 rooms have views of the city or the soaring interior courtyard. The rooms themselves are less inspired than the building they're in but are comfortable enough, with good beds, new air-conditioners, modern bathrooms, and large TVs. Rates include a full buffet breakfast. Casa Mexicana is affiliated with Suites Bahía and Hotel Colonial.

Studios and Condos

An easy 20-minute walk north of the center, **⋈ Condumel** (Box 142, tel. 987/872-0892, www.aquasafari.com, US$120) has 10 enormous one-bedroom apartments, each with air-conditioning, king-sized bed, sofa bed, marble bathrooms, and a large, fully equipped kitchen—the refrigerator even comes stocked with basic food and drinks (at regular prices) so you don't have to go shopping right away. Oversized sliding-glass doors offer awesome views of the ocean, sunsets, and incoming airplanes (the airport is a short distance inland). The shore is rocky here, but a small, semiprotected cove in front of the hotel is perfect for swimming and snorkeling. The hotel has created a pleasant sandy area with chairs, built steps and a ladder into the water, and even installed a diving board that screams cannonball. Owner Bill Horn also manages **Aqua Safari** (Av. Rafael Melgar at Calle 5, tel. 987/872-0101) and the adjacent **Safari Inn** (US$44 s/d); the shop opened in 1966 and is the oldest dive shop on the island; the hotel has large, clean, no-frills rooms that sleep up to six people.

Suites Bahía (Calle 3 between Avs. Rafael Melgar and 5 Sur, tel. 987/872-9090 or toll-free Mex. tel. 800/227-2639, U.S. tel. 877/228-6747, www.suitesbahia.com, US$57–78 s/d) and **Hotel Colonial** (Av. 5 Sur No. 9 between Calles 1 and Rosado Salas, same phone, www.suitescolonial.com, US$57 s/d, US$68 s/d with kitchenette) are sister hotels that both rent unremarkable but functional suites and studios, most with kitchenette. The Colonial is down a long vine-covered corridor and feels newer, but the rooms at the Bahía (especially the ocean-view ones) are roomier and get more natural light. Neither hotel will win any awards for charm, but the rooms are clean and reasonably comfortable, and a kitchen can definitely be nice for longer stays. Both come with cable TV, continental breakfast, and Internet service in the lobby.

⋈ Villas Las Anclas (Av. 5 Sur No. 325 between Calles 3 and 5, tel. 987/872-5476, U.S. tel. 866/779-9986, www.lasanclas.com, US$65–120 s/d, US$10 extra person, US$1,800/month) is a great option for those coming for long-term stays or who just want a little home away from home. Seven pleasantly decorated apartments each have air-conditioning, fully equipped kitchens, living room, and a loft master bedroom up a set of spiral stairs; utilities, purified water, and daily fresh-ground coffee are all included. Using the sofas as beds, the apartments can accommodate up to six people, making a good price even better. Apartments open onto a leafy, private garden. The friendly owner/operator is well-informed of local dive shops, restaurants, and activities, and can help guests organize their stays. A great value.

Outside of Town

The only hotel on the east side of the island, **Hotel Ventanas al Mar** (south end of Playa Tortugas, tel. 987/876-7687, ventanasalmar2@hotmail.com, US$89/150 d/q) has 24 large airy rooms with high ceilings and simple but well-kept furnishings. All units have small kitchenettes (microwave, refrigerator, coffeemaker, plates, silverware) and fantastic ocean views. Suites have two floors connected by a spiral staircase and can comfortably sleep four. You'll need a car to get to and from town, as there are no ATMs, Internet cafés, or grocery stores on the east side. There isn't even electricity—like many establishments on the east side, Ventanas del Mar is 100 percent wind- and solar-powered. Or you can embrace the isolation; many guests spend a week or more without going to town at all. Playa Tortugas is a scenic windswept beach that's good for surfing, but it is often too rough for swimming or snorkeling.

The **Fiesta Americana** (Carretera Sur Km. 7.5, tel. 987/872-9600, toll-free Mex. tel. 800/343-7821, or toll-free U.S. tel. 800/343-7821, www.fiestamericana.com, $133/203 European plan/all-inclusive) caters to divers, most of whom come on package tours arranged from the United States or Canada. Every afternoon, the pool area fills with divers relaxing and trading stories over beer and cocktails. Medium-sized standard rooms have decent though aging beds and furnishings; suites are larger with a sitting area and a small refrigerator and sink. All units have exterior terraces and excellent ocean views (plus air-conditioning, cable TV, and so on) and the lobby is large and welcoming. The beach is disappointing, however, constructed on a rocky shoreline with concrete barriers to hold in the imported sand. The hotel has a gym and a pricey but well-regarded dive shop.

The **M Presidente InterContinental** (Carretera Sur Km. 6.5, tel. 987/872-9500, toll-free Mex. tel. 800/503-0500, or toll-free U.S. tel. 800/317-0200, www.intercontinental.com, US$200–300) may well be the best hotel-resort in Cozumel, boasting the island's best beach and featuring spacious, classy rooms, a well-regarded dive shop, and two enjoyable restaurants. Rooms and suites are priced according to location; some are upstairs with garden or ocean views, some have private balconies, and still others—definitely the best—offer private patios opening right onto the beach. And speaking of the beach: Jagged rocks along the shore have thick white sand on one side and Cozumel's famously gorgeous water on the other; several sandy corridors make getting in

or out easy, or you can swim from a small pier with steps leading into the water. Snorkeling is great here; a full-service dive shop can rent gear or organize guided snorkel and dive tours and packages. The hotel has tennis courts, a kids' program, and special arrangements with the island's golf course. In December 2004, the hotel inaugurated a beautiful new full-service spa, with massage, yoga, water therapy, 24-hour gym, and *temazcal* (traditional Mayan steam bath).

Like many all-inclusives, the four-star **Occidental Allegro** (Carretera Sur Km. 16.5, tel. 987/872-9770 or tel. 987/872-9730, www.allegroresorts.com, US$100–150/night) has a fantastic beach and pool area but rather unremarkable rooms and meals. The wide beach has powdery white sand dotted with beach chairs and umbrellas. On one side is a watersports kiosk, where you can check out anything from snorkel gear (free) to small sailboats (extra charge). Two pools set end to end form a long corridor from the ocean toward the main building. Along the sides are two-story, palapa-roofed bungalows with four units apiece. Rooms are relatively large but showing their age, with outdated air-conditioners, furniture, and decor. The Occidental Grand, a five-star sister all-inclusive, is next door (US$125–180/night). The accommodations and installations are fancier there, but the beach is actually better at the Allegro. Daytime and nighttime activities include aerobics, cocktail parties, and theme nights. Town is a US$12 cab ride away.

North of town and near the country club, **Playa Azul** (Zona Hotelera Norte Km. 4, tel. 987/872-0033, www.playa-azul.com, US$150–210 s/d standard, US$160–250 suite, US$185–350 master) caters mostly to golfers, but it has packages for divers and honeymooners as well. Even if you don't golf much, you may as well get in a round or two if you stay here—guests pay no green fees. Medium-sized rooms have modern furnishings and large bathrooms; most have a terrace with chairs and excellent ocean views. Top-floor rooms have a little cupola on the bedroom, a nice touch. The pool is clean and attractive, but the beach (already small) can get crowded with day guests visiting the hotel's beach club. That said, the overall atmosphere here is calm and quiet, removed from the noise and activity downtown.

FOOD

As Cozumel is an island, seafood is without question the specialty here (although because of the marine park and its restrictions on fishing, much of the fish and virtually all the lobster served here is actually caught elsewhere, especially Isla Mujeres). *Huachinango Veracruz* (red snapper cooked with tomatoes, green pepper, onions, and spices), *camarones con ajo* (shrimp with garlic), and tangy *ceviche* (raw fish marinated in lime, vinegar, onions, tomatoes, and cilantro) are good and fresh just about anywhere you go. And Cozumel has a decent variety of non-seafood options as well, from waffles and crepes to Italian and Argentinean.

Breakfast Places

Once you eat a cream cheese muffin and a plate of eggs at **Los Cocos** (Av. 5 Sur between Calles Rosado Salas and 1, no phone, 6 A.M.–noon Tues.–Sun., US$3–6), it'll be tough to eat breakfast anywhere else. Just a block from the main plaza, this diner is popular among travelers and locals alike.

Owned and operated by a French couple, **M Crepería La Delicia** (Calle Rosado Salas between Avs. 10 and 15, no phone, 7:30 A.M.–noon and 5:30 P.M.–10:30 P.M. Mon.–Fri., 7:30 A.M.–2 P.M. Sat., 5 P.M.–10:30 P.M. Sun., US$3–5) is a whimsical little place, serving more than 20 different crepes—delicious and filling for a meal, a dessert, or both. Breakfast specials include three crepes of your choice, with coffee, tea, or hot chocolate (US$3–5). Three-item baguettes and omelets also are offered.

An old-time favorite, **Jeannie's Waffles and Raul's Tacos** (Av. Rafael Melgar near Calle 11, tel. 987/878-4647, 6 A.M.–11 P.M. daily, US$5–7) serves made-to-order waffles in every shape, way, and form—they even replace tortillas as the base for traditional *huevos rancheros*. Other breakfast options include

eggs, hash browns, and homemade bread. Portions are hearty so come hungry or be prepared to leave some for Mr. Manners. As the name suggests, the restaurant also serves decent tacos for lunch and dinner.

Once you get past the reluctant service, **The Coffee Press** (Av. 5 Norte No. 99 at Calle 6, tel. 987/872-1747, 7 A.M.–3 P.M. Mon.–Sat., US$2–4) is a charming place to have breakfast: painted tile floors, brightly colored walls, and lots of sun—the epitome of the Mexican Caribbean. The food isn't bad either—fruit shakes, lattes, and lots of waffles.

Vegetarian

In the mood for a big salad? How about a sandwich just like you'd make at home? **Garden of Eatin'** (Calle Rosado Salas between Avs. Rafael Melgar and 5, tel. 987/878-4020, 9 A.M.–6 P.M. daily, US$3–6) caters directly to your needs. Here, you can make your own salad from 21 types of vegetables, 11 types of cheeses, four types of meats, and six dressings. Sandwiches are a similar story: Just add your choice of five breads (the black olive bread is particularly good). Prefab sandwiches and salads are also sold if you're running to catch the ferry.

The New Age-y **M Restaurant Manatí** (Av. 10 Norte at Calle 8, tel. 987/100-0787, manati13@hotmail.com, 2–10 P.M. Mon.–Sat., US$4–14) is breezy place to get a creative meal. While not exclusively vegetarian, the menu certainly veers in that direction (think spinach and cheese pasta, mixed vegetables in mango sauce, curry shrimp). The filling *comida corrida* (fixed lunch menu) also is one of the best deals in town: soup, main dish, and all-you-can-drink fruit juices for US$4.50.

Mexican

Occupying a yellow clapboard house just steps from the main plaza, **Casa Denis** (Calle 1 between Avs. 5 and 10 Sur, tel. 987/872-0067, www.casadenis.com, 7 A.M.–11 P.M. Mon.–Sat., 5–11 P.M. Sun., US$1.50–14) has tables set up on its porch and the pedestrian walkway. Great for people-watching, it has an extensive

Yucatecan menu as well. A perfect place to have a cold beer and empanadas stuffed with fish.

Popular among locals, **Ⅳ Sabores** (Av. 5 No. 316 between Calles 3 and 5, no phone, noon–4 P.M. Mon.–Fri.) is a family-run restaurant operated out of a bright yellow house. *Comida corrida* (set lunch specials) is the M.O. here with an appetizer, main dish, and fruit drink running US$2.50–8.

Las Arracheras de Johnny Bravo (Av. 15 Sur No. 216 between Calles Rosado Salas and 3, tel. 987/872-3069, noon–2 A.M., US$1.25–10.50) is a popular taco joint, selling mouth-watering northern-style food. Tortillas are handmade and come filled with quality beef. Be sure to ask for a side order of *frijoles de la olla* (whole bean soup) for a traditional meal.

Mexican-food lovers pack **La Choza** (Av. 10 at Calle Rosado Salas, tel. 987/872-0958, lachoza_cozumel@hotmail.com, 7 A.M.–10:30 P.M., US$6–19), a simple restaurant with oilcloth-covered tables, painted concrete floor, and thatched roof. Always crowded with returning aficionados (with few vegetarians among them).

Restaurante del Museo (Av. Rafael Melgar and Calle 6, 7 A.M.–2 P.M. daily, US$3.50–7) is a little outdoor café on the roof of the Museo Cozumel. Great for a late breakfast after a morning at the museum or simply for a drink to watch the boats cruise past. Service is especially friendly.

With gurgling fountains, colonial-style decor, and marimba music, **Pancho's Backyard** (Av. Rafael Melgar 27 between Avs. 8 and 10 Norte, tel. 987/872-2141, 10 A.M.–11 P.M. Mon.–Sat., 5–11 P.M. Sun., US$10–17) is a great choice. Add top-notch Mexican cuisine such as *chiles rellenos* (peppers stuffed with bananas and walnuts, US$10) and *camarones a la naranja* (orange shrimp flambéed in tequila, US$16) and you've got a winner. Popular with cruise ship travelers, the restaurant is big enough that it never feels crowded.

Seafood

The nautical-themed **El Capi Navegante** (Av. 10 Sur No. 312 between Calles 3 and 5, tel. 987/872-1730, noon–11 P.M. daily, US$10–30) is a favorite on the island for some of the freshest seafood around. For a treat, try the *Parrillada Capi Navigante*—a delectable display of grilled fish, shrimp, octopus, conch, squid—you won't be disappointed (US$14). Friendly service.

The Caribbean chic **La Lobstería** (Av. 5 Sur at Calle 7, tel. 987/100-2510, noon–11 P.M. Mon.–Sat., US$4–12) is a good place to get a creative seafood dish such as fish sautéed in orange, garlic, and cumin (US$8), smoked marlin salad (US$4.50), and coconut shrimp (US$11.50). As the name suggests, lobster is a big seller as well but the smallish sizes don't quite merit the largish price tag. With a few tables outdoors, this makes for a great people-watching locale.

Just south of the Punta Langosta shopping center, **Acuario Restaurant** (Av. Rafael Melgar at Calle 11, tel. 987/872-1097, www.acuariorestaurant.com, noon–midnight daily, US$9–22) is an oceanfront place known for its romantic ambience and live lobster dinners. A decent wine cellar only adds to a special night out. The dress code is classy casual (no flip-flops or T-shirts) and the service is excellent.

International

In a nautical-style dining room overlooking the ocean, **Pepe's Grill** (Av. Rafael Melgar between Calles Rosado Salas and 3, tel. 987/872-0213, 5–11 P.M. daily, US$11–22) has long been noted for its relaxed atmosphere and sunset view. If you're in the mood for prime rib or a salad bar, this is the place. Excellent service.

For a tasty change of pace, head to **Ⅳ Especias** (Calle 5 at Av. 10 Sur, tel. 987/876-1558, especiascozumel@hotmail.com, 5–10:30 P.M. Mon.–Sun., US$5–10), a small restaurant serving Argentinean, Jamaican, and Thai specialties. The zucchini stuffed with cheese and tomatoes (US$3) and the *chistorro* (rolled thin sausage, US$4) are especially good ways to start your meal.

For a good hamburger and rock 'n' roll memorabilia, head to **Hard Rock Cafe** (Av. Rafael

Melgar between Calles 1 and 3, tel. 987/872-5271, 10 A.M.–1 A.M. daily, US$6–18). With views of the Caribbean during the day and live music at night (10 P.M.–1 A.M. Thurs.–Sat.) you're sure to enjoy your meal. You can even get a trendy T-shirt on your way out.

Italian

Specializing in northern Italian dishes, **Prima Trattoria** (Calle Rosado Salas at Av. 5, tel. 987/872-4242, prima@ecozu.com, 4:30–11 P.M. daily, US$7–23) serves handmade pastas and great salads in a charming rooftop garden.

With a delightful shady courtyard and a seemingly endless list of sauces, **M Guido's** (Av. Rafael Melgar No. 23 between Calles 6 and 8, tel. 987/872-0946, www.guidoscozumel.com, 11 A.M.–11 P.M. Mon.–Sat., US$10–12) is the place to head if you're in the mood for the perfect pasta dish. Add a glass of sangria and you've got the makings for a perfect Caribbean night out. Highly recommended.

At the island's finest hotel, **Restaurante Alfredo di Roma** (Presidente InterContinental, Carretera Sur Km. 6.5, tel. 987/872-9500, 6–11 P.M. daily, US$11–30) occupies a huge, brightly lit dining room, with high ceilings and large windows overlooking the beach and ocean. Fettuccini alfredo is the specialty here, and the menu is mostly northern Italian cuisine with Caribbean flair, especially incorporating fresh seafood. Service is impeccable and the decor impressive.

Sweets and Coffeehouses

Just off the bustling Avenida Melgar, **The Coffee Bean** (Calle 3 between Avs. Rafael Melgar and 5 Sur, tel. 987/100-8184, 7 A.M.–11 P.M. daily) is a soothing place to take a midafternoon break. Offering gourmet coffees, homemade pastries, and even bagels, this comfy coffee shop is sure to leave you rejuvenated and satisfied.

If you notice the aroma of roasting beans, follow your nose to **Café Chiapas** (Calle 2 No. 140 between Avs. 5 and 10 Norte, tel. 987/869-2042, 8 A.M.–8 P.M. Mon.–Sat.). With just one

stool and a countertop, this place sells some of the best coffee around—just take it to go.

Hands down, the best place to go for traditional Mexican baked goods is **Zermatt** (Av. 5 Norte No. 199 at Calle 4, tel. 987/872-1384, 7 A.M.–8:30 P.M. Tues.–Sat., 7 A.M.–3 P.M. Sun.–Mon.). And be sure to get a little something for the street dogs who like to sniff around outside—otherwise they'll follow you (and your bag of treats) back to your hotel.

For a refreshing treat, head to **La Michoacana** (Av. Juárez No. 299 between Avs. 10 and 15, 8:30 A.M.–11 P.M. daily). Here you can choose from eight flavors of *aguas* (fruit drinks), *nieves* (ice cream), and *paletas* (popsicles). The piña colada flavor is especially popular in these parts.

Groceries

If you are cooking for yourself, **Chedraui** (Av. Rafael Melgar between Calles 15 and 17, 8 A.M.–10 P.M. daily) is the largest supermarket on the island. For a traditional market experience—fresh produce and sides of beef hanging from hooks—head to the *mercado público* (Av. 25 between Calles 1 and Rosado Salas, 7 A.M.–3 P.M. daily).

INFORMATION AND SERVICES
Tourist Information Centers

On the second floor of the Plaza del Sol, the **city tourist office** (east side of the plaza, Av. 5 between Av. Juárez and Calle 1, tel. 987/869-0212, turismocozumel@quintanaroo.com, 9 A.M.–5 P.M. Mon.–Fri.) has a handful of brochures and maps. When it's actually open, an **information booth** on the plaza is more helpful. English is spoken at both places.

Medical Services

The **Hyperbaric Medical Center** (Calle 5 No. 21-B between Avs. Rafael Melgar and 5 Sur, tel. 987/872-1430 or tel. 987/872-2387, cozumel@sssnetwork.com) has very well-regarded emergency and nonemergency medical service for divers and can treat general nondiving ailments as well. English-speaking staff.

Clínica San Miguel and **Cozumel Hyperbarics** (Calle 6 No. 135 between Avs. 5 and 10 Norte, tel. 987/872-0103 or tel. 987/872-3070) are at the same location and offer both general and diver-related services. Most locals and long-time expats prefer this clinic for its competent doctors and reasonable prices. Spanish only.

Non-Spanish speakers may feel more comfortable at **Centro Médico de Cozumel** (CMC, Calle 1 No. 101 between Avs. 45 and 55 Sur, tel. 987/872-3545 or tel. 987/872-5664, www.centromedicodecozumel.com.mx, 24-hour emergency room). The clinic is affiliated with the South Miami Hospital and accepts most foreign insurance plans. Prices are higher here than elsewhere.

Dr. M. F. Lewis (Av. 50 bis Sur between Calles 11 and 13, tel. 987/872-1616, cell tel. 044-987/876-0914, cozumeldoctor@hotmail .com) is an American doctor with a private practice in town.

Those planning on doing a lot of diving (or even snorkeling) should consider buying divers insurance through DAN (Divers Alert Network, toll-free U.S. tel. 800/446-2671, www.diversalertnetwork.org). The basic plan provides medical and decompression coverage for dive accidents for only US$25/year. The Master and Preferred plans (US$35/year and US$70/year, respectively) offer additional protection, from lost equipment and vacation cancellation insurance, to accidental death and disability coverage. Though diving accidents are relatively rare on Cozumel, DAN is uniquely suited to handle them quickly and competently.

Pharmacies

Farmacia Portales (Calle 1 at Av. 10 Sur, tel. 987/872-1448, 7:30 A.M.–10:30 P.M. Mon.–Fri.) has a complete range of medication, plus sunscreen, film, and snacks. One of the largest pharmacies in town, **Farmacia Dori** (corner of Calle 7 and Av. 5 Sur, tel. 987/872-5518 or tel. 987/872-1439, 7:30 A.M.–10:30 P.M. Mon.–Fri.) has this and two other locations in town; delivery available. For 24-hour service, try **Farmacia Santa Fe** (Calle 2 at Av. 20 Norte,

tel. 987/869-1718), a well-stocked pharmacy a 10-minute walk from the main plaza.

Police

The police office (tel. 987/872-0409, tel. 987/872-0092, or dial 066 from any public phone) is in the Palacio Municipal on Calle 13 between Avenida Rafael Melgar and Avenida 5 Sur. Open 24 hours a day.

Newspapers, Radio, and Television

Pick up a copy of the *Free Blue Guide to Cozumel* (tel. 987/872-1451, freeblueguide@ demasiado.com) for a good map and listings for a range of services, from restaurants to dive shops. Look for the booklet with its bright blue cover as you get off the ferry and at many popular shops, hotels, and restaurants.

Money

Cash is not hard to find in this town, especially near the main plaza. **HSBC** (Av. 5 Sur at Calle 1, 8 A.M.–7 P.M. Mon.–Sat.) exchanges travelers checks and has one ATM; **Bancomer** (Av. 5 Sur between Av. Juárez and Calle 1, 8:30 A.M.–5 P.M. Mon.–Fri.) and **Banorte** (Av. 5 Norte between Av. Juárez and Calle 2, 9 A.M.–4 P.M. Mon.–Fri., 10 A.M.–2 P.M. Sat.) have similar services.

Post Office

The post office (Av. Rafael Melgar at Calle 7, 9 A.M.–5 P.M. Mon.–Fri., 9 A.M.–1 P.M. Sat.) is next to Punta Langosta.

Internet and Fax

For emailing, **Blau Net** (Calle Rosado Salas between Avs. 10 and 15, tel. 987/872-7673, 10 A.M.–10 P.M. Mon.–Sat., US$.90/hour, US$3.50 to burn CD) is a quiet and reliable place. You also can send faxes within Mexico for US$.45 per page, to the United States/Canada for US$.55 per page, and to most European countries for US$.70 per page.

Web Station (Av. 5 Sur No. 380 between Calles 3 and 5, tel. 987/872-3911, 9 A.M.–11 P.M. daily, US$1.35/hour, US$3.50 to burn CD) is another good choice. You also can send faxes within Mexico for US$.26 per minute and to the United States, Canada, and most European countries for US$.35 per minute.

Telephone

For phone calls, try **Blau Net** (Calle Rosado Salas between Avs. 10 and 15, tel. 987/872-7673, 10 A.M.–10 P.M. Mon.–Sat.). Calls within Mexico cost US$.22 per minute, to the United States /Canada US$.35 per minute, and to most European countries US$.45 per minute. **Web Station** (Av. 5 Sur No. 380 between Calles 3 and 5, tel. 987/872-3911, 9 A.M.–11 P.M. daily) has similar rates.

Laundry

Servi-Lav Lavandería (Av. 10 Norte No. 316 between Calles 6 and 8, tel. 987/872-3951, 9 A.M.–8 P.M. Mon.–Sat., US$.95/kilo—2.2 pounds) provides next-day service but if you drop off your clothes first thing in the morning, you can typically get them back—washed, dried, and folded—by the end of the day.

Lavandería Express (Calle Rosado Salas between Avs. 5 and 10, tel. 987/872-2932, 8 A.M.–9 P.M. Mon.–Sat., 8:30 A.M.–4:30 P.M. Sun.) is a convenient place to do your own laundry—US$1.75 per load to wash, US$1.25 every 10 minutes to dry. Full service (two hours, US$6.65 for up to four kilos) also is available.

GETTING THERE

Air

Cozumel International Airport (CZM) is approximately three kilometers (1.9 miles) from downtown San Miguel and is served by Continental (tel. 987/872-0487), Mexicana/Aerocaribe (tel. 987/872-0133 or tel. 987/872-0877), Aeromexico (tel. 987/872-3454), and AeroCozumel (tel. 987/872-0438). The airport has a Banamex ATM and a few magazine stands and duty-free shops. Taxis meet all incoming flights— fares to or from the airport are a ripoff (US$12).

Bus

Although there are no long-distance buses on Cozumel (it is a pretty small island, after all), you can buy tickets for buses leaving from Playa

del Carmen at **Ticket Bus** (Calle 2 at Av. 10 Sur, tel. 987/872-1706, 6 A.M.–9:30 P.M. daily). The office sells ADO, Riviera, and Cristóbal Colon tickets at no extra cost. You can even reserve your seats!

Ferry

Ferries to Playa del Carmen (US$8 each way, 25 minutes) leave from the main passenger pier opposite the plaza. Two companies **(UltraMar** and **Mexico Water Jets)** operate the boats; the service and fares are identical, though UltraMar's boats are somewhat newer. Between the two companies, there are 1–2 ferries leaving Cozumel every hour on the hour 7 A.M.–6 P.M., plus an early departure at 6 A.M. and later ones at 8 P.M. and 10 P.M. daily.

UltraMar has built a second ferry pier in Playa del Carmen at the end of Avenida Constituyentes, 10 blocks north of the present pier. When service begins there—it hadn't yet as we went to press—be sure to ask in Cozumel where your ferry is headed, as the company apparently intended to continue service to the main pier as well. If you're catching a bus straight from the ferry, the new pier will be more convenient to Terminal Alterna (long-distance service) while the main pier is just steps from Terminal Turística (for local service, including to Cancún and Tulum).

GETTING AROUND

In town, you can easily walk anywhere you like. However, the powerful taxi union has succeeded in quashing any and all efforts to start public bus service out of town and around the island. It is a shame, really, since it would be so easy and convenient to have a fleet of buses making loops around the island, or even just up and down the western shore. Until that changes (don't hold your breath), you'll need a car, bike, or rented scooter or car to explore the rest of the island.

Bike

A bike can be handy for getting to beach clubs and snorkel sites outside of town. Traffic on

Avenida Rafael Melgar can be heavy south of town. **Rentadora Cozumel** (Av. 10 Sur between Calle 1 and Av. Benito Juárez, tel. 987/869-2444) and **Sol y Mar** (Calle 2 between Avs. 5 and 10 Norte, tel. 987/869-0545) near Intermar car rental rent bikes for US$9–12/day as well as snorkel gear and scooters.

Taxis

Taxis are everywhere, and you can flag one down on Avenida Rafael Melgar, near the main passenger pier, and around the plaza. Finding one in the mornings can be a bit of a challenge, though, as virtually the entire fleet queues up at the cruise-ship piers. The taxi office is on Calle 2 Norte (tel. 987/872-0236 or tel. 987/872-0041) and any hotel will call a taxi.

Car and Scooter Rental

Renting a car is a nice way to get out of the downtown trap and see the rest of the island. It is virtually impossible to get lost, and you can visit all the main spots in a day, or two if you want to take it in the sights more thoroughly. Car rentals start at US$45–55/day (less in low season) for a basic VW bug or Chevy Pop, including insurance and taxes—ask for a convertible. Jeeps are popular, especially for trips organized for cruise-shippers, and cost a bit more. Many agencies also rent snorkel gear (US$7–10), which can be nice to have along.

Rentadora Isis (Av. 5 Norte No. 181 between Calles 2 and 4, tel. 987/872-3367, 8 A.M.–7 P.M. daily) has the island's best rates, and friendly service and reliable cars to boot. **Budget** (tel. 987/872-0903, budget7@prodigy.net.mx, www.budgetcancun.com, 7:30 A.M.–7:30 P.M. daily) is across the street from Isis, and **Intermar Cozumel Rent** (Calle 2 between Avs. 5 and 10 Norte, tel. 987/872-1098, ext. 108, 8 A.M.–7 P.M. daily) is around the corner. Another option is **Smart Rent A Car** (Corner of Av. 10 Sur and Calle 1, tel. 987/872-5651, smartrental@prodigy.net.mx, 8 A.M.–7 P.M. daily).

These agencies (except Budget) also rent scooters for around US$17–23/day. Other agencies include **Rentadora Cozumel** (Av. 10 Sur between Calle 1 and Av. Benito Juárez, tel. 987/869-2444) and **Sol y Mar** (Calle 2 between Avs. 5 and 10 Norte, tel. 987/869-0545) near Intermar car rental. Though fun to drive, scooters are involved in most of the accidents on Cozumel—and there are a lot. Speed bumps, uneven pavement, and windy conditions (especially on the far side of the island) can upend even experienced drivers.

Cozumel has three gas stations. Two are in town on Avenida Benito Juárez (at Av. Pedro Joaquín Coldwell and at Av. 75) and the third is four kilometers (2.5 miles) south of town on Avenida Rafael Melgar across from Puerta Maya, the main cruise-ship pier.

Cozumel has government-sponsored **Ángeles Verdes** (Green Angels) motorist assistance. If your car or scooter breaks down on the coastal highway, stay with it until they pass—they drive squat green and white trucks and are on the lookout for disabled vehicles. However, the Green Angels do not cover unpaved roads, or anywhere after dark. Service is free, but tips are appreciated.

Puerto Aventuras

One of the most ambitious (and obnoxious) developments on the Riviera Maya is Puerto Aventuras, a manicured condoville with time-shares, hotels, all sorts of resort amenities, and a large marina including a swim-with-dolphins area. It is a few minutes north of Akumal—you can't miss the huge signs alongside the highway. You'll see a sprinkling of trinket shops around the marina. Not much of interest, just lots of postcards and second-rate *artesanía*.

SIGHTS
Museo Sub-Acuatico CEDAM
Short for the Conservation, Ecology, Diving, and Archaeology Museum, CEDAM (Bldg. F, 9 A.M.–2 P.M., 3:30–6 P.M. Mon.–Sat., donation requested) is a worthwhile museum, displaying a wide variety of items: Mayan offerings that were dredged from the peninsula's cenotes, artifacts recovered from nearby colonial shipwrecks, early diving equipment, and

fascinating maps of the region before it was a major tourist destination. Makes a nice stop on a hot (or gray) day.

SPORTS AND RECREATION
Snorkeling and Scuba Diving
Aquanauts (tel. 984/873-5041, www.aquanauts-online.com, 8:30 A.M.–5:30 P.M. daily) is Puerto Aventuras's top dive center now that the famous diver, cave explorer, and filmmaker Mike Madden closed up shop and moved to Puerto Morelos. Not that Aquanauts is a step down—owner and instructor Mark McCraig runs a safe, professional, full-service shop that has many repeat guests. Divers can count on personal details (such as storing dry gear and loading it onto the boat for you) and guest-first practices (such as staying under as long as your air permits, not just the standard 45 minutes). The shop offers the full range of dives and courses; prices in 2005 included US$40/75

© LIZA PRADO CHANDLER

Dolphin swims are popular along the Riviera Maya.

one-/two-tank reef dives, US$75 one-/two-tank cenote dives, US$140/300 for packages of 4/10 dives, and US$385/414 group/private open-water certification course. Equipment rental (US$15/20 for one/two tanks) is not included in fun dives. The shop also offers a 2.5-hour snorkel tour (US$40, including equipment, snacks, and drinks, four people minimum) visiting two different reefs and has a good selection of new equipment for sale. Reservations recommended in high season

Swimming with Dolphins

Dolphin Discovery (Marina, tel. 984/873-5078, toll-free Mex. tel. 800/713-8862, www.dolphindiscovery.com) offers several dolphin-encounter activities, ranging in price and the amount and type of interaction you have. For the most contact, the Royal Swim program (US$125; 30 minutes' orientation, 30 minutes in water) includes two dolphins per group of eight people, with a chance to do a "dorsal tow," "footpush," and "kiss," plus some open swim time. The Swim Adventure (US$99) and Dolphin Encounter (US$69) have somewhat less direct contact. All-day programs also include interacting with stingrays and two rescued manatees named Romeo and Juliet.

Dolphin Discovery also offers an afternoon shuttle service to and from Playa del Carmen for its clients. The shuttle leaves Puerto Aventuras at 12:15, 2, 4, and 5:30 P.M. and returns at 12:40, 2:40, 4:40, and 6:15 P.M. To get a ride, shuttle-goers congregate in front of the gift shop in Puerto Aventuras. In Playa del Carmen, head to the main plaza and look for the shuttle sign.

Golf and Tennis

In town, the **Puerto Aventuras Club de Golf** (across from Bldg. B, tel. 984/873-5109, 7:30 A.M.–5:30 P.M. daily) offers a nine-hole, tournament-quality golf course (par 36). Rates include a golf cart and are US$75 pp before 3 P.M. and US$55 pp afterward. Two tennis courts are also available for US$20/hour. Need equipment? Golf club rentals cost US$24, tennis racquets run US$5.

Fishing

The best-known fishing outfit is **Captain Rick's Sportfishing Center** (past Omni Puerto Aventuras hotel, tel. 984/873-5195 or toll-free Mex. tel. 800/719-6439, www.fishyucatan.com, office 8 A.M.–7 P.M. daily). Trolling is the most popular sportfishing here as the Riviera Maya is known for its *dorado,* tuna, barracuda, sailfish, and even marlin. Bottom/drift fishing is also fun and targets "dinner fish" such as grouper, snapper, and yellowtail. Pleasure cruises are up to the guest and can involve visiting a deserted beach or Mayan ruin, snorkeling on the reef, or just cruising by upscale homes and hotels. You can also combine all three (trolling, bottom fishing, and a pleasure cruise) on a full-day trip or two parts on a half-day. As with most fishing operators, guests either charter a private boat or join a "shared" trip if they aren't traveling with a group. For charters, choose between a 21-foot boat (up to three passengers, US$220/420 half/full day) and 31-foot boats (up to eight passengers, US$350/600 half/full day). Shared trips are US$87 pp half day and US$174 full day. Full-day trips leave at 9 A.M. and return at 5 P.M.; half-day trips are 9 A.M.–1 P.M. and 1:30–5 P.M. There's good fishing year-round, but April, May, and June are the best months, especially for billfish.

Parasailing

Riviera Maya Parasail Adventures (past Omni Puerto Aventuras hotel, tel. 984/873-5623, www.rivieramayaparasail.com, office 8 A.M.–6 P.M. daily) offers three single and three tandem parasail trips daily (US$55/99 single/tandem, 9 A.M., 10 A.M., and 11 A.M.). The flights last 10–12 minutes (although the whole excursion takes about an hour) and you reach 250 feet in the air. Others can accompany you on the boat for US$10 pp. The agency may add extra flights in the high season, and it is a good idea to make reservations.

ACCOMMODATIONS

The main road bumps right into the **Omni Puerto Aventuras** (tel. 984/875-1950, toll-free U.S. tel. 800/843-6664, www.omnihotels.com, US$280 standard, US$359/319 adult/child all-inclusive), a small upscale hotel with the marina on one side and a fine, palm-shaded beach on the other. All 30 rooms have tile floors, one or two beds, colorful regional decor, and first-class amenities such as wireless Internet access, golf discounts, and a small compartment by the door where your breakfast is delivered each morning. All rooms have private patios with hot tubs; second- and third-floor rooms also have partial marina or ocean views. Large discounts in low season.

Amid all the plastic commercialism of Puerto Aventuras, **Casa del Aqua** (Punta Matzoma 21, tel. 984/873-5184, www.casadelagua .com, US$269/283 s/d with full breakfast, discounted for a week or more) is a beacon of class and charm. At the far southern end of town, the hotel's four gigantic suites—the bathrooms alone are bigger than some hotel rooms—all have king-sized beds, air-conditioning and fan, and come with a good breakfast. There is a small pool and the beach is quiet and reasonably nice, curving slowly northward all the way to town. Guests can arrange massages and body treatments, and the friendly owner gives good private tours in the area. The hotel caters to honeymooners and small yoga and meditation groups, so children are welcome if you rent the entire building; otherwise 12 and older only.

Real estate is a big business in Puerto Aventuras and gets bigger every year. If you are interested in buying or finding a longer-term rental, try **Paradise Beach Sales and Rentals** (next to Café-C@fé coffee shop, tel. 984/873-5029, www.puertaaventirasrentals.com, 7 A.M.–7 P.M. Mon.–Sat.) or **Costa Realty** (office next to Omni Hotel or ask in large kiosk in front, tel. 984/873-5110, www.puertaaventuras.com.mx, 8 A.M.–7 P.M. Mon.–Sat.).

FOOD

It is easy to find a place to eat in Puerto Aventuras: Stroll around the marina for a few minutes and you'll run into every restaurant in town. Unfortunately, the variety is slim—most menus have a similar selection of Americanized Mexican food, pastas, and grilled meats. A few oldies continue to stand out, though:

Café Olé International (Bldg. A, tel. 984/873-5125, 8 A.M.–10 P.M. daily, US$4–22) is known for its filet mignon and homemade desserts. Its tables, most of which are outdoors, have a great view of the dolphin shows.

If you're in the mood for a big salad or a pizza—thin, regular, or deep dish—try **Richard's Quarterdeck Steakhouse and Pizza** (Bldg. A, tel. 984/873-5086, 11 A.M.–10 P.M. daily, US$6–32). Opened in 1994 by a Chicago native, food here is especially good if you're missing flavors from home.

If you've gone fishing, bring your catch to **Gringo Dave's** (Bldg. C, 7 A.M.–11 P.M. daily, US$6–31). For US$3.50 pp, the chef will prepare your fish any way you want it and he'll even throw in rice, veggies, and a side of guacamole. Live music on weekends is also a great reason to drop in.

Super Akumal (across from Omni Puerto Aventuras hotel, 8 A.M.–8 P.M. Mon.–Fri.) is the local market and has a little of everything, including water, chips, sunscreen, toiletries, and so on.

INFORMATION AND SERVICES

Despite the numbers of tourists who frequent this town, the traveler services are still somewhat lacking. At the time of print, they included the following:

Conveniently situated on the marina, **First Aid Pharmacy** (ground floor of Bldg. A, tel. 984/873-5305, 24 hours daily) also delivers.

There is one **Banamex ATM** in town, which is on the ground floor of the Omni hotel, facing Building C.

The **post office** (10 A.M.–3 P.M. Mon., Wed., and Fri.) is in a large kiosk between Building B and the Golf and Racquet Club.

Along with two-for-one drinks all day long, **Azul Tequila Internet Bar** (Bldg. A, tel. 984/873-5673, 9 A.M.–11 P.M. daily) offers the best rates for Internet service (US$3.50/hour) and CD-burning (US$4 including CD).

For faxing and telephone calls, head to

Café-C@fé (Bldg. F, tel. 984/873-5728, www .cafecafe-pa.com, 8 A.M.–8 P.M. Mon.–Fri., 10 A.M.–5 P.M. Sat.). Calls cost US$.26 per minute within Mexico, US$.35 per minute to the United States and Canada, and US$.70 per minute to Europe. Faxing jumps to a whopping US$1.31 per page within Mexico, US$2.20 per page to the United States and Canada, and US$3.05 per page to Europe.

On the ground floor of Building B, **Lavandería Del Caribe** (8 A.M.–8 P.M. Mon.–Sat., 8 A.M.–3 P.M. Sun., US$1.30/kilo, minimum two kilos—4.4 pounds) is the only laundry shop in town.

Xpu-Há

A sleepy beachside community, Xpu-Há is made up of a sprinkling of hotels, a couple of restaurants, and a bunch of travelers just kicking back. On a spectacularly wide beach, it's definitely a known stop on the Riviera but it's managed to maintain a hideaway feel. Great for a couple of days (or weeks!) to catch up on that novel you've been meaning to read.

SPORTS AND RECREATION
Beach Activities
Just south of the all-inclusive Copacabana resort, the restaurant and beach club **La Playa** (tel. 984/877-8553, 9 A.M.–5:30 P.M. Mon.–Sat., 10 A.M.–6 P.M. Sun.) has a variety of beach and water sports, including parasailing, fishing, banana boats, snorkeling, and kayaking, all at pretty reasonable prices.

Cenotes
Near the entrances to Xpu-Há, look for the set of cenotes on the west side of Highway 307. For around US$2 each (cenote-keepers charge separate admission) you can swim and snorkel in any of these crystalline waters; divers pay US$7–9. (For more information on these once-sacred waters, see the *Cenotes: Sacred Swimming Pools* sidebar in the *Tulum and Southern Quintana Roo* chapter.)

Fishing
For any sort of sportfishing—deep-sea, troll-

GETTING THERE AND AROUND
By public transportation take a *combi* from Cancún, Playa del Carmen, or Tulum (US$2). Let the driver know where you're going and he'll drop you off on the side of the highway. You'll have to walk the 500 meters (0.3 mile) into town. Driving is much more convenient—take Highway 307 and turn east at the sign (you can't miss it—a huge gate slows traffic down).

Once here, walking is the best option in this small town since everything is centered around the marina.

ing, fly-, and bottom—head to the beachside reception desk of **Hotel-Villas del Caribe** (Xpu-Há X-4, tel. 984/873-2194). Here you can reserve a boat for US$70 per hour, two-hour minimum, six-person maximum.

Yoga
Hotel-Villas del Caribe (Xpu-Há X-4, tel. 984/873-2194) also offers yoga instruction under a huge round palapa just steps from the Caribbean. Classes are held 8:30–9:45 A.M. Monday–Friday and 5–6:15 P.M. Wednesday and Friday. Rates are US$6 per class. All levels are welcome.

ACCOMMODATIONS
Under US$50
Although slightly run-down, **Bonanza Xpu-Há** (entrance at Carr. Cancún-Tulum Km. 93, tel. 984/100-9821, US$3 pp camping, US$22 s/d with fan) offers eight clean rooms with private bath (cold water only) and decent campsites with electrical hookups. Right on the beach, these accommodations are a steal; perfect if you are traveling on a tight budget.

US$50–100
Down a tiny sand road next to the Copacabana resort, **M Hotel-Villas del Caribe** (Xpu-Há X-4, tel. 984/873-2194, www.xpuhahotel.com,

US$55–75 s/d with fan) is an oceanfront hotel with clean and comfortable rooms, some with terraces and hammocks. Rates vary according to the size and view: large or larger and garden or ocean. A great ocean breeze more than makes up for the lack of air-conditioning. Yoga classes and sportfishing (see *Sports and Recreation*) also are offered and a fantastic restaurant on-site makes this an especially comfortable place to wind down for a few days.

FOOD

Wiggle your toes in the sand as you await your meal at **M Café del Mar** (Hotel-Villas del Caribe, tel. 984/873-2194, 8 A.M.–9 P.M. Tues.–Sun., US$6–14). Right on the beach, this is an excellent open-air restaurant that offers an international menu made with the freshest of ingredients. Offering a full bar, this is also a great place to just sit for awhile and to take in the ocean air. Service is especially good.

A short distance south is the restaurant and beach club **La Playa** (tel. 984/877-8553, 9 A.M.–5:30 P.M. Mon.–Sat., 10 A.M.–6 P.M. Sun.). The buffet includes two drinks and costs US$13.

GETTING THERE AND AROUND

To get to this tiny beach community, take a *combi* (US$2) from Cancún, Playa del Carmen, or Tulum and let the driver know where you're going (if he's not sure, give him the name of your hotel). You'll get dropped off on the side of the highway and you'll have to walk about 10 minutes down a sand road before you hit the beach. If you're driving, take Highway 307 and turn east when you see the sign to your hotel. A good marker for Xpu-Há, which is very poorly signed, is the Copacabana resort.

Akumal

Unreachable by land until the 1960s, Akumal (literally, Place of the Turtle) is a low-key and upscale community that has developed on two bays: Akumal and Half Moon. It's a quiet place with sand roads and dozens of condominiums and rental homes. The beach in town is decent—if you can handle the boats parked on the sand—and the one around Half Moon Bay is calm but definitely rocky. What draws people here is a spectacular barrier reef, which protects Akumal's bays from the open sea and makes for ideal swimming and great snorkeling.

Down the beach about 45 minutes by foot, you'll find Aventuras Akumal—a small, upscale community on a breathtaking turquoise bay ringed by a tawny sand beach. Here, comfortable villas, condos, and hotels are perched all along the water's edge.

SIGHTS

Beaches

Akumal Bay—the one right in front of town—has a long, slow-curving shoreline, with soft sand shaded by palm trees. The water is beautiful but a bit rocky underfoot, and you should be aware of boat traffic when swimming or snorkeling. Half Moon Bay can also be nice for swimming and snorkeling, but the shoreline is rocky in many parts; where there is beach, it is mostly narrow and covered with sea plants that have washed ashore.

M Laguna Yal-Ku

A seemingly endless upwelling of fresh water from underground rivers and cenotes collides with the tireless flow of seawater at the mouth of an elbow-shaped channel/lagoon at the far north end of Akumal. The result is, among other things, a great place to snorkel, teeming with fish and plants adapted to this unique hybrid environment. You may even see sea turtles. Once a snorkeler's secret getaway, Laguna Yal-Ku (8:30 A.M.–5:30 P.M. daily, US$5.75 adult, US$3.50 child) now has a parking lot and a spot in every guidebook and is managed by a local organization to prevent misuse. (It must be the one that put up those peculiar statues....)

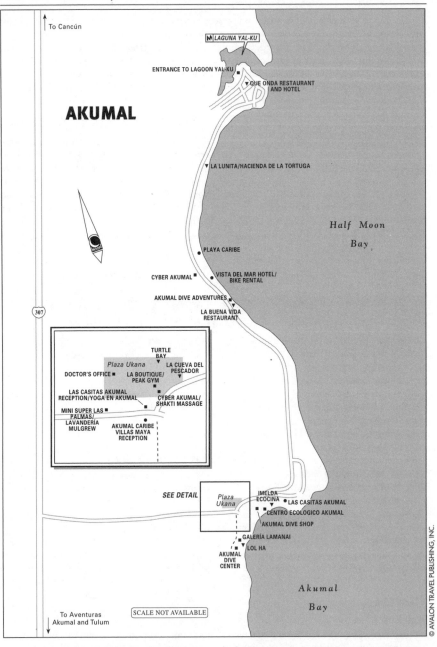

To Cancún

M *LAGUNA YAL-KU*

ENTRANCE TO LAGOON YAL-KU

▼ QUE ONDA RESTAURANT
AND HOTEL

AKUMAL

▼ LA LUNITA/HACIENDA DE LA TORTUGA

Half Moon
Bay

● PLAYA CARIBE

CYBER AKUMAL ■

● VISTA DEL MAR HOTEL/
BIKE RENTAL

AKUMAL DIVE ADVENTURES ▼

LA BUENA VIDA
RESTAURANT

307

TURTLE
BAY

Plaza Ukana

LA CUEVA DEL
PESCADOR ▼

DOCTOR'S OFFICE ■

LA BOUTIQUE/
PEAK GYM

LAS CASITAS AKUMAL
RECEPTION/YOGA EN AKUMAL

CYBER AKUMAL/
SHAKTI MASSAGE

MINI SUPER LAS ■
PALMAS/
LAVANDERÍA
MULGREW

AKUMAL CARIBE ●
VILLAS MAYA
RECEPTION

SEE DETAIL

*Plaza
Ukana*

IMELDA
ECOCINA ●

● LAS CASITAS AKUMAL

CENTRO ECOLOGICO AKUMAL

AKUMAL DIVE SHOP

GALERÍA LAMANAI

▼ LOL HA

AKUMAL
DIVE
CENTER

Akumal
Bay

SCALE NOT AVAILABLE

To Aventuras
Akumal and Tulum

© AVALON TRAVEL PUBLISHING, INC.

© GARY PRADO CHANDLER

snorkeling in Laguna Yal-Ku

As anywhere you snorkel or dive, do not touch plants or animals underwater and avoid kicking things with your fins. Try to use as little sunscreen as possible as the residues, even from the biodegradable kind, can collect on plants and sometimes coral. Of course, don't get sunburned either—many people snorkel in full or short wetsuits, but even a T-shirt and long shorts help. Rental gear is available at the entrance (mask and snorkel US$4.50, fins US$4.50, life vest US$4.50, locker US$1) as well as bathrooms, showers, and a small snack bar.

Centro Ecológico Akumal

From May to September, the Centro Ecológico Akumal (Akumal Ecological Center, on the beach next to Akumal Dive Shop, tel. 984/875-9095, www.ceakumal.org, 9 A.M.–5 P.M. Mon.–Fri. 9 A.M.–1 P.M. Sat.) offers nightly "turtle walks," where guests join volunteers on their patrols of Akumal's beaches, an important sea turtle breeding ground. After a 40-minute lecture/orientation, you'll cover around two kilometers (1.25 miles) of beach, looking for new turtle nests, checking existing ones, counting eggs, and even helping move some eggs to protected hatch-

eries. The walks can last less than a hour or until 2 A.M., and guests can stay (or return) as they like. The program begins at 7:30 P.M. and costs US$9 pp; sign up at least two days in advance as groups are limited to 10 people.

Founded in 1993, CEA is a well-regarded nonprofit organization that monitors the health and development of Akumal's ecosystems, particularly related to sea turtles and the coral reef. At the organization's spacious information center, visitors can sign up for turtle walks, look through interesting displays on ocean ecology, and attend weekly lectures held every Wednesday at 6:30 P.M. (high season only). CEA also has a number of long-term volunteer projects—besides serving as turtle monitors, volunteers have worked on water quality, wastewater management, and reef-monitoring projects. The organization has also introduced innovative composting toilets around town, which significantly reduce water usage and groundwater contamination. Definitely worth a stop, whether you're here for a couple of days or a couple of months.

Aktun Chen

Just south of the exit to Aventuras Akumal, look for the turnoff to Aktun Chen (Carr. Cancún-Tulum Km. 107, tel. 998/892-0662, www.aktunchen.com, 9 A.M.–5 P.M. daily, US$19 adults, US$10 children under 12). A nature preserve, it consists of 985 acres of rainforest with established paths, three caves with breathtaking stalactites and stalagmites, a 12-meter/39.4-foot-deep crystalline cenote, and a small zoo. A mandatory tour of the park, including a walk through the most accessible cave, leaves every 15 minutes and lasts 1.5–2 hours. The last tour leaves at 5 P.M. An easy walk, this is perfect for families and older travelers. Note: The entrance to the park is three kilometers (1.9 miles) from the highway. If arriving by bus, be prepared to walk or hitch a ride to the ticket counter.

SHOPPING

Akumal has a handful of shops, most of which sell regional clothing, leather sandals, and

Riviera Maya and Cozumel

CEDAM AND THE RIVIERA MAYA

In 1948, a small group of Mexican divers—active frogmen during World War II—organized themselves into a nonprofit organization called Club de Exploración y Deporte Acuáticos de México (Exploration and Aquatic Sports Club of Mexico)—CEDAM for short. Their mission was to actively promote the conservation of the ocean and to educate the population about its resources and treasures.

In 1958, the fledgling CEDAM salvaged the *Mantanceros,* a Spanish galleon that foundered off Palancar reef in 1741. The divers were allowed to camp on the deserted crescent beach of the then-private Akumal. The owner, Don Argimiro Arguelles, also leased CEDAM a work boat for their project. Lending his services as the captain of the boat as well, Don Argimiro and the divers of CEDAM became fast friends. It was this relationship that sealed Akumal's destiny (and arguably, the entire Riviera Maya's); during a relaxed evening around the campfire Don Argimiro sold Pablo Bush (the head of CEDAM) the bay of Akumal and thousands of acres of coconut palms north and south of it.

For the next 12 years, CEDAM continued its work in the rustic and beautiful environment—using the creaky SS *Cozumel* to ply the waters between the island of Cozumel and Akumal carrying divers, drinking water, and supplies (ironically, since there were no roads, the only way off the mainland was via the island). The only change to the bay was the addition of typical palapa huts, used as shelters by the CEDAM divers.

It was during this time that CEDAM began to gain fame as a preservationist organization in the diving world. As early as 1960, however, CEDAM had the idea of promoting tourism in the region. Pablo Bush and other area leaders began talking about a road and an airport.

In 1966, CEDAM International was born and gave new meaning to its initials: Conservation, Ecology, Diving, Archaeology, and Museums. As the name suggests, CEDAM was—and continues to be—an active part of the archaeological exploration of cenotes, where early Mayan artifacts have been retrieved. In 1968, a branch of CEDAM formed the nonprofit Club de Yates Akumal Caribe (Akumal Caribe Yacht Club). As a club, it turned over 5,000 acres of land to the government and donated the Cove of Xelha for a national park. The aim was to open the isolated area to tourists, and in so doing, create jobs for local residents. CEDAM provided housing, food, electricity, running water, a school for the children, and a first-aid station with a trained nurse. Word began to spread around the world about the spectacular Caribbean reef. Snorkelers and scuba divers were entranced. By the mid-1980s Cancún was born, Quintana Roo became a state, and Akumal finally bloomed.

Today, Akumal continues to be the main headquarters for CEDAM groups in the Caribbean. International symposiums and seminars are held here for divers from around the world. The bay itself also continues to grow; several condominiums, restaurants, and dive shops have popped up along the once deserted bay.

A worthwhile museum in Puerto Aventuras—Museo Sub-Acuatico CEDAM—also displays some incredible items that the group has recovered in the region's waters. Open 9 A.M.–2 P.M. and 3:30–6 P.M. Monday–Saturday, the museum is in Building F, just off the marina.

handmade jewelry. **Galería Lamanai** (tel. 984/875-9055, 9 A.M.–9 P.M. daily) is an exception, offering a good selection of Mexican crafts and folk art. It's on the beach near the Akumal Dive Center. **La Boutique** (Plaza Ukana, tel. 984/875-9208, 9 A.M.–5 P.M. Mon.–Sat.) is the best of a cluster of three shops in the plaza area.

SPORTS AND RECREATION

Scuba Diving

Mexico's first mainland diving group waded in from the shores of Akumal Bay, and the area has long held a special place among divers here. (See the sidebar *CEDAM and the Riviera Maya*). While not as spectacular as other areas along the Riviera Maya, Akumal's diving is easy and fun, with a mellow current and few profiles that go below 20 meters (65.6 feet). Visibility is decent by Caribbean standards—great by everyone else's—averaging 10–30 meters (32.8–98.4 feet). The reef is predominantly boulder coral, which isn't as picturesque as other types, but still it teems with tropical fish and plant life.

With more than 30 years' experience, **Akumal Dive Shop** (tel. 984/875-9032, www.akumal.com, 8 A.M.–7 P.M. daily, until 6 P.M. Sept.–Dec.) was not only the first dive shop in Akumal, but the first on mainland Mexico. Still right on the beach, the shop offers fun dives and various certification courses in both open water and cave/cavern diving. Divers can take one-/two-tank reef dives (US$45/60), cavern/cenote dives (US$65/120) or buy packages of 4/10 dives for US$120/250. Fun dives do not include equipment rental (US$21/day, US$50/week). Open-water certification courses take 3–4 days and cost US$420, equipment and materials included.

Down the beach a short distance, **Akumal Dive Center** (tel. 984/875-9025, www.akumaldivecenter.com, 8 A.M.–5 P.M. daily) has operated in Akumal almost as long and offers the same dives and courses at comparable prices.

On Half Moon Bay, **Akumal Dive Adventures** (next to La Buena Vida restaurant, tel. 984/875-9157, U.S. tel. 877/425-8625, www.akumaldiveadventures.com, 8 A.M.–5 P.M. daily) offers similarly priced diving and courses, as well as a package of three nights' lodging and four reef dives for US$230 pp single occupancy, US$343 pp double occupancy, with an option to extend your stay or swap reef dives for night or cenote dives (extra cost). Rooms are at the affiliated Vista del Mar hotel and condos, and all have private bath, air-conditioning, refrigerator, and a patio or balcony with ocean view.

On a calm bay with a healthy reef, Aventuras Akumal has good diving (and snorkeling) right at your doorstep. **Aquatech** (tel. 984/875-9020, U.S. tel. 866/619-9050, www.cenotes.com) is a full-service dive shop operated at the Villas DeRosa hotel, offering daily reef dives at 9 A.M. and 1:30 P.M. that cost US$40/60 one/two tanks (rates include tanks, air, weights, boat captain, and dive master). Night, cenote, and cave dives also are available and are easily arranged. PADI open-water courses and NADI cavern and cave certifications are offered as well at standard rates.

Snorkeling

Akumal has one of the best snorkeling spots in the Riviera Maya. **Laguna Yal-Ku** (see *Sights*) gets a lot of repeat visitors for its large area, calm water, and unique mix of fresh- and saltwater ecosystems. Look for several modern sculptures standing somewhat incongruously along the lagoon's edges.

The northern end of Akumal Bay also makes for fine snorkeling and you can wade in right from the beach. It's a great little nook of fairly shallow water, where tropical fish dart about a labyrinth of rocks, boulder coral, and plant life. Fishing boats do not pass through here (another reason it's good for snorkeling), but you should be careful not to drift out of the area and into boat channels. Many snorkelers make their way toward the large buoy at the edge of the bay, not realizing it marks a channel that boats use to get through the reef. Be smart and steer clear. Half Moon Bay has some good shore snorkeling as well.

You can rent snorkel gear at any of the dive shops and at the entrance of Laguna Yal-Ku for around US$9–10/day or US$40–50/week.

To snorkel on the reef, join a guided snorkel tour offered by all three dive shops. Tours typically visit 2–3 sites, last about two hours, and cost US$24–35, including gear.

Sailing

Akumal Dive Shop (tel. 984/875-9032, www .akumal.com, 8 A.M.–7 P.M. daily, until 6 P.M. Sept.–Dec.) offers a popular Robinson Crusoe cruise: a 5–6-hour excursion on a catamaran sailboat, with stops for fishing and snorkeling (US$65 including lunch and equipment). Other shops offer this tour, even by the same name, but Akumal Dive Shop was the only one at the time of research to do it on a sailboat— a big plus. If time is short, the Sunset Cruise (US$35, two hours) is also fun and beautiful.

Fishing

All three dive shops offer fishing tours for US$90–120/boat (US$45–50/hour extra, 1–4 passengers; Akumal Dive Adventures was the least expensive), including equipment and beverages. The best months for fishing are January–August, especially April and June when sailfish and marlin are most numerous and active.

Yoga

In a breezy studio in the archway to town, **Yoga en Akumal** (tel. 984/875-9114, www.yoga-in-akumal.com) offers classes and workshops for beginners and advanced students.

Gym

If you want to maintain your workout regime, head to **Peak Gym** (Plaza Ukana, 1st floor, tel. 984/875-9208, 8 A.M.–7 P.M. Mon.–Sat.). Although small, this place is *packed* with shiny weights and well-maintained cardio equipment. Plus (a major one), it's got air-conditioning. Day passes cost US$10, weekly rates rise to US$46, and the monthly membership is US$60.

Massage

For a breezy outdoor massage, try **Shakti Massage** (Plaza Ukana, 2nd floor, no phone,

heading out for an afternoon of fishing

Mon.–Sat., US$60/hour). The masseuse, Salvador, has two weeks' worth of sign-up sheets outside of his door; just stop by and sign up for an appointment.

ACCOMMODATIONS

Akumal's hotel prices are on the high end, with the big exception of the CEA dorms, which are a steal. There are many condos and villas for rent around the bend at Half Moon Bay, only about a kilometer (0.6 mile) from the main entrance to Akumal. At the right time and shared among several people, these can turn out to be reasonably affordable. To reserve, contact the rental agencies we've listed or simply do an Internet search.

In Town

M **Centro Ecológico Akumal (CEA)** (on the beach next to Akumal Dive Shop, tel. 984/875-9095, www.ceakumal.com, 9 A.M.–5 P.M. Mon.–Fri., 9 A.M.–1 P.M. Sat.) has a number of large dorm rooms sleeping 3–6 people at the awesome price of US$10 pp. The rooms surround the plaza and basketball court, and each has a clean private bathroom, lockers (bring your own lock), tile floors, and either concrete or palapa roof. Some rooms have air-conditioning, the rest have fans. Guests can use a large communal kitchen and there is a place to handwash your clothes. CEA's summer volunteers have priority for the rooms, but walk-ins are welcome if space is available.

The old thatch huts once used by the CEDAM diving club now form the core of the **Hotel Club Akumal Caribe Villas Maya** (reception in the arches at the entrance to town, tel. 915/584-3552, toll-free U.S. tel. 800toll-free U.S. tel. 800/351-1622, toll-free Can. tel. 800/343-1440, clubakumal@aol.com, www.hotelakumalcaribe.com, US$140 s, US$130 d hotel, US$100 s, $112 d bungalow). The bungalows have garden views and have been completely remodeled with private baths, tile floors, fans, small refrigerators, air-conditioning … even the lighting has been improved. Across the street from the bungalows are 21 ocean-

front hotel rooms, each with full bath, compact refrigerator, and small porch or balcony. The rooms look out over the Caribbean and the garden area, which has a swimming pool.

On the eastern end of the beach in town, **Las Casitas Akumal** (tel. 984/875-9071, toll-free U.S./Can. tel. 800/5-AKUMAL (800/525-8625), casitasakumal@prodigy.net.mx, www.lascasitasakumal.com) has 18 airy, furnished condominiums with two bedrooms, two baths, living room, fully equipped kitchen, and private patio. All have ocean views and direct access to a semiprivate section of the beach. Rates range US$250–285 per night. If you are traveling with a larger group, consider staying in a more expensive unit; they are two stories and can accommodate up to six adults (the less expensive units are one floor and sleep up to five). Note: Reservations must be made for a minimum of seven nights and begin on a Saturday.

Half Moon Bay

Along Half Moon Bay's sand road, **Hacienda de la Tortuga** (tel. 984/875-9068, htortuga@prodigy.net.mx, www.haciendatortuga.com, US$150 one bedroom, US$200 two bedroom) offers spacious one- and two-bedroom condos, all with huge windows overlooking the Caribbean. Although each is uniquely decorated, all units have a living room, kitchen, (at least one) full bathroom, and air-conditioning in the bedrooms. A nice pool and no televisions only add to the relaxed feel of the place.

Nearby **Playa Caribe** (tel. 984/875-9137, lunaakumal@prodigy.net.mx, www.amcakumal.com, US$250 one bedroom, US$275 two bedroom) offers a similar deal: one- and two-bedroom fully equipped condos with spectacular ocean views. The main difference here is twofold: Most—though not all—units have air-conditioning and all condos have satellite TV.

Just a block from Yal-Ku Lagoon, **M** **Que Onda** (Caleta Yal-Ku, tel. 984/875-9101, www.queondaakumal.com, US$85 s/d, US$130 suite) offers six rooms, each lovingly decorated with tile floors, beautiful fabrics, and unique works of art. One two-story suite with wood floors and a loft also is available and offers a spectacular view of the Caribbean and Yal-Ku. All face a verdant garden and a pool in the middle of the property. Use of bicycles and snorkel gear are included in the rates. A bit off the beaten track but worth it especially if you don't mind staying a few blocks from the ocean.

Aventuras Akumal

Villas DeRosa (tel. 984/875-9020, U.S. tel. 866/619-9050, www.cenotes.com, US$65 s/d, US$120 one bedroom, US$170 two bedroom, US$225 three bedroom) offers jungle-view hotel rooms and one-, two-, and three-bedroom condominiums with ocean views and private balconies. The spacious accommodations are comfortable and have air-conditioning in the bedrooms, cable TV, stereos, and, in condos, fully equipped kitchens. All are just steps from the Caribbean; you literally can snorkel in your backyard. The resort also boasts an excellent full-service dive shop; ask about the dive/accommodation packages—rates are decent.

Smaller and cozier than the DeRosa, **Villa Las Brisas** (tel. 984/875-9263, villa lasbrisas@hotmail.com, www.aventuras-akumal.com, US$78 room, US$89 studio, US$140 one bedroom, US$200 two bedroom) has just three units (two of which can be combined to make the two-bedroom condo), all spacious, spotless, and meticulously furnished, down to a stocked spice rack in the kitchen. Opened in 1998, the condos have large terraces with hammocks and stunning views; the smaller units have balconies that overlook a tidy garden. With comfortable beds, modern furnishings, and room to stretch out in, it's easy to feel at home here. Families are welcome, and the friendly owners can lend you a crib or car seat. Beach chairs and umbrellas are free, bikes and snorkel gear can be rented, and there's a simple mini-mart at the entrance (8 A.M.–4 P.M. Mon–Sat.). US dollars, euros, checks, and travelers checks okay.

Condos and Rental Properties

The great majority of rooms for rent in Akumal are in condos and privately owned homes along

Half Moon Bay. For information and online listings, contact **Caribbean Fantasy** (toll-free U.S. tel. 800/523-6618, www.caribbfan.com), **Akumal Villas** (tel. 984/875-9088, U.S. tel. 770/234-5708, www.akumal-villas.com, 8:30 A.M.–4:30 P.M. CST), or **Loco Gringo** (www.locogringo.com). For retail and some rentals, stop by the office of **Akumal Real Estate** (north of the arches at the entrance to town, tel. 984/875-9064, www.akumalrealestate.com, 9 A.M.–2 P.M. and 4–7 P.M. Mon.–Sat.).

FOOD

In Town

An Akumal institution, **Lol Ha** (on the beach, tel. 984/875-9013, 7–11 A.M. and 6:30–10:30 P.M. daily, closed Oct.–mid-Nov., US$12–30) burned down some time ago but has since reopened as a classy spot for live music and fine dining. The restaurant's beautiful wood and stucco dining room is topped with a high palapa roof and opens onto a pleasant patio for outdoor dining. Expect excellent seafood and Mexican and American specialties, including prime USDA steaks and daily specials. At breakfast, a basket of homemade sweet rolls comes immediately when you sit down, and the orange juice is fresh-squeezed. Flamenco dancers perform on Wednesday nights, while Fridays are for jazz. For something especially romantic, ask about arranging a private dinner on the beach.

Next door to the mother restaurant, **Snack Bar Lol Ha,** (same phone, 11 A.M.–9 P.M. daily, US$8–13) serves the best hamburgers on the beach, a fine guacamole, and *tacos cochinita,* a fusion of Mayan flavor and Mexican packaging. There's usually a game playing on the TV—this is the place to come for the Super Bowl—or ask about playing pool or Foosball in the adjacent pizzeria-turned-gameroom.

For a fresh, healthy breakfast or lunch, try **Imelda Ecocina** (no phone, 8:30 A.M.–3 P.M. Mon.–Sat., US$3–5) next to Centro Ecológico Akumal. Breakfast options include eggs, omelets, pancakes, French toast, and more. Lunch is usually *comida corrida* (set lunch menu). On Mondays and Thursdays the restaurant hosts a popular Mayan buffet (US$15; 6 P.M.) followed by *cumbia* tunes and dancing at 7 P.M.

In Plaza Ukana, **Ⓜ Turtle Bay** (tel. 984/875-9136, 7 A.M.–3 P.M. daily, 6–9 P.M. Thurs.–Sat., US$4–6 breakfast, US$5–7 lunch, US$9–18 dinner) offers spectacular vegetarian and light creations such as grilled portabella mushroom burgers, hummus pitas, and crab cakes with roasted corn salsa. Breakfasts—think French toast, eggs Benedict, fruit plate with yogurt and granola—are equally as tempting. You also can enjoy your meal surrounded by palm trees—either in the outdoor palapa-roofed dining room or on the porch of the main building.

For fresh seafood, check out **La Cueva del Pescador** (Plaza Ukana, tel. 984/875-9205, 11 A.M.–10 P.M. daily, US$7–26). Sink your teeth into fish kabobs, shrimp prepared nine different ways (e.g., grilled, à la tequila, with curry salsa, and so on), and lobster—all caught the day that you order it. The bar is an especially popular stop on weekends.

For groceries, try **Mini Super Las Palmas** (in front of the arches to town, tel. 984/875-9337, 7 A.M.–9 P.M. daily). Here, you'll find canned food, dried goods, and other basic needs (think sunscreen, booze, and film). For produce, check out the **farmers market** held Wednesdays and Saturdays in the plaza behind the Mini Super.

Half Moon Bay

A fantastical flying fish skeleton greets you at the oceanside **Ⓜ La Buena Vida** (tel. 984/875-9061, 11 A.M.–11 P.M. daily, US$4–10 lunch, US$6–26 dinner). Here, a varied menu offers something for everyone—from hamburgers to lobster. You can also just stop in for a drink at the (so to speak) swing bar, where swings serve as seats around the bar. Try the specialty—La Buena Vida—which is a smooth combo of Baileys, Kahlua, rum, coconut cream, and Grand Marnier (US$4.50). Look for the palapa-roofed restaurant/bar just past the Vista del Mar condos.

Also right on the ocean, try **La Lunita** (tel.

984/875-9068, 5–10 P.M. Mon.–Sat., US$8–20), a fine little dinner house with stained wood tables and candles on the ground floor of the Hacienda de la Tortuga (see *Accommodations*). It serves lobster worth stopping for and tasty fish dishes, inside or on the beach.

If you're in the mood for Italian, try the popular **Que Onda** (Caleta Yal-Ku, tel. 984/875-9101, www.queondaakumal.com, 4–10 P.M. Wed.–Mon., US$6–14). An outdoor café with wood tables, modern chairs, and a garden view, it's run by an Italian-Swiss couple who definitely know their way around an Italian kitchen. Try the lasagna for an especially good taste treat. The restaurant is in the front part of its hotel (see *Accommodations*), just a block from the Yal-Ku Lagoon.

Aventuras Akumal

Cooking your own meals is the only option in this condo community. Make sure to stop at a supermarket—Chedraui in Playa del Carmen or Super San Francisco in Tulum—before hunkering down here. Mini Super Las Palmas in Akumal town also has some basic groceries.

INFORMATION AND SERVICES
Tourist Information Centers

Akumal doesn't have an official tourist office, but it's a small town and you can probably find what you're looking for by asking the first person you see. If that fails, the folks at Centro Ecológico Akumal are friendly and awfully sharp; several speak English.

Medical Services

For an English-speaking physician, call or stop by the offices of general practitioner **Dr. Néstor Mendoza Gutiérrez** (Plaza Ukana, tel. 984/875-4051, dr_nestor_akumal@hotmail.com, 8 A.M.–4 P.M. Mon.–Sat., for emergencies 24 hours a day, call cell tel. 044-984/806-4616).

There is a private **pharmacy** in the part of town across the highway—call cell tel. 044-984/806-4072 for service. For **ambulance service** call cell tel. 044-984/876-2250.

Police

The police can be reached by calling tel. 984/875-9345 or cell tel. 044-984/875-9345.

Money

There is an ATM in Super Chomak, the fancier of the two grocery stores at the entrance of town, just outside of the arches.

Post Office

The post office (9:30 A.M.–3 P.M. Tues. and Thurs. only) is inside the Centro Ecológico Akumal, on the beach in the center of town.

Internet, Fax, and Telephone

Cyber Akumal has two locations in Akumal. The first one (Plaza Ukana, ground floor, tel. 984/875-9313, info@cyberakumal.com, 7 A.M.–9 P.M. daily) is just past the arches as you enter town. The second (Half Moon Bay, tel. 984/875 4219, 8 A.M.–8 P.M. daily) is 40 meters (131 feet) north of Vista del Mar hotel, about halfway around Half Moon Bay. At both locations, Internet runs a steep US$5.25 per hour and CD-burning costs US$4.35. Fax service is US$.90 per page within Mexico and to the United States and Canada. To Europe, rates rise to US$1.30 per page. Telephone calls also can be made from the shop: US$.45 per minute within Mexico, US$.52 per minute to the United States and Canada, and US$.62 to Europe.

Laundry

Next to the Mini Super Las Palmas, **Lavandería Mulgrew** (entrance to the village, no phone, 7 A.M.–1 P.M. and 5–7 P.M. Mon.–Sat., US$1.60/kilo, two kilos minimum—4.4 pounds) will provide same-day service if you drop off your load before 8 A.M.

GETTING THERE AND AROUND

As with so many other places on the coast, having a car will make getting to and around Akumal much easier. Vans and second-class buses pass the Akumal turnoff, going both north and south, throughout the day. (So do first-class buses but they don't stop.) It's about one kilometer (0.6 mile) to town—a hot haul if you're carrying luggage.

Once in town, you can get around the center area easily by foot, but walking to and from Half Moon Bay can be a hassle. A car is helpful, but a bike also works—the condo-hotel **Vista del Mar** (Half Moon Bay, tel. 984/875-9060, www.akumalinfo.com) rents decent bikes for US$5.25 per day.

A couple of **taxis** are usually waiting by their *sitio* (base) near the Super Chomak grocery store at the entrance of town, just outside of the arches. A ride from town to Laguna Yal-Ku costs US$2.50, significantly more for destinations out of town.

You can get to Aventuras Akumal by taking any *combi* from Cancún, Playa del Carmen, or Tulum (US$2). Just let the driver know where you are going—he'll drop you off on the side of the highway. You'll have to walk the 500 meters (0.3 mile) into the community since there is no taxi stand. A car makes getting there much easier. Take Highway 307 and turn east when you see the sign to Villas DeRosa (the community itself isn't well signed). The community is so small that walking is the best option. Bring your flip-flops—you'll never have to go very far.

Tankah Tres

Six kilometers (3.7 miles) north of Tulum ruins, the scattered condo/villas and private homes on this stretch of coast were once connected (together and to the highway) by a U-shaped access road. But new development cut the U right in half, and now you have to drive back out to the highway to get to either side of the community. The southern entrance is still marked Tankah Tres, but the northern entrance is indicated by a sign for Oscar y Lalo restaurant.

SIGHTS

Cenote Tankah

Across the street from Casa Cenote hotel, Cenote Tankah (no admission) forms a large lagoon perfect for snorkeling. The cenote's winding channels have crystal-clear water and a tangle of rocks, trees, and freshwater plants along their edges and bottoms. Look for schools of tiny fish near the surface, and some bigger ones farther down. Just a short distance inland, Cenote Tankah also has an underwater tunnel that empties into the ocean in front of the hotel, and scuba divers wow beachgoers by emerging Navy Seal–like a short distance offshore.

Playa Tankah

Casa Cenote hotel fronts a pretty little beach, which non-guests are free to use if you order something at the restaurant. With soft white sand, few tourists, good snorkeling in the cenote out back and in the ocean in front, this is one of the better places on the Riviera Maya to spend a relaxing beach day.

SPORTS AND RECREATION

There is excellent snorkeling and kayaking in the three bays that make up Tankah Tres. In the Tankah Inn, **Lucky Fish Diving** (southern entrance, cell tel. 044-984/804-5051, www.luckyfishdiving.com, 8:30 A.M.–6 P.M.

© GARY PRADO CHANDLER

contemplating the cool waters of Cenote Tankah

and 9 A.M.–4 P.M. Sun., US$75/95 two-tank reef/cenote dive) is a full-service shop offering guided trips and dive instruction, including open-water, technical, cave, and nitrox dives. Rates are a little higher than usual but include all equipment. The shop also rents snorkel gear for US$7.50 a day.

For cheaper snorkel gear, try the restaurant **Oscar y Lalo** (northern entrance, tel. 984/804-6973, 11 A.M.–8 P.M. daily), near the northern entrance to town. At US$2.50 for a mask and snorkel, the price is hard to beat. If you'd rather paddle than swim, it also rents sea kayaks for US$6.50 per day.

ACCOMMODATIONS

At the northern entrance to Tankah Tres the road forks; the road to the right goes into town, the road to the left leads you to **M Oscar y Lalo** (tel. 984/804-6973) a restaurant and campsite on an isolated palm tree–lined beach. Here, you can set up a tent among the coconut trees for US$2.50 pp and feel, if only for a night or two, that you are on a idyllic deserted island (that happens to have a bathroom with running water, of course). When the restaurant closes at 8 P.M. (see *Food*), the place is yours, starry night and all. Be sure to bring mosquito nets in the rainy season.

Casa Cenote (southern entrance, 1.5 km/0.9 mile from the turnoff, tel. 998/874-5170, www .casacenote.com, US$130 s/d including breakfast and free use of kayak and snorkel gear) was for many years the only life on the beach, and it is still a pleasant place to visit. All seven rooms have air-conditioning, one or two large beds, and fine views of the ocean. Cenote Tankah, great for snorkeling and a popular diving destination, is just across the street. You can rent snorkel gear (US$3.50/hour) or kayaks (US$6–8.50/hour) at the hotel's small retail shop.

Five rooms with murals of Mayan temples make up the **M Tankah Inn** (southern entrance, 1.5 km/0.9 mile from the turnoff, U.S. tel. 918/582-3743, bill@bill-in-tulsa.com, www.tankah.com, US$79–99 s/d). Right on

the beach, each room has tile floors, terraces, and ocean views. A healthy breakfast is included in the rate as is the use of sea kayaks. A full-service dive shop also is on the premises (see *Sports and Recreation*). It's a great place to hole up for a few days or more.

FOOD

Near the northern entrance to town, **Oscar y Lalo** (tel. 984/804-6973, 11 A.M.–8 P.M. daily, US$7–32) is an oceanside restaurant that serves excellent fresh seafood. While it's a little pricey, the view and the monster portions more than make up for it. If you're feeling a little flush, try the lobster ceviche.

The restaurant at **M Casa Cenote** (southern entrance, two km/1.25 miles from the turnoff, tel. 998/874-5170, www.casacenote.com, 8 A.M.–9 P.M. daily, US$6–15) has a breezy patio dining area just steps from the sea's edge. You can order beach food such as quesadillas or a guacamole plate, or something heftier—the seafood is always tasty and fresh. Every Sunday at noon, the hotel hosts an awesome Texas-style barbecue (US$8.50–10), which is popular with locals and expats up and down the Riviera Maya. All settle in for an afternoon spent over heaping plates of great food and boisterous conversation. The regular menu includes pork ribs, marinated chicken, beef, burgers, homemade potato chips, and nachos with all sorts of toppings.

INFORMATION AND SERVICES

There are no formal services here because it's not really a formal town. Head to Tulum for ATMs, medical services, Internet, groceries, and so on.

GETTING THERE AND AROUND

Arriving by car is definitely the best option—look for the Oscar y Lalo or Tankah Tres signs, depending which part you want to go to. By bus, get off at the turnoff and start walking.

Tulum and Southern Quintana Roo

The small but impressive ruins of Tulum, set on a bluff overlooking the turquoise Caribbean waters, are the bridge between the busy Riviera Maya and the state's decidedly less-traveled southern coast. Just south of Tulum (which has perhaps the finest beaches in the Yucatán Peninsula) is the pristine Sian Ka'an Biosphere Reserve, some 1.3 million acres of tropical forest, tangled mangroves, and the beautiful Ascension Bay. The bay's shallow waters teem with bonefish, tarpon, and permit, attracting anglers from all over the world who stay in fish-

ing lodges in and around the small town of Punta Allen.

South to the Belize border, the coast is mostly uninhabited save for a few small fishing villages. The coral reef runs close to shore here—and it is very healthy, owing to the paucity of tourist traffic—making for excellent snorkeling and diving. This area has been dubbed the Costa Maya, not by the locals but by advertisers selling cruise-ship vacations. As odd as it seems, huge cruise ships now dock at a specially made pier outside the tiny town of Mahahual,

Must-Sees

M Tulum Ruins: Location, location, location. Tulum may not be the biggest or baddest of the Mayan ruins, but with its own beach and stunning ocean views it is still one of the most memorable (page 184).

M Cenotes Outside Tulum: Explore an unforgettable realm of crystal-clear water and eerily beautiful stalagmites and stalactites in the world's longest underground river system—300 miles and counting (page 186).

M Tulum's Southern Beaches: Picture perfect, these beaches have the classic white sand, turquoise blue water, and palm tree–studded shores that make the Caribbean famous. The stretch between Kilometers 7–9 is particularly spectacular (page 188).

M Ascension Bay: Anglers from all over the world ply the shallow flats and mangrove islands of this bay in search of the grand slam of fly-fishing: hooking a bone fish, tarpon, and permit all in the same day (page 206).

© LIZA PRADO CHANDLER

one of the striking masks found in Kohunlich

M Fuerte San Felipe Bacalar: Re-opened in 2004 after extensive renovation, this star-shaped fort houses a small but excellent museum with state-of-the-art displays on piracy, the Caste war, and the area's history (page 222).

M Museo de la Cultura Maya: Chetumal's phenomenal museum has three levels (to mirror Mayan cosmology) and excellent exhibits on the religion, astronomy, writing, artwork, and daily life of ancient Mayans (page 227).

M Kohunlich Archaeological Zone: Large, well-preserved, and eerily compelling stucco masks are the highlight of this remote, seldom-visited archaeological site west of Chetumal (page 229).

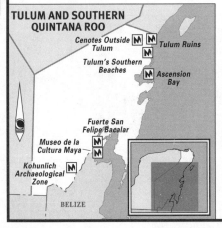

TULUM AND SOUTHERN QUINTANA ROO

Cenotes Outside Tulum **M**
M Tulum Ruins
Tulum's Southern Beaches
M Ascension Bay
Fuerte San Felipe Bacalar
Museo de la Cultura Maya **M**
Kohunlich **M** Archaeological Zone
BELIZE

Southern Quintana Roo

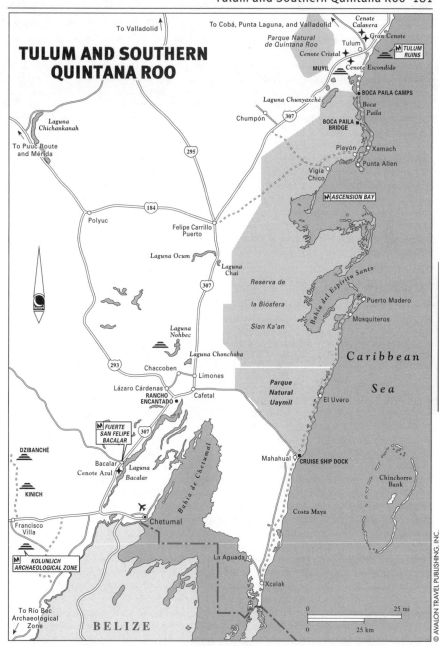

TULUM AND SOUTHERN QUINTANA ROO

To Valladolid

To Cobá, Punta Laguna, and Valladolid

Cenote Calavera

Parque Natural de Quintana Roo

Gran Cenote

Tulum

Cenote Cristal

TULUM RUINS

MUYIL

Cenote Escondido

BOCA PAILA CAMPS

Laguna Chunyaxché

Boca Paila

Chumpón

307

BOCA PAILA BRIDGE

Laguna Chichankanah

Playón

Xamach

To Puuc Route and Mérida

295

Vigia Chico

Punta Allen

ASCENSION BAY

184

Polyuc

Felipe Carrillo Puerto

Laguna Ocum

Laguna Chal

307

Reserva de la Biósfera

Bahía del Espíritu Santo

Sian Ka'an

Puerto Madero

Mosquiteros

Laguna Nohbec

Laguna Chonchoba

Caribbean

293

Chaccoben

Limones

Sea

Lázaro Cárdenas

RANCHO ENCANTADO

Cafetal

Parque Natural Uaymil

El Uvero

FUERTE SAN FELIPE BACALAR

307

DZIBANCHÉ

Bacalar

Cenote Azul

Laguna Bacalar

Mahahual

CRUISE SHIP DOCK

Chinchorro Bank

KINICH

Francisco Villa

Chetumal

Costa Maya

Bahía de Chetumal

KOLUNLICH ARCHAEOLOGICAL ZONE

La Aguada

To Río Bec Archaeological Zone

Xcalak

0   25 mi

BELIZE

0   25 km

Southern Quintana Roo

which installed phone and power lines only in early 2005. But while mass tourism is clearly on its way, Mahahual and the nearby town of Xcalak still retain a last-frontier feel and are a fine choice for people seeking peace and isolation (though surely something of a disappointment for party-minded cruise-shippers!).

Southern Quintana Roo is also home to Laguna Bacalar, a beautiful freshwater lagoon whose remarkable blue hues prompted the ancient Mayans to name it Lake of Seven Colors. Just south, the state capital—Chetumal—boasts an excellent Mayan museum and is a main gateway into Belize. Two intriguing archaeological sites are a day trip away from the city and along the same highway travelers can reach the remarkable Mayan sites of southern Campeche and Chiapas.

PLANNING YOUR TIME

Many travelers to Quintana Roo don't make it farther south than Tulum. It's not with-

out reason—the northern part of the peninsula boasts better beaches, more Mayan ruins, and cities and towns geared toward tourists. Still, southern Quintana Roo is a rewarding place to visit if you have the time. Tulum is definitely worth two or three days, not only to visit the ruins but also to enjoy the spectacular beaches and to experience snorkeling or diving in the many nearby cenotes. If you enjoy fly-fishing or want to explore the area's largest eco-reserve, head to Sian Ka'an—you may never leave! Otherwise, drive or take a bus south to Mahahual and Xcalak—either town makes for a relaxing two- or three-day stop, in which you can snorkel, kayak, and catch up on your reading. Take another day to visit Laguna Bacalar, which is great for swimming and has a surprisingly good piracy museum in its renovated fort. There's an equally impressive Mayan museum in Chetumal, a short distance south, which you can visit before or after going to the ruins just west of there.

Tulum

Tulum has long captured the imagination of independent, beach-loving travelers. Mayan ruins overlooking turquoise seas and picturesque cabanas set on deserted beaches were (and still are) the anti-Cancún for many. Tulum has definitely grown—there are 50-some hotels along the beach now—but it still offers remarkable natural beauty and isolated affordable charm.

Tulum has three distinct parts. The Tulum ruins are the popular Mayan temples. Tulum Pueblo (literally, Tulum Town) is 1.5 kilometers (0.9 mile) south of the ruins and three kilometers (1.9 miles) from the coast, and it is the commercial and residential center. The highway runs right down the center of town and the bus terminal plus various hotels, restaurants, Internet cafés, and other services are here. A road at the entrance of Tulum Pueblo heads east three kilometers (1.9 miles) to the Zona Hotelera (Hotel Zone), a 10-kilometer (6.2-mile) strip stretching from just south of the

ruins to the entrance to the Sian Ka'an Biosphere Reserve.

The Zona Hotelera used to be a haven for backpackers and other budget-conscious travelers, with cheap, simple, sand-floor cabanas facing beautiful untouched beaches. The beaches are still beautiful—and a few hotels still have sand floors—but you have to come in the low season to find anything decent for under US$50/night, and even those are few and far between. The Zona Hotelera now caters more to yoga and meditation groups—folks with a little more money but who still appreciate isolation and tranquility. And Tulum's hotel zone *is* still an isolated and tranquil place—if it's within your budget, a day or two here (or more) can be a real treat.

Tulum Pueblo used to be a small village of mostly Mayan farmers and workers from the ruins and the handful of hotels on the coast. As more and more tour buses arrived at the

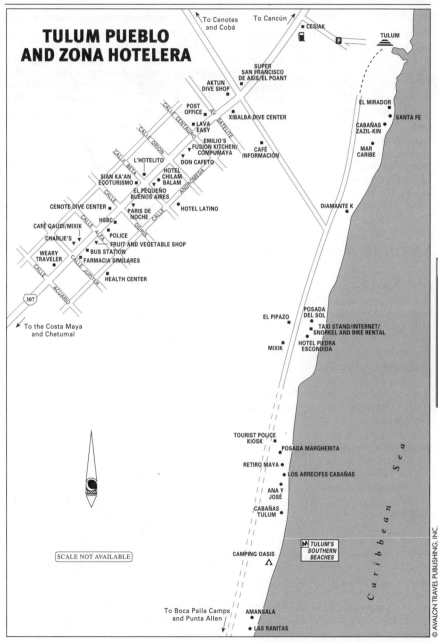

TULUM PUEBLO AND ZONA HOTELERA

To Cenotes and Cobá

To Cancún

CESIAK

TULUM

SUPER SAN FRANCISCO DE ASIS/EL POANT

AKTUN DIVE SHOP

POST OFFICE

XIBALBA DIVE CENTER

EL MIRADOR

SANTA FE

LAVA EASY

CABAÑAS ZAZIL-KIN

EMILIO'S FUSION KITCHEN/ COMPUMAYA

CAFÉ INFORMACIÓN

MAR CARIBE

L'HOTELITO

DON CAFETO

SIAN KA'AN ECOTURISMO

HOTEL CHILAM BALAM

EL PEQUEÑO BUENOS AIRES

CENOTE DIVE CENTER

PARIS DE NOCHE

HOTEL LATINO

DIAMANTE K

HSBC

CAFÉ GAUDÍ/MIXIK

POLICE

CHARLIE'S

FRUIT AND VEGETABLE SHOP

WEARY TRAVELER

BUS STATION

FARMACIA SIMILARES

HEALTH CENTER

307

To the Costa Maya and Chetumal

POSADA DEL SOL

EL PIPAZO

TAXI STAND/INTERNET/ SNORKEL AND BIKE RENTAL

MIXIK

HOTEL PIEDRA ESCONDIDA

TOURIST POLICE KIOSK

POSADA MARGHERITA

RETIRO MAYA

LOS ARRECIFES CABAÑAS

ANA Y JOSÉ

CABAÑAS TULUM

Caribbean Sea

TULUM'S SOUTHERN BEACHES

CAMPING OASIS

SCALE NOT AVAILABLE

To Boca Paila Camps and Punta Allen

AMANSALA

LAS RANITAS

MOON

N Southern Quintana Roo

© AVALON TRAVEL PUBLISHING, INC.

ruins from Cancún, and the hotels in the Zona Hotelera grew in number and category, Tulum Pueblo ballooned into a roadside tourist trap, with kitschy shops, haggling tour guides, and not much else.

But Tulum Pueblo is slowly coming into its own. More backpackers are staying there, pushed out of the Zona Hotelera by rising room rates. That has created a market for cool restaurants, small cafés, jewelry and crafts shops, tour operators, and more and better hotels, which in turn attract more midrange travelers, and so on. While the Zona Hotelera will always be the most appealing place to stay—the beach and ocean trump all else—staying in town is no longer the huge step down that it was.

◪ TULUM RUINS

Perched on a cliff 12 meters (39.4 feet) above the turquoise Caribbean waters, Tulum (8 A.M.–5 P.M. daily, US$3.30) is justly the subject of thousands of postcards and is one of Mexico's best-known archaeological sites. While the structures themselves lack the grandeur of ruins in the interior, they are still interesting and well worth a visit.

The most important advice regarding Tulum is **get there early.** Thousands of tourists arrive in tour buses from Cancún and Playa del Carmen and descend upon the ruins between 11 A.M.–12:30 P.M. and 2:30–4 P.M. Also consider wearing your swimsuit and bringing a towel—this may be the only Mayan ruin with a great little beach right inside the archaeological zone.

History

Tulum was part of a series of Mayan forts, towns, watchtowers, and shrines established along the coast as far south as Chetumal and north past Cancún. Measuring 380 by 165 meters (1,247 by 541 feet) it's the largest fortified Mayan site on the Quintana Roo coast, though it's small compared to other archaeological zones. The name Tulum (wall in Mayan) is probably a reference to the thick 3–5-meter (9.8–16.4-foot) stone wall that encloses the

site's 60 structures. The original name was Zama (sunrise).

Tulum emerges relatively late in the Mayan chronology, around A.D. 1200, during the time when Mayapán was the major power and this part of Quintana Roo was the province of Ecab. Many of Tulum's buildings show late Chichén Itzá, Mayapán, and Mixtec influences. The Spanish got their first view of the then-brightly colored fortress when Juan de Grijalva's expedition sailed past the Quintana Roo coast in 1518. This was also the Spaniards' first encounter with the indigenous people of the new continent, and according to ships' logs, the image was awe-inspiring. One notable entry describes "a village so large, that Seville would not have appeared larger or better."

The Structures

The Tulum ruins are made up of mostly small, ornate structures with stuccoed gargoyle faces carved onto their corners. By far the site's most impressive structure is **El Castillo** (The Castle), a large pyramid standing on the edge of a 12-meter (39.4-foot) limestone cliff overlooking the sea. The building was constructed in three different phases. A wide staircase leads to a two-chamber temple at the top; visitors are no longer allowed to climb this stairway, but the view from the hill on which the Castillo stands encompasses the sea, the surrounding jungle (with an occasional stone ruin poking through the tight brush), and scattered clearings where small farms are sprouting.

In the **Temple of the Frescoes,** looking through a metal grate you'll see a fresco that still bears a trace of color from the ancient artist. Archaeologically, this is the most interesting building on the site. The original parts of the building were constructed around 1450 during the late Postclassic period, and as is the case with so many Mayan structures, it was added to over the years.

Across the compound, the small off-kilter **Temple of the Descending God** has a palapa-cover to protect a carving of an upside-down winged creature on the main lintel. The name is purely descriptive: some archaeologists believe

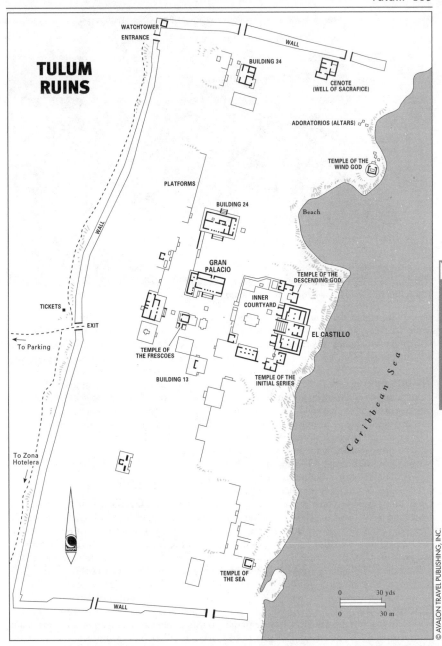

TULUM RUINS

WATCHTOWER
ENTRANCE

WALL

BUILDING 34

CENOTE
(WELL OF SACRAFICE)

ADORATORIOS (ALTARS)

TEMPLE OF THE
WIND GOD

PLATFORMS

Beach

BUILDING 24

GRAN
PALACIO

TEMPLE OF THE
DESCENDING GOD

INNER
COURTYARD

TICKETS

EXIT

To Parking

TEMPLE OF
THE FRESCOES

BUILDING 13

EL CASTILLO

TEMPLE OF THE
INITIAL SERIES

To Zona
Hotelera

Caribbean Sea

TEMPLE OF
THE SEA

WALL

| 0 | 30 yds |
| 0 | 30 m |

Southern Quintana Roo

© LIZA PRADO CHANDLER

The Tulum ruins are known for their spectacular setting.

the carving depicts the God of the Setting Sun, while others say it represents the bee; in pre-Hispanic times, honey was revered and valued almost as much as maize.

Visitors Center

Tulum's massive parking lot and mall-like visitors center ought to clue you in to the number of tourists that pass through here every day. (Did we mention to get here early?) The visitors center houses a museum and bookstore, plus a Subway sandwich shop, ATM machines that give U.S. dollars instead of pesos, and several snack shops. Sometimes the *voladores* (traditional pole flyers) put on a show. The site entrance and ticket booth are about one kilometer (0.6 mile) from the visitors center; if you don't feel like walking, a **trolley** ferries guests there and back for US$1.50.

Professional bilingual guides can be hired at the entrance for around US$30.

Getting There

Buses and shared vans pass the entrance to the ruins frequently. Upon arriving, be sure to ask the driver to let you off at *las ruínas,* as opposed to the town which is another 1.5 kilometers (0.9 mile) south. To return, vans may be waiting near the site exit; otherwise flag a bus or van down on the highway. They pass frequently well after the ruins have closed.

Tulum ruins are seven kilometers (4.3 miles) south of Akumal on Highway 307. As you drive south, the ruins are on your left (the ocean side) but the turnoff is to your right—the exit loops back and you cross the highway. Parking is US$2.25.

OTHER SIGHTS
Cenotes Outside Tulum

Some favorite cenotes are **Casa Cenote** (at Tankah Tres); **Car Wash, Kolimba/Kin-Ha, Cenote Grande,** and **Calavera Cenote** (all just west of Tulum on the road to Cobá), **Cenote Azul** and **Cristalina** (Hwy. 307 across from Xpu-Há). All can be visited on a tour or by yourself, and most have snorkel gear for rent (US$7). Most are on private or *ejido* (farmer-collective) land and charge admission fees, usually US$5–8 snorkelers, US$10 divers. If you take a tour, ask if admission fees are

CENOTES: SACRED SWIMMING POOLS

One of the Yucatán Peninsula's most intriguing features are its cenotes, large freshwater sinkholes. Cenotes owe their formation to the massive meteorite that hit the Yucatán Peninsula 65 million years ago, near present-day Mérida. The impact shattered the peninsula's thick limestone cap like a stone hitting a car windshield. Through millions of years, rainwater seeped into the cracks, forming what is today the world's largest underground river system. Cenotes are former caverns whose roofs collapsed. (Cave-ins are extremely rare today, however.) Cenotes can be hundreds of meters deep and are usually filled with fresh water (occasional seawater intrusion in some cenotes forms haloclines—a bizarre and interesting sight).

Cenotes were sacred to the Mayans, who relied on them for water. They also were seen as apertures to the underworld, and sacrificial victims were sometimes thrown into their eerie depths, along with finely worked stone and clay items. Archaeologists have learned a great deal about early Mayan rituals by dredging cenotes near ancient ruins.

Still revered by many Mayans, the peninsula's cenotes have attracted other worshippers: snorkelers and scuba divers. The unbelievably clear water—100-meter (328-foot) visibility in places—attracts many underwater enthusiasts. But the real joy of snorkeling or diving here comes from the amazing stalactite and stalagmite formations. Formed in the ice age when water levels were extremely low, they were submerged in water as the climate warmed. Today, you can snorkel and dive past beautiful formations that you would walk around in a dry cave.

Divers with open-water certification can dive in the cenotes. Though "full-cave" diving requires advanced training, most cenote tours are actually "cavern" dives, meaning you are always within 130 feet of an air pocket. It's a good idea to take some open-water dives before your first cenote tour—buoyancy control is especially important in cenotes, and you'll be contending with different weights and finning technique.

included in the rate. Most cenotes are open 9 A.M.–5 P.M. daily.

Hidden Worlds Cenotes Park (Hwy. 307 between Tulum and Akumal, tel. 984/877-8535, www.hiddenworlds.com.mx, 9 A.M.–5 P.M. daily) is an excellent place for first-timers to experience underground snorkeling or diving. Although sometimes crowded, Hidden Worlds earns its popularity by offering excellent tours and professional service. Snorkeling tours (US$40 pp for 2.5 hours, US$25 pp for 1.5 hours, gear included; 9 A.M., 11 A.M., 1 P.M., 2 P.M., and 3 P.M. daily) visit two different cenotes. You will explore huge caverns, see light beams penetrate distant pools, and (if you want) swim through channels with just a head's worth of air space. One- and two-tank cavern dives (US$50 one tank, US$90 two tank, gear rental US$5–15, four divers maximum, 9 A.M., 11 A.M., 1 P.M. daily) also visit two cenotes and follow guidelines set by cave explorers. Exploration is ongoing—ask about "Dreamgate," a stunning cavern opened

to divers in September 2003. Hidden Worlds offers free hotel pickup if you're staying in or between Puerto Aventuras and Tulum. Reservations strongly recommended.

Xel-Há

Snorkel in the ocean, around a lagoon, or down a river at Xel-Há (nine km/5.6 miles north of Tulum, www.xelha.com, 9 A.M.–sunset daily, US$29 adults and US$15 ages 5–12 Mon.–Fri., US$22 adults and US$11 ages 5–12 Sat.–Sun.). If you love the water and don't mind crowds, this park may be just right for you. (For details, see *The Riviera's Ecoparks* sidebar in the *Playa del Carmen* section.)

Tulum's Northern Beaches

Tulum has some great beaches but the nearly unbroken chain of hotels can make getting to the best spots a little challenging. A good easy option is **El Paraíso beach club** (between La Vita Bella restaurant and Mar Caribe, 7 A.M.–11 P.M.

a glorious stretch of sand on Tulum's southern beaches

daily) set on a long appealing stretch of sand on the northern section of the Zona Hotelera, just past La Vita Bella restaurant. Hammocks hung under an open-air palapa are free to use, and beach chairs just US$1.75/day. The restaurant serves breakfast, lunch, and dinner inside or on the beach (US$5–12), and the beach bar has cold beers and cocktails. A Tulum dive shop offers snorkel tours three times a day (US$20, 1.5 hour, 10 A.M., 12:30 P.M., and 2:30 P.M. Mon.–Sat.). The Weary Traveler hostel runs a daily bus to El Paraíso from town, leaving the hostel at 9:20 A.M. and returning at 5:20 P.M. (free for guests, otherwise US$1 each way).

Tulum's Southern Beaches

Tulum's very best beaches—thick white sand, turquoise blue water, no one around—are toward the southern end of the hotel zone. Not surprisingly, the most exclusive hotels are in the same area, and access to the beach can be difficult if you're not staying at one of them. That said, just south of the Zona Hotelera's "mini-village" is a rocky public beach, the end of which marks the beginning of the southern beaches; from here just walk down the shore until you find a spot that fits your fancy—hotels are allowed to restrict use of their chairs and umbrellas, but the beach itself is public.

ENTERTAINMENT AND EVENTS

Weary Traveler hostel hosts a **Sunday barbecue** in its backyard garden and restaurant area. A DJ provides hang-out and dancing tunes in the low season—in the high, expect a live band and even more atmosphere. Admission is free and the meals and drinks reasonably priced (US$3.50 vegetarian, US$8.50 meat plate). Popular with backpackers, but open and welcoming to all. Starts at 7 P.M.

SHOPPING

Mixik Artesanía Mexicana (Av. Tulum between Calles Alfa and Jupiter, tel. 984/871-2136, 9 A.M.–6 P.M. Mon.–Sat., high season until 9 P.M.) has a large selection of quality folk art, from green copper suns to carved wooden angels and masks, plus T-shirts, jewelry, cards, and more. There's a sister shop in the Zona Hotelera by the same name. Also in the hotel zone

© LIZA PRADO CHANDLER

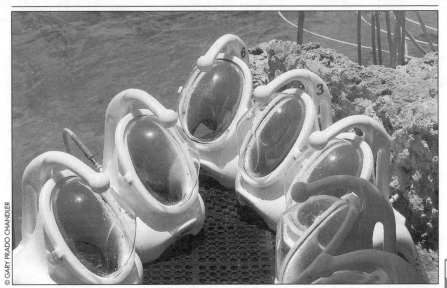

© GARY PRADO CHANDLER

snuba gear at the ready

and near Mixik's sister store, **Posada del Sol** (tel. 984/876-6206, 8 A.M.–10 P.M. daily) sells good handmade *artesanía* from a small shop at the hotel entrance.

SPORTS AND RECREATION

Diving

Cave and cavern diving is Tulum's recreational claim to fame, with a slew of diveable cenotes with easy reach. While full-cave diving requires advanced training and certification, divers with open-water certification can make cavern dives, which industry guidelines define as no more than 30 feet deep and no more than 130 feet from an air pocket. (Don't worry—it still *feels* as if you're in a full cave.) If you haven't dived in a while, it is a good idea to take a few open-water dives before your first cenote trip, as buoyancy control is especially important down there. (See the sidebar *Cenotes: Sacred Swimming Pools.*)

Prices are fairly uniform among the various shops, around US$60/100 one-/two-tank cenote dives, US$100/200 cave dives, US$7–25/day equipment. Tulum's shops also offer multidive packages and cavern, intro to cave, and full cave certification courses. As always, choose a shop and guide you feel comfortable with, not necessarily the least expensive one. (See the sidebar *How to Choose a Dive Shop* in the *Isla Cozumel* section.)

Aktún Dive Center (corner of Av. Tulum and the road to Zona Hotelera/Boca Paila, tel. 984/871-2311, www.aktundive.com, 8 A.M.–7 P.M. daily) is one of Tulum's most experienced cave and cavern diving shops, and it also offers reef-diving trips. The shop also has a small hotel and restaurant on-site and offers dive/accommodations packages. Credit cards accepted with 6 percent surcharge.

Cenote Dive Center (corner of Av. Tulum and Calle Osiris, tel. 984/871-2232, www.cenotedive.com, 9 A.M.–7 P.M. daily, low season closed Sun.) is affiliated with the Abyss Dive Center located by the turnoff to the Tulum ruins. No credit cards.

Named after the Mayan underworld, **Xibalba Dive Center** (Av. Tulum between Av. Satelite and the road to Zona Hotelera/Boca Paila, tel. 984/807-4579, www .xibalbadivecenter.com, 9 A.M.–7 P.M. daily) had just opened when we passed through, but the owner/operator has dived in Tulum for years and has a good reputation for safety and professionalism.

Snorkeling

You don't have to be a diver to enjoy the eerie beauty of the cenotes here—guided snorkel trips make a great introduction, and of course the ocean and coral reefs are minutes away. Most of the dive shops in town offer snorkel trips in the cenotes for around US$35. Thirteen kilometers (eight miles) north of Tulum, **Hidden Worlds Cenote Park** (Hwy. 307 Km. 243, tel. 984/877-8535, www.hiddenworlds.com.mx, 9 A.M.–5 P.M. daily) has excellent, if sometimes a bit crowded, cenote snorkeling tours visiting two different cenotes. Trips are 2.5 hours, cost is US$40 pp, and they leave at 9 A.M., 11 A.M., 1 P.M., 2 P.M., and 3 P.M. daily. Groups of 8–10 maximum, all equipment included; 1.5-hours, one-cenote tours also available for US$25 pp. (See the sidebar *Cenotes: Sacred Swimming Pools*.)

For reef snorkeling, **Abyss Dive Center** (Hotel El Crucero, turnoff to Tulum ruins, tel. 984/871-2608, www.abyssdiveshop.com, affiliated with Cenote Dive Center in town) conducts tours from El Paraíso hotel and beach club on the northern part of the Zona Hotelera (US$20, 1.5 hours, 10 A.M., 12:30 P.M., 2:30 P.M. Mon.–Sat.) Look for the sign on the beach near the bar.

Cabañas Zazil-Kin (northern section between Mar Caribe and Tulum ruins, tel. 984/871-2508) has snorkeling tours that leave from the hotel most days at noon (US$10.50 pp, 2.5 hours). The tours visit three different locations and the price includes equipment—a good value.

To rent snorkel gear ask at any of the dive shops in town. In the Zona Hotelera, try Cabañas Zazil-Kin and Cabañas Punta Piedra (tel. 984/876-9978, 8 A.M.–7 P.M. daily). Both rent snorkel kits for around US$4.50/day; both also rent bicycles for around the same price.

Spa

At the Ana y José hotel, **Om... Spa** (tel. 998/887-5470, 10 A.M.–6 P.M. daily) offers a full-service, open-air spa. Choose from a menu of massages (US$75–85) and body treatments (US$55–75) that are given in a beachfront, ultrachic setting.

ACCOMMODATIONS

Hotel options in town are still limited but have definitely improved through the years.

The Zona Hotelera has a short "northern section" (north of the turnoff to Tulum Pueblo) and a longer "southern section" (south of there). The northern section's roads are paved and perfect; the southern road (where most of the best hotels and beaches are, naturally) is unpaved and pretty rough in places. Any car can get through, but take it slow.

Note: Some hotels use generators for electricity. We've tried to note where this is the case, but it is definitely worth double-checking when you make your reservation. If your hotel has a generator, be sure to ask for a room as far away from it as possible. Nothing is a bigger killjoy than a giant diesel motor pounding outside your window, especially since the whole point of coming here is for the peace and quiet.

Under US$25

In Town: ◪ **Weary Traveler Hostel** (Av. Tulum between Calles Jupiter and Calle Acuario, tel. 984/871-2390, www.weary.intulum .com, US$7 pp) is Tulum's main backpacker gathering spot, and it has a number of useful services available to guests and nonguests alike. Those include cheap 24-hour Internet (US$.45/hour), luggage storage (US$1/day/bag, free for departing guests), daily bus service to El Paraíso beach club (free for guests, $1 each nonguests, leaves 9:20 A.M., returns 5:20 P.M.), and a popular Sunday barbecue with music and dancing (7 P.M., US$3.50 vegetarian, US$8.50 meat plate). In fact, the dorm rooms here—a bit grubby, not much natural light—are the only small disappointment, but they are adequate for most budget travelers. Each has four bunks (two singles and two doubles), okay private bath, fan, mosquito screens, and amateur new-age paintings on the walls.

Dive and Spanish-language packages are available, and come with lodging, two meals per day, and instruction/classes.

Rancho Tranquilo (two blocks south of Weary Traveler, tel. 984/871-2286, US$8.50 s, US$15 d, US$17.50 two beds) is operated by Weary Traveler and caters to budget travelers looking for more privacy and isolation than they get at the hostel. Individual cabins vary in size and amenities—the largest ones have private bath, patio, and hammock—and guests can use a large common kitchen and well-stocked library, and receive all the guest-only advantages at Weary Traveler (free luggage storage, free beach bus, and so on).

The rooms at **Hotel Chilam Balam** (Av. Tulum between Calles Beta and Orion, tel. 984/871-2042, US$24.50 s/d with fan, US$33 s/d with a/c) have somewhat saggy beds but otherwise are clean and fairly big, with high ceilings and large bathrooms. Most rooms could use more natural light—ask for one with extra windows. You can pay US$6 more to have breakfast included, but it doesn't make much sense with so many good cafés and restaurants around.

Zona Hotelera: Camping Oasis (between Cabañas Tulum and Los Lirios, no phone, US$4.50 pp camping) sits on one of the best stretches of sand in the Tulum hotel zone—ironic considering all the upscale resorts stacked up on either side. Campers set their tents up under palm trees near the beach, and there's usually a large mesh tent for storing food and other stuff that won't fit in the tent (no lock, though). The somewhat dodgy bathrooms and showers are closer to the road, near the house used by the owners and their family. Camp stoves and small fires are okay, and you can buy basic foodstuffs at two minimarts about a kilometer (0.6 mile) south. Don't expect much in the way of service, although the family may sell you a jug of water so you don't have to lug it from the store.

Mar Caribe (between El Paraíso and Tulum ruins, no phone, US$5 pp camping, US$13/18 cabana with sand/concrete floor, half-price in low season) occupies a broad, windswept beach with views of the Tulum ruins and usually a handful of fishing boats tied ashore. There are plenty of spots to set up a tent, as well as 30 extremely basic one-room wood cabanas with hammock hooks, grubby beds, and sand blowing through the gaps in the walls—none too pleasant, but a place to lock your stuff. The restaurant here (7 A.M.–midnight daily, US$5–15) is actually pretty good—run by the same people as Don Cafeto's in town—and with a bar and food service on the beach qualifies as downright luxury. Now if there were just electricity....

Cabañas Zazil-Kin (northern section between Mar Caribe and the Tulum ruins, tel. 984/871-2508, reception desk 8 A.M.–8 P.M. only, US$4.50 camping, US$4.50 dorm with hammocks, US$16.50 s with shared bath, US$20–26 d with shared bath, US$30 d with private bath) occupies a rambling beachside property criss-crossed with paths and dotted with cabins in varying states of repair. The newer cabins are rustic but adequate, with concrete floor, fresh paint, mosquito nets, and candles; some older ones feel musty. The shared baths are tolerable and the hotel restaurant (8 A.M.– 9 P.M. daily) serves standard Mexican and seafood dishes. The hotel provides free use of the safe-deposit box and rents bikes (US$5.25/day) and snorkel gear (US$4.50/day). This hotel also has the Zona Hotelera's only **disco,** which is open in the high season every day except Monday and can be loud and rambunctious well into the morning hours—unless you don't mind the noise, be sure to ask for a cabana as far away as possible. An on-site dive shop offers snorkeling tours (US$10.50 pp, 2.5 hours) at noon on most days, visiting three different locations—a great deal. The same shop has the lowest scuba diving prices around—US$30/50 one-/two-tank reef dives, US$50/90 one-/two-tank cenote dives, including full equipment but not entrance fees— but seemed overly casual. Be sure to check your gear carefully and quiz previous divers to see if you are comfortable diving with this shop.

US$25–50

In Town: At last, a genuinely classy place to stay in Tulum pueblo. On the street parallel to

Avenida Tulum one block east, **N Hotel Latino** (Av. Andrómeda s/n between Calles Orion and Beta, tel. 984/871-2674, tutlumhotellatino @hotmail.com, www.hotel-latino.com, US$16 dorm, US$39 s/d, US$49 suite) showcases modern Mexican architectural style, with clean lines, sturdy construction, and excellent use of natural light. The whole thing is whitewashed inside and out, with minimalist decor and an attractive square swimming pool in one corner. Cozy rooms have thick mattresses, spotless bathrooms with gleaming fixtures, and plenty of sunlight from the open-air corridor. Suites are roomier, with a private terrace, hammock, and free bottle of wine. The dorms hold six guests on double bunks and also have comfy mattresses, clean bathrooms, and secure lockers—a large aquarium with tropical fish was being installed in one of the dorms when we stopped by. Rates include use of a bicycle and a small but well-equipped kitchen.

L'Hotelito (Av. Tulum between Calles Beta and Orion, cell tel. 044-984/114-0147, hotelito@viaggiland.it, US$35 s/d with fan, US$40 s/d with a/c, US$4.50 extra person) has nine comfortable rooms that open onto wide wooden corridors and have colorful walls and various pieces of Mexican *artesanía*. Three of the rooms are large enough for five people; the others are much smaller but in a cozy way. About half the rooms have cable TV. Fan rooms upstairs have high palapa roofs and mosquito nets over the beds. The restaurant here is highly recommended.

If you plan on doing a lot of diving, **Aktún Dive Center** (corner of Av. Tulum and the road to Zona Hotelera/Boca Paila, tel. 984/871-2311, www.aktundive.com, US$30 s/d with fan, US$40 s/d with a/c) offers decent dive/ accommodations packages at its on-site hotel. Eight rooms have private bath, air-conditioning, and minifridge, and were being renovated and repainted when we were here. The ground-floor restaurant serves standard meals, and a large grocery store is across the street. Free Internet use for guests.

Zona Hotelera: North of the intersection, **N Diamante K** (just north of Cabañas Lol-

Tun, www.diamantek.com, US$30–$80) is a classic Tulum cabana hotel and a good mid-range option. More than a dozen clean wood bungalows each have concrete floor, fresh linens, and most have hanging beds—instead of legs, they are supported by ropes from the roof. The shore here is a jagged rocky shelf, and the hotel has various nooks and crannies with cushions, chairs, or hammocks set up where you can see the waves crashing ashore. For swimming or sandcastles, Diamante K has a tiny private beach and a path leads a few hundred meters north to a long broad unkempt beach, strewn with driftwood, seaweed, and (in some places) a fair amount of trash. Other than the litter, which is avoidable, it's all part of the rustic, unpolished charm. The hotel has a good restaurant and bar, and the clientele tends to be young and outgoing.

Behind a huge dune, **Cabañas Los Arrecifes** (just north of Ana y José, tel. 984/879-7307, www.losarrecifestulum.com) does a good job at catering to budget travelers; it offers sand-floored bungalows on the beach (US$30 s/d with shared bath) and simple thatch-roofed rooms with terraces and ocean views (US$60 s/d with private bath). Recently built and more modern rooms are offered as well but at US$100 are overpriced. The hotel also has hammocks strung from palm trees throughout the property—great for kicking back—and the beach is ample and clean. Electricity from 5 P.M.–midnight only.

US$50–100

Zona Hotelera: Posada del Sol (minivillage area, tel. 984/876-6206, posadadelsol@hotmail. com, US$50–75) has seven modern attractive rooms—with more being built—all with private bath, fan, and most with terrace and hammock. Some of the rooms have ocean views and others have huge artsy bathrooms. Built on a small lot, parts of the hotel can feel somewhat cramped and there's just a narrow path down to the beach. Stay here if you prefer a little more atmosphere—in this cluster of hotels are also a few restaurants, Internet access, a market and some stores, plus money exchange, taxi post, and a place to rent bikes; 24-hour solar-generated electricity.

Built in 1972, **Cabañas Tulum** (just south of Ana y José, tel. 984/879-7395, cabanastulum@hotmail.com, www.hotelstulum.com /cabañas_tulum/, US$60–70) was one of the first hotels here and is definitely old-school—in fact it looks a little like a school, with a big boxy main building and boxy two- or three-room units all in a row facing the beach. The rooms themselves are clean and fairly large, all with private bath, a seafront patio, and hammock hooks. The fans are pretty wimpy but a constant breeze off the water keeps things from getting musty (though the sea air gives the whole place a somewhat decaying look). Come here if you just want a "normal" room in the Tulum hotel zone, as opposed to the chi-chi accommodations that prevail. The main building has a cheap, basic restaurant (7 A.M.–9 P.M. daily, US$2–8), table tennis, and some board games. Rooms have electricity 7–11 P.M. and 5–11 P.M. only; ask for a room away from the generator.

⚅ Retiro Maya (between Ana y José and Maya Tulum, tel. 984/100-8940, www.retiromaya.com, US$75/100 shared/private bath) is a relative newcomer here, built in 2002. Cozy little cabins house smallish but charming and well-appointed rooms, each with a comfortable bed and concrete floor covered in a thin layer of sand. Six rooms share clean bathrooms and showers; the four rooms with private baths have the hotel's most striking feature—stout wooden canoes-cum-bathtubs, complete with plumbing and hot/cold water. All rooms are angled so you can see the ocean when you're lying on the lounge chair outside your door. The hotel has a pretty beach (seaweed raked off daily) and a small restaurant serving mostly seafood and vegetarian dishes (7 A.M.–10 P.M. daily). Retiro Maya caters to people and groups interested in "spiritual growth" and sometimes converts the restaurant into a meditation or yoga area. No children under 14. The hotel also has one four-person room with shared bath (US$100) and the owner rents a three-bedroom/three-bath house next door with kitchen and room for eight (US$3,000/week).

Over US$100

Zona Hotelera: Self-named "Bikini Boot Camp," **Amansala** (between La Zebra and Las Ranitas, tel. 984/100-0805, www.amansala. com, US$90–165 s/d) is an urban chic resort on a beautiful stretch of beach—think Soho meets the Caribbean. The 10 eclectic rooms are set in four beachfront palapas and are beautifully appointed with wood floors, stone-encrusted walls, paper lanterns, and the finest in linens. Balconies and terraces look out over the stunning white sand beach and turquoise waters. So why the bikini boot camp reference? Amansala caters to people—okay, women—who are looking to buff up in the sun. All-inclusive packages include yoga and Pilates instruction on the beach, outdoor cardio and strength workouts, and eating low-fat, low-carb meals at the vegetarian restaurant on-site. For (more) fun, biking and kayaking excursions are included as well as a tour to the archaeological site of Tulum. Popular—not surprisingly—with women in their 20s and 30s, but all are welcome and unlike in the Army, no one is forced to do push-ups.

A simple but classy option is **Hotel Piedra Escondida** (minivillage area, tel. 984/876-3226, piedraescondida@tulum.com, www.piedraescondida.com, US$135–160). On a small private beach, it offers eight ocean-view rooms in two-story palapa-roofed cabanas. Rooms are ample and clean and have details such as heavy wood furniture and *azulejo*-tiled bathrooms. Breakfast is included and served in a welcoming dining room. Be sure to ask about discounts in the low season.

Heading south toward Sian Ka'an, you'll hit **Ana y José** (just south of Cabañas Los Arrecifes, tel. 998/887-5470, www.anayjose. com), one of the few hotels in the area that offer 24-hour electricity, a spa, and a swimming pool. Its two-story buildings house 14 rooms (US$112 s/d) that are pleasant but impersonal; they have a Mexican cookie-cutter style—something you wouldn't expect when you walk past the beautifully minimalist entrance. The seven newly constructed beachfront suites (US$175–250 s/d) are a different story altogether—with king-sized beds, living

Southern Quintana Roo

rooms, ocean views, and chic decor, you'll feel like you're living the high life. Actually, you will be. A sand-floored restaurant with tree-trunk tables also is on-site; the food is good, but the service could be better.

Just one kilometer (0.6 mile) from the entrance to Sian Ka'an, **M Las Ranitas** (just south of Amansala, tel. 984/877-8554, www .lasranitas.com, US$150–350) is an upscale ecoresort on a huge stretch of beachfront property. Set in bungalows, the 17 rooms are ample and airy and have great terraces or balconies with hammocks. The decor is a little tacky (think ceramic frogs) but the rooms remain pleasant, comfortable, and are very private. Lush gardens also surround each bungalow and stone-encrusted walkways lead guests to an inviting pool, a paddle tennis court, and the delightful main house, where a lounge, reading room, and a good restaurant are found. And the beach. Hands down, it is the best we saw in Tulum—expansive white sand, huge palm trees, and a playful sea. With beach chairs and umbrellas, it is the Caribbean at its best.

FOOD

Most of the hotels in the Zona Hotelera have restaurants—handy for the days you don't feel like going anywhere. When you feel like venturing out, a few eateries in town and in the hotel zone definitely stand out from the crowd.

Mexican

Charlie's (Av. Tulum between Calles Alfa and Jupiter, tel. 984/871-2573, 11 A.M.–11 P.M. Tues.–Sun., US$5–12) is one of Tulum's most popular restaurants, with a large airy dining area under a high palapa roof. The menu has classic Mexican dishes, such as *chiles rellenos,* enchiladas, tacos, and even a vegetarian plate or two. The restaurant hosts live music on Saturday nights during the year-end high season.

As popular as Charlie's is, locals and visitors looking for truly *casera* (homemade) Mexican food head to **M Don Cafeto's** (Av. Tulum between Calles Centauro and Orion, tel. 984/871-2207, 7 A.M.–11 P.M. daily, US$5–9)

for fresh seafood and grilled meat platters and ceviche plates that are meals unto themselves. On a hot day, try a tall cold *superlimonada*.

For more contemporary Mexican fare, try the restaurant **M L'Hotelito** (Av. Tulum between Calles Orion and Beta, cell tel. 044-984/114-0147, 7:30–11 A.M. and 6–10:30 P.M. daily except Wed. and Sun., US$7–12). A half-dozen wooden tables occupy the hotel's airy entryway and the food is well-prepared and tasty; in addition to familiar Mexican dishes, look for fresh lobster and *oro negro* (literally, black gold) made with shrimp and *cuitlacoche.* (The latter, sometimes spelled *huitlacoche,* is a black corn fungus usually prepared with *chile* and considered a delicacy. It is definitely an acquired taste.)

In the Zona Hotelera, the roadside restaurant at **Cabañas Zahra** (8 A.M.–7 P.M. daily, US$5–12) is part of the minivillage partway down the strip. The menu includes a number of vegetarian options—not surprising considering the number of health-conscious travelers here—but overall the meals are simple Mexican fare.

International

El Pequeño Buenos Aires (Av. Tulum between Calles Orion and Beta, tel. 984/871-2708, noon–11 P.M. Mon.–Sat., US$5–15) serves excellent cuts of beef, plus an array of crepes and even a few vegetarian dishes—not exactly a norm for Argentinean grills! The *parrillada Argentina* (US$13 pp) comes piled with different cuts and sausages; a good daily lunch special (US$4.50) includes a main dish and a vegetarian crepe as an appetizer.

Speaking of crepes, that's the specialty at **M Paris de Noche** (Av. Tulum between Calles Beta and Osiris, no phone, noon–midnight daily, sometimes closed Mon., US$2–6) a half block farther south. This quaint, brightly painted eatery has tables in its small dining area or on the sidewalk in front, and it serves both *dulce* (sweet) and *salada* (literally salty, here it implies meal-like) crepes. Try spinach and goat cheese for dinner and strawberry and chocolate for dessert.

Café Gaudí (Av. Tulum between Calles Alfa and Jupiter, no phone, 7 A.M.–4 P.M. Tues.–Sun., US$1.50–5) is another small café-restaurant serving light fresh fare. Breakfast options include fruit and yogurt or eggs any way you like; the (real) Spanish tortilla and salami or roasted vegetable sandwiches make a good lunch. Right across from the bus terminal; useful traveler's bulletin board at the entrance.

Emilio's Fusion Kitchen (Av. Tulum between Calles Centauro and Orion, tel. 984/879-5742, US$5–15) won't win any prizes for its dining area, but the meals are popular with expats and other residents. Seafood and chicken dishes have a pre-Hispanic base with a colonial and international flare—coconut, tamarind, and tequila all figure prominently. It also has sushi (rolls and pieces US$5–9); it wasn't being served when we stopped in, but several regulars assured us it's first-rate. That would be no small feat—good sushi is amazingly hard to find here or anywhere in Mexico.

In the Zona Hotelera, **M Posada Margherita** (between Maya Tulum and Retiro Maya, tel. 984/100-3780, 7:30–10 A.M., noon–2:30 P.M., and 6–8:30 P.M. daily, US$5–10 breakfast, US$11–18 dinner) is an excellent Italian restaurant that serves fresh seafood and homemade pastas with a variety of delicious sauces. A *huge* tree-trunk plate of appetizers also comes with your meal (think olives, roasted red peppers, artichoke hearts, and nuts)—almost a meal in itself. The setting—a sand-floor, open-air restaurant with billowing white fabrics and candles—is enough to make you want to stay all night.

Just south of the Zona Hotelera and four kilometers (2.5 miles) into the Sian Ka'an Biosphere Reserve, **Boca Paila Camps** (tel. 984/871-2499, 8 A.M.–9 P.M. daily, US$5–15) serves excellent seafood dishes on the roof of its main building. The views of the lagoon to the west and the Caribbean to the east are breathtaking.

With indoor and outdoor dining, **Las Ranitas** (just south of Amansala, tel. 984/877-8554, www.lasranitas.com, 7 A.M.–11 P.M. daily, US$4–15) is a good choice anytime of the year. It serves a wide variety of tasty dishes, and you'll be sure to find something that satisfies your cravings.

Groceries

Tulum has a great open-air **fruit and vegetable shop** (6 A.M.–8:30 P.M. daily) on Avenida Tulum at Calle Alfa. For bread, cheese, canned food, and other groceries, head to the big new **Super San Francisco de Asis** (7 A.M.–10 P.M. daily) at the intersection of Avenida Tulum and the road to the Zona Hotelera/Boca Paila.

For basic groceries outside of the minivillage, head to **Abarrotes Sirenas** (in front of Viejo y El Mar, 7 A.M.–7 P.M. daily); it usually carries some produce, a little dairy, and lots of cans.

El Pipazo (9 A.M.–9 P.M. daily) is attached to Nohoch Tunich hotel and is the Zona Hotelera's largest market, with one room filled with essentials such as snack food, canned food, water, liquor, and sunscreen.

INFORMATION AND SERVICES

There is no official tourist office in Tulum pueblo. However, **Café Información** (road to Zona Hotelera/Boca Paila, 8 A.M.–8 P.M. daily) is a friendly café where you can get information about area ruins, cenotes, and beaches, plus arrange tours or airport transfer. The café is affiliated with Weary Traveler hostel, whose owner also operates InTulum.com, a website with up-to-date information and listings about the town and surrounding area. And there is an excellent InTulum.com city and hotel zone map which you can pick up at Café Información, Weary Traveler hostel, and at many shops and restaurants around town.

Tour Operators

CESiaK (Hwy. 307 just south of the Tulum ruins turnoff, tel. 984/871-2499, www.cesiak. org, 9 A.M.–2 P.M. and 4–8 P.M. daily) offers an excellent all-day trip that includes a stop at Muyil ruins and a boat tour of the lagoon, floating down the canal, and snorkeling in the cenote (US$68 pp from Tulum, US$80 from

Playa del Carmen, minimum four people, including transfer, box lunch, and bilingual guide). Ask about other tours, including fishing, mountain biking, kayaking, bird-watching, and tours of Punta Laguna or Cobá.

Sian Ka'an Ecoturismo (Av. Tulum between Calles Beta and Osiris, tel. 984/871-2363, siankaan_tours@hotmail.com, 10 A.M.–7 P.M. Mon.–Fri., 10 A.M.–2 P.M. Sat.) also offers an identical tour to Muyil and around the lagoon (these two used to be the same agency, in fact). This agency also offers a jeep tour to Punta Allen (US$85 pp, 9 A.M.–7 P.M. Tues., Thurs., and Sat., lunch not included) with stops for snorkeling, swimming, and boating.

Medical Services

Tulum's modest *centro de salud* (health center, tel. 984/871-2050) is more commonly known by the acronym CESA and is on Calle Andrómeda between Calles Jupiter and Alfa. For more serious medical matters, go to Playa del Carmen or preferably Cancún.

Pharmacies

Farmacia Similares (Av. Tulum next to bus terminal, tel. 984/871-2736) is open 8 A.M.–10 P.M. Monday–Saturday, 9 A.M.–3 P.M. Sunday.

Police

The police station is on Avenida Tulum and Calle Alfa next to the HSBC bank. Dial 066 from any public phone for emergency assistance.

Money

HSBC (Av. Tulum at Calle Alfa next to police station, 8 A.M.–7 P.M. Mon.–Sat.) has a reliable ATM machine and will change foreign cash and AmEx travelers checks 10 A.M.–5 P.M. Mon.–Fri. only.

An **exchange booth** (9 A.M.–9 P.M. daily) in the Zona Hotelera will change euros, U.S. dollars, and AmEx travelers checks.

Post Office

Send postcards at the easy-to-miss post office on the north end of Avenida Tulum between Avenida Satelite and Calle Centauro. Although

it's technically open 8 A.M.–4 P.M. Monday–Friday, come before 1 P.M. to catch the one postman before he leaves to deliver the day's mail.

Internet and Telephone

The Weary Traveler (south end of Av. Tulum between Calles Jupiter and Acuario, tel. 984/871-2390) has the cheapest Internet on the Riviera Maya—US$.45/hour, with a fast connection and open 24 hours to boot. International calls are US$.45/minute to the United States and Europe. Across the street, **Savana** (Av. Tulum next to the bus terminal, tel. 984/871-2091, 8 A.M.–9 P.M. Mon.–Sat., 8 A.M.–2 P.M. Sun.) charges US$1.25/hour for Internet, US$.45/minute for calls to the United States and US$.60/minute to Europe. Farther up, try **CompuMaya** (Av. Tulum between Calles Acuario and Orion next to Emilio's Fusion Kitchen, 9 A.M.–11 P.M. Mon.–Sat., US$1.30/hour Internet) or **El Point** (Super San Francisco de Asis shopping center, corner of Av. Tulum and road to Zona Hotelera/Boca Paila, tel. 984/871-2715, 8 A.M.–11 P.M. Mon.–Sat., 10 A.M.–10 P.M. Sun., US$1.40/hour, modern computers, fast connection).

In the Zona Hotelera, **Cabañas Zarha** has one computer with Internet access (US$2.75/hour). Two coin-operated public phones are just outside the front door of **El Pipazo** market.

Laundry

Lava Easy (Av. Tulum between Av. Satelite and Calle Centauro, no phone, 8 A.M.–8 P.M. Mon.–Sat.) charges a steep US$1.25/kilo (2.2 pounds) to have your clothes back the next day or US$2.25/kilo for two-hour rush service. Luckily, the minimum is just one kilo.

Storage

The **main bus terminal** (open 24 hours) has luggage storage for US$.45/.70 per hour per small/large bag.

GETTING THERE

Bus

Tulum's **main bus terminal** (Av. Tulum between Calles Alfa and Jupiter, tel. 984/871-2122) is at

TULUM BUS SCHEDULES

Departures from the **main bus terminal** (Av. Tulum between Calles Alfa and Jupiter, tel. 984/871-2122) include:

Destination	Price	Duration	Schedule
Cancún	US$5.50	2.5 hrs	2 A.M.*, 2:30 A.M., 3:30 A.M.*, 4:30 A.M.*, 6:15 A.M.*, 8:30 A.M.*, 10 A.M.*, 11 A.M., 11:30 A.M.*, 12:15 P.M.*, 12:30 P.M.*, 1 P.M.*, 2 P.M., 3 P.M., 4 P.M., 4:30 P.M.*, 5 P.M., 5:30 P.M.*, 6 P.M., 6:30 P.M.*, 7 P.M., 7:15 P.M.*, 8:15 P.M.*, 8:30 P.M.*, 9 P.M., 9:15 P.M.*, 10 P.M., 10:30 P.M.*, and 11 P.M.
Chetumal	US$10.50	3.5 hrs	10:15 A.M., 11:45 A.M., 12:45 P.M., 3:30 P.M., and 10 P.M.
Chichén Itzá	US$7	3 hrs	9 A.M. and 2:30 P.M.
Cobá	US$2.25	1 hr	7 A.M., 9:30 A.M., 11 A.M., and 6 P.M.
Felipe Carrillo Puerto	US$4.50	1 hr	11:45 A.M., 12:45 P.M., and 10 P.M.
Mérida	US$12	4 hrs	1:25 A.M., 2 A.M.*, 12:20 P.M., and 2:30 P.M.
Mexico City-TAPO	US$78	24 hrs	1:10 P.M.
Ocosingo	US$36	14 hrs	take any Tuxtla Gutiérrez bus
Palenque	US$30	12 hrs	take any Tuxtla Gutiérrez bus
Playa del Carmen	US$2.75	1 hr	take any Cancún bus
San Cristóbal de las Casas	US$40	16 hrs	take any Tuxtla Gutiérrez bus
Tuxtla Gutiérrez	US$43.50	18 hrs	4:15 P.M., 5:45 P.M.
Valladolid	US$4.50	2.5 hrs	1:25 A.M., 9 A.M., 12:20 P.M., and 2:30 P.M.
Veracruz	US$56	15 hrs	3 P.M.
Villahermosa	US$35	12 hrs	1:10 P.M. and 9:05 P.M.
Xpujil	US$16	5 hrs	1:10 P.M.

* Denotes second-class service; fares are lower but service is much slower.

Southern Quintana Roo

the south end of town, not far from the Weary Traveler hostel. See the *Tulum Bus Schedules* sidebar for departure times.

Colectivos also go to Cobá, albeit less frequently. Catch them at the intersection of Highway 307 and the Cobá/Boca Paila road (US$2, one hour).

Car

The town of Tulum is on Highway 307, just past the turnoff to Cobá. As you head south, it's a straight shot from Cancún—you can't miss it.

GETTING AROUND

On Foot

In town, you'll have no problem getting around by foot. Restaurants, hotels, and all traveler services are within a few blocks of one another.

If you're heading to the Zona Hotelera, you're better off getting a ride or renting a car.

Car

While not necessary in town, if you're staying in the Zona Hotelera—three kilometers (1.9 miles) away—you're better off on wheels (especially if your hotel is way down the coastal road). Once in the Zona Hotelera, a car is especially useful if you plan to check out the restaurants and beaches that line this 10-kilometer (6.2-mile) stretch of oceanfront properties.

Taxi

Taxis are plentiful in town, where rides cost around US$1.50. In the Zona Hotelera, there is a taxi stand at the minivillage area; rates are US$1.50–2.50 within the Zona Hotelera, US$2.75 to Tulum Pueblo, US$3 to Tulum ruins, and US$55 to the Cancún airport.

Cobá

It's 42 kilometers (26 miles) of good but speed bump–infested road from Tulum to Cobá (just hope you'll still have your muffler when you get there). Just outside of Tulum, you'll pass several well-marked cenotes—if you happen to have time, they are great for snorkeling.

COBÁ ARCHAEOLOGICAL ZONE

The Mayan site of Cobá (US$3.50, under 11 free, parking US$1.25, 7:30 A.M.–5 P.M. daily) was probably founded around A.D. 600 and reached its zenith around A.D. 800–900 before collapsing, along with so many Classic Mayan sites, by the turn of the millennium. Cobá covers 50 square kilometers (31 square miles) and contains more than 6,000 structures, including the second-highest Mayan pyramid and numerous stone roads connecting it to outlying cities. This was clearly a major political, economic, and social center and archaeologists believe that at its height Cobá had as many as 50,000 residents.

Much of our understanding of Cobá's im-

portance has emerged fairly recently, and some archaeologists now believe it could become one of the largest Mayan excavations on the Yucatán Peninsula. Thousands of structures remain unexcavated, clustered in groups up to two kilometers (1.25 miles) apart. Between the ruins is thick forest overgrown with vines, trees, and flowers.

Visiting the Ruins

It takes several kilometers of walking to see the whole site, or you can rent a bike near the entrance for US$2.25. Whether you walk or ride, don't forget a water bottle, comfortable shoes, bug repellent, sunscreen, and a hat. Watch for signs and stay on the designated trails. Guide service is available—prices are not fixed, but should be around US$15 for 1–6 people.

Ancient Highways

The remains of more than 50 *sacbes* (raised stone roads) crisscross the Yucatán Peninsula, and there are more here than in any other location, underlining Cobá's importance as a commercial

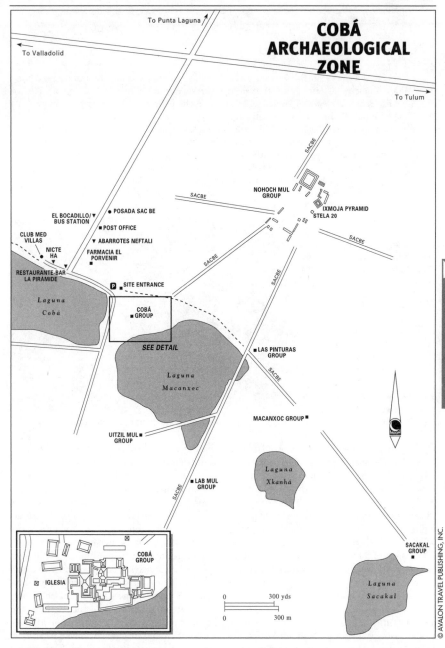

COBÁ ARCHAEOLOGICAL ZONE

To Punta Laguna

To Valladolid

To Tulum

SACBE

NOHOCH MUL GROUP

IXMOJA PYRAMID
STELA 20

SACBE

• POSADA SAC BE

EL BOCADILLO/ ▼
BUS STATION

■ POST OFFICE

▼ ABARROTES NEFTALI

CLUB MED
VILLAS

NICTE
HA ▼
•

FARMACIA EL
PORVENIR
■

RESTAURANTE-BAR
LA PIRÁMIDE

SACBE

SACBE

P ■ SITE ENTRANCE

*Laguna
Cobá*

COBÁ
■ GROUP

SACBE

SEE DETAIL

■ LAS PINTURAS
GROUP

SACBE

*Laguna
Macanxoc*

MACANXOC GROUP ■

UITZIL MUL ■
GROUP

*Laguna
Xkanhá*

■ LAB MUL
GROUP

SACBE

SACAKAL
GROUP
■

*Laguna
Sacakal*

COBÁ
GROUP

☒

IGLESIA
☒

| 0 | 300 yds |
| 0 | 300 m |

N Southern Quintana Roo

© AVALON TRAVEL PUBLISHING, INC.

DECIPHERING THE GLYPHS

Mayanist and scholar Michael D. Coe's *Breaking the Maya Code* (Thames and Hudson, 1992) is a fascinating account of the decipherment of Mayan writing.

For many years scholars could not agree that Mayan writing contained anything more than numbers and dates. Many thought the text was not "real writing" as it did not appear to reproduce spoken language. Even those who believed the writing to be more meaningful despaired at ever reading it.

In 1952, Russian scholar Yuri Valentinovich Knorosov jump-started Mayan scholarship by showing that Mayan writing did in fact convey spoken words. Using a rough alphabet recorded by Fray Diego de Landa (the 16th-century bishop who, ironically, is best known for having destroyed numerous Mayan texts), Knorosov showed that ancient texts contain common Yucatec words such as *cutz* (turkey) and *tzul* (dog). Interestingly, Knorosov conducted his research from reproductions only, having never held a Mayan artifact or visited an ancient temple. When he did finally visit Tikal in 1990, Coe writes, he wasn't very impressed.

By the mid-1980s decipherment picked up speed. One of many standouts from that era is David Stuart, the son of Mayan experts, who went to Cobá with his parents at age eight and passed the time copying glyphs and learning Yucatec words from local playmates. In high

© LIZA PRADO CHANDLER

Mayan glyphs were not fully deciphered until the 1980s.

and political center. The roads pass through what were once outlying villages and converge at Cobá—one extends in an almost perfectly straight line from the base of Nohoch Mul (Cobá's principal pyramid) to the town of Yaxuna, more than 100 kilometers (62 miles) away. Each *sacbe* was built with a base of stones 1–2 meters (3.3–6.6 feet) high and about 4.5 meters (14.8 feet) wide, which was covered with white mortar. (The literal translation of *sacbe* is white road.) In Cobá, ancient roads as wide as 10 meters (32.8 feet) have been uncovered, as well as mines where the raw materials were extracted and even a massive stone cylinder used to flatten the roadbeds.

The Pyramids

Cobá's principal pyramid, **Nohoch Mul,** is the second-highest Mayan pyramid, after the massive main structure at Calakmul in southern Campeche. But from 42 meters (137.8 feet) up (about 12 stories) the view of the Yucatán's thickly forested and incredibly flat landscape is second to none. A small temple at the top bears a fairly well-preserved carving of the Descending God, and a rope running down the stairs makes going up and down easier.

La Iglesia is the second-highest pyramid at the site (22.5 meters/73.8 feet) and also offers splendid views of the surrounding jungle and Lake Macanxoc from its summit. Scientists believe there might be a connection between the Petén Mayans (who lived hundreds of kilometers south in the Guatemalan lowlands) and the classic Mayans who lived in Cobá. Both groups

school he served as chief epigrapher on a groundbreaking exploration in Belize, and at age 18 he received a US$128,000 MacArthur Fellowship to, as he told Michael Coe, "play around with the glyphs" full-time.

Researchers now know that Mayan writing is like most other hieroglyphic systems. What appears at first to be a single glyph can have up to four parts, and the same word can be expressed in pictorial, phonetic, or hybrid form. Depending on context, one symbol can have either a pictorial or phonetic role; likewise, a particular sound can be represented in more than one way. The word cacao is spelled phonetically as "ca-ca-u" but is written with a picture of a fish (*ca*) and a comblike symbol (also *ca*, according to Landa) and followed by -u. One of David Stuart's great insights was that for all its complexity, much of Mayan glyphic writing is "just repetitive."

But how do we know what the symbols are meant to sound like in the first place? Some come from the Landa alphabet, others are suggested by the pictures that accompany many texts, still others from patterns derived by linguistic analyses of contemporary Mayan languages. In some cases, it is simply a hunch that, after applying it to a number of texts, turns out to be right. If this seems like somewhat shaky scientific ground, it is—but not without a means of being proved. The cacao decipherment was confirmed when the same glyph was found on a jar with chocolate residue still inside.

Hundreds of glyphs have been deciphered and most of the known Mayan texts can be reliably translated. The effort has lent invaluable insight into Mayan civilization, especially dynastic successions and religious beliefs. Some archaeologists lament, not entirely without reason, that high-profile glyphic studies have diverted attention from research into the lives of ancient ordinary Mayan people. Without question, there is much to be learned on that front. But it is hard not to marvel at how one of the great ancient civilizations is revealed in the whorls and creases of fading stone pictures.

built pyramids that are much taller than those found in Chichén Itzá, Uxmal, or elsewhere in the northern part of the peninsula.

Other Highlights

Numerous carved stelae dot the site; some are covered by palapas to protect them from the elements. One temple is named **Las Pinturas Group** (The Paintings Group) because of the stucco paintings that once lined the walls. Minute traces of the paintings, in layers of yellow, red, and blue, can still be seen on the temple's uppermost cornice. This small building is well preserved, and bright green moss grows up the sides of the gray limestone.

Flora and Fauna

Cobá (Water Stirred by the Wind in Mayan) is surely a reference to the group of shallow lagoons here (Cobá, Macanxoc, Xkanha, and Sacakal). The archaeological site and the surrounding wetlands and forest are rich with birdlife—herons, egrets, motmot, parrots, and the occasional toucan are not uncommon. In fact, some people come here more for the birdwatching than the ruins. Arrive early to see the most birds—at the very least you'll get an earful of their varied songs and cries. Later, as the temperature climbs, you'll start to see myriad colorful butterflies, including the large, deep-blue *morphidae* and the bright yellow-orange barred sulphur.

If you look on the ground, you'll almost certainly see long lines of leaf-cutter ants. One column carries freshly cut leaves to the burrow, and the other marches in the opposite direction, empty-jawed, returning for more. The vegetation decays in their nests, and the fungus that grows on the compost is an important staple of the ants' diet—a few scientists even claim

© LIZA PRADO CHANDLER

Dozens of *sacbes* crisscross the archaeological site of Cobá.

this makes leaf-cutter ants the world's second species of agriculturists. Only particular types of leaves will do, and the columns can be up to a kilometer (0.6 mile) long.

COBÁ VILLAGE

It should be immediately clear driving into this tiny town that Cobá has never regained the population (much less the stature) that the ancient city had at is peak, more than 1,000 years ago. Though the grandeur is gone, many of the traditional beliefs remain. Residents of the main village and smaller communities around the lagoon, many full Mayan, still plant their corn with traditional ceremonies and some villages appoint a calendar-keeper to keep track of the auspicious days that guide daily life, as early Mayans did. Tourism has helped Cobá's economy by providing a market for small artisans' shops, restaurants, and hotels, but it remains an isolated, one-road town.

Sights

About 17 kilometers (10.6 miles) north of Cobá, **Punta Laguna** (6 A.M.–6 P.M. daily,

US$2.75) is a forested area where spider and howler monkeys can be spotted and heard. While the admission fee grants access to the forest trails, your best chance of spotting these curious creatures is by hiring one of the guides near the entrance to the zone (US$26/group). The largest number of monkeys—as well as colorful birds—can be seen in the early morning and at dusk. Traveling by car, look for the cutoff road from Cobá toward Nuevo Xcan—that'll lead you straight to the entrance.

Entertainment

The main leisure activity here is paying a kid to feed an alligator off a pier near the site entrance (US$1) and tipping back beers at **Restaurante-Bar La Pirámide** (tel. 984/858-1450, 7:30 A.M.–9 P.M. daily) at the corner of the main road and the access road to Club Med Villa Cobá. It's got a good view of the lagoon and is not as dodgy as the bars up by the bus station.

Accommodations

There aren't many hotel options in this tiny town—three to be exact and only two worth

© LIZA PRADO CHANDLER

The steps of Nohoch Mul—the second-highest Mayan pyramid in the world—reach about 12 stories high.

considering. Be sure to call ahead to reserve a room if you want to guarantee a place to crash. (No worries if they're booked—Tulum, with its surplus of hotels, is just 40 minutes away.)

The modest **M Posada Sac Be** (Calle Principal s/n, tel. 984/206-7067, US$15–19 s/d with fan, US$26 s/d with a/c) offers five spotless rooms with two beds and a small desk. All have private bathrooms and nice yellow tile floors. If no one is around to show you a room, go two doors down to the no-name *artesanías* shop that doubles as the post office. Someone inside will be able to assist you. Very friendly service.

M Club Med Villas Cobá (facing the lagoon, tel. 984/206-7000, cobcchef01@clubmed.com, US$60 s/d) is one of three virtually identical Club Med mini-resorts at archaeological sites on the peninsula (the others are at Chichén Itzá and Uxmal). Small but attractive rooms surround a courtyard with an L-shaped pool. The restaurant serves good, somewhat overpriced meals indoors or outside beside the pool. The hotel has a library and reading room, with a good selection of books on Mayan culture and history, plus a billiards table and tennis court. The hotel faces Laguna

Cobá and a pretty pier and gazebo, though crocodiles make the swimming there unsafe (really).

Food

M Restaurante-Bar La Pirámide (tel. 984/858-1450, 7:30 A.M.–9 P.M. daily) is right at the corner of Calle Principal and the access road to Club Med Villas Cobá. With a large raised patio overlooking the lagoon, it's a nice place for lunch après-ruins or beer and snacks in the evening. The restaurant receives a number of tour groups, and it often has a buffet set up (US$8); otherwise, the menu has grilled fish, chicken, and meat dishes and other Mexican fare for US$4.50–11.

A few doors down and just before the entrance to Club Med Villa Cobá, **Nicte Ha** (facing the lagoon, tel. 984/206-7025, 8 A.M.–7 P.M. daily) is a small restaurant serving tacos, enchiladas, and various pork dishes, all under US$4. The name Nicte Ha (Flower of the Water) may refer to the eyes of a hungry resident crocodile the restaurant owner feeds occasionally—raw chicken is his favorite, apparently.

The restaurant at **Club Med Villas Cobá**

(7:30 A.M.–10 P.M. daily, US$4.50–12) definitely has the most comfortable setting and the best and largest selection of dishes in town, including pasta, seafood, and Yucatecan dishes. But the prices are a bit high, making it a poor value for some. Depending mostly on your mood, eating here is a worthwhile splurge or an unnecessary expense.

Across the street from a peach-colored church, **Abarrotes Neftali** (Calle Principal s/n, 7 A.M.–11 P.M. daily) sells canned goods, bread, and some fresh produce.

Information and Services

Cobá has neither an official tourist office nor recommended medical services beyond the pharmacy. You should be able to get most questions answered at the Club Med Villas Cobá hotel or at one of the listed restaurants. Otherwise, try Tulum, which has basic medical services. For serious medical matters, go to Cancún or Valladolid.

Pharmacies

Facing the lagoon, **Farmacia El Porvenir** (Calle Principal s/n, 9 A.M.–1 P.M. and 2 A.M.–9 P.M. Mon.–Sat.) is a small shop selling basic medicines, toiletries, and film.

Police

Impossible to miss, the police station is halfway down the main drag, before you hit the lagoon.

Money

There were no banks or ATMs when we passed through. The nearest banking services are in Tulum and Valladolid.

Post Office

You can buy stamps and drop off mail for pickup at a tiny, no-name *artesanías* shop. Look for it across the street from the bus station on Calle Principal. Open 8 A.M.–9 P.M. daily.

Getting There and Around

Getting to Cobá is easiest by car, of course, but buses and *combis* do come here from via Tulum, Pisté, and Valladolid. The roads in all directions are smooth and fast, if a bit narrow in places, cutting though pretty farmland and small towns; watch for *topes* (speed bumps). Just outside of Cobá village is a large roundabout—head south a few hundred meters to town and the ruins; west via Chemex to get to Valladolid, Chichén Itzá, and Mérida; north for Punta Laguna and Cancún; or east to Tulum. For Playa del Carmen, go via Tulum.

A tiny **bus station** operates out of El Bocadillo restaurant (Calle Principal s/n, tel. 985/852-0052). At the time of research, only second-class buses serviced the station. Destinations included:

Cancún, US$6.50, 3.5 hours, 10:30 A.M., 3:30 P.M., and 6 P.M.

Chichén Itzá, US$4.90, 2.5 hours, 9:30 A.M.

Playa del Carmen, US$4.10, 2.5 hours, 9:30 A.M., 10:30 A.M., 3:30 P.M., and 6 P.M.

Tulum, US$2.25, one hour, 10:30 A.M., 3:30 P.M., 4:30 P.M., and 6 P.M.

Valladolid, US$2.50, one hour, 7:30 A.M., 9:30 A.M., noon, and 7 P.M.

You can easily walk to any of the listed hotels, restaurants, and services in town, and the ruins are just a five-minute walk down the main road alongside the lagoon.

Punta Allen and the Sian Ka'an Biosphere Reserve

Sian Ka'an is Mayan for "where the sky is born," and it's not hard to see how the original inhabitants arrived at such a poetic name. The unkempt beaches, blue-green sea, bird-filled wetlands and islets, and humble accommodations are manna for bird-watchers, artists, snorkelers, and kayakers. But most of the visitors here come for the fishing—Sian Ka'an is one of the best fly-fishing spots in the world, especially for the "big three" catches: bonefish, tarpon, and permit.

The reserve was created in 1986, designated a UNESCO World Heritage Site in 1987, and expanded in 1994. It now encompasses around 1.3 million acres of coastal and mangrove forests, wetlands, and some 70 miles of pristine coral reefs just offshore. A huge variety of flora and fauna thrive in the reserve, including four species of mangrove, many medicinal plants, and about 300 species of birds, including toucans, parrots, frigate birds, herons, and egrets.

Crocodiles are common, and boa constrictors can be spotted occasionally, growing to lengths up to four meters (13 feet). Manatees and jaguars are even more reclusive, but definitely there, along with monkeys, raccoons, foxes, and various rodents. More than 20 Mayan ruins are found in the reserve, though most are unexcavated.

Tiny **Punta Allen** (pop. 400, also known as Rojo Gomez) is the peninsula's only real town and is situated at the far southern tip of the peninsula. About 100 families survive mostly by lobster fishing, though tourism is growing and many local young men have proved excellent and uncannily sharp fly-fishing guides (no surprise).

Spending a few days in Sian Ka'an is the best way to really appreciate its beauty and pace. Hotels and tour operators there can arrange fishing, bird-watching and other tours, all with experienced local guides. But if time is short, a number of tour operators in Tulum offer day trips into the reserve as well (see *Tour Operators* in that section).

SIGHTS

Muyil Archaeological Zone

The most accessible Mayan site within the Sian Ka'an reserve is Muyil (8 A.M.–5 P.M., US$3), on the western side of the park. Also known as Chunyaxche, the ruins stand on the edge of a limestone shelf near Laguna Chunyaxche and was at one time an ancient Mayan seaport. It was probably settled about A.D. 1 and occupied continuously until just before the Spanish conquest.

A large *sacbe* (raised stone road) runs at least a half kilometer (third of a mile) from the center of the site to near the edge of the lagoon, and in the other direction through a mangrove swamp. Six structures are spaced along the roadway approximately every 120 meters (394 feet), ranging from two-meter/6.6-foot-high platforms to the impressive **Castillo** (Castle).

© LIZA PRADO CHANDLER

sunset on the shores of Boca Paila Camps in Sian Ka'an

At 21 meters (68.9 feet), it is one of the tallest structures on the peninsula's Caribbean coast. The Castillo is topped with a solid round masonry turret, unique to ancient Mayan structures, from which you can see the waters of the Caribbean.

Muyil is about 25 kilometers (15.5 miles) south of Tulum; look for the signs on the highway toward Felipe Carrillo Puerto.

Ⓜ Ascension Bay

Ascension Bay covers about 20 square kilometers (12.4 square miles) and its shallow flats and tangled mangrove islands teem with bonefish, tarpon, and huge permit—some of the biggest ever caught, in fact. It is a fly fisher's dream come true, and it has been attracting anglers from around the world since the mid-1980s. And not just guys in waders—the spin fishing is fantastic, too, and the offshore reef yields plenty of grouper, barracuda, *dorado*, tuna, sailfish, and marlin.

SPORTS AND RECREATION

Fishing

Ascension Bay has world-class fishing. All of the hotels listed in this section arrange tours, and most specialize in it, using their own boats and guides. See *Accommodations* for information about fishing packages.

Bird-Watching and Ecotours

Sian Ka'an is also an excellent place for bird-watching. Trips to Bird Island and other spots afford a look at various species of water birds—in the winter, male frigates show off their big red balloonlike breasts. Tours often combine bird-watching with time snorkeling and walking around one or more bay islands. All the hotels can arrange tours, which typically cost US$35–65 pp.

ACCOMMODATIONS

Punta Allen is the only real town on the peninsula and has the most options for lodging, food, tours, and other services, but it is not the only place to stay. Boca Paila is a tiny settlement a short distance past Tulum's Zona Hotelera with a good ecolodge and probably the most upscale of the various fishing lodges. As you move south, there's a whole lot of nothing until you get close to Punta Allen, where you'll find a few scattered lodges outside of town.

Boca Paila

If you love the outdoors but don't like roughing it, Ⓜ **Boca Paila Camps** (four km/2.5 miles south of the entrance to the reserve, tel. 984/871-2499, www.cesiak.org, US$72–92) is an excellent choice. Here, spacious tent cabins (tents set on raised platforms) with surprisingly comfortable beds (real ones!), chairs, and spectacular views are distributed within the oceanfront jungle. Tents have private terraces that overlook the Caribbean or the lagoon and are lit by candles only—at night, the stars seem just beyond your fingertips. All share spotless and very modern compost bathrooms and there is a rainwater/gray-water system in place. The welcoming main building, which is solar- and wind-powered, houses a great restaurant and tends to be the social center of the place. Bicycles, kayaks, and boogie boards are available for guest use and a healthy reef just a few meters from shore makes for fantastic snorkeling. Guests who stay here also have ready access to the excursions offered by CESiaK, an environmental preservation and education foundation that runs the camp (see *Tour Operators* in the *Tulum* section). Continental breakfast is included in the rate.

On the Road to Punta Allen

About eight kilometers (five miles) from town, **Rancho Sol Caribe** (fanny@cancun.net, US$106 s/d, meal packages available; free in/out transfer for four-plus nights all-inclusive or seven-plus nights room only) has four comfortable cabanas, each with two double beds, private bath, patio with hammocks, and 24-hour electricity. The hotel owners organize guided fishing trips with a maximum of two anglers per boat, departing from a private pier on the lagoon. Fishing trip prices vary with the season and can be combined with lodging and meal packages—email for rates and availability. Boat tours through the mangroves can also be arranged.

Also north of town is **Let It Be Inn** (tel. 984/877-8506, www.letitbeinn.com, three nights/two days fishing US$2,195 s, US$1,495 pp d; seven nights/six days fishing US$2,195 pp d, US$3,595 s) which has just three palapa-roofed cabanas, each with a double bed, private bath, tile floors, and porch with chairs and hammocks and view of the beach and water. With a maximum of just six people at any one time, the hosts give friendly and personalized service. Visits are typically Friday-to-Friday, including airport pickup in Cancún; shorter stays should end on Friday. Everything here is geared toward anglers, down to rod racks in your cabin and beers and fly-tying in the main cabin. Fishing trips begin at 7:30 A.M. and don't return until the late afternoon, with a prepacked lunch and a cooler full of drinks onboard.

Punta Allen

One of the original fishing lodges in town, **Cuzan Guesthouse** (www.flyfishmx .com, tel. 983/834-0358, US$35–80) still has a loyal following despite the ever-growing pool of competitors. Basic palapa-roofed cabanas made of wood and stucco have private bath and ocean views from their front patios. The sand-floor restaurant may be the best in town, serving fresh seafood (the ceviche is famous) and a number of other Mexican and Yucatecan dishes. Daily fishing rates for two people are US$350 including box lunch; single, half-day and multiday fishing and lodging packages are also available. The hotel can arrange bird-watching, snorkeling, and combination outings as well; prices vary according to the number of passengers.

Also in town, **Posada Sirena** (tel. 984/877-8521, www.casasirena.com, US$30–50 s/d) has large, simple "Robinson Crusoe-style" bungalows at the very end of the road, about 100 meters (328 feet) from the beach. The cabins sleep up to 6–8 people and have private bathrooms and fully equipped kitchens. Half- and full-day tours of the bay, including snorkeling, bird-watching, and exploring various islands, can be arranged (US$40 half-day, US$60 pp full day,

Southern Quintana Roo

© LIZA PRADO CHANDLER

a little-visited stretch of coastline in southern Quintana Roo

minimum two people). All-day fishing trips go for US$130 pp or US$165 for solo anglers. Room rates do not include airport pickup; contact Javier Gonzales (agitours@agitours.com) if you don't feel like renting a car.

For something with your own kitchen, try **Serenidad Shardon** (tel. 984/876-1827, http:// shardon.com, US$100 lower part, US$150 upper part, US$250 both).

FOOD

Cuzan Guest House (8 A.M.–9 P.M. daily, US$5–$15) has the best restaurant in town, and there are a half dozen or so other little eateries. At all, fresh seafood and lobster (in season) are the specialties. Most of the hotels include meals in their packages.

Punta Allen also has three small **markets** and a good **bakery.**

INFORMATION AND SERVICES

Don't expect much in the way of services—if there is something you can't do without, definitely bring it with you. There is no ATM and none of the hotels or tour operators accept credit cards. Punta Allen has an understocked **pharmacy** and a modest **clinic** with a resident doctor and nurse. A few local entrepreneurs buy gas in Tulum and sell it for a small premium, and most hotels offer laundry service. Punta Allen's first and only **Internet café** has expensive and not terribly fast service.

GETTING THERE

Many of the hotels include airport pickup/ drop-off, which is convenient and helps avoid paying for a week's car rental when you plan on fishing all day. That said, a car is useful if you'd like to do some exploring on your own.

Car

There are two good ways to enter the reserve. The first entrance is about eight kilometers (five miles) south of the Tulum ruins on the Zona Hotelera/Boca Paila road. From the control kiosk—where you're supposed to pay a US$2 entrance fee—it's almost 60 kilometers (37.3 miles) of unpaved and sometimes muddy road to Punta Allen, passing the small settlement of Boca Paila along the way. The drive is slow going and bumpy, but any decent vehicle can make it if it's not raining. (4WDs do best, of course.) Take it slow and be sure to fill up on gas before leaving Tulum.

The other entrance is from the west, off Highway 307 between Tulum and Felipe Carrillo Puerto. From Tulum, go south of Highway 307 for 45 kilometers (27.9 miles) to the Playón/Punta Allen turnoff—it's a tiny road and tiny sign, so keep your eyes peeled. (The turnoff is about two kilometers/1.25 miles past a much more visible road and sign to the right for Chaccoben.) This is also a rough and sometimes muddy road but it's much shorter than the northern route. You weave through tangled wetlands, past the park entrance, to the town of Playón. From there, ferries take passengers across the bay to Punta Allen. You have to leave your car—there is a fellow there who watches the cars and theft isn't common, but it still makes sense not to leave anything valuable in plain view.

Bus

There are two *combis* daily from the market area in Felipe Carrillo Puerto to Playón (US$10, two hours, 10 A.M. and 3 P.M.). From there you take a ferry across to Punta Allen (US$10, 10 minutes, 6 A.M.–10 P.M. daily). On the return trip, *combis* leave Playón at 6 A.M. and 6 P.M.

Felipe Carrillo Puerto

Highway 307 from Tulum to Chetumal passes through Felipe Carrillo Puerto, a small city with little of interest to most travelers (except to fill up on gas) but plays a central role in the history of Quintana Roo and the entire peninsula. As the Mayans lost more and more ground in the War of the Castes, two indigenous leaders in the town of Chan Santa Cruz (present-day Felipe Carrillo Puerto) enlisted a ventriloquist to introduce—or invent, to some—the **Cruz Parlante** or Talking Cross. The cross "spoke" to the battle-weary population, urging them to continue fighting, even issuing tactical orders and predicting victory in the long, bitter conflict. Thousands joined the sect of the cross, calling themselves Cruzob (People of the Holy Cross, a conflation of Spanish *cruz* or "cross" and the Mayan pluralization *-ob,* in this case, "people of"). Some accounts portray the talking cross as little more than political theater for a simple-minded audience, but it seems likely that many or most of the Cruzob understood the ruse behind the Talking Cross and saw it as a form of channeling or simply much-needed motivation. Whatever the case, it reinvigorated the Mayan soldiers, and Chan Santa Cruz remained the last redoubt of organized indigenous resistance, finally submitting to federal troops in 1901.

But Mayan nationalism has not died here, nor is it blind to the sometimes invasive effects of mass tourism. A mural in the town center reads: *La zona Maya no es un museo etnográfico, es un pueblo en marcha* (The Mayan region is not a ethnographic museum, it is a people on the march).

And get this: The church in Felipe Carrillo Puerto was built by slaves, but they weren't Mayan or African. During the War of the Castes, indigenous troops captured many Spaniards and white Mexicans, some of whom they enslaved and forced to work.

The town's current name is in honor of a former governor of Quintana Roo, much revered by indigenous and working-class people for his progressive reforms, for which he was ultimately assassinated.

SIGHTS

Despite its unkempt appearance, the **Santuario de la Cruz Parlante** (Calle 69 at Calle 60) is a sacred place where the Talking Cross (along with two smaller ones) is housed in a small wooden church. Shoes and hats must be removed before entering. Ask permission before snapping any photographs.

ENTERTAINMENT AND EVENTS

If you're stuck here overnight, catch a movie at **Ca' Azhil Cine** (Calle 69 s/n, US$1.75 Fri.–Mon., US$.90 Wed.), which features mostly Hollywood films—just be sure to check whether it's dubbed or in English with Spanish subtitles.

ACCOMMODATIONS

Owned and operated by one of the founding families of the city, **Hotel Esquivel** (Calle 65 No. 746 between Calles 66 and 68, tel. 983/834-0344, US$30 s/d, US$45 s/d with kitchenette) offers 37 spotless rooms in four buildings, each with private bathroom, cable TV, and air-conditioning. Some second-story rooms in the main building have small balconies overlooking the pedestrian walk to the main plaza. The property across the street—once a hacienda called La Casona—houses guests in what once was the family quarters.

FOOD

El Faisán y el Venado (Av. Benito Juárez s/n, kitty-corner from the Pemex station, tel. 983/834-0043, 6 A.M.–10 P.M. daily, US$5–7) is Felipe Carrillo Puerto's best-known restaurant, as much for its location and longevity than any particular noteworthiness of its food. The menu is mostly reliable Yucatecan standards, including 8–10 variations each of fish, chicken, and beef, plus soup and other sides.

Southern Quintana Roo

FELIPE CARRILLO PUERTO BUS SCHEDULES

Destination	Price	Duration	Schedule
Bacalar	US$4	1.5–2 hrs	take any Chetumal bus
Cancún	US$9.50	3 hrs	12:10 A.M.*, 1:15 A.M., 2:15 A.M.*, 3:30 A.M.*, 5 A.M.*, 5:15 A.M., 6:30 A.M., 7:10 A.M.*, 7:30 A.M., 8:30 A.M.*, 8:45 A.M., 9 A.M.*, 10:15 A.M.*, 11 A.M.*, 11:30 A.M.*, noon, 12:45 P.M., 1:30 P.M., 2:15 P.M., 2:45 P.M.*, 3:15 P.M.*, 3:45 P.M., 4 P.M.*, 5 P.M.*, 5:45 P.M., 7 P.M.*, 8 P.M.*, 9 P.M.*, and 9:45 P.M.
Chetumal	US$6.50	2 hrs	1:30 A.M.*, 3:30 A.M.*, 5:45 A.M.*, 7:30 A.M.*, 8:15 A.M., 9:15 A.M., 9:45 A.M.*, 10:30 A.M.*, 12:30 P.M.*, 12:45 P.M., 1:45 P.M., 2:30 P.M.*, 3:15 P.M., 3:45 P.M.*, 5 P.M.*, 5:30 P.M.*, 7:30 P.M.*, 9:40 P.M.*, and 11:15 P.M.
Limones	US$2.50	45 min.	take any Chetumal bus
Mérida	US$10.50	5 hrs	12:30 A.M.*, 3 A.M.*, 4 A.M.*, 5:30 A.M.*, 6:30 A.M.*, 8:30 A.M.*, 11 A.M.*, 11:30 A.M.*, 3 P.M.*, 4:30 P.M.*, 7 P.M.*, 8:40 P.M.*, and 10:40 P.M.*
Mexico City-TAPO	US$74	22 hrs	9:15 P.M.
Oxkutzcab	US$7	3.5 hrs	take any Mérida bus
Playa del Carmen	US$7	2 hrs	take any Cancun bus
Ticul	US$8	4 hrs	take any Mérida bus
Tizimín	US$7	4 hrs	9:30 A.M.* and 4:30 P.M.*
Tulum	US$4.25	1 hr	take any Cancún bus
Valladolid	US$5.50	2 hrs	take any Tizimín bus
Veracruz	US$52	17 hrs	4 P.M.
Villahermosa	US$30.50	10 hrs	9:15 P.M.
Xpujil	US$11.50	5 hrs	9:15 P.M.

* Denotes second-class service; fares are 10–20 percent lower, travel time can be significantly slower.

There is also nearby **van service** to Chetumal (US$4.50, 2 hrs) from the small terminal on Calle 66 next to the Palacio Municipal. Vans leave when they are full 6 A.M.–8 P.M. daily.

Southern Quintana Roo

THE CASTE WAR

On July 18, 1847, a military commander in Valladolid learned of an armed plot to overthrow the government that was being planned by two indigenous men—Don Miguel Antonio Ay and Cecilio Chí. Ay was arrested and executed. Chí managed to escape punishment and on July 30, 1847, led a small band of armed men into the town of Tepich. Several officials and Euro-Mexican families were killed. The military responded with overwhelming force, burning villages, poisoning wells, and killing scores of people, including many women, children, and the elderly. The massacre galvanized indigenous people across the peninsula, sparking what came to be called the Caste War.

Supplied with arms and ammunition from Britain, the indigenous troops tore through colonial cities, killing and even enslaving terrified non-Mayans. Valladolid was evacuated in 1848 and was left abandoned for nearly a year. By 1849, the peninsula's indigenous people, drawing on centuries of misery and abuse, were close to expelling the colonial elite. However, as they were preparing their final assaults on Mérida and Campeche, the rains came early, forcing the Mayan soldiers to choose between victory and famine. The men returned to their fields to plant corn.

Mexican troops immediately took advantage of the lull, and the Mayans never regained the upper hand. For the next 13 years, indigenous soldiers (and increasingly *any* indigenous person) captured were sold to slave brokers and shipped to Cuba. Many Mayans eventually fled into the forests and jungles of southern Quintana Roo. The fighting was rekindled when a wooden cross in the town of Chan Santa Cruz (today, Felipe Carrillo Puerto) was said to be channeling the voice of God, urging Mayans to keep fighting. The war ended, however, when troops took control of Chan Santa Cruz in 1901. An official surrender was signed in 1936.

On the opposite corner, **El Mirador de la Iguana** (Av. Benito Juárez, tel. 983/834-0266, 11 A.M.–7 P.M. daily) is a classic *centro botanero* (a beer garden, essentially) where beers and drinks come with a hefty supply of appetizers. You can order more meal-like dishes such as ceviche and shrimp cocktail, but most people just fill up on the *chicharron, taquitos,* and other finger foods. Like at the popular *salones familiares* in Mérida, a family atmosphere reigns here and travelers should feel very welcome.

La Casona (5 P.M.–1 A.M. daily, US$5–10) opens right onto the main plaza and offers good Mexican fare at reasonable prices. Although it's not obvious, this is actually part of the Hotel Esquivel—you can reach the restaurant from the plaza or from the other side by going through the hotel.

SERVICES
Money
Next to the Pemex station, **HSBC** (Av. Benito Juárez at Calle 69, 8 A.M.–7 P.M.

Mon.–Sat.) is the only bank in town. It has one 24-hour ATM.

Post Office
The post office (Calle 69 at Calle 68) is open 9 A.M.–4 P.M. weekdays.

Internet and Fax
Facing the main plaza, **Balam 'Nah Internet** (tel. 983/834-1026, 8 A.M.–8 P.M. daily) offers reasonably fast Internet at great prices (US$.70/hour) and burns CDs for US$3. Fax service to the United States or Canada is US$1.35 per page and within Mexico for US$.60 per page.

GETTING THERE
Bus
Felipe Carrillo's **main bus terminal** (tel. 983/834-0815) is just off the main plaza. The majority of buses shuttle between Cancún and Chetumal; connect to Campeche and Chiapas from the latter. First-class service is faster

and more comfortable than second-class, which makes many intermediate stops.

Car

Fill your gas tank in Felipe Carrillo Puerto, especially if you're headed to Mahahual or Xcalak, where you'll appreciate having plenty of gas on the long stretches of empty highway. The next gas station is just before you enter Mahahual, but it occasionally runs dry for a day. Xcalak does not have a gas station, but a few locals do sell marked-up gas there.

La Costa Maya

This low-lying limestone shelf—bounded by Bahía Espíritu Santo to the north, Bahía Chetumal to the south, and the Caribbean Sea to the east—holds a mosaic of savannas, marshes, streams, and lagoons, dotted by islands of thick jungle. The coastline is a series of sandy beaches and dunes interrupted by rocky promontories, some of which connect with the offshore Belize Reef. A few still-healthy coconut plantations from the early 20th century dominate the shore.

Mayan sites have been discovered on the peninsula's shores and in its jungles, but little is known about the area's preconquest history; the peninsula was already abandoned when the Spaniards unsuccessfully tried to settle Bahía Espíritu Santo in 1621. Later, however, the peninsula became a sanctuary for indigenous refugees fleeing Spanish control in the interior, as well as a haven for pirates, British logwood cutters, and Belizean fishermen.

In 1910 the village of Xcalak (shka-LAK), at the peninsula's southern tip, held a population of 544; a few additional people were scattered among the *cocales* (small coconut plantations) and ranchos along the coast. In the ensuing years, the population fluctuated. The major industries—coconuts and fishing—have been periodically disrupted by hurricanes and, more recently, a yellowing disease that has decimated the state's coconut trees.

Xcalak and Mahahual (the other main town here) were long isolated by virtue of there being no paved roads from the highway to or along the coast. Starting in 1993, the state government started encouraging tourist development in the area, starting with the all-important task of renaming it "La Costa Maya." Now Mahahual has a major cruise-ship port and passenger-only commercial center with hundreds of shops, and a new road to Xcalak has slashed the drive time from Mahahual from half a day to less than an hour. That's not to say this is the next Playa del Carmen—at least not yet. The one-lane sand road connecting the two towns—the Carretera Antigua—is very much in use, both towns were just installing telephone and power lines when we visited, and many of the outlying homes and hotels still rely on solar, wind, and generator power for electricity. The state government has vowed to control development so it doesn't overly damage the environment, such as by limiting the height and size of hotel-resorts and closely regulating septic systems and water use. Time will surely tell.

MAHAHUAL

Mahahual is a place of two faces—cruise ship days, when the town's one road is packed with day trippers looking to buy T-shirts and throw back a beer or two; and non-cruise ship days, when Mahahual is sleepy and laid-back and the narrow, seaweed-strewn beaches are free to walk for miles. Whether you stay here a night or a week, you're likely to see both. It's a good thing. You can be in a major party zone one day, and the next be the only snorkeler in town—all without changing hotels. If what you seek are long quiet days every day, definitely stay outside of town. You'll see a few ATVers flying by now and again but that's as much partying as you'll see.

© LIZA PRADO CHANDLER

Mahahual's town beach

Sports and Recreation

Blue-Ha Dive Center (Carr. Antigua Km. 2.7, no phone, www.bluehadiving.com) is Mahahual's best-known dive shop. Though it got new owners in 2004, the shop still enjoys a good reputation. Prices for one-/two-/three-tank dives are US$40/70/100, plus US$10 for full gear rental if you need it. Since the reef is so close, you spend most surface intervals on-shore; dives are scheduled for 10 A.M., noon, 2 P.M., and 4 P.M. Night and sunrise dives can also be arranged (US$50/one-tank).

Maya Palms Resort (Carr. Antigua Km. 9.5, tel. 983/831-0065, U.S. tel. 888/843-3483, www.mayapalms.com) has a well-run dive shop, managed by the former co-owner of Blue-Ha. Two-tank reef dives are US$65, plus US$15–20 for equipment rental. By the time you read this the shop will be operating day trips to Chinchorro Bank, including transport on the shop's 48-foot dive boat (two hours each way), three tanks of diving, and lunch (US$235 pp, minimum six people, equipment not included, snorkelers US$140 pp).

For **snorkeling,** the folks at Luna de Plata restaurant can arrange a trip for US$30/

hour for the boat. Most hotels in town can do the same.

Accommodations

Under US$25: Although the rooms at this place leave something to be desired, **Las Cabañas del Doctor** (Av. Mahahual No. 6, tel. 983/832-2102, primomm@hotmail .com) offers camping and hammock sites with very clean shared bathrooms. Tent sites run US$2.25 per person (BYO tent), hammock sites cost US$2.65 per person (US$5.25 pp with hammock).

A good budget option if you don't mind roughing it a bit, **Kaba-Nah Cabañas** (Carr. Antigua Km. 8.5, US$18 s/d with shared bath, US$26 s/d with private bath, including breakfast) has five palapa-roofed cabins, each with two beds, concrete floors, and good mosquito nets. Three have clean, brightly painted private bathrooms; the other two share a bathroom. The cabins have no electricity but there are plenty of candles for nighttime (all the better for stargazing). Bring a good book as you'll surely while away an afternoon or two in the hotel's shaded hammocks and chairs.

The beach here isn't fantastic—few in this area are—but the seaweed and driftwood manage to complement the hotel's rustic, laid-back atmosphere. Breakfast is included, and a simple restaurant can stir up your other meals.

US$25–50: On a decent swimming beach, **Ⓜ Kohun Beach Cabañas** (Carr. Antigua Km. 7, no phone, kohunbeach@hotmail.com, US$31–35 s/d) offer excellent accommodations, privacy, and friendly service. Three spacious and modern cabanas have comfortable queen beds with beautifully hand-carved headboards, curtained windows with views of the Caribbean, and tile floors. Each is spotless and sleeps up to three (cabanas have a small sitting area with a sofa bed). An extensive library also is open to guests. Continental breakfast is included in the rate and is served under a huge palapa. Discount of up to 15 percent for stays of one week or longer. Be sure to email well in advance if you want reservations—the owner doesn't check email daily.

Ⓜ La Cabaña de Tío Phil (Carr. Antigua Km. 2.2, tel. 983/835-7166, tiophilhome@ hotmail.com, US$35 up to four people) is a friendly Mahahual fixture. Seven free-standing cabanas all have two beds, fan, wood floors, mosquito nets, 24-hour electricity, and a private front patio with table and chairs where— yes—your free continental breakfast is served. The operators are conscientious about cleanliness: All the sheets, pillowcases, and bed stands had just been replaced when we visited. Not much of a beach here, but a good one in town is a short walk away.

The **Luna de Plata** restaurant (Carr. Antigua Km. 1.7) has four rooms for rent for US$35/43.50 for two/three people in the high season. Built behind the restaurant, the rooms are a bit small but have a queen-sized bed, private bath with hot water, 24-hour electricity, fan, and a porch. The restaurant owners have also converted a large atticlike space over the restaurant into a large suite—worth asking about if you want the space and don't mind the noise.

Opened in March 2004, **Ⓜ La Posada de Los 40 Cañones** (center of town, tel. 983/834-5803, los40canones@hotmail.com, www .los40canones.com, US$35–43.50 s/d with fan, US$52–65 s/d with a/c) promises to fare better than its namesake, the best-known shipwreck off Chinchorro Bank. Smallish standard rooms have comfy beds, modern baths, and a clean, bright feel. Superior rooms and two huge suites have more artful decor—the hanging beds are very Tulumesque—and added amenities such as minisplit air conditioners, king-sized or multiple beds, indoor jet baths, and (for one) a big private patio. The rooms form a horseshoe around an attractive entrance and patio area. The hotel restaurant has tables on the patio or in a tasteful dining area and serves Mexican food during the day and Italian at night. The hotel operates the beach bar across the street (a small beach but the best in town) and rents kayaks and snorkels in addition to mixing good drinks.

US$50–100: Balamkú (Carr. Antigua Km. 5.7, tel. 983/838-0083, www.balamku .com, US$60 s, US$70 d including breakfast; closed September) was Mahahual's finest hotel-resort when we came though, although it may have some competition by the time you read this considering the breakneck pace of construction here. Not to worry: You can count on comfortable lodging and excellent service at the Balamkú. Run by a friendly Canadian couple, rooms here are spacious, super-clean and artfully decorated with Mexican and Guatemalan *artesanía*. All have modern ecofriendly bathrooms, ceiling fans, queen and twin beds (and available inflatable mattress), and 24-hour electricity (totally sun- and wind-generated). A full breakfast is included. The rooms occupy a series of circular two-story buildings—both levels have high ceilings and upstairs rooms look up into the palapa roofs. Guests have free use of the hotel's kayaks and library, with plenty of books, board games, and music, and yoga classes and other activities can be arranged. Popular with yoga groups; credit cards accepted online only, with 8 percent surcharge.

Over US$100: Those seeking the ultimate in outdoorsy relaxation should check out the intimate **Kailuum Cito III** (12 km/7.5 miles north of Mahahual, toll-free U.S. tel. 800/538-6802, info@turqreef.com, www.kailuum.com). Those who remember **Kailuum I** or **Kailuum II** just north of Playa del Carmen will recognize the features: nine beachfront *tentalapas* (wood-floor tents under protective palapas), each with comfortable beds, pillows and linens, hammocks on the front porch, and daily maid service. You'll also find very clean shared bathrooms, a sand-floored dining room serving family-style meals, an honor bar (with purified water and ice), and great snorkeling a few steps from your tent. This is about as quiet and away-from-it-all as you can get. Rates are US$140 per guest and include breakfast, dinner, tips, and taxes. Lunch also is available for an extra charge. Closed September and October.

Formerly the Maya-Ha Resort, the **Maya Palms Resort** (Carr. Antigua Km. 9.5, tel. 983/831-0065, U.S. tel. 888/843-3483, www .mayapalms.com, US$145 s/d) has new owners and let's hope a new outlook on life. The restaurant has been renovated, the dive shop is under new management, and all 16 large, clean rooms have air-conditioning (at night only), private bath, and comfortable beds. However, the new owners inherited a somewhat boxy and charmless place, and new paint and bedspreads go only so far. The resort has 200 meters (656 feet) of coastline and a great reef just offshore, but the beach is narrow and covered in seaweed. The large pool is appealing, but the expanse of concrete and tile surrounding it is not. The big pseudopyramid—well, Lord Pakal would not have been pleased. The dive shop (open to nonguests as well) is a definite bright spot, run by the well-regarded former co-owner of Blue-Ha Dive Center.

Food

N Luna de Plata (Carr. Antigua Km. 1.7, south of center, noon–midnight daily, US$4–15) serves tasty and well-prepared Italian dishes, from a slice of good, crispy pizza to fresh-made pasta with shrimp or lobster. There are a few international variations as well, such as veggie curry pasta, and full bar. Run by a friendly Italian couple, Luna de Plata is one of Mahahual's best watering holes, proved by the number of loyal cruise-ship staff people who eat here. You should also ask here about rooms for rent, if you need one, and scenic flights and snorkel tours.

Across the street, **Casa del Mar** (casadel mar@mahahual.biz, 7 A.M.–3 P.M. daily) is a modest snack- and juice-bar; pancakes, eggs, and other breakfasts cost US$2–3), sandwiches are US$2.50, fresh-squeezed juices US$1–2.

Specializing in Thai and Italian dishes, dinner at **Tirovino Club Parrilla** (Carr. Antigua Km. 1.4, no phone, 6–10 P.M., US$5–9) is a great change of pace. The palapa-roofed dining room, with tile floors and heavy wood tables, is especially pleasant.

The restaurant at **La Posada de Los 40 Cañones** (center of town, 7:30–10:30 A.M., 12:30–2:30 P.M., 7–9 P.M. Mon.–Sat., 7:30 A.M.–11 P.M. Sun., US$5–15) is also recommended, serving familiar Mexican breakfasts and lunches, and well-prepared Italian food for dinner. The outdoor patio seating is nice, weather permitting.

N Travel In' (Carr. Antigua Km. 6, no phone, 8 A.M.–late night Mon.–Sat., US$2–4.50 breakfast, US$6–8 lunch/dinner) is a great little restaurant a few kilometers down the coastal road. Fresh breads—particularly pitas—are baked daily and the international menu focuses on curries and Mexican food. Daily specials vary depending on the day's catch and what's available in town. Known for making a mean sandwich and creative dinners, this is well worth the walk (or ride) down the coast.

For groceries, try **Mini Super El Caribeño** (just before La Posada de Los 40 Cañones, 8 A.M.–8 P.M. Mon.–Sat., 8 A.M.–3 P.M. Sun.). It's a tiny place but it has the basics.

Information and Services

Despite the weekly barrage of cruise-shippers, Mahahual still has limited tourist services: no information or medical centers, no police (although the army has a posting near the gas station), no bank or post office, and forget about laundry service. The town is growing by leaps and bounds, though. By the time you read this, there may be additional services to those listed below.

At the time of research, the only place to surf the Internet was at the restaurant **Tirovino Club Parrilla** (Carr. Antigua Km. 1.4, no phone, 6–10 P.M., US$3.50).

Public satellite telephones can be found at **Mini Super El Caribeño** (just before La Posada de Los 40 Cañones, 8 A.M.–8 P.M. Mon.–Sat., 8 A.M.–3 P.M. Sun.). Calls are a whopping US$.75 per minute within Mexico and US$2.65 per minute to the United States/Canada. Note: Phone lines were being put in when we passed through town, so by the time you read this, there may be other (cheaper) options.

Getting There and Around

Just south of the grubby roadside town of Limones, a good paved road with signs to Mahahual breaks off Highway 307 and cuts through 57 kilometers (35.4 miles) of coastal forest and wetlands tangled with mangroves. It's a scenic stretch, whether in car or bus, along which you should see egrets, herons, and other water birds.

At the time of research, all the **buses** in Mahahual were either going to or coming from Chetumal, always with a stop in Limones. There was discussion of establishing a Mahahual-Limones-Felipe Carrillo Puerto route, but no firm plans. Change buses in Limones if you are coming from (or going to) anywhere other than Chetumal. Bear in mind that Mahahual is growing extremely fast, and service is sure to change or expand—call ahead to be sure of making the smoothest connection.

There is no fixed bus terminal in Mahahual—just flag the bus down anywhere on the main road. Buses going to Chetumal (US$5.25, three hours) making a stop in Limones (US$2.50, one hour) depart Mahahual at 8 A.M., 3 P.M., and 5 P.M. If you are headed up the coast, switch buses in Limones. Buses to Cancún pass every 1–2 hours and can drop you anywhere along the way. The last northbound bus passes at 11:30 P.M.; the ones that pass at 7:30 P.M. and 9 P.M. are first-class.

To get to Mahahual from Chetumal (same prices and duration), buses leave the main terminal at 4 A.M., 6 A.M., and 10:55 A.M., and sometimes 3:15 P.M. If you are coming from the north, you can catch those same buses when they pass Limones at 6 A.M., 7:30 A.M., 12:30 P.M., and 4:30 P.M.

If you're **driving,** there is one gas station on the main road to Mahahual, just east of the turnoff to Xcalak. It runs out of gas now and again, so definitely fill your tank in Felipe Carrillo Puerto or Chetumal before heading out here.

The town of Mahahual is definitely walkable—just follow the sandy road through the small town. If you're staying outside of town, though, you'll definitely need some wheels—car, scooter, bike, or taxi—to get back and forth.

XCALAK

The tiny fishing village of Xcalak lies just a short distance from a channel that separates Mexico from Belize's Ambergris Caye, and a blessed long ways from anything else. The town was founded in 1900 by the Mexican military, and its first real hotel was Costa de Coco, which opened in 1988. Until the late '90s the only way in or out of town was by boat or via 55 kilometers (34 miles) of rutted beach road. Electrical lines were installed in 2004 but only in the village proper, so many outlying areas (including most of the better hotels) still rely on solar, wind, and diesel generators. The town has no bank, no public phones, and no gas station, although at least two families make side money by reselling gas bought in Mahahual.

But there are big plans for little Xcalak. The area doesn't have much beach, but it makes up for it with world-class fly-fishing, great diving and snorkeling, and a healthy reef and lagoon. The new road makes getting to Xcalak much, much easier, and no one should be surprised to find tourism on the rise and most of the beachfront property already bought up. A growing contingent of expats, mostly American and Canadian, have built homes, some for personal use, others for rent, others as small hotels. But large-scale tourism here is still a way off, and though the armies of development (and guidebook writers) march ever nearer, Xcalak

© LIZA PRADO CHANDLER

Brightly painted clapboard homes are the norm in Xcalak.

remains a small and wonderfully laid-back place, perfect for those looking for some honest-to-goodness isolation.

Sports and Recreation

Xcalak has great **diving and snorkeling** opportunities, many right from the shore. The main reef is 100–200 yards from shore and the water is less than five feet deep virtually the whole way out. Many snorkelers prefer the coral heads even closer to shore, which have plenty to see and much less swell than the main reef. Be alert for boats, though the shallow waters keep boat traffic to a minimum and fishermen are good about steering clear of snorkelers. The reef took a beating from Hurricane Mitch in 1998 and again from Hurricane Keith in 2000 but it has rebounded and is once again healthy, vibrant, and teeming with sealife.

Divers and snorkelers can also explore the reef at around 20 official sites and many more unofficial ones. Most are a short distance from town, and shops typically return to port between tanks. "La Poza" is one of the more unique dives, drifting through a trench where hundreds, sometimes thousands, of tarpon congregate, varying in size from three-foot "juveniles" to six-foot behemoths.

And, of course, there is **Banco de Chinchorro** (Chinchorro Bank), which is by some measurements the largest coral atoll in the Northern Hemisphere and a paradise for divers and snorkelers alike. About 35 miles northeast from Xcalak, Chinchorro is a marine reserve and is known for its spectacular coral formations, massive sponges, and abundant sealife. Scores of ships have foundered on the shallow reefs through the years, but the sunken remains are rarely dived: Almost all the wrecks are on the rough eastern side, they are mostly debris fields with few intact structures, and the reserve has banned diving on them to prevent looting. The famous "40 Cannons" wreck, in about 10 feet of water on the atoll's northwest side, is a good snorkeling site though there are many fewer than 40 cannons left, thanks to past looters.

To get to Chinchorro, it's a 1.5–2-hour boat ride, which can be pretty punishing depending on conditions. You typically set out around 8 or 9 A.M., dive three or four tanks (air or nitrox), have lunch onboard, and return to port around

© LIZA PRADO CHANDLER

kayaking along the Costa Maya

4:30 or 5 P.M. There are small government and fishermen's huts on one of the cays, but as of 2005 it was not possible for tourists to stay the night. Dive shops usually require at least four divers (or eight snorkelers) and may not go for days at a time if the weather is bad.

XTC Dive Center (far north end of town, across bridge, tel. 983/831-0461, info@xtc divecenter.com, 9 A.M.–5 P.M. daily) is a full-service dive shop that specializes in trips to Chinchorro Bank; its acronym officially stands for "Xcalak to Chinchorro," though the ecstasy-inducing dives here surely figured into the name. As of 2005, reef dives cost US$35/ tank for a single dive or US$26/tank for a package of four or more. Chinchorro trips are US$150 for three air tanks, US$175/200 for three/four nitrox tanks. Snorkelers and passengers pay US$75. Equipment rental is US$15 for buoyancy control device (BCD) and regulator; US$8 for mask, snorkel, and fins; weekly rentals available. The shop also has two-, three-, and five-hour snorkel tours for US$25/35/50 per person, with discounts for groups of four or more. The longer trips include jaunts into the lagoon and Bird Island, which can be fas-

cinating, especially in January and February when the birds are most plentiful.

Costa de Cocos, Casa Carolina, and **Sandwood Villas** also have dive operations. Costa de Cocos was in the process of getting a Chinchorro license and should be taking divers there by the time you read this. Prices at all three shops are comparable, so ask around and pick a shop based on whom you feel comfortable with. (See *How to Choose a Dive Shop* in the *Isla Cozumel* section for additional tips.)

Xcalak also has world-class **fishing,** with skilled local guides, easy access to ocean, bay, and lagoon environments, and plentiful tarpon, bonefish, barracuda, snook, and more. All the dive shops listed above arrange guided fishing tours. XTC takes fly fishers out for US$150/half day or US$250/full day; trolling runs US$90 for two hours and US$35 each additional hour (maximum four people). Costa de Coco has similar trips, and also offers six-day/seven-night packages with full room and board, airport pickup, open bar, and daily fishing for around US$2,500/person (double occupancy). Other hotels also arrange packages, and all can contact the local guides directly—

Nato and Victor were considered the best when we came through.

Accommodations

Under US$50: There are a few good options in the village, but most of Xcalak's most appealing accommodations are on the beach road heading north out of town. Few places accept credit cards on-site, but many have payment systems on their websites. Prices listed are for high season, roughly December to May; expect a 10–25 percent discount otherwise.

If you can handle sketchy bathrooms, **Maya Village** (Calle Principal, just after the bridge, no phone) has a decent beachside lot where you can camp (US$2.65 pp). It also has three *rustic* sand-floored bungalows with hammocks but—at US$13—they're not worth it.

Marina Mike's (Calle Principal, just before the bridge, tel. 983/831-0063, U.S. tel. 877/877-3529, www.xcalak.com, studio with kitchen US$110, with minifridge and sink only US$67) is a boxy, modern condo-hotel with four comfortable attractive suites big enough for two couples and outfitted with in-room cable and wireless Internet for those who can't

quite disconnect. All have 24-hour electricity, two have air-conditioning, and three have a full (but small) kitchen. Rates include use of a two-person kayak. There's a separate palapa-roofed cabin that also has a kitchen and is a bit more spacious, but it was once a restaurant and still kind of looks the part. Weekly and monthly rates available.

Over US$50: Tierra Maya (2.1 km/1.3 miles north of town, tel. 983/831-0404, toll-free U.S. tel. 800/480-4505, fantasea@xcalak .com, www.tierramaya.net, US$70–75 single, US$75–85 double, US$12 extra for a/c) is a low-key hotel on a nice stretch of beach. Its seven rooms are ample and nicely decorated with simple wood furniture, *talavera* accents, and bright Mexican blankets. All rooms also have glorious views of the Caribbean from their private terraces or balconies. Breakfast is included in the rate and is served in the hotel's charming palapa-roofed restaurant (see *Food*).

Four bright units with fully equipped kitchenettes make **Casa Carolina** (2.5 km/1.6 miles north of town, tel. 983/831-0444, www .casacarolina.net, US$85 s/d) a fine choice. Add perfect ocean views from the private balconies,

© LIZA PRADO CHANDLER

view of Xcalak's coastline from one of Sin Duda's roof decks

free use of kayaks and bicycles, and a wide beach with palm trees, and you've got the formula for a relaxing beach vacation. Co-owner Bob Villier also is an experienced NAUI dive instructor trainer and offers personalized classes and fun dives (see *Sports and Recreation*). Continental breakfast included.

Advertised as a place where "all you need is your smile," **Playa Sonrisa** (6.9 km/4.3 miles north of town, tel. 983/838-1872, playa sonrisa@yahoo.com, www.playasonrisa.com, US$85–125 s/d) is a clothing-optional resort on a palm tree–strewn beach. The grounds are ample and private and there are bicycles, kayaks, and snorkel gear for guest use. Rooms here are divided between nice beachfront bungalows and very rustic garden view cabins. The units are adequate but pricey for the area. What you pay for here is the freedom to enjoy the Caribbean in the buff without being ogled or disrespecting local mores. Continental breakfast included.

Our favorite place on the Costa Maya is without a doubt—no pun intended—**M Sin Duda** (eight km/five miles north of town, tel. 983/831-0006, www.sindudavillas.com, US$75–125 s/d). As soon as you walk through the front door, owners Margo and Robert (and their three corgis) make you feel as if you've walked into your own home—they show you around the delightful villa, tell you where to find the snorkel gear, kayaks, and bicycles, point out the best spots on the reef to explore, and leave you to unwind. That is, of course, until the nightly cocktail hour, when guests can join the hosts for a "margo-rita" in the delightful lounge that doubles as a common kitchen and library. (When we visited, our party ended up on an unforgettable night snorkeling trip in the backyard reef—after the effects of our drinks had subsided, of course.) And the units? The three standard rooms, one studio, and two full-sized apartments are charmers: beautifully furnished, whimsically decorated, and with breathtaking views of the turquoise Caribbean sea outside (except the studio). Also, don't miss the two roof decks, which have breathtaking 360-degree views of the jungle, lagoon, sea, and reef. A home away from home for sure.

Other comfortable options on this stretch of the coast include **Villa La Guacamaya** (8.5 km/5.3 miles north of town, tel. 983/831-0334, www.villalaguacamaya.com, US$80 s/d), which has comfortable rooms with a great shared kitchen; **Sand-Wood Villas** (7.9 km/4.9 miles north of town, tel. 983/831-0034, scubadad12007@yahoo.com, www.sandwood .com, US$89 s/d) with two apartments; and **Costa de Cocos** (2.9 km/1.8 miles north of town, tel. 983/831-0110, www.costadecocos. com, US$84), which is especially popular with divers and fishermen.

Food

M Taquitos (near the entrance of town, tel. 983/838-0318, 11 A.M.–midnight daily, US$3–18) is a popular eatery with a few tables set up on the front porch of a clapboard house. Fresh fish—caught by the owner himself—is served in tacos, fillets, whole… you name it, you got it. Highly recommended.

On the beachside road in town, **The Leaky Palapa Restaurant/Conchitas** (no phone, 11:30 A.M.–9 P.M. Sat.–Mon., US$4–16) is a bohemian palapa-roofed restaurant run by two Canadian expats. Menu items change depending on the day's catch and what the food truck brings by. Check out the blackboard menu in back for options.

On Friday and Saturday nights, head to **Maya Village** (Calle Principal, just after the bridge, no phone), where locals and travelers alike come together for finger-lickin' good barbecue chicken and a few cold beers. Come early—around 5:30 P.M.—to get the best drumstick.

Costa de Cocos (2.9 km/1.8 miles north of town, tel. 983/831-0110, 7 A.M.–10 P.M. daily, US$5–18) has the only hotel restaurant where you don't need dinner reservations. That said, ask your hotel owner to radio ahead in the morning if you know you'll be there that night. The resort caters to sportspeople, so the food is good, solid fare: from fresh fish and lobster to hamburgers and New York strip steak. There are a few vegetarian options and a full bar.

M Tierra Maya (2.1 km/1.3 miles north of town, tel. 983/831-0404, 5–8 P.M. daily,

US$12–18) has a delightful beachside restaurant that offers an almost entirely grilled-food menu. You'd think your dad was hired as the chef, funny apron and all. Be sure to call for reservations so that the cook can stock up on fresh items for the night's menu. Highly recommended by locals and travelers alike.

If you are cooking for yourself, a **food truck** passes through town and down the coastal road almost every day. It comes stocked with eggs, yogurt, grains, basic produce, fresh meats, and canned food. You can also buy a broom or two.

Information and Services

At the time of research there was no bank, ATM, or currency exchange office in Xcalak, and few places take credit cards. Plan accordingly!

There is **Internet access** at XTC Dive Center (9 A.M.–5 P.M. daily) for a hefty US$8.75 per hour. The Leaky Palapa restaurant was planning to set up a few terminals when we passed through, and many hotel owners will let you use their computers in a pinch.

A basic **health clinic** is near the entrance of town and is staffed by a doctor and one nurse. Office hours are 8 A.M.–noon and 2–6 P.M. Monday–Friday. If you need immediate attention during off-hours, you can receive 24-hour emergency care by banging on the door (the doctor sleeps in the clinic on weeknights). Closed weekends.

Getting There and Around

All **buses** leaving Xcalak go to Mahahual, Limones, and then Chetumal. All buses coming here follow the same route in reverse. Note that this area is growing fast and service will likely have expanded by the time you read this—you may want to call your hotel to double-check the

schedule. If you are staying at one of the hotels north of town, you should also ask if someone can pick you up at the bus stop. Otherwise, you'll have to bum a ride or ask around for a cab (US$5).

Buses leave Xcalak at 5 A.M. and 2:30 P.M. You can catch it in the center of town. Coming here, buses leave the main terminal in Chetumal at 5:40 A.M. and 3:15 P.M. Coming from the north, you can meet those same buses as they pass Limones at 7:30 A.M. and 4:30 P.M.

A **car** certainly makes your life easier around here, but it's not an absolute necessity. It used to be that you really needed a four-wheel drive car or truck to safely navigate the rutted coastal road to Xcalak (or do as locals have for years and go by boat). All that changed with the new inland road, built in 1996, which cut a five-hour bone-jarring adventure to a one-hour walk in the park.

The only guaranteed **gas station** is in Felipe Carrillo Puerto. There is another one on the main road to Mahahual, right after the turnoff for Xcalak, but it runs out of gas now and again. If you remember, be sure to top off at both places to keep your vacation on track—getting stranded on the dark road to Xcalak is no fun. If you do end up with an empty tank in Xcalak, you can usually buy some—at a small premium—from locals. A popular place for gas is at the house next door to Taquito's restaurant; the folks there helped us in a jam.

The town of Xcalak is small enough that getting around on foot is easy. If you're staying at a hotel outside of town, however, you'll definitely need a set of wheels (the farthest hotel is 8.5 kilometers/5.3 miles from the edge of town). You'll have no worries about getting around once you're out there—many of these hotels lend bicycles to their guests.

Laguna Bacalar

Almost 50 kilometers (31 miles) long, Laguna Bacalar is the second-largest lake in Mexico (after Lago de Chapala in Jalisco) and certainly among the most beautiful. Okay, it's not technically a lake: A series of waterways do eventually lead to the ocean, making Bacalar a lagoon. But it is fed by springs and the water on the western shore, where the town and hotels are, is 100 percent *aqua dulce* (fresh water; literally "sweet water").

The Mayan name for the lagoon means Lake of Seven Colors. It is an apt description, as you will see on any sunny day. The lagoon's sandy bottom and crystalline water turn shallow areas a brilliant turquoise, which fades to deep blue in the center. If you didn't know better, you'd think it was the Caribbean.

The little roadside town of Bacalar won't win any prizes for charm, but it does have a terrific museum, several good hotels, and of course views of the lagoon. Cenote Azul, a giant cenote (which you could also mistake for a lake) is a few kilometers south and has great swimming.

SIGHTS

⋈ Fuerte San Felipe Bacalar

The 17th-century Fuerte San Felipe Bacalar (northeast side of the main plaza, 9 A.M.–8 P.M. Tues.–Sun., US$1.75) was built by the Spanish for protection against the bands of pirates and Mayans that regularly raided the area. In fact, attacks proved so frequent (and successful) that the fort was destroyed in 1858 during the Caste War. Today, the star-shaped stone edifice has been restored to its former glory: drawbridge, cannons, moat, and all. The fort also houses the excellent **Museo de la Piratería.** Housed in two rooms, it has state-of-the-art displays on the history of the area with a focus on the pirates who gained so much fame for their attacks. Well worth a stop.

Cenote Azul

As good or better than the lagoon for swimming, Cenote Azul (two km/1.25 miles south

Fuerte San Felipe Bacalar was beautifully renovated in 2004.

© LIZA PRADO CHANDLER

of town, Carretera Chetumal-Bacalar Km. 15, tel. 983/834-2460, 8 A.M.–8 P.M. daily, free) is a huge circular cenote 61 meters (200 feet) deep, 185 meters (607 feet) across, and filled to the brim with brilliant blue water. Short ladders make getting into the water easy, and the cenote has no hidden rocks or shore grass to contend with along its edges. A rope stretches clear across, so even less-conditioned swimmers can make it to the other side. A large, breezy restaurant (US$6–15) has smallish portions and unremarkable food, but the pretty waterside tables are perfect for fries and a beer.

ENTERTAINMENT AND EVENTS
Fiesta de San Joaquín
Every July, Bacalar celebrates San Joaquín, its patron saint, for a whopping nine consecutive days. Local unions and workers' cooperative organize exuberant celebrations in different neighborhoods each night, each trying to outdo the other for the year's best party. Visitors are welcome and if you're in Bacalar at the time, definitely join the fun—expect plenty of food, music, dancing, and performance of all sorts. Cockfights are also popular, and a three-day hydroplane race usually follows the festivities in early August.

SPORTS AND RECREATION
Swimming and Kayaking
On a choice piece of waterfront property, the **Club de Vela Bacalar** (Av. Costera s/n, tel. 983/834-2478, 9 A.M.–5 P.M. daily) is one of the best places to swim in town; a wooden footbridge leads water babies from land to a swimming dock, where the water is crystal clear and deep. Use of the dock is free. The club also rents sea kayaks (US$8.75/hour) and has a pricey restaurant that serves mostly seafood and regional treats (see *Food*).

Other good swimming spots on the lagoon can be found at Rancho Encantado and Hotel Laguna (see *Accommodations*), though nonguests should order something at the restaurant to use the waterfront.

ACCOMMODATIONS
Under US$50
All things considered, **M Casita Carolina** (Blvd. Costero 17, 1.5 blocks south of the plaza, tel. 983/834-2334, casitacarolina@aol .com, www.casitacarolina.com, US$22–39 s/d, camping US$4.50 pp) has Bacalar's most charming and convenient accommodations. It's 100 meters (328 feet) from the center of town, and the fort, restaurants, ATM, cybercafé, bus terminal, and so on. Three of the rooms (there are only five) occupy a converted family home and share a common living room and aging kitchen. The other units—a cozy apartment and a medium-sized palapa-roofed casita—face a large grassy garden that runs to the lakeshore. (You can swim here, but water grass and sharp rocks can be off-putting; try the boat club a few lots down.) The rooms vary in size, decor, and price, but all have private bath, fan, and a homey feel. Campers set up on the grass near the lake—only one or two tents are allowed at a given time, which suits everyone. American host and owner Carolyn Niemeyer Weiss lives on-site and loves to visit with guests; she also hosts a weeklong painter's retreat in February. Kayaks can be rented for US$4.50 per day.

Hotelito Paraíso (end of Calle 14 at Blvd. Costero, tel. 983/834-2787, hotelito paraiso@hotmail.com, US$31 s/d, camping US$4.50 pp) has six aging but clean rooms surrounding a large grassy area that runs right to the lakeshore. One of the rooms is quite big, the others midsized; all have private bathrooms and full kitchens with gas stoves and dishes. That said, the beds are a bit saggy, and there's a generally downtrodden feel about the place. Campers can set up on the grass near the lake and use collective showers and toilets in the main building.

Built on a bluff overlooking Laguna Bacalar, **Hotel Laguna** (Blvd. Costero 479, tel. 983/834-2206 or toll-free Mex. tel. 800/713-6947, US$34 s/d with fan, US$46 s/d with a/c) has large clean rooms, most with balcony and a beautiful view of the lake. The decor is seriously dated—seashells and animal prints figure prominently—but in an endearing way. Several worn but clean bungalows have two bedrooms, living room, small kitchen, and patio with barbecue grill and great lake views. Stairs zig-zag down to the water, where a pier, ladder, and even a diving board make swimming here easy and fun. Otherwise, there's a small pool (filled only during high season) up by the rooms. The hotel restaurant serves basic, predictable meals. From the highway, look for the large sign and white and green structure on the south side of town.

Over US$100

Rancho Encantado (two km/1.25 miles north of town, tel. 983/831-0037, U.S. tel. 505/894-7074, www.encantado.com, US$150/180 garden/lagoon view, including two meals) is a pleasant, new-agey hotel and spa on the edge of Laguna Bacalar. Fourteen spacious casitas are set in a lush lakeside property, replete with coco palms, fruit trees, and native birds. The units have windows on all sides and feature Mexican tile floors, clean bathrooms, and a small porch (with hammock) looking onto either the garden or the lagoon. Paintings of Mayan scenes cover some outdoor walls. At the lake, a pier leads to a shady dock area strung with hammocks—it's the hotel's prettiest spot and perfect for swimming and relaxing. The charming honeymoon suite has its own stairs into the water and trees lend extra privacy. Rancho Encantado also has a large open-air yoga and mediation area, and a small kiosk built over the lake was especially designed for massages and treatments, complete with a ladder descending discreetly into the lagoon. There's an outdoor whirlpool tub, good restaurant (prices include two full meals), and kayaks available to guests. The hotel offers a number of guided tours, from a lake and fort tour to all-day visits to Mayan ruins in Campeche and even Belize. Persistent noise from the highway is the one drawback.

FOOD

For a town that is somewhat touristed, the restaurant options are quite limited and what there is closes early. On the main plaza, you'll find two hole-in-the-wall options: a **hamburger joint** that doubles as an ice cream parlor and a popular **rotisserie chicken place.** For a sit-down lunch, the lagoonfront **Club de Vela Bacalar** (Av. Costera s/n, tel. 983/834-2478, 9 A.M.–5 P.M. daily) serves seafood and regional food in its open-air restaurant. The prices are somewhat inflated for what you get (US$7–14) but the view and the variety are welcome.

INFORMATION AND SERVICES

Medical Services

A basic health clinic is across the street from the post office.

Pharmacies

Farmacia Guadalupe (Calle 14 s/n, 7 A.M.–8:30 P.M. daily) is just a couple of blocks from the main plaza.

Police

The police station is just off the plaza, across the street from the Fuerte San Felipe Bacalar.

© LIZA PRADO CHANDLER

Rancho Encantado's pier makes a great swimming spot.

LAGUNA BACALAR BUS SCHEDULES

Destination	Price	Duration	Schedule
Cancún	US$13	5–6 hrs	12:45 A.M., 5:30 A.M., 7:15 A.M., 9:15 A.M.*, 9:45 A.M., 11 A.M., 12:45 P.M., 2:15 P.M., 3:15 P.M.*, 5:15 P.M., 6:15 P.M., 7:15 P.M., and 10:45 P.M.
Chetumal	US$1.50	45 min.	every 30–60 min. 5 A.M.–1 A.M.
Felipe Carrillo Puerto	US$4	2–2.5 hrs	7:45 A.M., 2:45 P.M., 4:15 P.M., and 9:45 P.M.
Playa del Carmen	US$13	4–5 hrs	take any Cancún bus
Tizimín	US$11	6 hrs	7:45 A.M., 2:45 P.M.
Tulum	US$10	4–4.5 hrs	take any Cancún bus
Valladolid	US$9	4 hrs	take any Tizimín bus

* Denotes first-class ADO service; fares are 10–30 percent higher and travel time is much shorter.

Money

There is no bank in town but there is a brand-spanking-new **Banorte** ATM on the west side of the main plaza. If you need any other services or the ATM has run out of cash, the closest bank is in Chetumal.

Post Office

The post office (10 A.M.–2 P.M. Mon.–Fri.) is in the center of town, just east of Fuerte San Felipe Bacalar.

Internet

The most convenient place to email is the **Nave de Papel Internet** (west side of the main plaza, 9 A.M.–10:30 P.M. Mon.–Sat., 3–10:30 P.M. Sun., US$.90/hour).

Telephone

Two blocks north of the main plaza, look for the **Telefónica** sign. Here, calls can be made within Mexico (US$.22/minute) and to the United States and Canada (US$.70/minute). It's open 8:30 A.M.–2 P.M. and 5–9 P.M. Monday–Saturday, 8:30 A.M.–2 P.M. Sunday.

GETTING THERE

Bus

Bacalar's modest **bus terminal** (one block south of center, tel. 983/834-2517) has mostly second-class *de paso* (passing) service, which means you have to wait for the bus to arrive before buying your ticket, space permitting. A few first-class buses do stop, but you may consider going into Chetumal to catch a bus from there. For Chetumal, you can also take a **shared taxi** (US$1.75) or *combi* (US$1.25); pick up either in front of Iglesia San Joaquín on Avenida 7, one block up from the lake. You can also flag down Chetumal-bound buses along the highway, if your hotel is closer to there than the terminal. They pass every half-hour or so.

GETTING AROUND

You can easily walk to all the sites of interest in Bacalar, with the exception of Cenote Azul. A taxi there from town costs US$1.50; you can usually find one around the main plaza or on Avenida 7.

Chetumal

Chetumal is the capital of Quintana Roo and the gateway to Belize. Many signs and restaurant menus are in both Spanish and English (English is Belize's official language), and the government and commercial traffic lends Chetumal a businesslike atmosphere. But like all border towns, Chetumal has its seedy side too. Be alert for scams—sly Belizeans with little or no accent sometimes pass themselves off as American or Canadian tourists in need.

Most guidebook-toting travelers here are just passing through, headed to or from Guatemala or southern Campeche (and Chiapas beyond). However, Chetumal's modern Mayan museum is one of the best you'll find, and well worth a visit. In fact, more and more tour groups stop here just to visit the museum. And if you're dying to see the Guatemalan ruins of Tikal, a shuttle from Chetumal can get you there in eight hours (cutting through Belize), and back again just as fast. The beautiful Laguna Baca-

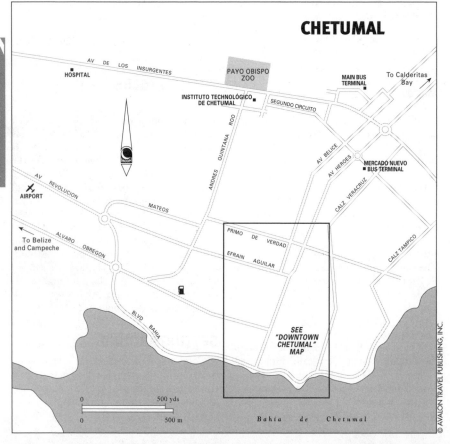

CHETUMAL

© AVALON TRAVEL PUBLISHING, INC.

lar, north of town, and intriguing Kuhunlich and Dzibanché ruins, west of town, make for easy day trips (sans border crossings).

SIGHTS

 Museo de la Cultura Maya

Museo de la Cultura Maya (Av. de los Héroes at Calle Cristóbal Colón, 9 A.M.–7 P.M. Sun. and Tues.–Thurs., 9 A.M.–8 P.M. Fri.–Sat., closed Mon., US$4.50) is organized on three levels—the upper level is the world of gods, the middle the world of humans, and the lower level is Xibalabá, the underworld. An oversized Mayan world tree—which to Mayans represented the much-revered ceiba tree and which the Spanish mistook for a Christian cross when they arrived—extends through the three levels just as it does (in a larger sense) in Mayan cosmology. Interesting and well-designed displays explain Mayan spiritual beliefs, agricultural practices, astronomy and counting, and more, all in English and Spanish. The exposition area past the ticket booth usually has good temporary art shows.

Museo de la Ciudad

The city museum (Calle Héroes de Chapultepec between Avs. Juárez and de los Héroes, tel. 983/832-1350, ext. 116, 9 A.M.–7 P.M. Tues.–Sun., US$1) is a small, well-organized museum with interesting displays (in Spanish only) of the political, economic, and cultural history of Chetumal, from its founding as the town of Payo Obispo, to its elevation in 1915 to capital of the then-federal territory of Quintana Roo, and on up to present day. There's a small art exposition space at the end.

Monument to the Mestizo

In front of the Museo de la Cultura Maya, note the Monument to the Mestizo, an interesting sculpture symbolizing the joining of Spanish shipwrecked sailor Gonzalo Guerrero and a Mayan princess—the birth of the mestizos.

Boulevard Bahía

This breezy bayside promenade lacks beaches but makes for a fine bayfront stroll. Along it you'll find cafés, sculptures, monuments, a

© LIZA PRADO CHANDLER

The Monument to the Mestizo adorns downtown Chetumal.

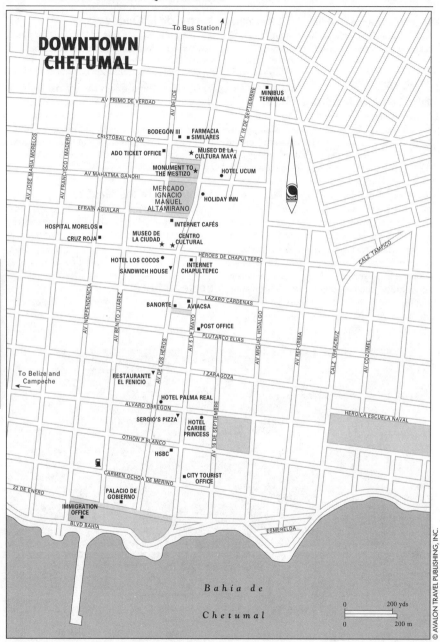

DOWNTOWN CHETUMAL

To Bus Station

AV PRIMO DE VERDAD

AV BELICE

AV 16 DE SEPTIEMBRE

MINIBUS TERMINAL

BODEGÓN III

FARMACIA SIMILARES

CRISTÓBAL COLÓN

ADO TICKET OFFICE

MUSEO DE LA CULTURA MAYA

AV JOSE MARIA MORELOS

AV FRANCISCO I MADERO

MONUMENT TO THE MESTIZO

HOTEL UCUM

AV MAHATMA GANDHI

MERCADO IGNACIO MANUEL ALTAMIRANO

HOLIDAY INN

EFRAIN AGUILAR

HOSPITAL MORELOS

INTERNET CAFÉS

CRUZ ROJA

MUSEO DE LA CIUDAD

CENTRO CULTURAL

HÉROES DE CHAPULTEPEC

CALZ TAMPICO

HOTEL LOS COCOS

SANDWICH HOUSE

INTERNET CHAPULTEPEC

AV INDEPENDENCIA

AV BENITO JUÁREZ

LÁZARO CÁRDENAS

BANORTE

AVIACSA

AV 5 DE MAYO

POST OFFICE

PLUTARCO ELIAS

AV MIGUEL HIDALGO

AV REFORMA

CALZ VERACRUZ

AV COZUMEL

AV DE LOS HÉROS

To Belize and Campeche

I ZARAGOZA

RESTAURANTE EL FENICIO

HOTEL PALMA REAL

ALVARO OBREGON

SERGIO'S PIZZA

HOTEL CARIBE PRINCESS

HEROICA ESCUELA NAVAL

OTHON P BLANCO

AV 16 DE SEPTIEMBRE

HSBC

CARMEN OCHOA DE MERINO

CITY TOURIST OFFICE

22 DE ENERO

PALACIO DE GOBIERNO

IMMIGRATION OFFICE

BLVD BAHIA

ESMERELDA

Bahía de Chetumal

0   200 yds
0   200 m

lighthouse, and, you'll hope, a cooling breeze. The backstreets harbor pastel-colored, worn wooden buildings with an old Central American/Caribbean look. Where Avenida de los Héroes meets the water is **Plaza la Bandera,** where Sunday concerts and city celebrations are held, and the site of newly renovated **Palacio de Gobierno.**

Kohunlich Archaeological Zone
The archaeological site of Kohunlich is outside Chetumal. Neither as grand as Calakmul nor as glorious as Uxmal, it is still worth a trip if only to visit the compelling **Temple of the Masks.** Dedicated to the Mayan sun god, this stone pyramid features haunting stucco masks with star-incised eyes, mustaches, and nose plugs. Standing two meters (6.6 feet) tall, these masks are rarities, to say the least. Be sure to wander through the jungle site; you'll be rewarded with more than 200 structures, stelae, and uncovered mounds that date to late Preclassic (A.D. 100–200) through the Classic (A.D. 600–900) periods. Open 8 A.M.–5 P.M. daily, US$3.

Dzibanché Archaeological Zone
If you have time and want to explore a semi-excavated site, your admission ticket to Kohunlich also will get you into Dzibanché (8 A.M.–5 P.M. daily), a site that dates to A.D. 300–600. Lesser visited than the little visited Kohunlich, this site was once a major Mayan city extending 40 square kilometers (24.9 square kilometers).

SHOPPING
There is a fine **bookstore and giftshop** (tel. 983/832-3049, 9 A.M.–8 P.M. Mon.–Fri., 9 A.M.–3 P.M. Sat.) at the Instituto Quintanaroense de la Cultura (Quintano Rooan Institute of Culture) on the corner of Avenida de los Héroes and Calle Héroes de Chapultepec. (The sign reads "Centro Cultural de las Bellas Artes" for some reason.) You'll find good maps, posters, T-shirts, and Spanish-language books and magazines.

Across from the Museo de Cultura Maya, **Mercado Ignacio Manuel Altamirano** (Efraín Aguilar between Avs. Belice and de los Héroes)

sells items geared toward locals, such as clothing, electronics, and kitchenware.

ACCOMMODATIONS
Although Chetumal is not considered a tourist resort, its status as the state capital and its location on the Belize border make it a busy stopover for both Mexicans and Belizeans. Arrive as early in the day as possible to have your choice of hotel rooms. During the holiday season, definitely make a reservation.

Under US$50
The basic but very clean **Hotel Ucum** (Av. Mahatma Gandhi No. 167 between Avs. 5 de Mayo and 16 de Septiembre, tel. 983/832-0711, US$17.50 s/d with fan, US$20 s/d with fan and cable TV, US$26 s/d with a/c and cable TV) is the best budget option in town. Just half a block from the excellent Museo de Cultura Maya, rooms are decent-sized, beds are comfortable, and there's a great pool with a separate wading pool for smaller children. The parking lot also is secure. Ask for a room on the top floor for the best breeze.

With tile floors, wood furniture, and flower bedspreads, the **Hotel Caribe Princess** (Av. Alvaro Obregón No. 168 between Avs. 5 de Mayo and 16 de Septiembre, tel. 983/832-0900, caribe_princess@hotmail.com, US$34 s with a/c, US$40 d with a/c) has very pleasant rooms. They are on the small side, but they're definitely more than adequate. Ask for a room facing the interior of the building—the avenue in front is a busy one.

Newcomer **Hotel Palma Real** (Av. Alvaro Obregón No. 193 at Av. de los Héroes, tel. 983/833-0964, htldenegocios@yahoo.com.mx, US$37–40 s/d with a/c) is another bright spot on the hotel scene. Rooms here are spacious, clean, and have brand-new furniture and amenities. Some also have balconies that face the main drag—a somewhat loud but interesting bird's-eye view of the hubbub downtown.

US$50–100
Having undergone a major renovation, **Hotel Los Cocos** (Av. de los Héroes No.

134 at Calle Héroes de Chapultepec, tel. 983/832-0544, www.hotelloscocos.com.mx, US$58 s/d standard, US$74 s/d premiere, US$77 s/d villas) is a stylish surprise in this small town. With its urban-chic look, you'll feel as if you're in Playa del Carmen or Cancún. Renovated rooms—premiere and villas only—are absolutely worth the price: sleek furniture, gleaming tile floors, and the newest in amenities. Older rooms—standards—are overpriced: outdated white furniture, bathrooms that are begging for new tiles, and air-conditioning units that could use a tuneup. Whichever room you choose to book, however, all guests have access to the lush garden and inviting pool area. Free Internet also is offered and there is a good open-air restaurant on-site.

If Los Cocos is full, try the **Holiday Inn** (Av. de los Héroes No. 171-A, tel. 983/835-0400, holimaya@msn.com, www.holiday-inn.com/Chetumal) across the street.

Over US$200

On the road to Kohunlich is the luxurious **Explorean Kohunlich** (toll-free Mex. tel. 800/366-6666, www.theexplorean.com, US$209 pp). This Fiesta Americana all-inclusive resort boasts 40 deluxe suites set in 30 hectares (74 acres) of jungle property. Each has gleaming stone floors, high palapa ceilings, elegant furnishings, and private stone-walled yards for sunbathing. Breakfast is served in a private outdoor living room or—if you prefer—in the indoor sitting area. At the main building, a fine restaurant serves delicious regional fare (9 A.M.–11 P.M. daily, US$9–14, open to nonguests), a full-service spa is at the ready, and a sleek lap pool overlooks the jungle below (you can even see the ruins at Kohunlich from here). An excursion a day—including rappelling in the jungles of Campeche, kayaking through a crocodile reserve, or mountain biking through forgotten forests—also is included in the rate. Add in all your meals, drinks, and taxes and this is simply a spectacular place to spend a few days.

FOOD

Restaurante El Fenicio (Av. de los Héroes at Calle Zaragoza, no phone, open 24 hours, US$3–8) is our favorite restaurant in Chetumal, not only because it's open late when practically everything else closes by 7 P.M., but also for its careful service and tasty, reliable meals. Be sure to try the "make you own taco" dish (US$11.50 for two), a platter stacked with chicken, chorizo, beef, and melted cheese, and served with tortillas and all the fixings.

Simple and clean, **Sandwich House** (Av. de los Héroes, next to Hotel Los Cocos, 9 A.M.–4 P.M. Mon.–Sat., US$3–6) serves sandwiches, baguettes, and hamburgers from a streetside stand with a counter and barstools. Good spot for a quick bite, and there's a juice bar one stand over.

Set in a dark wood, dimly lit, faux-Tiffany lamp dining room, **Sergio's Pizza** (Av. 5 de Mayo at Av. Alvaro Obregón, tel. 983/832-2991, 7 A.M.–midnight daily, US$3.50–5 breakfast, US$4–16 lunch/dinner) serves much more than pizza—the extensive menu covers the gamut of Italian and Mexican dishes—from meat lasagna to *molletes rancheros*. Meals are tasty and service is excellent. Popular with families.

Bodegón III (Calle Cristóbal Colon between Avs. Belice and de los Héroes, no phone, 5 A.M.–9 P.M. Mon.–Sat., 5 A.M.–3 P.M. Sun.) is a large grocery store with a decent selection of canned and dry foods and a huge display of fruits and veggies in front. Nos. I and II are nearby.

INFORMATION AND SERVICES

Tourist Information Center

Near the waterfront, the city tourist office (Av. 5 de Mayo at Carmen Ochoa de Merino, 8:30 A.M.–4 P.M. Mon.–Fri.) has a decent selection of brochures and maps.

Medical Services

Cruz Roja (Red Cross, corner of Av. Independencia and Calle Héroes de Chapultepec, tel.

983/833-0223 or dial 065 from any pay phone, open 24 hours) is the local ambulance dispatch and first-response center. Next door on Avenida Independencia is **Hospital Morelos** (tel. 983/832-1977, open 24 hours), which is primarily a maternity hospital but it has a full-service emergency room. **Hospital General de Chetumal** (corner of Avs. Andrés Quintana Roo and Juan José Isiordia, tel. 983/832-3932, open 24 hours) is the city's main hospital and is about two kilometers (1.25 miles) from the center.

Pharmacies
Cruz Roja (corner of Av. Independencia and Calle Héroes de Chapultepec, tel. 983/833-0223) has a pharmacy open 8 A.M.–9 P.M. Monday–Friday, and 8 A.M.–7 P.M. Saturday. **Farmacia Similares** (Calle Cristóbal Colón between Avs. Belice and de los Héroes) is behind the Mayan museum and open 24 hours. There's another branch of the same pharmacy at Avenida de los Héroes 101 at Calle Plutarco Elias Calles (tel. 983/833-2331, 8 A.M.–9 P.M. Mon.–Sat., until 8 P.M. Sun.).

Money
HSBC (Othon P. Blanco No. 184 between Avs. 5 de Mayo and Av. de los Héroes, 8 A.M.–7 P.M. Mon.–Sat.) has two ATMs as does **Banorte** (9 A.M.–4 P.M. Mon.–Fri.), on a pedestrian walkway off Avenida de los Héroes between Lázaro Cárdenas and Plutarco Elias. There is also an ATM at the bus station.

Post Office
The post office (Av. Plutarco Elias Calles between Avs. 5 de Mayo and 16 de Septiembre, 8 A.M.–6 P.M. Mon.–Fri., 9 A.M.–1 P.M. Sat.) is just a block off the main drag.

Internet
A string of Internet cafés are conveniently lined up across from the **Mercado Ignacio Manuel Altamirano** (Efraín Aguilar between Avs. Belice and de los Héroes). Charging around US$.90/hour, most are open 7 A.M.–2 A.M. Monday–Saturday and 8 A.M.–midnight on Sunday. If those are full, try the reliable **Internet Chetumal** (Calle Héroes de Chapultepec at Av. 5 de Mayo, tel. 983/833-4475, 8 A.M.–midnight daily, US$.90/hour, US$3.15 to burn CDs).

Telephone and Fax
At least one of the listed Internet cafés ought to have cheap international telephone service via the Internet by the time you read this—it was just being set up when we passed through. For faxing, try the **Telecomm/Telegrafos** (Av. Plutarco Elias Calles between Avs. 5 de Mayo and 16 de Septiembre, 8 A.M.–6 P.M. Mon.–Fri., 9 A.M.–12:30 P.M. Sat.–Sun.) next to the post office, which sends faxes for US$1.50/page to the United States and Canada, US$2.40/page to Europe, and US$1.45/page within Mexico.

Immigration Office
The immigration office (Calzada del Centenario 582, tel. 983/832-6353) is open 9 A.M.–1 P.M. Monday–Friday. A cab from here from the center is US$1.25.

Storage
Conveniently located in the bus station, **Revistas and Novedades Laudy** stores bags for an amazing US$.45 per hour. Open 24 hours.

GETTING THERE
Air
Chetumal's small modern airport still has only a few flights each day. **Aviacsa** (corner of Calle Lázaro Cárdenas and Av. 5 de Mayo, tel. 983/832-7676 or 832-7787 at airport, 9 A.M.–7 P.M. Mon.–Fri., 9 A.M.–2 P.M. Sat.) and **Aerocaribe** (Av. de los Héroes in front of Mayan museum, tel. 983/833-5334, at airport tel. 983/833-4781, 9 A.M.–7 P.M. Mon.–Fri.) both have flights to Mexico City, with onward connections from there.

Bus
Most first- and second-class buses leave from the **main bus terminal** (Av. Insurgentes at Av. de los Héroes, tel. 983/832-5110,

CHETUMAL BUS SCHEDULES

Main bus terminal (Av. Insurgentes at Av. de los Héroes, tel. 983/832-5110, ext. 2404) departures include:

Destination	Price	Duration	Schedule
Bacalar	US$1.50	20 min.	8:30 A.M. and 2:30 P.M., or take local bus at Minibus terminal
Campeche	US$18	7 hrs	4:15 A.M.**, noon, and 2:15 P.M.**
Cancún—1st class	US$16	5.5 hrs	1 A.M., 2:30 A.M., 4 A.M., noon, 11 P.M., and midnight*
Cancún—2nd class	US$13.50	6.5 hrs	4:45 A.M., 6:30 A.M., 9 A.M., 10:15 A.M., noon, 1:30 P.M., 2:30 P.M., 4:30 P.M., 5:30 P.M., 6:30 P.M., 10 P.M., and midnight
Ciudad Cuauhtémoc (Guatemalan border)	US$40	16 hrs	1:30 A.M.
Felipe Carrillo Puerto	US$6.50	2 hrs	noon, 11 P.M., or take second-class Cancún bus (US$4.50; 2.5 hrs)
Mahahual	US$3	4 hrs	4 A.M., 6 A.M., 10:55 A.M., and 3:15 P.M.
Mérida	US$17	6 hrs	7:30 A.M., 8 A.M.**, 11:30 A.M.**, 1:30 P.M., 5 P.M., 11 P.M.**, and 11:30 P.M.
Mexico City—Norte	US$68	20 hrs	8 P.M.
Mexico City—TAPO	US$68	20 hrs	11.55 A.M., 4:30 P.M., and 11 P.M.
Palenque	US$21	7 hrs	7:45 P.M. and 9:15 P.M.
Playa del Carmen	US$13	4.5 hrs	noon, 11 P.M., and midnight*, or take second-class Cancún bus (US$10; 5.5 hrs)

ext. 2404). You can buy tickets there or at a **ticket office** (Avs. Belice and Cristóbal Colón, tel. 983/832-0639) just west of the Mayan museum. Two other terminals—the Minibus terminal and Mercado Nuevo—have service to Bacalar and the Zona Libre and to Belize, respectively.

Going to Guatemala

Getting to the famous Guatemala Mayan ruins of **Tikal** is easier than you may realize—and worth the trip. Take the Mundo Maya shuttle (US$22 plus border fees, eight hours, departs 6 A.M. daily) from Chetumal's main terminal, which passes through Belizean and Guatemalan border posts en route to the charming island town of Flores. Flores has numerous hotels and services, including many daily buses to and from the ruins. Mundo Maya has daily return service to Chetumal when (or if!) you decide to return to Mexico.

Going to Belize

Buses to Belize leave from the Mercado

Destination	Price	Duration	Schedule
Puebla	US$61	18 hrs	10 P.M.
San Cristóbal de las Casas	US$30	12 hrs	1:30 A.M., 7:45 P.M., and 9:15 P.M.
Tapachula (Guatemalan border)	US$47	20 hrs	1:30 A.M.
Tulum	US$11	3.5 hrs	1 A.M., noon, and 11 P.M., or take second-class Cancún bus (US$8.50; 4.5 hrs)
Tuxtla Gutiérrez	US$33	14 hrs	7:45 P.M. and 9:15 P.M.
Veracruz	US$46	16 hrs	6:30 P.M.
Villahermosa	US$24	8 hrs	4:30 P.M., 6:30 P.M., 8 P.M., 9 P.M., and 10:30 P.M.
Xcalak	US$5	5 hrs	5:40 A.M. and 3:15 P.M.
Xpujil	US$5.50	2 hrs	6:10 A.M.**, noon, 6:10 P.M.**, 6:30 P.M., and 8 P.M.

*Denotes ADO-GL deluxe service. Rates are 10–30 percent higher; travel time is the same.
**Denotes second-class service. Rates are 25–30 percent lower; travel time can be significantly longer.

Minibus terminal (Av. Primo de Verdad at Av. Miguel Hidalgo, no phone) departures include:

Bacalar	US$1.25	20 min.	every hour on the hour 9 A.M.–6 P.M.

Mercado Nuevo (Av. de los Héroes and 2 Circuito, no phone) departures include:

Zona Libre (duty-free shopping zone)	US$.75	30 min.	every 15 min. 6:30 A.M.–8 P.M.

Southern Quintana Roo

Nuevo (Circuito Segundo at Av. de los Héroes), about a dozen blocks north of the museum. A few of the first-class buses (marked below with an asterisk) also stop at the main bus terminal. After crossing the border, first-class buses stop only at Corozal, Orangewalk, and Belize City. Second-class buses cost slightly less but make many intermediate stops. First-class rates and travel times are: Belize City (US$7, three hours), Orangewalk (US$3.50, two hours), and Corozal (US$1, one hour).

First class: 5 A.M., 6 A.M., 10:30 A.M.*, 1:45 P.M.*, 3 P.M., and 4:45 P.M.*

Second class: 10 A.M., 11 A.M., noon, 1 P.M., 2:15 P.M., 3:15 P.M., 4:30 P.M., 5:30 P.M., and 6:30 P.M.

Car

The highways in this area have improved immensely in recent years. The roads from Chetumal to Mahahual, Tulum, and Xpujil have transformed from isolated adventure roads to modern highways with very few potholes.

GETTING AROUND

Chetumal is a relatively large city, but the parts most travelers will be interested in are all within easy walking distance—mostly along Avenida de los Héroes in fact. The exception is the main bus terminal and Mercado Nuevo (where you catch buses to Belize), both of which are 10–12 grubby blocks from the center. A cab to either terminal, or anywhere around town, costs US$1.25.

There is no public transportation to either archaeological zone. Highway 186, however, leads you past both turnoffs. The bumpy turn-off to **Dzibanché** is about 50 kilometers (31 miles) east of Chetumal and runs north for 24 kilometers (14.9 miles) before getting to the site. The turnoff to **Kohunlich** is three kilometers (1.9 miles) farther west on Highway 186. This paved road runs a smooth 8.5 kilometers (5.3 miles) south before getting to the site.

The State of Yucatán

Yucatán is a state that clings to its past, and not without reason—it is home to a stunning array of Mayan ruins and fascinating colonial-area haciendas, beautiful city-bound *casonas* (colonial mansions), and traditional indigenous villages. Visitors come to be awed by centuries-old churches, to climb ancient stone pyramids, and to marvel at Mayan hieroglyphics. Many travelers are surprised by parts of the story they did not know—the vast henequen plantations where indigenous people labored in slave-like conditions and the massive uprising in the mid-1800s in which well-organized Mayan rebels nearly expelled white colonizers from the Yucatán Peninsula altogether.

This is the place where a massive asteroid hit the earth 65 million years ago, killing the dinosaurs and opening the ecological door to mammals and eventually humans. It is also home to an intriguing array of flora and fauna; almost 500 species of birds (including the world's largest colony of nesting American flamingos) and one of the continent's most beautiful orchids *(Rhyncholaelia digbyana)* are found here.

Yucatán state is a triangle-shaped area bordered by the Gulf of Mexico to the north, the

Must-Sees

M **Museum of Anthropology and Museo MACAY:** In Mérida, two of the Yucatán's best museums span the ages from the carved stone and painted pottery of ancient Mayans to the molded bronze and painted canvases of modern-day Yucatecan artists (page 242).

M **Domingo en Mérida:** Sunday in Mérida is a weekly celebration of the city and by the city. Locals and tourists alike throng to the main plaza for street food, music and dance performances, and the simple joy of being there (page 245).

M **Cenotes de Cuzamá:** Ride a rickety horse-drawn trolley through abandoned henequen fields to three spectacular cenotes perfect for swimming. At two of them, you climb down ladders through openings in the cavern roof to the iridescent blue water below (page 274).

M **Uxmal Archaeological Zone:** Soaring graceful structures built on rolling terrain make this one of the most beautiful Mayan ruins that

you'll ever see. Be sure to stick around for the sound and light show—it beats the one at Chichén Itzá (page 275).

M **Labná Archaeological Zone:** The best of the four smaller Puuc route sites, this set of ruins features a famous stone archway and an impressive palace covered in ornate stone masks (page 285).

M **Hacienda Tabi:** Sweeping stone stairs frame the entryway of this grand hacienda and former sugar plantation, a relic of Yucatán's fascinating but little-discussed boom years. Not far from Loltún caves, but seldom visited (page 288).

M **Flamingo Tours:** Yucatán is home to the largest colony of the biggest and pinkest flamingos in the world. Boat tours in Celestún (page 290) and Río Lagartos (page 329) and an observation platform at Uaymitún Reserve (page 301) get you close to these peculiar birds.

M **Convento de San Antonio de Padua:** This stately and distinctive yellow church and convent in Izamal was built on top of—and with stones taken from—one of the three most important Mayan temples. Glyphs on some of the pilfered stones are still visible in the convent walls (page 304).

M **Chichén Itzá Archaeological Zone:** One of the most well-known ancient ruins is also one of the most heavily visited. Arrive early to enjoy the site's awesome scale and superlative design, including the largest ball court in the Mayan world (page 310).

M **Ek' Balam Archaeological Zone:** Growing in popularity but still relatively unknown, this small site features a spectacular stucco mural with winged angel-like figures (page 323).

THE STATE OF YUCATÁN

Museum of Anthropology and Museo MACAY

Flamingo Tours

Domingo en Mérida

Convento de San Antonio de Padua

Flamingo Tours

Cenotes de Cuzamá

Ek' Balam

Uxmal

Chichén Itzá

Hacienda Tabi

Labná

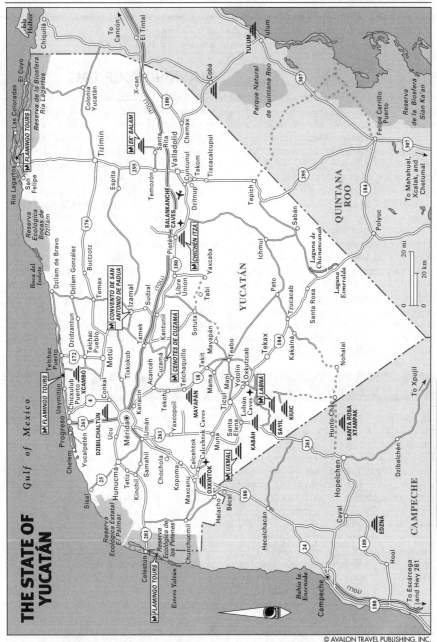

THE STATE OF YUCATÁN

state of Quintana Roo to the east, and the state of Campeche to the west. It occupies 38,508 square kilometers (14,868 square miles) and boasts a population of more than two million people. The state has virtually no hills, surface lakes, or rivers—rainwater seeps down through cracks in the peninsula's thick limestone cap into underground rivers and natural wells called cenotes. Mérida—Yucatán's capital city—is famous across Mexico for being a hot place, and justifiably so. The average daytime temperature April–July is 37°C (97°F) and humidity is high; but the same season is marked by almost daily rain showers, which provide cooling relief, and most travelers adapt quickly to the climate.

Tourism is the state's principal industry. Though Mérida has long been a vibrant city, the state (and peninsula as a whole) was a virtual backwater until well into the 20th century when the advent of beach resorts along the Caribbean coast brought foreign tourism to the region. But this remains Mayan country and many Yucatecans speak the same language and pursue the same industries that their predecessors have for millennia, including fishing, salt and honey production and small-scale agriculture. In some cases, even the methods and technologies remain the same.

PLANNING YOUR TIME

The state of Yucatán has the peninsula's best and biggest colonial city, Mérida, the most-famous Mayan ruins, and great bird-watching and other outdoors activities. You can sample a little of everything in five days, but you won't be sorry to have a week or more. Mérida is an attractive and interesting city; budget at least two days to see the museums and churches and to soak up its famously rich cultural scene. Next, hit the ruins. You'll want at least two days for this—one to visit the Puuc Route and another to visit Chichén Itzá and its surroundings. That said, you can easily spend four full days exploring the ruins, plus the many caves, haciendas, and colonial towns in the area. (And some people spend weeks!) Finally, leave a day to visit the flamingos, either in Celestún or Río Lagartos—this is one of the best places in the world to observe these bright pink birds.

Mérida

Mérida bursts with art and culture, in a way unrivaled by any other city on the Yucatán Peninsula (and few in the whole country). The city's rich artistic and architectural heritage can be enjoyed in its museums, monuments, churches, colonial mansions, and beautiful government buildings, while tree-lined parks and plazas offer a peek into ordinary Mexican life. But it is the city's commitment to music and dance that really sets it apart, with city-sponsored performances held every single day, all year long. *Ballet folklórico*—regional dances performed to orchestral music and featuring traditional costumes—is especially popular, with music from the town's professional band; performances are always well attended by locals and tourists alike. Every Saturday night one of Mérida's main avenues is closed and a series of live bands play salsa and merengue while people dance in the street. Modern music, dance, film and art performances, and expositions are held in three different theaters and numerous galleries and performance spaces—and that's just in the center of town. Mérida is known around the state and the country as *la Ciudad Blanca* (the White City) in reference to the once-whitewashed buildings and traditional white cotton clothing worn by residents.

With a million residents, Mérida is the largest city on the Yucatán Peninsula. Although one of the loveliest colonial cities in the region and in the country, the state capital harbors an oppressive and brutal past. Mérida was founded January 6, 1542, by Francisco de Montejo "El Mozo" (The Younger) to celebrate his victory over indigenous defenders after 15 years of conflict. Enslaved Mayans were forced to dismantle their temples and palaces and use the materials to build homes, offices, cathedrals, and parks they were not permitted to enjoy.

SIGHTS

Plaza de la Independencia

Surrounded by aristocratic colonial buildings, the large green central plaza is an oasis in the middle of this busy town. This is a city where people stroll the streets after dark and feel safe

and comfortable. Men in woven panama hats and guayaberas gather in the morning; women in colorful *huipiles* sit in the shade or tend small sidewalk stands, and white, S-shaped chairs are quaint reminders of former courtship rituals.

La Catedral

The most prominent building on the plaza is the cathedral. Built from 1561 to 1598 with stones taken from Mayan structures on-site, it's one of the oldest buildings on the continent. The architecture prevalent in Spain at

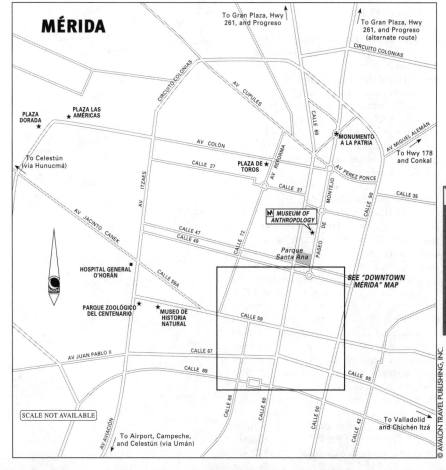

the time is reflected in the Moorish style of the two towers. Overall, though, the exterior and interior are stark in comparison to some of the ornately adorned churches in other parts of Mexico—this is partly owing the traditional austerity of Franciscan design, and partly to damage and looting that took place during the Caste War and the 1910 revolution. In the right-hand nave, near the altar, note the painting of the meeting between the nobles of the Mayan Xiu clan and the Spanish invaders in 1541. This solemnly portrays the Xiu tribe joining the Spaniards as allies—a trust that was violated, marking the beginning of the end of the Mayan regime.

On the left side of the church, a small but elaborately decorated iron and glass chapel houses a revered image of Christ called **El Cristo de las Ampollas** (Christ of the Blisters), carved from a tree in Ichmul that is said to have been engulfed in flames but remained undamaged. Reportedly the wooden statue then went through another fire in a church, this time developing blisters as living skin would. Though the statue is honored with a fiesta each September, every Sunday sees the devout crowding around to touch the statue and sigh a brief prayer.

Los Palacios Gobernales

On the northeast corner of the Plaza de la Independencia is the **Palacio de Gobierno,** the seat of government offices for the state of Yucatán. Inside and in the upper galleries, you'll find striking abstract paintings created by the famous Mérida-born artist Fernando Castro Pacheco. Created between 1971 and 1974, these works of art depict the history of the region—from the time of the ancient Mayans to modern-day Mexico. Restoration of these works—under the supervision of Pacheco himself—was completed in 2004 by four professional restoration artists from the Centro de Restauracion de Bellas Artes in Mexico City. The building is open to the public from 8 A.M.–10 P.M. daily and entry is free of charge.

On the west side of the Plaza de la Independencia you'll find the **Palacio Municipal.** This architectural beauty dates from 1543 and

The State of Yucatán

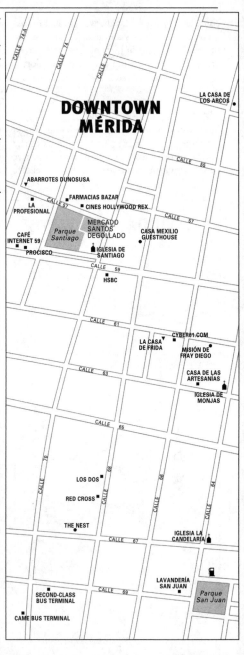

DOWNTOWN MÉRIDA

LA CASA DE LOS ARCOS

CALLE 71-A
CALLE 74
CALLE 72
CALLE 55
CALLE 57

ABARROTES DUNOSUSA

FARMACIAS BAZAR
CALLE 57
CINES HOLLYWOOD REX
LA PROFESIONAL

CAFÉ INTERNET 59
Parque Santiago
MERCADO SANTOS DEGOLLADO
CASA MEXILIO GUESTHOUSE
PROCISCO
IGLESIA DE SANTIAGO

CALLE 59
HSBC

CALLE 61

CYBER81.COM
LA CASA DE FRIDA
MISIÓN DE FRAY DIEGO

CALLE 63
CASA DE LAS ARTESANÍAS
IGLESIA DE MONJAS

CALLE 65

CALLE 70
LOS DOS
CALLE 68
RED CROSS
CALLE 66
CALLE 64
THE NEST
IGLESIA LA CANDELARIA
CALLE 67

LAVANDERÍA SAN JUAN
Parque San Juan
SECOND-CLASS BUS TERMINAL
CALLE 69
CAME BUS TERMINAL

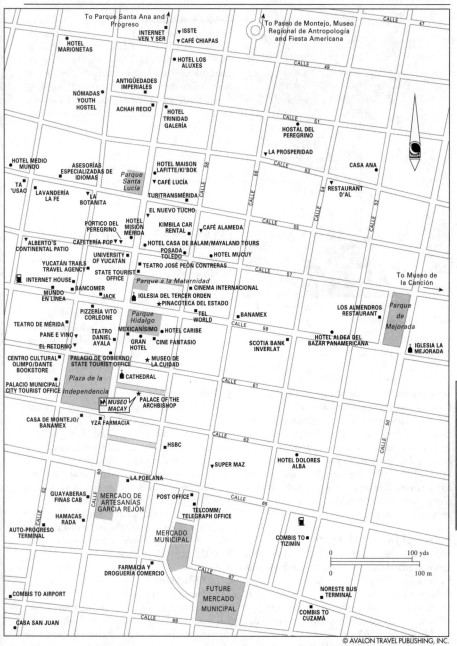

To Parque Santa Ana and Progreso

INTERNET VEN Y SER

ISSTE
CAFÉ CHIAPAS

To Paseo de Montejo, Museo Regional de Antropología and Fiesta Americana

HOTEL MARIONETAS

HOTEL LOS ALUXES

ANTIGÜEDADES IMPERIALES

NÓMADAS YOUTH HOSTEL

ACHAH RECIO

HOTEL TRINIDAD GALERÍA

HOSTAL DEL PEREGRINO

LA PROSPERIDAD

HOTEL MEDIO MUNDO

ASESORÍAS ESPECIALIZADAS DE IDIOMAS

Parque Santa Lucía

HOTEL MAISON LAFITTE/KI'BOK

CAFÉ LUCÍA

CASA ANA

TA 'USAO

LAVANDERÍA LA FE

LA BOTANITA

TURITRANSMÉRIDA

RESTAURANT D'AL

EL NUEVO TUCHO

PÓRTICO DEL PEREGRINO

HOTEL MISIÓN MÉRIDA

KIMBILA CAR RENTAL

CAFÉ ALAMEDA

CAFETERÍA POP

HOTEL CASA DE BALAM/MAYALAND TOURS

ALBERTO'S CONTINENTAL PATIO

UNIVERSITY OF YUCATAN

POSADA TOLEDO

HOTEL MUCUY

YUCATÁN TRAILS TRAVEL AGENCY

STATE TOURIST OFFICE

TEATRO JOSÉ PEÓN CONTRERAS

To Museo de la Canción

INTERNET HOUSE

Parque a la Maternidad

CINEMA INTERNACIONAL

BANCOMER

JACK

IGLESIA DEL TERCER ORDEN

MUNDO EN LÍNEA

PINACOTECA DEL ESTADO

PIZZERÍA VITO CORLEONE

Parque Hidalgo

TEL WORLD

BANAMEX

LOS ALMENDROS RESTAURANT

Parque de Mejorada

TEATRO DE MÉRIDA

PANE E VINO

TEATRO DANIEL AYALA

MEXICANÍSIMO

HOTEL CARIBE

GRAN HOTEL

CINE FANTASIO

SCOTIA BANK INVERLAT

HOTEL ALDEA DEL BAZAR PANAMERICANA

EL RETORNO

CENTRO CULTURAL OLIMPO/DANTE BOOKSTORE

PALACIO DE GOBIERNO/ STATE TOURIST OFFICE

MUSEO DE LA CIUDAD

IGLESIA LA MEJORADA

PALACIO MUNICIPAL/ CITY TOURIST OFFICE

Plaza de la Independencia

CATHEDRAL

MUSEO MACAY

PALACE OF THE ARCHBISHOP

CASA DE MONTEJO/ BANAMEX

YZA FARMACIA

HSBC

SUPER MAZ

HOTEL DOLORES ALBA

LA POBLANA

GUAYABERAS, FINAS CAB

MERCADO DE ARTESANÍAS GARCÍA REJÓN

POST OFFICE

TELCOMM/ TELEGRAPH OFFICE

HAMACAS RADA

AUTO-PROGRESO TERMINAL

MERCADO MUNICIPAL

COMBIS TO TIZIMÍN

COMBIS TO AIRPORT

FARMACIA Y DROGUERÍA COMERCIO

FUTURE MERCADO MUNICIPAL

NORESTE BUS TERMINAL

COMBIS TO CUZAMÁ

CASA SAN JUAN

0   100 yds
0   100 m

CALLE 47
CALLE 49
CALLE 51
CALLE 53
CALLE 55
CALLE 57
CALLE 59
CALLE 61
CALLE 63
CALLE 65
CALLE 67
CALLE 69

CALLE 58
CALLE 56
CALLE 54
CALLE 52
CALLE 60
CALLE 62
CALLE 50

The State of Yucatán

Mérida's cathedral is home to the revered El Cristo de las Ampollas.

serves as Mérida's city hall. The building was renovated in the mid-1800s.

One of the most outstanding structures in Mérida sits on Paseo de Montejo: the **Palacio Cantón** (Paseo de Montejo at Calle 43). Designed by the same architect who built the Teatro Peón Contreras, this impressive rococo-facade building was built 1909–1911 for Gral. Francisco Cantón Rosado, a former governor of Yucatán. It served as the official state residence 1948–1960 and in 1977 became the city's **Museo Regional de Antropología** (Regional Museum of Anthropology). (See *Museum of Anthropology.*)

Palace of the Archbishop

Adjacent to the cathedral facing the plaza, this sprawling building has gone through various incarnations. Originally the home of the archbishop, it became the local military post after the revolution, and eventually—after being remodeled—transformed into its current state: the **Museo MACAY** or the museum of contemporary art. (See *Museo MACAY.*)

Casa de Montejo

Facing the southern edge of the central plaza is the Banamex Bank building, once the home of Francisco de Montejo "El Mozo" (The Younger). The building was constructed in 1542 by Mayan slaves. Note the carvings of Spaniards standing at attention with their feet planted firmly on the heads of the Mayans—a lasting reminder of Spanish tyranny. It is said that 13 generations of Montejos lived in the house until it was sold to Banamex in 1980. Today the bank takes up the entire structure, including a large second floor. You can see the enormous patio during normal bank hours (9 A.M.–4 P.M. Mon.–Fri., 10 A.M.–2 P.M. Sat.).

Museum of Anthropology

In a beautifully renovated *casona,* the Museo Regional de Antropología (Palacio Cantón, Paseo de Montejo No. 485 at Calle 43, tel. 999/923-0557, palacio.canton@inah.gob.mx, 8 A.M.–8 P.M. Tues.–Sat., 8 A.M.–2 P.M. Sun., US$3) houses one of the finest collections of Mayan artifacts in the Yucatán Peninsula, including objects brought up from the sacred well at Chichén Itzá. An excellent complement to a visit to any of the archaeological sites in the region.

Museo MACAY

Museo MACAY (Pasaje Revolucion between Calles 58 and 60, tel. 999/928-3236, www .macay.org, 10 A.M.–6 P.M. Wed.–Mon., US$2) is a fantastic modern art museum housed in a rambling building that was once physically connected to the cathedral. It boasts an impressive collection of Yucatecan modern art, including works by Fernando Castro Pacheco and Fernando García Ponce, and has 11 rooms that are dedicated to displaying visiting works of art. To arrange a free private tour, call tel. 999/928-3191. Worth a stop.

Other Museums

The **Museo de la Cuidad** (Calle 58 at Calle 61, 8 A.M.–8 P.M. Tues.–Fri. and 8 A.M.–2 P.M. Sat. and Sun., free) is a museum dedicated exclusively to the history of the development of Mérida. Housed in a former colonial church,

© LIZA PRADO CHANDLER

The State of Yucatán

a section of the ornate Casa de Montejo

the exhibits include Mayan artifacts, antique weapons and maps, photographs, and various scale models. Explanations are in both Spanish and English (the latter are surprisingly well translated) and staff members happily answer questions.

The **Museo de la Canción** (Calle 57 No. 464-A at Calle 48, tel. 999/923-7224, 9 A.M.–5 P.M. Tues.–Fri. and 9 A.M.–3 P.M. Sat. and Sun., free) is dedicated to teaching the public about the development of Yucatecan music and its artists. Divided into five areas, the first provides a historical explanation of the region's music, from its beginnings in the late 1800s to present day. The remaining areas are homages to Yucatan's most famous composers, singers, and musicians and contain portraits, instruments, and some personal belongings. Explanations—unfortunately—are only in Spanish. The museum also hosts a free concert on the last Wednesday of every month. Beginning at 9 P.M. and continuing until 10:30 P.M., the music featured is dedicated to Yucatecan musicians born in that month.

Easy to miss, the **Pinacoteca del Estado Juan Gamboa Guzman** (Calle 59 be-

tween Calles 58 and 60, tel. 999/924-5233, 8 A.M.–8 P.M. Tues.–Sat. and 8 A.M.–2 P.M. Sun., US$2.50) is on two floors of an annex to an abandoned church. It houses works by the famous Yucatecan painter Juan Gamboa Guzman, bronze statutes by Enrique Gottidiener, an influential Mexican artist who lived and died in Mérida, and a series of anonymous paintings and busts dating from the 19th century, including several of Yucatecan governors and Mexican presidents.

Not really worth a visit, the **Museo de Historia Natural** (Calle 59 No. 648 between Calles 84 and 84-A, tel. 999/924-0994, museo hn@merida.gob.mx, 9 A.M.–3 P.M. Tues.–Sun., US$1, free Sun.) is a museum with exhibits that look as if they were mounted in the early '70s and haven't been touched since. That said, the museum does a decent job of explaining the basics of the solar system, the development of Earth, and the animals and environments that make up the planet. Explanations, however, are in Spanish only.

Conkal, a small town a few minutes northeast of Mérida, is home to the **Ex-Convento de San Francisco de Assisi: Museo de Arte**

SIGN LANGUAGE

As you navigate through the numbered streets of Mérida, you'll soon begin noticing whimsical street signs—carved pictures of animals, household items, people—adorning street corners. Recently affixed, these signs pay homage to Mérida's past when, because of the high illiteracy rate, the city government hung painted wooden signs of familiar figures so that every inhabitant could find an address. Typically, these signs directly related to establishments or sights nearby: a pair of nuns to signal a convent, a violin to indicate an instrument maker, a bull to direct people to the Plaza de Toros (bullring). Look around, and you'll not only get a flavor of where things were in Mérida's past, but also where they still might be today.

© LIZA PRADO CHANDLER

Signs like these can be seen throughout downtown Mérida.

Sacro en Yucatán (behind the church in the main plaza, tel. 999/912-4198, 10 A.M.–6 P.M. Mon.–Sat., free), a museum opened in 2001 and housed in a beautifully remodeled ex-convent. While its permanent collection of sacred art is far from impressive and almost not worth a side trip, it often has excellent visiting exhibits. Call or check with the tourist office in Mérida.

Dzibilchaltún

A quick 25-minute trip from Mérida on Highway 261 will bring you to the important but somewhat underwhelming archaeological site of Dzibilchaltún (dzee-beel-chawl-TOON) (turnoff at Hwy. 261 Km. 15, 8 A.M.–5 P.M. daily, US$5, US$2.60 fee for video camera use). Recognized as the oldest continuously used Mayan ceremonial and administrative center on the peninsula, it was inhabited as early as 1000 B.C. through to the arrival of the Spanish. The intriguing **Temple of the Seven Dolls** is the only known Mayan temple with windows, and its orientation suggests it was used for astronomical observations. The temple is named for a set of small clay figures that were found inside during excavation. The seven dolls and other artifacts are displayed in

the site's exceptional **Museo del Pueblo Maya** (8 A.M.–4 P.M. Tues.–Sun.), which focuses not only on the archaeology of Dzibilchaltún but the area's cultural and economic development from ancient times to today; explanations are in Spanish and English. A 350-meter/1,148-foot-long ecological path joins the museum to the ruins. Along the way, trees and plants are labeled and small palapa-roofed billboards provide explanations of local flora and fauna. The cenote on-site—Xlacah—is still used as a swimming hole, although when we stopped by, it was filled with a few too many water lilies for comfort.

If you don't have a car, you can catch a *combi* (Volkswagen minivan) in Parque San Juan (Calle 69 between Calles 62 and 64) that will drop you off in front of the site (US$1). You also can take a bus headed to Progreso, which will drop you off on the highway about one kilometer (0.6 mile) away (US$1; see *Getting There*). In either case, be sure to double-check when the last *combi* or bus passes on its way back to Mérida.

Locals and tourists alike take to dancing in the streets every Saturday night.

ENTERTAINMENT AND EVENTS

As one of Mexico's colonial shining stars, Mérida also is the region's cultural supernova. With fantastic museums, free nightly performances around town, four theaters, five cinemas, art galleries, a planetarium, and a bullring, there is absolutely something for everyone.

Music and Dance

Music is heard all over Mérida, and dancing is a way of life. Informal free concerts and other entertainment are regularly presented for Mérida's residents and visitors at parks and plazas throughout the city. Every Saturday night, Calle 60 is closed from the main plaza past Parque Santa Lucía and bands hired by the various restaurants play salsa and merenque and everyone dances in the streets. Sunday, of course, features traditional music and dance performances in the center. In fact, all of the regularly scheduled events throughout the week involve music and dancing in some way, whether to watch or to join in. (See the *Mérida's Weekly Cultural Events* sidebar for details.)

 Domingo en Mérida

Sunday is a wonderful day in Mérida. The streets in the heart of the city around the plazas are closed to traffic. Everyone dresses in their Sunday best and comes downtown, where sidewalk cafés do a lively business, as do the dozens of pushcarts selling drinks, *tortas* (sandwiches), *elote* (corn on the cob), and sweets. There are two excellent folkloric dance performances in the main square at 1 and 3 P.M.—for a good seat, grab some street food and stake out a spot on the bleachers a half hour early. At Parque Santa Lucía, a miniflea market is followed by a performance of Yucatecan music. Parque Hidalgo often has art displays and marimba music.

Theater

Built during Mérida's boom in the early 1900s, **Teatro José Peón Contreras** (Calle 60 at 57, tel. 999/924-3954, box office hours 9 A.M.–9 P.M. Tues.–Sat., 9 A.M.–3 P.M. Sun.) is a beautiful and mammoth building: The main staircase is made of Carrara marble and various murals and paintings adorn the walls

MÉRIDA'S WEEKLY CULTURAL EVENTS

Sunday

Domingo en Mérida: shopping and entertainment near the main plaza (10 A.M.–6 P.M.)
Parque Santa Lucía: antiques bazaar and live regional music
Plaza Independencia: handicrafts market
Parque Hidalgo: live marimba music
Palacio Municipal: regional dance performances (1 and 3 P.M.)

Monday

Palacio Municipal: regional dance performance (9 P.M.)

Tuesday

Parque Santiago: live big band music and dancing (8:30 P.M.)
Centro Cultural de Mérida Olimpo: classical guitar and ballad performance (8:30 P.M.)

Wednesday

Jardín de los Compositores: spoken-word performance (9 P.M.)

Thursday

Parque Santa Lucía: regional dance, music, and spoken-word performances (9 P.M.)

Friday

Universidad de Yucatán: live regional music performance (9 P.M., US$1)

Saturday

Paseo de Montejo at Calle 47: Noche Méxicana—food stalls, handicrafts booths, live music, and dance performances (7–11 P.M.)
Calle 60 (between Plaza Independencia and Calle 53): Corazón de Mérida—street closes for live bands, dancing, and outdoor eating (8 P.M.–1 A.M.)

and ceiling. Today, the theater hosts mostly musical concerts and *ballet folklórico* performances. For a listing of events, ask at the box office or check with the city's tourist information center, at the corner of the theater building. When there aren't rehearsals, you also can take a look around the theater for free from 9 A.M.–6 P.M.

Teatro Mérida (Calle 62 No. 495 between Calles 59 and 61, tel. 999/924-0040, 9:30 A.M.–9 P.M. Tues.–Sun.) is an art-deco venue housing a main theater and two smaller ones. It's an alternative artsy place—productions vary from modern dance festivals to international art films. Definitely worth stopping to check out what's playing.

Teatro Daniel Ayala (Calle 60 No. 499 between Calles 59 and 61, tel. 999/924-0277, 9 A.M.–9 P.M. Tues.–Sun.) is a huge but modest theater used mainly for dramatic performances. Prices tend to be very accessible.

Cultural Center and Planetarium

Centro Cultural de Mérida Olimpo (Calle 61 at 62, tel. 999/942-0000, ext. 477, 10 A.M.–10 P.M. Tues.–Sun.) is a cultural center housed in an award-winning ultramodern building. Here, there are exhibition halls, a research li-

© LIZA PRADO CHANDLER

Ballet folklórico is performed several times per week in Mérida.

brary, a planetarium, and theaters where films are shown and concerts are held. The programming is chock-full each month—check the bulletin board at the entrance for listings. One concert that never fails is the *Noche de Trova,* which takes place every Tuesday at 8:30 P.M. and is free.

City Tours

There are two city bus tours that you can choose from to get a good lay of the land when you first arrive in Mérida. Transportadora Turistica Carnaval's **Camioncitos Multicolores** (Calle 55 at Calle 60, tel. 999/927-6119, US$7 adult, US$4 child) offers a two-hour guided driving tour of the city in English and in Spanish. Drive-bys include the historical center as well as outlying neighborhoods. Tours leave at 10 A.M., 1 P.M., 4 P.M., and 7 P.M. Monday–Saturday, 10 A.M. and 1 P.M. Sunday. Look for the multicolored bus in front of Parque Santa Lucía on Calle 55. Reservations accepted but not necessary.

Turibus Ciruito Turístico (US$9 adult, US$4.50 child, 9 A.M.–9 P.M. daily, www.turibus.com.mx) operates a fleet of big red modern double-decker tourist buses that have all-day

"hop-on hop-off" service along a preset route; the stops include, in this order, Fiesta Americana Hotel/Shopping Area, the main plaza, Museum of Anthropology, Itzimná church and park, Gran Plaza mall, and the Monumento a la Patria. The tour includes multilingual recorded explanations of various historical buildings and points of interest along the way. Buses should pass by any given stop every 45 minutes.

The **city tourist office** (Palacio Municipal, Calle 62 between 61 and 63, tel. 999/942-0000, ext. 133, 8 A.M.–9 P.M. Mon.–Sat., 8 A.M.–2 P.M. Sun.) offers a free walking tour Monday–Saturday at 9:30 A.M. in English and Spanish. The tour lasts 1.5 hours and focuses on the buildings around the Plaza de la Independencia. To sign up, just go to the tourism office at 9:20 A.M. on the day you'd like to join the group.

La Calesa

Mérida's narrow streets were originally designed for *calesas* (horse-drawn buggies) and you can still ride one through the old aristocratic neighborhoods where mansions with carved facades, stone gargoyles, and wrought-iron fences still stand (although some much better than others). Sunday is the best day to hire a *calesa* as many streets are closed to vehicular traffic and the rest are relatively quiet; other days, you'll have to share the streets with the exhaust from passing cars. The easiest places to hire a *calesa* is on Calle 61 at Plaza de la Independencia and in front of the Hotel Fiesta Americana (Paseo de Montejo at Av. Colón). Drivers are typically at both sites 8 A.M.–midnight daily. Prices range US$17–26 and tours last 40 minutes–one hour. Definitely negotiate and agree upon a price before sitting down for the ride.

Bullfights

Interested in what makes this sport so popular in Mexico? You can catch a *corrida* (literally, a running) at the **Plaza de Toros** (Calle 72 at 33). Unless you want to work on your tan, opt for the premium *sombra* (shade) seats—the extra charge is worth every bead of sweat you save. You can buy tickets at the bullring's ticket office the day of the event or from a table that's set up next to

The State of Yucatán

the entrance to the Olimpo—they typically cost US$3.50–5.25 but can run a little higher depending on the caliber of the bullfighter. Look around the Plaza de la Independencia for posters advertising the next *corrida* or ask at the tourist office for more information.

Bars and Discos

La Botanita (Calle 62 at Calle 55, tel. 999/928-1867, noon–1 A.M. Mon.–Sat., noon–7 P.M. Sun., no cover) is a small local hangout where you can sit back, drink a few beers, and listen to the live *trova* (guitar ballads) played 3–4 P.M. and 9 P.M.–midnight Tues.–Sunday. Free appetizers are brought with each round of drinks.

Popular with travelers, **Amaro** (Calle 59 No. 507 between 60 and 62, tel. 999/928-2451, 11 A.M.–midnight daily, no cover) is a great place to get a drink and to listen to music—candlelit tables surround a charming courtyard while live *trova* is played Wednesday through Saturday beginning at 9:30 P.M. And the food? It's overpriced—mostly small portions of shredded veggies in various incarnations.

Azul Picante (Calle 60 between Calles 53 and 55, 9 P.M.–3 A.M. Wed.–Sat., US$2.75) is a hot Latin music dance spot—live salsa and merengue bands keep the crowd moving into the wee hours of the night. On Saturdays, live bands often play outdoors—you'll be sure to see a few people spinning on Calle 60—experts and novices alike. Popular with both locals and travelers.

KY60 (Calle 60 between Calles 53 and 55, tel. 999/924-2289, 10 P.M.–3 A.M. daily, free) is a hipster bar with a DJ spinning everything from Mexican rock to hard-core rap. (And in case you were wondering—"KY" refers to the pronunciation of those letters in Spanish, which sounds like "Calle.")

Ay Caray!(Calle 60 between Calles 53 and 55, 9:30 P.M.–3 A.M. daily, US$4.50 women, US$10.50 men) is a rock bar and disco that gets especially busy on Saturday nights when live bands are typically featured. Open bar comes with the cover. For a great deal, get there before 10:30 P.M. on Fridays and Saturdays—men get in for US$9, women walk in for free.

For Kids

Sunday is family day in Mexico, and Mérida is no exception. The tree-shaded parks are popular for picnicking, playing ball, and buying giant colorful balloons and other fanciful goods sold by vendors.

Parque Zoológico del Centenario (Av. Itzaes at Calle 59, 8 A.M.–5 P.M. Tues.–Sun., free) is the city zoo and a popular spot for families, especially on weekends. The park has kiddy rides, playgrounds, and an overwhelming number of concession stands. The zoo has a decent selection of animals but the somewhat cramped quarters can be upsetting if you're used to seeing animals housed in more spacious conditions. The aquarium, with its extensive goldfish wing, is skippable. On Sundays, magicians, clowns, puppets, and theater groups come out in full force to entertain children and their parents.

Titeradas (Calle 55 No. 514-A between Calles 62 and 64, tel. 999/923-0705) is a popular puppet theater that has performances every Sunday at 11 A.M. and 5 P.M. While it's geared toward children, parents seem to enjoy the shows tremendously. The season runs September–January. Prices vary widely depending on the show; reservations recommended.

Cinema

Just up the street from the Plaza de la Independencia, **Teatro Mérida** (Calle 62 No. 495 between Calles 59 and 61, tel. 999/924-0040) often shows international and alternative art films.

In Parque Hidalgo, **Cine Fantasio** (Calle 59 at Calle 60, tel. 999/942-1414, US$3, US$2 all day Tues. and Wed., and first show on Mon. and Thurs.) is the most centrally located of the cinemas featuring current films.

Nearby, the easy-to-miss **Cinema Internacional** (Calle 58 between Calles 55 and 57, tel. 999/923-0250, US$3, US$2 all day Tues. and Wed.) has one screen.

Cines Hollywood Rex (Calle 57 between Calles 70 and 72, tel. 999/928-5980, US$3, US$2 all day Tues. and Wed., first show on Mon. and Thurs., and before 3 P.M. on Sun.)

© LIZA PRADO CHANDLER

Teatro Mérida is an art deco beauty in its own right.

shows films from the United States and Mexico on its two screens.

For a megaplex, head to either of the two shopping malls: Gran Plaza houses **Hollywood Cinema** (tel. 999/944-7890, US$4 Fri.–Tues., US$2 Wed.–Thurs.) and **Hollywood Cinema Platinum VIP** (tel. 999/942-1429 for reservations, US$7 Thurs.–Tues., US$4 Wed.), with its comfy seats, extensive menu, and waiters. A little closer to the center of town, Plaza America has the popular **Cinepolis** (tel. 999/987-6003, US$4 Thurs.–Tues., US$3 Wed.) inside its doors.

Bird Festival

Since 2001, an **Annual Bird Festival** has been held in Mérida. For a week, birders from around the world gather to attend conferences, to see exhibits, and to observe (or at least get a glimpse of!) the 430 bird species registered in the state. It's a well-attended conference and one that welcomes amateurs and experts alike. It's a great way to see the state and to learn about its myriad birds. For more information, check out www.yucatanbirds.org.mx

or contact **Ecoturísmo Yucatán** (Calle 3 No. 235 between 32A and 34, Col. Pensiones, tel. 999/920-2772, www.ecoyuc.com.mx).

SHOPPING

If there is any place in the Yucatán Peninsula where you are guaranteed to find something that you absolutely cannot resist, it'll be in Mérida. From small family-run stores to rambling *artesanía* markets, Mérida attracts the treasures of the region: hammocks, *guayaberas, huipiles,* handcrafted toys, ceramic figurines, *jipi* hats, Mayan replicas…this town will have it. Explore the markets, peek into sidewalk stores, and enjoy the beauties that are made in this part of the world.

Markets

The **Mercado Lucas de Galvez** (Calle 67 between Calles 56 and 58, 8 A.M.–8 P.M. daily)—better known as the **Mercado Municipal**—is a blockwide, two-story building bustling with vendors of all sorts. Here you'll find everything from shoelaces to live chickens. It's an experience all its own, and one worth taking a camera to. The first floor—with its myriad of colors and layers of scents—is where the main action is: You'll see rows of neatly stacked fruits and vegetables, flowers of all hues, beef and pork in discernible forms (you're sure to see a fair share of heads, hooves, and stomachs), mounds of herbs and spices, incense and religious icons, children's toys, rows of women's shoes, stand upon stand of gold jewelry—you name it, you'll probably find it here. The second floor is quieter and directed at tourists: There are Yucatecan handicrafts—*guayaberas,* hand-woven hammocks, sandals, *huipiles*—and also *artesanía* from other parts of the country—silver from Taxco, pottery from Puebla, and masks from Guerrero. And if you get hungry and aren't a stickler about hygiene (it's on the edge, to say the least), there are dozens of restaurants serving cheap local fare on both floors; *comidas corridas* (two-course meals with a drink) cost between US$1–3 but you can also order tacos, tamales, ceviche, and *tortas* for around

The State of Yucatán

US$1 each. In early 2005, the city opened a huge new market building (Calle 54 between Calles 67 and 69), occupying a full city block right behind the old market. The long-term plan is to move all the vendors from the old building to the new one, and tear down the old one to build a park. However, that may take years to complete; for now and the foreseeable future, both buildings are open and functioning as market areas.

An **open-air market** by Parque Maternidad (Calle 60 between Calles 57 and 59, sunset–11 P.M. daily) is often set up in the evenings. Here, you'll find handmade jewelry, batik fabrics, feather art, and clothing from Chiapas and Guatemala.

Artesanía

The superb **Casa de las Artesanías del Estado de Yucatán** (Calle 63 No. 503-A between Calles 64 and 66, tel. 999/928-6676, 9 A.M.–8 P.M. Mon.–Sat., 9 A.M.–2 P.M. Sun.) is a state-owned arts and crafts shop run out of a converted convent. All items—including jewelry, sisal liquor, leather goods, clothing, books, and toys—are bought directly from local artisans and are of the highest quality. Definitely worth a stop.

Near the Mercado Municipal, the **Artesanías Bazar Garcia Rejon** (Calle 60 at Calle 65, 9 A.M.–8 P.M. daily) is a market devoted entirely to local arts and crafts. You'll find a good selection of sandals, clothing, hammocks, and other regional items. Remember to bargain! All items have been marked up in anticipation of the customary exchange. There also is a parking lot conveniently situated underneath the market that charges US$.70 per hour.

Miniaturas (Calle 59 No. 507-A4 between Calles 60 and 62, tel. 999/928-6503, 11 A.M.–9 P.M. Mon.–Sat.) is an eclectic shop devoted to selling *tiny* arts and crafts from every state in Mexico. The selection is excellent and the atmosphere is interestingly strange. Be sure to check out the whimsical papier-mâché skeletons.

Traditional Clothing

The *huipil* (wee-PEEL) is a beautiful type of dress first worn by Mayan women at the insis-tence of hacienda *patrones*. The squared neck and hem are edged with brightly colored embroidery, and a lace-finished petticoat peeks out at the bottom. The similar, long *terno* (TARE-no) is more elaborate than the *huipil* and is worn at parties and celebrations. Both are practical and cool and are worn by many Yucatecan women. Prices vary considerably for these dresses (US$10–550) and depend upon the fabric (cotton, linen, or synthetic) and whether they have been hand-embroidered or machine-made. As with most Yucatecan goods, you'll see them everywhere. Excellent stores to stop by for *huipiles* and *ternos* include **Casa de las Artesanías del Estado de Yucatán** (Calle 63 No. 503-A between Calles 64 and 66, tel. 999/928-6676, 9 A.M.–8 P.M. Mon.–Sat., 9 A.M.–2 P.M. Sun.), **Mexicanísimo** (Parque Hidalgo, Calle 60 No. 496 between Calles 59 and 61, tel. 999/923-8132, www.mexicanisimobymasud.com.mx, 9 A.M.–8:30 P.M. Mon.–Sat.), and **Camisería Camul** (Calle 62 No. 484 between Calles 57 and 59, tel. 999/923-0158, guayaber@sureste.com, 8:30 A.M.–8 P.M. Mon.–Sat., 10 A.M.–1 P.M. Sun.). If the price tags at these stores stop you in your tracks, head to the Mercado Municipal and the **Artesanías Bazar Garcia Rejon** (Calle 60 at Calle 65, 9 A.M.–8 P.M. daily)—both are good options for less expensive dresses.

Guayaberas—button-down shirts with piping—are a staple of menswear in the Yucatán. You'll see them everywhere—from storefronts to market stalls. Typically, *guayaberas* are white, cotton, and short-sleeved, but you'll also find them in pastel tones, in linen or silk, and long-sleeved. If you're in the market for one, head to **Jack** (Calle 59 No. 507-A between Calles 60 and 62, tel. 999/928-6002, www.guay-aberasjack.com.mx, 10 A.M.–9 P.M. Mon.–Sat., 10 A.M.–3 P.M. Sun.), a well-respected maker and vendor of *guayaberas*. The prices are a bit higher than most (US$13–120—prices not ne-gotiable), but the quality of the product is excellent. Jack has a second store nearby on the corner of Calle 61 and 60. Other good options are **Canul Jr.** (Calle 59 No. 507 between Calles 60 and 62, tel. 999/923-1811, 9 A.M.–2 P.M. and 4–8 P.M. Mon.–Fri., 9 A.M.–8 P.M. Sat.,

YUCATECAN HAMMOCKS

Yucatecan *hamacas* (hammocks) have the reputation of being the best in the world. Many locals sleep in them and love it. Cool and easy to store, they make great traveling beds and wonderful souvenirs.

Be sure to look around and try out a few before buying. The vendor will stretch out the hammock if asked. Feel the different types of thread, look at different patterns and color schemes, check out the different sizes, and ask about prices (definitely bargain). You'll soon hone in on one that you like.

Nylon, cotton, or a blend of the two are the typical materials used to make hammocks. Nylon is more resilient but cotton is typically more comfortable. Check out a few to see if you have a preference. If you're ambivalent, consider how much you'll be using it and which serves your needs best. Beware of vendors selling hammocks supposedly made of henequen; unless there has been a major innovation since our research, henequen hammocks (outside of miniature ones that hold fruit) don't exist. Even if they did, they would be incredibly itchy.

Size is another important factor. Hammocks typically come in *individual* (twin), *matrimonial* (queen), and *familiar* (king). While twins may be snug for a person taller than five feet, queen-sized hammocks are roomy enough for most people. Be sure to stretch out a hammock before buying it—a good size is approximately five meters (16.4 feet) in length (one-half of which is the woven section) and 3–5 meters (9.8–16.4 feet) wide. To judge whether a hammock will be long enough for you, hold one end of the body of the hammock to the top of your head and let it drop. The other end of the body should be touching the floor for you to be comfortable (a little extra on the floor is better).

Be sure to check the end strings, which are called *brazos* (arms); there should be at least 100–150 triple loops for a *matrimonial*.

10 A.M.–1 P.M. Sun.) and **Guayaberas Finas Cab** (Calle 60 No. 517 between Calles 65 and 67, tel. 999/928-5127, 8 A.M.–7:30 P.M. Mon.–Fri., 8 A.M.–4 P.M. Sat.)—both have a good variety of well-made shirts. Want one custom-made in red silk with lighting bolts stitched in? Typically a *guayabera* can be made in about a week for off-the-rack prices. Ask a salesperson for details at any of the shops listed above.

If you're in the market for a hat, *jipi* (HE-pee) hats are what you'll find in this town. Made in several villages in the states of Yucatán and Campeche, the finest are made of the jipijapa fiber. They can be folded and stuffed in a pocket and then will pop back into shape when needed. But buyer beware: Many cheaper palms are used and will be ruined if folded. Browse around **Artesanías Bazar García Rejon** (Calle 60 at Calle 65, 9 A.M.–8 P.M. daily) or **Casa de las Artesanías del Estado de Yucatán** (Calle 63 No. 503-A between Calles 64 and 66, tel. 999/928-6676, 9 A.M.–8 P.M. Mon.–Sat., 9 A.M.–2 P.M. Sun.) where you'll see various qualities. Not cheap, *finos* (the most supple) can run as high as US$80.

Hammocks

Yucatán is renowned for producing some of the best hammocks in Mexico. As soon as you arrive, you'll see them everywhere in a variety of colors, lengths, and materials.

If you want a sure thing, head to **La Poblana** (Calle 65 No. 492 between Calles 58 and 60, tel. 999/928-6093, www.poblanahammocks.com.mx, poblanahammocks@hotmail.com, 8:30 A.M.–6:30 P.M. Mon.–Sat.). Run by the Sazu family for more than 70 years, it is one of the most respected hammock shops in the city. It sells excellent hammocks at decent prices and has hundreds in stock. Another great option is **Hamacas Rada** (Calle 60 No. 527 between Calles 65 and 67, tel. 999/924-1208, rada@sureste.com, www.cmerida.com/rada, 9:30 A.M.–6 P.M. Mon.–Fri., 9:30 A.M.–2:30 P.M. Sat.), a wholesaler of cotton hammocks. Just inside the entrance to a parking garage, the third-floor warehouse has piles upon piles of hammocks from which to choose.

Antiques Shops

Antigüedades Imperiales (Calle 51 No. 501 between Calles 60 and 62, tel. 999/923-8087, 10 A.M.–2 P.M. and 5–8 P.M. Mon.–Fri., 10 A.M.–2 P.M. Sat.) specializes in furniture, chandeliers, and bronze sculptures from the 17th to the mid-20th century. Shipments of small items can be handled by the store. Larger items, such as furniture, must be arranged directly by the customer. Remember—it's illegal to export antiques from Mexico without special written permission.

Each Sunday, an **Antique and Artesanía Bazaar** is held at Parque Santa Lucía as part of the weekly city-sponsored Domingo en Mérida. Booths wind through the park and are packed with all sorts of antique tchotchkes, local crafts, and tempting fried *antojitos*. Live Yucatecan music also is played throughout the day and chairs are set up so that you can take it all in. A great place to spend the morning.

Shopping Centers and Malls

Facing the plaza and next to the Palacio de Gobierno, the **Pasaje Picheta** (Calle 61 between Calles 60 and 62, 8 A.M.–midnight daily) is a small shopping center with a few shops selling trendy items, a couple of overpriced Internet cafés, and a handful of fast-food eateries. The food court in the center is a good place to rest if it's raining outdoors and the small art gallery on the mezzanine has interesting and changing expositions. There is also a clean public bathroom on the second floor (US$.25).

Gran Plaza (Calle 50 Diagonal No. 460, tel. 999/944-7658, 10 A.M.–9:30 P.M. daily) is the city's largest and fanciest mall with dozens of upper-end stores and boutiques. The main reason to head out here, though, are the movie theaters: **Hollywood Cinema** (2nd floor, tel. 999/944-7890, US$4 Fri.–Tues., US$2 Wed.–Thurs.) and **Hollywood Cinema Platinum VIP** (2nd floor, tel. 999/942-1429 for reservations at no cost, US$7 Thurs.–Tues., US$4 Wed.), which have mostly standard Hollywood movies.

Plaza America (Calle 56-A No. 451 at Av. Colón, tel. 999/920-2196, 10 A.M.–9:30 P.M. daily) is a standard mall with a J. C. Penney, lots of ATMs, and a **Cinepolis** movie theater, also with Hollywood fare.

Books, Magazines, and Newspapers

Next to the Palacio Municipal, **Dante Olimpo** (Calle 61 No. 502, tel. 999/928-2611, 8 A.M.–10:30 P.M. daily) has an excellent selection of reading material, tapes, and CDs in English. It also has two smaller downtown locations: **Dante 59** on—yes—Calle 59 (between Calles 60 and 62) and **Dante Centro** on Parque Hidalgo.

Librería Juan García Ponce (Calle 60 No. 499 at Calle 61, tel. 999/930-9485, 9 A.M.–9 P.M. daily) is another option for English reading materials. Though small, this shop has a good variety of books, especially regional travel guides and books on the Mayans.

The **Mérida English Library** (Calle 53 No. 524 between Calles 66 and 68, tel. 999/924-8401, englishlibrary@prodigy.net.mx, 9 A.M.–1 P.M. Mon.–Fri. plus 4–7 P.M. Tues.–Thurs., 10 A.M.–1 P.M. Sat.) has a huge selection of English-language books. It is mostly set up for long-term visitors—only registered members can check out books—but tourists can read books in the library's quiet reading area, buy books from the for-sale rack, and join weekly programs and get-togethers. Those include monthly socials, English-Spanish conversation exchanges, AA meetings (in English), and children's story hour—call or email for the current schedules. There is also an excellent bulletin board with postings of tours, short- and long-term housing, items for sale, and so on.

Colloquial Spanish for "It's Used," **Ta 'Usao** (Calle 64 at Calle 55, tel. 999/928-6130, 8:30 A.M.–7 P.M. Mon.–Fri., 8:30 A.M.–2 P.M. Sat.) has a small collection of used books in English thrown in with its bulky collection of used furniture.

If you're looking for English-language newspapers, your best bet is the **Sanborn's** restaurant in front of the Fiesta Americana (Paseo de Montejo at Av. Colón)—it's the only place in town we've seen the *New York Times* sold.

SPORTS AND RECREATION

Golf

Just a 20-minute drive outside of Mérida is the **Club de Golf La Ceiba** (Carr. Mérida-Progreso Km. 14.5, tel. 999/922-0053, 6:30 A.M.– 8 P.M. daily). At the far end of an upscale, gated community, the golf course is open to the public and costs US$60 per person. The green fee includes use of the gym and pool. Clubs also can be rented for an additional US$17.50.

ACCOMMODATIONS

Accommodations suited to all tastes and budgets are in Mérida, from backpacker hostels to high-rise hotels to small boutique inns.

Under US$25

Nómadas Youth Hostel (Calle 62 No. 433 at Calle 51, tel. 999/924-5223, www.nomadastravel.com, camping US$4.25/person, dorm US$5.25, US$14 d with shared bath, US$17.50 d with private bath) is an excellent hostel six blocks north of the plaza. Dorms are clean and comfortable, especially the spacious women-only room. All bunks have an individual light, fan, and locker, and the bathrooms are spotless. Private rooms are medium-sized and have fans—no air-conditioning. Bread, fruit, and coffee are available every morning, and guests can use the fully equipped kitchen (also very clean) at any time. The hostel offers free salsa class 3–7 nights a week and organizes trips to nearby sights for less than you'll find elsewhere. Nómadas also functions as a full-service travel agency (selling, among other things, international plane tickets and ISIC and IH cards) and has tons of info on do-it-yourself excursions. All in all, a great place for backpackers.

M Hostal del Peregrino (Calle 51 No. 488 between Calles 54 and 56, tel. 999/924-5491, www.hostaldelperegrino.com, dorms US$10.50/person, d with private bath and fan US$23.50, with a/c US$28.50, extra person US$6) opened in August 2004—just a week before we passed through, in fact. Operated by two young, friendly Mexico City transplants, this well-recommended hostel occupies a gorgeously refurbished colonial home—the original tile floors are especially fine—and offers spacious fan-cooled dorm rooms and comfortable private rooms, new clean bathrooms, and a TV room and small rooftop bar. Dorm rooms have lockers and mostly single beds (not bunks). A good, and good-sized, breakfast is included, and the bar serves light fare—no kitchen access, however. You can rent bikes (US$2.50/day) and arrange tours, such as mountain biking and snorkeling in cenotes. It's a bit of a walk from downtown (though the owners will collect you at the bus terminal if you call ahead) and prices are higher than the competition's. Still, you'll likely find less of a "scene" here, which older backpackers may appreciate. Show this guidebook for a 10 percent discount.

Another hostel is **The Nest** (Calle 67 No. 547-B between Calles 68 and 70, tel. 999/928-8365, www.nesthostel.com, dorm with fan US$8/person, with a/c US$10/person). Two blocks from the first- and second-class bus stations, dorm rooms have two levels of semiprivate cubicles, each with mattress, locker, fan, light, and a draw curtain. The cubicles are comfy enough but are crammed into rooms too small for the purpose—claustrophobics won't get much sleep here. The hostel has a fully equipped kitchen, a women-only dorm, continental breakfast, and several nice common areas, indoors and out. The Internet café is open 24 hours for guests. Most backpackers still go to Nómadas, but The Nest is a good, clean, convenient alternative.

Other than the hostels, **Hotel Mucuy** (Calle 57 No. 481 between Calles 56 and 58, tel. 999/928-5193, US$15.50 s with fan, US$17.50 d with fan, US$20 s with a/c, US$22 d with a/c) is one of the few decent hotels in this category. The rooms are small and a bit musty but clean. There's a sunny courtyard area where you can lounge and dig into a book from the hotel's large English-language exchange shelf. The owner is a delight and has earned many repeat guests since the hotel opened in 1974.

Hotel Trinidad Galería (Calle 60 No. 456

at Calle 51, tel. 999/923-2463, www.hotel estrinidad.com) and its sister establishment **Hotel Trinidad** (Calle 62 No. 464 at Calle 55, tel. 999/924-2033) are owned by a local art collector, and both are a peculiar blend of budget hotel and modern art gallery. The Galería has a coffee shop, pleasant swimming pool (open to guests of both hotels), and a fine collection of modern art—paintings, sculptures, and carvings crowd the lobby and just about every bit of wall and floor space. However, rooms at both places are fairly dim and musty. Doubles with fan or air-conditioning, some with TV, range US$20–30 and the Hotel Trinidad has a few dorm beds for US$7 a person, all with continental breakfast. (There are also suites, but for the price you'll find better options elsewhere.)

US$25–50

A excellent deal in this range is the 🔃 **Hotel Dolores Alba** (Calle 63 No. 464 between Calles 52 and 54, tel. 999/928-5650, www .doloresalba.com, US$38 s/d). Rooms are immaculately clean, with tile floors, firm beds, and small table and chairs; those on the middle and upper floors get more sunlight. In the courtyard, beach chairs and tables with umbrellas surround a genuinely inviting (and well-used) outdoor swimming pool. The hotel's only (small) drawback is its location—3.5 blocks east of the plaza through a busy market area. Free parking and very friendly service. Cash only.

Another pleasant, affordable option is the **Posada Toledo** (Calle 58 No. 481 at Calle 57, tel. 999/923-1690, US$26 s/d with fan, US$30 s/d with a/c), occupying an old spacious mansion a few blocks from the main park. Older rooms have high ceilings and somewhat aged furniture; newer rooms have better furnishings and modern bathrooms, but not the high ceilings. See if the junior suite is available—two enormous rooms elaborately decorated in blue and violet with a bathroom as big as some of the other bedrooms.

Casa Ana (Calle 52 No. 469 between Calles 51 and 53, tel. 999/924-0005, www.casaana .com, US$30–45) is in a residential neigh-borhood almost 10 blocks from the central park—good if you want a smaller place and don't mind the walk. Four large, airy rooms have simple, attractive decor and face an interior garden with a small pool and artificial waterfall. The rooms have prefabricated bathrooms, with plastic walls and open at the top—a bit less private than some may be accustomed to. The hotel has a pleasant sitting room and very friendly owners.

The lobby at **Hotel Aldea del Bazar Panamericana** (Calle 59 No.455 between Calles 52 and 54, tel. 999/923-9111, www.aldeadelbazar .com, US$36.50 s/d, US$49 s/d with breakfast) has an impressive colonial entrance with columns, carved wood trim, and an ornate statue and fountain. Unfortunately, the rest of the hotel doesn't measure up to the gloriousness of the entryway. Occupying a modernish high-rise in back, rooms are large with black and white tile floors, but they have somewhat drab decor and utilitarian bathrooms. They're not bad, just not as charming as they could be. The swimming pool is long and clean, and the hotel was planning to build a spa for massages, steam baths, and other *tratamientos* (treatments). Note the prices here are "promotional," but are in effect almost year-round. Good thing, as the rooms aren't worth the "real" prices, about US$30 more. Visa, MC, and AmEx accepted.

US$50–100

Three blocks from the main plaza and just up from Parque Santa Lucía, 🔃 **Hotel Maison Lafitte** (Calle 60 No. 472 between Calles 53 and 55, tel. 999/928-1243 or toll-free Mex. tel. 800/711-5048, www.maisonlafitte.com.mx, US$65 s, US$70 d, breakfast included) is more intimate than a high-rise but less homey than a bed-and-breakfast. Rooms, though somewhat small, are modern, spotless, and comfortable; air-conditioning and cable TV are standard. Ground-floor rooms get a fair amount of foot traffic in front—if you don't mind the climb, ask to be placed upstairs, where you should have a view of the hotel's leafy courtyard and clean, welcoming pool. Service is impeccable, and an excellent breakfast buffet is included. The live trio plays tunes in the lobby and restaurant Thursday–Friday evenings and Saturday–Sunday mornings.

Misión de Fray Diego (Calle 61 No. 524 between Calles 64 and 66, tel. 999/924-1111, toll-free Mex. tel. 800/221-0599, www .lamisiondefraydiego.com, US$86 s/d standard, US$96 s/d superior, US$126 s/d junior suite, US$136 s/d master suite) is a former monastery converted into a classy colonial hotel—you'll find some fine religious art here. Rooms have heavy wood furnishings, large marble bathrooms, and, in some cases, the original high ceilings. The hotel has two courtyards—the first has an attractive garden and fountain and the next a small clean pool and deck chairs. A quiet restaurant serves good Spanish food—paella is the specialty—with seating either in the garden or a small, bistrolike dining area. Guests enjoy free green fees at the Club de Golf La Ceiba, and reception can arrange massages, car rental, and area tours. This is a sister hotel to Hotel Caribe.

Hotel Caribe (Calle 59 No. 500, tel. 999/924-9022, toll-free Mex. tel. 800/555-8842, U.S./Canada tel. 888/822-6431, www.hotelcaribe.com .mx, US$43 s/d with fan, US$50 s/d with a/c, US$56 deluxe) has an ideal location on Hidalgo Park, just one block from the main plaza with dramatic views of the cathedral from the rooftop swimming pool area. The deluxe rooms are, of course, the most pleasant, having been recently remodeled and outfitted with cable TV and modern air conditioners. They are also on the third floor, with direct access to the small pool. Standard rooms are clean but aging; all units open onto wide tiled corridors with archways and overlook a spacious courtyard. (The building itself is quite impressive; built in 1650, it has 55 rooms and served as a convent, a Catholic high school, and private apartments before being converted into a hotel.) Guests play for free at the Club de Golf La Ceiba and can check email at a lobby computer at no cost—a small donation to a local children's AIDS foundation is requested. All in all, a good value.

Also facing Parque Hidalgo, the **Gran** Hotel (Calle 60 No. 496 at Calle 59, tel. 999/924-7730, granh@sureste.com, www .granhoteldemerida.com.mx, US$44 s, US$49 d, US$66 junior suite, US$75 master) is a classic colonial hotel, with Corinthian columns, painted tile floors, and a soaring atrium surrounded by several floors of wide airy corridors set with armchairs and low tables. Opened in 1901 and restored in the 1980s, it's worth peeking into even if you don't stay. If you do stay, junior suites are spacious and attractive (corner rooms have four patios and great park views) but the master is poorly conceived. Some of the standard rooms also have good views while others have no windows at all—look at a few before deciding; all have air-conditioning and TV. Visa and MC accepted.

A few blocks' walk from the central plaza, **Hotel Los Aluxes** (Calle 60 No. 444 between Calles 49 and 51, tel. 999/924-2199, toll-free Mex. tel. 800/712-0444, toll-free U.S. tel. 800/782-8395, www.aluxes.com.mx, US$68 s/d, US$104 suites) is a multistoried hotel with quite comfortable rooms, notwithstanding the 1970s-style building and slightly dated decor. Suites are the highlight here, offering significantly more space, including a separate sitting area, terrace, and good views. Nos. 317, 417, 517, and 617 are the best, with cool, triangular glassed-in patios—you'll see them as you walk or drive up to the hotel. All rooms have air-conditioning and cable TV, and the hotel has a pool, restaurant, travel agency, and Internet café.

Over US$100

The charming **☒ Hotel Casa del Balam** (Calle 60 No. 488, tel. 999/924-2150, balamhtl@finred.com.mx, www.haciendachichen.com, US$115 s/d) occupies a 15th-century structure—the café and courtyard area used to be where the horse-drawn carriages would pull in and park. Structures have been added, but the large, clean rooms maintain their colonial character, with tile floors, wrought-iron fixtures, and heavy, dark-wood furniture. Of course, modern touches such as new bathrooms, central air-conditioning, satellite TV, super-comfortable beds and double-paned glass let you enjoy colonial times without actually living in them. Five honeymoon suites and three master suites occupy original rooms and have antique decorations. Diners can eat in the shady courtyard café, with a splashing fountain and lush tropical plants; the tiled corridor has wide arches and comfortable, private chairs. A small pool in back is nice on hot days. This hotel is affiliated with the Hacienda Chichén and (by family connections) with Mayaland, both at Chichén Itzá archaeological zone.

Hotel Misión Mérida (Calle 60 s/n between Calles 55 and 57, tel. 999/923-9500, toll-free Mex. tel. 800/712-0098, ventamda@prodigy .net.mx, US$90 standard, US$116 superior, US$168 junior suite, $203 master) occupies one of Mérida's tallest buildings, just blocks from the central plaza. Rooms and furnishings are a bit dated but by no means lacking. The standard rooms are narrow and a bit dim; superiors are a better deal, with more space and better views. The best views are in the master suite, however, where the living room has floor-to-ceiling windows overlooking the park, cathedral, and university. Two bedrooms with king-sized beds and private baths make the master a decent deal for two couples traveling together. The interior courtyard has a nice pool and lawn area, and table tennis and billiards tables under covered archways. There's live marimba in the lobby bar every night, and classic guitar in La Trova, the hotel music lounge (9:30 P.M. to 2 A.M. Mon.–Sat., US$10 minimum consumption).

The **Fiesta Americana** (Paseo de Montejo at Av. Colón, tel. 999/942-1111, www .fiestamericana.com, suites US$120–$570) is Mérida's top luxury hotel, assuming you aren't interested in Mérida's many fine boutique guesthouses. Suites here are modern and well appointed, though some at the standard and executive levels had strangely saggy beds—you may want to see your room before deciding. Governor and presidential suites are huge and luxurious, with private terraces with city views and lounge chairs for sunbathing. The highlight of the place may be the building itself, with a soaring lobby, attractive spa area, and upscale shopping center below. ADO offers first-class and deluxe long-distance bus service, including to Cancún, directly from the hotel.

A block from the Hotel Fiesta Americana, another favorite is **Hotel Villa Mercedes** (Av. Colón 500, tel. 999/942-9000, toll-free Mex. tel. 800/216-7628, www.hotelvillamercedes .com.mx, US$155–180 s/d). The original structure was built in French art-nouveau style (including stained glass, wrought iron, marble floors, and chandeliers), which the proprietors of this fine 84-room hotel complement with modern amenities such as air-conditioning, direct-dial phones, a business center, and an elegant restaurant.

Small Inns and Bed-and-Breakfasts

Mérida has a profusion of charming little inns and bed-and-breakfasts, and staying in one is a highlight for many visitors. Virtually all are restored *casonas* (large colonial homes) whose resurrection has been a labor of love for an expatriot couple. The inns vary from faithful replicas of colonial residences to miniature museums full of folk and modern art, but all are very comfortable and classy. Most listed here have fewer than 10 rooms, so it's best to call ahead or reserve online.

The award-winning **Ⓜ Casa Mexilio Guesthouse** (Calle 68 No. 495 between Calles 57 and 59, tel. 999/928-2505, U.S./Canada tel. 877/639-4546, www.casamexilio.com, US$47–75 s/d, penthouse US$125) is one of Mérida's finest and most memorable accommodations, occupying a gorgeous colonial *casona* and operated like a European-style inn. The interior courtyard is like a piece of rainforest, with lush tropical plants surrounding a crystal-clear pool and jet pool. Eight guest rooms and a penthouse are tucked into the home's many nooks and crannies; a series of stairways and short bridges connect the rooms to various outdoor patios, as well as to the first-floor vestibule, second-floor dining room, and quiet rooftop bar. The guest rooms vary from cozy fan-cooled units to the penthouse, with air-conditioning, king-sized bed, and large private terrace; all have spotless tile bathrooms and comfortable beds. The rooms and common areas are literally brimming with eclectic and high-quality artwork from Mexico and around the world. Continental breakfast—juice, fresh bread, and homemade jams—is included, but you can also order a full breakfast for just US$3. The atmosphere is elegant and discreet and the service superb. Visa and MC accepted; reserve online.

Another excellent choice is **M Hotel Medio Mundo** (Calle 55 No. 533 between Calles 64 and 66, tel. 999/924-5472, www.hotelmedio-mundo.com, US$45 s/d with fan, US$60 s/d with a/c, US$65 t with a/c), a more hacienda-style guesthouse just a few blocks away. Within high, cheery, blue-painted walls are an attractive courtyard with fountain and a small inviting pool and patio area, where a bar serves light fare and fresh juices. All 12 rooms are simple but far from plain, with thick, brightly painted walls, deep beds, and large spotless bathrooms (and no TVs or telephones). Beautiful tile floors are from the original construction. The friendly owners can arrange various trips, including such alternative options as Mayan shamans, and natural medicine, or nighttime cantina tours around town. Visa and MC accepted.

Hotel Marionetas (Calle 49 No. 516 between Calles 62 and 64, tel. 999/928-3377, www.hotelmarionetas.com, US$70 s/d, US$15 extra person) gets its name from the building's former tenant—a well-known puppet theater company. All eight guestrooms are large and brightly painted, with beautiful tile floors and attractive understated decor. There's a sunny dining area and small, somewhat austere pool in the interior courtyard—a full fresh breakfast comes with the room. The energetic owners operate a small café in front, with light fare, juices, and highly recommended cappuccinos. Guests can use the Internet free and even hook up their own laptops.

La Casa de Los Arcos (Calle 66 No. 496 between Calles 51 and 53, tel. 999/928 0214, www.losarcosmerida.com, US$70 s, US$90 d, US$15 extra person) takes a very different approach to decor than does Hotel Marionetas. Virtually every inch of wall space (and a good deal of floor space) is filled with artwork, some from Mexico, some from Africa and elsewhere, some painted by the owners themselves. Add potted houseplants, a small swimming pool in a leafy garden, and a troop of tiny dogs, and Los Arcos is one of the more eclectic guesthouses you may ever find. The rooms—there are only two—are very comfy, with high ceilings, canopy beds, throw rugs, and big bathrooms, and they come stocked with robes, sarongs (to use poolside), and CD players. All in all, it's a unique, private, homey place. Big breakfast included.

Ángeles de Mérida (Calle 74-A No. 494-A between Calles 57 and 59, tel. 999/923-8163, U.S. tel. 713/208-2482, www.angelesdemerida.com, US$70 s, US$85 d) is west of Parque Santiago, about eight blocks from the city center. The four spacious rooms are each decorated with the work of a different artist (one of the co-owners is an art collector from Houston) and have large bathrooms and comfortable beds. There's a clean pool in the courtyard, and full breakfast is included.

Casa San Juan (Calle 62 No. 545-A between Calles 69 and 71, tel. 999/923-6823 or tel. 999/986-2937, www.casasanjuan.com, info@casasanjuan.com, US$35s/d with fan, US$45 s/d with a/c, US$55 suite, two-night minimum stay, reservations required) occupies an antiquated townhouse built in 1850 and renovated in 1980; ask Pablo, the owner, to tell you the history of the place. A small semishaded patio in back offers tables and chairs for reading or eating continental breakfast (included). Guestrooms have comfy beds, chairs and a table, and impressive five-meter (16.4-foot) ceilings. Those with air-conditioning have attached bathrooms; fan-cooled rooms have open-topped bathrooms built into the rooms when the home was converted into a hotel. Two recently built suites have fridge, microwave, and a connecting door that can be opened for groups or families; bathrooms are open at the top. The area around Casa San Juan is pleasant during the day but a bit grimy at night—solo women may consider taking a cab from the center. Note: Be sure taxi drivers don't confuse this with *Hotel* San Juan, near Parque Santa Lucía.

Outlying Haciendas

Yucatán is rife with abandoned colonial haciendas, yet only relatively recently did anyone think to turn them into hotels. You can hardly blame would-be hoteliers—most of these old structures are severely decayed and overgrown with vegetation, yet they remain subject to strict historic preservation laws limiting reconstruction. But more than a few entrepreneurs have persevered and tourists reap the benefit in the form of beautiful accommodations in unique colonial settings.

Once one of the most important sisal-producing haciendas in the region, **La Hacienda Xcanatún** (Carr. Mérida-Progreso Km. 12, tel. 999/941-0213, U.S. tel. 888/883-3633, www .xcanatun.com, US$240–290 s/d suites) is now a luxury hotel that boasts 18 beautifully restored and decorated suites set in lush tropical gardens. Rooms have Lebanese-style floors, hand-carved furnishings, Mexican and Far Eastern antiques, and original oil paintings. Most also enjoy private sitting areas, king-sized beds, and whirlpool tubs. To add to the absolute comfort and tranquility of guests, the hacienda has two pools, a full-service spa, and one of the best restaurants in the area, the Casa de Piedra. Rates include continental breakfast.

(See *Hacienda Tabi* and *Other Haciendas* in *The Puuc Route* section for more details.)

FOOD

Mérida has a rich selection of restaurants, from great hole-in-the-wall pizza joints to award-winning restaurants. Yucatecan as well as Mexican food predominates, but you can also find excellent Arabic, Chinese, and European food around town.

Salones Familiares

A classic Meridian experience, the *salon familiar* is a place where locals head for regional food, drink, and entertainment at reasonable prices. Performances typically include live music, comedy acts, and *ballet folklórico*. It's a place where everyone is welcome and a party atmosphere rules. On weekends and during vacation periods, you'll see lots of families inside. The most popular *salones* downtown are: **La Prosperidad** (Calle 53 No. 491 at Calle 56, tel. 999/926-1402, 11:30 A.M.–8 P.M. daily, US$4–6)—a big, noisy, friendly place with a stage. Performances run daily 2 P.M.–7:30 P.M. While you enjoy the entertainment, try the Yucatecan *botanas* (appetizers) or a one of the huge entrées, most of which are pork- or chicken-based; and **El Nuevo Tucho** (Calle 60 No. 482 between Calles 55 and 57, tel. 999/928-2858, eltucho@prodigy.com.mx, www .eltucho.com.mx, 11:30 A.M.–11:30 P.M. daily, US$5–7) with performances featured 1:30–9 P.M. While it's a good introduction to regional food and entertainment, don't expect much conversation at this place—the speakers blast away any possibility of interaction. You'll even have to yell your order although pointing is easier.

Mexican

La Casa de Frida (Calle 61 No. 26 at Calle 66, tel. 999/928-2311, 6–11 P.M. Tues.–Sat., US$5–11) is an eclectic restaurant with bright pink walls and loads of Mexican art hung and strung throughout the place. Excellence should be the motto here—meals are creative and delicious and service is top-notch. Be sure to try the *crepas huitlacoche* (crepes stuffed with corn fungus—a delicacy, really!) or the *flan de berejena* (eggplant flan) for a tasty spin on traditional Mexican fare. Seating is open-air, either in the softly lit courtyard or the colorful interior room.

With comfy couches and tables overlooking Calle 60, **Ki'bok** (Calle 60 between Calles 53 and 55, tel. 999/928-5511, kibokcafe@hotmail .com, 6 P.M.–2 A.M. Thurs.–Sat., 6 P.M.–1 A.M. Sun.–Wed., US$6–8) is a welcoming place that offers contemporary Mexican meals (think rabbit-based dishes and cactus stuffed with *huit-*

lacoche), fresh pastries, and a wide variety of coffee drinks. Check out the daily three-course specials before you decide on an entrée—they are a great deal (around US$9, including a cocktail)—or just stop by for dessert. Live *trova* (guitar ballads) is featured at 10 P.M. until 2 A.M. Thursday–Sunday.

With funky '70s decor and a retro mural on the back wall, **Cafetería Pop** (Calle 57 No. 501 between Calles 60 and 62, tel. 999/928-6163, 7 A.M.–midnight Mon.–Sat., 8 A.M.–midnight Sun., US$2–4 breakfast, US$2.50–6.50 lunch and dinner) seems like a total hipster throwback but in fact it has just maintained its look since it opened three decades ago. Friendly waiters serve simple Mexican food in this all-welcoming place—you'll find everything from guayabera-clad locals arguing over politics to five-year-old tourists munching on cornflakes. Breakfast specials are particularly good.

Yucatecan

On Parque La Mejorada, **Los Almendros** (Calle 50 No. 493 between Calles 57 and 59, tel. 999/928-5459, 10 A.M.–11 P.M. daily, US$3.50–4.50 breakfast, US$4–8 lunch and dinner) is a must if you're interested in classic Yucatecan food. This established Mérida restaurant offers the best of the region's cuisine, including meats prepared in *poc chuc, pollo pibil,* and homemade tortillas. The setting—with hand-painted chairs and attentive staff—is casual and family-oriented. A branch of the restaurant, **Gran Almendros** (Calle 57 No. 468 at Calle 50, tel. 999/923-7091) is nearby and offers the same menu.

Pórtico Del Peregrino (Calle 57 No. 501 between Calles 60 and 62, tel. 999/928-6163, noon–midnight daily, US$5–14) is an intimate and upscale restaurant offering excellent Yucatecan dishes in a vine-covered patio or two air-conditioned dining rooms. Be sure to try the house specialties—*sopa de lima* (lime soup), *pollo pibil* (chicken with Mayan spices wrapped in banana leaves), and *berenjenas al horno* (slices of eggplant layered and baked with chicken and cheese). Reservations recommended for outdoor evening dining.

For huge portions in a locals environment, head to **Ñ Restaurant D'Al** (Calle 54 No. 545 at Calle 53, tel. 999/923-7012, 9 A.M.–7 P.M. Mon.–Fri., 9 A.M.–4 P.M. Sat., US$1–2 breakfast, US$2.50–4.50 lunch). Here, you will undoubtedly leave stuffed with delicious local eats and drinks. Daily specials are especially good deals—for US$3–4, you'll get a big entrée with a bunch of sides. You'll leave wishing you had a fridge in your hotel room for leftovers.

Café La Habana (Calle 59 at Calle 62, open 24 hours daily, US$2–4 breakfast, US$4–10 lunch and dinner) is a classic greasy spoon diner with a Yucatecan twist: Legions of waiters in crisp white shirts and dark bow ties serve strong and hot coffee along with local and Cuban fare. The *chilaquiles con huevo* (fried corn tortillas in tomato sauce and cheese with a fried egg on top) is excellent. The large smoking section—with its clouds of cigarette and cigar smoke—is always bustling; nonsmokers are segregated to the far end of the room with a handful of air conditioners.

Middle Eastern

Ñ Alberto's Continental Patio (Calle 64 No. 482 at Calle 57, tel. 999/928-5367, alberto@albertoscontinental.com, 1–11 P.M. daily, US$11–24) is a superb restaurant specializing in Lebanese and Yucatecan dishes. The Middle Eastern food is refreshingly different—start off with tasty tabbouleh or hummus before moving on to grilled kabobs and cabbage rolls. It's housed in a *casona* built in 1727. The walls are 1.5 meters (4.9 feet) thick and the stones used to build the columns apparently were taken from Mayan ruins. You can't go wrong for a romantic ambience—choose between dining at a candlelit table in a vine-covered patio or in a softly lit dining room decorated with antique furnishings. Service is top-notch.

Café Alameda (Calle 58 between Calles Calles 55 and 57, tel. 999/928-3635, 8 A.M.–5 P.M. daily except Tues. and Sun., US$2–5) is a simple restaurant serving inexpensive Lebanese and Yucatecan food. Popular with locals and travelers alike, the food is excellent. Be sure to try the *baba ghanouj* (an eggplant dish)—it's one of the best we've ever had.

Asian

Well off the beaten track, **Thai Mid Restaurant** (Calle 31 No. 101 at Calle 20, tel. 999/927-2551, www.thaimid.com, 1 P.M.–1 A.M. Tues.–Sun., US$8–16) is a chic place with authentic Thai dishes. Meals are beautifully presented and service is cool but good. There are lots of vegetarian options, including tofu appetizers that are meals in themselves. Outdoor and indoor seating available.

A couple of doors down, **La Nao de China** (Calle 31 No. 113 between Calles 22 and 24, tel. 999/926-1441, 7:30 A.M.–9 P.M. daily, US$5–10) is a good place to head for Chinese food. Particularly popular are the lunch and dinner buffets, which are offered 1–5 P.M. Friday, and 1–6 P.M. Saturday and Sunday. Standard Chinese dishes are offered à la carte the rest of the week.

Italian

Café Lucía (Calle 60 No. 474-A between Calles 53 and 55, tel. 999/928-0740, www.hotelcasalucia.com, noon–midnight daily, US$5–8.50) is a chic restaurant featuring light Italian dishes in a space beautifully decorated with fine art—much of it for sale. On Thursday evenings, the restaurant sets up tables just outside of its doors in the Parque Santa Lucía, where you can enjoy the weekly *serenata* sponsored by the city (see the sidebar, *Mérida's Weekly Cultural Events*) while eating a fine meal or dessert.

Facing Teatro Mérida, **Pane e Vino** (Calle 62 No. 496 between Calles 59 and 61, tel. 999/928-6228, lunamay@prodigy.net.mx, 6 P.M.–midnight Tues.–Sun., US$6–11) is a simple but classy restaurant offering a good variety of imported and homemade pasta dishes. If you want more than just an entrée, stick to appetizers or desserts, as side dishes tend to be small.

Arguably the best pizzeria in all of Mexico, **⋈ Pizzería Vito Corleone** (Calle 59 No. 508 between 60 and 62, tel. 999/923-6846, 9:30 A.M.–11 P.M. daily, US$2–7) is not much to look at: a true hole-in-the-wall with tables crammed into two floors and a handful of fans furiously blowing hot air around. The phenomenal slices are worth every bead of sweat though:

The thin-crust pizza comes smothered in cheese and red sauce and loaded with toppings of your choice. Made in four sizes, a medium is enough for two hungry travelers. Come with an appetite, order a couple of cold beers, and remember to wear a tank top. Call for delivery.

International

Half an hour from Mérida and well worth the trip is the ⋈ **Casa de Piedra** (Carr. Mérida-Progreso Km. 12, tel. 999/941-0213, www.xcanatun.com, 7 A.M.–11 P.M. Mon.–Wed., 7 A.M.–midnight Thurs.–Sat., 7 A.M.–6 P.M. Mon.–Sun, US$9–25). In the renovated luxury hotel Hacienda Xcanatún, this award-winning restaurant serves exquisite French-Caribbean fusion cuisine. Service in the classy dining room is first-rate. An excellent choice if you're craving something a little different.

At Misión de Fray Diego hotel, **Restaurante el Convento** (Calle 61 No. 524 between Calles 64 and 66, tel. 999/924-1111, 7 A.M.–11 P.M. daily, US$3–14) specializes in Spanish food, including Spanish tortillas for breakfast and paella for dinner. The dining area is a cozy, wood and glass dining room opening on the hotel's pretty central courtyard.

Pastry Shops and Coffeehouses

Café Chiapas (Calle 60 No. 440-A at Calle 49, tel. 999/928-2864, 9 A.M.–8 P.M. Mon.–Sat.) is a tiny place offering fantastic coffee drinks made from Chiapanecan beans. Order a cold cappuccino to go or enjoy a flavored coffee at one of the three tables. Ground coffee and beans are also sold in pretty boxes for US$6 per kilo (2.2 pounds).

El Retorno (Calle 62 No. 500 between Calles 59 and 61, tel. 999/928-5634, 7 A.M.–9 P.M. daily) is one of the city's best bakeries with one shop half a block from the Plaza de la Independencia and several others throughout the city. Here you'll find cookies, cakes, and breads of all tastes and shapes.

Groceries

Near Parque Santiago, **Abarrotes Dunosusa** (Calle 74 No. 575 at Calle 57, tel. 999/929-9181,

8 A.M.–8 P.M. Mon.–Sat., 8 A.M.–2 P.M. Sun.) is a small grocery store offering basic foodstuffs along with fresh meats and dairy products.

Just south of Parque Santa Ana, **ISSTE** (Calle 60 between Calles 47 and 49, 8 A.M.–9 P.M. Mon.–Sat., 9 A.M.–7 P.M. Sun.) is a state-run supermarket with a warehouselike atmosphere. Fully stocked, it has a clothes section on the second floor and a small pharmacy at the entrance.

The **Mercado Municipal** (Calle 67 between Calles 56 and 58, 8 A.M.–8 P.M. daily) is a rambling, two-story market offering every fruit, vegetable, and meat sold in this region. Upstairs, you'll also find a few cheap eateries—not the cleanest but the bustling shoppers and yelling vendors are definitely an experience. (For a full description, see *Shopping.*)

For fresh fruit, vegetables, and meats without the hustle-bustle of the larger Mercado Municipal, head to the ◪ **Mercado Santos Degollado** (Calle 57 between Calles 70 and 72, 6 A.M.–2 P.M. daily). On Parque Santiago, this market gives you a taste of how the locals shop with its myriad of fruit and vegetable stands, *tortillerías,* shoe repair shops, and flower sellers. Stay for a meal—the handful of small restaurants are known citywide for their excellent seafood tacos and *tortas.* Prices run US$1–3 for a full meal.

INFORMATION AND SERVICES
Tourist Information
When you get to Mérida, pick up a copy of *Yucatán Today,* one of the most helpful tourist magazines anywhere in Mexico. Published monthly and distributed free at hotels, shops, and tourist offices, the magazine has maps, suggested itineraries, short articles, and lists of upcoming events. While focusing on Mérida, *Yucatán Today* also covers Progreso, the Puuc Route, Izamal, Valladolid, and Campeche. The hotel and restaurant listings are paid—and therefore not comprehensive—but it's a fine complement to this or other guidebooks.

The city and state tourism boards (**Información Turística del Ayuntamiento** and **Departamento de Turismo del Estado de Yucatán,** respectively) maintain a total of five tourist offices in Mérida. At any one of them, you'll find a wide selection of maps, brochures, and usually someone who speaks English. That said, we found the staff at the city offices much more helpful for specific questions and any information not found in the brochures. The best (and most convenient) city tourist office is in the Palacio Municipal on the main plaza (Calle 62 between Calles 61 and 63, tel. 999/942-0000, ext. 133, 8 A.M.–9 P.M. Mon.–Sat., 8 A.M.–2 P.M. Sun.). There are two other locations—a sidewalk kiosk (8 A.M.–8 P.M. daily) at the corner of Paseo de Montejo and Avenida Colón near the U.S. Consulate and Hotel Fiesta Americana, and a booth in the arrivals *(llegadas)* area of the CAME first-class bus terminal (Calle 70 between Calles 69 and 71, 8 A.M.–2 P.M. Mon.–Fri.). The state tourist offices are two blocks apart, one adjacent to the Teatro José Peón Contreras (Calle 60 between Calles 55 and 57, tel. 999/924-9290, 8 A.M.–9 P.M. daily) and the other just inside the front doors of the Palacio de Gobierno (Calle 61 at Calle 60, tel. 999/930-3101, 8 A.M.–9 P.M. Mon.–Sat., 8 A.M.–8 P.M. Sun.).

Medical Services
Hospital General O'Horán (Av. Itzaes and Calle 59-A, tel. 999/928-5707, ext. 300) has 24-hour emergency service. **Cruz Roja** (Red Cross, Calle 68 between Calles 65 and 67, tel. 999/924-9813) provides first-aid and ambulance service.

Pharmacies
On the Plaza de la Independencia, **Yza Farmacia** (Calle 63 No. 502-A, between Calles 60 and 62, tel. 999/926-6666, yza@farmacias .com, 24 hours daily) is an excellent choice—not only is it a fully stocked pharmacy but it also makes deliveries.

Across the street from the Mercado Municipal, **Farmacia y Droguería Comercio** (Calle 67 at Calle 57-A, tel. 999/928-1489, 7 A.M.–9 P.M. Mon.–Sat., 9 A.M.–3 P.M. Sun.) is a popular pharmacy selling medicine, toiletries, and film.

Facing Parque Santiago, **Farmacias Bazar** (Calle 57 No. 555, between Calles 70 and 72, tel. 999/928-5454, 8 A.M.– 9 P.M. Mon.–Fri., 8 A.M.– 8:30 P.M. Sat., 8 A.M.– 2 P.M. Sun.) is a fully stocked pharmacy that offers delivery service.

Police

The police station is on Calle 61 between Calles 52 and 54. In emergencies, call tel. 999/925-2034 or tel. 999/930-3200, ext. 462.

Money

You'll have no problem getting access to your money in Mérida. Every bank in town has a 24-hour ATM, virtually all of which accept foreign debit cards and offer good exchange rates. (Note that a small fee, typically US$.65 per withdrawal, is charged in addition to whatever fees your own bank charges.) Many convenience stores also have cash machines. Most banks exchange AmEx travelers checks and U.S. dollars, most accept euros, and a few will change other currencies. You can also try changing cash at a *casa de cambio* (currency exchange office), or the front desk of an upscale hotel, but the rates at either are rarely good. **American Express** (Paseo de Montejo No. 492 between Calles 43 and 45, tel. 999/942-8200, 9 A.M.–6 P.M. Mon.–Fri., 9 A.M.–1 P.M. Sat.) has an office across from the Anthropology Museum, sells travelers checks, and replaces those that are lost or stolen.

Most of the banks and ATMs are on or near the Plaza de la Independencia and along Calle 59. Among many others are: **Banamex** (inside Casa de Montejo, Calle 63 between Calles 60 and 62, 9 A.M.–4 P.M. Mon.–Fri., 10 A.M.–2 P.M.Sat.); **HSBC** (Calle 60 No. 515 between Calles 63 and 65, 8 A.M.–7 P.M. Mon.–Sat.; there's another on Calle 58 around the corner); **Bancomer** (Calle 59 at Calle 62, 8:30 A.M.–4 P.M. Mon.–Fri.); and **Scotiabank Inverlat** (Calle 54 at Calle 59, 9 A.M.–4 P.M. Mon.–Fri., exchange until 1 P.M. only).

Near the Mercado Municipal, **HSBC** (Calle 54 No. 521 between Calles 65 and 67, 8 A.M.–7 P.M. Mon.–Sat.) has one ATM.

If you need money wired to you, Western Union has an outpost at **Telcomm/Telegrafos** (Calle 56 at Calle 65, tel. 999/928-5979, 8 A.M.–7 P.M. Mon.–Fri., 9 A.M.–1 P.M. Sat., 9 A.M.–noon Sun.).

Post Office

The post office (Calle 65 at Calle 56, tel. 999/928-5404, 8 A.M.–4:30 P.M. Mon.–Fri., 9 A.M.–1 P.M. Sat.) is in front of the Mercado Municipal.

Internet

Internet cafés are in almost every block surrounding Plaza de la Independencia. As you venture farther afield, however, they are harder to find. Below are the best-priced Internet cafés in town, including a few that we found outside of the core touristed area. Remember—these businesses are highly competitive, so if you see a better rate, take it.

Near Plaza de la Independencia: **Mundo En Línea** (Calle 59 No. 515 between Calles 62 and 64, tel. 999/928-7936, 9 A.M.–11 P.M. Mon.–Sat., 9 A.M.–9 P.M. Sun.) is a cool place with fast connections and good Internet specials. Standard rates are US$.90 per hour, US$.90 for two hours on Wednesday, and US$1.10 per 1.5 hours on Sunday. Other services include CD-burning (US$2.20) and fax service (US$.86 per page within Mexico and US$2.20 per page outside of Mexico).

Internet House (Calle 62 No. 487 between Calles 57 and 59, tel. 999/928-1531, 9 A.M.–10 P.M. Mon.–Sat.) is a quiet and friendly place that charges US$1 per hour and burns CDs for US$2.60. Fax service also is available for US$.90 per page within Mexico and US$1.30 per page outside of Mexico.

Cyber61.com (Calle 61 No. 524 between Calles 66 and 66A, tel. 999/928-7116, 9 A.M.–9 P.M. Mon.–Sat., 10 A.M.–5 P.M. Sun.) is a true Internet café since you can order (and eat!) sandwiches and sodas while you work. Rates are US$.90 per hour and US$2.60 for CD-burning.

A half-block from Parque Santiago, **Café Internet 59** (Calle 59 No. 576 between

MÉRIDA CONSULATES

Mérida's consulates include:

Belgium: Calle 25 No. 155 between Calles 28 and 30, tel. 999/925-2939, 8 A.M.–noon and 2–5 P.M. Monday–Friday. (Emergencies only; this is the private residence of Mérida's former Belgian consul.)

Belize: Calle 53 No. 498 between Calles 56 and 58, tel. 999/928-6152, 9 A.M.–1 P.M. Monday–Friday.

Cuba: Calle 42 No. 200 between Calles 1-D and 1-E, tel. 999/944-4216, 8:30 A.M.–1:30 P.M. Monday–Friday. (Call ahead; it was closed for a month's vacation when we passed by.)

France: Calle 33-D No. 528 between Calles 62-A and 72, tel. 999/925-2886. (French citizens with emergencies can call 24 hours; for all other matters call for an appointment.)

Netherlands: Calle 64 No. 418 between Calles 47 and 49, tel. 999/924-3122, 9 A.M.–5 P.M. Monday–Friday. (Appointment only.)

Spain: Calle 8 No. 101 between Calles 5 and 7, tel. 999/984-0181, 9:30 A.M.–1 P.M. Monday–Friday.

United States: Paseo de Montejo No. 453 at Av. Colón, tel. 999/925-5011, 8:30 A.M.–5:30 P.M. Monday–Friday.

Calles 72 and 74, tel. 999/924-3040, 8 A.M.–10:30 P.M. Mon.–Sat.) charges an amazing US$.45 per hour during the summer, *Semana Santa* (the week before Easter Sunday), and the week between Christmas and New Year's Day. The rest of the year, the price rises to US$.90 per hour; two doors down, **Procisco** (Calle 59 No. 571-A between Calles 72 and 74, tel. 999/928-8445, 9 A.M.–10 P.M. Mon.–Fri., 9 A.M.–2 P.M. Sat.) charges US$.50 per hour and burns CDs for US$.45.

By Parque Santa Ana, try **Internet Ven y Ser** (Calle 60 between Calles 47 and 49, tel. 999/928-8135, 7 A.M.–10 P.M. Mon.–Sat.). It charges US$.90 per hour and US$2.20 to burn CDs. Sometimes it closes early on weekends.

Telephone and Fax

Tel World (Calle 59 at Calle 58, tel. 999/928-6856, 8 A.M.–9 P.M. Mon.–Fri., 8:30 A.M.–8 P.M. Sat., 9 A.M.–8 P.M. Sun.) offers domestic (US$.33/minute) and international (US$.60/minute to the United States/Canada, US$1.13 to Europe) telephone service. The same rate per minute plus a US$.26 service charge applies to

send faxes; to receive faxes, the cost is US$.08/minute plus US$.26/page.

In the same building as the post office, **Telcomm/Telegrafos** (Calle 56 at Calle 65, tel. 999/928-5979, 8 A.M.–7 P.M. Mon.–Fri., 9 A.M.–1 P.M. Sat., 9 A.M.–noon Sun.) is the official Mexican fax service. Sending to or receiving faxes from the United States and Canada costs US$1.50 per page, to/from Europe costs US$2.40 per page, and within Mexico costs US$1.45 per page.

Immigration Office

The immigration office (Av. Colón No. 507 at Calle 8, Colonia García Gineres, tel. 999/925-5009, 9 A.M.–1 P.M. Mon.–Fri.) is four long blocks west of the Hotel Fiesta Americana. The most common reason to visit is to extend your visa—to do so, you'll fill in several forms (usually available in Spanish and English), go to a bank to pay the US$18.25 fee, and then return to the office to get the extension. For every 30 days you request, you'll have to prove you have US$1,000 on hand—a current credit card will do the trick. Be sure to bring your passport and current visa, both of which must still be valid, of course. If you go early, you should be able to complete everything by the time the office closes at 1 P.M.

Consulates

Many European countries have closed their Mérida consulates and moved services to their offices in Cancún. A number of countries still maintain "honorary" consulates, often in private homes or offices and whose services vary from emergency-only assistance to basic passport and visa matters. Call ahead to see if the consulate can help you or if you're better off going to Cancún. Canada and the United Kingdom do not have any representatives in Mérida.

Laundry

Centrally situated, **Lavandería La Fe** (Calle 64 at Calle 55, tel. 999/924-4531, 8 A.M.– 6 P.M. Mon.–Fri., 8 A.M.–2 P.M. Sat.) charges US$3.50 for the first three kilos (6.6 pounds), and US$1.75 for each additional kilo (2.2 pounds). Same-day service is typical if you drop off your clothes in the morning. Pickup and delivery service can also be arranged around the center of town, including hotels near Paseo de Montejo, for US$2.60.

Half a block from Parque Santiago, **La Profesional** (Calle 57 No. 562, tel. 999/924-8712, 9 A.M.–7 P.M. Mon.–Fri., 9 A.M.–2 P.M. Sat.) is a friendly place offering same-day service with a smile. Bargain rates begin at US$2.35 for a minimum of three kilos (6.6 pounds) and US$.80 for each additional kilo (2.2 pounds). Sneakers and daypacks also can be washed separately for US$1.50 apiece.

Near the bus terminals, try **Lavandería San Juan** (Calle 69 between Calles 64 and 66, 9 A.M.–6 P.M. Mon.–Fri., 9 A.M.–1 P.M. Sat., US$.80/kilo—2.2 pounds).

Storage

Store your bags at **Guarda Plus** (across from CAME bus terminal, Calle 70 between Calles 69 and 71, 6 A.M.–10 P.M. daily) for US$.45/ hour per bag (backpack size; more for large suitcases). There is no daily rate.

Spanish Schools

The **Centro Idiomas del Sureste** (Calle 52 between Calles 49 and 51, tel. 999/926-9494, cis@sureste.com. www.cisyucatan.com.mx) is a great place to perfect your Spanish while living with a local family. The school is a favorite with Spanish teachers from the United States, Mayan scholars, and archaeologists who get intensive training in the language with classes geared to their area of interest. Classes are held at two locations: one in the downtown historical district and another in a residential area north of downtown. Prices vary.

Asesorías Especializadas de Idiomas (Calle 55 No. 529-A between Calles 62 and 64, tel. 999/928-7389, aeiyucatan@yahoo .com, www.yucatantoday.com/ads/aei/aei .htm, 8 A.M.–1 P.M. and 5–9 P.M. Mon.–Fri., 8 A.M.–noon Sat.) is a language school offering beginning- to conversation-level Spanish in classrooms no larger than six students. Prices vary from US$4.50 per hour to US$313 for 96 hours of instruction. Ask for a discount if you can't swing the cost or if you're signing up with a group of fellow travelers.

Cooking Classes

A great way to spend a half or full day in Mérida is learning Yucatecan cuisine at **Los Dos** (Calle 68 No. 517 between Calles 65 and 67, tel. 999/928-1116, www.los-dos.com) cooking school and guesthouse. American David Sterling, a Manhattan transplant and accomplished chef, conducts fun and informative classes at his gorgeously refurbished colonial home. The full-day course starts at Los Dos at 8 A.M. with pastries and coffee and a short introduction to Mayan and modern Yucatecan cuisine. Then it's off to the market with David to buy fresh vegetables, fish, meat, corn dough for tortilla chips or tamales, *chiles,* cilantro— anything and everything you'll need. Back at the kitchen you don a Los Dos denim apron (yours to keep) and David helps you prepare the items in the personalized cookbook (also yours to keep), which you will have helped to select in the days before your class. You take short breaks for lunch and while things are cooking—bring your swimsuit to cool off in the pretty courtyard pool—and finish the day off with cocktail hour and a grand, white-tablecloth dinner. Prices are US$50 pp half-day group class, US$75 pp full-day group class, US$300 1–3 people private class; multiday courses, including lodging in Los Dos's two beautiful guestrooms, can be arranged. Friends can join you for drinks and dinner for US$35 pp. Reserve as far in advance as possible, as the schedule fills up fast.

Tour Operators and Travel Agencies

There is a *lot* to see and do around Mérida, including Mayan ruins and villages, colonial towns and convents, cenotes, caves, birdwatching, mountain biking, snorkeling, and rappelling. Many people rent a car for a few days or a week—this is definitely the way to go if you want to see it all, or if you like to visit the sights at your own pace. Another advantage is you can arrive at the popular sights early, before they are crowded with tour groups. For the most educational experience, consider hiring a private guide or taking a specialized tour. Prices are higher, of course, but you'll get personal attention and a trip customized to your interests and stamina; transportation is usually included. For a pain-free look at the principal sights, an basic organized tour might make the most sense. Tours range US$30–50 per person, and include transportation (from your hotel and back), buffet lunch, and a guide. Be sure to check if the price includes entrance to the sites, which can be as high as US$8. Most operators offer a standard selection of trips, including Chichén Itzá, Uxmal, and Kabah, Uxmal evening show, Celestún, the Puuc Route, Progreso, and Dzibilchaltún, and a cenote tour. Expect larger groups and heavier crowds at the sites. If you are continuing to Cancún, most agencies also offer a "Cancún Drop-Off," which lets you visit Chichén Itzá before continuing to Cancún, where you are dropped at your hotel.

Ecoturísmo Yucatán (Calle 3 No. 235 between 32A and 34, Col. Pensiones, tel. 999/920-2772, www.ecoyuc.com.mx) is a well-run and highly recommended tour operator that offers a range of tours around Mérida and the peninsula. Day trips include a snorkel tour to three different cenotes plus visits to a Mayan village and small archaeological site (US$40 pp, transport and equipment included) and a mountain-biking tour that includes visiting a cave, two archaeological sites, a henequen hacienda, and two cenotes (US$85 pp, including equipment). The flamingo and bird-watching tour to Celestún gets rave reviews, especially for the quality of the guides. But Ecoturísmo Yucatán's forte is all-inclusive multiday customized tours to the greater Yucatán Peninsula. It has 7-, 10-, and even 15-day tours that range as far as the Río Bec archaeological sites in southern Campeche and Akumal on the Caribbean coast. Choose from an itinerary designed by the agency or one customized to your interests. Prices vary according to the number of days and places you go, but average around US$150–175/day with lodging, meals, transportation, and guide service included.

Deep Rock Adventures (tel. 999/987-8040 or cell tel. 044-999/110-6835, deeprockadventures@yahoo.com.mx) offers rappelling tours to various caves in the area, including Calcetok and Tecoh, and into cenotes around Valladolid. Besides the adventure, you'll get an interesting and unique insight on the ecology and geology of the Yucatán Peninsula, and a bit of culture as well. Tours include transportation, equipment, and guide and do not require previous experience.

Iluminado Tours (tel. 999/923-3455, trudy@iluminado-tours.com) is run by Canadian expat Trudy Woodcock, who designs and conducts weeklong specialized tours. The "Discover the Magic" tour is designed as an introduction to Mérida and the Yucatán, including visits to Uxmal and Chichén Itzá, plus a bird and nature reserve, Mayan villages, and colonial haciendas and churches. The "Women's Discovery Tour" (US$1,390 pp, double occupancy) is for women only, while the "Mayan Wisdom Tour" includes a shaman-guide and delves into Mayan beliefs and cosmology with visits to spiritually significant

FLYING TO MÉRIDA

The following airlines service Mérida's **Crescencio Rejón International Airport** (MID):

Aerocalifornia (Hotel Fiesta Americana, tel. 999/920-3855 or tel. 999/946-1682 at the airport)

Aerocaribe (Paseo de Montejo No. 500-B, tel. 999/928-6790 or tel. 999/946-1365 at the airport)

Aeromexico (Hotel Fiesta Americana, tel. 999/237-1786 or tel. 999/237-1740 at the airport, toll-free Mex. tel. 800/021-4000)

Aviacsa (Hotel Fiesta Americana, tel. 999/925-6890 or tel. 999/946-1850 at the airport)

Continental Airlines (Paseo de Montejo 427, tel. 999/926-3100 or tel. 999/946-1888 at the airport, toll-free Mex. tel. 800/900-5000)

Magnicharters (Calle 21 No. 104-B between Calles 22 and 24, tel. 999/926-1616 or tel. 999/946-2122 at the airport)

Mexicana (Paseo de Montejo No. 498 between Calles 43 and 45, tel. 999/924-1772 or tel. 999/946-1332 at the airport, toll-free Mex. tel. 800/502-2000)

sites such as Izamal, Chichén Itzá, and Loltún caves (US$1,790 pp double occupancy). Prices include transport, lodging, guides, and some meals. Tours have limited space and are offered periodically according to a set schedules; check well in advance for the upcoming schedule.

Yucatán Backroads Tours (Calle 53 No. 508 between Calles 66 and 68, tel. 999/924-0117, www.yucatanbackroads.com) is a one-man tour agency operated by seventh-generation Meridiano Ivan R. de Leon. His all-day "Yucatán Insider" tour (US$180 1–3 people, US$300 4–6 people, US$400 7–11 people, including private car or van, snacks, and drinks) visits various villages, cenotes, and small Mayan ruins, usually off the standard tourist route. Ivan is friendly, professional, and extremely knowledgeable about the area, and he can tailor the tour to your interests, from bird-watching to contemporary Mayan culture to colonial churches and haciendas. And he does not combine groups, so you are sure to get the trip you want with the people you want. Lunch not included; US$40–135, discount if you have your own vehicle.

Nómadas Travel (Calle 62 No. 433 at Calle 51, tel. 999/924-5223, www.nomadastravel.com) is the travel agency run out of Nómadas Youth Hostel. While most of its business comes from the hostel, it is a full-service tour operator and travel agency offering affordable trips to anyone who is interested. You'll find some of the best prices on standard trips here, and an even better deal on "last-minute" fares—you don't get confirmation until the morning of the trip, but you get it for almost half off. Nómadas also sells international student and hosteling cards and has good rates on international plane tickets.

Yucatán Trails Calle 62 No. 482 between Calles 57 and 59, tel. 999/928-2582 or tel. 999/928-5913, yucatantrails@hotmail.com, 9 A.M.–6:30 P.M. Mon.–Fri., 9 A.M.–1 P.M. Sat.) is a reliable agency offering all the standard trips. It uses vans and Suburbans, so groups tend to be a more manageable size. Air tickets and tour packages also available; it's operated by long-time Canadian expat Denis Lafoy.

Turitransmérida Calle 55 No. 495-A between Calles 58 and 60, tel. 999/924-1199, www.turitransmerida.com.mx, 8 A.M.–1 P.M. and 4–7 P.M. Mon.–Fri., 8 A.M.–1 P.M. Sat.)

is one of the largest tour operators in Mérida, with a fleet of buses, vans, and more than 20 guides speaking a half dozen languages. Many hotels and smaller agencies subcontract here, but you'll get a better price going to the office yourself. Minimum is four people, but popular trips during the high season can have as many as 40.

Carmen Travel Service (Pasaje Picheta, facing the plaza next to Palacio Municipal, Calle 61 between Calles 60 and 62, tel. 999/928-3060, www.carmentravel.com, 9 A.M.–7:30 P.M. Mon.–Fri., 9 A.M.–2 P.M. Sat.) sells ADO bus tickets, so you don't have to go all the way to the terminal to reserve a seat; air and hotel reservations also available. Carmen sells area tours, but the prices are much higher than you can find elsewhere.

Achah Recio (Calle 60 No. 457 at Calle 51, tel. 999/923-1557, ventas@achachortiz.com, 9 A.M.–8 P.M. Mon.–Fri., 9 A.M.–2 P.M. Sat.) is a regular travel agency handling national and international tickets, plus hotel and package reservations.

GETTING THERE
Air
Planes fly into Mérida's **Crescencio Rejón International Airport** (MID) from most cities in Mexico and from a few outside the country. There is a US$17 departure tax when you fly out of Mexico—most airlines incorporate the tax into their tickets, but it's worth setting some cash aside just in case. The airport has several car rental agencies, a 24-hour ATM, and a bank that changes foreign cash and AmEx travelers checks 8 A.M.–7 P.M. daily.

The airport is on Avenida de Itzaes (Highway 180), seven kilometers (4.3 miles) southwest of town. Taxis charge a fixed US$9.50 from the airport into town, while the other direction is around US$5—agree on a price beforehand. There is no airport bus, per se, but vans marked "UMAN" leave every 10 minutes from Parque San Juan (Calle 69 between Calles 62 and 64) and pass the airport entrance road (US$.35, 25 minutes). Be sure to ask the driver to let you off at *el aeropuerto;* it's a quarter-mile walk from the stop to the terminal. From the airport, you can walk to Avenida de Itzaes and catch an UMAN van to Parque San Juan—there is a bus stop just to your right when you reach the main road. Or wait for a "79-Aviación" bus (US$.30, 30 minutes) in front of the Budget office just outside the terminal—they pass less frequently (every 15–20 minutes) but you don't have to walk so far. Bus No. 79 goes to Parque San Juan as well, passing the first- and second-class bus terminals along the way. Note the UMAN vans don't have much room for luggage—if you are loaded down, consider springing for a cab.

Bus
Mérida has four bus stations. The main first-class station is known by the acronym **CAME** (KAH-may, Calle 70 No. 555 between Calles 69 and 71, tel. 999/924-8391, toll-free Mex. tel. 800/702-8000) and has ADO, ADO-GL, OCC, and UNO service. Most of your bus travel, especially long-distance, will be from here. Around the corner, the **second-class bus terminal** (Calle 69 between Calles 68 and 70, tel. 999/923-2287, Clase Europea tel. 999/924-4275) serves many of the same destinations as are offered at CAME, but the added comfort and safety of a first-class bus are definitely worth the few extra pesos. Note that the all-day Puuc Route Tour bus leaves from here as do buses to Chiquilá, where you catch the ferry to Isla Holbox. **Terminal Noreste** (Calle 67 between Calles 50 and 52, Noreste tel. 999/924-6355, Oriente tel. 999/928-6230, Lineas Unidas tel. 999/924-7865) is the base for regional bus lines. Most tourists using this terminal are headed to Río Lagartos to see the flamingos, or to Cuzumá to visit the cenotes; other destinations include Mayapán and Izamal. **Terminal Auto-Progreso** (Calle 60 between Calles 65 and 67) serves Progreso only (US$1, 50 min.), with departures every 10–20 minutes 5 A.M.–10 P.M.

Car
Good highways approach Mérida from all directions. Be prepared for one-way streets and

The State of Yucatán

MÉRIDA BUS SCHEDULES

Main first-class bus station **CAME** (Calle 70 No. 555 between Calles 69 and 71, tel. 999/924-8391, toll-free Mex. tel. 800/702-8000) departures include:

Destination	Price	Duration	Schedule
Campeche	US$8	2.5 hrs	every 30–60 min., 6 A.M.–11:45 P.M. (except 8:50 A.M.–10:30 A.M.)
Cancún	US$16	4 hrs	5:30 A.M., 6:30 A.M.**, 7 A.M., 8 A.M., 8:30 A.M.*, 9 A.M., 10 A.M., 10:30 A.M.*, 11 A.M., noon, 12:30 P.M.*, 1:30 P.M., 2 P.M., 3 P.M., 4 P.M., 4:30 P.M.*, 5 P.M., 6 P.M., 6:30 P.M., 6:45 P.M.*, 7:30 P.M.*, 8 P.M., 9 P.M., 9:15 P.M.*, 11.30 P.M., and midnight
Chetumal	US$17	5.5 hrs	7:30 A.M., 1 P.M., 6 P.M., and 11 P.M.
Chichén Itzá	US$6	1.75 hrs	6:30 A.M., 9:15 A.M., and 1 P.M.
Mexico City	US$71	18–20 hrs	10 A.M., 12:05 P.M., 2 P.M.*, 4:20 P.M., 5:30 P.M.*, and 9:15 P.M.
Oaxaca City	US$58	19–20 hrs	7:10 P.M. Friday only
Palenque	US$24	9 hrs	8:30 A.M., 7:15 P.M., 9 P.M.*, 10 P.M., and 11:30 P.M.
Playa del Carmen	US$18	5 hrs	6:45 A.M.*, 7:40 A.M.*, 9:45 A.M., 11 A.M., noon, 1 P.M., 2 P.M., 4 P.M., 6 P.M., 11 P.M., and midnight
Puebla	US$64	16–18 hrs	2 P.M.* and 6:30 P.M.
San Cristóbal	US$33	14 hrs	take Tuxtla Gutiérrez bus
Tulum	US$12	4 hrs	6:30 A.M., 11 A.M., and 1 P.M.
Tuxtla Gutiérrez	US$36	16 hrs	7:15 P.M. and 9 P.M.*
Valladolid	US$8	2 hrs	5:30 A.M., 6:30 A.M., 7:40 A.M., 8 A.M., 9:15 A.M., 11 A.M., 1 P.M., 3:25 P.M., 4 P.M., and 6:05 P.M.
Veracruz	US$50	15–16 hrs	10:30 A.M., 7:15 P.M.*, and 9 P.M.
Villahermosa	US$47	9 hrs	7:15 A.M., 9 A.M., 12:05 P.M., 4:20 P.M., 6:15 P.M., 7:15 P.M.*, 7:30 P.M., 9 P.M., 9:15 P.M., 9:30 P.M., 10:30 P.M., and 11 P.M.

*Denotes deluxe ADO-GL or UNO service; prices are 10–30 percent higher.

The State of Yucatán

Second-class bus terminal (Calle 69 between Calles 68 and 70, tel. 999/923-2287, or tel. 999/924-4275 for Clase Europea) departures include:

Destination	Price	Duration	Schedule
Campeche (semidirect)	US$7	3 hrs	6:30 A.M., 11 A.M., 1 P.M., 2 P.M., 3:10 P.M., 4 P.M., 5 P.M., 7 P.M., and 9 P.M.
Cancún**	US$11	6.5 hrs	every hour on the hour 6 A.M.–midnight
Chichén Itzá/Pisté	US$4	2.5 hrs	6 A.M., 6:30 A.M., 7 A.M., 7:30 A.M., 8 A.M., 9 A.M., 9:30 A.M., 10 A.M., 11 A.M., noon, 1 P.M., 2 P.M., 3 P.M., 4 P.M., 5 P.M., 6 P.M., 7 P.M., 8 P.M., 10 P.M., 11 P.M., and midnight
Chiquilá	US$11	5.5 hrs	11:30 P.M.; or connect via El Ideal
Dzibalché	US$3.50	2.5 hrs	every 30–60 min., 5 A.M.–9 P.M.
El Ideal	US$10	4 hrs	take any Oriente bus toward Cancún; frequent connecting service to Chiquilá
Oxkutzcab	US$4	2 hrs	8:30 A.M., 12:30 P.M., and 9 P.M.
Puuc Route (ATS bus line)	US$10 (round-trip)	8 hrs	leave 8 A.M. and return to Mérida 4 P.M. (30 min. at Kabah, Sayil, Xlapak, and Labná, and 2 hrs at Uxmal; entrance fees not included)
Ticul	US$3	1.5 hrs	8:30 A.M., 12:30 P.M., and 9 P.M.
Uxmal (ATS bus line)	US$6 (round-trip)	1.5 hrs each way	leave Mérida 8 A.M. and return to Mérida 2:30 P.M.
Valladolid	US$6	3 hrs	take any Oriente bus toward Cancún

**Be sure to take an Oriente bus, not Mayab, which goes through Felipe Carrillo Puerto and takes several hours more.

Terminal Noreste (Calle 67 between Calles 50 and 52, Noreste tel. 999/924-6355, Oriente tel. 999/928-6230, Lineas Unidas tel. 999/924-7865) departures include:

Celestún	US$3.50	2 hrs	hourly 5 A.M.–8:30 P.M., except 7 A.M.
Chiquilá	US$10	6 hrs	10:30 A.M.

continued next page

The State of Yucatán

MÉRIDA BUS SCHEDULES (cont'd)

Destination	Price	Duration	Schedule
Cuzamá (bus)	US$.90	1.25 hrs	7:45 A.M., 9:15 A.M., 10:45 A.M., 12:30 P.M., and 2:30 P.M.
Cuzamá (combi)	US$1.25	1 hr	every 30 min., 5 A.M.–8 P.M.; vans queue up on Calle 67 in front of terminal
Izamal	US$2.50	1.5 hrs	hourly 4:45 A.M.–9 P.M.
Mayapán Ruínas	US$1	1.25 hrs	hourly 5:30 A.M.–8 P.M.
Río Lagartos and San Felipe	US$9	3.5 hrs	5:30 P.M.
Tizimín (bus)	US$7	2 hrs	6:45 A.M., 9 A.M., noon, 2 P.M., 5:30 P.M., and 8 P.M.
Tizimín (combi)	US$6	2 hrs	approximately 11 A.M., 12:30 P.M., 2 P.M., 3:30 P.M., 5 P.M., and 6 P.M. (Mon.–Sat. only; vans queue up on Calle 52 between Calles 65 and 67)

avoid arriving on Sunday—a large area in the center of town is closed to vehicles. If you don't know the city, it can be a real headache to drive to your hotel, since many are downtown. The *periférico* is a wide, freshly paved traffic loop that circumscribes the city, making it possible to bypass the congested downtown streets if you're headed from Chichén Itzá to Celestún, for example.

The eight-lane toll highway (180D) from Mérida to Cancún cuts the driving time by 30–60 minutes. The highway, called an *autopista,* begins about 16 kilometers (10 miles) east of Mérida at Kantunil; from Mérida take Highway 180 toward Valladolid. Tolls to Chichén are about US$5, to Cancún about US$20. The toll road is in great condition, with rest stops, gas stations, and clearly marked exits; it's also nearly empty since most bus and trucking companies choose to take the *libre* (free road). It's slower and positively teeming with speed bumps, but it also takes you through many small villages and past fields of henequen and corn.

Ferry

A luxury ferry operates October–April from Tampa, Florida, to the port town of Progreso, north of Mérida. You can bring your car and even your boat for quite reasonable fares, especially compared to what you'll spend on airfare and car rentals. However, service had been halted indefinitely, but the agency was hoping to recommence service in November 2005. (See *Getting There* in the *Progreso* section for more information.)

GETTING AROUND

Mérida is laid out in a neat grid pattern of one-way numbered streets. The even-numbered streets run north and south, the odd east and west. The central plaza is the center of town and you can easily walk to most downtown attractions, shops, and marketplaces. Buses provide frequent service in and around the city and outlying areas, and cabs are plentiful.

On Foot

The best way to see Mérida is on foot. Granted, some of the sidewalks are narrow, and the traffic can be thick, but the city is a pleasure to wander. Look up for street names, which are usually found at the intersection on the building corners, high up.

Bicycle

Although drivers are somewhat aggressive, getting around town on bike is relatively easy if you stay off the main drags. **Hotel Meridiano** (Calle 54 No. 478 between Calles 55 and 57, tel. 999/923-2614) rents bikes for US$4.50 per day. Just be prepared to leave your passport as a deposit.

Bus

The most useful city buses are the ones that go between downtown and points along Paseo de Montejo. Downtown, catch an "Itzmna" bus on Calle 59, between Calles 56 and 58. You can catch the same bus all along Paseo de Montejo, including right in front of the U.S. Consulate.

Taxis

Taxis are generally found at taxi stands in most neighborhoods and there's almost always a queue at any one of the parks. If it's late, any hotel, café, or disco will call one for you. Some taxis are metered, but most aren't, so establish your fare in advance. Taxi fares are higher than in other cities, averaging US$3–5 around town. Bargaining still helps. A cab to the airport is US$8–10.

Car Rental

Mérida has a number of car-rental agencies. Rates fluctuate with the season and according to competition, but start at US$30–35/day for a basic Volkswagen bug, including tax and insurance. Don't hesitate to ask for a discount off the listed price—10–15 percent is common, especially in the low season or if you are renting for a week or more.

For the best deals and the friendliest service in town (if not the newest cars...), head to **Tourist Car Rental** (Calle 60 No. 421 between Calles 45 and 47, tel. 999/924-9471, harrycaam@hotmail.com, 8 A.M.–7 P.M. daily). Rates range US$30–60, including taxes and insurance. For rentals of a week or longer, discounts apply. Other shops offering decent rates include **Kimbilá Car Rental** (Calle 58 No. 485 between Calles 55 and 57, tel. 999/923-9316, www.kimbila.com, 8 A.M.–10 P.M. daily) and **Mexico Rent-A-Car** (tel. 999/923-3637, mexico rentacar@hotmail.com, 8 A.M.–12:30 P.M. and 6–8 P.M. Mon.–Sat., 8–10 A.M. Sun.), which is just down the short pedestrian walkway by Teatro José Peón Contreras, between Calles 58 and 60. **Budget, Hertz,** and several other agencies are on Calle 60 between Calles 55 and 57.

At the airport are **Avis** (tel. 999/946-1524, 6 A.M.–11 P.M.; office at Hotel Fiesta Americana, tel. 999/925-2525, 7 A.M.–9 P.M. daily); **Executive** (tel. 999/946-1387, 7 A.M.–11:30 P.M.; office at Hotel Fiesta Americana, tel. 999/920-3732, 7 A.M.–10 P.M. daily); **Europcar** (tel. 999/946-0971, 7 A.M.–midnight daily; office at Hotel Fiesta Americana tel. 999/925-3548, 7 A.M.–10 P.M. daily); and others.

The Puuc Route

You can easily spend a day or two in this region south of Mérida, with its rich concentration of Mayan ruins, caves, and small appealing towns. The Puuc ruins are the main attraction of course, from the stunning size and accomplishment of Uxmal (easily one of the best ruins in the Mayan world) to the fantastic artistry of smaller sites such as Labná and Kabah.

The Loltún caves are a great introduction to the Yucatán's vast underground world, and a tour of nearby Hacienda Tabi reveals the splendor (and pervasive inequality) of the state's colonial era. And in case you wondered, *puuc* is Mayan for "hilly area" and the modest rollers that inspired the name are the largest hills in the pancake-flat Yucatán Peninsula.

Getting There

An ATS bus headed for the Puuc Route leaves Mérida's second-class bus terminal every day at 8 A.M. and returns around 4 P.M. You can either do the Puuc Route tour (US$10; half hour at Kabah, Sayil, Labná, and Xlapak, and two hours at Uxmal) or spend the whole day at Uxmal (US$6 round-trip; bus leaves the Uxmal parking lot at around 2:30 P.M.). Entry fees are not included. If you are going to Uxmal only, be sure to notify the driver so he'll drop you off first.

If you miss the 2:30 P.M. bus from Uxmal, you can also walk out to the highway and flag down a second-class bus (the first-class buses won't stop). They pass at around 3–3:30 P.M., 5–5:30 P.M., and 7:30–8 P.M. Obviously this does not allow you to stay for the sound and light show; for that you have to have come on a tour or in your own car. There are also relatively frequent *colectivos* (public minibuses) headed toward Muna, where there are many more departures to Mérida. One leaves at 12:30 P.M. from the Uxmal parking lot; otherwise flag one down on the highway.

BETWEEN MÉRIDA AND MUNA

Yaxcopoil

Just off Highway 261 between Mérida and Uxmal, **Hacienda Yaxcopoil** (tel. 999/910-4469, Hwy. 261, 33 km/20.5 miles south of Mérida, 8 A.M.–6 P.M. Mon.–Sat., Sun. 9 A.M.–1 P.M., US$3.50) was one of dozens of huge henequen (aka sisal, a type of cactus) estates that dotted the Yucatán Peninsula. Built in the

MÉRIDA TO THE PUUC ROUTE

© AVALON TRAVEL PUBLISHING, INC.

17th century, Yaxcopoil (yawsh-ko-po-EEL) grew to encompass 11,000 hectares (27,181 acres), reaching its zenith during World War I, when rope made from the thorny, fibrous henequen plant was in great demand. A visit to the hacienda today leaves much to be desired—guide service or written descriptions for starters—but you can stroll through the grand old rooms, whose antique furniture, old photos, and original tile floors give a sense of the life the *patrones* (wealthy landowners) must have enjoyed. Don't leave without visiting the machine room out back (you may have to ask for it to be unlocked). There, huge machinery once used to extract fiber from the henequen leaves and bind it into bales still stands. The high brick chimney is from the days of steam power (notice the narrow tubes running underfoot) while the massive diesel engine was added in 1913 and used until the hacienda stopped production in 1984. Admission to Yaxcopoil is a bit steep considering how little formal information there is, but if you speak any Spanish, definitely chat up whoever is there—they likely either worked the hacienda, or their parents or grandparents did, and many have fascinating stories. The history of henequen production—the grandeur of the estates, the cruel exploitation of indigenous workers, the political and economic influence wielded by hacienda owners—is as fascinating as it is little understood.

Muna

This small town is home to many of the people who work at or around the Uxmal archaeological site. For travelers, there's not much reason to stop, and now that the highway loops around it, many people don't make it into town even if they want to! But Muna does have a nice 17th-century Franciscan church, whose facade is adorned with lacy belfries and glows a mellow gold in the late afternoon. People are friendly and the plaza has a number of fruit stands. This is also a good place to fill up on gas if you have a rental car and to pick up the ATS Puuc Route bus from Mérida if you don't. There is a promising **campground, cabanas,** **and trailer park** complex about a kilometer (0.6 mile) south of town, on the road toward Uxmal. It was closed every time we passed, but it looked well-kept.

There was no bank or ATM that accepted foreign cards in Muna at the time of research.

For Internet and a tank of gas, head to the PEMEX station in front of the church. On the second floor of the white building in back, you'll find **Internet Zone** (Calle 26 s/n, 8 A.M.–10 P.M. daily, US$1/hour). The gas is out in front.

There is no bus station in Muna, so buses stop at the northwest corner of the plaza, near the church. There is usually a bus representative hanging around selling tickets—the poor guy doesn't even get a kiosk to call his own. Buses to Mérida (US$1.75, one hour) leave frequently 5:30 A.M.–midnight. Buses to Uxmal (US$.90, 25 minutes) leave at 7 A.M., 9 A.M., 10 A.M., 11:30 A.M., 1 P.M., 3:45 P.M., 6 P.M., and 7 P.M.

The ATS Puuc Route bus from Mérida arrives here around 8:45–9 A.M. daily.

WEST OF MUNA
Oxkintok Archaeological Zone
The Oxkintok ruins (8 A.M.–6 P.M. daily, US$2.50) don't have the "wow-factor" of better-known ruins, but it's a beautiful, well-maintained site that can make an extra day on the Puuc Route so rewarding. The site is big and varied, with pyramids, plazas, and palaces scattered amid high grass and trees. Best of all, you'll probably have it completely to yourself. The ruins sit in a fertile plain at the edge of the hilly Puuc region and may have been connected to Uxmal by a limestone *sacbe*. Oxkintok has attracted a fair amount of attention in the past few years, as archaeologists uncover an urban center at least three square miles. Tombs have been found in a number of the structures, though many of the artifacts were lost to looters. To reach Oxkintok, follow the signs eastbound from Highway 180. Consider combining a visit here with a tour of the Calcehtok caves.

Calcehtok Caves

These may be the most adventure-oriented of the *grutas* (caves) along the Puuc Route. Up to four kilometers (2.5 miles) of the cave can be visited, during which you squeeze through narrow gaps, teeter along slippery pathways, and crawl and clamber through muddy passageways. Along the way are huge chambers filled with stalactites and stalagmites, and tiny rooms where archaeologists have found human bones and other remains of pre-Hispanic Mayan ceremonies. Calcehtok's caves are definitely less commercialized than other caves—you don't need any technical experience, but be prepared to get dirty.

To get here, follow the signs on Highway 184 until you reach a turn-off that leads to a small parking lot. A guide should be waiting up the short path. (If not, it means he is with other people and you can either wait or come back later. *Never* enter this or any cave without a guide.) A full tour takes 2–3 hours, and costs US$9/hour for up to three people. Before going in, agree with the guide how long the tour will last and how far into the cave you will get. The price is probably negotiable in the low season. If you have a flashlight of your own, bring it as a backup. Do not wear flip-flops—tennis shoes or boots are best, although sandals with a heel strap should be fine.

BETWEEN MÉRIDA AND MAYAPÁN

Located along (or just off) Highway 18, these sights are easily reached by car and make for interesting stops between Mérida and the Puuc Route.

Ruínas de Acancéh

These ruins (8 A.M.–5 P.M. Mon.–Sat., 8 A.M.–3 P.M. Sun.) are mainly notable for being right in the middle of the small town of Acancéh—they literally face the plaza with a church on one side and TV-repair shop on the other. Not really worth a stop or the US$2 admission, they serve best as window-candy on the way to Cuzamá.

Cenotes de Cuzamá

This was one of our favorite nonarchaeological outings from Mérida. When the henequen plantations were functioning, the harvest was stacked on small trolleys that were pulled by horses over long networks of lightweight rails. The residents of the small town of Cuzamá have put their trolleys back to use, outfitting the carts to hold 1–4 people and offering tours to three beautiful cenotes along the rail line. The trip is half the fun—there is only one set of rails and there's evidently an etiquette as to which driver has to pull over, which in this case entails unloading the passengers and hoisting the cart off the tracks before the other guy clatters past. With a few starts and stops, you make it the cenotes. The first is the largest and easiest to get into, with concrete stairs leading to a cavernous pool. The second two are more challenging—in both you have to negotiate a steel ladder from the cavern roof down to the water. Wear sandals with heel straps, if not tennis shoes or boots. But once there, swimming in the crystalline water with sunlight and tree roots angling down though the roof…well, it's simply sublime. The whole trip takes 2–3 hours and costs US$10 per trolley (1–4 people). Horseflies (*tábanos* in Spanish) are the one annoyance, buzzing around the horse and cart. They have a nasty bite, so be careful not to let one land on you.

Tecoh Caves

The Tecoh caves (10 A.M.–5 P.M. Mon.–Fri., 8 A.M.–5 P.M. Sat.–Sun., US$2.50) is something of a mixed bag: A 1.5-hour tour leads you past a dozen crystalline underground cenotes, but the walls and limestone formations are marred with the spray-painted messages of local kids and couples. The payoff is a 50-meter (164-foot) crawl to the last and largest cenote, which has pretty beams of light entering from two holes in the roof and makes for a refreshing swim.

Mayapán Archaeological Zone

Mayapán (8 A.M.–5 P.M. daily, US$2) is thought by some to have been one of the most impor-

© LIZA PRADO CHANDLER

the observatory at Mayapán

tant cities in the pre-Hispanic Mayan world, although you'd never know from the trickle of visitors the site gets nowadays. Mayapán is not on any tour-group itineraries, and independent travelers tend to skip it going to or from the "main" Puuc sites farther south. While not as grand as Uxmal or Chichén Itzá, people who do stop are rarely disappointed. Mayapán is a compact, immaculately maintained site with two primary pyramids, an observatory, cenote, and excellent fresco paintings and stucco masks. It was founded around A.D. 1000 after the powerful Cocom dynasty left Chichén Itzá to establish the region's capital here. (Chichén Itzá was subsequently abandoned except as a place for religious worship and pilgrimages.) Mayapán dominated northern Yucatán almost until the mid-15th century, when it was abruptly abandoned, perhaps because of an internal revolt. The first indigenous people met by the Spanish newcomers still called themselves *maya uinic* (Mayan men) in reference to their former capital, and it is from there that modern use of the word Maya emerged. Unfortunately, there are few explanatory plaques on-site.

Second-class buses from Mérida's Noreste terminal pass the ruins' entrance in both directions; just be sure you get on one for Mayapán ruins, not Mayapán town, which is in an entirely different area.

UXMAL ARCHAEOLOGICAL ZONE

History

Eighty kilometers (49.7 miles) south of Mérida in a range of low hills covered with brush, Uxmal is the greatest Mayan city of the Puuc region. Some believe it was founded by Mayans from Guatemala's Petén region in the 6th century. Others contend it dates back even further, perhaps to the Preclassic period. Unlike most of northern Yucatán, the Puuc region has good soils, allowing for greater population density than other areas. Uxmal emerged as the dominant city-state between A.D. 850 and 900, when the House of the Magician, the Great Pyramid, and the Nunnery were built, and is believed to have been the hub of a district of about 160 square kilometers (100 square miles) encompassing many sites, including the lesser sites in the area: Kabah, Sayil, Labná, and Xlapak.

The State of Yucatán

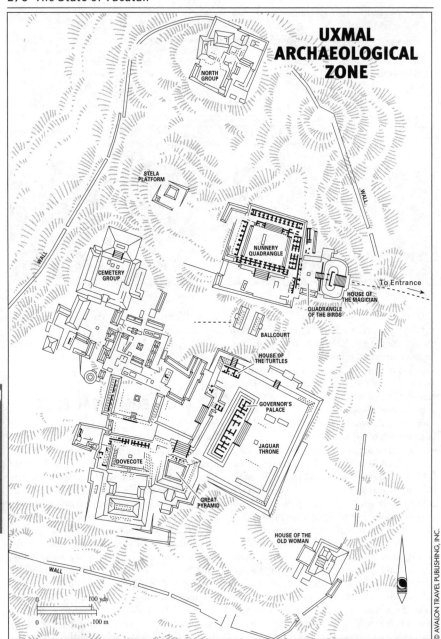

UXMAL ARCHAEOLOGICAL ZONE

NORTH GROUP

STELA PLATFORM

CEMETERY GROUP

NUNNERY QUADRANGLE

WALL

WALL

To Entrance

HOUSE OF THE MAGICIAN

QUADRANGLE OF THE BIRDS

BALLCOURT

HOUSE OF THE TURTLES

GOVERNOR'S PALACE

JAGUAR THRONE

DOVECOTE

GREAT PYRAMID

HOUSE OF THE OLD WOMAN

WALL

0   100 yds
0   100 m

© AVALON TRAVEL PUBLISHING, INC.

STEPHENS AND CATHERWOOD

The Mayan ruins of the Yucatán Peninsula were all but unknown in the United States and Europe until well into the 19th century. Although Spanish explorers and colonizers had occupied the peninsula for more than two centuries, conflicts with local Mayans and Catholic antipathy for all things "pagan" probably account for the Spaniards' lack of research or even apparent interest. To be fair, the immensity of the task was surely daunting—by the time the Spanish reached the Yucatán in the early 1500s, the majority of sites had been abandoned for at least 300 years and in some cases double or triple that. Many were piles of rubble, and those still standing would have been covered in vegetation. Just getting to the sites was a task in itself.

Between 1839 and 1841, an American explorer and diplomat named John Lloyd Stephens and an English artist and architect named Fredrick Catherwood conducted two major explorations of the Mayan region, including present-day Yucatán, Chiapas, and Central America. Stephens, an amateur archaeologist, kept a detailed account of their travels and the ruins they visited, while Catherwood made incredibly precise drawings of numerous structures, monuments, hieroglyphs (then unreadable), and scenes of peasant life. They published their work in two volumes, made a sensation in the United States and Europe, and awakened outside interest in ancient Mayan civilization. Their books now are condensed into a single, very readable volume, *Incidents of Travel in Yucatan* (Panorama Editorial, 1988), available in English and in many bookstores in the Yucatán. It makes for fascinating reading, not only for the historic value, but also as a backdrop for your own travels through the Yucatán.

On discovering a red handprint on the rear wall of the Governor's Palace structure at Uxmal:

The seams and creases of the palm were clear and distinct in the impression. There was something life-like about it that waked exciting thoughts, and almost presented the images of the departed inhabitants hovering about the building.

On the House of Turtles at Uxmal:

It wants the rich and gorgeous decoration of the [Governor's Palace], but is distinguished for its justness and beauty of its proportions, and its chasteness and simplicity of ornament.

However, in the mid-10th century, Uxmal was abruptly abandoned, probably after being defeated by armies from Chichén Itzá and as part of a pan-Mayan collapse around that time. During the Postclassic era, the Xiu clan based in the nearby town of Mani spuriously claimed to be descended from Uxmal's rulers and occupied the ruins. All that said, however, relatively few stelae have been found at Uxmal, so less is known about the ruling dynasties here than at other major sites.

The Mayan word Uxmal (oosh-MAHL) means Thrice Built. The name notwithstanding, it is believed that Uxmal was built five times, each time over top of the last. Puuc architecture is one of the major achievements of Mesoamerica, whose hallmarks include thin squares of limestone veneer, decorated cornices, boot-shaped vault stones, rows of attached half columns, and heavily decorated upper facades. The constant threat of drought also inspired the Mayans to adorn their structures with hundreds of stone masks and carvings representing the rain god, Chac, easily identified by his prominent hooked nose. Unlike most Mayan centers in Yucatán, Uxmal was not built around a cenote, since there are none in this arid part of the peninsula. Rainwater was collected in *aguadas* (natural holes in the ground) as well as in man-made *chultunes* (cisterns) built into the ground, sometimes right inside a house or under a patio.

Visiting the Ruins

Uxmal's tallest structure is the demi-pyramid **House of the Magician** (38 meters/124.7 feet). It's shaped in a distinctive elliptical form, rather than a true pyramid, which has a square or rectangular footprint. The west staircase, facing the Nunnery Quadrangle, rises at an imposing 60-degree angle. (You used to be able to climb to the top, where there is another temple—the Temple of Five—and stunning views of the site and surrounding forest, but the ascent has been closed.) Five temples were built one over the other on this site. Under the west stairway you can see parts of the oldest one; a date on a door lintel is A.D. 569.

The **Nunnery Quadrangle** is the courtyard to the northwest of the House of the Magician. Covering an area of 60 by 45 meters (197 by 148 feet), the square is bounded on each side by a series of buildings constructed on platforms of varying heights during different periods of time. The buildings, which contain numerous small rooms, reminded the Spaniards of the nunneries in Spain, hence the name.

A path leads south from the Nunnery to the **House of the Turtles,** a simple 11- by 30-meter (36- by 98.4-foot) structure. The lower half is very plain, but the upper part is decorated with a frieze of columns; a cornice above that has a series of turtles along its facade.

Just south of the House of the Turtles, the **Governor's Palace** is considered by some to be the finest example of pre-Hispanic architecture in Mesoamerica. It sits on a platform measuring almost 100 meters (328 feet) long, 12 (39.4 feet) meters across, and 8 meters (26.2 feet) high. The lower facade is plain, but the upper section is a continuous series of ornate carvings and mosaics of geometrical shapes and Chac masks. Two arrow-shaped corbel arches add to the delicate design of this extraordinary building. A double-headed jaguar in front of the palace (presumed to be a throne) was uncovered by John Stephens in 1841, who tried to take it with him but found it "too heavy to carry away."

Another large structure is the **Great Pyramid** (30 meters/98.4 feet), originally terraced with nine levels and a temple on the top. According to early explorers, at one time four small structures sat on each of the four sides of the top platform, described as palace-like. The top story is decorated in typical Puuc fashion, with ornate carvings and stonework depicting flowers, masks, and geometric patterns.

Walking through the grounds, you'll find many other structures and a ball court. Visit the **Dovecote, House of the Old Woman, Cemetary Group, North Group,** and other structures large and small, and as-yet-unexcavated mounds.

Light Show

Every evening a sound and light show is presented at the ruins overlooking the Nunnery Quadrangle, similar to the one at Chichén Itzá. If you've never seen one of these shows, it's worth checking out. Yes, some of the narration is either corny or unintelligible, but being at the archaeological site at night, with the ancient stone structures looming around you and the occasional flash of lightning in the distance, is undeniably impressive. You can't help but cast your mind back to ancient times, to imagine living in these awesome and (to us) mysterious cities or spending a warm dark night gazing at the stars, the same ones we see today.

Practicalities

The ruins and museum are open 8 A.M.– 5 P.M. daily; the sound and light show takes place at 7 P.M. in the winter (October–April) and at 8 P.M. in the summer (May–September). General admission, which includes the sound and light show, is US$7.50. Admission to just the sound and light show is US$2.50, plus US$2.25 for headphones with the translation from Spanish. It's possible to go to the sound and light show the night before you visit the park for the single general admission price, but you must tell the attendant that is what you're doing. You will buy part of the general admission ticket for US$4.50 (plus the headphones if you want them) and then pay the remaining US$3.50 the next day—don't lose your ticket from the show, though, as you must show it the next morning. Note there are no reduced or refunded tickets if you don't plan on going to the sound and light show, or if it is cancelled because of rain or other reasons. Parking is US$.90 per car; use of a video camera is US$2.50.

Guides to the ruins charge fixed prices and can be hired right at the entrance. Prices vary according to the language you prefer: Spanish or English US$30, Italian or French US$34.50, German US$39.

In addition to the museum and gift shop, the visitor/entrance center has an ATM, snack bar, postal drop box (buy stamps at the small just past the entrance), and an excellent Dante bookstore.

Accommodations

The following upper-end hotels (all with restaurants) are clustered right around the entrance to Uxmal, and a few others are down the highway, also within walking distance. There are few services.

If you've seen the Club Med in Cobá or Chichén Itzá, then walking into **Club Med Villas Uxmal** (Carr. Mérida-Campeche Km. 76, tel. 997/974-6020, villauxmal@prodigy .net.mx, www.clubmed.com, US$ US$67–112 s/d with a/c) will be like dejá vu. Actually, it *is* dejá vu: these Club Meds are clones of one another. Constructed around a tropical courtyard with a pool, the resort has small, attractive, and functional rooms with beds set on built-in concrete platforms. A reading room with a complete library on the history and culture of the Mayans, a billiards table, and tennis court add to an already restful stay. A good restaurant also is on-site (see *Food*). Friendly service.

The original residence of the first archaeologists to excavate Uxmal, **Hotel Hacienda Uxmal** (Carr. Mérida-Campeche Km. 78, tel. 997/976-2012, uxmal1@sureste.com, www .mayaland.com, US$88–188 s/d with a/c) is now a colonial hotel offering 80 charming rooms. Units are decorated in a Yucatecan style with striking tile floors, heavy carved furniture, and ironwork beds. All offer modern amenities. The lush grounds also include a pool, tennis court, and nice jogging trails. A spacious dining room offers decent but unremarkable meals.

Just 30 meters (98.4 feet) from the entrance to Uxmal, **M The Lodge at Uxmal** (tel. 997/976-2010, toll-free U.S. tel. 800/235-4079, uxmal1@sureste.com, www.mayaland .com, US$105–122 s/d with a/c) is the most luxurious of the hotels in this area. Surrounded by lovely gardens that hold two inviting pools, bungalow rooms are well appointed, ample, and have comfortable beds. Most rooms have whirlpool tubs and (somewhat gaudy) stained-glass windows as well. Free access to Hacienda Uxmal's tennis court and pool also is offered. A relaxing spot, this is hands down the most comfortable hotel in the area. A palapa-roofed restaurant serves good meals (see *Food*).

Food

Set in a lovely Mexican-style dining room, the restaurant at **Club Med Villas Uxmal** (Carr. Mérida-Campeche Km. 76, tel. 997/974-6020, villauxmal@prodigy.net.mx, www.clubmed .com, 7:30 A.M.–10 P.M., US$5 breakfast, US$7–17 lunch and dinner) offers a decent international menu. A good place to relax after a day at the ruins.

Conveniently situated just outside of Uxmal's entrance is the restaurant at **The Lodge at Uxmal** (tel. 997/976-2010, uxmal1@sureste .com, www.mayaland.com, 7:30 A.M.–10 P.M., US$5 breakfast, US$7–20 lunch and dinner). Although it's often busy with tour groups, here you can order Mexican specialties, pastas, sandwiches, and a good selection of Yucatecan dishes. Live music and dance troupes often perform at peak hours.

Getting There

Note that most buses do not go onto the ruins road (where the hotels also are), but stop on the highway at the Uxmal turnoff. If you're driving from Mérida, the drive to Uxmal takes about one hour; from Campeche allow two hours.

SANTA ELENA

This peaceful community of 4,000 people lies smack-dab in the middle of the Puuc Route, just 16 kilometers (9.9 miles) east of Uxmal and 7 kilometers (4.3 miles) north of Kabah, the first of the smaller sites. It is a pleasant and convenient base for exploring the entire region, with two fine lodging options, a good restaurant, and an impressive church.

Sights

Long before reaching Santa Elena, you can see its imposing **Iglesia de San Mateo** rising like a misplaced airplane hangar from a small tree-covered hill. (Some say it was built atop a Mayan ruin—not at all uncommon—but locals dispute that.) A huge pinkish stone box standing 35 meters (114.8 feet) high, 50 meters (164 feet) long, and 20 meters (65.6 feet) wide, the church has almost no exterior adornment. The cavernous nave is also austere, with thick, whitewashed walls, wood pews, and a simple altar, but it features exquisite and unique wooden *retablos* (hand-carved religious scenes depicted in ornate boxes) hanging on the walls. Be sure to ask the church attendant (he's usually hanging out in the nave) to let you up to the roof, reached via a rickety spiral staircase. Near the top is the organ platform (sans organ) with a dizzying view down into the nave from a wooden patio and narrow corridors along the sides. The roof affords an awesome vista of the surrounding countryside. Don't go up during a lightning storm, of course.

A small **museum** alongside the church (8 A.M.–7 P.M., US$.50) has detailed and somewhat disturbing displays of the well-preserved remains of 4 of 11 children uncovered in the church floor during renovations in 1980. (The others, including the "best" ones, were taken to Mérida and never returned; it used to be common to bury the deceased in church floors.) The corpses are displayed in cases and beneath a glass floor in the same form they were found. They date from the 1800s and may have been children of German transplants brought during the French occupation who died (or were killed) during the Caste War.

Accommodations and Food

Once a water-purification plant, ℕ **The Flycatcher Inn** (on the southern end of town, 100 m/328 feet before Hwy. 261 to Kabah, no phone, flycatcherinn@yahoo.com, www.geocities.com/flycatcherinn/index.html, US$35–44 s/d with fan) now is a tranquil bed-and-breakfast set in a tropical garden. Lovingly transformed, the four comfortable units are spotless and have tile floors, ironwork beds, and local artwork displayed on the walls. The owners, Kristine Ellingson and Santiago Domínguez, also are incredible founts of information about the region and the Yucatán Peninsula as a whole, and they are regularly involved in historical and restoration projects around town. A large and healthy breakfast is included in the rate; the owners were installing a nature and bird-watching trail through a lush, four-hectare (9.9-acre) lot behind the inn. Reservations recommended.

One kilometer (0.6 mile) south of town, ℕ **Camping-Bungalows Sacbe** (Hwy. 261 toward Kabah, tel. 985/858-1281, sacbe bungalow@hotmail.com, www.sacbebungalows.com.mx) is an excellent (and affordable!) option with camping (US$3 pp, no equipment available to rent), trailer space (US$3 pp, electrical hookups US$4.50 extra), and bungalows with private bath, sturdy mosquito screens, and porches (US$20 s/d). The grounds are well-kept and the amenities and accommodations are incredibly clean (although with corrugated tin roofs, private rooms and bathrooms may heat up on summer days). Owned and run by a friendly French-Mexican couple, this is a welcoming place. Well worth staying a few days if you have the time.

The best restaurant in town is **El Chac-Mool** (Calle 18 No. 211-B, tel. 997/971-0191, 8 A.M.–8 P.M. daily, sometimes open later) serving good cheap Yucatecan dishes.

Information and Services

There is almost nothing in the way of traveler services in this town; it's still very much a small

Yucatecan village without the hubbub often found in touristed towns. Count yourself lucky, then, if the **Cibernet** is open when the sign says it is: 1:30 P.M.–4:30 P.M. and 6:30–9 P.M. daily. Internet costs US$1/hour, CD-burning runs US$2.65. Look for it at the bottom of the hill to the left of the church facade.

Getting There and Around

Like almost everywhere on the Puuc Route, Santa Elena is easiest to reach and negotiate if you have a car. That said, a number of people do visit by bus and do just fine. To get here, take a Campeche-bound bus from Mérida's second-class bus station. To get back to Mérida, you'll catch the same bus on its return trip—there are seven total, and the most convenient are at 9 A.M., noon, and 3 P.M. daily.

To see the ruins, the ATS Puuc Route bus from Mérida passes on Highway 261 (a few blocks from the Flycatcher Inn and right in front of Camping-Bungalows Sacbe) at 9:15–9:30 every morning. It stops for 25–30 minutes at each of the four smaller Puuc ruins, before returning to Uxmal, passing back by Santa Elena. You can get off at that point, or continue to Uxmal and catch a Campeche-bound bus back to Santa Elena later in the afternoon.

TICUL

Northeast of Santa Elena, the small, pleasant city of Ticul (pop. 30,000) is an agricultural zone, pottery town, and shoemaking center. An elaborate, high-domed 18th-century cathedral faces the plaza; next to it is a Franciscan monastery built 200 years earlier. Like Santa Elena, Ticul is a good place to base yourself if you think you'll want more than one day along the Puuc Route. You'll avoid the long drive back to Mérida after the first day of ruins and get an earlier start the next day.

Sights and Entertainment

Ticul's **main church** has a beautiful stained-glass window over an arched doorway framed by simple columns. Other than those flourishes, the structure possesses the pleasant unadorned

© LIZA PRADO CHANDLER

Ticul's main church

The State of Yucatán

austerity typical of so many Franciscan churches in this region.

Cine Plus Ideal (Calle 23 at Calle Comp. Sergio Esquivel) usually has a somewhat outdated Hollywood flick showing around 9:15 P.M. nightly. Admission is US$1.75.

Shopping

The hills and riverbeds around Ticul have great clay, and the town has long been famous for its pottery. Perhaps the most highly regarded studio here is **Arte Maya** (Calle 23 No. 301 between Calles 46 and 46-A, tel. 997/972-1669, 8 A.M.–8 P.M. daily) on the west side of town on the highway toward Muna. The studio was founded by the late Wilbert González and now operates as an art school, women's cooperative, and pottery store. The shop specializes in high-quality reproductions of classic Mayan art, using laboriously prepared clay and all-natural "paint" made from local soils and minerals. The artists typically model their work from photographs of pieces found during excavations—the finished products are by no means cheap, but they are remarkable in their faithfulness to the originals. In fact, the shop holds a license from INAH—the government body that oversees all things Mayan—to make such exact copies, and all pieces bear a special mark to distinguish them from actual artifacts. Short tours (in Spanish) are given on request, and if someone is working you are usually free to watch. The shop is most active between November and April.

Accommodations

Across from the church, the recently opened **N Hotel San Antonio** (Calle 25-A No. 202 between Calles 26 and 26-A, tel. 997/972-1893, US$15 s, US$25 d) is an excellent value. Bright rooms with balconies, cable TV, in-room phones, air-conditioning, and a good, inexpensive restaurant guarantee a restful stay. Rooms above the entrance to the hotel have king-sized beds and the best views in the place. Off-street parking also is available.

Posada El Jardín (Calle 27 No. 216 between Calles 28 and 30, tel. 997/972-0401, US$26 s/d with fan, US$35 s/d with a/c) is a charming, family-run hotel offering three secluded rooms—one a large bungalow—surrounding a lush garden and small pool. Accommodations are brightly painted and are decorated with Yucatecan curios. Continental breakfast is included in the rate. A great place to unwind after a day or two (or three) of ruin-hopping.

Food

Restaurante Los Almendros (Carretera a Chetumal; 997/972-0021; 9:30 A.M.–9 P.M. daily, US$5–12) is a Ticul institution and one of the best *típico* eateries in town. The restaurant literature claims this is where *poc chuc,* a very popular meat dish served all over the Yucatán Peninsula, was invented. True or not, the food here, mostly Mayan-influenced, is excellent and the service prompt. The restaurant used to be in the center but has moved to a larger location (with parking) near the southern entrance to town.

Right on the corner facing the plaza, **N La Carmelita** (Calle 23 No. 201 at Calle 26, tel. 997/972-0515, 8:30 A.M.–6 P.M. daily, US$2–8) serves good, no-frills meals to a loyal local clientele. The breakfasts are reliable and the fish plates and shrimp cocktail quite tasty—and we don't often order seafood this far from the coast. Look for the tinted windows.

Pizzería La Gondola (Calle 23 at Calle 26-A, tel. 997/972-0112, 8 A.M.–1 P.M. and 6–11 P.M. daily, US$5–10) may have somewhat reluctant service, but the pizza and pasta dishes are well prepared and make a nice culinary alternative to Mexican food, if you need it. On the corner, a few doors down from the movie theater.

Super Solomon (Calle 23 No. 214 between Calles 28 and 30, tel. 997/972-0081, 8 A.M.–2:30 P.M. and 5:30–10 P.M. daily) is a large supermarket with produce, canned food, munchies, and more. Across the street, the small town **mercado** (6 A.M.–5 P.M. daily) has fresh fruits, vegetables, and small lunch stands dishes, plus clothes, shoes, and other doodads.

Information and Services

For a 24-hour pharmacy, head to the reliable and well-stocked **YZA Farmacía** (Calle 23 No. 217-D at Calle 28, tel. 997/972-1080).

The **police station** (tel. 997/972-0210) faces the plaza and is staffed 24 hours a day.

On the main plaza, you'll find an ATM at **Banamex** (Calle 26 between Calles 23 and 24, 9 A.M.–4 P.M. Mon.–Fri.). It exchanges travelers checks and cash but only until 3 P.M. For another option, try **HSBC** (Calle 23 195-B between Calles 24 and 26, 8 A.M.–7 P.M. Mon.–Sat.), which has an ATM as well but exchanges money until 6 P.M.

The **post office** (Calle 23 at Calle 26, 8 A.M.–2:30 P.M. Mon.–Fri.) is right on the main plaza.

Across from the amphitheater, **Camheros.com** (Calle 26 at Calle 23, 9 A.M.–2 P.M. and 4 P.M.–midnight daily, US$.90/hour, US$2.50 to burn CDs) is a reliable and breezy place. Equally as convenient, but open much later, is **Café Internet** (Main Plaza at Calle 25, 9 A.M.–3 A.M. daily, US$.90/hour, US$3.50 to burn CDs).

For faxing, head to pricey **Telecomm/Telefax** (Calle 23 between Calles 24 and 26, tel. 997/972-0146, 9 A.M.–3 P.M. Mon.–Fri.) where

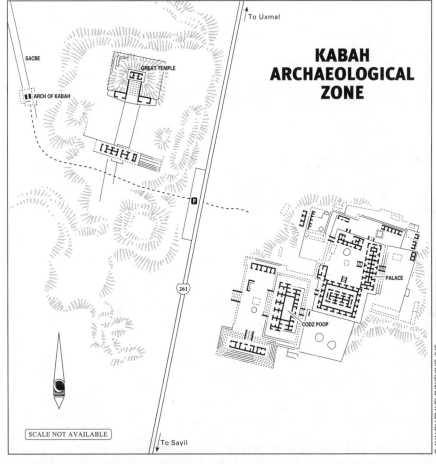

SACBE

ARCH OF KABAH

GREAT TEMPLE

To Uxmal

KABAH ARCHAEOLOGICAL ZONE

P

261

PALACE

CODZ POOP

SCALE NOT AVAILABLE

To Sayil

faxes to the United States and Canada cost US$1.50/page, to Europe US$2.40/page, and within Mexico US$1.45/page.

Getting There

Ticul has a smallish bus terminal and largeish *colectivo* terminal, almost across the street from each other on Calle 24 behind the church and main plaza. Going to Mérida, buses (US$2.75, 1.5 hours) leave every 30–60 minutes 5 A.M.– 9:30 P.M. and *colectivos* (US$2.50, 1.5 hours) leave whenever they are full in the same span. There is bus service to Chetumal (US$11, 6.5 hours) and to Felipe Carrillo Puerto (US$7, four hours) with connections from there to Tulum, Playa del Carmen, and Cancún. *Colectivos* are better for Oxcutzcab (US$.50, 30 minutes), Muna (US$.75, 45 minutes, board on Calle 23 at Calle 28), and Santa Elena (US$.50, 20 minutes; board on Calle 30 at Calle 25). You can catch the ATS Puuc Route bus at either of the latter two, passing Muna at 8:45–9 A.M. and Santa Elena at 9:15–9:30 A.M.

KABAH ARCHAEOLOGICAL ZONE

Twenty-two kilometers (13.7 miles) south of Uxmal, Kabah ruins (8 A.M.–5 P.M., US$2.50) include structures on both sides of Highway 261. Kabah's temples were constructed in A.D. 850–900, though the area was probably first settled as far back as 300 B.C.–A.D. 250 (Late Preclassic era). **Codz Poop** is Kabah's most ornate building. Dedicated to the rain god, Chac, and measuring nearly 45 meters (147.6 feet) long and 6 meters (19.7 feet) high, the temple's entire west facade is a series of 250 masks with the typical elongated, curved nose, some almost a complete circle. It's thought that small pits on each mask were used to burn incense or oil; if true, Codz Poop must have shone like a lighthouse in the rolling countryside. Inside Codz Poop are two parallel series of five rooms each, and part of the original rooftop comb (at one time three meters/9.8 feet high) can still be seen.

West of the road is the impressive **Arch of Kabah.** It is presumed that this arch marks the end of a ceremonial Mayan *sacbe* extending from Uxmal to Kabah. A few more structures have been partially restored—look for the **Great Temple** and the **Temple of the Columns.** Already impressive, Kabah is undergoing additional restoration that will make it even more so.

SAYIL ARCHAEOLOGICAL ZONE

The several hundred known structures uncovered at Sayil (8 A.M.–5 P.M., US$2.50) illustrate a technical progression from the earliest, unornamented buildings to the later, ornate **Chultun Palace,** constructed in A.D. 730. The Palace is a large, impressive building, more than 60 meters (197 feet) long, with three levels. The second level is decorated with columns and a multitude of rich carvings, including the ever-present rain god and one distinctive portrayal of a descending god (an upside-down figure sometimes referred to as the bee god). By A.D. 800 this site was abandoned.

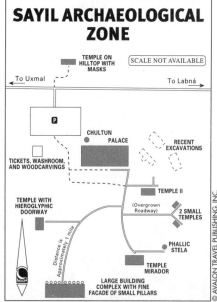

© LIZA PRADO CHANDLER

the small but impressive archaeological site of Sayil

Because of the lack of rainfall in this area, *chultunes* are found everywhere, including the sites of the ceremonial centers. One example of a *chultun* that holds up to 7,000 gallons of water can be seen at the northwest corner of the Palace. The fast-decaying **Temple Mirador** (on a path going south from the Palace) and the monument of a human phallic figure lie beyond.

XLAPAK ARCHAEOLOGICAL ZONE

Xlapak (8 A.M.–5 P.M., US$2) is the most "skippable" of the four smaller Puuc ruins. Its restored building has curious carvings of masks, curled Chac noses, and geometric stepped frets. It's easy (a little too easy, in fact) to pick out the light-colored areas of restoration compared to the darker weathered stones that were covered with bushes and soil oxides for so many years. The word Xlapak in Mayan means Old Walls.

N LABNÁ ARCHAEOLOGICAL ZONE

Three kilometers (1.9 miles) past Xlapak, Labná (8 A.M.–5 P.M., US$2.50) is for many people the best of the four smaller Puuc ruins. Dating to around A.D. 850, Labná is famous for the beautiful **arch** (or, more accurately, portal vault) at the south side of the site. The arch forms a 3- by 6-meter (9.8- by 19.7-foot) passageway, one of the largest ever built by the Mayans. It is also one of the most ornate—the northeast side of the arch has two outstanding representations of thatched Mayan huts, one on each side of the portal. Nearby, the stark, square **El Mirador** building stands on a tall mound with a roof comb gracing the top. The comb was originally decorated with a carved seated figure and a series of death heads.

Closer to the entrance, the elaborate multiroom **Palace** is an impressive 135 meters (443 feet) long and 20 meters (65.6 feet) high and sits on an immense 165-meter (541.3-foot) platform. A *chultun* is built into the second story of the Palace; at least 60 *chultunes* have been found in the Labná area, indicating a population of about 3,000 residents within the city.

LOLTÚN CAVES

Seven kilometers (4.3 miles) southwest of Oxkutzcab, the Loltún *grutas* (caves) are the largest known caves in Yucatán. This

The State of Yucatán

vast underground network first served ancient Mayans as a source of water and pottery clay and later developed in the Classic era into an important pilgrimage and ceremonial space. (Caves typically represented fertility and the entrance to *xibalbá,* the underworld.) Researchers working in Loltún also uncovered bones belonging to mammoths and other extinct mammals—evidently dragged to the cave by early hunters. Dated to 9000–7500 B.C. they are the earliest evidence yet found of human presence on the peninsula. Ceramics and carved reliefs from the Early Preclassic era (2000–1250 B.C.) have been discovered here too, including some in the style of southern Mayan cities such as Tikal.

Visiting the Caves

A route through caverns has been wired for lights, which are turned on and off by the guide

LABNÁ ARCHAEOLOGICAL ZONE

TICKETS

PALACE

SACBE

EAST TEMPLE

SACBE

EL MIRADOR

ARCH

0   50 yds

0   50 m

© AVALON TRAVEL PUBLISHING, INC.

as groups move through. Loltún means Rock Flower in Mayan and in the caves you'll see carvings of small flowers. One of the more intriguing sights are dozens of handprints on the cavern walls, either in silhouette or negative outline, whose meaning remains a mystery. Early Mayans also placed stone cisterns *(chultunes)* under the dripping stalactites to catch "virgin water," important in ceremonies honoring Chac, the rain god. But the most important archaeological find here is the relief dubbed "The Warrior," which is carved on a rock face just outside the Nahkab entrance to Loltún. Strangely, it appears to follow the Izapan style of Kaminaljuyú, the enormous Preclassic city near Guatemala City. Toward the end of the hour-long tour you come to an opening in the roof of an enormous two-story-high cavern. The sun pours into the room, creating dust-flecked shafts of golden light. The gnarled trunk of a towering tree grows from the floor of the cave, reaching hundreds of feet up through the sunny opening, and flocks of birds twitter and flit in and around the green leafy vines that dangle freely into the immense chamber from above.

Practicalities

Wear decent walking shoes in the caves. For the most part it's an easy two-kilometer (1.25-mile) walk; however, it's dark and damp, and in a few places the paths between chambers are steep, rocky, and slippery.

For safety reasons, you may enter the caves only at set times with a guide. Tours begin daily at 9:30 A.M., 11 A.M., 12:30 P.M., 2 P.M., 3 P.M., and 4 P.M., and last about an hour. Entrance fee is US$4.50 (children under 13 are free), but none of that goes to the guides—budget another US$2–5 per person for tip. Tours are given in English or Spanish—let the ticketseller know which language you prefer so you are paired with the right guide.

There is a small restaurant across the street from the caves, with friendly service, basic meals, and nice cold beer.

By far the easiest way to get to Loltún is by car, though a few tour operators from Mérida include Loltún in select trips. With a car, you can also visit Hacienda Tabi, the road to which is adjacent to the Loltún entrance area. Alternatively, take a bus to Oxkutzcab (US$4, two hours, 8:30 A.M., 12:30 P.M., 9 P.M. from Mérida's second-class terminal) and take a cab or a relatively frequent *combi* (shared van) to the caves. To get back to town, you should be able to flag down a *combi* if its not too late.

OXKUTZCAB

The small village of Oxkutzcab has at least one good hotel and is conveniently near the Loltún caves, Hacienda Tabi, and the Puuc Route. The land here is extremely fertile—besides high healthy fields of corn, you'll pass through fields of bananas, coconut palms, and citrus groves. Oxkutzcab is the orange capital of the Yucatán Peninsula, and a huge citrus processing plant nearby employs many area residents (and buys produce from local farmers).

Oxkutzcab's central plaza is bordered by a large Franciscan church (the Templo y Exconvento San Francisco) and an attractive arched building, which holds municipal offices. The plaza itself has concrete benches, a gazebo, and a painted plaster statue of a woman carrying a load of oranges on her head. Kitty-corner to the plaza is the town market, Mercado 20 de Noviembre.

Oxkutcab's two-week-long **Orange Festival** is celebrated in late October or early November and is renowned throughout Yucatán. Definitely stop by if you are in the area, although don't expect to find any empty hotel rooms.

Just north of Oxkutzcab, Mani is a quiet, peaceful town with few tourists and a gas station. But Mani's history is less benign—it is most likely the location of Friar Diego de Landa's infamous *auto-da-fé* in 1562 in which he burned untold number of Mayan codices, pottery, and other records because he deemed them works of the devil. Mani was also the scene of an early surrender by the *Xius* (prominent Mayan rulers with descendants still living in the state of Yucatán), which allowed Francisco Montejo the Elder to gain control of the area. Montejo quickly had a huge church/monastery complex built—it was completed in just seven months using the forced labor of 6,000 enslaved Mayans under the direction of Fray Juan de Mérida, who also designed and built the famous monastery at Izamal.

Sights

Leonardo Paz is an accomplished painter and muralist and an Ozkutzcab native son. He painted the long, beautiful mural above the market and several smaller works around town. In the plaza, look on the backside of the gazebo to see paintings depicting the War of the Castes and the infamous *auto-da-fé*, when in 1562 Franciscan priest Fray Diego de Landa burned scores of irreplaceable Mayan codices and sculptures.

Mercado 20 de Noviembre is worth a quick exploration. Paz's ingenious mural mirrors the scene just below it, with indigenous women sitting in front of huge piles of fruit and packing boxes stacked in every free space. Most memorable is the incredible assortment of colorful citrus fruits, including oranges, limes, grapefruit, gaudy pink *pitayas,* and little yellow *nanzim.*

Accommodations and Food

On the road that leads out of town toward Loltún Caves, **Hotel Puuc** (Calle 55 No. 80 at Calle 44, tel. 997/975-0103, US$17.50 s, US$20 d) has 25 rooms, all large, clean, and pleasant with air-conditioning and cable TV. The hotel has a good restaurant and some parking. The friendly owners also run a tour agency and have plenty of information and advice about area ruins, churches, caves, and more.

At the Hotel Puuc, **Restaurante El Peregrino** (8 A.M.–4 P.M., 6–10 P.M. Mon.–Sat., 8–10 P.M. Sun., US$2–10) serves regional food in a simple, brightly decorated dining area attached to the hotel. The breakfast and lunch buffets run US$4.50–8. Menu items include Yucatecan-style chicken and pork, plus Mexican standards such as quesadillas (tortillas with melted cheese) and grilled beef.

Facing the plaza, **Pizza Express** (no phone, 3–11 P.M. daily, US$4–15) is a small eatery where you can get all sorts of pizza (naturally) as well as pasta, hamburgers, fries, and other artery-hardening treats.

Information and Services
Banamex (main plaza, tel. 997/975-0135, 9 A.M.–4 P.M. Mon.–Fri.) was the only bank in town when we passed through. It has an ATM machine and you can change cash and travelers checks inside.

Check your email at **Compured** (main plaza, tel. 997/975-1018, 9 A.M.–10:30 P.M. daily, US$1/hour, US$1.25 to burn CDs) or InterCafé (Calle 52 at Calle 51, no phone, 8:30 A.M.–10 P.M. Mon.–Sat., 8:30 A.M.–5 P.M. Sun., US$1.25/hour, US$1 to burn CDs).

Across from InterCafé is **Farmacia María del Carmen** (Calle 51 No. 106 at Calle 52, tel. 997/975-0165, 8 A.M.–midnight Mon.–Sat., 8 A.M.–2 P.M. Sun.)

Getting There
Oxkutzcab's **main bus terminal** (Calle 51 between Calles 52 and 54) has service on Mayab and ATS buslines. Both are second-class but ATS service is slightly faster and more expensive. Destinations include:

Cancún, US$15, 7–7.5 hours, 5 A.M., 6:30 A.M., 7:20 A.M., 8 A.M., 11:30 A.M., 3:15 P.M., 4 P.M., 10 P.M., and midnight.

Chetumal, US$11, five hours, 1 A.M., 4 A.M., 9 A.M., 10:45 A.M., 1:30 P.M., 7 P.M., and 11 P.M.

Felipe Carrillo Puerto, US$7, 3.5 hours, 5 A.M., 6:30 A.M., 8 A.M., 10 A.M., 11:30 A.M., 4 P.M., 6 P.M., 10 P.M., and midnight.

Mérida, US$3.50, 2.5 hours, every 30–45 minutes 5:30 A.M.–7:30 P.M., stopping in Uman, Muna, and Ticul.

Playa del Carmen, US$12.50, 6.5–7 hours, take any Cancún bus.

Tulum, US$10.50, 5.5–6 hours, take any Cancún bus.

You can also catch *colectivos* to Tecax (US$.75, 25 minutes) every 30–45 minutes 6:30 A.M.–7 P.M., until 5 P.M. only Sunday, from outside the terminal; and to Ticul

(US$.75, 30 minutes) every 10–15 minutes 6 A.M.–8:30 P.M. daily from the corner of Calles 51 and 54.

To get to Loltún Caves, flag down a *combi* outside Hotel Puuc.

◪ HACIENDA TABI

Seven kilometers (4.3 miles) northwest of the Loltún caves, Hacienda Tabi (8 A.M.–4 P.M. daily, US$1, contact Leticia Roche at leta@fcy .org.mx) makes for an interesting side trip if you have some extra time and enjoy old haciendas. The soaring 22,000-square-foot main structure has 24 rooms and faces a huge grassy area, with a windmill, stables, rum distillery, and sugar mill along the edges. Through the trees in front are a massive, beautifully decaying chapel and two stout chimneys. Tabi was founded in 1750 and operated for nearly 200 years—at its height, Tabi encompassed 14,000 hectares (35,000 acres) and is unique for cultivating sugar rather than henequen. The hacienda finally closed in 1948, and was declared a protected zone in 1997. A team of researchers sponsored by the Cultural Foundation of Yucatán in Mérida have been studying the hacienda since 1996—with so much attention paid to the Yucatán's ancient ruins, relatively little is known about life on the colonial-era haciendas, despite the fact that poor working conditions there helped spark the Caste War and later the Mexican Revolution. Hacienda Tabi is the first and only hacienda in the Yucatán to be excavated using archaeological methodology. There is a small museum on-site, and you may be able to get a guided tour from the guard/docent—email ahead if you can. You can also stay the night (US$47 s/d, including breakfast and dinner) in one of five large, drafty, none-too-fancy rooms in the main building—reservations required. To get here, follow the signs from Loltún caves; the last half kilometer (third of a mile) is dirt.

OTHER HACIENDAS

After lying abandoned for decades or even centuries, the Yucatán Peninsula's old henequen haciendas are returning to (and surpassing) their former colonial glory. In particular, the powerful Hernández family of Monterrey is behind the renovation of five (and counting) beautiful haciendas, reopening them as isolated, deluxe hotels. Rates aren't cheap, but the setting and service are unforgettable.

Gloriously restored, the **N Hacienda Temozón** (Off Hwy. 261, tel. 999/923-8089, reservations1@thehaciendas.com, www.luxurycollection.com, US$300–586 s/d with a/c) is a gem of a hotel. Boasting 28 beautifully decorated rooms and suites, attention to detail is paramount. Each has 5- to 7-meter (16.4- to 23-foot) ceilings, gleaming tile floors, luxurious linens, and elegant furnishings; some also have outdoor whirlpool tubs and the master suite enjoys a private pool. Outside, the lush grounds feature a spectacular stone pool, a cenote, walking trails, tennis courts, and stables. The original machinery used on the hacienda to work the once-valuable henequen is on display beside the full-service spa and the tracks that were used to move the product is now used to give hayrides around the property. A gourmet restaurant in the main building (US$8–28) simply completes a lavish stay. It's about 45 minutes south of Mérida.

About eight kilometers (five miles) off Highway 180 to Campeche, **Hacienda Santa Rosa** (tel. 999/923-8089, reservations1@thehaciendas.com, www.luxurycollection.com, US$300–586 s/d with a/c) is another elegant option. The sister hotel of Hacienda Temozón, it is equally as classy although less splendid: The rooms are similarly decorated but there are only 11 of them, there is a large botanical garden to wander in but the grounds are much smaller, and spa services are offered but there is no spa (treatments are given inside guest rooms or in common areas). What you get at Santa Rosa is privacy and excellent service in a fine hotel. There definitely aren't the bells and whistles that you'd find at Temozón, but you get a lot of bang for your buck.

Hacienda Santa Cruz (Cuxtal Ecological Reserve, tel. 999/910-4549, www.hacienda santacruz.com) was warmly recommended by expats in Mérida.

Celestún

Celestún is a small fishing village on the northwest shoulder of the Yucatán Peninsula on the mainland side of a 22-kilometer/13.7-mile-long inlet-estuary known as the Ría Celestún. The shallow super-salty waters are an ideal breeding and feeding area for *Phoenicopterus ruber ruber,* the largest and pinkest of the five flamingo species. The peculiar pink birds—along with dozens of other species of waterfowl that live in the inlet—are Celestún's primary attraction; in fact, this is one of the best bird-watching areas in Mexico and is known by bird enthusiasts worldwide.

Though tourism is growing, Celestún's coastal waters teem with fish and octopus, and catching them is still the main industry of locals here. The town has about 8,000 permanent residents but 10,000 fisherman ply the coast from here to Río Lagartos during octopus season (August–December). Celestún is also an important salt extraction area, producing 21,000 tons of salt every year. Salt production has been a vital industry since A.D. 600, and fishing goes back even further, of course.

If you're not a hard-core birder, a trip to the flamingo reserve is about the only reason to come to Celestún, and the town is just close enough to Mérida (96 kilometers/59.7 miles) to make day trips possible. Numerous tour operators offer tours here from Mérida, or you can do it yourself relatively easily by bus—either way it's a pretty long day. If you have some time and a car, staying a night or even two lets you visit the reserve pressure-free and to check out some additional tours and a great eco-lodge.

FLAMINGO RESERVE

The Reserva Ecológica de los Petenes (Petenes State Ecological Reserve; the reserve's little-used official name) is one of just a few breeding areas in the Northern Hemisphere for the American flamingo, and it is home to the species' largest colony—15,000–20,000 birds can gather here in the November–February mating season. Hundreds of other birds and waterfowl nest in the wetlands and mangrove forests—about 300 of the 509 identified bird species in the Yucatán Peninsula can be spied here. It's not unusual to see a blue heron or an anhinga perched on a tree stump with wings stretched to dry in the sun.

One reason for the diversity of bird life is the diversity of habitat, which includes mangrove forests, coastal dunes, savannas, low deciduous forest, and hummocks (small islands of mangroves in the wetlands), and of course seashore and the Celestún estuaries.

⋈ Flamingo Tours

No matter how you do it (there are a couple of ways), a standard flamingo tour unfolds in four parts: a stop at the "petrified" forest (a stand of ghostly, leafless trees killed by salt-water intrusion), then to the flamingo feeding grounds, followed by a short ride through the mangroves, and then a stop at an *ojo de agua* (freshwater spring; literally, an "eye of water") to go swimming. Because the sites are relatively far apart—the petrified forest is at the mouth of the *ría* while the flamingos congregate near its top, around 15 kilometers (9.3 miles) away—you spend a good amount of time motoring from one place to the next. In a 2–2.5-hour trip, you'll spend 20–30 minutes observing the flamingos (and somewhat less at the other spots). It doesn't sound like much, but most people find it sufficient. If you want more time with the flamingos—especially if the flock is at its height—private guides are the most flexible. With either the state guide service or the fishermen's cooperative, you'll have to get everyone in the boat (and the guide) to agree to adjust the schedule.

The **Parador Turístico Cultur** is the rather inelegant name for the pier and visitor center where the state-sponsored guide service is based. It is two kilometers (1.25 miles) from Celestún,

flamingos in flight

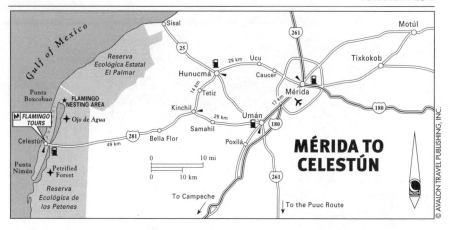

on the west side of the highway bridge spanning the *ría*. A standard tour (petrified forest, flamingos, mangroves, and swimming hole) has an official price of US$90 plus US$26 for the guide, for 1–6 people. A shorter, 80–90 minute tour, which doesn't include the petrified forest, costs US$56 plus US$17 for the guide. The people at the visitors desk won't necessarily offer to put small groups together; the best way to join other travelers is to arrive around 10 A.M. (if you're coming from Mérida by bus, take the 8 A.M. departure) and ask around. You may get a lower price by negotiating directly with the guide or boatman, but only do so if you really need to—the profit margin is already low and part of the money goes to environmental preservation. Guide service is available in Spanish, English, and Italian.

The **fishermen's cooperative** has a stand on the beach, at the end of Calle 11. Trips taken from here are basically the same except for one element: the cost. Trips are a little more expensive because of the gas used to travel up the coast to the entrance of the *ría*. A typical tour will run a party of up to six US$105 plus US$26 for the guide. If you end up waiting for more than an hour for a group to develop, captains often will take groups of 2–4 people for US$78 (not including the US$26 guide fee).

Celestún Expeditions (southeast corner of main park, tel. 999/916-2049, celexp@sureste .com, 8 A.M.–5 P.M. daily) is operated by David Bacab and a team of trained naturalist-guides. Their flamingo tour is US$110 for 1–5 people and follows the standard tour. Guides speak Spanish, English, and some Italian and French.

Other Tours

Celestún Expeditions offers several alternative ecological tours as well. Bacab is an expert birder and his long-running "Morning Bird Walk" (US$35/person, two hours, binoculars included) includes a walk to the *ría;* starting at 6:30 A.M., it is a great introduction to birding. A kayak and bike tour (US$35/person, 2.5 hours, all equipment included) starts with a five-kilometer (3.1-mile) ride to the abandoned salt-producing village of Hacienda Real de Salinas and a kayak trip through the mangroves. A newer tour is the "Butterfly Walk" (US$35/person, two hours) and is for those interested in the region's numerous species of butterflies and moths. Other tours include crocodile spotting, fly-fishing, visiting area haciendas, and a shoreline tour. Bacab also is interested in involving tourists in environmental efforts, such as collecting trash along the highway—he did not have a fixed program when we came through, but that's another option worth asking about.

In Mérida, **Ecoturismo Yucatán** (Calle 3 No. 235 between Calles 32A-34, Col. Pensiones, tel. 999/925-2187) is one of several agencies

the petrified forest in the Reserva Ecológica de los Petenes

that offer ecological tours to the area, especially for those interested in birding.

ACCOMMODATIONS
Under US$50
In a watermelon-colored building, the new **Hostal Ría Celestún** (Calle 12 No. 104-A at Calle 13, tel. 988/916-2222, hostalriacelestun@hotmail.com, US$3.50 pp hammock spot/tent site, US$5.25 pp dorm, US$13 s/d with shared bath) was still working out the kinks when we passed through. Accommodations were dark and in need of a serious wipe-down, bathrooms were approaching the edge of decency, and the outdoor kitchen, while fully equipped, was somewhat suspect. That said, the common areas were very inviting with hammocks and comfy chairs, there was a growing book exchange, Internet access was available (US$1.75), and there were plenty of bicycles to rent (US$2.60/hour, US$4.50/day). Guests also seemed quite content.

Just one block from the beach is  **Posada Sofia** (Calle 12 No. 100 between Calles 9 and 11, tel. 999/990-7707, US$9 s, US$18 d,

US$22 s/d and cable TV), a clean and simple hotel offering rooms with fans and private bathrooms. At reasonable prices—especially for solo travelers—this is a fine choice.

Half a block from the pier, **Hotel María del Carmen** (Calle 12 No. 106 between Calles 13 and 15, tel. 988/916-2170, US$26 s/d with fan, US$31 s/d with a/c) is a reliable option on a spectacular stretch of beach. Each of the nine simple rooms has sturdy window screens, two double beds, and a balcony or terrace. Most also have ocean views. If your budget permits, the air-conditioned rooms are worth the extra five bucks.

Near the northern edge of town, **Ecohotel Flamingo Playa** (Calle 12 No. 67-C between Calles 3 and 5, tel. 988/916-2133, flamingo_hotel@hotmail.com, US$35–44 s/d) offers beachside rooms with tile floors, air-conditioning, and cable TV. The ocean is right in front, and you also can take a dip in the small but inviting pool.

US$50–100
Hotel Manglares (Calle 12 No. 63, tel.

988/916-2063, www.hotelmanglares.com, US$65 s/d, cabana US$110) had not opened yet when we passed through but was clearly shaping up to be one of the better hotels in Celestún. It's expected to open in the fall of 2005, and will include 24 double rooms with a/c, satellite TV, and telephone, and four beachfront cabanas, each with a small living room, bedroom, and kitchenette. A pool, restaurant, and bar were planned as well. The hotel is at the north end of Calle 12 and is owned by the same two brothers who operate Restaurante La Palapa.

Over US$100

North of town in the middle of the flamingo reserve, you'll find the classy **N Hotel Eco Paraíso Xixim** (Antigua Carretera a Sisal Km. 10, tel. 988/916-2100, www.ecoparaiso .com, US$159 s, US$99 pp double occupancy). This hotel boasts 15 oceanfront palapa-roofed bungalows that rest on 61 acres of land. Each private unit has a sitting area, comfortable beds, and an ample hammock-hung patio right outside the door. A short walk brings you to a modern pool, an immense shade palapa, and a tall lookout platform that affords views of the sea and coast for miles. Walk a bit farther and you will hit four ecologically diverse trails (two for walking, two for biking). As the name suggests, it also is an eco-friendly hotel: Solar energy is used, all water is recycled (as is waste), and the topography of the land has been kept intact by building upon only 1.2 percent of the property. No question, it's a long way from city life. And it's a perfect retreat away from it all, with sun, white sand, and the emerald sea at your doorstep. Be sure to ask about the educational (and excellent!) ecotours that are offered. Rates include a full breakfast and dinner, all taxes, and tips.

For longer stays, consider **Playa Maya Resorts** (Antigua Carretera a Sisal s/n, tel. 999/944-2901, playamaya@prodigy.net.mx, www.playamaya.net). In construction when we passed through, it is a condominium complex—with one and two bedroom units, a few pools, and stores. Call or check the website for more information.

FOOD

N Restaurante La Palapa (Calle 12 No. 105 between Calles 11 and 13, tel. 988/916-2063, 11 A.M.–7 P.M. daily, US$5–10) is easily the best and most reliable restaurant in Celestún, serving tasty seafood, plus various chicken and beef dishes, beneath a soaring palapa roof. Whereas other restaurants in town have a somewhat liberal approach to appearance and cleanliness (we tracked down one restaurant owner chopping chicken in the kitchen with no shirt on) the service, facilities, and food prep at La Palapa are impeccable. The restaurant burned down in December 2003, but reopened—bigger and more modern—in July 2004. Tour groups often eat here, but the dining area is large enough to give everyone space.

Restaurante Boya (Calle 12 No. 99 at Calle 11, tel. 988/916-2129, 9 A.M.–6 P.M. daily, US$4–8) serves a standard seaside menu of fillet, shrimp, seafood soup, and more, plus cheap beer and a full bar. Eat in a somewhat dim indoor dining area or at shady tables set up in the sand on the beach. Friendly service.

Restaurante El Lobo (corner of Calles 10 and 13, no phone, 8 A.M.–noon and 6–11 P.M. daily, US$2.50–5) has great breakfast options, including Belgian waffles and yogurt with mixed fruit. For dinner, the pizza is good and a welcome alternative if you are seafooded out.

The **mercado municipal** (north side of park, 7 A.M.–6 P.M. daily) has a decent selection of fruit, veggies, bread, and other stuff, plus several taco stands near the entrance.

INFORMATION AND SERVICES

There are no banks, ATMs, or currency exchange offices in Celestún, and few places accept credit cards. Until this changes, be sure to take out enough cash beforehand to cover housing, food, and excursions. There is also no post office.

Celestún's **Centro de Salud** (health center, Calle 5 between Calles 8 and 10, tel. 988/916-2046, 8 A.M.–4 P.M. Mon.–Fri., emergency services available daily) is a very basic operation.

If possible, serious injuries should be treated in Mérida.

Farmacia Similares (south side of park, next to the *palacio municipal,* no telephone, 9 A.M.–9 P.M. daily) has a modest selection of medications and other items.

The **police** (tel. 988/916-2025) are stationed in the *palacio municipal,* on the south side of the park. Note that the phone number is the general number to city hall, so you may not get an answer after hours or on weekends.

You can surf the net at **Hostal Ría Celestún** (Calle 12 No. 104-A at Calle 13, US$1.75/hour), although the connection is often down.

GETTING THERE AND AROUND

Bus

Buses to Celestún leave from Mérida's Noreste bus terminal every hour every day 5 A.M.–8:30 P.M. (except 7 A.M.). In Celestún, the small bus terminal (tel. 988/916-2067) is at the southeast corner of the main park, near the Celestún Expeditions office. There are buses to Mérida (US$3.50, two hours, hourly 5:30 A.M.–8 P.M.) as well as to many of the intermediate towns. If you want to go directly to a flamingo tour, ask the driver to let you off at the visitor center instead of going all the way into town.

Car

From Mérida, there are two routes to Celestún: The southern route goes through Umán while the northerly one passes through Hunucma. Both routes lead to Kinchil, where you pick up Highway 281 direct to Celestún. We find the southerly route to be more convenient, as long as you don't get lost in Umán. Entering town, you'll come to a broad three-way intersection, often packed with cars, *triciclos* (three-wheeled bike taxis), pedestrians, and one overworked traffic cop. Bear right there, and look for signs to Celestún.

Getting Around Town

You can walk just about anywhere in Celestún, although when it's hot many locals prefer to take a *triciclo;* a ride in town costs US$.50. If you don't have a car, you'll probably have to take a *triciclo* to the river port where flamingo trips start, about three kilometers (1.9 miles) back down the highway. The fare there is US$1.

Bicycling is another possibility, mostly to visit Hacienda Real de Salinas. You can rent bikes (or arrange bike tours) at Restaurante El Lobo, Hostel Ría Celestún, and Celestún Expeditions; the cost is around US$1.50 per day.

Progreso

On the Gulf of Mexico, Progreso (pop. 55,000) is Mérida's closest access to the sea, an easy 33-kilometer (20.5-mile) drive on Highway 261. Meridianos flock here in summer to escape the intense heat and sticky humidity—as many as 150,000 during July and August weekends. The whole town comes to life; all the restaurants are open, usually quiet shops hustle, the beaches are filled with families enjoying the surf and sea. Cruise ships also land here twice a week (maybe more by the time you read this) disgorging several thousand passengers each. Many of those passengers take buses straight to Mérida and the Puuc Route, but Progreso has made a number of improvements to its waterfront in an attempt to entice cruise-shippers to stick around (and to please the Meridianos too). The *malecón* (concrete boardwalk) in particular is reasonably pleasant. One drawback the town fathers can't do anything about is the constant and sometimes powerful wind, which buffets the entire northern coast. Mexico sent two windsurfers to the Olympics; they trained in nearby Chicxulub Puerto. Ironically, you'll see little wind-sport activity right in front of Progreso as the long pier disrupts the airflow.

Progreso was founded in 1856, and during the halcyon days of the henequen industry, huge ships were a regular feature of the town

a windy day in Progreso

waterfront and its then-amazing two-kilometer/1.25-mile-long wharf. (It's now about seven kilometers/4.3 miles long.) Henequen entrepreneurs built mansions east of town; there are still mansions there, albeit more modern constructions befitting their current owners, mostly Canadians and Mérida's well-to-do. Many are for rent by the week or month.

SIGHTS

La Playa

Travelers arriving from the Caribbean side of the peninsula will find the Gulf coast rather underwhelming. The sand is coarser, and the water doesn't have the flamboyant shades of blue that make the Quintana Roo coast justly famous. But the beach at Progreso is still fairly broad and clean and will do in a pinch. The water stays shallow a long way out and is relatively calm, although expect some chop during the stormy season (June–October) and know that the wind never really dies down. The beach is dotted with palapa sun shelters; across the street are a line of restaurants and cafés.

El Faro

Built between 1885 and 1891 on the site of an earlier lighthouse, today's 40-meter/131-foot-high *faro* (lighthouse) was originally lit with kerosene. It was converted to electricity in 1923; a 1,000-watt light bulb and a backup generator ensure there's always light to lead sailors through the shallow Gulf waters into Progreso. Even Hurricane Gilbert didn't knock this old-timer down. It's not officially open to tourists, but lighthouse buffs may be able to finagle a visit by asking at the tourist office, just down the street.

The Wharf

At the turn of the 20th century, Progreso's two-kilometer/1.25-mile-long pier was the longest stone wharf in the world. It had to be—the Yucatán Peninsula sits on a long limestone shelf that drops ever-so-gradually into the Gulf, making this and most bays here extremely shallow. Some geographers conjecture that at one time Yucatán, Cuba, and Florida were all one long extension of land.

For being so long, the original pier was still in only six meters (19.7 feet) of water, which

The State of Yucatán

© LIZA PRADO CHANDLER

Progreso's pier is one of the longest in the world.

proved insufficient for larger container ships and, more recently, modern cruise ships. During the henequen days, Progresso and its pier were the scene of heavy international shipping. That activity has declined greatly, especially since an alternative pier was built in 1968 in the protected Yucalpetén harbor, six kilometers (3.7 miles) west of Progreso. However, in addition to cruise ships, some ships still call at Progreso to pick up Mexican exports such as honey, cement, fish, salt, and steel. The pier was extended to accommodate the traffic (and in hopes of attracting more), and now stretches 4.3 kilometers (2.6 miles) into the gulf. There's an artificial island and fleet of trucks and buses to ferry cargo and cruise-shippers back and forth. Tourists used to be able to walk or take a ride to the end of the pier, but that has been halted out of safety and (improbably) antiterrorism concerns.

Parque Marino Nacional Arrecife Alacranes

Formed in June 1994, this marine park is made up of five islands 125 kilometers (78 miles) straight out into the gulf north of Pro-

greso. Covering nearly 300 square kilometers (186 square miles, although the islands themselves make up only a fraction of that), the reserve is a haven for a variety of marine birds, plus turtles, lobster, conch, shark, grouper, and other species under population pressure. There were no organized visits to the reserve at the time of research, and the distance from Progreso and the relative murkiness of Gulf water don't exactly recommend the reserve for future snorkeling or diving excursions. Still, the folks at the tourist office seemed to think trips to the reserve were in the making, so you can try asking them for additional info.

ENTERTAINMENT AND EVENTS

Cinema

Cines Hollywood (Plaza Del Mar, Calle 27 between Calles 76 and 78, tel. 969/934-4200, US$3, US$1.50 Tues.–Wed.) is centrally located and shows U.S. and Mexican films on its two screens. **Cine Teatro Variedades** (Calle 80 between Calles 29 and 31, tel. 969/935-0085, US$2) also runs recently released movies in

English and Spanish and has occasional live theater productions.

Bars

La Ferretería (Calle 80 between Calles 27 and 29, noon–1 A.M. Tues.–Sun.) is a dimly lit, air-cooled, bistrolike bar with ornate wood floors and chrome chairs and tables. Amid a bunch of classless places, this is a great spot for a beer and bar-food specials.

SHOPPING

For the best selection of *artesanía* and traditional clothing, head to the plaza in front of the Casa de la Cultura (Calle 80 at Calle 25), where every Tuesday and Thursday 7 A.M.–4 P.M. an **open-air market** is held for tourists arriving by cruise ship.

Plaza Del Mar (Calle 27 between Calles 76 and 78, 8 A.M.–10 P.M.) is a small shopping center with T-shirt shops, a few boutiques, a food court, a pharmacy, and a supermarket. The movie theater on the second floor is the main reason to visit.

SPORTS AND RECREATION

You can rent **personal watercraft** (US$30/half hour) and kayaks (US$3/half hour) or take a **banana boat ride** (US$3 pp, 20 minutes) from the beach in front of El Viejo y El Mar restaurant (Calle 19 at Calle 78, tel. 969/935-2299). The equipment is available roughly 10 A.M.–4:30 P.M. daily, but the boats are operated by the restaurant, so ask there if you don't find anyone on the beach.

The Gulf coast is a great area for **sailboarding, sailing,** and **kiteboarding.** However, Progreso proper isn't the best spot, as the pier disrupts the wind flow. Better to head to **Marina Silcer** (tel. 969/934-0491) in Chicxulub Puerto a few kilometers east.

ACCOMMODATIONS

Progreso has a growing but still limited selection of accommodations. Finding a room

can be hard in July or August and on high-season weekends.

Camping

At the time of research, there were no formal campsites in Progreso. That said, there are miles of beach where you can set up a tent for free and not be bothered. Just be sure to stop in at the Tourist Information office to double-check that camping is still legal (and safe) before you set down your stakes.

Under US$50

Hotel Embajadores (Calle 64 No. 130 between Calles 21 and 23, tel. 969/935-5673, www.progresohotel.com, US$6 dorm with fan, US$18 s/d with fan, US$22–40 s/d with a/c) has a decent variety of rooms—from a dorm with shared bath to a suite with a view—that were being renovated when we stopped in; at that time, the accommodations were a little run-down but relatively clean. The hotel also has a good-sized communal kitchen, lots of books to borrow or exchange, and Internet access on-site (guests receive 30 minutes free per day). There were plans to rent bicycles and provide laundry service.

Near the center of town, **Hotel San Miguel** (Calle 78 No. 148 between Calles 29 and 31, tel. 969/935-1357, US$20 s/d with fan, US$25 s/d with a/c) is a simple and clean hotel offering rooms with private bathrooms, hot water, and cable TV. Rooms are about US$4 less during the low season.

Just a block from the beach, **M Casa Isadora** (Calle 21 No. 116 between Calles 58 and 60, tel. 969/935-4595, www.casaisadora.com, US$33–44 s/d with a/c and cable TV) is a converted *casona* housing six spotless rooms with high ceilings and beautiful tile floors. The hotel boasts a nice pool area with lots of comfy chairs and greenery. Breakfast also is included in the rate. There were plans to build two rooms poolside.

US$50–100

Condhotel Progreso (Calle 21 No. 150 between Calles 66 and 68, tel. 969/935-5079, www.condhotelprogreso.com, US$40 s/d,

US$50–55 one bedroom, US$75–85 two bedrooms) offers 23 condos, all equipped with full kitchen, satellite TV, and air-conditioning as well as seven hotel rooms without the kitchen amenities. Some condos have balconies and ocean views—ask to look at a few before choosing. There is also a small but clean pool. Discounts available for weekly/monthly rentals.

Although a little far from the action, **M Hotel Casa Quixote** (Calle 23 No. 64 between Calles 48 and 50, tel. 969/935-2909, casaquixote@prodigy.net.mx, www.casaquixote.com, US$40 s/US$55 d with fan, US$70 s/US$80 d with a/c) is worth the extra time it takes to walk to town. Within a converted home, rooms vary significantly in size and decor but all are nicely appointed and have Yucatecan tile floors. A huge and well-maintained lawn in back surrounds an inviting pool. A two-bedroom/two-bath house is also available for US$85 (US$125 Easter and July–Aug.).

West of Progreso in Yucalpetén, **Sian-Ka'an** (Calle 13 Poligono III No. 252, tel. 969/935-4017, www.hotelsiankaan.com, US$48–78 s/d) is a quiet hideaway on a nice stretch of beach with palapas. While all nine rooms have kitchenettes and cable TV, they vary greatly in style, view, and comfort; rooms 1 and 4 are particularly coveted because of their fantastic ocean views and nice decor. Take a look at a few before choosing. A small clean pool also faces the ocean. For eats, Sian-Ka'an boasts a glass-enclosed restaurant, **Yikil-Ha** (8 A.M.–8 P.M. daily), which serves local and international food for US$3–5 breakfast, US$3–14 lunch and dinner.

Yucalpetén can be reached easily by public transportation; go to the corner of Calles 82 and 29 in Progreso, where you'll find a small parking lot filled with *combis* (Volkswagen minivans) that leave about every five minutes for Yucalpetén and cost US$.25. By car, take Highway 261 north out of Mérida. Before you hit Progreso, take the turnoff for Yucalpetén.

FOOD

Progreso's restaurants are typical of Mexican seaside resorts: If you like fresh-caught fish

you're in luck, but it's hard to find much else. The following is just a sampling; you can walk up and down the waterfront and pick the restaurant that appeals to you the most.

Flamingos (Calle 19 at Calle 72, tel. 969/935-2122, 8 A.M.–midnight daily, US$6–12) serves big portions under a breezy palapa roof. Shrimp, fish fillets, and ceviche are the most popular, but you'll also find brochettes, meat and chicken dishes, and even a few Chinese options. Nice views of the beach and waterfront.

Next door, **Shark Restaurant** (Calle 19 at Calle 72, tel. 969/935-2116, 11 A.M.–7 P.M. daily, US$5–8) is a somewhat newer, hipper place, specializing in seafood *carpacho*—a version of carpaccio made from thinly sliced fish, octopus, or conch served in an olive oil, vinegar, and white wine sauce. The restaurant also has shrimp, chicken, beef, and pasta options, and it offers specials on a different beer every month. It was open only until 7 P.M. when we came through, which makes it best as a lunch spot.

Le Saint Bonnet and **El Viejo y El Mar** (Calle 19 at Calle 78, tel. 969/935-2299, 8 A.M.–11 P.M. daily, US$5–15) are sister restaurants right next to each other on the *malecón*. They keep the same hours (more or less) and share a menu of mostly international seafood: Try the three-person seafood platter or the *filete de mero empapelado,* fresh grouper baked in aluminum foil with shrimp. There are also pizza, pasta, and standard Mexican plates. Le Saint Bonnet has tablecloths and is a bit classier, while El Viejo y el Mar caters to a slightly younger crowd with drink specials and DJ music Friday and Saturday nights. There also is a small swimming pool (and changing area) that guests of either place can use.

All the way at the east end of the waterfront, **M Viña del Mar** (Calle 19 between Calles 60 and 62, tel. 969/934-4747, 8 A.M.–1 A.M. daily, US$5–10) is worth the walk. The dining room is pretty plain, but the dishes are creative and tasty, such as the *filete viña,* prepared with shrimp and a cilantro, *chaya* (a spinachlike plant) and *xtabentún* flower sauce, and the coconut shrimp made with fresh coconuts and a mango-apple dressing. And don't leave without trying an *Azul Progreso,* the house cocktail.

Mercado Municipal (Calle 80 between Calles 25 and 27, 7 A.M.–3 P.M. daily) is a place where locals come to shop for their daily needs: fruits, veggies, fresh meats, clothes, toiletries, and other personal items. There are also a handful of eateries offering cheap local eats and *antojitos*.

Super San Francisco de Asis (Calle 80 between Calles 29 and 31, 7 A.M.–9 P.M. daily) is a large modern supermarket across from HSBC bank.

INFORMATION AND SERVICES

Tourist Information

The **tourist office** (Calle 80 and Calle 25, tel. 969/935-0104, www.puertoprogreso.com, 8 A.M.–8 P.M. Mon.–Sat. and 8 A.M.–1 P.M. Sun.) is in the Casa de Cultura; the main doors are on Calle 25 but you can also cut through the large courtyard fronting Calle 80. Not everyone working there is altogether helpful, but asking a few people usually works.

Medical Services

Centro Médico Americano (Calle 33 between Calles 80 and 82, tel. 969/935-0769 or tel. 969/935-0951) is the best hospital in Progreso, with a 24-hour emergency room.

Farmacia Yza (Calle 78 at Calle 29, tel. 969/935-0684) is open 24-hours daily; use the walk-up window on Calle 78 11 P.M.–7 A.M. Delivery is available 8 A.M.–9:30 P.M. You may find better prices around the corner at **Farmacias Similares** (Calle 29 between Calles 78 and 80, tel. 969/934-4205, 7:30 A.M.–9:30 P.M. Mon.–Sat., 8:30 A.M.–8:30 P.M. Sun.).

Police

There is a police station on Calle 19 at Calle 66. The phone number is tel. 969/935-0026.

Money

A block apart, **Banamex** (Calle 80 between Calles 27 and 29, tel. 969/935-0312, 9 A.M.–4 P.M. Mon.–Fri.) and **HSBC** (Calle 80 No. 144 between Calles 29 and 31, 8 A.M.–7 P.M. Mon.–Sat.) both have reliable ATMs and change cash and travelers checks.

Post Office

The post office (8:30 A.M.–3 P.M. Mon.–Sat.) is just east of Parque Independencia on Calle 31 between Calles 78 and 80.

Internet, Telephone, and Fax

Consorcio Navarro Bolio (Calle 80 at Calle 29, tel. 969/935-3174, 8 A.M.–8:30 P.M. Mon.–Sat., 8 A.M.–2 P.M. Sun.) is a casual lottery and betting house that moonlights as an Internet and long-distance phone center. Check your email for US$.90/hour; call the United States and Canada for US$.45/minute.

Across the street and next to the movie theater, **Inter Coffee** (Calle 80 between Calles 29 and 31, tel. 969/934-4558, 8 A.M.–2 A.M. daily) also has Internet access (US$.90/hour) and will burn CDs for US$1.75.

The **telephone office** (Calle 31 between Calles 78 and 80, tel. 969/935-0128, 8 A.M.–7 P.M. Mon.–Sat. and 9 A.M.–12:30 P.M. Sat.–Sun.) is in the same building as the post office; send faxes for US$3/page and receive them for US$.60/page.

Laundry

Lavandería Caremi is at the back of Consorcio Navarro Bolio (Calle 80 at Calle 29) and is open 8 A.M.–1 P.M. Monday–Saturday. Wash, dry, and fold is US$.90/kilo (2.2 pounds), with a three-kilo minimum (6.6 pounds); drop your clothes off by 8:30 A.M. to have them back by the afternoon (you hope).

GETTING THERE

Bus

From Mérida, buses leave the Auto-Progreso terminal on Calle 62 between Calles 65 and 67 every 10–20 minutes 5 A.M.–10 P.M. daily (US$1.50, one hour). You'll be dropped off at the bus station in Progreso (Calle 29 between Calles 80 and 82, tel. 969/935-3024), a few blocks from the center of town and a short walk from the *malecón*. To return, buses leave the Progreso station for Mérida every 15–20 minutes 5:20 A.M.–10 P.M. daily.

Vans also make the round-trip from Mérida to Progreso, leaving Mérida from a small station at Calle 60 between Calles 65 and 67 every 15 minutes or so (when full). In Progreso, the same vans head back to Mérida from the corner of Calles 31 and 82.

Car

From downtown Mérida, drive north on Paseo de Montejo or Calle 60. The two streets eventually merge and become Highway 261, which leads directly to Progreso.

Ferry

Yucatán Express (Mex tel. 800/514-5832, U.S. tel. 866/670-3939, www.yucatanexpress .com) operates a luxury car ferry from Tampa, Florida, to Progreso. The ferry usually operates twice weekly October–April, but it was suspended in 2003 and had not been restarted at the time of research. It is worth checking into though, considering what you spend on airfare and rental car otherwise. (The agency had plans to restart service in November 2005.) Round-trip passage is US$120 pp, extra for a vehicle (you can even bring a fishing boat!), and various vacation packages are available starting at US$229. Ask for info on car insurance companies before you buy your ticket—it is required in Mexico, and U.S. and Canadian insurance are not recognized.

GETTING AROUND
Golf Cart and Scooter
Rentadora Damson (Calle 19 at Calle 70, 8 A.M.–5 P.M. daily) rents *carritos de golf* for US$13/hour or US$39/day. Look for a sandwich-board sign on the corner. Down a few blocks, **Rentadora Big Banana** (Calle 19 between Calle 66 and 68, 11 A.M.–midnight daily) rents scooters for US$9/hour until 6 P.M. They also rent small lockers for US$1.75/day, with use of the changing room.

Bus
To head a few kilometers east or west of Progreso, go to the corner of Calles 82 and 29, where you'll find a small parking lot filled with *combis* (Volkswagen minivans) headed to destinations such as Chicxulub Puerto and Yucalpetén. *Combis* leave about every five minutes and cost US$.25.

To get as far as Telchac Puerto, cross the street from the *combis* to a run-down bus stop with benches. Here at 7 A.M. and 2 P.M. you can catch a bus out (one hour) for US$1.50.

East of Progreso

CHICXULUB PUERTO

East of Progreso, the coastal road wanders behind a long string of summer houses for seven kilometers (4.3 miles) to the small fishing village of Chicxulub Puerto. The town is run-down, has few hotels, and the beach is always filled with boats—not too appealing for most travelers. (The town was pummeled by Hurricane Isadora in 2002 and has yet to fully recover.) However, the strong, steady wind and shallow, obstacle-free shoreline make for ideal sailing, windsurfing, and kiteboarding conditions, and wind-sport athletes come to Chicxulub from all over the world to play and train. The town is home base for two of Mexico's 2004 windsurfing Olympians.

Sights
You can't really *see* it, but Chicxulub is inside (and is the namesake of) a massive **crater** left by a meteorite that hit Earth 65 million years ago. Geologists and paleontologists believe the impact and its aftermath killed most of the world's dinosaur species and ushered in the age of mammals and eventually humans. Chicxulub Puerto may be barely a blip on most travelers' radar screens, but it is oddly compelling to find yourself at ground zero of arguably the most important and cataclysmic event of all time.

Chicxulub's town beach

Sports and Recreation

Unless you are a scientist studying the crater, the best (and maybe only) reason to visit Chicxulub Puerto is for the wind sports. And for that, all roads lead to **Marina Silcer** (turn at the old gasoline station, tel. 969/934-0491, 10 A.M.–6 P.M. Tues.–Sun.). One-on-one instruction is available for all levels in windsurfing (US$17.50/1.5-hour session), sailing (US$35/two-hour session), and kiteboarding (US$35/two-hour session), or sign up for a complete four- or eight-part course. You can also rent gear by the hour and use the marina's small swimming pool. Restaurant on-site. The best wind is from September to May.

Food

On the main drag, **Los Barriles** (Calle 19 No. 48, between Calles 16 and 18, tel. 969/934-0403, 11 A.M.–10 P.M. daily, US$5–8) is hard to miss with the entryway in the shape of two enormous barrels, hence the name. The main restaurant in town for almost a quarter century, Los Barriles serves good, reliable seafood dishes such as fish fillets, shrimp platters, and ceviche.

Information and Services

The **post office** is on Calle 21 between Calles 10 and 12. There were no banks or ATMs in Chicxulub Puerto when we came through, so it's best to take out cash in Progreso.

Getting There

By car, take Highway 261 north out of Mérida. As you approach Progreso, follow signs east (or right) to Chicxulub. By public transportation, go to the corner of Calles 82 and 29 in Progreso, where you'll find a small parking lot filled with *combis* (Volkswagen minivans) that leave about every five minutes and cost US$.25.

UAYMITÚN RESERVE

Farther east, you'll pass the small town of Uaymitún (why-mih-TOON), which, in addition to a number of upscale summer houses and rental properties, is home to the interesting **Mirador Ecoturístico Uaymitún** (Uaymitún Ecotouristic Viewpoint, Carretera Chicxulub-Telchac Puerto Km. 15, 8 A.M.–6 P.M. daily, open until 7 P.M. during summer, free, binocular

The State of Yucatán

CHICXULUB CRATER

Sixty-five million years ago, a meteorite more than 10 kilometers (6.2 miles) wide collided with the Earth. It was traveling at 20 kilometers (12.4 miles) per second and at the time of impact its temperature was 18,000°C (32,432°F)—three times that of the sun's surface. This massive meteor created a colossal crater—more than 2.5 kilometers (1.6 miles) deep and about 200 kilometers (124.3 miles) in diameter—the largest and best-preserved crater on Earth. It caused volcanoes to erupt, the earth to tremble, and tidal waves more than 500 meters (0.3 mile) high. The turmoil then sent millions of tons of pulverized rock into the atmosphere, plunging the earth into darkness. The lack of sun eventually led to the demise of more than 70 percent of all living things on the planet, including the dinosaurs.

All very interesting, but why mention it here? Because this is where the meteor hit—in what is today the coastal town of Chicxulub, just east of Progreso (this is why the crater is known as Chicxulub Crater). In 1981, scientists from PEMEX (Mexico's national petroleum company) were drilling in the Yucatán Peninsula when they discovered gravitational anomalies near the town of Chicxulub. The scientists took core samples and soon concluded that the meteor that had changed the face of the planet crashed in the Yucatán. It provided an explanation as to why the limestone-covered peninsula had eroded so dramatically, creating a ring of caves and cenotes in numbers found nowhere else on Earth. In 1991, UNAM (the National Autonomous University of Mexico) in cooperation with NASA confirmed the theory.

The Yucatán Peninsula is well known as one of the richest parts of the world; what many do not know, however, is that life as we know it began here.

rental US$.90). A high wooden platform overlooks a protected part of the extensive marshland that runs just inland along much of the Gulf coast. Thousands of flamingos come here to feed, and with binoculars you can get a decent look at these beautiful, peculiar birds in their natural habitat. If you're lucky, some may come closer to the platform, and you're sure to see other bird species as well. May to November has the highest flamingo population, but the mirador is worth a stop at any time. Tip: Another spot to see flamingos is along the road to Xtambó ruins; the road cuts across the marshland and the birds are sometimes feeding quite close by.

XTAMBÓ

A few kilometers inland from Telchac Puerto, on the road to Tixkokob, are the not-too-exciting Mayan ruins of Xtambó (Carretera Dzemul-Xtambó Km. 14, 8 A.M.–6 P.M. daily, free). Various low-lying structures without surface ornamentation surround two plazas. On a clear day, you can see the coast from the top of the highest point, Pyramid of the Cross. More than 600 skeletons were unearthed during excavations here, but there is no museum and the reconstruction was overzealous, leaving the ruins very artificial looking. The Catholic chapel on a small rise nearby was built from stones of the dismantled pyramids.

TELCHAC PUERTO

Continuing along the coast east from Chicxulub Puerto, the road parallels the sea for 75 kilometers (46.6 miles) to Dzilam de Bravo. Along the way are several small villages, all tuned in to life on the sea. The largest of these villages is Telchac Puerto, about 40 kilometers (25 miles) east of Progreso.

Accommodations

On the main road into town, **Posada Liz** (Calle 23 between Calles 30 and 32, tel. 991/917-

4125, US$12 s/d with fan) offers eight basic and cleanish rooms two blocks from the beach. Rooms are little stuffy on the first floor—ask for one upstairs to catch the evening breeze.

Across the street, **Hotel Principe Negro** (Calle 23 No. 90 between Calles 30 and 32, tel. 999/141-3389, toll-free Mex. tel. 800/505-8028, US$22–30 s/d with fan, US$39 s/d with a/c) has clean rooms with cable TV and small refrigerators. There also is an inviting pool if you tire of the ocean. Discounts are available during the low season and for extended stays.

Reef Club (Carretera Progreso-Telchac Puerto Km. 32, tel. 999/948-4848, toll-free Mex. tel. 800/000-7333, www.reefyucatan .com, US$95 pp single occupancy, US$77 pp double occupancy) is an all-inclusive resort just outside of Telchac Puerto. Rooms are unremarkable although all have a terrace or balcony. The main restaurant also feels more like a school cafeteria than a resort with its plastic chairs and fluorescent lights. That said, the beach is one of the best on this coast—wide, clean, and overlooking the emerald ocean—and everything *is* included: meals, snacks, drinks, nightly shows, tennis courts, and kayaks. There are also two pools and a discotechque on-site. If you don't want to stay the night but do want some R&R on the beach, the Reef Club offers a **day pass** (US$35 men, US$26 women, US$9–17 children between the ages of 5–15). The day pass is good 9 A.M.–6 P.M. and includes breakfast, lunch, open bar, and use of all the amenities.

Food

Restaurante Miramar (Calle 19 at Calle 99, no phone, 10 A.M.–6 P.M. daily, US$5–15) is a big, basic eatery with plastic tables, a palapa roof and a menu full of—what else?—seafood. *Pulpo en su tinta* (octopus cooked in its ink) is sure to be fresh, and the large ceviche platter would feed a hungry basketball team. The restaurant actually has a large, decent section of beach, which you are free to use if you order something.

Information and Services

There are no services to speak of here—withdraw cash and take care of any other business in Progreso.

Getting There

Having your own car is by far the easiest and surest way to see this lonely stretch of coast. From Mérida, take Highway 261 north toward the coast; as you approach Progreso, follow signs east (or right) to Telchac Puerto. If you want public transportation, buses theoretically leave Progreso at 7 A.M. and 2 P.M. daily and cost US$1.50 (one hour). You can catch a bus at the run-down bus stop at the corner of Calles 82 and 29.

Izamal

The pope managed to visit Izamal, so you surely can find a day or two to look around as well. North of Highway 180 between Mérida and Chichén Itzá, Izamal is a fine old colonial city with a beautiful convent and several Mayan ruins right in town, plus quiet plazas, friendly residents, and two excellent lodging options (and other more than adequate ones). Most tourists arrive here on a tour bus, visit the convent and the city center for an hour or so, and then motor off again. But Izamal is a great place for independent travelers to stay a night or two, soaking in atmosphere and rich history of this classic Yucatecan town.

HISTORY

Pope John Paul II visited Izamal in August 1993, instantly transforming the city and cathedral into places of high Catholic symbolism. But it has been an important religious site since the time of the ancient Mayans—it was one of three major pilgrimage sites in pre-Colombian Yucatán, along with Chichén Itzá and San Gervasio on Isla Cozumel. Spanish priests and colonizers recognized the area's importance and lost little time constructing a magnificent convent and church atop the existing

Mayan pyramids, even using the same stones as building materials. Fray Diego de Landa, who would later gain notoriety for burning dozens of Mayan codices, oversaw the church.

SIGHTS

 Convento de San Antonio de Padua

The most imposing structure in this small town is the mustard-colored Convento de San Antonio de Padua (Parque la Estrella, 8 A.M.–9:30 P.M. daily). Constructed between 1533 and 1562 under the direction of Fray Diego de Landa, the convent was built upon what was once the immense Mayan temple Pap-Hol-Chac. If you look closely, you'll even see some Mayan glyphs in the church walls themselves. A 7,806-square-meter (25,610-square-foot) grassy atrium enclosed by 75 arches sits at the front of this beautiful complex. It's the largest atrium in the Americas and arguably the second-largest in the world (the largest is at Saint Peter's in the Vatican)—an impressive photo-op to say the least. On-site, there also is a small

museum (10 A.M.–1 P.M. and 3–6 P.M. Tues.–Sat., 9 A.M.–4 P.M. Sun., US$.45), which commemorates Pope John Paul II's 1993 visit to the convent.

Town Plazas

Izamal's two, adjoining plazas—Parque la Estrella and Parque 5 de Mayo, also known as Parque Zamná—are pleasant enough, though many trees were removed before the pope's visit in 1993 so the masses of the faithful would have a better look at the pontiff. Small stands sell street food and other knick-knacks.

Archaeological Zones

Kinich Kak Moo (also known as Kinich-Kakmó, entrance on Calle 27 between Calles 28 and 30, 8 A.M.–5 P.M. daily, free) is one of a dozen Mayan ruins right in Izamal. While the others are relatively modest, Kinich Kak Moo is a whopping 195 meters (639.8 feet) long, 173 meters (567.6 feet) wide, and 34 meters (111.5 feet) at its highest point, making it the largest pyramid in the state of Yucatán, and the third- to fifth-largest in Mexico, depend-

The Convento de San Antonio de Padua welcomed Pope John Paul II in 1993.

ing on how you calculate it. Built around A.D. 400–600, the pyramid was dedicated to the sun god, or Fire Macaw, and was the principal structure of a massive plaza that extended over much of present-day Izamal. Interestingly, it was once a deeply important site for Mayan shamans and worshipers, just as Izamal's Convento de San Antonio de Padua has become for Mexican Catholics today. Kinich Kak Moo is only partially restored and is therefore less impressive than even smaller structures, but it is still worth a climb, if only for the views of the city and surroundings. On a clear day, you can see Chichén Itzá, 50 kilometers (31 miles) to the east.

Museums

The **Museo Comunitario** (Calle 30, north side of convent, no phone, 8 A.M.–1 P.M. and 4–6 P.M. daily, free) is a small museum with modest displays on Izamal's ancient, colonial, and modern-day history.

There is also a small museum at the Convento de San Antonio de Padua (see listing).

Distillery Tour

About two kilometers (1.25 miles) from the center of town is the **Destilería Sisal** (end of Calle 42, tel. 999/925-9087, www.licoresdehenequen.com, 8 A.M.–7 P.M., free), where sisal, a variation of tequila made from the henequen, or sisal plant, is produced. A visit here includes a tour of the distillery and a tasting, both rather brief. Although henequen is closely related to the agave cactus and distilled in the same way, this new liquor cannot be called tequila owing to trademark restrictions of the sort France placed on sparkling wines produced outside the region of Champagne. ("Real" tequila is produced only in and around the town of Tequila in the western state of Jalisco and a few other locations.) Sisal looks and tastes very much like tequila—the main difference is that you won't find the rich, ultra-aged variations because the plant has been open only since September 2003. A 750-milliliter bottle sells at the plant for around US$12 and for slightly more in town.

SHOPPING

Hecho a Mano (Calle 31 No. 308 at Parque 5 de Mayo, tel. 988/954-0344, 10 A.M.–2 P.M. and 4–7 P.M. Mon.–Sat.) is a recommended folk-art and photography shop owned and operated by the collector-photographer team of Hector Garza and Jeanne Hunt. The pieces and photos are beautiful and museum quality, with prices to match. Or at least that's what everyone says: It was never open when we passed through, and even the shop's flyers list the hours as *más o menos* (more or less).

For a more reliable and affordable option, browse the *artesanía* tables set up in Parque Zamná most days around 8 A.M.–3 P.M.

The nearby town of Kimbilá is known as the place to go for fine *guayaberas* and *huipiles* (typical Yucatecan dresses) at wholesale prices—many of the shops in Mérida stock up there. **Exclusivas Addy** (Calle 20 No. 49, tel. 988/916-3016, 6 A.M.–10 P.M. daily) is one of a handful of family shops in the center of town—just follow the main road to the plaza. Both hand- and machine-stitched items are available. Prices still aren't rock-bottom, especially if you're only buying one, but the selection is quite large.

SPORTS AND RECREATION

You can go **horseback riding** at Hacienda San Antonio Chalanté (see *Accommodations*), about 11 kilometers (6.8 miles) south of Izamal. Well-marked dirt roads and trails lead from the hacienda to abandoned churches, caves, and cenotes, where the guide can help you clamber down for a swim in the cool clear waters; US$7/hour.

ACCOMMODATIONS

Housing is somewhat limited in Izamal, mainly because until recently few travelers stayed the night. Even today, most visitors arrive on large tour buses and stay just long enough to visit the convent and maybe climb the pyramid. Yet one of the Yucatán's most charming restored haciendas is a few miles away, and there are a couple of decent options in town. There are rumors, too, that the famous Hernández family is buying property to build another luxury hacienda-like hotel here—true or not, there is no doubt that Izamal is rising fast as a tourist destination and accommodations of all sorts aren't far off.

Under US$50

Easily the best place to stay in town is the **Hotel Macan-ché** (Calle 22 No. 305 between Calles 33 and 35, tel. 988/954-0287, macanche_86@hotmail.com, www.macanche .com, US$22–26 s/d with fan, US$35–57 s/d with a/c). Set in a lush garden that is overflowing with local fruit trees, the 12 bungalows are unique in size and style but each is comfortable and very clean. Most also have inviting patios to while away a lazy afternoon or—if you prefer to work on your tan—there is a small pool at the back of the property. A hearty breakfast is included in the rate.

Posada Flory (Calle 30 No. 267 at Calle 27, no telephone, US$13 d with fan, US$17.50 with a/c) is the least-worst of the remaining budget options. Run out of a family home— you have to walk through the family hair salon to get inside—rooms here are simple and rundown but fairly clean, all with okay private bathrooms and cable TV. The upstairs units get a bit more light—look at a few before deciding. The owner is friendly and the atmosphere pleasant.

US$50–100

About 11 kilometers (6.8 miles) south of town is the charming **M Hacienda San Antonio Chalanté** (outskirts of the town of Sudzal, tel. 999/109-4092, reservations@janus-research.com, US$35–50 s/d with fan, US$50–70 with a/c). Originally built as a Franciscan monastery and later transformed into a henequen farm, today it has been lovingly restored into a colonial-style bed-and-breakfast. Here, two manor houses hold nine uniquely named rooms, all of which have seven-meter (23-foot) ceilings, beautifully tiled bathrooms, and an-

tique furnishings. The main house also has a warmly decorated salon that begs you to stay late into the night, flipping through one of the many archaeology books while you lounge on one of the overstuffed couches. Fifteen horses also call the hacienda home—you'll be sure to see a few of them wandering untethered throughout the grounds. And if you enjoy riding, horseback tours of the backcountry are offered for US$7/hour (includes guide). A stone-floored swimming pool and a *temascal* (Mayan sauna) also are on-site. Rates include a full (and tasty!) breakfast. A taxi here from Izamal is about US$4.50.

FOOD

Near the ruins, **Kinich Kakmó** (Calle 27 No. 299 between 28 and 30, tel. 988/954-0489, 9 A.M.–6 P.M. daily, US$4–7) is a pleasant palapa-roofed place that serves regional dishes, including a full meal of *poc-chuc* (marinated grilled pork), beans, salad, and tortillas for US$5. And if you've never seen tortillas being made, check out the tiny palapa in back, where two women often can be found sitting around a small fire, patting and cooking them into shape for your meal.

Near the main plaza, **El Toro Restaurante** (Calle 33 No. 303 between Calles 30 and 32, tel. 988/967-3340, 8 A.M.–11 P.M. Tues.–Thurs., 8 A.M.–midnight Fri.–Sun., US$5–8) is a good place for a cool drink and a plate of *salbutes, papadzules,* or quesadillas. Friendly service.

Mercado Municipal (facing Parque la Estrella, 6 A.M.–2 P.M. daily) is where you'll find fresh produce, dairy, and meats.

If you have a car, head to the renovated **Hacienda San Antonio Chalanté** (outskirts of the town of Sudzal, tel. 999/109-4092, US$3.50–4.50 breakfast, US$6–8 lunch/breakfast). Here in a beautifully renovated hacienda, the cook serves Yucatecan specialties and a few international dishes that will leave you wanting to come back for more. Special meals—low cholesterol, low sodium, meatless—are prepared without a fuss; just be sure to let the staff know before you arrive. Reservations required.

YUCATECAN CUISINE

Considered among the most distinct cuisines of the country, Yucatecan food reflects the influences of its Mayan, European, and Caribbean heritage. Some popular menu items include:

Cochinita Pibil (coh-chee-NEE-ta pee-BEEL): pork that has been marinated in achiote, Seville orange juice, peppercorn, garlic, cumin, salt, and pepper, wrapped in banana leaves, and baked. Typically served on weekends only.

Dzoto-bichay (diz-OH-toe beech-EYE): tamales made of *chaya* (a leafy vegetable similar to spinach) and eggs. Comes smothered in tomato sauce.

Empanizado: slices of pork or chicken that has been breaded and fried. Often served with salad, rice, and beans.

Panucho (pahn-OO-choh): handmade tortilla stuffed with refried beans and covered with shredded turkey, pickled onion, and slices of avocado. Like a *salbute* plus!

Papadzules: hard-boiled eggs chopped and rolled into a corn tortilla. Comes smothered in a creamy pumpkin-seed sauce.

Poc-Chuc (pohk-CHOOK): slices of pork that have been marinated in Seville orange juice and coated with a tangy sauce. Pickled onions are added on the side.

Salbute (sahl-BU-teh): handmade tortilla covered with shredded turkey, pickled onion, and slices of avocado. Served hot and fast.

Sopa de Lima: a turkey-stock soup prepared with shredded turkey or chicken, fried tortilla strips, and lemon juice.

INFORMATION AND SERVICES

Tourist Information Center
The friendly city **tourist office** (tel. 988/954-0692, 9 A.M.–6 P.M. daily) is in the Palacio Municipal, facing Parque la Estrella. Theoretically you can be attended in English, French, German, or Italian, in addition to Spanish—at the very least you can pick up brochures, maps, and other info. There are public bathrooms here as well.

Medical Services
Izamal's **public hospital** (Calle 24 between Calles 35 and 37, tel. 988/954-0241 or toll-free 114) has a 24-hour emergency room and can handle minor emergencies, but those with major ailments should head to Valladolid. Note the phone is answered only 8 A.M. to 8 P.M. daily; after hours, go directly to the clinic.

Pharmacies
Farmacia Yza (Calle 28 No. 300 at Calle 31, tel. 988/954-0600) is the only pharmacy in town open 24 hours. It faces Parque Zamná, between the bank and the movie theater.

Police
The tourist police in Izamal may be the friendliest in the Yucatán Peninsula—one officer flagged us down just to ask if we needed directions. One or more officers are usually stationed at intersections around the center or ask at the tourist office in the Palacio Municipal.

Money
Banorte (corner of Calles 28 and 31, 8 A.M.–3 P.M. Mon.–Fri.) was the only bank in town when we passed through, but that seems destined to change. It has an ATM that accepts most foreign debit cards.

Post Office
The post office (8 A.M.–3 P.M. Mon.–Fri.) is on Calle 31 at Calle 30-A, next to the Palacio del Gobierno.

Internet and Fax
Cibernet (Calle 34 between Calles 29 and 31,

8:30 A.M.–10:30 P.M. daily, Internet US$.90/ hour) is the best of three Internet cafés clustered at this corner, near the gas station. It's slightly more expensive, but the connection is much faster. You also can burn CDs here for US$.90—bring your own blank disk.

You can send faxes and telegrams at the **telégrafos office** (Calle 31-A at Calle 32 No. 300 at Calle 31), in the Palacio Municipal.

Telephone
Pay phones are oddly hard to find in Izamal. There is one affixed to a support column in the Mercado Municipal, on the south side of Parque la Estrella—there may be a line to use it.

Laundry
Lavandería María José (Calle 30 No. 277-A between Calles 27 and 29, no telephone, 7:30 A.M.–1:30 P.M. and 3:30–7:30 P.M. Mon.–Fri., 7:30 A.M.–8:30 P.M. Sat.) is close to the center of town and charges US$.60 per kilo (2.2 pounds), with a three-kilo minimum (6.6 pounds).

Lavandería Burbujas (Calle 21 No. 285 at Calle 26-B, tel. 988/954-0659, 8 A.M.–7 P.M. Mon.–Sat.) is a bit farther away but can clean, dry, and fold your duds in two hours flat and charges US$.50 per kilo (2.2 pounds), with a two-kilo minimum (4.4 pounds). If no one is at the desk, ask at the house next door.

GETTING THERE
Bus
Izamal's bus terminal is one block west of the Palacio Municipal, at the end of Calle 31-A. **Oriente** (tel. 988/954-0107) and **AutoCentro** (tel. 999/101-9167) offer identical second-class service to surrounding destinations. Hours listed below are for both lines—ask at the terminal which bus is leaving at the hour you need.

Cancún, US$8, five hours, 1:15 A.M., 5 A.M., 6 A.M., 6:15 A.M., 6:30 A.M. 7 A.M., 8 A.M., 10 A.M., 11:30 A.M., 2 P.M., 2:30 P.M., 4 P.M., 4:45 P.M., 6 P.M., 7:30 P.M., and 10:30 P.M.

Mérida, US$2.50, 1.5 hours, every 30–45 minutes 5 A.M.–7:30 P.M.

Tizimin, US$4.75, 2.5 hours, 7:30 A.M., 8:35 A.M., and 6:15 P.M. only.

Valladolid, US$3, two hours, all Cancún departures plus 1:45 P.M.

Car
From Mérida, the road to Izamal (via Hoctún) is well marked. If you are going directly to Hacienda Chalanté, stay on the highway (which turns into the toll road, but you'll just be on for a few kilometers so it doesn't cost anything) and take the Izamal exit at Km. 68. (Take the same exit if coming from the other direction.) Headed north, it's four kilometers (2.5 miles) to the small town of Xanaba and another four kilometers (2.5 miles) to Sudzal. There, look for the sign to the hacienda, which is another 2.7 kilometers (1.7 miles) out of town.

GETTING AROUND
Izamal is easy to navigate on foot: The bus terminal, major sights, and a handful of hotels and restaurants are all within easy walking distance. Then again, having a car will allow you to stay at Hacienda San Antonio Chalanté (or at least go there for a meal or a horseback ride) as well as visit the sisal distillery and the small town of Kimbilá, where you can buy good *huipiles* and guayaberas for less.

Bicycle
The only place to rent a set of wheels is the **Hotel Macan-ché** (Calle 22 No. 305 between Calles 33 and 35, tel. 988/954-0287). Bicycle rentals run US$.90/hour. Stop by or call to check on availability.

Horse Carriages
At any hour of the day, you'll find a queue of *calesas,* here more commonly referred to as *victorias,* parked along the long northern wall of the convent. Ostensibly for tourists—a half-hour ride around town runs around US$4.50— these tiny, horse-pulled buggies do an active business carrying locals (often whole families) from place to place. It is one of relatively few cities in Mexico where this is the case.

Car

As in so many towns throughout the peninsula, street signs here are inconsistent and one-way streets—of which there are many—are not always marked. (When they are, it is usually with a small black arrow with a red circle and line through it; note that many streets turn from two-way to one-way as you approach the center.) Fortunately, folks are fairly good-natured about foreigners who make wrong turns—if you are heading the wrong direction someone will likely call out *"sentido contrario!"* (wrong way!), which is your cue to pull a U-turn.

Chichén Itzá and Pisté

Chichén Itzá is one of the finest Mayan archaeological sites in the northern part of the peninsula, and in all of Mesoamerica. It is also one of the most visited—just three hours from Cancún (and two hours from Mérida), the site is inundated by bikini-clad tourists in huge tour groups. That fact should not dissuade independent travelers from visiting—crowded or not, Chichén Itzá is a truly magnificent ruin and a must-see on any archaeology tour of the Yucatán. Arrive early, and you can see the big stuff first and be exploring the outer areas by the time the tour buses roll in.

Pisté is a one-road town that is strangely underdeveloped considering it is just two kilometers (1.25 miles) from such an archaeologically important and heavily touristed site. The hotels and restaurants here are unremarkable and there's not much to do or see other than the ruins. In fact, only a fraction of tourists here spend the night.

There are numerous shops along the main road through town selling souvenirs, mostly stone Mayan reproductions and carved wooden masks. Although most are of average quality, the better ones make nice gifts for back home.

HISTORY

Some of the structures at Chichén Itzá were built as early as the 2nd or 3rd century, but

Some of the structures at Chichén Itzá date back to the 2nd century.

© LIZA PRADO CHANDLER

The State of Yucatán

the main period of construction began in mid-9th century, or Late Classic period, when Chichén had eclipsed Cobá as the dominant power in the region. Early constructions follow classic Puuc and Putun Mayan styles. (The Nunnery and the Akab Dzib in the "Old Chichén" part of the site exemplify this era.) Later (and most striking) structures and adornments bear a striking resemblance to those at the ancient Toltec capital of Tollan, today called Tula, 1,200 kilometers (745 miles) away in the state of Hidalgo. Similarities include the reclining *chac mool* figures, warrior columns, skull platforms, feathered serpents, and the cult of Tlaloc. There must have been contact between these far-removed centers, but the precise circumstances of that contact remain unclear and are the source of a running dispute among Mayanists. Traditionalists stick to a long-held theory that Toltec warriors invaded the Yucatán, bringing certain architectural and decorative styles with them. Revisionists suggest the reverse, that Chichén's great influence reached all the way to Tula.

What we call Chichén Itzá surely had another name when it was founded. The name means Mouth of the Well of the Itzá, but the Itzá, a seminomadic group probably related to the Putún Mayans, didn't arrive here until the 12th century. The Itzá were apparently the *last* occupants, which is why their name was the one that stuck. (The Itzá also founded Mayapán, which ruled much of the Yucatán almost to the arrival of the Spanish.) Whatever its name, present-day Chichén Itzá was a typical Late Classic city of the northern region, featuring Puuc-influenced architecture and hieroglyphs commemorating important political events.

At the end of the 10th century—in A.D. 987 to be exact—a king named Topiltzin Quetzalcoatl in the far-off Toltec capital of Tula (just north of Mexico City) was expelled from his realm after a power struggle with the warrior caste. He was last seen departing from the Gulf coast on a raft of feathered serpents heading east. In the same year, the *Books of Chilam Balam* record the arrival on Yucatán's shores of a king named Kukulcán, identifying him, like Tolpiltzin Quetzalcoatl, with the Feathered Serpent. Kukulcán gathered an army that defeated the Puuc city-states of northwestern Yucatán and made Chichén Itzá his capital, rebuilding it in a mixed Toltec-Mayan style that we see today. As in Tula, hieroglyphs were absent from the art, and reliefs show bloody battle scenes celebrating Toltec victories.

A rival theory holds that influence flowed the other direction—that the traits we identify as Toltec are actually Putún Mayan in origin and were brought to Tula and the rest of Central Mexico by far-ranging Yucatecan traders. Adherents to this theory point to the fact that Chichén Itzá is far more splendid than anything the Toltecs created and argue that Chichén, and not Tula, must have been more influential. Then again, history is rife with cases in which "rude" invading forces defeat, occupy, and influence cities and peoples more magnificent and creative than themselves.

After dominating northern Yucatán for more than two centuries, Chichén Itzá fell into decline after an internal dispute and the subsequent rise of Mayapán. The city was all but abandoned by the early 1200s, though it remained an important pilgrimage site long after the arrival of the Spanish. Restoration of Chichén Itzá began in 1923 and has continued in one form or another for most of the time since—even today, mounds are being uncovered and excavated.

CHICHÉN ITZÁ ARCHAEOLOGICAL ZONE

Chichén Itzá is a monumental archaeological site, remarkable for both its size and scope. The ruins include impressive palaces, temples, and altars, as well as the largest known ball court in the Mayan world. One of the most widely recognized (and heavily visited) ruins in the world, it was declared a World Heritage site by UNESCO in 1988.

The grounds are open daily 8 A.M.–6 P.M., although some of the structures have special hours (posted on the buildings or ask at the entrance). Admission is US$7.75 pp, US$3

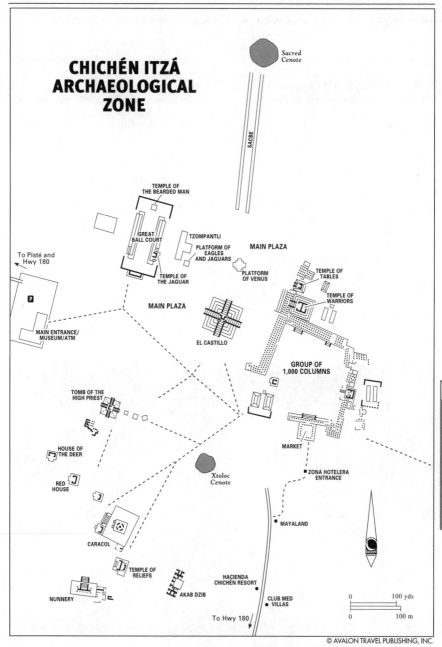

CHICHÉN ITZÁ ARCHAEOLOGICAL ZONE

Sacred Cenote

SACBE

TEMPLE OF THE BEARDED MAN

GREAT BALL COURT

TZOMPANTLI

PLATFORM OF EAGLES AND JAGUARS

MAIN PLAZA

To Pisté and Hwy 180

TEMPLE OF THE JAGUAR

PLATFORM OF VENUS

TEMPLE OF TABLES

TEMPLE OF WARRIORS

MAIN PLAZA

MAIN ENTRANCE/ MUSEUM/ATM

EL CASTILLO

GROUP OF 1,000 COLUMNS

TOMB OF THE HIGH PRIEST

HOUSE OF THE DEER

RED HOUSE

MARKET

Xtoloc Cenote

ZONA HOTELERA ENTRANCE

MAYALAND

CARACOL

TEMPLE OF RELIEFS

AKAB DZIB

HACIENDA CHICHÉN RESORT

NUNNERY

CLUB MED VILLAS

To Hwy 180

0   100 yds

0   100 m

The State of Yucatán

© AVALON TRAVEL PUBLISHING, INC.

additional if you bring a video camera. This fee entitles you to visit the ruins, the museum, and to return for the light show, which is presented nightly at 7 P.M. (winter hours) and 8 P.M. (summer hours).

Guides can be hired at the entrance according to fixed and clearly marked prices: US$35 for a 1.5- or 2-hour tour in Spanish, US$42 in English, French, Italian, or German. Prices are per group, which can include up to eight people. Tips are customary and not included in the price. The visitor center also has clean restrooms, ATM, luggage storage, a café, bookstore, gift shop, and information center.

Buses often drive right to the archaeological site entrance. Otherwise it is about a 1.5-kilometer (.9-mile) walk from the center of town.

El Castillo/Temple of Kukulcán

The most breathtaking structure in Chichén Itzá—and best vantage from which to appreciate the whole site—is El Castillo (the Castle), also known as the Temple of Kukulcán. At 24 meters (78.7 feet) it's the tallest and most dramatic structure on the site, and one of the most

impressive Mayan structures anywhere. Made of one pyramid atop another, El Castillo was constructed around A.D. 850, probably to commemorate the end of a 52-year cycle and to honor the gods for allowing the world to survive into the next one.

El Castillo was built according to strict astronomical guidelines. Each of the four sides has 91 steps. Including the platform on top, that makes for a total of 365 steps—one for each day of the year. On the spring and autumn equinoxes (March 21 and September 22), the sun lights up a bright zigzag strip on the outside wall of the north staircase and the giant serpent heads at the base, giving the appearance of a serpent slithering down the steps. The effect was discovered relatively recently and, truth be told, we cannot be certain the original builders built the pyramid with that effect in mind. Nor, since this is a reconstruction, that it even occurred in the original structure. Still, Chichén Itzá is mobbed during those periods, especially by spiritual-minded folks seeking communion with the ancient Mayans. The effect also oc-

the famous Temple of Kukulcán at Chichén Itzá

© ILZA PRADO CHANDLER

The State of Yucatán

curs in the days just before and after the equinox, and there are many fewer people blocking the view.

Be sure to make the climb into the inner structure of El Castillo where you'll see a red-painted, jade-studded sculpture of a jaguar, just as it was left by the Mayan builders more than 1,000 years ago. Check the visiting hours since the inner chamber is not always open.

Group of a Thousand Columns

It isn't hard to see how this cluster got its name—reminiscent of Egypt's Karnak, the number of columns may actually get to 1,000 someday as archaeologists continue to reconstruct. Many of the square and circular stone columns have carvings still in excellent condition. Adjacent to this, on a three-tiered platform, is the impressive **Temple of the Warriors,** where some of the famous, reclining *chac-mool* figures are found. In 1926, during restoration, a subtemple found underneath was named **Chacmool Temple.** The former color on the columns of the inner structure is still barely visible.

Great Ball Court

Of several ball courts at Chichén Itzá (some archaeologists say nine), the most impressive is the Great Ball Court, the largest found yet in Mesoamerica. On this field, life-and-death games were played with a 12-pound hard rubber ball, in the tradition of the Roman Coliseum. The playing field is 135 meters (443 feet) by 65 meters (213 feet), with two eight-meter/26.2-foot-high walls running parallel to each other on either side. On these walls, note the reliefs that depict the ball game and sacrifices. The players were obliged to hit the ball into carved stone rings embedded in the vertical walls seven meters (23 feet) above the ground using only their elbows, wrists, or hips. The heavy padding they wore indicates the game was dangerous; it was also difficult and often lasted for hours. The winners were awarded jewelry and clothing from the audience. The losers were decapitated as sacrifices to the gods.

Temple of the Bearded Man

At the north end of the ball court sits the handsome Temple of the Bearded Man. Two graceful columns frame the entrance to a small temple with the remains of decorations depicting birds, trees, flowers, and the earth monster. Standing in the temple you can speak in a low voice and be heard a good distance down the playing field, well beyond what is normal (much like in the dome of St. Peter's Cathedral in Rome). Was this the "dugout" from which the coach whispered signals to his players downfield? Some believe that only the upper class actually watched the game, and that the masses remained outside the walls and listened. We will likely never know if the effect is the result of advanced acoustical design or simply an accident of construction.

Temple of the Jaguar

On the southeast corner of the ball court, the upper temple was constructed A.D. 800–1050. To get there you must climb a steep stairway at the platform's south end. Two large serpent columns, with their rattlers high in the air, frame the opening to the temple. The inside of the room is decorated with a variety of carvings and barely visible remnants of what were likely colorful murals.

The Platforms

Strolling the grounds, you'll find the **Platform of Venus** and **Platform of Eagles and Jaguars,** among others. The flat, square structures, each with low stairways on all four sides, were used for ritual music and dancing, and, according to Diego de Landa (the infamous 16th-century Franciscan bishop), farce and comedy were presented for the pleasure of the public.

Sacred Cenote

This natural well is 300 meters (984 feet) north of the main structures, along the remains of a *sacbe* (raised stone road) constructed during the Classic period. Almost 60 meters (197 feet) in diameter and 30 meters (98.4 feet) down to the surface of the water, this impressive sinkhole is where early Mayans believed the rain god

Chac lived; to ask him produce rain, sacrifices of children and young adults were made, evidenced by human bones found here. On the edge of the cenote is a ruined sweat bath, probably used for purification rituals before sacrificial ceremonies.

Observatory

One of the most graceful structures at Chichén Itzá is the **Caracol,** a two-tiered observatory shaped like a snail, where advanced theories of the sun and moon were calculated by Mayan astronomers. Part of the spiral stairway into the tower/observatory is closed to tourists in an effort to preserve the decaying building. The circular room is laid out with narrow window slits facing south, west, and toward the summer solstice and the equinoxes. The priests used these celestial sightings to keep (accurate) track of time in their elaborate calendrical system.

Other Structures

The largest building on the grounds is the **Nunnery,** so-named by Spanish explorers who thought it looked like convents back home. Judging from its size, location, and many rooms, the Nunnery was probably a palace for Mayan elite.

Tzompantli (Wall of Skulls) is a platform decorated on all sides with carvings of skulls, anatomically correct but with eyes staring out of large sockets. This rather ghoulish structure also depicts an eagle eating a human heart, a common image in Toltec design and clear evidence of Mayan-Toltec contact. It is presumed that ritualistic music and dancing on this platform culminated in a sacrificial death for the victim, the head then left on display, perhaps with others already in place. It's estimated that the platform was built A.D. 1050–1200.

A much-damaged pyramid—**Tomb of the High Priest**—is being taken apart piece by piece and rebuilt. The ruin is intriguing because of its inner burial chamber. Sometimes referred to as **Osario** (Spanish for "ossuary," a depository for bones of the dead), the pyramid at one time had four stairways on each side and a temple at the crest. From the top platform, a vertical passageway lined with rock leads to the base of this decayed mound. There, from a small opening, stone steps lead into a cave about three meters (9.8 feet) deep. Seven tombs were discovered containing skeletons and the usual funeral trappings of important people, in addition to copper and jade artifacts.

Museum

In the entrance and visitor services area, Chichén Itzá's museum (8 A.M.–5 P.M. daily) is curiously small for a site as important and oft-visited as this one, but it's worth visiting nonetheless. An air-conditioned auditorium nearby shows films (circa 1971, apparently) on Chichén Itzá and other sites.

Light Show

The site puts on a nightly high-tech sound and light show at 7 P.M. (winter hours) and 8 P.M. (summer hours). The fee to enter is included in the general admission, although if you'd like to see the show the night before you visit the ruins, you can pay for the light show part of the ticket (US$4.50) in advance. Just be sure to let the salesperson know that you would like to buy a half ticket and be sure to save the stub so that you're not double-charged the next day. The show is presented in Spanish. For an additional US$2.25 you can rent earphones with translations in English, French, and German.

OTHER SIGHTS

Balankanche Caves

Six kilometers (3.7 miles) east of Chichén Itzá, **Grutas de Balankanche** (8 A.M.–5 P.M., US$4, children under 13 free) are disappointing. The 1959 excavation of the caves by prominent archaeologist Dr. E. Wyllys Andrews uncovered numerous artifacts and ceremonial sites and gave researchers a better understanding of ancient Mayan cosmology, especially related to caves and the notion of *xibalbá* (the underworld). Nowadays, the caves are basically a tourist trap—a wide path meanders 500 meters (0.3 mile) down a tunnel-like cavern with urns

© LIZA PRADO CHANDLER

Mayan artifacts on display at Balankanche Caves

and other artifacts supposedly set up in their original locations. Wires and electric lights illuminate the path, but the recorded narration does nothing of the sort—you can hardly understand it, no matter what language it's in.

Entry times are fixed according to language: Spanish at 9 A.M., noon, 2 P.M., and 4 P.M.; English at 11 A.M., 1 P.M., and 3 P.M.; French at 10 A.M.

Parque Ecológico y Cenote Ik Kil

Three kilometers (1.9 miles) east of Pisté, the centerpiece of the Parque Ecologico y Cenote Ik Kil (across from Hotel Dolores Alba Chichén, 8 A.M.–6 P.M. daily, US$5.50 adults, US$2.50 children) is an immense, perfectly round cenote with a partial stone roof. Although real, the alterations to the cenote's natural state—supported walls, a set of stairs leading you in, a waterfall—make it feel pretty man-made. While not representative of the typical cenote experience, this is a good option if you are traveling with small children and need a spot to cool off. The cenote and on-site restaurant get packed with tour groups 12:30–2:30 P.M.; try visiting outside those times for a mellower visit.

ACCOMMODATIONS
Camping

At the eastern end of Pisté, **Pirámide Inn** (Calle 15 No. 30, tel. 985/851-0115, piramide inn@yahoo.com, www.chichen.com, US$3.50 s/d) is the closest hotel to the ruins, about one kilometer (0.6 mile) away. In back, there's a grassy garden for camping and several open-air palapas with concrete floors where you can hang hammocks. Shared bathrooms are clean. The price is US$3.50 per person (US$3.50/night extra to rent a hammock) and you can use the swimming pool.

Under US$25

Posada Olalde (Calle 6 s/n at Calles 17, tel. 985/851-0086, US$13 s, US$17.50 d with fan only) is the best budget option in town. Rooms are simple and bit musty, but they're brightly painted and facing a leafy courtyard. Additional rooms were being built at the time of research. The hotel also has four "bungalows," which sound nice (and cost the same) but are inferior to the rooms, with saggy beds, bad light, and a dank feel about them. The posada is a little hard to find—coming from Mérida, turn right on a narrow dirt alley across from El Pollo Mexicano restaurant. From there it's two blocks down.

Posada Flamboyanes (Calle 15 s/n, no phone, US$13 s/d with fan only) has only three small simple rooms, and the low price and welcoming exterior means they are often taken. If you do manage to get one, it should be relatively clean and will open onto a breezy covered corridor. Coming from Mérida, look for it on your right, just beyond the Hotel Chichén Itzá.

Posada Chac Mool (Calle 15 No. 15-G, tel. 985/851-0270, US$14 s, US$15.30 d with fan, US$26/28.50 with a/c) is a last resort if you're on a budget and everything else is full. The owners are friendly but the rooms are dark and humid, with saggy beds and mediocre bathrooms. Rooms with air-conditioning are way overpriced.

US$25–50

If you have a car, the **M Hotel Dolores Alba Chichén** (Carretera Mérida-Cancún Km. 122, tel. 985/858-1555, www.doloresalba.com, US$34.50 s/d, US$5 extra person, cash only) is hands-down the best deal in the area. Three kilometers (1.9 miles) east of the ruins, rooms here are spotless and decent-sized, with good beds and simple tile work to spiff up the floors and walls. The hotel has a pleasant outdoor restaurant (open 7–10 A.M., 12–4 P.M. and 6–10 P.M. daily) and two large swimming pools—the one in back has a (mostly) natural stone bottom, with holes and channels reminiscent of an ocean reef. Ask at reception about joining other guests to share a guide at Chichén Itzá. When making reservations online, be sure to specify that you want a room in the hotel at Chichén, as the website also handles guests to the sister hotel in Mérida.

Pirámide Inn (Calle 15 No. 30, tel. 985/851-0115, piramideinn@yahoo.com, www.chichen.com, US$35.50 s/d), on the eastern end of Pisté, is a low sprawling hotel with large rooms that are clean though a bit dark. The decor is distinctly '70s den, down to the lac-

quered bricks on one wall. The pool in back faces a pleasant garden; the restaurant (open 7 A.M.–10 P.M. daily) serves standard meals. Visa and MC accepted.

US$50–100

A handful of upscale hotels make up a small Zona Hotelera (Hotel Zone) on the far side of Chichén Itzá, complete with its own entrance. The access road is a few kilometers east of Pisté. Tour buses from Cancún can clog up the parking area and roadway in front of the hotels, but typically they don't arrive until midmorning and are gone by the end of the day. Rooms fill up around the equinoxes.

Renovated in 2001, **Club Med Villas Chichén Itzá** (Zona Hotelera, Carr. Mérida-Valladolid Km. 120, tel. 985/856-6000, chic crec01@clubmed.com, www.clubmed.com, US$67–112 s/d with a/c) is a pleasant two-story hotel with a lighthearted ambience. Boxy—though nice—rooms are set around a lush courtyard with an inviting L-shaped pool in the center. A library/TV room with comfy couches and a variety of books—from romance novels to archaeology books—also faces the courtyard. A decent restaurant (see *Food*) and a somewhat neglected tennis court are on-site as well. A 10 percent discount is given upon showing this book. Often closed in June.

Once the headquarters for the Carnegie Institute's expedition to Chichén Itzá, the 16th-century **Hacienda Chichén Resort** (Zona Hotelera, Carr. Mérida-Valladolid Km. 120, tel. 999/924-2150, balamhtl@finred.com.mx, www.haciendachichen.com, US$120–190 s/d with a/c) is now a tranquil hotel set in a lush tropical garden. Rooms—most in the original cinder-block cottages used by the archaeologists—have colonial tile floors, wood beam ceilings, simple furnishings, and terraces with hammocks. Ask for a newer room when making reservations as some of the older ones suffer from the intense humidity and have a slight mildewy smell. Also be sure to wander the hacienda grounds; you're sure to run across the narrow-gauge railroad tracks that were used for transportation to and for hauling artifacts from

Chichén Itzá, the original chapel, and the striking stone gate. A pool and a fine dining room (see *Food*) also are at guests' disposal.

The **M Hotel and Bungalows Mayaland** (Zona Hotelera, Carr. Mérida-Valladolid Km. 120, tel. 985/851-0100, mayaland@chichen .com.mx, www.mayaland.com, US$138–340 s/d with a/c) is literally at the Zona Hotelera's entrance to Chichén Itzá (visitors must pass through Mayaland—and by two of its gift shops—to get to the ticket booth). A popular stop for tour buses, the 98 rooms, three restaurants, and four pools are spread out over 100 acres of tamed tropical jungle. Even when fully booked it's easy to find a quiet (and beautiful) place away from the crowds. The ample accommodations—both rooms and suites—are in the main house and in private bungalows; each has tile floors, stained-glass windows, regional hardwood furniture, and terraces. Suites have whirlpool tubs and a few of the rooms even have a view of Chichén Itzá's Observatory. If you really want to splurge, ask about the Pavarotti Suite, a luxurious suite that was expressly built for the corpulent tenor when he sang in concert at Chichén Itzá.

In a former life, the **Hotel Chichén Itzá** (Calle 15 s/n, tel. 985/851-0022, info@ mayaland.com, US$40–83 s/d) was the Hotel Misión Chichén, before being bought and renovated by the hotel/tour conglomerate Mayaland. It is now the nicest place in Pisté proper, toward the east end of Pisté about a mile from the ruins. All rooms have artful decor, comfortable beds, and large modern baths; the least expensive rooms face the street and can be noisy, while the top ones are larger and overlook the hotel's attractive garden and pool area. Visa and MC accepted.

FOOD

Eating options are pretty limited in Pisté but improve somewhat if you have a car and can get to and from the large resorts.

M Restaurante Las Mestizas (Calle 15-I, across from Hotel Chichén Itzá, tel. 985/851-0069, 7 A.M.–10 P.M. Tues.–Sun., breakfast US$2.25–4, lunch/dinner US$4–7) is probably the best place in town, with a high palapa roof, airy interior, and friendly service. The food is good, classic Yucatecan fare, from *panuchos* to *pollo pibil*.

Clean and friendly, **Restaurante El Paso** (Calle 15 s/n, next to Hotel El Paso, no phone, 8 A.M.–10 P.M. daily) is one of the best of the simple, cheap eateries that line Calle 15, serving basic meals such as omelets, quesadillas, and fresh-squeezed orange juice. The service is a bit slow because nothing is premade.

As its name suggests, **Restaurante Pizzería Mr. Tacos** (Calle 15 s/n, across from Restaurante Fiesta, tel. 985/851-0079, 2–11 P.M. daily) offers an eclectic menu of tacos (US$1 apiece), pizzas (US$7.50–10), plus hamburgers and other standards.

Abarrotes Alba (Calle 15 s/n, 50 m/164 feet east of the plaza, 6 A.M.–10 P.M. daily) and **Super and Farmacia Lidia** (Calle 15 s/n, 75 m/246 feet east of the plaza, 6:30 A.M.–10:30 P.M. daily) are Pisté's two main supermarkets, where you can stock up on fruit, snack foods, canned food, water, sodas, and some toiletries.

Set in the original house of a 16th-century hacienda, the **M Hacienda Chichén Resort's restaurant** (Zona Hotelera, tel. 999/924-2150, balamhtl@finred.com.mx, www.haciendachichen.com, 7 A.M.– 10:30 P.M. daily, US$10–14) is a pleasant place to have a meal after a visit to the ruins. The menu is varied—Yucatecan specialties, pastas, sandwiches—and in the evenings, a trio plays regional music. Reservations recommended.

Although often inundated by day-trippers from Club Med Cancún, the restaurant at the **Club Med Villas Chichén Itzá** (Zona Hotelera, Carr. Mérida-Valladolid Km. 120, tel. 985/856-6000, chiccrec01@clubmed.com, www.clubmed .com, 7:30 A.M.–10:30 P.M. daily, US$6–15) is a good option. With an international menu, there's something for everyone.

If you can stand the tour groups who descend upon the place, the buffet at **Hotel and Bungalows Mayaland** (Zona Hotelera, Carr. Mérida-Valladolid Km. 120, tel. 985/851-0100,

mayaland@chichen.com.mx, www.mayaland
.com, noon–3 P.M. daily, US$10) is a popular
choice. With its huge variety of hot and cold
dishes, live music, and outdoor seating under a
massive palapa, you definitely will find something good to fill you up.

INFORMATION AND SERVICES

There is no tourist office in Pisté. We found
the folks at Hotel Dolores Alba Chichén and
Club Med Villas Arqueológicas to be the most
helpful and informative.

Medical Services

Clínica La Promesa (Calle 14 s/n between
Calle 13 and 15, tel. 985/851-0005, open 24
hours) is the only clinic in town. There's a doctor on call, but for anything serious you are better off going to Valladolid.

Farmacia Isis (Calle 15 s/n, tel. 985/851-
0216, 8 A.M.–midnight) is on the west end of
town across from the church and Restaurante
El Atrio. It is one of several pharmacies in town
but the only one on call 24 hours a day.

Police

The police have an office in the Palacio Municipal (City Hall), facing the church. At the
time of research they did not have a working
telephone, but someone should be at the office
24 hours a day.

Money

Pisté does not have a bank, but there are reliable ATMs in the visitor complex at Chichén
Itzá ruins and at Mayaland Resort (Chichén
Zona Hotelera, turnoff five km/3.1 miles east
of Pisté).

Internet and Fax

Internet Hardsoft (Calle 15 s/n, 100 m/328
feet east of plaza, tel. 985/851-5057, 10 A.M.–
11 P.M. daily, US$.90/hour Internet, US$1.75
to burn CDs) has a fast connection. Sometimes
filled with kids, it's on the second floor of a long
commercial building, over a jewelry shop.

La Red.com (Calle 15 s/n, 50 m/164 feet from

plaza across from Abarrotes Alba, no phone,
10 A.M.–3 P.M. and 5:30 P.M.–11 P.M. Mon.–Sat.,
5:30 P.M.–11 P.M. Sun., US$1.25/hour Internet)
is a tiny concrete cube with three or four computers in it, next to the public library.

Tienda San Antonio (Calle 15 31-B, across
from bus station, tel. 985/851-0089, 9 A.M.–
9 P.M. daily, US$1.25/hour Internet) is an-
other option.

Laundry

Lavandería Calle 13 (Calle 13 s/n between
Calle 8 and 10, one block east of the park, open
8 A.M.–6 P.M. Mon.–Sat.) changes US$.90 per
kilo (2.2 pounds) to wash and dry; if you drop
your clothes off first thing in the morning, they
should be ready by early afternoon. If no one
is at the shop, ask in the house to the left. The
large hotels all offer laundry service as well.

GETTING THERE AND AROUND

Buses from all directions converge on Chichén Itzá and Pisté, especially from Cancún
and Mérida (see *Getting There* sections in those
cities). Many of the buses to and from Mérida
and Cancún will drop passengers right at the
main entrance to the ruins, which is about 1.5
kilometers (0.9 mile) west of town. If you are
in Pisté, you can hop a ride to the entrance
on just about any bus passing by (US$.50) or
just walk.

Bus

Pisté's bus station (tel. 985/851-0052,
7:30 A.M.–6:30 P.M. daily, cash only) is at the
far east end of town, next to the Pirámide Inn.
That said, you can flag down buses anywhere
along Calle 15 and there is usually a uniformed
representative selling tickets in the plaza. Most
service is on Oriente, a second-class line operated by ADO, but there are a few direct/first-
class buses as well, which are worth the extra
cost. There was talk of installing a computer
system that will allow you to buy long-distance tickets; until then, make all connections
in Cancún, Mérida, or Valladolid.

To Mérida, first-class buses (US$5.75, two

hours) leave Pisté at 2:30 P.M. and 5 P.M. only, while second-class buses (US$4, 2.5 hours) leave hourly 6:30 A.M.–9:30 P.M.

To Cancún, first-class buses leave (US$10.50, 2.5 hours) at 4:30 P.M. and take the fast toll road. Second-class buses (US$7, 4.5 hours) use the free road and leave hourly 8:30 A.M.–9:30 P.M. Take a second-class Cancún bus to get to Valladolid (US$1.50, one hour).

Direct buses to Tulum and and Playa del Carmen cut south before reaching Cancún. First-class buses to Tulum (US$6.25, 2.5 hours) leave Pisté at 8 A.M., 2:45 P.M., and 4:30 P.M., and there's one second-class departure at 7:30 A.M. (US$5, three hours). The 2:45 P.M. and 4:30 P.M. first-class departures continue to Playa del Carmen (US$13.25, 3.5 hours) as does the 7:30 A.M. second-class bus (US$7.50, five hours).

To get to Cobá town and archaeological site, take the second-class Tulum/Playa del Carmen bus (US$3.50, 2.5 hours).

Car

Chichén Itzá lies adjacent to Highway 180, 120 kilometers (75 miles) east of Mérida, 200 kilometers (124 miles) west of Cancún, and 40 kilometers (25 miles) west of Valladolid. An eight-lane highway known as the *cuota* (toll road) connects Cancún and Mérida; exit at Pisté. Tolls from Mérida are US$5, from Cancun it's a whopping US$18.50. The *libre* (free road) is slower but also in good condition, pass-

ing through numerous villages and past simple farms. Watch for *topes* (speed bumps) before and after villages—there are 83 in all between Mérida and Cancún, and hitting one at anything faster than a crawl can jar you to the bones (not to mention your car).

Plane

Aeropuerto Internacional Chichén Itzá (tel. 985/851-0408) is 16 kilometers (9.9 miles) east of Pisté, between the towns of Xcalacot and Kaua. Inaugurated in April 2000, it is one of the most modern airports in the region, if not the country, with an 1,800-meter (5,905-foot) runway capable of receiving 747 jets. Initially, the airport received dozens of regular and charter flights every week (even some international arrivals), but on September 12, 2001, a day after the attacks in New York City, a small plane crashed here, killing around 20 people. The federal government immediately suspected terrorism and though it was eventually deemed an accident, the incident cooled private and public enthusiasm for the new airport. Today it stands virtually empty, with no regular service and only a smattering of charters. Aerocaribe (a division of Mexicana; toll-free Mex. tel. 800/502-2000, www.mexicana.com) is the largest airline with service here, plus there are smaller outfits such as AeroSaab, SkyTur, and EcoTour. Most flights come from Playa del Carmen and Cancún, with a few from Cozumel and Mérida.

Valladolid

Valladolid is gaining attention from tourists because of its colonial atmosphere and its central location: 30 minutes from the archaeological zones of Chichén Itzá and Ek' Balam, an hour from the ruins at Cobá and the Flamingo reserve on the Gulf Coast, and two hours from both Mérida and Cancún. It's an easy bus or car ride to any of these destinations, restaurants and hotels are reasonably priced, and you have the advantage of staying in a colonial Mexican town. If you're en route between Cancún and

Mérida or simply want to have a small-town experience, consider spending a night here—you're sure to be happily surprised.

HISTORY

The site of several Mayan revolts against the Spanish, Valladolid was conquered in 1543 by Francisco de Montejo, cousin of the likenamed Spaniard who founded Mérida. It was once the Mayan city of Zací; Montejo

VALLADOLID

SCALE NOT AVAILABLE

To Cobá and Cancún (free highway)

CALLE 34

CALLE 36

CALLE 38

CALLE 40

CALLE 42

CALLE 44

CALLE 46

CALLE 48

CALLE 33

CALLE 35

CALLE 37

CALLE 39

CALLE 41

CALLE 43

CALLE 45

CALLE 47

CALLE 49

CALLE 41-A

CALLE 43-A

CALLE 50

CALLE 62

CALLE 45

CALLE 47

✦ CENOTE ZACI

LAVANDERÍA LUYSO ■

HOTEL LA CANDELARIA ●

PLAZA CANDELARIA

▼ LA CASA DEL CAFÉ KAFFE

HOTEL ZACI ●

MAIN BUS TERMINAL ■

BICICLETAS SILVA ■

AGUILAR DEPORTES ■

MERCADO DE ARTESANÍAS ■

▼ SUPERMERCADO LA FAVORITA ■

BANAMEX ■

HSBC ■

HOTEL SAN CLEMENTE ●

INTERNET CAFÉ ■

HOTEL EL MESÓN DEL MARQUÉS ●

■ BANCOMER
■ POST OFFICE
PALACIO MUNICIPAL ■
MUSEO SAN ROQUE ■

▼ FARMACIA YZA
■ CINE UNIVERSAL

Park

RESTAURANTE LOS PORTALES ■
TOURIST OFFICE

To Cancún, Chichén Itzá, and Mérida (toll highway)

To Cenotes de Dzitnup, Chichén Itzá, and Mérida (free highway)

IGLESIA SAN BERNARDINO DE SIENA Y EX-CONVENTO DE SISAL

MUSEO ATL ★

To Cenotes de Dzitnup (bike route)

To Red Cross

© AVALON TRAVEL PUBLISHING, INC.

brutalized its inhabitants and crushed their temples, building large churches and homes in their place. It is perhaps not surprisng, then, that the Caste War started in Valladolid, and that the city played an important role in the beginning of the Mexican Revolution. Today, Valladolid is a charming colonial town with a rich history and strong Mayan presence.

SIGHTS

Iglesia San Bernardino de Siena y Ex-Convento de Sisal

In a well-kempt colonial neighborhood several blocks southwest of the *parque central,* Iglesia San Bernardino de Siena (end of Calle 41-A, tel. 985/856-2160, 8 A.M.–noon and 5–7 P.M., daily except Tues., free) is one of Valladolid's most attractive churches. The entrance is through a series of arches, and the facade, covered in a checkerboard-like stucco pattern, rises into a squat tower complete with turrets. The convent has rooms radiating from a center courtyard, which features, uniquely, a cenote in the middle. Visits to the convent are by special permission from the priest; call ahead or ask in the office. Mornings are best.

Museo ATL

This museum hadn't opened yet when we passed through, but we heard about it before we even got to Valladolid. Across the large grassy plaza in front of Iglesía San Bernardino de Siena, the museum will display its owner's large collection of traditonal folk masks from around Mexico. If the beautiful carved wood door is any indication, this will be a worthwhile stop.

Museo San Roque

Just one long high-ceilinged room—this used to be a church—the Museo San Roque (Calle 41 between Calles 38 and 40, 9 A.M.–9 P.M. daily, free) is a worthwhile stop, with fascinating, modern displays (all in Spanish, however) on Valladolid's history, especially relating to the Caste War and the beginning of the Mexi-

can Revolution. Interestingly, both conflicts, so important to Mexican history, grew out incidents in and around Valladolid. Be sure to peek to the pretty courtyard in back before leaving.

Palacio Municipal

On the second floor of the city hall (7 A.M.–7 P.M. daily, free) is a large balcony overlooking the plaza, with four large paintings by local talent Manuel Lizama. The paintings depict events in Valladolid's history: pre-Hispanic communities, the city's founding, the Caste War, and the Mexican Revolution. Not spectacular, exactly, but something to see.

Cenote Zaci

Cenote Zaci (Calle 36 s/n, between Calles 37 and 39, no telephone, 8 A.M.–7:30 P.M. daily, US$1.25, under 13 US$.90) is in the middle of town and often pooh-poohed in comparison to the cenotes at Dzitnup. But it's a peaceful, attractive spot, especially if you have it to yourself, and a whole lot easier to get to than the others. (You can scope out the scene before going in by looking over the wall halfway down Calle 37, around the corner from the entrance.) A dark natural pool lies in a huge cavern with a bank of trees on one side and a path looping down from the entrance. You may find leaves and pollen floating on the water's surface, but it's still clean and refreshing. Few tourists bother to visit, and not many locals either. There's a small open-air zoo/museum and a simple eatery.

Cenotes de Dzitnup

Four kilometers (2.5 miles) west of Valladolid on Highway 180 is the small community of Dzitnup, home to two appealing underground cenotes. Both make for a unique and refreshing swim—in fact on warm days both can be somewhat crowded with locals and visitors alike. At both cenotes, there are a parking lot and many small *artesanía* stands at the entrance, and you'll be aggressively pursued by indigenous children offering to watch your car or sell you a postcard.

The State of Yucatán

EK' BALAM
ARCHAEOLOGICAL ZONE

THE ACROPOLIS

INNER WALL

OUTER WALL

MOON

STRUCTURE II

STRUCTURE III

BALL COURT

STRUCTURE X

STRUCTURE XVII

OVAL PALACE

INNER WALL

OUTER WALL

OUTER WALL

ENTRANCE

SACBE

SACBE

SCALE NOT AVAILABLE

© AVALON TRAVEL PUBLISHING, INC.

Although the two are across the street from each other, **Cenote Xkeken** (8 A.M.–7 P.M. daily, US$1.75, video cameras US$2.50) has been open longer and is better known; many postcards and travel guides show it as "Cenote Dzitnup." After a reasonably easy descent underground (in a few places you must bend over because of a low ceiling; there's a hanging rope to help), you'll come to a circular pond of clear, cool water. It's a pretty, albeit damp, place, with a high dome ceiling that has one small opening at the top letting in a ray of sun and dangling green vines. Often an errant bird can be seen swooping low over the water before heading to

the sun and sky through the tiny opening. Stalactites and at least one large stalagmite adorn the ceiling and cenote floor.

At **Cenote Sakmu'ul-ja** (7 A.M.–6:30 P.M., US$1.75, video cameras US$2.50) tree roots dangle impressively from the roof (that is, ground-level) all the way down to the water. Enter through a narrow tunnel, which opens onto a set of stairs that zig-zag down to the water. Fearless little kids jump from the first or even second switchback, into the clear turquoise water below.

Many people ride their bikes here—a bike path parallels the highway, making it a pleasant

the one-of-a-kind winged figures at Ek' Balam

trip. Private taxi to the cenotes runs US$4.50. You can also catch a shared taxi on Calle 44 between Calles 39 and 41—the fare is US$1 pp but there have to be at least four people to go.

Ek' Balam Archaeological Zone

Thirty kilometers (18.6 miles) north of Valladolid, Ek' Balam (8 A.M.–5 P.M., US$2) is a unique and fascinating site that has only recently been appreciated by researchers and tourists. Restoration began in the mid-1990s, during which a remarkable and incredibly well-preserved stucco mural was uncovered partway up the site's main structure. Especially notable are the beautiful winged figures, reminiscent of angels and unique in Mayan art and design. A corbeled arch covers the entrance to the site, which is surrounded by an unusual double wall. To date, about 45 structures have been excavated in this commercial city that thrived about A.D. 700–1100, including a ball court, two residences, and a circular building believed to be a watchtower.

There are no guides at the entrance to the ruins, but the owner of Genesis Ek' Balam can arrange one if you call ahead.

Accommodations and Food: The best place to stay in town (and until recently the only place) is definitely **Genesis Ek' Balam** (tel. 985/852-7980, www.genesisretreat.com, US$15–30 pp). Eight cabanas occupy a small leafy property with a welcoming natural pool in the middle. All the rooms are different—our favorite was the "Birdhouse," a second-floor room with screened windows on all sides and a small balcony overlooking the pool and center area. All the rooms share large, clean bathrooms and outdoor (but private) showers. The hotel restaurant (8 A.M.–5 P.M. daily, US$4–9) functions more like a family kitchen and serves great vegetarian meals; *chaya,* a rich spinachlike plant used in many pre-Colombian dishes and still very popular today, is picked fresh from the garden and used in most dishes. The Canadian expat owner and operator organizes interesting excursions in the area, including mountain biking to nearby cenotes, haciendas, and unexcavated Mayan ruins. A personal tour of the village is free for all guests. Ask about lodging/tour specials. The owner has a number of friendly dogs that roam and lounge

The State of Yucatán

about the property. Fine if you like dogs, but it may not be everyone's thing. Say hi to Mango the toucan.

Much more rustic accommodations are available at **Uh Najil Ek' Balam** (tel. 999/994-7488, US$13 d), a community-run complex a short distance from Genesis Ek' Balam. Ten wood cabanas have very basic furnishings and share fairly scary bathrooms and showers. The idea is great—a cooperative of more than 20 local people share in the camp's operation and profit—but the place could use a little better upkeep. Bikes are for rent (US$.75/hour) and there is a simple restaurant on-site (US$2–5).

Getting There and Around: To get here from Valladolid by car, head north on Highway 295 toward Tizimín. About 17 kilometers (10.6 miles) north, turn right (east) onto a turn-off (there's a sign to Ek' Balam). From there, it's another 11 kilometers (6.8 miles) to the ruins. You can take a *combi* from Valladolid to the town of Santa Rita, which leaves you a few kilometers from the ruins. A cab here will cost around US$8 or US$17 round-trip with an hour at the ruins. Genesis Ek' Balam can arrange guest pickup in Valladolid for US$5.

Once there, the tiny village is easily covered on foot. The ruins are a pleasant two kilometers (1.25 miles) from the village.

ENTERTAINMENT AND EVENTS

Open in the evenings only, **Cine Universal** (Calle 40 No. 200 between Calles 41 and 43, tel. 985/856-2040) shows mostly Hollywood films on its two screens. Tickets cost US$3, US$2.25 on Wednesdays.

SHOPPING

Mercado de Artesanías (corner of Calles 39 and 44; 8 A.M.–8 P.M. Mon.–Sat., 8 A.M.–2 P.M. Sun.) has a pretty good variety of guayberas, embroidered *huilpiles,* hammocks, and other popular items. The selection isn't as large as at most markets—there are only about a dozen shops here—but be sure to bargain.

ACCOMMODATIONS

Valladolid offers a good choice of simple and midrange hotels. All are convenient to the central plaza.

Under US$50

Affiliated with Hostelling International, **M Hostel La Candelaria** (Calle 35 No. 201-F between Calles 42 and 44, tel. 985/856-2267, candelaria_hostel@hotmail.com, www.hostellingmexico.com, US$6.75 pp dorm, US$16.50 s/d with shared bath) is a colorful hostel that offers clean accommodations to budget travelers. Dorm rooms and private rooms alike come with sheets, fans, and private lockers. Additional facilities include a fullyequipped outdoor kitchen, an awesome lounge decorated with Mexican art, and a nice garden area with hammocks, tables, and chairs. The hostel staff also is a wonderful source of information about tours in the area—don't hesitate to ask for suggestions. Breakfast is included in the rate. Slight discounts for HI members or ISIC card holders.

Just across from the cathedral is the **Hotel San Clemente** (Calle 42 No. 206 between Calles 41 and 43, tel. 985/856-2208, www.hotelsanclemente.com.mx, US$24 s with fan, US$26 d with fan, US$26 s with a/c, US$30 d with a/c). The 64 rooms surround a pleasant courtyard with an inviting pool. The rooms themselves are spacious and clean although some units' bathrooms could use a scrub-down.

With spotless rooms set along a grassy, flower-lined courtyard, **Hotel Zaci** (Calle 44 No. 191 between Calles 39 and 41, tel. 985/856-2167, US$26 s with a/c, US$31 d with a/c) is a good option. Rooms are upkept nicely and have details such as stencilings on the walls and iron-work furnishings. A small pool in back is a plus.

US$50–100

Originally a 16th-century home, the **M Hotel El Mesón del Marqués** (main plaza, Calle 39 No. 203, tel. 985/856-2073, www.mesondelmarques.com, US$53–63 s/d with a/c) is now without a doubt the nicest hotel in town. With lush courtyards, a gurgling fountain, arches upon arches, it's no wonder that it's a favorite. Rooms themselves are decorated in a simple Mexican style: heavy wood furniture, iron headboards, and brightly colored woven bedspreads. They vary in size significantly but all are comfortable. A well-tended pool in the garden only adds to the relaxed atmosphere. Breakfast is included in the rate and (lucky for you!) the restaurant here is considered one of the best in town (see *Food*).

FOOD

La Casa del Café Kaffé (Calle 35 No. 202 at Calle 44, tel. 985/856-2879, 8 A.M.–1 P.M., 7–midnight Mon.–Sat., 8 P.M.–midnight Sun., US$1.35–4) is a fantastic place to get breakfast or a late-night snack. Owned and run by a welcoming Chilean couple, the menu features empanadas, quesadillas, sandwiches, fruit shakes, and a nice variety of coffee drinks. With tables on the lovely Parque Candelaria, tasty food, and great service, you can't go wrong.

Restaurante Los Portales (southeast corner of plaza, tel. 985/856-3243, 8 A.M.–11 P.M. daily, US$2.50–8) has a popular *comida corrida* (lunch special) with soup, entrée, dessert, and drink for under US$3. Though it's a bit noisy, outdoor tables are set up in a pleasant covered walkway and have a nice view of the plaza through a set of arches.

Right on the main plaza, the restaurant at the **Hotel El Mesón del Marqués** (main plaza, Calle 39 No. 203, tel. 985/856-2073, 7 A.M.–11 P.M. daily, US$4–10) is considered by many as the best place in town. Here tables fill an interior courtyard with a lovely colonial-style fountain and masses of fuchsia-colored bougainvillea that drape from the surrounding balconies. The ambitious yet successful menu features scrambled eggs with *chaya* (a local green that's similar to spinach), marinated chicken breast salad, and yogurt cucumber soup; some items are marked as low calorie. There's also a decent wine list.

La Favorita (Calle 39 between Calles 42 and 44; tel. 985/856-2036, 8 A.M.–2 P.M., 5–9 P.M. Mon.–Sat., 8 A.M.–2 P.M. Sun.) is a medium-sized supermarket.

INFORMATION AND SERVICES
Tourist Information Centers
You may be able to pry some useful information from Valladolid's **city tourist office** (next to the Palacio Municipal, Calle 40 No. 200 at Calle 41, tel. 985/856-2063, ext. 211, 9 A.M.–8 P.M. Mon.–Sat., 9 A.M.–1 P.M. Sun.) but it's not easy.

Medical Services
For medical assistance, head to the **Cruz Roja** (Red Cross, Calle 63-A at Calle 40, tel. 985/856-2413) or **Hospital General** (facing Parque de Sisal, Calle 49 s/n, tel. 985/856-2883).

Pharmacies
Farmacia Yza (Calle 41 No. 201 at Calle 40, tel. 985/856-4018) is open 24 hours and accepts credit cards.

Police
The **Policía Municipal** (facing Parque Bacalar, Calle 41 s/n) can be reached by dialing tel. 985/856-2100.

Money
Half a block from the main plaza, **HSBC** (Calle 41 No. 201-D between Calles 42 and 44, 8 A.M.–7 P.M. Mon.–Sat.) has one ATM. Across the street, **Banamex** (9 A.M.–4 P.M. Mon.–Fri.) has one as well. On the main plaza, you'll also find **Bancomer** (Calle 40 between Calles 39 and 41, 8:30 A.M.–4 P.M. Mon.–Fri., 10 A.M.–3 P.M. Sat.), with—you got it—one ATM.

Post Office
On the main plaza, the tiny post office (Calle 40 No. 195-A between Calles 39 and 41) is open 8:30 A.M.–3:30 P.M. Monday–Friday.

Internet and Fax
@.com (Calle 42 s/n, between Calles 41 and 43, no telephone, 8 A.M.–2 A.M. daily) is one

VALLADOLID BUS SCHEDULES

Departures from Valladolid's **bus station** (Calle 39 No. 221 at Calle 46, tel. 985/856-3448) include:

Destination	Price	Duration	Schedule
Campeche	US$15.65	4 hrs	2 P.M.
Cancún	US$5.75	3 hrs	1:15 A.M., 2:15 A.M., 3:15 A.M., 6 A.M., 6:45 A.M., 7:45 A.M.*, 8:45 A.M., 9:30 A.M., 10 A.M., 10:15 A.M.*, every 30 min. 10:30 A.M.–1 P.M., 1:15 P.M.*, 1:30 P.M., 2:30 P.M., 3:30 P.M., every 30 min. 4:30 P.M.–6 P.M., 6:15 P.M.*, 6:30 P.M., 7 P.M., 7:30 P.M., 8:30 P.M., 9:30 P.M., and 10:30 P.M.
Chetumal	US$10.65	5 hrs	5:30 A.M., 7:30 A.M., and 2:30 P.M.
Chichén Itzá	US$1.50	45 min.	7:15 A.M., 8:15 A.M., 8:45 A.M., 9:30 A.M., 10:30 A.M., 10:45 A.M.*, 11:15 A.M.*, 11:20 A.M., 12:30 P.M., 1:30 P.M.*, 2 P.M., 2:30 P.M., 3:30 P.M., 4:20 P.M.*, 4:30 P.M., and 5:30 P.M.
Chiquilá	US$5.45	3 hrs	2:45 A.M.
Cobá	US$1.85	1 hr	9:30 A.M., 2:45 P.M., and 5:15 P.M.
Izamal	US$3.15	1.5 hrs	12:45 P.M., 3:50 P.M., 5:15 P.M., and 9 P.M.

of several cybercafés on and around the central plaza. Internet access was a bargain at US$.90/1.5 hour when we passed through.

Telephone
Dial Mex (Calle 42 No. 206 between Calles 41 and 43, tel. 985/856-3977, 7 A.M.–10 P.M. daily) provides long-distance service within Mexico (US$.45/min.), to the United States (US$.80/min.), Canada (US$1/min.) and Europe (US$1.45/min.). Rates drop about 30 percent 4–9 P.M. Fax service also is offered for the per minute price listed above plus US$.10/page to send, US$.35/page to receive.

Laundry
The welcoming but busy **Lavandería Luyso**

(Calle 40 No. 172 at Calle 33, tel. 985/856-3542, 8 A.M.–8 P.M. Mon.–Sat., 8 A.M.–2 P.M. Sun., US$.65/kilo—2.2 pounds) offers next-day service only.

GETTING THERE AND AROUND

Valladolid's **bus station** (Calle 39 No. 221 at Calle 46, tel. 985/856-3448) is an easy walk from the main plaza, or if you have a lot of bags, a cheap (and quick) taxi ride. While first-class service is recommended, please note that most buses leaving from this station are second class.

The city is easy to get around. It's laid out in a grid pattern with even-numbered streets running north to south, odd-numbered streets running east to west. The *parque*, at the cen-

Destination	Price	Duration	Schedule
Mérida	US$6.15	3 hrs	12:15 A.M., 2:15 A.M., 3 A.M., 3:45 A.M., 5 A.M., 6 A.M., 6:30 A.M., 7:15 A.M.*, 8:15 A.M., 8:45 A.M.*, 9:30 A.M., 10:15 A.M.*, 10:30 A.M., 10:45 A.M.*, 11 A.M., 11:30 A.M., 12:30 P.M., 1:30 P.M.*, 2 P.M., 2:01 P.M.*, 2:30 P.M., 3:30 P.M., 4:15 P.M.*, 4:20 P.M.*, 4:30 P.M., 5:30 P.M., 5:45 P.M.*, 6:30 P.M., 7:30 P.M., 8:30 P.M., 9:15 P.M.*, and 10:30 P.M.
Playa del Carmen	US$6	3 hrs	8:30 A.M., 9:30 A.M., 2:45 P.M., and 5:15 P.M.
Tizimín	US$1.35	1 hr	5:30 A.M., 6:45 A.M., 8 A.M., 8:45 A.M., 9 A.M., 9:15 A.M., 10:30 A.M., 11:15 A.M., 11:45 A.M., noon, 1 P.M., 1:45 P.M., 2:15 P.M., 3:30 P.M., 4:45 P.M., 5:30 P.M., 6 P.M., 7:15 P.M., and 8 P.M.
Tulum	US$4	2 hrs	8:30 A.M., 9:10 A.M.*, 9:30 A.M., 1:15 P.M.*, 2:45 P.M., 3:50 P.M.*, 5:10 P.M.*, and 5:15 P.M.

* Denotes first-class service; prices are slightly higher but service is much faster.

ter of the city, is bordered by Calles 39, 40, 41, and 42.

You can bike to the cenotes at Dzitnup, or to the San Bernardino de Sienna church and convent. Bikes are for rent at **Antonio "Negro" Aguilar Deportes** (tel. 985/856-2125, 7 A.M.–noon and 4–7 P.M. daily) or **Refraccionía de Bicicletas Silva** (9 A.M.–8 P.M. Mon.–Sat, 9 A.M.–2 P.M. Sun.) The shops are a few doors apart on Calle 44 between Calles 39 and 41 and both charge around US$3.50/day. The former is run by "El Negro," a voluable Valladolid native and former baseball star who played in the minor leagues in the United States for several years in the 1950s.

If you need a taxi, call **Catedral** (tel. 985/856-2090) or **Maria de Luz** (tel. 985/856-2046).

Río Lagartos and San Felipe

A little more than 100 kilometers (62 miles) north of Valladolid, on the northernmost point of the Yucatán Peninsula, Río Lagartos is justly famous for the huge colonies of flamingos that nest and feed here.

Nearby San Felipe is a much more pleasant place to spend an afternoon or night, and it's still convenient to the tours from Río Lagartos. If you have a car, consider staying in San Felipe and driving into Río Lagartos in the morning for a flamingo tour.

Why are the two towns so different? Both are simple fishing villages—San Felipe has access to a few popular beaches, but Río Lagartos gets all the flamingo business and is closer to the salt factory. We asked a few locals and got mixed answers. One was that San Felipe's leaders mostly belong to the PAN political party, while Río Lagartos is more closely affiliated with the PRI. As PAN's fortunes rise state- and nationwide, San Felipe may have had easier access to outside development money. Culture, for lack of a better word, seems to play a role too. While Río Lagartos has a large number of semipermanent workers from all over, San Felipe's residents are long-settled and tightly knit. After Hurricane Isadora, San Felipe's residents organized cleanup and restoration projects within a few days, and today little evidence of the destruction remains. Río Lagartos is still picking up the pieces more than two years later, with no real apparent urgency. Neither of these explanations tells the whole story, of course, but the towns do present an interesting study of contrasts.

RÍO LAGARTOS

Tens of thousands of pink and cerise *Phoenicopterus ruber ruber* flamingos throng to the area's *ría* (saltwater lagoon), which winds many kilometers east of the town of Río Lagartos. In addition to the flamingos, bird-watchers will spot plover, white egret, heron, cormorant, hawks, and pelican.

Río Lagartos itself is an isolated, rather dumpy town that would not merit a visit were it not for the flamingo and bird-watching tours. The town was pummeled by Hurricane Isadora in 2002 and has yet to fully

Flamingos can be seen year-round in Río Lagartos.

recover. Houses without roofs—even foundations without houses—line the main street, which was only just being repaved in 2004. The population is a mix of longtime local families and itinerant workers from across the state and as far away as Chiapas and Veracruz. Besides fishing and tourism—the main industries—many people here come to work at the salt factory 16 kilometers (9.9 miles) east in Las Coloradas. Interestingly, salt has been produced here, and across much of the Yucatán's Gulf coast, since pre-Hispanic times. You'll see the factory's huge mounds of salt during the flamingo tour.

N Flamingo Tours

While a group of flamingos remains in Río Lagartos year-round, you'll see the highest concentration April, June, and July. From November to March, the young are just beginning to color. At hatching, flamingos are mostly white, and at three months the black feathers along their wings begin to grow.

The locals and government are both very protective of the flamingos. During the April–June brooding season, visitors are not allowed to approach the nesting area, as the skittish birds sometimes knock their eggs out of their nests (they lay only one per year). You can still visit the feeding area.

Although you'll be constantly approached by local fishermen offering flamingo tours—even flagged down as you drive into town—the most-recommended operator is the **Restaurant Isla Contoy** (end of Calle 19, tel. 986/862-0000). Trips take 2–2.5 hours and cost US$44 for 1–6 people, plus a US$1.75 pp natural reserve fee. If you ask ahead of time, the guides will usually merge smaller groups to save you money. Tours are offered 6 A.M.–7 P.M. daily. The guides at Isla Contoy always recommend going as early as possible—although you can

FLAMINGOS

The wetlands along the Yucatán's northern coast are shallow and murky and bordered in many places by thick mangrove forests. The water content is unusually high in salt and other minerals—the ancient Mayans gathered salt here, and several salt factories still operate. A formidable habitat for most creatures, it's ideal for *Phoenicopterus ruber ruber*—the American flamingo, the largest and pinkest of the world's five flamingo species. Nearly 30,000 of the peculiar birds nest here, feeding on algae and other tiny organisms that thrive in the salty water. Flamingos are actually born white, but they turn pink from the carotene in the algae that they eat.

For years, flamingos nested only near Río Lagartos, on the peninsula's northeastern tip. But in 1988, Hurricane Gilbert destroyed their nesting grounds (not to mention the town of Río Lagartos) and forced the birds to relocate. They are now found all along the north coast, including three major feeding and reproduction grounds: Río Lagartos, Celestún, and Uaymitún.

The best way to observe flamingos is on a sunrise boat tour. That's when the birds are most active, turning their heads upside down and dragging their beaks along the bottom of the shallow water to suck in the mud containing their food. (In the morning you should see dozens of other birds too, such as storks, herons, kingfishers, and eagles.) If you go in the spring, you may see the male flamingos performing their strange mating dance, craning their necks, clucking loudly, and generally strutting their stuff.

All three sites have flamingos year-round, but you'll see the highest numbers at Río Lagartos in the spring and summer and at Celestún in the winter. Uaymitún stays pretty uniform but has no boat tours—instead you observe the birds through binoculars from a raised platform. No matter when you go, make as little noise as possible and ask your guide to keep his distance. Flamingos are nervous and easily spooked into flying away en masse. While an impressive sight—some guides scare the birds deliberately—this interferes with feeding and may cause the birds to abandon the site altogether.

The State of Yucatán

see the flamingos all day, it takes almost 45 minutes to get to the flamingo sites and leaving early means seeing other waterbirds along the way. The water is also calmer in the morning, as the afternoon can bring wind. It is best to arrange your trip the day before; English- and Italian-speaking guides available. Binoculars aren't absolutely necessary but nice to have; bring your own or ask to borrow a pair.

Sociedad Flamingo Tours (Calles 9 and 12, tel. 986/862-0158, 6 A.M.–6 P.M.) is a group of former Isla Contoy guides who have set up their own tour operation. You can find them at their office in the two-story kiosk on the waterfront—look for their green polo shirts. They offer the same tour (US$40 for up to six people; English and Italian spoken) but recommend taking it in the afternoon—"You're on vacation, why would you want to wake up at 5 in the morning?"

Accommodations

Posada Leyli (Calle 14 No. 104-A at Calle 11, tel. 986/862-0106, US$10.50 s/d with shared bath, US$13–17.50 s/d with private bath) is a very basic hotel in Río Lagartos offering the minimum in facilities: old beds, toilets without seats, one bare fluorescent bulb per room, walls that are begging for a coat of paint. In this town, though, this is the cream of the crop in budget accommodations—sad but true. Acceptable for a night's stay.

If you're able to spend a bit more, **Ꮓ Hotel Villa de Pescadores** (Calle 14 No. 93, tel. 986/862-0020, villade_pescadores@yahoo.com.mx, US$26 s with fan, US$31 d with fan) is worth every extra penny. Right on the Río Lagartos waterfront, the nine rooms have spectacular views of the estuary and the Gulf of Mexico beyond it. Although some rooms were still being painted when we passed through, all were clean, spacious, and had balconies or terraces. Owner Felipe González Rodríguez is a fount of information about the region's treasures.

Food

Restaurante Isla Contoy (end of Calle 19, 8 A.M.–9 P.M. daily, US$4–9) is a good spot to get breakfast after an early-morning tour, and a decent option at any time. Breakfast specials mostly include eggs, beans, and coffee (US$2–3) and for lunch or dinner the specialty is seafood, including *filete,* shrimp cocktail, ceviche, and more.

Los Negritos (Calle 10 s/n, 9 A.M.–6 P.M., US$4–10) is on the main road near the entrance of Río Lagartos and serves standard Mexican fare.

Information and Services

There is no tourist office in Río Lagartos, though the people at Isla Contoy have a fair amount of information. There was no bank nor ATM when we visited, and no immediate plans for either. For medical attention, it is best to head to Tizimín or Valladolid. For package tours, inquire at the tour agencies listed in the Mérida section.

Getting There and Around

Noreste has service from Río Lagartos from its terminal a few blocks from Isla Contoy—ask for directions there as most of the streets here are not signed. Service includes:

Mérida, US$8.50, 2.5 hours, 5:30 A.M., 11 A.M., 12:30 P.M., and 4 P.M.

San Felipe, US$.40, 15 minutes, 7:30 A.M., 10:15 A.M., 11:30 A.M., 12:30 A.M., and 5:30 P.M.

Tizimín, US$1.75, one hour, 5:30 A.M., 6:30 A.M., 7 A.M., 9 A.M., 11 A.M., 11:30 A.M., 12:30 P.M., 2:30 P.M., 3:30 P.M., 4 P.M., and 5:30 P.M.

SAN FELIPE

While Río Lagartos is quite downtrodden, San Felipe has well-maintained streets and sidewalks, brightly painted houses, and a clean, attractive waterfront promenade. The hotels and restaurants are nicer, and the atmosphere much more agreeable.

Accommodations

Ꮓ Hotel Posada La Hacienda (Calle 12 No. 32 between Calles 15 and 17, tel. 986/862-

The San Felipe waterfront is often crowded with fishing boats.

2037, US$22 s/d with fan, US$26 s/d with a/c) is a charming hotel just four blocks from the oceanfront. Rooms are nicely decorated in a Mexican style: adobe-colored tile floors, heavy wood furniture, and *talavera* sinks. They also are very clean. With cable TV, they are a steal in this part of the state.

Right on the waterfront, **Hotel San Felipe** (Calle 9 between Calles 14 and 16, tel. 986/862-2027, hotelsf@hotmail.com, US$24–34 s/d with fan, US$29–39 s/d with a/c) is a pleasant hotel with 18 rooms. Each room is slightly different, but all are clean and comfortable. Rooms with views are especially nice—inside and out. If you're interested in **fly-fishing** be sure to ask about trips at the front desk; this hotel is recommended as *the* operator in these parts. Trips last eight hours and cost US$350 (includes drinks and a meal too).

Food

The oddly named **M Restaurant El Popular Vaselina** (The Popular Grease Restaurant, Calles 9 and 12, tel. 986/862-2083, 8 A.M.–7 P.M., sometimes until 9 P.M., US$3–9) serves excellent, super-fresh seafood in a big, airy dining area. Try the ceviche—usually an appetizer, the servings here are big enough to make a meal, and then some. Fronting San Felipe's pleasant promenade, some of the tables have nice views and get a breeze off the water. Service is friendly and prompt. (A smaller restaurant-bar by the same name next door can get a bit rowdy, especially when a soccer game is on. During lunch, we saw a guy—rooting for the wrong team?—get tossed headfirst right out the door onto the street.)

Information and Services

Although more polished than Río Lagartos, San Felipe had no bank or ATM and no tourist office when we visited. A small **clinic** is on Calle 15 at Calle 10-A but was open 8 A.M.–1 P.M. and 5–8 P.M. Tuesday–Thursday only. Bring money and moleskin from Valladolid or Tizimín.

Getting There

The **Noreste** bus terminal is on the main street entering town. It is closed when there is no bus leaving or arriving. Service includes:

Cancún, US$9, 2.5 hours, 6:45 A.M., 12:30 P.M., and 5:30 P.M.

Mérida, US$8.50, 2.5 hours, 6:45 A.M.,

TIZIMÍN BUS SCHEDULES

Noreste terminal (tel. 986/863-2034, Calle 47 between Calles 46 and 48) has three levels of service: *económico* (slow and cheap), *semi-directo* (slightly faster), and *ejecutivo* (almost first class). For short trips, prices vary little and travel times are comparable. However, for long trips such as to Mérida, Cancún, or Chetumal, *ejecutivo* buses are much faster and definitely recommended.

Destination	Price	Duration	Schedule
Cancún	US$7	3.5–4.5 hrs	3 A.M., 5:45 A.M., 6:45 A.M.*, 7:30 A.M., 9:30 A.M., 10 A.M.* (Saturday only), 11 A.M., 12:30 P.M.*, and 1 P.M.
Chiquilá	US$4.25	2.5 hrs	4:30 A.M., 11 A.M., 12:15 P.M., and 2:15 P.M.
Colorados	US$3	2 hrs	10:30 A.M., 12:30 P.M., and 7:15 P.M.
El Ideal	US$4	1.5 hrs	US$3 A.M., 5:45 A.M., 7:30 A.M., 9:30 A.M., and 11 A.M.
Izamal	US$4	2.5 hrs	11 A.M. and 4 P.M.
Mérida	US$6.50	2–4 hrs	5:30 A.M.*, 5:45 A.M., 6:45 A.M.*, 7:30 A.M.*, 10 A.M., noon*, 1 P.M., 1:15 P.M.* (Friday only), 2 P.M.*, 2:30 P.M. (Friday and Monday only), 4:30 P.M., 5 P.M.* (daily *económico* service, *ejecutivo* service Friday–Sunday), and 6:30 P.M.
Río Lagartos	US$1.75	1 hr	5 A.M., 6:30 A.M., 9:15 A.M., 10:30 A.M., 11:15 A.M., 2:15 P.M., 4:15 P.M., and 7:45 P.M.

7:30 A.M., noon, 1:15 P.M. (Friday only), 2 P.M., 5 P.M. (Friday–Sunday) and 6:30 P.M.

Río Lagartos, US$.40, 15 minutes, 6:15 A.M., 8:30 A.M., 10:30 A.M., 2 A.M., 3 P.M., and 9 P.M.

Tizimín, US$1.75, one hour, 5:45 A.M., 7 A.M., 8:30 A.M., 10:30 A.M., 11:45 A.M., 2 P.M., 3:30 P.M., and 6 P.M.

You can also catch a **minibus to Río Lagartos** (US$1.75, one hour) across the street and closer to the promenade at 7 A.M., 8 A.M., and 5:30 P.M. The last minibus continues to Mérida (US$8.50).

The cutoff to San Felipe is a few kilometers before entering Río Lagartos and well signed.

TIZIMÍN

A busy grubby town, there's no real reason to stop here, though you'll likely pass through (and possibly switch buses) on your way to/from Río Lagartos.

Accommodations and Food

Just a couple of blocks from the bus station is the **M Hotel 49** (Calle 49 No. 373-A between Calles 46 and 48, hotel49tizimin@hotmail.com, US$17.50 s/d with fan, US$22 s with a/c, US$26 d with a/c). The tile-floored rooms are absolutely spotless, well kept, and very comfortable. Cable TV and secure parking make

Destination	Price	Duration	Schedule
San Felipe	US$1.75	1.5 hrs	9:15 A.M., 10:30 A.M., 11:15 A.M., 2:15 P.M., 4:15 P.M., and 7:45 P.M.

*denotes *ejecutivo* service; prices are 10–25 percent higher.

The **Oriente/Mayab terminal** (tel. 986/863-2424, Calle 46 between Calles 45 and 47) is just around the corner and has semidirect and executive service only. Destinations include:

Destination	Price	Duration	Schedule
Cancún	US$7.50	3–3.5 hrs	3:30 A.M., 5:15 A.M., 8:30 A.M., 2:30 P.M., 5:15 P.M.
Chetumal	US$12	5 hrs	4:30 A.M., 1:30 P.M.
Felipe Carrillo Puerto	US$7	3.5 hrs	take any Chetumal bus
Izamal	US$4.50	2 hrs	take any Mérida bus
Mérida	US$5.50	3.5 hrs	5:30 A.M., 11 A.M., 4 P.M.
Playa del Carmen	US$9.50	4 hrs	8:30 A.M.
Valladolid	US$1.25	1 hr	5:30 A.M., 6:45 A.M., 7:30 A.M., 8 A.M., 9:15 A.M., 10 A.M., 10:30 A.M., 11:45 A.M., 12:30 P.M., 1 P.M., 2:15 P.M., 3 P.M., 3:30 P.M., 4:45 P.M., 6 P.M., 7:30 P.M.

To Río Lagartos, you can also catch a colectivo (public minibus) at the corner of Calles 47 and 48. Buses depart daily at 5 A.M., noon, and 4 P.M., returning from Río Lagartos to Tizimín at 7 A.M., 2 P.M., and 5 P.M. (US$1.75, one hour).

The State of Yucatán

it even that much better. A great option if you have to stay the night.

About two blocks from the cathedral, **Restaurant Candy** (Calle 52 No. 446 between Calles 55 and 57, tel. 986/863-4058, 7 A.M.– 4 P.M. daily, US$3–8) is a popular spot in town for regional fare.

Getting There

Tizimín takes its role as a transporation hub very seriously—maybe too seriously. There are two terminals and numerous *colectivo* stops, all with overlapping services. Fortunately, everything is close together so you don't have to lug bags back and forth across town.

Like many towns in this area, Tizimín has many one-way streets. Coming from Valladolid, the highway feeds onto the main street through town, which becomes one-way (the other way, of course) a few blocks before the center. You have to jog one street up; the sign is hard to spot, so look carefully.

The State of Campeche

It's not easy having to compete for attention when your neighbors are cultural and natural powerhouses such as Quintana Roo, Yucatán, and Chiapas. Campeche doesn't have Cancun's beaches, Mérida's charm, or San Cristóbal's indigenous presence. It really can be no surprise that it is by far the least visited of the states on the Yucatán Peninsula. Which means, it's a great time to go there! Few people realize just how incredible Campeche's archaeological sites are—from Edzná and Santa Rosa Xtampak on the way toward Mérida, to the awesome cluster of ruins in the Río Bec region farther south. Campeche city, the state's attractive but somewhat underwhelming capital, was recently named a UNESCO World Heritage site. Archaeological and colonial museums there befit Campeche's intriguing history, which is populated by pirates and businessmen, conquistadors and Mayan warriors.

PLANNING YOUR TIME

Having a car will make your visit to Campeche considerably more rewarding. While you can get to (and explore) Campeche city and Edzná

Must-Sees

Look for **M** to find the sights and activities you can't miss and **M** for the best dining and lodging.

M Fuerte de San Miguel and Museo Arqueológico de Campeche: On a bluff overlooking the gulf, San Miguel Fort houses Campeche's outstanding archaeological museum. Exquisite urns, tiny figurines, and jade funerary masks are highlights, and the view from the fort walls isn't bad either (page 340).

M Edzná Archaeological Zone: A convenient stop if you're driving between Campeche and Mérida, and a worthwhile excursion even if you're not. Survey your domain from the top of the Temple of Five Stories (page 353).

M Calakmul Archaeological Zone and Reserve: Home of the tallest known Mayan temple and situated deep in a biosphere reserve, this mega-ruin puts you at eye level with howler monkeys and parrots. A few very lucky people have even spotted jaguars and pumas (page 358).

© LIZA PRADO CHANDLER

Fuerte de San Miguel

M Chicanná Archaeological Zone: Much smaller than Becán or Calakmul, Chicanná features the exquisite stonework and ghoulish "serpent mouth" facades typical of Río Bec architecture (page 360).

M Becán Archaeological Zone: Palaces, pyramids, tunnels, and hidden passageways make this a great site for people who like to explore and clamber around ruins. A recently discovered 1,500-year-old mask is an added bonus (page 360).

M Bat Caves: Known as the "black cloud," hundreds of thousands of bats emerge every night from a cave at the bottom of a huge sinkhole near Xpujil. An awesome sight, and not a mosquito for miles (page 362).

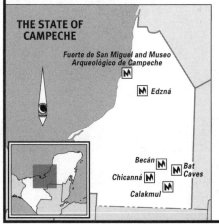

THE STATE OF CAMPECHE

Fuerte de San Miguel and Museo Arqueológico de Campeche **M**

M Edzná

Becán **M**

Chicanná **M**

M Bat Caves

Calakmul **M**

M The State of Campeche

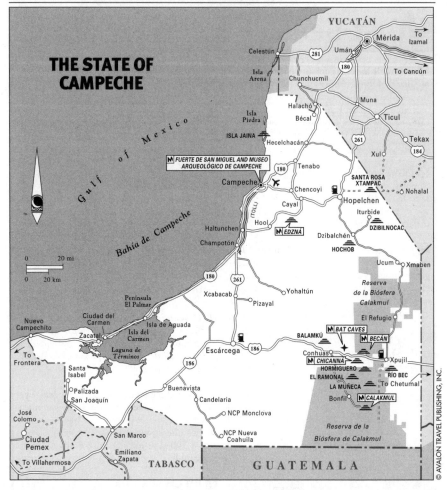

THE STATE OF CAMPECHE

YUCATÁN

To Izamal

Mérida

Celestún

Umán

281

180

To Cancún

Isla Arena

Chunchucmil

Muna

Isla Piedra

Halachó

Bécal

Ticul

ISLA JAINA

Hecelchacán

261

Tekax

Xul

184

M FUERTE DE SAN MIGUEL AND MUSEO ARQUEOLÓGICO DE CAMPECHE

180

Tenabo

SANTA ROSA XTAMPAC

Nohalal

Campeche

Chencoyi

Hopelchen

Cayal

Iturbide

DZIBILNOCAC

Hool

Haltunchen

M EDZNÁ

Dzibalchén

HOCHOB

Champotón

Ucum

Xmaben

180

261

Xcabacab

Yohaltún

Reserva de la Biósfera Calakmul

Pizayal

El Refugio

Peninsula El Palmar

M BAT CAVES

BALAMKÚ

M BECÁN

Nuevo Campechito

Ciudad del Carmen

Isla de Aguada

Xpujil

Zacatal

Isla del Carmen

Escárcega

186

Conhuas

HORMIGUERO

RÍO BEC

To Frontera

Laguna de Términos

186

M CHICANNÁ

EL RAMONAL

To Chetumal

Santa Isabel

LA MUÑECA

Palizada

San Joaquín

Candelaria

Bonfil

M CALAKMUL

José Colomo

Buenavista

NCP Monclova

Ciudad Pemex

San Marco

NCP Nueva Coahuila

Reserva de la Biósfera de Calakmul

To Villahermosa

Emiliano Zapata

TABASCO

GUATEMALA

Gulf of Mexico

Bahía de Campeche

0   20 mi

0   20 km

© AVALON TRAVEL PUBLISHING, INC.

by bus, service in the Río Bec region is too infrequent to be practical. You will probably want two days in Campeche city, though it is possible to see the main sights in one full day. Edzná and Santa Rosa Xtampák are on the way between Campeche city and Mérida, and it is tempting to visit both in one day as stop-overs on the way from one city to the other. However, the road to Xtampák is long, slow, and bumpy and neither ruin is the sort you will want to rush. To do this, leave very early in the morning and be ready for a long day. Also, consider

starting from (or going to) Santa Elena or Ticul instead of Mérida—it trims an hour off your drive and is more convenient to Uxmal and the Puuc Route.

If you love to visit ruins, you will want at least three days in the Río Bec area—a full day for Calakmul and Balamkú, another for Becán, Chicanná, and Xpujil, and a third for El Hormiguero, the Bat Caves, and to just relax a bit. If you have only one day, you have to make a hard choice—Calakmul is definitely the alpha-ruin and it's hard to say you've been to Río Bec without visiting there. Then again, the other ruins are extremely interesting and rewarding, and being close to the highway and Xpujil town, they make for a less tiring day.

Río Bec is a convenient and logical stop if you are going between Palenque and the southern Caribbean coast, though you'd never know it from the tour buses that whiz by without so much as a blink. (This may change soon, however, as Xpujil town gets more group-friendly hotels. Better get here quick!) Between Palenque and Mérida, Río Bec is definitely a detour but a worthwhile one if your time permits.

HISTORY

Present-day Campeche—a Spanish corruption of the Mayan place-name *Ah Kim Pech*—was an important indigenous commercial center and trade route between northern and eastern parts of the Yucatán Peninsula and a gateway to central and southern Mexico. It took a series of Spanish conquistadors a quarter century and fierce and bloody fighting to overcome the Mayan defense of this vital coastal region. The Spanish had the favor returned, however, as Campeche endured frequent (and frequently brutal) pirate attacks for nearly 200 years.

Campeche City

HISTORY

Spanish explorers first arrived at the Mayan town of Ah Kim Pech on March 22, 1517, with intentions of conquest, but a number of decisive and demoralizing defeats sent several would-be conquerors back to their ships. The Spanish kept returning, though, and after 23 years, under the leadership of Francisco de Montejo, finally conquered the region and founded the city of Campeche on October 4, 1540. The Spanish valued Campeche for much the same reason the Mayans did, and it wasn't long before Campeche was once again the region's major port and trade center, though now for Spanish galleons instead of Mayan canoes.

But the ships and port facilities (laden with, among other things, *palo de Campeche,* a highly valued tropical wood used to make fabric dyes) were easy target for pirates, many supported by Spain's archenemies England and France. For almost two centuries the city of Campeche was harassed, burned, and sacked by ne'er-do-wells and scalawags—there was even a whole community of buccaneers on the Island of Tris, today's Ciudad del Carmén, only 208 kilometers (129 miles) away. On February 9, 1663, pirates nearly destroyed Campeche, killing men, women, and children in the worst massacre in the city's history. Another infamous assault was

led by Laurent Graff, also known as Lorencillo, who attacked Campeche with an army of 700 men on July 6, 1685. They didn't stop with just sacking the city—they also took dozens of prisoners and demanded the city leader pay an exorbitant ransom. After two months of occupation, the city hadn't paid—it didn't have the money or goods—so the pirates planned a mass execution. After the first round of killings, a city representative talked the pirates out of the plan, and even out of the city. The ordeal prompted a push to abandon Campeche; in the end, though, the Spanish crown agreed to help fund fortifications that would eventually bring relative peace and protection to Campeche.

In 1999, Campeche was named a UNESCO World Heritage Site for its famous walls, fortifications, and numerous historically significant buildings.

SIGHTS
The Walled City

The wall that surrounded Campeche was built of stone and mortar, eight meters (26.2 feet) high, three meters (9.8 feet) thick, and with four gates placed strategically around the city. The builders also extended the wall into the sea, with huge gates that allowed ships to swiftly unload their cargo into the protected fort, often

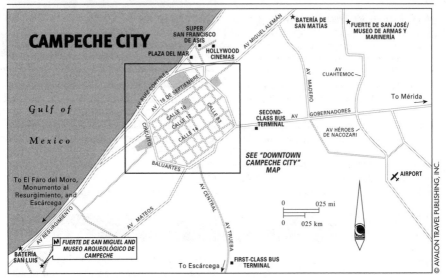

with a brigantine in pursuit. Though finishing touches weren't made until 1704—and isolated attacks lasted until 1717—the wall served its purpose and ended the era of invasion.

The old city within the ramparts of the ancient wall is well laid out and once you become comfortable with the numbering system for the 40 square blocks, getting around is easy. The streets that run southeast to northwest—perpendicular to the Gulf of Mexico—are odd-numbered from 51 to 65. Streets running northeast to southwest—parallel to the Gulf—are even-numbered from 8 to 18. Most of the touristed sights and services lie within these ancient boundaries, set off by the seven remaining *baluartes* (bastions) built by Spanish settlers. This old part of the city is surrounded by Circuito Baluartes on three sides and by Avenida 16 de Septiembre on the Gulf side. The city outside the walls is creeping ever outward toward the mountains, north and south, up and down the coast.

City Center

Since being named a World Heritage site in 1999 (and in the years beforehand, in an effort to secure the designation), Campeche has

undertaken extensive renovations of its city center, most notably in the freshly painted facades of virtually every building. (The insides are another matter....) Campeche's **main plaza** is bordered by Calles 8, 10, 55, and 57 and is a pleasant, shady spot to rest your feet between walking tours around the city. On one side of the plaza is **Catedral de la Concepción Inmaculada** (Calle 55 between Calles 8 and 10), the city's cathedral and one of the oldest churches on the Yucatán Peninsula. Construction was ordered by Francisco de Montejo in 1540 and completed in 1760 (and here you thought it took the contractor a long time to finish your deck). On another side, an arcaded passageway known as **Los Portales** provides an airy shaded corridor for a number of small shops and restaurants.

Housed in a restored colonial-era home, the **Centro Cultural Casa No. 6** (Calle 57 No. 6 between Calles 8 and 10, tel. 981/816-1782, 9 A.M.–9 P.M. daily, free) is a venue for cultural events, both public and private. Inside you'll find four rooms that have been meticulously decorated in 19th-century style, a pleasant café on the back patio that serves regional treats (9 A.M.–3 P.M. and 6–9 P.M. daily, US$1–2), an artsy bookstore off the main patio, and a tourist information desk (beware—it's sometimes manned by travel agents trying to sell tours). Live *trova* music is presented 8:30–9:30 P.M. Thursdays, and for a raucous game of *lotería* (bingo), drop by 6–10 P.M. on Saturdays.

The **Mansion Carvajal** (Calle 10 No. 584 between 51 and 53, tel. 981/816-7419, ext. 101, 8 A.M.–2:30 P.M. Mon.–Fri., free) is another old mansion that has been restored to its original beauty. Built at the beginning of the 1800s by the wealthy Carvajal family as a home, by the late 1900s it had been converted twice—once into a hotel, later into a dance hall. Today, it houses the offices of DIF (the family services branch of the state government). Open to the public, it is well worth a quick visit: Check out the Moorish-style architecture, art nouveau staircase with Carrara marble steps, iron balustrade, and the black-and-white tile floors.

Galería de Arte Joaquin Clausell (Calle 12 No. 139 between 51 and 53, tel. 981/811-3653, 9 A.M.–2 P.M. and 4–8 P.M. Mon.–Fri., 9 A.M.–2 P.M. Sat., free) is a small gallery featuring rotating works of art by regional artists.

Built by the Jesuits in 1700, the **Ex-Templo de San José** (Calle 10 at Calle 63) is a beautiful structure, decorated with an impressive blue and yellow tile facade. The history of the building is as varied as that of the city of Campeche: It has gone from being a church to being the first lighthouse in Campeche (check out the spires!) to library to warehouse to—today—an art museum.

The **Archivo General del Estado de Campeche** (Calle 12 No. 159 between Calles 57 and 59, tel. 981/816-0939, 8 A.M.–3 P.M. and 6–8 P.M. Mon.–Fri., free), the state archives building, reserves part of its first floor for the exclusive purpose of mounting educational and artistic exhibits. INAH (Insituto Nacional de Antropología) or the Insituto de Cultura typically sponsors the displays, which often are excellent.

The modern concrete and glass building near the waterfront with the colorful mosaic is the **Palacio de Gobierno** (Calle 8 between Calles 61 and 63). The strange concrete building next to it—yep, the one that looks like a UFO—is the **Palacio Legislativo.**

© LIZA PRADO CHANDLER

La Catedral de la Concepción Inmaculada is one of the oldest churches on the Yucatán Peninsula.

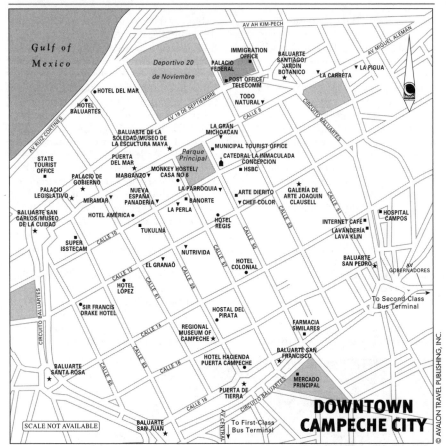

Gulf of
Mexico

**DOWNTOWN
CAMPECHE CITY**

SCALE NOT AVAILABLE

© AVALON TRAVEL PUBLISHING, INC.

Ⓜ Fuerte de San Miguel and Museo Arqueológico de Campeche

If you go to only one sight, make it Fuerte de San Miguel/Museo Arqueológico de Campeche (Av. Escencia s/n, 9 A.M.–7:30 P.M. Tues.–Sun., US$2), about 2.5 kilometers (1.6 miles) south of the center. Built in the 18th century, the fort sits atop a large hill and includes a moat, draw-bridge, and a breathtaking view of the Gulf. The museum here is the real highlight though, housing a truly fantastic collection of Mayan artifacts from around the state, including several pieces from the ruins at Isla Jaina, six spec-

tacular jade funeral masks found at Calakmul, and urns decorated with tapirs, monkeys, and turtles from Río Bec. If using public trans-portation, take a "Playa Bonita/Lerma" bus in front of the post office (US$.25). The bus will drop you off at the turnoff to the fort, which is about another 500 meters (0.3 mile) up a steep hill.

Other Baluartes and Forts

Neglected for years and with sections destroyed to make way for trolley tracks, Campeche's bas-tions have managed to survive and today lend a wonderful old-world ambience to the city. Six

Campeche City was named a UNESCO World Heritage Site in 1999.

of the nine original bastions—San Miguel, San Carlos, Soledad, Santiago, San Juan, and San José—are open to the public. You can easily visit them on your own or on one of the popular **cable car tours** (9 A.M.–1 P.M. and 5–8 P.M. daily, US$6). Leaving from the main plaza and with explanations in English and Spanish, they are informative and convenient.

Adjacent to the modern Palacio Legislativo, **Baluarte San Carlos** (Calle 8 at Circuito Baluartes, 8 A.M.–8 P.M. Tues.–Sun., US$2) was the first of the nine fortresses in the city to be completed. Today it houses a modest but excellent city museum. Exhibit pieces include suits of armor, antique weapons, navigational tools, period furniture, and colonial paintings. Explanations of Campeche's development are incredibly detailed but—alas—are in Spanish only.

Completed in 1690, **Baluarte Nuestra Señora de la Soledad** (Calle 8 at Calle 57, 8 A.M.–7 P.M. daily, US$2) is the largest of the city's bastions. Today, it houses the **Museo de las Estelas,** a four-room museum containing many of the stelae found in Campeche's ar-

chaeological sites. Explanations are basic and in Spanish only. Interestingly, there is a section for the visually impaired with reproductions of the stelae on-site that can be touched, which also can be great for curious kids. Braille (Spanish) explanations are provided.

The last of the bastions completed, **Baluarte Santiago** (Calle 49-C at Calle 8, 8 A.M.–8 P.M. Mon.–Sat., 8 A.M.–2 P.M. Sun., free) closed the hexagonal wall around Campeche in 1704. Destroyed in the early 1900s to make room for the public health-services building, it was reconstructed on-site in 1955. Today, this tiny fort houses the **Jardín Botánico Xmuch'haltun,** a small garden with more than 200 species of tropical plants surrounding a gurgling fountain.

Near the *mercado principal,* **Baluarte San Pedro** (Calle 16 at Calle 51) was built in the last decade of the 17th century. It was recently used as an arts and crafts market. When we passed, however, it was closed with no reopening in sight.

Close by is **Baluarte de San Juan** (Calle 63 at Calle 18, 9 A.M.–9 P.M. daily, free), a massive fortification with a long inland wall

the view from Reducto de San José El Alto

that seems impenetrable even today. It's accessible through the **Puerta de Tierra,** and visitors can walk atop the eight-meter/26.2-foot-high walls, look out over the city, and imagine what it must have been like to defend it. A tour also is offered as part of the **Espectáculo de Luz y Sonido** (8:30 P.M. Tues., Fri., and Sat., US$2.50), a light show that tries to transport the audience back into Campeche's violent past via a few colored lights, blasting speakers, some firecrackers, and a sword fight or two atop the wall. Needless to say, it's kind of cornball but if you have kids with you, it may be fun for them. Offered in Spanish, subtitles are projected onto a tiny screen in English and French upon request—just be sure to sit in the front and near the center to be able to read them.

Off the northern coastal road and at the top of the *Cerro de las Tres Piedras* (Hill of the Three Stones) is **Reducto de San José El Alto** (Av. Francisco Morazan s/n, 8 A.M.– 8 P.M. Tues.–Sun., US$2), a well-renovated fort complete with cannons, rifle slits, and thick walls and—impossible to overlook—a spectacular view of the Gulf of Mexico. It

also houses the small **Museo de Armas y Barcos,** a maritime and weaponry museum where you'll find model ships, 18th-century weapons, and a few other colonial-era artifacts. Explanations in Spanish only. To arrive by public transportation, catch a bus marked "Morazán/Bella Vista" in front of the post office (US$.25).

ENTERTAINMENT AND EVENTS

On weekends, traffic is blocked off around the main plaza and the streets and pathways fill with food carts and local families who come meet, eat lunch, and stroll about. Concerts are held in and around the kiosk; don't be surprised to hear an oompah band—with French horns, flutes, violins, and tubas—blaring forth with the energy of a great orchestra. In the evening during certain months, tens of thousands of swallows gather in the trees, making an impressive racket and prompting not a few people to carry umbrellas.

Run by the Restaurante Faro del Moro, **Barco Pirata Lorencillo** (Av. Resurgimiento No. 120, tel. 981/816-1990, departures at noon and 6 P.M.

daily, US$8.75) is a 90-minute boat ride up and down the coast with a pirate show as the highlight. Catch the boat at the fishing pier in Lerma, several kilometers south of Campeche.

Fronting the Gulf of Mexico, a three-kilometer/1.9-mile-long *malecón* (boardwalk) has been redone over the course of several years. Overlooking the sea, it lures dog-walkers, joggers, and inline skaters, as well as those out for a simple evening stroll. With several modern fountains and benches for resting, it's a great place to enjoy the breeze. Especially popular at dawn and dusk.

Campeche's bars and clubs are open Thurs.–Sat.; other days, there's really not much going on. The most popular spots when we visited were **KY8** (Calle 8 at Calle 59), **JAXX** (Av. Resurgimiento, near El Faro del Moro restaurant), and believe it or not **Lafitte's,** the pirate-theme restaurant that turns into a nightclub at the Hotel del Mar (Av. Ruiz Cortinez No. 51).

Near the convention center just outside the city walls, **Cines Hollywood** (Av. Ah-Kin-Pech s/n, tel. 981/816-1500, US$3.50, US$2.25 on Wed.) plays Mexican films and relatively new U.S. releases on its six screens.

SHOPPING

Shopping in Campeche is a limited sport. Most shops are geared toward local needs, so you'll find lots of paper stores, teen clothing boutiques, and shoe shops. Those stores that are geared toward tourists often are kitschy, offering a smattering of T-shirts, ashtrays, and key chains. That said, Campeche is a fast-growing town. By the time you read this, there may be more from which to choose.

Arguably the best shopping spot in the city, **Tukulná: Casa de Artesanías** (Calle 10 No. 333 between Calles 59 and 61, tel. 981/816-9088, www.tukulna.com, 9 A.M.–8 P.M. Mon.–Sat.) is a state-run shop that offers top-notch items that it buys directly from local artisans. Inside, you'll find every type of Campechano handicraft—from handmade clothing to rocking chairs. In the back, you'll

also find a re-creation of a Mayan home as well as a *jipi* hat cave.

Arte Dieriv (Calle 55 No. 13-B between Calles 10 and 12, tel. 981/816-1360, arte_dieriv@hotmail.com, 10 A.M.–10:30 P.M. daily) is a small shop that sells handicrafts and artwork from all over Mexico. If something catches your eye, show this guide for a 10 percent discount.

For a quick mall fix, head a block behind the post office and you'll find the **Plaza del Mar** (end of Calle 53 between Adolfo Ruiz Cortinez and Pedro Sainz de Baranda, 9 A.M.–2 P.M. and 5–9 P.M. Mon.–Sat., 9 A.M.–2 P.M. Sun.), a half-baked shopping center with lots of clothing shops, knickknack stores, and a video arcade.

ACCOMMODATIONS

Campeche has two good hostels and several nice high-end hotels (including two beautiful hotels in the Starwood Luxury Collection, one in town and the other a short drive away) but relatively few reliable midrange options. Like so much in Campeche, a pleasant outward exterior is often belied by an unimaginative and poorly maintained interior.

Under US$50

N Monkey Hostel (Parque Principal, Calle 57 and Calle 10, tel. 981/811-6605 or toll-free Mex. tel. 800/CAMPECHE (tel. 800/226-7324), www.hostalcampeche.com, US$7–7.50 pp dorm, US$15.50–17.50 s/d) has a great location overlooking the main park—be sure to go up to the roof—and it is a good place to meet other backpackers and get info. Dorm rooms are large and airy; the US$7.50 beds are in a corner room with more windows. Private rooms are small, simple, and clean; all have shared bath, while the more expensive ones have small balconies. A large bright common area has computers with Internet, plus board games and a book exchange. Continental breakfast is included, and there's a full kitchen.

Hostal del Pirata (Calle 59 No. 47 between Calles 14 and 16, tel. 981/811-1757, piratehostel@hotmail.com, www.hostelcampeche.com, dorm US$6.50, d with shared bath

US$16.50) is in a quiet area a block from the Puerta de Tierra. Continental breakfast is included, served in a pleasant interior courtyard. There are mixed and women-only dorm rooms, and all beds have individual lights, fans, and lockers. The "private" rooms aren't exactly private—more like stalls with three-quarter walls, plastic doors, and a double bed. There is a roomful of these, plus two more stuck in the back of the women's dorm. Overall, though, it's a comfortable, friendly place. Kitchen access, laundry service, and bike rentals available; room discounts for HI members.

Hotel Colonial (Calle 14 No. 122, tel. 981/816-2230, US$15 s, US$18 d, US$29 s/d with a/c) is very popular, especially with European tour groups, but we don't see the appeal. Yes, the rooms are clean, economical, and have private bathrooms with hot water, but they're also dim and have a moist air typical of old buildings with poor ventilation. The common area is nice.

The **N Hotel Regis** (Calle 12 No. 148 between Calles 55 and 57, tel. 981/816-3175, US$22.50 s, US$27 d, extra person US$5) is the best mid-range option in town. Occupying an old two-story colonial building with a wide entryway and foyer, the Regis's seven rooms vary from big to huge, with high ceilings, black-and-white tile floors, one or two double beds, and cable TV. The bathrooms are a bit small and the air-conditioning is controlled at the front desk (off or Arctic), but it's still a comfy hotel and a good value.

Hotel López (Calle 12 No. 189 between Calles 61 and 63, tel. 981/816-3344, hotlpez@prodigy.net.mx, US$39 s/d, extra person US$4) gets points for renovating its rooms—many hotels in Campeche don't seem to see any need—but it's more expensive than it ought to be. Until all the rooms are done, definitely ask for one of the new ones, which are medium-sized and have comfortable beds, tile bathrooms and quiet air conditioners; some have cable TV.

Hotel América (Calle 10 No. 252 between Calles 59 and 61, tel. 981/816-4588, US$26 s with fan, US$36 d with fan, US$39 s/d with a/c) is set in a pleasant old three-story mansion, but unfortunately it is somewhat overpriced (notice a theme?). The best rooms are those on the second floor (which has a nice, breezy corridor compared to the third floor's closed-in hallway) and a view of the interior courtyard—try Nos. 117 or 118. Otherwise, see a few rooms before deciding, as not all are worth the price. Continental breakfast is included and guests get one free hour of Internet. Note that in Spanish the *primer piso* (first floor) is what English-speakers would call the second floor. The first floor in English is known here and elsewhere as the *planta baja* (ground floor).

US$50–100

Many travelers end up staying at a slightly fancier hotel since the midrange options in Campeche aren't stellar.

N Sir Francis Drake Hotel (Calle 12 No. 207 between 63 and 65, tel. 981/811-5626, www.hotelfrancisdrake.com, US$43 s, US$50 d, US$57 junior suite, US$65 master suite) is a cozy, classy hotel at the south end of the center. All 24 rooms and suites have comfortable beds, modern bathrooms and furnishings, and air-conditioning and minibars; the suites have extras such as desks, sofas, and sitting rooms. Some of the units lack natural light, but others have small balconies and a view of the street. Guests can use the Internet for free in the hotel's small business center; printing and fax service are additional. Small restaurant, good service, parking.

Hotel Baluartes (Av. 16 de Septiembre No. 128 at Av. Ruiz Cortinez, tel. 981/816-3911 or toll-free Mex. tel. 800/667-1444, www.baluartes.com.br, US$59 s, US$66 d) is a modern, high-rise hotel fronting the *malecón* (seaside promenade). The hotel has 102 clean, well-furnished rooms with air conditioning and cable TV, and there are a swimming pool, sidewalk café, bar, dining room, banquet facilities, travel agency, car rental, and ample parking. Ask for one of the slightly larger oceanfront rooms; the views are superb and they cost the same as those facing the parking lot.

Over US$100

The **Hotel del Mar** (Av. Ruiz Cortinez 51, tel. 981/811-9191, www.hoteldelmar.com.mx, US$80 d with city view, US$98 d with ocean view, US$109–137 suites) is considered by some as Campeche's finest hotel, though those at the Hotel Hacienda Puerta Campeche would certainly beg to differ. (It's really a case of apples and oranges: The Puerta Campeche is a boutique luxury hotel while the Hotel del Mar is designed for business travelers.) Rooms here are medium-sized, with comfortable beds and modern furnishings. Those on the ocean side have small balconies to better enjoy the view and are worth the extra cost. The hotel's **Lafitte's** restaurant, open for lunch and dinner, has a pirate theme and costumed waiters; at night it becomes a disco. Travel agency, car rental, and parking.

Opened in June 2004, the **Ⓜ Hotel Hacienda Puerta Campeche** (Calle 59 No. 71 between Calles 16 and 18, tel. 981/816-7508, toll-free U.S. tel. 800/545-7802, puertacampeche@thehaciendas.com, www.luxurycollection.com, US$300–550 s/d) is one of the more inventive luxury hotels around and certainly the classiest in Campeche. Several adjoining colonial houses were gutted and transformed into an intimate 15-room hotel. (From the outside, the houses still appear separate.) The guest rooms have the same, high-quality decor as at fellow Starwood Luxury Collection haciendas, including deep beds, high ceilings, large marble bathrooms, and artful decorations. We actually preferred the junior and deluxe suites to the master suite—they're larger and have private open-air patios. But the swimming pool is the hotel's most memorable feature: It weaves through several enclosed rooms of the original houses, complete with doorways and brightly painted walls. The restaurant is recommended and the service, of course, is impeccable.

Twenty minutes outside Campeche city, along the road to Edzná archaeological site, **Hacienda Uayamón** (Carretera a Edzná Km. 20, tel. 981/829-7527, www.luxurycollection.com, US$250–300) is a sister hacienda of Hotel Hacienda Puerta Campeche in town. The hacienda was built in 1700 and has 12 freestanding units, each with deluxe furnishing and amenities, including thick beds, large bathrooms, high ceilings, and private terrace. The grounds are gorgeous, and several unused buildings have been left in a state of semi-disrepair to create a more authentic ambience. The pool is ensconced within the two remaining walls of the once-elegant ballroom; the dining room's large picture window looks out over former henequen fields. The restaurant (7:30 A.M.–11:30 P.M. daily, US$9–30) specializes in seafood and is recommended. Breakfast, lunch, and dinner can be arranged for nonguests with reservations.

FOOD

It seems only a matter of time before Campeche gets some cozy cafés, funky eateries, and classy Mexican and international restaurants to go along with the freshly painted façades and newly renovated parks and museums. But that time hasn't come yet—with a few exceptions, most restaurants here serve ordinary seafood and Mexican dishes in uninspired dining areas. That doesn't mean the food or service is bad—it's just nothing spectacular.

Seafood

The restaurant at the **Hotel Hacienda Puerta Campeche** (Calle 59 No. 71 between Calles 16 and 18, tel. 981/816-7508, 7:30 A.M.–11:30 P.M. daily, US$9–25) is Campeche's most upscale restaurant. Modern wood and steel tables are set up in attractive dining areas looking onto the restaurant's fine interior courtyard. Seafood is the specialty, of course, but you'll also find well-prepared beef and chicken dishes, accompanied by impeccable service.

Opened in 1947, **Miramar** (Calle 8 at Calle 61, tel. 981/816-2883, 8 A.M.–10 P.M. Mon.–Fri., 8 A.M.–3 A.M. Sat., 8 A.M.–7 P.M. Sun., US$4.50–9.50) is a popular Campechano restaurant with no frills, good food, and quick service. Be sure to try the specialties—*pan de cazón* (basically a baby shark tortilla lasagna) and *arroz con mariscos* (a large, tasty dish of rice with clams, shrimp, and conch).

Set in a bright and attractive dining room, **N Marganzo** (Calle 8 No. 267 between Calles 57 and 59, tel. 981/811-3898, 7 A.M.–11 P.M. daily, US$4–15) is known for its seafood but also offers excellent meat-based dishes. *Pampano relleno de mariscos* (white fish filled with seafood) is a favorite among regulars.

Open 24 hours a day, the diner-style **N La Parroquia** (Calle 55 No. 8 between 10 and 12, tel. 981/816-2530, US$2.50–10) is always busy. Here, along with either soap operas or televised soccer games, you'll find good seafood dishes and a smattering of traditional Mexican meals. Service is excellent.

Considered one of the best eateries in town, **La Pigua** (Av. Miguel Alemán No. 179-A, tel. 981/811-3365, 8 A.M.–6 P.M. daily, US$7–15) is an upscale restaurant and popular lunchtime stop for professionals and couples. The food is excellent—coconut shrimp with apple chutney is the specialty—although somewhat overpriced for the setting; tables are set in a sunless, palapa-roofed dining room with a view of neighboring concrete walls. Leafy plants between the two help, but not much. Bottom line—if you don't mind the lack of ambience, the food is a cut above the norm.

Steps from the Monumento al Resurgimiento and just below Fuerte de San Miguel, **El Faro del Moro** (Av. Resurgimiento No. 120, tel. 981/816-1990, noon–8 P.M. Tues.–Sun., US$5–15) doesn't look like much from the outside but gets rave reviews from people who visit Campeche frequently. Tables are on a patio overlooking the water—strangely enough, it's one of the few places in this seaside town where you can have a meal with an ocean view. Tortillas filled with cheese and shrimp are one of several favorites.

Mexican

For home cooking, cafeteria style, check out **Chef Color** (Calle 12 at Calle 55, tel. 981/811-1616, 10 A.M.–6 P.M. Mon.–Sat., US$2–3). A standard meal includes rice, beans, fried plantains, tortillas, and a choice of entrée. Good, cheap eats.

On a street lined with a string of cheap eats,

El Granaö (Calle 12 No. 179-A between 59 and 61, 8 A.M.–4 P.M. Mon.–Fri., 8 A.M.–2 P.M. Sat., US$.75–1.25) is a popular stop. Good chicken tacos in a bright, fast-food atmosphere.

Across from the Jardín Botánico, **La Carreta** (Calle 49-C No. 25 at Miguel Alemán, tel. 981/816-2942, 9 A.M.–5 P.M. and 7:30 P.M.–12:30 A.M. daily, US$.90–1.30 breakfast, US$2–11 lunch and dinner) is a local greasy spoon, offering—among other heart-stopping temptations—tacos, *flautas,* and juicy hamburgers.

Vegetarian

Nutrivida (Calle 12 No. 167 between Calles 57 and 59, tel. 981/816-1221, 8 A.M.–2 P.M. and 5:30–8:30 P.M. Mon.–Fri., 8 A.M.–2 P.M. Sat., US$.50–2) is a popular joint offering great soy-based meals, lots of veggie burgers, yogurt, and fruit dishes. Standing-room only indoors, although in back, there is a nice outdoor courtyard with tables.

N Todo Natural (Calle 8 between 51 and 53, cell tel. 044-981/107-8532, 8 A.M.–4 P.M. and 6–10 P.M. Mon.–Sat., 8 A.M.–4 P.M. Sun., US$1–3) is a cheerful place offering fantastic vegetarian and low-cholesterol meals at its tiny counter. Try the gazpacho or the *huevos sinco* (egg-white scramble with carrots, zucchini, bell peppers, *chaya,* tomatoes, onion, and cheese).

The small, vegetarian-friendly **La Perla** (Calle 10 No. 323 between Calles 57 and 59, tel. 981/816-2703, 7 A.M.–9 P.M. Mon.–Sat., US$1–2.50 breakfast, US$3–6 lunch and dinner) is a student hangout with low-priced, filling meals and great *licuados* (milk- or water-based fruit shakes) and fruit salads.

Sweets

La Nueva España Panadería y Pastelería (Calle 59 No. 7-A at Calle 10, tel. 981/816-2887, 6:30 A.M.–9:30 P.M. daily) offers great egg breads and sweet breads. Be there 12:30–1 P.M. and again at 5 P.M. to get the goods hot and fresh.

Just north of the main plaza, **La Gran Michoacán** (Calle 8 between 53 and 55, 7 A.M.–11 P.M. Mon.–Sat., 8 A.M.–11 P.M.

CHILE PEPPERS

Ever taken a bite out of a seemingly innocent quesadilla and ended up with your mouth on fire, throat burning, eyes watering, and no relief in sight? Throughout the kitchens of the Yucatán Peninsula a wide variety of *chile* peppers are used to spice food. Some, such as the *pimiento,* are benign and others, such as the habanero, can pack a wallop. Before you load up on that mystery salsa, check out this list to see what you're in for:

Pimiento (bell pepper): benign
Chile Dulce (literally, sweet pepper—small, pumpkin-shaped, and light green): benign
Güero (literally, light-skinned—long, light green): mildly hot
Chile Seco (literally, dried pepper—typically *pasilla* and *ancho*): mildly hot
Poblano (medium-sized, dark green): benign to deadly
Serrano (small torpedo-shaped peppers, typically green or red): medium hot
Puya (small, thin, red peppers): hot
Jalapeño (small to medium-sized, hard and green): hot
Chipotle (medium and rust-colored, often seen dried): hot
Morita (smoked and red): very hot
Piquín (tiny, red, and torpedolike): very hot to deadly
De Árbol (literally, from a tree—long, red, and very thin): very hot to deadly
Habanero (roundish, small and typically green, orange, or yellow): deadly

If you do get burned (pun intended), you'll find some quick relief in a glass of milk, a bite of banana, a pinch of salt, or a glass of beer. *Buen Provecho!*

Sun., US$.60–2.50), is the place to head for a refreshing fruit treat—you'll find homemade popsicles, ice cream, and juices in a huge variety of flavors.

Groceries
For the freshest fruits and vegetables, check out the **mercado principal** (Circuito Baluartes Este at Costa Rica), which is open daily 7 A.M.–2 P.M. There also are food stands inside that sell cheap, local fare.

Super San Francisco (end of Calle 51 between Av. Adolfo Ruiz Cortínez and Av. Pedro Sainz de Baranda, 7 A.M.–10 P.M. daily) is a big supermarket that, along with all the usual foods and household items, sells clothes, appliances, and furniture. There also is a small pharmacy just inside the entrance.

Super Isstecam (Calle 63 between Calles 8 and 10, 8 A.M.–4 P.M. Mon.–Fri., 8 A.M.–2 P.M. Sat.) is a basic grocery store selling mostly canned and dry foodstuff. For fresh produce, head to the *mercado principal.*

INFORMATION AND SERVICES
Tourist Information Centers
Behind the Palacio Legislativo is the **state tourist office** (Plaza Moch-Couoh, Av. Ruiz Cortines between Calles 63 and 65, tel. 981/816-6767 or tel. 981/811-9229, turismo@campeche.gob.mx, www.campechetravel.com, 8 A.M.–9 P.M. Mon.–Fri., 8 A.M.–2 P.M. and 5–8 P.M. Sat.–Sun.). A knowledgeable and friendly staff gives detailed information about local and regional sites. The office also provides guides that will give you a private tour of the city or a combo fort and city tour for about US$45 per small group. Ask about prices for personalized statewide trips. All tours must be booked in advance, preferably with one week's notice. English is spoken.

© LIZA PRADO CHANDLER

Campeche's main government buildings

On the main plaza, the **Municipal Tourist Office** (Calle 55 No. 3 between Calles 8 and 10, tel. 981/811-3989, www.campeche.gob.mx /dirturismo, 9 A.M.–3 P.M. and 5–9 P.M. daily) begrudgingly answers questions but has plenty of maps and brochures that may be more helpful. Theoretically, you can be attended in English, German, and French.

For information on cultural events in and around town, check out the bulletin boards in the entrance of the **Instituto de Cultura de Campeche** (Calle 12 between Calles 59 and 61). Postings tend to be extensive.

Medical Services

The main hospital is the public **Hospital Dr. Manuel Campos** (Calle 49 at Calle 14, tel. 981/816-2409 or 816-1709); it has a 24-hour emergency room. You can also call the **Cruz Roja** (Mexican Red Cross, Av. Las Palmas at Av. Ah-Kim-Pech, 065 or tel. 981/815-2411 for emergencies, tel. 981/815-2378 for nonemergencies).

Pharmacies

The most convenient 24-hour pharmacy is the one at **Hospital Dr. Manuel Campos** (Calle 49 at Calle 14, tel. 981/816-2409 or 816-1709, ext. 132). You may get better prices at **Farmacia Similares** (Calle 18 No. 99 at Calle 55, tel. 981/816-3316, 8 A.M.–9 P.M. Mon.–Sat.,8 A.M.–8 P.M. Sun.). **Farmacia Canto** (tel. 981/816-3165, 7 A.M.–10 P.M. Mon.–Sat., 8 A.M.–8 P.M. Sun.) is next door.

Police

You can reach the police by dialing 060 or 066 from any public phone.

Newspapers

The three main newspapers covering Campeche are *Tribuna de Campeche, Novedades Campeche,* and *El Sur de Campeche,* available at most newsstands in the capital and statewide.

Money

There are plenty of banks in the city center, including **Banorte** (Calle 57 at Calle 10, 9 A.M.–4 P.M. Mon.–Fri., currency exchange 9 A.M.–2 P.M. only), which is on the main plaza and has one ATM, and **HSBC** (Calle 10 No. 31 between Calles 53 and 55, 8 A.M.–7 P.M. Mon.–Sat.), which is open late and has two ATMs.

For currency exchange only, try **Centro Cambiario Canto** (Calle 18 between Calles 51 and 53, 10 A.M.–6 P.M. Mon.–Fri., 8 A.M.–12:45 P.M. Sat.). U.S. and Canadian dollars, euros, British pounds, and yen are accepted.

Post Office

In the Palacio Federal (Av. 16 de Septiembre at Calle 53, tel. 981/813-2245), the post office is open 9 A.M.–3 P.M. Monday–Friday.

Internet and Fax

The best Internet place in town is a **no name Internet café** across the street from the hospital (Calle 49 between Calles 14 and 16, 9 A.M.–11 P.M. daily). Connections are fast, service is friendly, and there's air conditioning. Rates are US$.80/hour, US$2.65 to burn CDs. **Ciber Chat** (Calle 59 at Calle 12, 9 A.M.–10 P.M. Mon.–Sat.) offers decent Internet connections for US$1 per hour. CD-burning costs US$1.75 and includes the CD.

Next to the post office, **Telecomm/Telegrafos** (Av. 16 de Septiembre at Calle 53, tel. 981/816-5210, 8 A.M.–7 P.M. Mon.–Fri., 9 A.M.–3 P.M. Sat.–Sun.) has fax service. Sending to or receiving faxes from the United States and Canada costs US$1.50 per page, to/from Europe costs US$2.40 per page, and within Mexico costs US$1.45 per page.

Telephone

Contrary to the name, **Compufast** (Calle 10 No. 280 between 65 and Circuito Baluartes, tel. 981/816-1617, 8 A.M.–9 P.M. Mon.–Fri., 9 A.M.–2 P.M. Sat.) has an excruciatingly slow Internet connection, but it does offer good but pricey international telephone service. Calls to the United States or Canada cost US$.90 per minute, domestic calls cost US$.35. International fax service costs US$1 per page, domestic faxes cost US$.70 per page.

Immigration Office

In the same building as the post office, **Migración** (Av. 16 de Septiembre at Calle 53, 1st floor, tel. 981/816-0369 or tel. 981/816-2868, 9 A.M.–1:30 P.M. Mon.–Fri.) is the place to head if you have to extend your visa or have any immigration questions you need answered. Extending your visa typically entails filling in several forms, going to a bank to pay the US$18.25 fee, and then returning to the office for the extension. For every extra 30 days, you have to prove you have US$1000 on hand, either in cash, travelers checks, or by simply showing a current credit card.

Laundry

Lavandería Lava Klin (Calle 49 between Calles 14 and 16, no phone, 8 A.M.–6 P.M. Mon.–Fri., 8 A.M.–4 P.M. Sat.) has same-day service for US$1.15/kilo (2.2 pounds).

Travel Agencies and Tour Operators

The following agencies are useful for tours to Edzná (around US$20 pp transport only, US$30 pp including guide) and nearby ecotourism activities, but they also arrange marathon one- and two-day visits to Calakmul and other ruins in the Río Bec region in southern Campeche: **Picazh** (Calle 16 No. 348 between Calles 57 and 59, tel. 981/816-4486); **Xtampak** (Calle 57 No. 14 between Calles 10 and 12, tel. 981/811-6473, www.xtampak.com); **Chito's Tours** (Calle 51 between Calles 8 and 10, tel. 981/811-4700, chitotours@hotmail.com).

Eco-Kayak (www.eco-kayak.com.mx) is the ecotourism wing of the national travel agency group **Intermar** (Hotel Baluartes, Av. 16 de Septiembre No. 128 between Calles 59 and 61, tel. 981/816-9006, campeche@travel2mexico .com, www.travel2mexico.com, 8 A.M.–9 P.M. Mon.–Fri., 9 A.M.– 8 P.M. Sat., 8 A.M.–5 P.M. Sun.); the former arranges kayaking and other nature tours, while the latter handles national and international air travel tickets.

GETTING THERE

Campeche city is on the Gulf coast, 190 kilometers (118 miles) southwest of Mérida and 444 kilometers (276 miles) northeast of Villahermosa, Tabasco. On the main highway, Campeche is a natural stopover for the trip between these two capitals.

CAMPECHE BUS SCHEDULES

First-class bus station (Av. Central at Av. Casa de Justicia, tel. 981/811-9910, toll-free Mex. tel. 800/702-8000) departures include:

Destination	Price	Duration	Schedule
Cancún	US$24	7 hrs	2:15 A.M., 8:30 A.M., 10:50 A.M., 11 P.M., and 11:45 P.M.
Chetumal	US$18	7 hrs	noon only
Ciudad del Carmén	US$10	3 hrs	8 A.M., 8:50 A.M., 10 A.M., 11:45 A.M., noon*, 1 P.M., 2 P.M., 2:50 P.M., 3:15 P.M., 4 P.M., 6:30 P.M., 7 P.M., 8:25 P.M., 9 P.M., 9:10 P.M., 9:15 P.M., and 10:30 P.M.
Escárcega	US$7	3 hrs	2 A.M., 11 A.M., noon, 12:30 P.M., 7 P.M., and 11:30 P.M.
Mérida	US$8	2.5 hrs	every 30–60 min. 1:15 A.M.–11:30 P.M.; deluxe service at 5 A.M. and 6:45 P.M. (US$10; 2 hrs).
Mexico City (TAPO)	US$63	16 hrs	12:30 P.M., 4 P.M.*, 7 P.M., 10:10 P.M., and 11:45 P.M.
Mexico City (Norte)	US$63	16 hrs	2 P.M. and 2:50 P.M.
Oaxaca	US$50	18 hrs	9:55 P.M. Friday only
Ocosingo	US$21	10 hrs	9:45 P.M. only
Palenque	US$16	6 hrs	12:30 A.M., 2 A.M., and 11 A.M.
Playa del Carmen	US$27	8 hrs	11:45 P.M. only
Puebla	US$56	15 hrs	9:15 P.M. only
San Cristóbal	US$23	11 hrs	9:45 P.M. and 11:30 P.M.*
Tuxtla Gutiérrez	US$29	12 hrs	9:45 P.M. and 11:30 P.M.*
Veracruz	US$40	12 hrs	1 P.M., 9 P.M., and 10:30 P.M.*
Villahermosa	US$20	6 hrs	2:15 A.M., 10 A.M., 11:45 A.M., 12:30 P.M., 2 P.M., 2:50 P.M., 4 P.M.*, 7 P.M., 9:10 P.M., and 10:30 P.M.

* Denotes ADO-GL deluxe service. Prices are 15–25 percent higher and travel time may be slightly faster.

Second-class bus station (Av. Gobernadores at Calle Chile, 981/816-3445 or 816-2633) departures include:

Destination	Price	Duration	Schedule
Ciudad del Carmén	US$7.75	3 hrs	5:30 A.M., 6:25 A.M., 10:45 A.M., 1:45 P.M., 3:30 P.M., 5:30 P.M., and 9:40 P.M.
Escárcega	US$6	2.5 hrs	every hour 4 A.M.–10 P.M. and 6:30 P.M.
Hecelchakán	US$2.35	1 hr	8:15 A.M.
Mérida	US$6.50	3 hrs	every 30 min. 3:45 A.M.–9:15 P.M., and 6 A.M., noon, 2:30 P.M., 5 P.M., and 5:30 P.M.
Santa Elena	US$5.65	3 hrs	6 A.M., 9:15 A.M., noon, 2:30 P.M., and 5 P.M.
Uxmal	US$6.15	2.5 hrs	6 A.M., 9:15 A.M., noon, 2:30 P.M., and 5 P.M.
Villahermosa	US$16	6 hrs	9:05 A.M. and 9:40 P.M.
Xpujil	US$10.25	6 hrs	5:15 A.M., 8:15 A.M., 6:30 P.M., and 8 P.M.

Terminal Autobuses Ejidales (Av. República No. 167, tel. 981/811-7265) departures include:

Edzná ruins	US$1.50	60–90 min.	7 A.M., 10 A.M., 11 A.M., noon, 12:30 P.M., 1 P.M., 2 P.M., 3 P.M., 3:30 P.M., 4 P.M., 5 P.M. and 6 P.M. (more or less).

Air

Aeromexico (toll-free Mex. tel. 800/816-5678, reservations 5:30 A.M.–7 P.M. daily) is the airline serving Campeche, with just three flights daily to Mexico City (US$175, 7 A.M., 12:15 P.M., and 6:10 P.M.). The tiny airport was being expanded when we came through, and there was talk of another airline offering service—call ahead. There are no convenient bus routes to or from the airport, which is about two kilometers (1.25 miles) northeast of the city. To get there, a taxi costs US$5.25 and takes about 15 minutes; from the airport, taxis meet most flights.

Bus

Campeche has three main bus terminals: the

first-class ADO station, known as *la terminal nueva* (the new terminal); the second-class station, known as *la terminal antigua* (the old terminal, as it was the original ADO terminal), and the Terminal de Autobuses Ejidales, which serves regional destinations. For departure times from these terminals, see the *Campeche Bus Schedules* sidebar.

The **first-class bus station** is used exclusively by ADO (tel. 981/811-9910, toll-free Mex. tel. 800/702-8000) and its affiliates, which together serve most major destinations. It is on Avenida Central at Avenida Casa de Justicia, about seven kilometers (4.3 miles) from the city center. A taxi between the terminal and the center runs about US$2.25, slightly more at night.

The **second-class bus station** (981/816-3445 or 816-2633) is four long blocks northeast of the city, at the corner of Avenida Gobernadores and Calle Chile. It's not too far from the center of town—about a 25-minute walk. It is served primarily by Sur bus line, although ATS Sur and UTCR bus lines also use the station. Note: We've heard several reports of robberies on Elite bus line, which sometimes operates here as well.

Terminal Autobuses Ejidales (tel. 981/811-7265) is next to a Sur ticket office on Avenida República No. 167, across from the purple-and white-painted Alameda Francisco de Paular Toro beside the market. The main reason to use this terminal is to get to the Edzná ruins, 52 kilometers (32.3 miles) southeast of Campeche city. Ask the driver to drop you at the *desvío Edzná* (turnoff to Edzná); from there, it's 200 meters (656 feet) to the entrance. The last bus back to Campeche passes the turnoff at 3 or 4 P.M.—ask the driver before getting off.

Car

Two good highways link Campeche and Mérida. Highway 180 is known as the *vía corta* (the short route) and goes north from Campeche through Hecelchakán, Bécal, and Umán, while Highway 261 is known as *vía larga* (the long route) because it veers east through Hopelchen and then north through Santa Elena and the Puuc region. Driving time is about the same (2–2.5 hours) their monikers notwithstanding. From Campeche south to Champotón, you can take Highway 180-Cuota (toll road) or Highway 180-Libre (free road); the former is a wide, fast highway and costs US$4; the latter goes nearer the ocean (but not always right alongside it) and passes through several small towns with their ubiquitous speed bumps. At Champotón, you can continue on Highway 180 to Ciudad del Carmen and on to Tabasco state, or take Highway 261 farther south to Escárcega, where you turn right for Palenque and the highlands of Chiapas or left for Calakmul and the Caribbean coast.

GETTING AROUND

Campeche's city center is small and very easy to navigate on foot, but unless you have a bike or rental car, you will need a taxi or local bus to get to and from the bus terminals, airport, and some of the outlying sights.

Bus

The first-class bus station is the only place that you can't walk to that has convenient local bus service. To get there, take an "S.E.P./Av. Central" bus or minivan (US$.30, every 15 minutes) from in front of the market on Calle 18 at Calle 53; the trip takes about 20 minutes. To get to the Fuerte de San Miguel and the Museo de Cultura Maya, take a "Lerma/Playa Bonita" bus (US$.30, every 30 minutes) from Calle 55 (on the market side) or from in front of the post office on Avenida 16 de Septiembre (also known as Circuito Baluartes) at Calle 53; ask the driver to let you off at *la subida San Miguel* (the road up to San Miguel), about four kilometers (2.5 miles) south of town. From there, it's a tough half-kilometer (one-third mile) climb to the fort. You can take the same bus to Playa Bonita, Campeche's best (but still rather sad) public beach. The stop-and-go trip takes about an hour; the last bus returns around 9 P.M.

Taxis

Taxis are relatively easy to flag down around town but if you want to guarantee a ride, head to a taxi stand: next to the cathedral, Calles 8 at Calle 55; near the *mercado principal,* Costa Rica at Circuito Baluartes; in front of the first-class bus station, Avenida Colosio at Avenida Central; in front of the second-class bus terminal, Avenidas Gobernadores at Calle Chile; near the Puerta de Tierra, Central and Circuito Baluartes, or call tel. 981/816-6666, tel. 981/815-5555, tel. 981/813-1333, or tel. 918/813-3540. Although there are set prices posted in cabs, be sure to agree upon the price before you close the door.

Car Rental

Maya Car Rental (Hotel del Mar, Av. Ruiz Cortinez No. 51, tel. 981/816-0670, viasetur@yahoo.com.mx, 9 A.M.–9 P.M.

Mon.–Sat., 9 A.M.–2 P.M. Sun.) operates with the Viasetur travel agency in the hotel lobby. A compact car with air conditioning starts at around US$60/day. You'll find lower prices, but a much smaller selection, around the corner at **Rentamar** (Prolongación Calle 59 s/n, tel. 981/811-6461, rentamar@aol.com), next to the Hotel Baluartes.

Bicycle Rental

Bikes can be a fun way to see the *malecón* and the outlying sights, although the latter involve some serious climbs. Rent some wheels at **Monkey Hostel** (Parque Principal, Calle 57 and Calle 10, tel. 981/811-6605) or **Hostal del Pirata** (Calle 59 No. 47 between Calles 14 and 16, tel. 981/811-1757) for around US$1/hour or US$5/day, or at **Rentamar** (Prolongación Calle 59 s/n, tel. 981/811-6461, rentamar@aol.com) for around US$3.50/day or US$12/day. It's worth asking about a helmet, but don't count on getting one.

Archaeological Zones near Campeche City

◪ EDZNÁ ARCHAEOLOGICAL ZONE

The most ambitious building program at Edzná (8 A.M.–5 P.M. daily, US$3) began in the early 7th century, though the area was settled as an agricultural zone around 600 B.C. and the first structures were built as early as 300 B.C. The site covers 25 square kilometers (15.5 square miles) and contains some of the earliest examples of the Puuc styles, though elements of Petén (probably via Cobá), Chenes, and Río Bec influence also exist. The city prospered until A.D. 900, when it (along with many other Classic centers) suddenly collapsed and the population dispersed.

As you approach Edzná on the road from Cayal, a tall pyramid rising from thick vegetation on the valley floor is visible from a long distance. The site is in the midst of a wide

© GARY PRADO CHANDLER

the Temple of Five Stories at Edzná

valley of cultivated land and scrub forest bordered by a low range of mountains. A network of drainage and irrigation canals 22 kilometers (13.7 miles) long was dug around the settlement's center and extended into agricultural zones. The canals were used as highways to transport canoe-borne goods and probably played a role as defensive moats as well. Also found here are 70 *chultunes* (man-made water-storage tanks), as well as 13 principal water canals. The remains of several *sacbes* (raised stone roads) that connected important buildings and extended to outlying towns are visible throughout the site.

The Temple of Five Stories

This is the largest and most impressive structure at Edzná, standing 31 meters (101.7 feet) high on a 60- by 58-meter (196.9- by 190.3-foot) base. The first four levels were probably used by priests as living quarters; a shrine and altar are on the highest level, with a roof comb—a decorative element built to make the pyramid appear even higher—rising over that. At one time this comb was covered with ornate stucco carvings, and the rest of the building's stones were coated with smooth stucco and painted brilliant colors. Some archaeologists and epigraphers believe

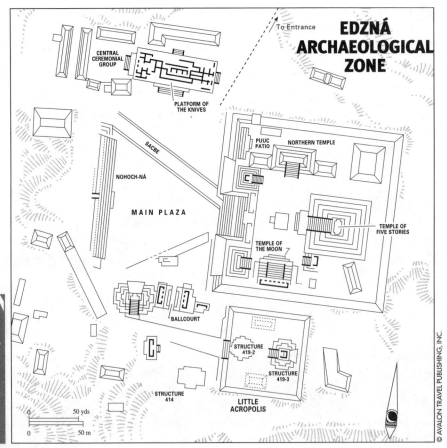

EDZNÁ ARCHAEOLOGICAL ZONE

To Entrance

CENTRAL CEREMONIAL GROUP

PLATFORM OF THE KNIVES

PUUC PATIO

NORTHERN TEMPLE

SACBE

NOHOCH-NÁ

MAIN PLAZA

TEMPLE OF FIVE STORIES

TEMPLE OF THE MOON

BALLCOURT

STRUCTURE 419-2

STRUCTURE 419-3

STRUCTURE 414

LITTLE ACROPOLIS

0   50 yds
0   50 m

the name Edzná comes from a Mayan phrase meaning "House of Grimaces" and possibly refers to the masks that decorated the comb of the Temple of Five Stories. Under the first-floor stairway is a corbel-vaulted tunnel that leads to an inner chamber.

Surrounding Temples

On the south side of the plaza is the restored **Temple of the Moon** (Paal u'na), across from the **Northern Temple.** Adjacent to these two are, respectively, the **Southwestern Temple** and the **Northwestern Temple** with the ruined sweat bath next door.

Another plaza contains the **Central Ceremonial Group,** with the **Great Acropolis, Great House, Platform of the Knives,** and **Southern Temple.** Part of Edzná is below sea level but the residents solved the drainage problem by building a complex system of underground canals and holding basins.

Just east of the ball court, the **Temple of the Masks** has carved stone masks at its east and west ends. Representing the rising and setting sun respectively, they have scarifications on the cheeks, large ear ornaments, and teeth filed to a point— all characteristics of the Mayan nobility.

Tours

Several agencies in Campeche offer transportation and/or tours to Edzná, which can be convenient if your time is short or you don't want to risk missing the bus home. (See *Travel Agencies and Tour Operators* in the *Campeche City* section for details and contact information.)

Getting There

If you're driving from Campeche, take Highway 180 east to Chencoyil, then go east on Highway 261 to Cayal, where you turn right and continue to the Edzná site. The 60-kilometer (37.3-mile) drive takes about one hour. Second-class buses leave Campeche's **Terminal Autobuses Ejidales** (tel. 981/811-7265, Av. República No. 167 across from Alameda Francisco de Paular Toro) at 7 A.M., 10 A.M., 11 A.M., noon, 12:30 P.M., 1 P.M., 2 P.M., 3 P.M., 3:30 P.M., 4 P.M., 5 P.M. and 6 P.M. (US$1.50, 60–90 minutes; departure time may vary somewhat). Ask the driver to drop you at the *desvio Edzná* (turnoff to Edzná); from there, it's 200 meters (656 feet) to the entrance. The last bus back to Campeche passes the turnoff at 3 or 4 P.M., but double-check with the driver on your way there.

SANTA ROSA DE XTAMPAK ARCHAEOLOGICAL ZONE

One of Campeche's most exciting new digs is Santa Rosa de Xtampak (8 A.M.–5 P.M. daily, US$2.50), which lies about 30 kilometers (18.6 miles) down an on-again/off-again paved road (when we visited it took us a painful 1.5 hours to make it). Its buildings date to 400 B.C., and many archaeologists believe that this old city was once the heart of the Chenes empire. Although rediscovered by John Stephens in the mid-1800s, major excavation didn't begin until the mid-1990s and it still continues. So far, only about half a dozen of the scores of major

Excavation and rebuilding are ongoing at Santa Rosa de Xtampak and most other archaeological sites.

© GARY PRADO CHANDLER

buildings here have been uncovered and excavated. Among the most important is the three-story **Palace**. With 27 rooms and 11 staircases, it is considered one of the best-designed buildings in Chenes zone. Today only a few staircases remain, including two internal ones that lead to underground chambers.

Getting There

Driving from Campeche, take Highway 261 past Hopelchén to a turnoff just north of town (about a 20-minute drive). Just look for the sign to Xtampak and cross your fingers that the road leading to the ruins has been recently patched up.

ISLA JAINA

Forty kilometers (24.9 miles) north of Campeche city, near the coast, the swampy island of Jaina holds the largest known Mayan burial ground on the Yucatán Peninsula; more than 1,000 interments have been found inside the two imposing pyramids on the island: **Zacpol** and **Sayasol**. According to the archaeologist Sylvanus Morley, who discovered the impressive site in 1943, Jaina was used by the Mayan elite—probably Puuc nobility—beginning in A.D. 652. Bodies were carried in long, colorful processions to this island and were interred in burial jars in crouched positions, their skin often stained red and bodies wrapped in either a straw mat or white cloth. Some were found with a jade stone in their mouths. Plates with food, jewelry, weapons, tools, and other precious items were placed on the heads of the dead to accompany them to the afterlife. Small figurines (4–10 inches tall) also were buried, resting on the deceased's folded arms. These finely crafted ceramic sculptures now are considered masterpieces of Mesoamerican art. They portray the buried in ritual costumes, like those of warriors and ball players, and are frozen in ritual positions, including as captives

being tortured. These tiny sculptures also often doubled as rattles, with clay balls rolling around the hollow interiors. Interestingly, to build the pyramids and the other ceremonial structures on the island, the Mayans raised the low elevation of the island by building platforms made of *sascab* (limestone material) brought from the mainland in canoes. This material covered the brittle coral of the island.

Visiting the Ruins

Although Isla Jaina is not officially open to the public, INAH (Insituto Nacional de Antropología) often gives special permission to those requesting entry. Permission can be granted by applying in person at the INAH office in Campeche (Calle 59 between Calles 14 and 16 (tel. 981/816-9111, tel. 981/816-9136, or tel. 981/811-1314).

The restaurant-marina **El Faro del Moro** (Av. Resurgimiento No. 120, tel. 981/816-1990, noon–8 P.M. Tues.–Sun.) offers guided charter trips to Isla Jaina (US$400, up to 10 people, eight hours). The boat ride is two hours each way, with the balance spent on the island. Reserve well in advance to give the boat captain time to obtain the necessary permits.

HECELCHAKÁN

About 60 kilometers (37.3 miles) north of Campeche on Highway 180 toward Mérida, the small town of Hecelchakán has some fine sculptures and Jaina burial art at the **Museo Arqueológico del Camino Real**. The bad news is that the place seems never to be open—official business hours are 10 A.M.–1 P.M. and 4–7 P.M. Tuesday–Saturday, and 4–7 P.M. Sunday. The good news is that a large part of the collection is displayed in a small garden along the street and is perfectly visible through the fence. If you're traveling by bus, you can catch a second-class bus from Campeche—one leaves daily at 8:15 A.M. (US$2.35, one hour).

Southern Campeche State

East from Escárcega, Highway 186 leads to the small town of Xpujil and the remarkable—and remarkably untouristed—Río Bec region. Here you'll find the awesome Calakmul ruins, which are deep in a nature reserve and include the highest and largest known Mayan structure, plus smaller but equally compelling sites of Chicanná, Becán, Balamkú, Hormiguero, among others. Most share the distinctive Río Bec architectural style, with meticulous stonework and high steeplelike towers.

Don't be surprised to find military and/or police checkpoints in this area, especially near the border with Quintana Roo east of Xpujil. The army and police are looking for drug smugglers and most tourists are waved through. If you're stopped, they will likely ask for I.D. and may want to search your trunk or glove box. Friendly cooperation is the best way to get through as quickly as possible.

ESCÁRCEGA

Escárcega, 150 kilometers (93 miles) south of Campeche, is an unremarkable town at the junction of Highways 186 and 261. For tourists, it is mainly a gas stop for those headed west to Palenque or east to the Río Bec area (150 kilometers/93 miles) and Chetumal (270 kilometers/167.8 miles). Escárcega has a reputation for being a rough-and-tumble place; true or not, there is little reason to linger here.

Accommodations and Food

On the main drag and impossible to miss with its bright purple and peach paint job, **Hotel Escárcega** (Av. Justo Méndez No. 87, tel. 982/824-0188, hotelescarcega@hotmail.com, US$16 s with fan, US$17.50 d with fan, US$23.50 s with a/c, US$26 d with a/c and cable TV) offers 64 basic rooms with private bathrooms and hot water. Rooms aren't spectacular but are decent for a night's stay if you get stuck in town.

There are a few taco stands on the main drag—you can't miss 'em.

Information and Services

There is a **launderette** (tel. 982/822-3141, 6 A.M.–2 P.M. and 4–8 P.M. daily, US$2.75/kilo—2.2 pounds) and an **Internet café** (Calle 28, tel. 982/824-1380, 9 A.M.–10 P.M. daily, US$.90/hour) a few blocks apart on Avenida Hector Perez Martínez, south of the main road into town not far from the Hotel Escárcega.

Getting There and Around

The **ADO bus terminal** (tel. 982/824-0144) is at the intersection of Highway 261 and Justo Sierra; if you're coming from Campeche, it is at the main intersection entering town. Buses here are all *de paso* (passing through), which means you can't technically make reservations and the schedules can be screwy. There are usually plenty of open seats, but you can call or stop by beforehand and put your name on the waiting list; be at the terminal 30 minutes early in case the bus arrives ahead of schedule. Long-distance destinations include Villahermosa, Mexico City, Mérida, Tulum, and Playa del Carmen, but more common ones for travelers include:

Campeche, US$6.50, 2.5 hours, 1:30 A.M., 4:30 A.M., 11:30 A.M., 4:15 P.M., 5 P.M., 11:35 P.M.

Cancún, US$27, nine hours, 12:05 A.M., 12:30 A.M., 1 A.M., 2 A.M., 5 A.M., 8:30 P.M., and midnight.

Palenque, US$9, three hours, 4 A.M. and 1 P.M.

San Cristóbal, US$18.50, 8–9 hours, 12:15 A.M.

Xpujil, US$6.50, two hours, 4:30 A.M., 8:30 A.M., 12:40 P.M., and 2:30 P.M.

The **second-class bus station** is in town at Justo Sierra and Calle 31. Buses to Xpujil (US$5, 2.5 hours) leave from there at 12:30 A.M., 7:45 A.M., 11 A.M., and 10:30 P.M.

The gas station is kitty-corner from the ADO terminal.

RÍO BEC ARCHAEOLOGICAL ZONE

The earliest occupation of the Río Bec area occurred between 1000 and 300 B.C., though the height of construction was much later, between A.D. 550 and 830. Then the population gradually dwindled and by the time of the Spanish conquest the sites were completely abandoned. The Río Bec sites were rediscovered early in the 20th century by chicle tappers and are still being explored and excavated. Many of the most noteworthy archaeological discoveries in the last few decades have been made here.

Calakmul is the mother of Río Bec sites, and of the Mayan world in fact, with the tallest pyramid, the most number of stelae of any ruin, and possibly the greatest number of total structures—they are still being mapped and counted. It is deep in a nature preserve, which makes the drive there pretty long but the bird- and wildlife-viewing that much better. Near the turnoff for Calakmul is Balamkú, a small site with a remarkably well-preserved stucco relief (and not much else). The sites of Chicanná,

Becán, and Xpujil are nearer the village of Xpujil (the only town of any size in the area) and are just off the highway and easy to get to. El Hormiguero is more of a challenge, about 15 kilometers (9.3 miles) down a rough dirt road, but rewarding for its detailed adornment.

 Calakmul Archaeological Zone and Reserve

In the Calakmul biosphere reserve and just 35 kilometers (21.7 miles) from the Guatemalan border, Calakmul (8 A.M.–5 P.M. daily, US$3) ruins are the center of what archaeologists now believe may have been the largest city-state in the Mayan world; as many as 60,000 people may have lived in or around the principal area at its height A.D. 300–700, with many more thousands in its surrounding sphere of influence. Approximately 6,750 structures have been mapped to date, including **Structure II**—at 53 meters (173.8 feet) high with a footprint of more than five acres, it is the tallest and largest Mayan pyramid yet discovered. Thousands more structural remains are believed to be hidden in the thick surrounding forest.

Over 6,700 structures have been mapped in Calakmul.

THE MAYAN COLLAPSE

Something went terribly wrong for the Mayans between the years A.D. 800 and 900. Hundreds of Classic Mayan cities were abandoned, monarchies disappeared, and the population fell by the million, mainly by death and plummeting birth rates. The collapse was widespread but was most dramatic in the Southern Lowlands, a swath of tropical forest stretching from the Gulf of Mexico to Honduras and including once-glorious cities such as Palenque, Tikal, and Copán. (Archaeologists first suspected a collapse after noticing a sudden drop-off in inscriptions; it has been confirmed through excavations of peasant dwellings from before and after that period.)

There are many theories for the collapse, varying from climate change and epidemic diseases to foreign invasion and peasant revolt. In his carefully argued book *The Fall of the Ancient Maya* (Thames and Hudson, 2002), archaeologist and professor of anthropology at Pennsylvania State University David Webster suggests it was a series of events, not any single event, that led to the collapse. Webster argues that a population boom just before the collapse left agricultural lands depleted just as demand was at its highest. Mayan farmers probably did not have large stores of corn and other food, as their farming methods—and especially the lack of draft animals—kept productivity relatively low. Even if they could generate large surpluses, storage was difficult in the lowlands' humid climate. And with so many rival states (whose populations were also increasing) there was little new undepleted land to cultivate. When "too many farmers grew too many crops on too much of the landscape," as Webster puts it, the population would have suffered malnutrition, disease, lower birthrates, increased infighting, and it would have been especially vulnerable to a large-scale catastrophe such as drought or epidemic disease. Whatever blend of social stress existed—and they surely varied somewhat from kingdom to kingdom—it seems clear that in the 9th century ordinary Mayans finally lost all faith in their leaders who, after all, legitimized their rule by being able to please or appease the gods. When the elites abandoned their positions, large-scale collapse was not far behind.

Nine jade funeral masks and around 120 stelae—the earliest dated A.D. 495, the latest A.D. 909—have been found here, more than at any other Mayan site. (Several of the masks are displayed at the museum at Fuerte de San Miguel in Campeche, though they are frequently—and frustratingly—on loan to other museums.) Calakmul is also referred to more frequently than any other city in the stelae of other ancient sites, especially Tikal, its great rival, yet another proof of Calakmul's once-high stature. More recently, archaeologists discovered and excavated a smaller temple deep inside the massive hulk of Structure II—it wasn't open yet when we passed, but by the time you read this visitors should be able to view the temple via a narrow tunnel about halfway up Structure II's main stairway (à la Rosalila temple in Copán, Honduras).

Calakmul has been excavated in the fashion of Tikal and Cobá, where a minimum of trees and vegetation has been removed and you feel as if you are in a forest. You don't get the clean sightlines and all-encompassing views that you do at totally cleared sites such as Chichén Itzá or Uxmal, but it's obviously much better for the environment. And the animals: Look for monkeys, toucans, parrots, and other assorted birds and rodents at the site—including a family of black howler monkeys that often hangs out in the trees in the Grand Plaza—and as you drive through the biosphere reserve on the way there and back. The reserve is home to five of Mexico's six wild cat species—some people have seen jaguars, and we drove around a bend to see a large puma (mountain lion) trotting down the road. It was a wonderful stroke of luck and extremely uncommon. Early morning and late afternoon are best for animal-viewing. From the top of the pyramids, you'll get a glorious view of the jungle and—on a clear day—even **Danta Structure** at El Mirador in Guatemala.

Calakmul is a good two hours' drive from Xpujil. From the turnoff on Highway 186, it's 60 kilometers (37.3 miles) of a paved but narrow and winding road to the archaeological zone. Drive carefully and be ready to pull over, whether for other cars or animals in the road.

Balamkú Archaeological Zone

For years archaeologists and the area's few tourists paid scant attention to little old Balamkú (8 A.M.–5 P.M. daily, US$2.50) preferring instead to focus on Calakmul, Becán, and the grander sites of this region. But in 1990 archaeologists uncovered a fantastic stucco frieze inside a ruined pyramid here, and Balamkú instantly became a must-see on the southern Campeche Mayan route. The frieze is huge and extremely well preserved, and it depicts a bizarre combination of anthropomorphic creatures quite different from those appearing at surrounding sites. In fact, archaeologists are still pondering a good explanation for them. The chamber where the frieze was found has been carefully reconstructed to protect the fragile stucco and preserve the appearance of the surrounding structure and plaza—from the outside you can hardly tell anything is there. It is accessible through a side door that is kept locked—the attendant is usually not far away and can open the door to give you a peek.

M Chicanná Archaeological Zone

Roughly 120 kilometers (75 miles) east of Escárcega and 270 kilometers (168 miles) southeast of Campeche city, the Mayan site of Chicanná (8 A.M.–5 P.M. daily, US$2.75) is about a half kilometer (third of a mile) off Highway 186. The small city includes five structures encircling a main center. Look for the impressive serpent mask that frames the entry of the main palace, the aptly named **House of the Serpent Mouth.** Across the plaza lies **Structure I,** a typical Río Bec-style building with twin false-temple towers. Several hundred meters south are two more temple groups.

a representation of Chac, the god of rain, at Chicanná

If you're curious to compare the subtle differences of design and architecture of the ancient Mayans throughout the peninsula, this group is worth a visit.

M Becán Archaeological Zone

Another five kilometers (3.1 miles) along Highway 186 is the turnoff to Becán (8 A.M.–5 P.M. daily, US$3). Dating to 600 B.C., Becán is notable for the large moat (15 meters/49.2 feet wide and 4 meters/13.1 feet deep) that encircles the city, probably for defensive purposes. **Structures IX and X** are huge pyramids—IX is more than 30 meters (98.4 feet) high—and afford excellent views of the surrounding countryside (and each other). There is an excellent, and only recently uncovered, mask depicting the sun god Kinichna on the south side of Structure X. **Structure VIII,** just off the southeast plaza, offers a labyrinth of underground rooms, passageways, and artifacts, indicating that it was an important religious ceremonial center. **Structure II** is easiest to climb from the back, where a rope hangs down a steep set of stairs. At the top, look for narrow doorways

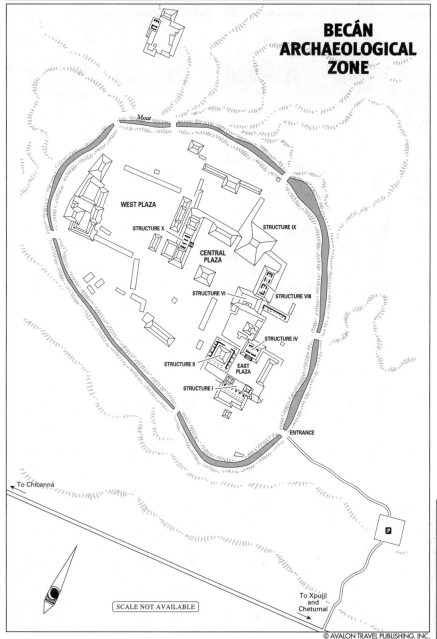

BECÁN
ARCHAEOLOGICAL
ZONE

Moat

WEST PLAZA

STRUCTURE X

STRUCTURE IX

CENTRAL
PLAZA

STRUCTURE VI

STRUCTURE VIII

STRUCTURE IV

STRUCTURE II

EAST
PLAZA

STRUCTURE I

ENTRANCE

← To Chicanná

To Xpujil
and
Chetumal

P

SCALE NOT AVAILABLE

© AVALON TRAVEL PUBLISHING, INC.

The State of Campeche

© LIZA PRADO CHANDLER

Structure X at Becán Archaeological Zone

on either side of the platform leading to spiral staircases down to the lower floors. This is a great site if you enjoy climbing and clambering around.

Xpujil Archaeological Zone

Right in the village of Xpujil, the Xpujil ruins (8 A.M.–5 P.M. daily, US$2.75) are small but well preserved. Its three towers (a tall central one flanked by two smaller ones) are built in classic Río Bec style, but are unusual in their number—most temples here have only two towers. On the back of the central tower, check out what's left of two huge inlaid masks.

El Hormiguero Archaeological Zone

Spanish for "The Anthill," El Hormiguero (8 A.M.–5 P.M. daily, US$2.50) was until relatively recently extremely hard to get to, requiring a heavy-duty 4WD vehicle and a lot of time. The road has improved significantly, and though it is still no autobahn, just about any car can get through as long as you go slow and it hasn't been raining. The site is notable for its ornate main facade, a classic serpent mouth doorway.

Bat Caves

At about Km. 107 on Highway 186 there is a small turnoff on the north side of the road, just big enough to pull your car off the road. From there, a couple of hundred meters' walking through the trees and up a small hill brings you to a huge sinkhole, at the bottom of which is a narrow cave opening. At dusk every night, hundreds of thousands of small black bats emerge from the cave in an endless whirling rush. Known locally as the *nube negro* (black cloud), it is an incredible spectacle and unlike no other. At the height, you can feel the wind from their collective wings and winding upward flight—a few may even crash into you or stop for a rest on your pant leg (they are completely harmless). Although you may be able to find it on your own, it's better to stop in the morning at Río Bec Dreams and arrange for one of the workers to guide you—if you come early, the outing can also include a short stop at **Mano Roja,** an unexcavated Mayan ruin about halfway to the caves. There's no fixed fee, but a US$10 tip seems about right.

XPUJIL TOWN
Accommodations

Xpujil has some basic, affordable hotels, but the area's best lodging options are west of town near the ruins. If you are coming from Campeche, look for them before reaching Xpujil proper.

In Town: Mirador Maya (tel. 983/871-6005, US$26/35 d/t) looks like a Girl Scout camp transplanted from the shores of an Alpine lake to a grubby lot in Xpujil overlooking the highway. That said, the cabins are clean, with high A-frame ceilings, a fairly large bathroom, and two double beds that take up most of the floor space. (A few even have satellite TVs.) Not a bad budget option overall—try to get a cabin that's set a bit off the roadway and make sure it has a working fan and good mosquito net. The hotel is a short walk from town and has a utilitarian restaurant, money exchange booth, and taxi service to area ruins (see *Getting Around*). Visa, MC, and AmEx accepted.

On the same side of the highway a bit closer

to town, **Hotel Calakmul** (tel. 983/871-6029, with private bath US$35/43 d/t, US$17.50/26 shared bath) is a step up. Small rooms have air conditioning and cable TV, and are clean and comfortable although a bit sterile. Several small wooden units in back are the cheapest rooms in town, with two beds, fan, and mosquito nets; the communal showers and toilets are pretty clean. Cash only.

Near the Ruins: Inside the Reserva de la Biosfera de Calakmul, **Ⓜ Calakmú Yaxche** (Carr. Calakmul Km. 6.5, no phone, camping US$13 pp including all equipment, US$4.50 pp without equipment, US$3 pp five or more people) is one of the few honest-to-goodness campgrounds you'll find here or just about anyplace in Mexico. A short distance off the road to Calakmul, campsites are scattered in a pleasant wooded area, with clean toilets and showers, a large fire pit, and a camp house serving good, basic meals (US$3–5). Rental equipment is quite nice, and the staff will set it up for you. The campground is run by a friendly Xpujil couple with incredible knowledge of, and passion for, the reserve. Bike and walking tours of the reserve cost around US$20 per person and come well recommended.

Just inside the entrance to the toll road that leads to Calakmul, **Puerta Calakmul** (Carr. Escárcega-Chetumal Km. 98, tel. 998/898-1641, www.puertacalakmul.com.mx, US$70 s/d) offers 15 well-spaced and higher-end cabins in a wooded area a half kilometer (third of a mile) from the road. All of the cabins have a palapa roof, mosquito nets, and private bathrooms. A pool is also on the premises but was empty when we visited. Cash only.

Ⓜ Río Bec Dreams (Carr. Escárcega-Chetumal Km. 142, www.riobecdreams.com, US$26 s/d) is a good choice if you don't mind sharing outdoor bathrooms or the sound of an occasional truck passing late into the night. Four "jungalows"—small cabins with good screens and nice touches such as curtains, hand-painted sinks, and purified water—are scattered in the woods behind a well-tended jungle garden. A cabana, with private bathroom and its own firepit, was on the brink of

completion when we passed through (US$60 s/d); a bookstore and information center were also in the works. The hotel restaurant is one of the best in the area and owners Diana and Rick are founts of information.

Across from the ruins by the same name, **Chicanná Ecovillage** (Carr. Escárcega-Chetumal Km. 144, tel. 983/871-6075, chicanna@campeche.sureste.com, US$89 s with fan, US$98 d with fan) is an oasis in the middle of the arid Río Bec region. Here one- and two-story solar-powered stucco villas rest on manicured grounds; all are ample, boast modern amenities, and are nicely appointed with Mayan replicas. All also have an inviting terrace or balcony with lounge chairs—a great place to relax after a day of ruin sightseeing. The resort also offers a small, solar-heated pool, and a dining room with an international menu. With just the song of the birds and the rhythmic swish of the broom on the stone walkways, this is a true retreat.

Food

The best restaurants in town are actually out of town at Río Bec Dreams and Chicanná Ecovillage hotels. The hotels in town have basic restaurants and there's one bakery.

In town, **Mirador Maya** (tel. 983/871-6005, 7 A.M.–midnight daily, US$4–9) serves standard Mexican food.

Kitty-corner from the taxi stand in the middle of town, **Expendido de Pan San Martín** (Av. Calakmul s/n, 6 A.M.–10 P.M. daily) sells fresh bread and pastries. Whether it's open on weekends is a crapshoot.

A classy open-air dining room at **Ⓜ Río Bec Dreams** (Carretera Escárcega-Chetumal Km. 142, www.riobecdreams.com, 8 A.M.–10 P.M. daily, breakfast US$4.50–7, lunch/dinner US$5.50–8) offers an excellent international menu. Fresh vegetables, good-sized portions, and excellent service make this a first-rate stop. Be sure to try the Indian curry chicken if you want a change of pace.

Choose between dining inside or out at the **Chicanná Ecovillage** (Carr. Escárcega-Chetumal Km. 144, tel. 983/871-6075, 7 A.M.–10 P.M. daily, breakfast US$5–7, lunch/dinner

US$8–12). With its varied menu, you'll be sure to find something that appeals to you. Service is upscale.

Information and Services

As of this writing, there was no bank, ATM, or currency exchange agency. Though this is bound to change, be sure to arrive with enough cash to make it through your visit. Otherwise you may have to take an unexpected trip to Chetumal.

Centro de Salud (Av. Siluituc between Balakbal and Av. Becan, tel. 983/871-6100) is a basic clinic with 24-hour emergency service. Alternatively, **Dr. Máximo Pucheta Quino** is a family practice doctor who runs the only private medical office in town (halfway down Av. Calakmul s/n, tel. 983/871-6132 during business hours, tel. 983/871-6013 in case of emergency). Office hours are 8 A.M.–8 P.M. daily but he is available 24 hours a day in case of emergency.

There's a fully stocked **pharmacy** attached to Dr. Pucheta Quino's clinic, or try **Farmacia Mérida** (Av. Calakmul s/n, 7 A.M.–11 P.M. daily) two doors down from the bus station.

When there is electricity in town, the most reliable Internet place is **Internet La Selva** (across from the health clinic, Calle Becan s/n, tel. 983/871-6071, 8 A.M.–11 P.M. Mon.–Sat., US$1/hour, US$2.25 to burn CDs). Next door, and run by the same owners, the **Lavandería La Selva** (tel. 983/871-6071, 8 A.M.–11 P.M. Mon.–Sat., 1–8 P.M. Sun.) charges US$1 per kilo (2.2 pounds) next-day service, US$1.30 per kilo same-day service.

Next to the bus station, the **Caseta Telefónica Becán** (Calle Calakmul s/n, tel. 983/871-6133, 7 A.M.–11 P.M. daily) is a quiet place to make calls (US$.90/minute to United States/Canada, US$.45 within Mexico) and to send faxes (US$.45/page within Mexico, US$.90/page worldwide).

The **post office** (Av. Calakmul s/n, 9 A.M.–3 P.M. Mon.–Fri.)—one man and his desk—is in a tiny building, a couple of doors up from the bakery.

Getting There and Around

Having a rental car is all but essential to enjoy the ruins here. Without one, you'll either spend a lot of time waiting for rides, or a lot of money on taxi service, or both. Hitching is possible to and from Calakmul but not a sure thing. **Private taxi service** is available at Mirador Maya hotel (tel. 983/871-6005). Round-trip to Calakmul and Balamkú for 1/2/3/4 people is US$60/80/90/100; to Chicanná, Becan, and Xpujil US$30/40/45/50 ; and to Kohunlich and Dzibanché US$60/80/90/100. You'll get about the same rates from the drivers in town.

There's a **gas station** about five kilometers (3.1 miles) east of Xpujil. Note that frequent power outages also affect the gas pumps, so fill up when you can.

First-class—ADO and OCC—and second-class—Sur and TRT—bus lines service the small **bus station** (Av. Calakmul s/n, tel. 983/871-6027) in the center of town. An asterisk denotes second-class service. Departures include:

Campeche, US$13, five hours, 4 A.M.*, 6:15 A.M.*, 10:30 A.M.*, and 1:45 P.M.

Cancún, US$21, seven hours, 6 A.M. and 10 A.M.

Chetumal, US$5.30, two hours, 1 A.M.*, 3 A.M.*, 7 A.M., 11:30 A.M., 1 P.M.*, 3:30 P.M., and 4:30 P.M.

Ciudad del Carmén, US$11, four hours, 2:15 P.M.*

Escárcega, US$6.50, two hours, 12:05 A.M., 6:15 A.M.*, 10:30 A.M.*, 2:15 P.M.*, 4:15 P.M.*, and 9:45 P.M.

Mexico City, US$62, 18 hours, 1:45 P.M., 5:30 P.M., and 1:15 A.M.

Palenque, US$16, five hours, 9 P.M.

Playa del Carmen, US$18.25, six hours, 6 A.M. and 10:45 A.M.

Puebla, US$56, 17 hours, midnight.

San Cristóbal, US$23, five hours, 9 P.M.

Tuxtla Gutiérrez, US$26.25, six hours, 9 P.M.

Veracruz, US$40.25, nine hours, 8:20 P.M.

Villahermosa, US$19, seven hours, 12:15 A.M., 7:30 A.M.*, 1:45 P.M., 5:30 P.M., and 9:45 P.M.

The State of Tabasco

Tabasco is not technically part of the Yucatán Peninsula—that would be just the states of Campeche, Yucatán, and Quintana Roo. But this marshy Gulf state is the birthplace of the Olmecs, the first advanced civilization in Mesoamerica, and it gave rise to at least one important Mayan city. Tabasco is where cacao was first harvested and chocolate first brewed—though chocolate manufacturers in other countries have eclipsed Tabasco in terms of taste and quality, the state remains an important chocolate producer.

Tabasco is definitely off the main tourist route and not without reason—the relatively few sights here mean travelers with limited time are better off spending it elsewhere. But those who intrigued by the little-understood Olmec people, or who are committed to seeing less-traveled Mayan ruins, will find some places of interest here.

PLANNING YOUR TIME

Two to three days are enough to visit in Villahermosa and Comalcalco, the state's main destinations. In Villahermosa, spend the

Must-Sees

Look for M to find the sights and activities you can't miss and Ⓜ for the best dining and lodging.

an Olmec sculpture in Parque-Museo La Venta

© LIZA PRADO CHANDLER

M Parque-Museo La Venta: Huge stone heads and other sculptures from Mesoamerica's first civilization are displayed in this leafy park and zoo (page 368).

M Comalcalco Archaeological Zone: These grand pyramids were built from baked bricks rather than stone, making them unique among all Mayan ruins (page 377).

M Chocolate Haciendas: Tabasco is where it all began, and the state is still producing chocolate 400 years after introducing it to Columbus and the world. Learn how chocolate is made—from juicy green fruit to sweet brown candies (page 378).

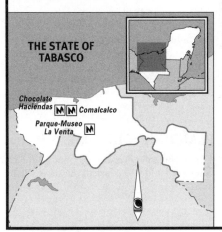

THE STATE OF TABASCO

Chocolate Haciendas Ⓜ Ⓜ Comalcalco
Parque-Museo La Venta Ⓜ

morning at Parque-Museo La Venta and the afternoon checking out sights in the Zona Remodelada, such as the Centro Cultural, Plaza de las Armas, Torre del Caballero, or the anthropology museum. There are also a number of small art galleries that host shows now and again—look for them as you wander the pedestrian walkways. The next

day hop on a *colectivo* to Comalcalco, where you can easily visit the ruins and a chocolate factory as a day trip. Tabasco 2000 is a modern but unremarkable mall, although the nearby planetarium, city hall, and fountains are pleasant enough. For a more interesting shopping experience, try the José María Suárez market.

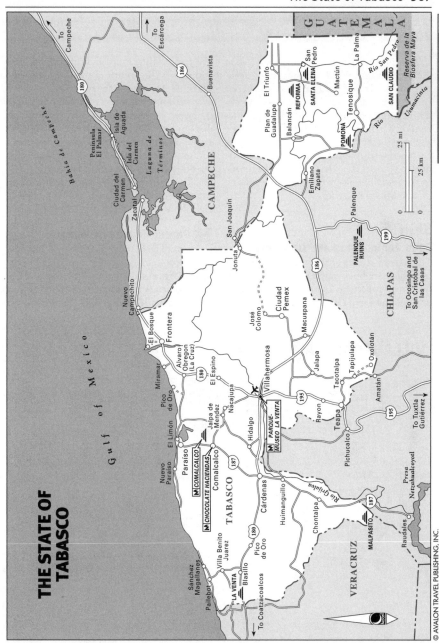

THE STATE OF
TABASCO

© AVALON TRAVEL PUBLISHING, INC.

Villahermosa

Villahermosa may not, at first glance, seem to deserve its name, which is Spanish for "beautiful town." Traffic snarls many of the streets and the buildings are plain compared to cities such as San Cristóbal and Mérida. Villahermosa's best feature is its lakes, which angle and elbow their way over much of the city. A few hotels—the Graham and Cencali in particular—have pretty lake views and a lemonade by the water is a nice way to rest after visiting Parque-Museo La Venta.

SIGHTS

Zona Remodelada and Downtown

The narrow streets of the original town center, which are brick-paved and closed to traffic, are referred to as the **Zona Remodelada** or the **Zona Luz.** The tree-lined streets bring you past bustling shops and tiny cafés packed with locals. Just south of the Zona Luz, the **Plaza de Armas** is a pretty park surrounded by government buildings on a slight rise above the zone. It boasts the **Puente de Solidaridad**—a footbridge that spans the Río Grijalva and allows the residents of Colonia Las Gaviotas to cross to the town center. Partway across the bridge, the **Torre del Caballero** (8 A.M.–5:30 P.M. daily, free) is a concrete lookout tower with 211-step spiral staircase leading to a windy platform with fine views of the city and river.

Parque-Museo La Venta

La Venta (The Marketplace) is one of the great Olmec communities, built on an island in the middle of the vast Río Tonolá marshland about 129 kilometers (80 miles) west of present-day Villahermosa. It was probably founded around

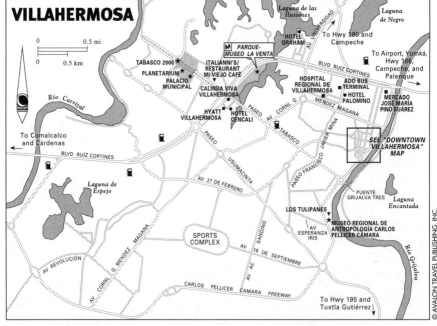

© LIZA PRADO CHANDLER

Parque-Museo La Venta has an excellent collection of Olmec stone sculptures.

900 B.C. and functioned primarily as a ceremonial center until it was abandoned around or before 300 B.C. The main structure was a 34-meter/111.5-foot-high pyramid made of clay; a stunning cache of jade figurine burial offerings found there are now on display in Mexico City's Museo Nacional de Antropología. But La Venta is best known for the massive stone heads more than two meters (6.6 feet) tall and weighing more than 15 tons each found throughout the site. No one has yet figured out how the Olmecs (without the wheel) managed to move these giant pieces of rock, since the raw material comes from an area almost 100 kilometers (62 miles) distant. Frans Blom—who is more famous for his work with the Lacondóns in eastern Chiapas—first investigated the ruins in 1925. It was the intrusion of the Pemex oil drills, however, that brought the Olmec ceremonial center back to national attention. A local poet named Carlos Pellicer Cámara arranged to have virtually the entire complex—including the stone heads—moved to a park on the outskirts of Villahermosa. There the artifacts were laid out in the precise configuration in which they were found.

Today, Parque-Museo La Venta (Blvd. Ad-olfo Ruíz Cortines s/n, tel. 993/314-1652, 8 A.M.–5 P.M. daily, zoo closed Mon., US$2.50) lies on the lovely Laguna de las Ilusiones and is now a combination outdoor museum and zoo—you will likely see a number of "escaped" monkeys and other creatures hanging around the park's thick trees and brush. A self-guided tour (brochures with explanations are available at the entrance) leads you through the trees and tropical foliage past numerous sculptures; in addition to the famous heads, look for large stones with finely carved deities emerging from niches, and smaller carvings of animals, including dolphins and monkeys. There are also a café, bookstore, and gift shop on-site.

Museo Regional de Antropología Carlos Pellicer Cámara

Part of larger complex known as CICOM (Spanish for the Center for Research of Olmec and Mayan Cultures) the Museo Regional de Antropología Carlos Pellicer Cámara (Regional Anthropology Museum—Av. Carlos Pellicer Cámara 511, tel. 993/312-6344, 9 A.M.–5 P.M. Tues.–Sun., US$2) is an aging but interesting museum with artifacts from Olmec, Toltec,

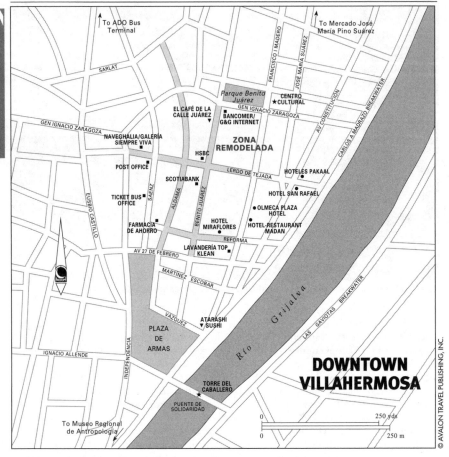

DOWNTOWN
VILLAHERMOSA

© AVALON TRAVEL PUBLISHING, INC.

and Mayan sites. The pieces are quite impressive, including pottery, clay figurines, stone carvings, and delicate pieces of carved jade, but the explanations and displays don't seem to have been updated since the 1970s. Part of the same complex is the 1,300-seat **Teatro Esperanza Iris** (tel. 993/314-4210), which has regular dance, music, and theater performances. Check at the Centro Cultural or in the box-office window for upcoming events.

Yumká

Next to the airport, Yumká (Las Barrancas s/n, tel. 993/356-0115, yumka@prodigy.net.mx,

www.yumka.org, 9 A.M.–5 P.M. daily, US$4 adults, $3 children) is Villahermosa's stab at an ecopark. Meaning "the elf that watches over the plants and animals in between the wetlands and the jungle" (big translation for such a small word, eh?), Yumká is basically a glorified throwback to the "African Safari" parks that were so popular in the United States in the 1970s. It's divided into three 30-minute segments—a guided walk through the jungle, a ride through the savanna on a tractor-pulled trolley, and a boat ride on a lagoon—and visitors pay to view monkeys, jaguars, hippos, giraffes, elephants, and birds. Between the

© LIZA PRADO CHANDLER

Tabasco 2000 has several pleasant fountains.

bullhorns, the tractor, and the 747s taking off next door, however, it's not exactly an eco-adventure. A taxi to the park from downtown costs a steep US$13 each way.

ENTERTAINMENT AND EVENTS

Centro Cultural Villahermosa

Out of place on a busy downtown street corner, the Centro Cultural Villahermosa (Avs. Francisco Madero and Zaragoza, tel. 993/314-5552, ccvhsa@hotmail.com, 10 A.M.–8 P.M. Tues.–Sun., free) is a sleek, modern building with a sloping glass facade and gleaming white walls inside and out. The cool main lobby doubles as an exhibition space—there was a fine photography exhibit when we passed through—and a small theater hosts occasional performances. You can also come here to get information about other expositions and cultural events around town. The café at the back has fresh coffee and good, light fare.

Tabasco 2000

This set of new buildings is developing into an impressive cultural center with a series of

lovely fountains and walkways that make for a pleasant stroll. Along with Villahermosa's most modern mall (Paseo Tabasco s/n, 10:30 A.M.–8:30 P.M. daily) with its polished marble floors and glass-enclosed shops, you'll find city and state government offices, a huge convention center, and a **planetarium** (tel. 993/316-3641, planetariot2000@hotmail.com, www.secured .gob.mx). The planetarium's observatory closed years ago, but the Omnimax theater has one show at 6:30 P.M. Tuesday through Friday and two shows at 5 and 6:30 P.M. on Saturday and Sunday. Tickets cost US$2.20. Cultural and art exhibits also are often displayed in the foyer.

SHOPPING

Villahermosa is by no means a shopping mecca for tourists; it's geared toward locals and their daily needs. One shop definitely worth noting, though, is **Artesanías de Tabasco**—a state-run business that sells some of the best handicrafts made in Tabasco. You can check out its products at www.ifat.gob.mx. There are five shops around Villahermosa: inside La

Venta (tel. 993/315-3421, 9 A.M.–5 P.M. daily), the Museo Regional de Antropología e Historia (no phone, 9 A.M.–5 P.M. Mon.–Sat.), the Casa de los Azulejos (Av. Juárez at 27 de Febrero, no phone, 9 A.M.–9 P.M. Tues.–Sun.), Tabasco 2000 (2nd floor, tel. 993/316-2822, 10:30 A.M.–8:30 P.M. daily), and at the airport (tel. 993/356-0196, 7 A.M.–9 P.M. daily).

If you need a mall fix, head to the sleek **Tabasco 2000** (Paseo Tabasco s/n, 10:30 A.M.–8:30 P.M. daily), a huge shopping center (*sans* cinema) with large department stores, clothing boutiques, and a food court (see *Sights*).

ACCOMMODATIONS

As one of the state's main commercial centers, Villahermosa's hotels are geared toward business travelers. The result is twofold. In the budget-room category, prices are inflated and the best of the rooms get taken early. In the mid- to high-range category, services are amplified; hotels often have business centers and restaurants and they typically offer courtesy airport shuttles. Regardless of the hotel, however, prices fall by about 25 percent on weekends. The best weekend deals are on the Internet—take a look before you head to town.

Under US$50

One of the first hotels in Villahermosa (and showing it) is the **Hotel San Rafael** (Av. Constitución No. 240, tel. 993/312-0166, US$9 s, US$13 d). It's a basic hotel offering relatively clean rooms with fans, private bath (cold water only), and a communal TV room. Ask for a room with a view of the river—they are quieter and feature balconies.

Directly in front of the ADO bus station, **Hotel Palomino** (Av. Francisco Javier Mina No. 222, tel. 993/312-8431, US$28 s/d with fan and a/c) has dark, cleanish rooms with cable TV. A tolerable option if you've arrived on a late bus or need to catch an early-morning one.

Hoteles Pakaal (Lerdo de Tejada No. 106, tel. 993/314-4648, US$35 s with a/c, US$39 d with a/c) offers rooms with cable TV and pri-

There are beautiful city parks near Parque-Museo La Venta and the city's top hotels.

© LIZA PRADO CHANDLER

vate bath just a block from the river. Rooms on the upper floors are more spacious. Beds are slightly springy.

Hotel Madan (Madero No. 408, tel. 993/314-0524, madanvhsa@prodigy.net.mx, US$42 s/d with a/c) is one of the best values downtown. Although rooms are small, they are very clean, feature TVs, and have in-room phones. A sweeping *azulejo* staircase leads you to your floor. Ask for a room in back for a more restful stay—rooms near the front are affected by the street noise and by the on-site bar.

Hotel Miraflores (Reforma No. 304, tel. 993/312-0054, www.miraflores.com.mx, US$46 s with a/c, US$51 d with a/c) is along a pedestrian walkway, making it a bit quieter than most downtown hotels. Accommodations are modern and ample. Rooms facing the river have balconies and are especially sunny. The hotel also features a restaurant and video bar.

On a peaceful curve of the Laguna de las Ilusiones, the **M Hotel Graham** (Rosendo Taracena s/n, tel. 993/312-7744, www.hotel-graham.com.mx, US$45 s/d with a/c) is an excellent option if you don't mind taking a taxi to and from city sights. Rooms are spacious, spotless, and have cable TV, phones, and pleasant views of the lagoon. The hotel also features a small pool and a good restaurant. A full breakfast is included in the rate.

US$50–100

In the heart of the city center, the **Olmeca Plaza Hotel** (Av. Madero No. 418, tel. 993/358-0102, www.hotelolmecaplaza.com, US$89 s/d, US$131 s/d deluxe) has not only changed its name for the third time (formerly known as the Casa Inn and before that the Hotel Don Carlos) but also has completely overhauled its accommodations and installations. Rooms feature brand-new furniture and fixtures, have electronic door keys, satellite TV, small writing desks, and telephones. Deluxe rooms—with marble floors and thick glass shower walls—are on a separate floor. A small but very nice rooftop pool and two-story gym also have been added. A full breakfast is included in the rate. Be sure to ask about specials: Standard room rates often drop to US$64, and deluxe rooms can go for as little as US$75.

Over US$100

Friendly and understated, **M Hotel Cencali** (Av. Juárez and Paseo Tabasco, tel. 993/315-1999, www.cencali.com.mx, US$113 s/d, US$130 junior, US$156 master) is the most unusual of Villahermosa's upper-end hotels. Instead of a boxy high-rise, the hotel's 160 rooms occupy long low buildings with curved walkways and broad sloping clay roofs. A huge mural adorns the lobby and many of the rooms have lovely views of Laguna de las Ilusiones. Rooms in the new wing are a bit nicer, but all are large and have modern furnishings. There are a pool and restaurant and Parque-Museo La Venta is a short walk away.

A gleaming lobby welcomes you at the **Calinda Viva Villahermosa** (Av. Adolfo Ruíz Cortínez at Paseo Tabasco, tel. 993/315-0000, U.S. tel. 877/657-5799, www.hotelescalinda .com.mx, US$142 s/d), where rooms are

smallish but very nice. A welcoming pool, good restaurant, and fully equipped business center are also at each guest's disposal. Parque-Museo La Venta and Tabasco 2000 are both a 10- to 15-minute walk away. Be sure to ask about specials, which feature room rates for as low as US$96 and often include a breakfast buffet.

Next door, the **Hyatt Villahermosa** (Av. Juárez at Paseo Tabasco, tel. 993/310-1234, toll-free Mex. tel. 800/004-9872, www.villa-hermosa.regency.hyatt.com, US$90–124 s/d) has elegantly furnished rooms and five-star amenities, including a large swimming pool and patio area, laundry, two tennis courts, and a car-rental agency. For a bit more, the hotel's Regency rooms include continental breakfast and afternoon drinks along with a private lounge.

FOOD

No one could call Villahermosa a culinary hot spot, but it does have a few restaurants worth noting. There are also a number of good, cheap, no-name eateries downtown, especially on Calle Francisco Madero between Lerdo de Tejada Zaragoza and throughout the pedestrian-only zone.

Mexican

Near CICOM and the anthropology museum, **Los Tulipanes** (Carlos Pellicer Cámara 511, tel. 993/312-9209, 8 A.M.–10 P.M. Tues.–Sat., 8 A.M.–6 P.M. Sun., 1 A.M.–10 P.M. Mon., US$6–15) serves good if not spectacular regional food, from baked fish to grilled chicken. The dining area is large and colorful, and there's live music every day but Monday, usually in the morning and the evening. It's a little hard to find: Take the wide passageway south of the theater toward the river.

International

Part of the Hotel Madan, **Restaurant Madan** (Av. Madero 408, tel. 993/312-1650, 7 A.M.–11 P.M. daily) is a no-frills hotel restaurant, filled day and night with locals and visiting businesspeople clustered over never-ending cups of coffee. Try for a table by the front windows, where you can watch the action on the street. Breakfast runs US$2.50–3.50, and the *comida corrida* lunch special is a good deal, with soup, salad, entrée, dessert, and drink for US$3–4.

Bugambilia (tel. 993/315-1234, 1 P.M.–1 A.M. Mon.–Sat., US$15–25) is the Hyatt Villahermosa's upscale restaurant. Excellent but pricey international meals are served with low-key elegance, complete with mellow live jazz. A good place to treat yourself to a nice dinner.

Italian

Ⓜ Italianni's (Paseo Tabasco at Av. Ruíz Cortines, tel. 993/317-7258, 1–11 P.M. Mon.–Wed., 1 P.M.–1 A.M. Thurs.–Sat., 1–10 P.M. Sun., US$6–15) features well-prepared Italian fare and a relaxed but classy bilevel dining area. Many of the dishes (including excellent salads and desserts) are designed for two people, and sharing plates is encouraged. The result is you can have a varied and satisfying meal for comparatively little. (And since you're saving all that money, be sure to try a "watermelontini," "appletini," or another of the creative mixed drinks.)

Asian

Tucked into the northeast corner of the Plaza de Armas, **Ⓜ Atarashi Sushi** (Vasquez Norte 203, tel. 993/314-7025, noon–midnight daily, US$3–5) is a pleasant surprise, especially if you are getting tired of Mexican food. Choose from about 20 different rolls, all tasty, well prepared, and—with 10 hefty pieces—a good value. Two or three rolls, a big order of veggie or seafood tempura, and some miso soup is more than enough for two. Other options include fried rice, noodles, curry dishes, and, of course, sushi.

Cafés and Breakfast Places

Next door to Italianni's, **Restaurant Mi Viejo Café** (Paseo Tabasco at Av. Ruíz Cortines, tel. 993/317-7267, 7 A.M.–midnight daily, US$4–11) is another classy but affordable place to eat, especially for breakfast or lunch. Morning specials (served until 12:30 P.M.) vary from scrambled eggs to quiche Lorraine, and they come

with fresh-squeezed juice and endless cups of finely brewed coffee. For lunch or dinner, try sandwiches, pasta, grilled chicken, or one of several cuts of beef.

If you just need a break, the **Centro Cultural** (Av. Francisco Madero at Zaragoza, tel. 993/314-5552, 10 A.M.–8 P.M. Tues.–Sun, US$2–6) has pleasant lobby café, with good coffee and light appetizers and pastries.

El Café de la Calle Juárez (Calle Juárez between Avs. Zaragoza and Lerdo de Tejada, tel. 993/312-3454, 7 A.M.–10 P.M. Mon.–Sat., until 9 P.M. Sun.) is one of several cafés along Calle Juárez with smoky, air-cooled indoor seating and street-side outdoor seating. Like the others, this one serves good basic breakfast and lunch specials (US$2.50–4) and is usually filled with old guys arguing politics and drinking coffee. Foreigners are almost as rare as women are, and the atmosphere is brusque but comfortable.

Groceries

The **Mercado José María Pino Suárez** (José María Pino Suárez at Av. Ruíz Cortines, 7 A.M.–6 P.M. daily) offers the freshest produce, dairy, and meats around. Check it out, even if just to experience the local market scene.

INFORMATION AND SERVICES

Tourist Information Centers

The state tourism board operates a tourist information booth at Parque-Museo La Venta (Blvd. Adolfo Ruíz Cortines s/n, tel. 993/314-1652). It's open 9 A.M.–4 P.M. daily and is much more helpful and convenient than the main offices near Tabasco 2000. There's another booth at the airport, open 9 A.M.–7 P.M.

Medical Services

Hospital Regional de Villahermosa (corner of Calles Lino Merino and Gil y Saenz, tel. 993/312-8607) is a busy public hospital with a 24-hour emergency room and pharmacy; expect lines. Pemex, the state oil company with major operations in the state, sponsors this hospital.

Pharmacies

Farmacia Reforma (tel. 993/312-1438, 7 A.M.–10:30 P.M. daily) and **Farmacia de Ahorro** (tel. 993/315-6606, 6 A.M.–11 P.M. daily) are both on Avenida Reforma at the corner of Calle Saenz. Both have a large selection of medicines as well as toiletry items. The latter will deliver to your hotel 8 A.M.–8 P.M.

Police

If you need help, you can reach the police by dialing 066 from any public phone.

Newspapers

EnterARTE is a small glossy magazine published monthly by the state culture and recreation office. It has listings of events taking place at Villahermosa's many private galleries and public museums and cultural centers. You'll find complete listings of upcoming music, theater, and art shows, plus special events and lectures at local colleges, museums, and libraries.

Money

In the Zona Remodelada, you'll find reliable ATMs at **Bancomer** (Av. Zaragoza at Parque Juárez, 9 A.M.–4 P.M. Mon.–Fri., 10 A.M.–2 P.M. Sat.), **HSBC** (Calle Juárez at Av. Lerdo de Tejada, 8 A.M.–7 P.M. Mon.–Sat.), and **Scotiabank Inverlat** (Calle Juárez between Reforma and Av. Lerdo de Tejada, 9 A.M.–5 P.M. Mon.–Fri.). Outside of the center of town, **Tabasco 2000,** with its handful of ATMs, is your best bet.

Post Office

The post office is at the corner of Avenidas Saenz and Lerdo de Tejada and is open 9 A.M.–5 P.M. Monday–Friday and 9 A.M.–1 P.M. on Saturday.

Internet

Busy **G&G Internet** (Av. Zaragoza at Parque Juárez, tel. 993/131-0915, 8 A.M.–1 A.M. daily) has Internet access for US$.70/hour and will download digital pictures and burn them onto a CD for US$2.50. **Naveghalia** (Av. Lerdo de Tejada at Av. Zaragoza, tel. 993/312-7216, 8 A.M.–3 A.M. daily) is less crowded and slightly more expensive, charging US$.85/hour and US$3.50 to burn a CD.

Laundry

On the main drag downtown, **Lavandería Top Klean** (Av. Madero No. 303-A, tel. 993/312-2856, 8 A.M.–8 P.M. Mon.–Sat., US$1.45/kilo—2.2 pounds) provides same-day service if clothes are dropped off in the morning. Tuesday through Thursday loads cost only US$.90/kilo.

Storage

The **ADO bus terminal** (open 24 hours) has luggage storage for US$1–1.50/hour.

GETTING THERE

Considered a gateway to Central Mexico, Villahermosa is easily reached by many means. A fine transportation network connects it with Mexico City, Chiapas, Guatemala, the Quintana Roo coast, and the rest of the Yucatán Peninsula.

Air

Villahermosa has a busy, compact airport (Aeropuerto Capitán Carlos Rovirosa Pérez) about 12 kilometers (7.5 miles) east of the city. Inside there is a bank with ATM and exchange services, a tourist information booth, restaurant, and a few gift shops. Flights arrive daily from many cities in Mexico—including Mexico City, Mérida, and Tuxtla Gutiérrez—and there are often nonstop flights from Houston, Texas. The following airlines currently service Villahermosa:

Aeroméxico (CICOM, Periferico Carlos Pellicer Cámara No. 511-2, tel. 800/021-4000, www.aeromexico.com, 9 A.M.–7 P.M. Mon.–Sat.), **AeroCalifornia** (Tabasco 2000, Calle Via 3 No. 120, tel. 993/316-8000), **AeroMar** (at airport only, tel. 993/356-0360, toll-free Mex. tel. 800/237-6627, www.aeromar.com.mx), **Aviacsa** (Tabasco 2000, Calle Via 3 No. 120, tel. 993/356-0133, toll-free Mex. tel. 800/711-6733, www.aviacsa.com), and **Mexicana** along with its affiliate **Aerocaribe** (Tabasco 2000, Calle Via 3 No. 120, tel. 993/316-3132 office, tel. 993/356-0101 airport, toll-free Mex. tel. 800/502-2000 reservations, www.mexicana.com).

Bus

The **ADO bus terminal** (Paseo Francisco Javier Mina at Calle Merino, tel. 993/312-8313) is large and loud, with first-class and deluxe service (here, denoted by an asterisk). Destinations include:

Campeche, US$19, six hours, 3 A.M.*, 9:10 A.M., 12:50 P.M., 8 P.M., 9 P.M., 9:40 P.M., 10:10 A.M., and 10:50 P.M.

Cancún, US$40, 12 hours, 12:10 A.M., 1:10 A.M., 3:35 A.M., 7:30 A.M., 8:45 P.M.*, and 9:15 P.M.*

Chetumal, US$24, eight hours, 9:20 P.M.

Ciudad de Carmen, US$7.50, three hours, every 30–45 minutes 5 A.M.–11 P.M. except 7:30–9:30 A.M.

McAllen, Texas, US$80, 24 hours, 4 P.M. and 8 P.M.

Mérida, US$27.50, nine hours, 12:50 P.M., 7:10 P.M., 8:45 P.M.*, 9 P.M., 9:15 P.M.*, 9:40 P.M., 10 P.M.*, and 10:50 P.M.

Mexico City-TAPO, US$43, 10 hours, 1:30 A.M.*, 12:10 P.M., 5:25 P.M., 6:25 P.M., 7 P.M.*, 8 P.M.*, 8:10 P.M., 8:30 P.M.*, 8:45 P.M.*, 9 P.M., 9:30 P.M.*, 9:35 P.M.*, 10 P.M., 10:15 P.M.*, 10:30 P.M.*, and 11:30 P.M.

Mexico City-Norte, US$43, 10 hours, 9:05 A.M., 7:15 A.M., 7:30 P.M.*, 8 P.M.*, 8:35 P.M., 9:30 P.M., and 11:15 P.M.—Thursday–Sunday only.

Palenque, US$6, 2.5 hours, 9:30 A.M., 11 A.M., noon, 1:50 P.M., 4:40 P.M., 7:40 P.M., and 9:15 P.M.

Playa del Carmen, US$37, 11 hours, 8 P.M. and 10:10 P.M.

San Cristóbal, US$14, seven hours, 9:30 A.M. and noon.

Tapachula, US$37, 12 hours, 7:15 P.M.

Tulum, US$35, 10 hours, 12:10 A.M.

Tuxtla Gutiérrez, US$15, five hours, 10:30 A.M., 2:30 P.M., 3:30 P.M., 10:30 P.M.*, 11:45 P.M. and midnight* (take the "via Raudales" bus).

Colectivos to Comalcalco

Near the ADO bus station and a block apart, **Comali Plus** (Calle Reforma at Calle Bravo) and **Transportes Torruco** (Calle Reforma at La Arboleda) provide identical service to and from Comalcalco. Operating vans that accommodate 12 comfortably (or in our case, 14 uncomfortably), service runs every 20 minutes, 4:30 A.M.–9 P.M. daily ($US2.25, 45 minutes).

Car

Driving into Villahermosa is easy from both north and south. From Campeche and points east take Highway 186. From Campeche along the coastal route take Highway 180. From Veracruz along the coast take Highway 180 east. From San Cristóbal de las Casas and points south take Highway 199 to Highway 186. These all converge in Villahermosa.

GETTING AROUND

On Foot

Navigating downtown Villahermosa on foot is easy, especially as several streets are pedestrian-only. You can conceivably walk from the large hotels to the downtown area, but it's a long haul.

Taxis

Around town, white radio taxis cost around US$2.50 while the yellow *colectivo* cabs (which may pick up several passengers along the way) cost around US$1.50. If you're arriving at the airport, the only way for you to leave it is by taxi or by rental car. A taxi into town runs US$13—vouchers are sold at a booth near the main exit (airport cabbies don't accept cash).

Car Rental

Three car-rental agencies are inside the airport terminal and are open as early as the first flight and as late as the last flight: **Budget** (tel. 993/356-0118, toll-free Mex. tel. 800/700-1700, www.budget.com.mx), **Dollar** (tel. 993/356-0211, toll-free Mex. tel. 800/222-8524, www.dollar.com), and **Hertz** (tel. 993/316-4400, ext. 7960, toll-free Mex. tel. 800/709-5000, www.hertz.com.mx).

Comalcalco

Anything but charming, this dusty town is the gateway to the ruins at Comalcalco and to the chocolate haciendas. It is just 45 minutes from Villahermosa, and it is rare for tourists to stay the night. If you do, no worries; there is at least one decent hotel in town.

SIGHTS

Comalcalco Archaeological Zone

Meaning, "place of the house with the grills," Comalcalco (10 A.M.–5 P.M. daily, US$3) is an early Mayan ruin set in the lush green hills of Tabasco's countryside. It is unique among the Mayan archaeological sites because instead of using heavy cut stone to build their structures, the Mayans built the city using thousands of kiln-fired bricks that bear a striking resemblance to those made today. (In fact that is exactly what archaeologists used to restore some sections.) There's no stone in the middle either—turns out there was none in this marshy region to use.

The original occupants—Chontal Mayans dating from A.D. 250—built these early temples out of dirt mixed with oyster shells for strength and cohesion. Comalcalco's distinctive bricks were developed A.D. 500–700 and were used to expand and elaborate the packed-dirt temples. Many of the bricks were incised with designs, including animals, humans, glyphs, and patterns, though for the most part the bricks themselves were covered in a thick layer of stucco painted red, blue, green, yellow, and black, which has long since eroded away.

Temple I, the immense structure on the left as you walk in from the entrance, has the best remaining example of the stucco high relief that once covered most of the structures. Look for the animal figures along the pyramid's southeast corner as well as a molded skull about halfway up the main stairway. Today these valuable remnants of history are covered with glass and have been roofed over to deter any further deterioration. The facial features of these figures are unique, with thick, strangely shaped lips, somewhat resembling the colossal heads in La Venta, yet vastly different in style.

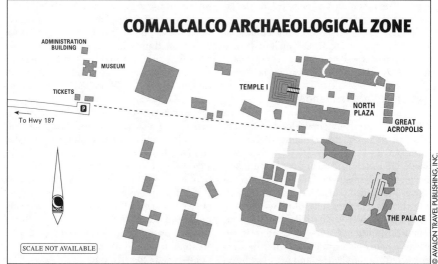

COMALCALCO ARCHAEOLOGICAL ZONE

ADMINISTRATION BUILDING

MUSEUM

TICKETS

To Hwy 187

TEMPLE I

NORTH PLAZA

GREAT ACROPOLIS

THE PALACE

SCALE NOT AVAILABLE

© AVALON TRAVEL PUBLISHING, INC.

CACAO BEANS

Although Christopher Columbus first encountered the cacao bean in 1502, it had been a coveted item in the New World for centuries. In Aztec mythology it was believed to have been given as a gift to humans by the Aztec god, Quetzalcoatl, to make a divine bitter drink. As the story goes, Quetzalcoatl scattered the seeds over Tabasco and, eventually, after the god was lost at sea (perhaps not used to the winds off the Gulf?), reappeared in the Mayan world as the god Kukulcán, beans and all.

For Mayans, cacao was as precious as gold; in fact, it was used as currency as late as the 1840s in isolated villages. Today, it continues to be coveted in the culinary delight of chocolate. An excellent source of energy, rich in vitamins, minerals, and antioxidants, it also just plain tastes good.

© LIZA PRADO CHANDLER

a cacao tree and its fruit—where chocolate begins

Opposite Temple I, the **Great Acropolis** sits 80 meters (262 feet) long and has a stucco mask of the Kinich Ahau, the sun god. To the right, walk up a hill to the **Palace,** which reveals a panoramic view of the countryside, including unexcavated mounds and a chocolate plantation in the distance.

A small but very interesting **museum** sits at the entrance to the site. Inside you'll find excellent artifacts as well as a few human skeletons found by workers while excavating the site.

Ⓜ Chocolate Haciendas

Traveling north on Highway 187, **Finca Cholula** (Carretera Comalcalco-Paraíso, tel. 933/334-3815, chocolate_elchontal@hotmail .com, 9 A.M.–4 P.M. daily, US$2.15) is located about 500 meters (0.3 mile) past the turnoff to the ruins on the east side of the road. It offers an interesting guided tour of its *finca* (plantation) and chocolate factory. The visit lasts about an hour, during which you'll stroll through the verdant fields, filled not only with cacao trees, but bananas, coffee plants, tall "shade" trees—cacao grows best in the shade—and even bee boxes

and cinnamon trees. If you're lucky, you'll spot some toucans or the resident troop of howler monkeys. Next, you visit the processing area, where the seed is separated from the shell (which is composted and sold as fertilizer) and the sweet white fruit (used to make cacao liqueur) and then dried in the sun, toasted, ground up, mixed with cacao butter and sugar, and poured into candy molds. There's lots to taste and smell along the way, and you can buy various chocolate products at the end. Cacao trees produce fruit year-round but the best time to visit is April–May and November–December, which are considered the peak harvest seasons.

If you haven't had your fill of chocolate by the end of the tour, the **Hacienda La Luz,** often referred to as **Wolter's** (next to the Tereno de la Fería, tel. 933/334-1126, US$3), offers a similar, and equally popular, tour. You'll need an appointment, however, to view its operation—be sure to call ahead.

ACCOMMODATIONS AND FOOD

If you miss the last *combi* to Villahermosa, stay the night at **Hotel Plaza Broca** (Blvd. Adolfo López Mateos at Nicolas Bravo, tel. 933/334-4060, US$21 s, US$22–31 d). It offers simple but very clean rooms in the heart of town; all rooms have air-conditioning, cable TV, phone, and 24-hour hot water. With a private parking garage, this is one of the best deals around. Ask for a room in back, as the road in front can get loud.

Taco and hotdog stands rule in this town. While not the healthiest of options, these will definitely keep your belly full for the night. Look for them around the main plaza, just half a block from the *combi* station.

GETTING THERE

Colectivos to Comalcalco

Near the ADO bus station and a block apart, **Comali Plus** (Calle Reforma at Calle Bravo) and **Transportes Torruco** (Calle Reforma at La Arboleda) provide identical service to and from Comalcalco. Van service runs every 20 minutes 4:30 A.M.–9 P.M. daily ($US2.25, 45 minutes). Passengers are dropped off in the center of Comalcalco.

Car

If driving from Villahermosa, head west on Highway 180 toward the city of Cárdenas. When you come to the junction with Highway 187, take it north to Comalcalco.

GETTING AROUND

Foot

Getting around downtown Comalcalco is easy on foot. Though there's not much to look at, everything you might need—vans to Villaher-mosa, banks, hotels, taco stands—all are concentrated a few blocks from each other.

Once you're at Comalcalco ruins, you also can walk to Finca Cholula (or visa versa). It takes about 10 minutes to walk from the ruins to the highway, where you turn right and walk another 10 minutes. The *finca* entrance is around the first large curve; of course, take care walking along the highway as the shoulder is soft and the traffic is fast.

Bus

To head to the ruins or to the Finca Cholula by bus, take any bus headed north on Carretera Comalcalco-Paraíso (US$.40, 10 minutes). Ask the driver to let you off at the *ruinas* or the Finca Cholula. Both are on the outskirts of town, about 10 minutes from the center of town. Please note that if you're heading to the ruins by bus, you'll get dropped off at the turnoff to the entrance. It's another 10-minute walk to the entrance down a paved road. To return, a bus will probably pass before an empty cab does—flag down either on the highway opposite from where you were let off.

Car

If traveling by car to the ruins or Finca Cholula, continue north past the town of Comalcalco on Carretera Comalcalco-Paraíso. You'll see signs for the ruins near the outskirts of town and about 500 meters (0.3 mile) past that, you'll find Finca Cholula.

Taxi

Taking a cab is the easiest of all options. A ride to or from either the chocolate hacienda or the ruins runs US$2.50 from the center of town. For Hacienda La Luz (Wolter's), this is the best option, as walking is a bit long and driving or taking a bus confusing.

The State of Chiapas

True, Chiapas is not part of the Yucatán Peninsula, which technically comprises Quintana Roo, Yucatán, and Campeche states. Yet the history, culture, and present circumstances of the peninsula are so deeply intertwined with those of its mountainous southern neighbor as to make them inseparable. You cannot discuss Mayan archaeological ruins without mentioning Palenque (considered by some to be the greatest of the Mayan sites). You cannot make a list of Mexico's great colonial cities and leave out San Cristóbal de las Casas. And you can hardly discuss contemporary Mayan life and conditions without examining the Zapatista uprising in 1994, which sent ripples throughout Mexico and Central America. (Indeed, you can argue that Guatemala ought to be included here as well for many of the same reasons, but we had to draw the line somewhere.) On a more practical level, it makes sense to include Chiapas in a guide to the Yucatán because those who enjoy the Yucatán are virtually guaranteed to *love* Chiapas.

That said, Chiapas and the Yucatán Peninsula are very different places. Chiapas's two main destinations—Palenque and San Cristóbal—are set in high pine forests with ample

Must-Sees

M Palenque Archaeological Zone: Arguably the most beautiful and compelling of Mayan ruins, with graceful buildings and well-preserved carvings (page 386).

M Yaxchilán Archaeological Zone: Although it was once an adventure route, you can now take interesting tours to Yaxchilán and nearby Bonampak. Both are deep in the Lancandón forest and feature delicate carvings, amazing frescoes, and an occasional howler monkey swinging through the trees (page 400).

M Parque Central: In San Cristóbal, this is an ideal place to just sit and watch life and people go by, from indigenous children selling bracelets to backpack-toting foreigners. If you're hungry, street carts sell corn on the cob with mayo and parmesan cheese—a Mexican classic (page 409).

the Palace tower at Palenque Archaeological Zone

© LIZA PRADO CHANDLER

The State of Chiapas

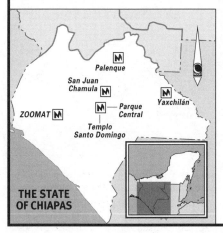

THE STATE OF CHIAPAS

M Templo Santo Domingo: This grand old church and former convent has a great *artesanía* market out front and an excellent museum and community folk art store alongside (page 409).

M San Juan Chamula: Learn about indigenous social and spiritual customs on a fascinating tour to this autonomous indigenous village just a few kilometers north of San Cristóbal (page 428).

M ZOOMAT: Tuxtla Gutiérrez's zoo has members of every mammal species found in Chiapas, from jaguars to armadillos, and dozens of birds, reptiles, and insects. It is considered one of the best in Latin America (page 439).

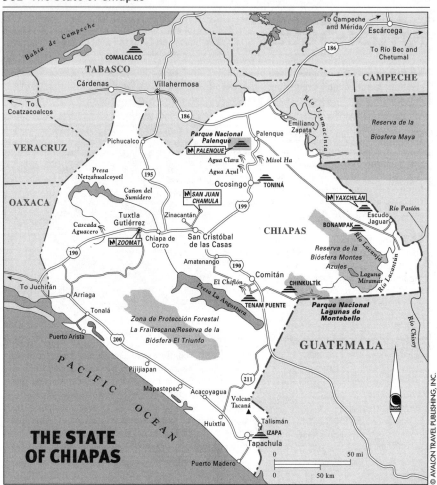

THE STATE OF CHIAPAS

rainfall and surprisingly chilly weather, especially in the winter. Chiapanecan Mayans are more visible than their Yucatecan counterparts, both in literal terms, with richly colored traditional clothing, and in their relative empowerment, maintaining autonomous villages and exercising (in some spheres) considerable political clout. They are also more desperate, with many thousands of dispossessed men, women, and children filling squatter camps on the outskirts of San Cristóbal and Tuxtla Gutiérrez or leaving the state for uncertain futures in Mex-

ico City, Cancún, and other metro centers. Persistent poverty and poor living conditions were among the rationales given by the Zapatistas for their armed uprising. Where Yucatán is inextricably linked to the sea that surrounds it on three sides, much of Chiapas is bound to the mountains and forest that preserve its rich native traditions.

Travelers in Chiapas can expect to see stunning archaeological ruins, one of Mexico's great colonial cities, fascinating insights on indigenous life and culture, and plenty of opportunities for adventure- and ecotourism. It is a safe place to visit, though you should take some extra precautions such as not traveling at night and favoring organized trips to overly ambitious indy ones. (Those are still a few years off.) And while Chiapas is firmly on the tourist route, prices here are still considerably lower than in most of the Yucatán Peninsula.

PLANNING YOUR TIME

Give yourself at least five days to visit Chiapas and preferably longer—you can easily and happily stay for weeks, and many people do just that. Assuming you're coming from the north, your first stop is Palenque. Give yourself a half day or more to visit the ruins and the museum, which are among the most impressive you'll find on the Mayan route. There are also a number of easy one- and two-day trips you can take from Palenque, most notably to the Yaxchilán and Bonampak ruins, and to three picturesque sites along the Yax-Ha River south of town.

Some people stay many extra days at Palenque, but the town really doesn't have much to offer beyond the ruins and the side trips—you're much better off spending your time in San Cristóbal, a beautiful and incredibly rich colonial city. You will want at least three days there, to visit the museums and churches, to take a tour to surrounding indigenous villages, and above all, to have time to write postcards in little cafés, to people-watch in the main plaza, and to browse in the market—in short, to soak up all the atmosphere you can in this charming little city. If you can drag yourself away from San Cristóbal, you may want to spend a day visiting Comitán and the Lagunas de Montebello, or to head the other direction to Sumidero Canyon and Chiapa de Corzo or the excellent zoo in Tuxtla Gutiérrez. (These are also doable as day trips from San Cristóbal.) Most people leave Chiapas wishing they had more time there, which is worth bearing in mind when you plan your trip.

HISTORY

The earliest inhabitants of the Chiapas area are presumed to be the Olmecs. The Mayans settled in during the Preclassic period and during the Classic age created their most outstanding structures. Present-day Chiapas was occupied by many groups, most of whom spoke in Mayan-derived tongues. The Choles inhabited the jungle; the Tojolabales lived in the plains between the valley of the Chiapas River and jungle; the Chiapanecans occupied the central part of the valley; the Mames lived along the coastal regions; the Zoques lived on the hillsides of the highlands; and the Tzotziles and Tzeltales cultivated the highlands. Today the largest of these linguistic groups are the Tzotziles and Tzeltales, and they are familiarly referred to as the Chamulans, Zinacantecos, Oxchuqueros, and San Pedranos.

After the intrusion of the Spaniards in 1519 many years of fighting ensued. It was a fight that cost the Spanish dearly—conquistador Bernal Díaz described the native people here as "the most courageous warriors [he] encountered in the new world." The first Spanish army, a mix of Spaniards and their indigenous allies, the Tlaxcaltecans, arrived in 1524 and were soon driven off by the Chiapanecans. In 1527, a Spanish army from Guatemala tried to take over but it too was sent running. Only in 1530, when Diego de Mazariegos arrived, were the outsiders able to assume control of the area and, as in all Spanish conquests, the natives were subjugated and made virtual slaves on their land.

When Bartolomé de las Casas became bishop in 1544, he tried to abolish slavery and managed to convince the Spanish crown to provide legal protection for native people throughout the New World. For his efforts—only marginally successful—Bishop de las Casas was and is held in great respect by the local indigenous peoples.

Palenque

The town of Santo Domingo de Palenque, usually just called Palenque, is eight kilometers (five miles) from the Palenque archeological zone. It is the county seat, with about 20,000 people in town and another 50,000 in the surrounding area. Much of the fine mahogany forest around Palenque has been stripped by lumber companies who buy (or else finagle) timber rights from indigenous people. Large areas of forest have also been converted to pastures for cattle grazing.

But tourism is without question Palenque's main industry. The town is rather nondescript, but it bulges at its seams with tourists coming to visit the ruins. Avenida Juárez is the main drag through town, and most hotels, restaurants, and shops, including travel agencies and the tourist office, are there. A large Mayan warrior's head stands at the entrance to town (and marks the cutoff to go to the ruins) and a medium-sized, elevated plaza sits at the other end. Hotels and restaurants in town aren't a great value—it is definitely a seller's market here—and many travelers find the leafy neighborhood of La Cañada and the hotels along the road to the ruins to be more pleasant options.

Like most Mayan ruins, Palenque holds a special draw for bohemian travelers, more so because of the prevalence of psychedelic mushrooms in the area. Suffice it to say that being caught with mushrooms (or any drug) is an extremely serious offense in Mexico. It is also quite taboo among ordinary Mexicans, making it not just risky but rude.

History

Scholars have been able to decipher enough of the many glyphs to construct a reasonable genealogy of the Palenque kings, from the rule of Chaacal I (A.D. 501) to the demise of Kuk (A.D. 783). But it was during the reign of Lord Pakal and his son, Chan Bahlum (A.D. 615–701) that Palenque grew from a minor city to an important ceremonial center.

K'inich Janaab Pakal was born in A.D. 603 and ascended to the throne in A.D. 615, at just 12 years of age. During his long rule—he died in A.D. 684 at age 81—Pakal expanded Palenque's influence throughout the western Mayan lowlands. He built the Temple of the Inscriptions to house his own elaborate tomb, which was decorated with deifications of his life and ancestors. Pakal was succeeded by his son, Chan Bahlum, who was noteworthy for having six digits on his hands and feet. (To maintain the royal bloodline, Mayan rulers sometimes took relatives as their wives, eventually leading to birth defects. Pakal himself had a club foot, and some archaeologists believe his mother and father were siblings. Likewise, Pakal may have married his sister, leading to Chan Bahlum's defects.) Chan Bahlum reigned for 18 years and built the temples of the Cross, Foliated Cross, and Sun to prove the preordination of his rule. After he died in A.D. 702, his younger brother, Kan Xul, took the reins of power. His rule was Palenque's apogee; the Palace was enlarged and the city's power reached its greatest extent. Kan Xul's heirs were less successful, and Palenque's prominence and glitter gradually faded. The last historical record found in the city is dated A.D. 799; it is a blackware vase from Central Mexico that with crude hieroglyphs celebrates the accession of a king named 6 Cimi to Palenque's throne.

The earliest Spanish-recorded comments on Palenque were made by a Spanish army captain, Antonio del Río, who passed through in March 1785. (Two centuries earlier, Hernán Cortés came within a few dozen kilometers of the ruins but apparently never knew they were there.) Del Río drew maps and plans and eventually received a royal order to excavate the site for a year. But the Spaniard's "excavation" was amateur and brutish and led to the destruction of a number of structures. Captain del Río also broadcasted wild and fantastic assumptions about the beginnings of the Mayans. It wasn't long before Europeans envisioned Palenque as the lost city of Atlantis or a sister civilization to the ancient Egyptians. A

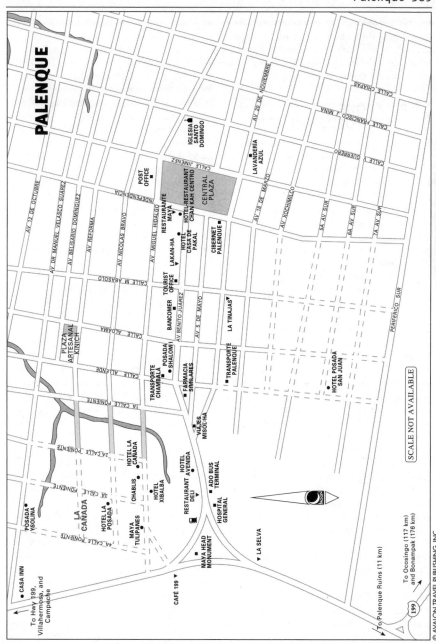

PALENQUE

The State of Chiapas

SCALE NOT AVAILABLE

© AVALON TRAVEL PUBLISHING, INC.

To Hwy 199,
Villahermosa, and
Campeche

To Ocosingo (117 km)
and Bonampak (176 km)

To Palenque Ruins (11 km)

199

true picture of Palenque didn't emerge until the mid-1800s, when the American diplomat John L. Stephens and English artist Frederick Catherwood visited the site and wrote and drew realistic and detailed accounts of what they saw.

Ⓝ PALENQUE ARCHAEOLOGICAL ZONE

Palenque is a must-see on any itinerary of Mayan ruins. The setting, on a lush green shelf at the edge of the Sierra de Chiapas forest, adds to the serenity of this noble archaeological compound of ornate carvings and graceful design. The ruins lie in the north-central part of Chiapas, about 150 kilometers (93 miles) southeast of Villahermosa or a seven-hour bus ride from Chetumal on the Caribbean coast. About eight kilometers (five miles) from the town of Palenque, the ruins are served by frequent and inexpensive *colectivos* (public minibuses). The archaeological site's excellent modern museum opened in May 1993 on the main road about a kilometer (0.6 mile) before (and down a steep hill from) the ruins. Most visitors take the bus directly to the ruins and walk down to the museum afterward, bearing in mind the museum closes an hour before the site.

The ruins are open 8 A.M.–5 P.M. daily; admission is US$3. (The museum is open 10 A.M.–4:30 P.M. Tues.–Sun. and is free with admission to the ruins—hang onto your ticket!) You can hire a guide at the entrance to the ruins for about US$39 for a 2–2.5 hour tour in English, about US$30 in Spanish. The tour includes a "ruins" part and a "nature" part; you should get a lower price if you want only the ruins part (about 1.5–2 hours). Be sure to go with a licensed guide—they have photo badges prominently displayed. If you get a guide at only one Mayan site, let Palenque be the one.

Temples XII and XIII

Through the entrance you follow a short road and a few steps up to Palenque's main plaza. The first two temples on your right are Temple XII and XIII. Temple XII is also known

as Temple of the Skull—look for the carved stone skull about halfway up the steps. Temple XIII is just beyond. Both temples were the sites of major excavation in the early 1990s. In Temple XII, archaeologists discovered a long passageway leading from the top of the pyramid to a sarcophagus. Inside were the remains of an unidentified leader, plus several other bodies, most likely the leader's servants. The passage and tomb are at present off-limits to visitors. In Temple XIII, a maintenance worker discovered a loose stone, behind which archaeologists found a passageway and a massive tomb, painted a brilliant red inside and holding the remains of a woman. The tomb has few markings, so archaeologists have dubbed the deceased the "Red Queen." It seems likely that the woman was Pakal's mother, but that has not been proven.

Temple of the Inscriptions

Just beyond XIII you'll come to the Temple of the Inscriptions, also on your right. At the top of the 24-meter/78.7-foot-high pyramid is the temple, where magnificent tablets of glyphs tell the ancestral history of the Palenque rulers. It was toward the rear of the gallery that Mexican archaeologist Alberto Ruz L'Huillier first uncovered, in 1949, a secret stairway cleverly hidden under a stone slab. The stairs were intentionally jammed with rubble and debris, clearly to prevent access to whatever lay beneath.

It took Ruz three years to excavate the stairway, which descended in several sections all the way to ground level. At the foot of the stairs Ruz found another sealed passage, in front of which were clay dishes filled with red pigment, jade earplugs, beads, a large oblong pearl, and the skeletons of six sacrificial victims. A final large stone door was removed, and on June 15, 1952, Ruz made what many consider to be the greatest discovery of Mayan archaeology: the untouched crypt of K'inich Janaab Pakal, or Lord Shield Pakal.

The centerpiece of the chamber is the massive sarcophagus, hewn from a single stone and topped by a flat, four-meter/13.1-foot-long,

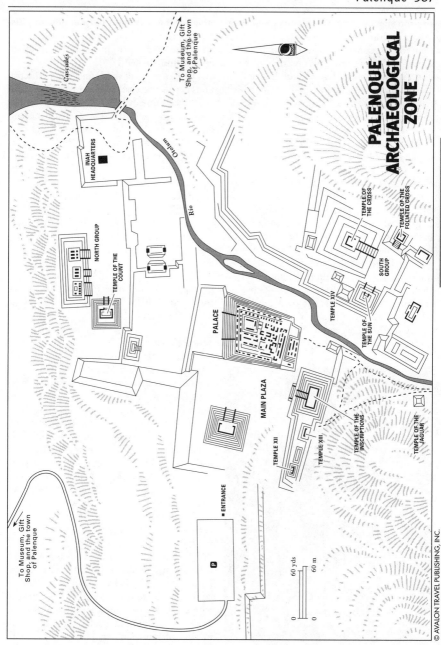

PALENQUE
ARCHAEOLOGICAL
ZONE

The State of Chiapas

Cascades

To Museum, Gift
Shop, and the town
of Palenque

INAH
HEADQUARTERS

Río Otulum

NORTH GROUP

TEMPLE OF THE COUNT

PALACE

TEMPLE OF THE CROSS

TEMPLE OF THE FOLIATED CROSS

SOUTH GROUP

TEMPLE XIV

TEMPLE OF THE SUN

MAIN PLAZA

TEMPLE XII

TEMPLE XIII

TEMPLE OF THE INSCRIPTIONS

TEMPLE OF THE JAGUAR

To Museum, Gift
Shop, and the town
of Palenque

■ ENTRANCE

P

0   60 yds
0   60 m

© AVALON TRAVEL PUBLISHING, INC.

five-ton slab of stone. The slab is beautifully carved with the figure of Pakal in death, surrounded by monsters, serpents, sun and shell signs, and many more glyphs that recount death and its passage. The walls of the chamber are decorated with various gods, from which scientists have deduced a tremendous amount about the Palencanos' theology.

Working slowly to preserve everything in its pristine state, Ruz didn't open the lid of the sarcophagus for six months. It took a week of difficult work in the stifling, dust-choked room to finally lift the five-ton slab. On November 28, 1952, the scientists had their first peek inside. In the large rectangular sarcophagus they found another, body-shaped sarcophagus (a first in Mayan history), within which was Pakal's skeleton, with precious jewelry and special accoutrements to accompany him on his journey into the next world. A jade mosaic mask covered the face, under which his own teeth had been painted red. (The mask was exhibited at the Anthropological Museum in Mexico City until December 24, 1985, when it was stolen along with several other precious historical artifacts. The mask was recovered in an abandoned house in Acapulco in 1989, mostly undamaged.)

The excavation of the Temple of the Inscriptions began a new concept in Mayan archaeology. It was formerly believed that the pyramids had served a single function, as a base for temples brought closer to the heavens. But now it's known that pyramids were used as crypts for revered leaders as well. All of this bears a resemblance to the culture and beliefs of the Egyptians, and imaginative students of history have tried to link the two cultures—so far unsuccessfully.

You used to be able to climb the Temple of the Inscriptions and even descend the passageway to just outside Pakal's tomb. However, erosion caused by thousands of hands and feet moving up and down the corridor prompted archaeologists to close the whole thing indefinitely—you can't even climb the pyramid anymore.

The Palace

Palenque's Palace is one of the most compelling structures among Mayan ruins. Directly in front of you as you walk up the main pathway with the Temple of the Inscriptions on your right, the Palace occupies the unusually large space of a city block. The four-story tower, another rarity of the Classic Mayans, will immediately catch your eye. The top of the tower had collapsed by the time it was rediscovered, so the original height and appearance could only be guessed from the pattern of rubble. Archaeologists believe the tower was constructed to give a good view of the winter solstice (December 22), when the sun appears to drop directly into the Temple of the Inscriptions. It probably was also used to make astronomical calculations, an important part of Mayan religious rites. The Palace has a large, sunken courtyard, surrounded by steps and adorned with excellent stone and stucco bas-reliefs. The large figures on the east side depict important prisoners captured in war. The entire Palace sits on a platform 10 meters (32.8 feet) high; stairs

© LIZA PRADO CHANDLER

a royal bedroom in Palenque

© LIZA PRADO CHANDLER

Palenque's Palace boasts a rare four-story tower.

lead into a labyrinth of rooms and passageways that served as royal sleeping quarters.

South Group

Just east of the Temple of the Inscriptions, you come to the South Group, which includes the Temple of the Cross, the Temple of the Foliated Cross, and the Temple of the Sun, all built around a plaza on the edge of the jungle. The Temple of the Sun is the first of these, with tablets at the top depicting Lord Pakal and Chan Bahlum. The Temple of the Cross is the largest of this group and contains tablets of Chan Bahlum wearing the full paraphernalia of royalty after his accession and accompanied by the cigar-smoking God L, a lord of the underworld, in an owl-feather headdress. The small Temple of the Foliated Cross against the jungle wall to the right holds more tablets celebrating the succession of Chan Bahlum. A team of Mexican archaeologists excavating the South Group found a major tomb at the base of the Temple of the Cross, containing the headless body of an official, perhaps the governor of a neighboring city, and 630 pieces of jade. They

have also found five perfectly preserved incense burners and some extremely fine ceramic figurines. One of these figurines, on display in the museum, is considered one of the finest Mayan sculptures yet found; it depicts a man seated on a square bench. His head has been broken off, but his helmet, in the form of a bird, was found nearby.

East of these structures (behind the palace), you'll find a well-marked path that leads past several smaller structures down to the main road. You can also enter this way, but the path is steep in places and makes a much nicer descent than ascent. You may see some birds or even monkeys. The path opens onto the road a short distance from the museum.

Museum

Definitely leave time to visit Palenque's museum (10 A.M.–4:30 P.M. Tues.–Sun., free with your ticket into the ruins), which contains artifacts and replicas of the carvings and murals from the ruins. Inaugurated in May 1993, it is not huge (an hour is enough time for most people) but it contains some truly incredible stucco and stone sculptures, all superbly displayed with explanations in Spanish and English. There's a restaurant and folk art shop in the same complex. The *colectivos* will stop here coming and going, and there is a short but steep path up to the ruins (one kilometer/.6 mile).

Getting There

Vans and minibuses operated by **Transportes Palenque** (Calle Allende between Avs. 20 de Noviembre and 18 de Marzo) and **Transportes Chamula** (Calle Allende between Avs. Juárez and Hidalgo) go to and from the ruins every 10–15 minutes 6 A.M.–6 P.M. daily. The fare is US$.80 each way and you can board in town (at their individual bases, across from the main bus terminal, and at the Mayan Head monument— all are good spots) or anywhere along the road to the ruins. The bus will pass through a gate set up by the national park service in 2004, at which foreigners are charged a park entrance fee of US$.80. The museum is a short distance beyond the park gate, and the ruins another short (but steep) way from there. Most people take the bus all the way to the ruins,

© LIZA PRADO CHANDLER

bas relief of a royal prisoner

and then take a forest path from inside the site down to the museum. Note: If you buy your bus ticket at the terminal in town, the cashier will almost certainly try to sell you a round-trip ticket. Don't be fooled: This saves you no money and no time; on the contrary, it means you have to wait for a bus from that specific company when you're ready to leave.

There is parking at the ruins, although on busy days drivers end up parking well down the access road. A taxi between town and the ruins costs around US$5.

OTHER SIGHTS

The following three sights are along the Yaks-Ha (Blue Water) River along the highway to Ocosingo and San Cristóbal. The name is apt—the river's water has a striking blue-green hue, almost like the Caribbean but less transparent. A popular tour from Palenque stops at all three spots, typically spending 30 minutes at the first, an hour at the second, and four hours at the last and most dramatic, Agua Azul falls. It's the surest, most convenient way to see the area in a day—the half hour at Misol Ha goes by too fast, but you still don't get back until after 4 P.M. Doing it by rental car is easy enough; to do it by public transport, catch any second-class bus or *colectivo* (usually a pickup truck) headed to Ocosingo or San Cristóbal and ask to be dropped at the turnoffs. You may or may make it to all three in one day; it's not recommended to travel this road at night.

Misol Ha

Mayan for "waterfall," Misol Ha (7 A.M.–6 P.M. daily, US$1) is indeed a waterfall, and a beautiful one at that, falling 30 meters (98.4 feet) into a shimmering pool. The fine spray in the air keeps everything cool and pleasant, and the swimming could hardly be better. Concrete stairs lead around behind the waterfall and pool; you can continue over some slippery rocks into a nearby cave. The falls are about 20 kilometers (12.4 miles) south of Palenque on the road toward Ocosingo, down a 1.5-kilometer (0.9 mile) side road. There's a small res-

the beautiful waterfall at Misol Ha

taurant here and even a few cabanas, although it doesn't seem like a terribly convenient place to set up camp.

It's 30 minutes here by bus or *colectivo* (US$1.25). There may be a truck waiting to ferry travelers to the falls (US$.50); otherwise you can walk. It's an easy distance, but we did hear of one traveler getting robbed, so maybe leave your camera at the hotel this time.

Agua Clara

Another pretty spot, and it's different from Misol Ha or Agua Azul. Here, the river slows into a long, wide pool between sloping stone banks. It's a good spot to appreciate the river's famous turquoise color. A long rope bridge spans the river from a high bluff, and one or two tourists usually dare each other into making the long, whooping plunge from the middle of the span into the water below.

Agua Clara (7 A.M.–6 P.M. daily, US$1) is another 20 kilometers (12.4 miles) beyond Misol Ha, down a 2.5-kilometer (1.6-mile) access road. There is usually a truck waiting at the turnoff to ferry travelers to the entrance (US$1 each way).

Agua Azul

Twenty kilometers (12.4 miles) farther—60 kilometers (37.3 miles) from Palenque now—is the most famous stop on the route, Agua Azul (7 A.M.–6 P.M. daily, US$1.75). Designated a national park, more than 500 hefty falls crash and boil down several kilometers of limestone riverbed. When it's not a frothy white, the water is a distinctive blue. A few pools are calm and large enough for swimming—needless to say, there is a current and you should be very careful, even near the shore. Trails alongside the river lead quite far upriver and mostly are used by locals (including youngsters) to carry wood, sweet potatoes, bananas, and other goods to and from the tiny villages upriver. As you climb higher, crossing rickety bridges and at some points just a log or two, you'll get beautiful views of the green valley below, criss-crossed by bluish brooks and rivers. We have heard a few reports of robberies here as well, unfortunately. Ask at the entrance about recent incidents, or about hiring a guide; avoid going alone or carrying any valuables.

Agua Azul is four kilometers (2.5 miles) down an access road from the highway. *Colectivos* wait at the turnoff to bring visitors to the entrance (US$1). Inside the park, you'll find a number of small eateries, snack shops, and places to sit and to change. Note that on Mexican holidays, especially Semana Santa, Agua Azul turns into a madhouse—really and truly. Better to wait for a different weekend.

SHOPPING

Unremarkable shops line the main streets of Palenque selling postcards, T-shirts, and arts and crafts. They're good if you're running short on time or if you want something particularly kitschy to take home. One place, however, stands out above the rest—the **Plaza Artesanal Kinich** (Calle Aldama at Av. Reforma, 10 A.M.–10 P.M. daily). Off the main drag, this indigenous market mostly sells the colorful fabrics and beautiful hand stitching that Chiapas is famous for. You'll also see some handcrafted toys, Mayan replicas, and even a few Guatemalan goods. Take your time looking around—this is as good as it gets in this town.

ACCOMMODATIONS
In Town

The main reason to stay in town is convenience. Rooms here are within a few blocks of restaurants, banks, Internet, and telephones—services you may need while you're on the road. That said, rooms near the main plaza are a little run-down for the money—adequate for a night or two but not especially pleasant. If you like the idea of being near town and don't mind walking a few extra blocks, consider staying in La Cañada district. On the edge of Palenque town, this jungly neighborhood has several fine hotel options, a couple of restaurants, and easy access to the ruins. It's also just a 10- to 15-minute walk to the main plaza.

Under US$50: On a dirt road just a couple of blocks from the center of town, **Hotel Posada San Juan** (Allende at Av. Emilio Rabasa, tel. 916/345-0616, hotel_san_juan@hotmail.com, US$5 pp dorm, US$13–16 s/d with fan, US$30 s/d with a/c) is a good budget travelers' place. The mixed-sex dorm consists of an open-air room with 22 twin wood frames set side by side, each with a futonesque pad that serves as the mattress. The single-sex bathrooms—with hot water no less—are acceptable. Sheets and communal lockers are provided (the reception holds the keys to the lockers) but that's about it. If you are looking for more privacy, the single/double rooms are decent: basic but spotless. Be sure to ask for one in the back as the *tortillería*, which faces the hotel, is pretty noisy in the morning.

A block from the ADO bus station, **Hotel Avenida** (Av. Juárez No. 173, tel. 916/345-0598, marcokichan@hotmail.com, US$13 s/d with fan, US$26 s/d with a/c) is a welcome surprise. Once you get past the dingy-looking lobby, the hotel opens onto a good-sized (and refreshing) pool with a jungle backdrop. Rooms are simple but are very clean and all have a television (local channels only) and screened windows. Many have porches looking out into the wilderness. There's also a secure parking lot. A great value.

Posada Shalom I (Av. Juárez No. 156, tel. 916/345-0944, US$17.50 s/d with fan, US$22 s/d with a/c) is in the heart of downtown and offers small but good rooms with hot water, TV, and—yes—matching bedspreads. Most rooms have windows that open onto an interior hallway. If it's full, try its sister hotel, the creatively named **Posada Shalom II** (Corregidora at Abasolo, tel. 916/345-2641).

In La Cañada district, **Hotel La Posada** (Av. Nicolas Bravo at Calle 3 Poniente, tel. 916/345-0437, US$18 s/d with fan, US$26 s/d with a/c) is a clean and friendly, if simple, hotel. Its 16 rooms are set far back from the road, away from the disco and restaurant noise that oppresses some of the neighboring hotels. Rooms on the second floor are larger, though all have plenty of hot water and portable fans. Tables and chairs also are set out on a wide lawn in front of the rooms, where travelers often can be found relaxing.

On a quiet street behind La Cañada neighborhood is the excellent **ᴍ Posada Ysolina** (Av. Manuel Velasco Suarez No. 51, tel. 916/345-1524, US$19–23 s/d with fan, US$26 s/d with a/c). Rooms are lovingly decorated with simple Mexican furniture, *talavera* tiles, and stenciled walls. Some have balconies and a couple even have bathtubs. Coffee and an assortment of breads are available each morning in the lobby. Worth every extra step it takes to get to the center of town, this place is a find.

Chablis (Calle Merle Green No. 7, tel. 916/345-0870, US$26 s/d with a/c) offers 19 spacious and spotless rooms with cable TV and air conditioning. Top-floor rooms have balconies—a definite plus. There also is a laid-back palapa-roofed lounge that is great for relaxing, reading, or—as the hotel name suggests—enjoying a glass of wine or two.

Across the street, **ᴍ Hotel Xibalba** (Calle Merle Green No. 9, tel. 916/345-0411, xibalba02@prodigy.net.mx, www.palenquemx.com/shivalva, US$33 with a/c) is another excellent choice; rooms here are distributed in two buildings but all are cozy, clean, and comfortable. The ones in the Mayan temple replica have A-frame ceilings (second floor only) and overlook a tropical forest. There also are a travel agency and a first-rate restaurant onsite (see *Food*).

US$50–100: Hotel Chan Kah Centro (Av. Juárez No. 2 at Independencia, tel. 916/345-0318, US$47 s with a/c, US$53 d with a/c) is a reasonably clean and modern hotel offering acceptable—though somewhat cramped—accommodations. Some rooms have balconies overlooking the main plaza, which is a plus for people-watching. The hotel also offers parking and a decent restaurant. Be sure to confirm your stay before arriving—some readers have complained of lost reservations.

Just past the entrance to La Cañada neighborhood on a busy street, **Casa Inn** (Blvd. Aeropuerto Km. 0.5, tel. 916/345-0104, www.hotel-casainntulija.com, US$52 s/d with a/c) is a good value if you can handle the tour groups; rooms are plain but they are ample, clean, and have cable TV. A billiards table and a pool (if it's filled) are nice additions. Breakfast also is included in the rate.

The best high-end choice in town, Ⓜ **Maya Tulipanes** (Merle Green No. 6, tel. 916/345-0201, www.mayatulipanes.com.mx, US$82 s/d with a/c) is a very comfortable hotel offering modern amenities and excellent service in a jungly setting. A welcoming pool and a good restaurant are added bonuses to a restful stay. Tour groups often stay here but it doesn't seem to affect the service or experience that independent guests receive. A fine choice, budget permitting.

Near the Ruins

On the road to the Palenque ruins, a cluster of hotels and restaurants known collectively as El Pachán offers an appealing alternative to staying in town. Amid a laid-back bohemian atmosphere, the options range from camping to upscale lodging. Here you can walk through jungle paths to get to your bungalow room, see countless stars in an expansive night sky, and be the first to walk through Palenque on a glorious spring morning.

Under US$50: At the far end of El Panchán

district, Ⓜ **Rakshita's Cabañas and Dormitorios** (El Panchan, Carr. Ruinas Km. 4.5, tel. 916/100-7557, jako_malck@hotmail.com, www.rakshita.com, US$1.75 pp camping or hammock, US$4.50 pp dorm, US$10.50 s cabana with private bath, US$13 d cabana with private bath, US$18 pp casita) is a new-agey place in the middle of the jungle offering a wide range of accommodations—from a huge palapa under which to hang your hammock to well-kept (and colorful) cabanas with rustic private bathrooms. You'll also find a two-story yoga and meditation palapa, where free instruction is often given, a small massage hut next to a gurgling stream (massage around US$20/hour), a small pool, and a fantastic vegetarian restaurant (see *Food*). It's a great place to kick back for a day or two or three....

Named after the welcoming owner, **Chato's Cabañas** (El Panchán, Carr. Ruinas Km. 4.5, tel. 916/341-4846, elpanchan@yahoo.com, www.elpanchan.com, US$12.50 d, US$14 d) offers clean cabanas of various sizes, all set deep in the jungle of El Panchán neighborhood. All have private bath, fans, and great views of the flora. Be sure to ask for a newer cabana, as the older ones are showing their age. A nice pool and a popular restaurant—Don Mucho—(see *Food*) add to an already fine choice. If the place is full, ask about availability at Chato's other Panchan establishment—**Jungle Palace.** The 18 simple cabanas are set throughout a lovingly manicured section of the jungle and have shared bathrooms. Some have porches and hammocks—a definite plus. Cabanas here run US$7 singles, US$9 doubles and camping and hammock space also is available at the back of the property for US$2.25 per person.

If El Panchán isn't quite your scene but you'd like to stay near the ruins, try Chato's newest cabanas and tent grounds across the highway from the neighborhood—**Cabañas y Camping Jaguar** (Carr. Ruinas Km. 4.5, tel. 916/341-4846, elpanchan@yahoo.com, US$2.50 pp camping, US$7 s cabana with shared bath, US$9 d cabana with shared bath, US$12.50 s cabana with private bath, US$14 d cabana with private bath). Although not as alluring as staying in the thick of the jungle, the cabanas are quite nice and the grounds offer spectacular stargazing.

The most modern place in El Panchán, **N Margarita and Ed** (El Panchán, Carr. Ruinas Km. 4.5, tel. 916/341-0063, edcabanas@yahoo.com, US$12 s cabanas, US$13 d cabanas, US$13 s with fan, US$14 d with fan and kitchenette, US$19 s/d deluxe with fan, US$26 s/d deluxe with a/c) offers a different sort of jungle accommodation. Rooms—both with kitchenette and deluxe—are tile-floored, spotlessly clean, and have the personal touches you would expect in a midrange hotel room in town. A perfect option if you like being in the wild with the comforts of the modern world. Rooms with kitchenettes are rented *without* use of the kitchen amenities if stays are less than a few days. A couple of rustic cabanas also are available near the entrance.

Another option is **Maya Bell Trailer Park** (500 m/1,640 feet from museum, tel. 916/345-1465, US$2.50 pp camping or hammock, US$7–9 s/d shared bath, US$13/trailer, US$35 s/d private bath with fan, US$48 s/d private bath with a/c), a sprawling budget lodging complex with a laid-back backpacker ambience. A large grassy area has room for tents and camper-trailers, and a small hillside in back has simple platforms with palapa roofs for setting up a tent or hanging a hammock (you can rent hammocks for US$1.25/night if you don't have one). Shared bathrooms are kept relatively clean and there are basins and clotheslines for hand-washing your clothes. Lockers are US$1/day—recommended for campers. Private rooms are fairly new and surprisingly nice, with low comfortable beds and windows facing the grassy center—note there are only two tiny private rooms with shared bath, which are usually occupied. The hotel swimming pool is somewhat grubby but makes a nice afternoon beer-and-music spot, and the restaurant (7:30 A.M.–10 P.M., US$3–8) serves reliable affordable meals. Some people walk here for lunch after visiting the ruins and museum.

Over US$100: For guaranteed tranquility, try the **Chan-Kah Resort Village** (Carr. Ruinas Km. 3, tel. 916/345-1100, chan-kah@palenque.com.mx, www.chan-kah.com.mx, US$106 s with a/c, US$112 d with a/c). Set in a manicured jungle environment, this resort boasts 67 spacious junior suite *casitas,* each with stone-encrusted floors, porches, and views of the thick jungle or a gurgling creek—one even has a Mayan ruin in its backyard! While all the rooms are excellent, ask for one toward the back of the property, which are the newest and away from the access road. An immense pool with a stone-floor bottom and two bridges also provide plenty of space for cooling off. The restaurant, which has live music in the evenings, is quite good as well.

FOOD

As with hotels, Palenque has a large but not particularly inspiring selection of restaurants. With a few exceptions, expect standard Mexican dishes at moderate prices.

Mexican

Upstairs from a 24-hour mini-mart and across from the bus terminal, you'd expect **N Restaurant Deli** (Av. Juárez s/n, tel. 916/345-2511, 7 A.M.–midnight daily, delivery noon–midnight only, US$2–8) to be selling hot dogs and Big Gulps. In fact, this bright new eatery is a surprisingly pleasant place to eat. With plenty of empty corners to stack your bags, it's an ideal spot for breakfast or lunch before a long bus ride. Try the pancakes with peach topping or the *huevos habañil* (literally worker's eggs), served with a terrific habanero and cilantro sauce. If you had a long day at the ruins, the restaurant also delivers, including whatever snacks from the mini-mart you may be craving.

Lakan-Ha (Av. Juárez 20, between Calles Abasolo and Independencia, tel. 916/345-0011, 7:30 A.M.–10 P.M. daily, US$2.50–10) is a local breakfast favorite, with a variety of inexpensive combo plates, but it can be counted on for a decent, reasonably priced meal anytime. The pleasant dining room is on the second floor, away from the hubbub on Avenida Juárez.

The restaurant at **Hotel Chan Kah Centro** (Av. Juárez No. 2 at Independencia, tel. 916/345-0318, 1–11 P.M. daily, US$3–12) has tables on two breezy floors—the ones upstairs have views of the plaza. The *comida corrida* (lunch specials) are varied, good, and inexpensive.

For a little splurge, try **La Selva** (tel. 916/345-0363, 11:30 A.M.–11:30 P.M. daily, US$8–18) on the road to the ruins, about a 10-minute walk from the Mayan Head statue. The traditional Mexican, seafood, and international dishes are good (if a bit overpriced), the mixed drinks are great, and everything is served beneath a high palapa roof. You'll find indigenous artisans here, along with *típico* music.

International

Las Tinajas (Calle 20 de Noviembre at Calle Abasolo, no phone, 7:30 A.M.–10 P.M. daily) is one of the better options in town. In addition to standard fish, chicken, and beef dishes, you can also order basic pastas, sandwiches, and salads. The main dining area is right on the corner with tables looking onto both streets, while the tiny original location is a few doors down. Service is friendly and the portions hefty—big *jarras* (pitchers) of fruit drinks are a good deal for the very, very thirsty.

Restaurante Maya (corner of Avs. Independencia and Hidalgo facing the park, tel. 916/345-0042, 7 A.M.–11 P.M. daily, US$3–12) is another old standby, with pink table cloths and a mural on the back wall. Reputation lets it get away with somewhat inflated prices, but the location facing the plaza is good and the meals—standard chicken, fish, and beef dishes—reliable. A newer, brighter sister restaurant of the same name in La Cañada area has similar fare plus live marimba music most nights.

In La Cañada, **Don Carlos Restaurant-Bar** (Hotel Xibalba, Calle Merle Green 9, tel. 916/345-0411, 7 A.M.–10 P.M. daily, US$3.50–9) has thick wooden tables and high bright walls. It's a very peaceful spot for breakfast or lunch; nighttime can be somewhat noisier (but not unpleasantly so), thanks to live marimba at the restaurant across the street. Choose from pasta, several vegetarian dishes, and Mexican dishes, all well prepared and graciously served.

M Café 199 (intersection of Av. Juárez and the road to the Palenque ruins, no phone, 7 A.M.–11 P.M. daily, US$3–8) is very out of place in the restaurant scene in town, and that's a good thing! The boxy modern structure has outdoor tables downstairs and a comfortable dining room upstairs, with traditional but fresh decor and a hip, understated feel. Come here for coffee or drinks and a bit of light fare. The full bar makes great mixed drinks—the *mojitos* even came with fresh mint—and food is creative and tasty, from sandwiches to crepes.

Italian

Café Restaurante Don Mucho (El Panchan, Carr. Ruinas Km. 4.5, tel. 916/341-4846, 9 A.M.–11 P.M. daily, US$3–10) is another popular place in the jungle neighborhood of El Panchán. Specialties here are the homemade pastas, wood oven–baked pizzas, and the *comida típica*. This place gets especially going 9–11 P.M., when live music and a fire show (performers swinging/juggling fire balls) are featured.

Vegetarian

For excellent vegetarian food, head toward the ruins and **M Rakshita's** (Carr. Ruinas Km. 4.5, tel. 916/100-7557, 7 A.M.–8 P.M. daily, US$2–3). Light meals—think eggs, sandwiches, salads—along with a creative juice menu are served on a jungle-enclosed terrace. Live acoustic music also is played weekend nights. Highly recommended.

INFORMATION AND SERVICES

Tourist Information Centers

The **Tourist Office** (Av. Juárez at Abasolo, no phone, 9 A.M.–9 P.M. Mon.–Sat., 9 A.M.–1 P.M. Sun.) is decent for a handful of maps and basic answers to travelers' questions.

Medical Services

The **Hospital General** (Av. Juárez s/n, tel. 916/345-1443 or tel. 916/345-1433) is a large blue building just west (uphill) from the ADO bus terminal and across the street from the Pemex station. It is a public hospital, so service can be slow in coming, but there is a 24-hour emergency room. For an ambulance, contact the **Cruz Roja** (Red Cross) at Mex. cell tel. 044-916/341-0025. **Farmacia Similares** (Av. Juárez 185 at Calle Allende, tel. 916/345-2250) is open 24 hours.

Police
The police station (tel. 916/345-0141) is in city hall, facing the plaza.

Money
Banamex (9 A.M.–4 P.M. Mon.–Fri.) and **Bancomer** (8 A.M.–4 P.M. Mon.–Sat.) are both on Avenida Juárez, have reliable ATMs, and cash travelers checks.

Post Office
The post office is a half block off the Central Plaza on Avenida Independencia at Calle Bravo.

Internet and Telephone
Check email and call home at **Cibernet Palenque** (Av. Independencia at Av. 5 de Mayo, no phone, 9 A.M.–11 P.M. daily). Prices are US$.90/hour for Internet, US$2.50 to download digital pictures and burn them onto a CD, US$.35/minute to call the United States and Canada, and US$.55/minute to Europe. Another Internet option is **Compuciber** (Av. Juárez between Calles Aldama and Abasolo, tel. 916/345-3658, 8 A.M.–10 P.M. daily, US$.70/hour, US$3.50 to burn CDs).

Near the ruins, try El Panchán's no-name **Internet and long-distance café** (entrance to El Panchán, Carr. Ruinas Km. 4.5, 9 A.M.–11 P.M. daily). Internet runs US$1.30/hour and it costs US$4.50 to burn CDs. Calls to the United States and Canada cost US$.35 per minute, to Europe US$.52.

Laundry
Lavandería San Francisco (Calle Abasolo at Av. 20 de Noviembre, tel. 916/345-3732, 8 A.M.–1 P.M. and 5–8 P.M. Mon.–Sat., 8 A.M.–2 P.M.

Sun.) is a tiny hole-in-the-wall and charges US$.70/kilo (2.2 pounds). Or try **Lavandería Azul** (Av. 20 de Noviembre between Calles Jiménez and Guerrero, tel. 916/345-2692, 8 A.M.–9 P.M. Mon.–Sat., 10 A.M.–4 P.M. Sun., US$.80/kilo for 3–5-hour service, US$1.30/kilo for 1–2-hour service).

Near the ruins, your best bet is El Panchan's **Jungle Palace Lavandería** (El Panchan, Carr. Ruinas Km. 4.5, 7 A.M.–3 P.M. Mon.–Sat.), where same-day and next-day service alike run US$2.25/three kilos.

Storage
You can store bags at the **ADO bus terminal** for US$.35/hour 6 A.M.–10 P.M. A few doors down, **Kukulcán Travel Agency** (Av. Juárez 8, tel. 916/345-1506, 10 A.M.–6 P.M. daily) charges US$.25/hour or US$3/day.

Tour Operators
A great many travel outfits want your business. Almost all offer the same tours at pretty much the same prices. The most popular trips are to Misol Ha, Agua Clara, and Agua Azul (US$10 pp, 9 A.M.–4:30 P.M.); day-trips to Bonampak and Yaxchilán ruins (US$45 pp, 6 A.M.–7:30 P.M.); and two-day excursions to Bonampak, Yaxchilán, and the Lancandón forest (US$78 pp, including meals and lodging). (See the *Archaeological Zones of the Rio Usumacinta Valley* section for more details on what you'll see on those trips.)

Tour operators have also begun offering combination trips, such as a morning tour of Palenque ruins followed by an afternoon at Misol Ha and Agua Azul (US$10 pp). New, convenient "drop-off" tours include spending a day visiting Bonampak and Yaxchilán, overnighting in Frontera Corozal, then taking a boat to Betel, Guatemala, to catch the bus there to Flores (US$78 pp, including transport, lodging, and meals).

Longtime operators include friendly **Na Chan Kan** (Av. Juárez next to Hotel Avenida, tel. 916/345-0263 or tel. 916/346-2154, 8 A.M.–10 P.M. daily), **Viajes Misol Ha** (Av. Juárez 148 at Av. 20 de Noviembre 8, tel.

916/345-2271, 7 A.M.–9 P.M. daily), and **Kukulcán Travel Agency** (Av. Juárez 8 next to the ADO terminal, tel. 916/345-1506, 10 A.M.–6 P.M. daily). For air tickets, try **Viajes Caribe** (Av. Hidalgo 98 between Calles Allende and Aldama, tel. 916/345-2568, 9 A.M.–2:30 P.M., 5–9 P.M. Mon.–Sat.).

GETTING THERE

Plane

Palenque has a small modern airport, but there was no regular passenger service there at the time of research.

Bus

The **ADO bus terminal** (Av. Juárez s/n, tel. 916/345-1344) is on the west side of town, about 100 meters (328 feet) from the turnoff to the Palenque ruins. A number of second-class bus stations are scattered nearby, but ADO service is significantly better and not much more expensive. An asterisk denotes deluxe ADO-GL service; fares are 10–30 percent higher. Destinations include:

Campeche, US$16.50, eight hours, take any Mérida bus.

Cancún, US$38, 12–13 hours, 5:30 P.M., 8 P.M., 8:15 P.M., 9 P.M., and 10:45 P.M.*

Chetumal, US$22, seven hours, take any Cancún bus.

Mérida, US$25, 8–9 hours, 12:30 A.M., 8 A.M., 9 P.M., and 11 P.M.*

Mexico City-TAPO, US$52, 12–13 hours, 6 P.M. and 9 P.M.

Mexico City-Norte, US$52, 12–13 hours, 9 P.M.

Oaxaca, US$39, 15 hours, 5:30 P.M.

Ocosingo, US$5, three hours, take any San Cristóbal bus except 4:45 and 6:30 A.M.

Playa del Carmen, US$35, 12 hours, take any Cancún bus.

San Cristóbal, US$9, five hours, 3 A.M., 3:30 A.M., 4 A.M., 4:45 A.M.*, 6:30 A.M.*, 9:30 A.M., 11:45 A.M., 2:15 P.M., and 11 P.M.

Tapachula, US$27, 12 hours, 9 A.M.

Tulum, US$33, 11.5 hours, take any Cancún bus except 9 P.M.

Villahermosa, US$6.50, 2.5 hours, 7 A.M., 8 A.M., 11:45 A.M., 1:30 P.M., 3 P.M., 4:20 P.M., 5:30 P.M., 6 P.M., 7 P.M., 8 P.M., and 9 P.M.

Car

There were no car rental agencies in Palenque as of 2005, the nearest being in Villahermosa. The road from Villahermosa (about 150 kilometers/93 miles, two hours) is safe and pleasant. However, armed robberies, some of them violent, have occurred on the highway south toward San Cristóbal and east toward Bonampak and Yaxchilán. Do not drive at night, and if possible drive in a group with other vehicles. Fill up whenever you can, as gas stations can be few and far between.

GETTING AROUND

Palenque town is easy to navigate on foot. To get to the ruins or accommodations outside of town, bikes would be a good option but no one seems to have them. *Colectivos* shuttle between town and the ruins every 10–15 minutes 7 A.M.–7 P.M.; the fare is US$.80 and you can flag them down anywhere along the road.

Archaeological Zones of the Río Usumacinta Valley

Visiting Yaxchilán and Bonampak archaeological zones used to be something of an adventure—a long, bumpy drive from Palenque into the heart of the lush forest, followed by a hike and boat ride through lands inhabited by reclusive Lacondón indigenous communities. Nowadays, most tour operators offer day trips to the sites, or two-day trips that include sleeping in rustic lodges and hiking through the forest.

While the challenge of getting to the ruins certainly added to their mystique, Yaxchilán and Bonampak are no less impressive for being more accessible. Here visitors are treated to fantastic painted frescos, huge stelae, finely carved lintels, and plenty of howler monkeys and huge river crocs along the way.

BONAMPAK ARCHAEOLOGICAL ZONE

In 1946 a young American conscientious objector, Charles Frey, took refuge in the jungles of eastern Chiapas in a small village called El Cedro. He soon struck up what would become a very close friendship with a Lacondón man named Kayon from a small village between the Lacanjá and Usumacinta Rivers. At some point, Kayon led Frey deep into the thick forest to an ancient—and until then, secret—Mayan ceremonial center. Frey reported having seen nine structures and stelae scattered around the overgrown site, including a long three-room structure whose interior was covered with brilliantly colored fresco paintings.

Apparently this discovery was too much for Frey to keep to himself, and he told Mexican federal authorities of the magnificent find. At first his news met with little enthusiasm, probably because getting there was a treacherous jungle trek through land occupied by Lacandóns, who were known to be fiercely defensive of their lands. (That Frey was so accepted into a Lacondón community was itself remarkable.) But with the help of another American, John

Bonampak's Acropolis

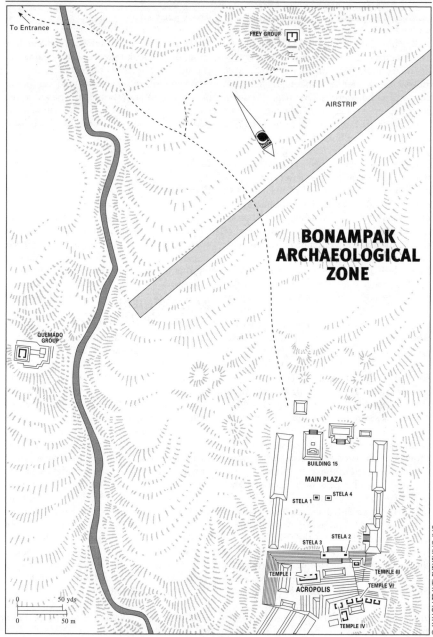

To Entrance

FREY GROUP

AIRSTRIP

BONAMPAK ARCHAEOLOGICAL ZONE

QUEMADO GROUP

BUILDING 15

MAIN PLAZA

STELA 1   STELA 4

STELA 3   STELA 2

TEMPLE I   TEMPLE III

ACROPOLIS   TEMPLE VI

TEMPLE IV

0   50 yds
0   50 m

Bourne, Frey managed to pique the interest of several Mexican archaeologists, who made several preliminary expeditions to the site, known as Bonampak, or "painted walls." In 1949, he organized an expedition of Mexican artists, archaeologists, architects, photographers, and chemists to Bonampak. That trip, sponsored by the Mexican National Institute of Fine Arts, would pave the way for future scientific research at the site, but it cost Frey his life—he drowned trying to rescue an engraver, Franco Lázaro Gómez, when their canoe overturned in the rapids of the Lacanjá River.

Bonampak was a small Late Classic (A.D. 600–800) center in the orbit of the nearby city of Yaxchilán. Bonampak's murals are housed in **Temple I,** which stands on a low level of the **Acropolis,** a large stepped structure that backs onto a jungle-covered hill. In front of the Acropolis is a plaza with low buildings around the other three sides. Researchers believe that the story told through the murals should be read from left to right, from Room 1 to Room 3. The setting of Room 1's mural is the palace, where the child-heir is presented to the court and 336 days later is the focal point of a celebration with actors and musicians. Room 2 is set in the jungle and on a flight of stairs. These murals tell the story of a jungle battle, probably in honor of the heir, led by Chaan-Muan. This is considered the greatest battle scene in Mayan art.

Next the scene moves to a staircase, where the captives are ritually tortured while Chaan-Muan watches from above. In Room 3 the setting is a pyramid, where costumed lords dance and a captive awaits his death. To the side, noblewomen ritually let their blood, while a pot-bellied dwarf is presented to the court. Anthropologists believe that the child-heir never ruled Bonampak, because there is evidence that the site was abandoned before the murals were even completed. The murals have faded with time and were damaged when the first researchers used kerosene to clean them—the kerosene brought out the colors but weakened the paints' adhesion and hastened the flaking and decay. The Museo Nacional de Antropología, in Mex-

ico City, has a reproduction of how the murals likely looked in their full glory, and lesser copies are found in Tuxtla Gutiérrez and Villahermosa. But, though they are old and damaged, you still can't beat the originals.

When visiting Bonampak (and Yaxchilán) be sure to look at the beautifully carved scenes on the underside the lintels (the slab of stone that forms the top of a doorway). Their location makes them easy to miss, but they are truly some of the best Mayan relief carvings you'll see outside of a museum.

Practicalities

If you take a tour—most people do—be sure to ask if the price includes entry to the archaeological sites. Otherwise, the cost is US$3; it's open 8 A.M.–5 P.M. daily. (See *Getting There and Away* in the *Frontera Corazal* section for information on getting here independently.)

▼ YAXCHILÁN ARCHAEOLOGICAL ZONE

The Yaxchilán ruins lie on the Río Usumacinta, Mexico's largest river and the border between Mexico and Guatemala. Archaeologists have found at least 35 stelae, 60 carved lintels, 21 altars, and 5 stairways covered with hieroglyphs—a treasure trove for epigraphers. Yaxchilán's rulers were obsessed with venerating their dynasty and legitimizing their rule and endowed a major monument-carving operation to achieve these goals. The site's hieroglyphs provided much of the raw material that led to the deciphering of the Mayan writing system.

Yaxchilán was a powerful city-state during the Classic era, ruled by the Jaguar dynasty, which traced its roots to A.D. 320 and a lord named Yat Balam (Jaguar Penis). The earliest recorded date at the site is from A.D. 435, and the first major monuments appeared early in the 6th century. Yaxchilán's greatest ruler was Shield Jaguar, who was born in A.D. 647 and ruled more than six decades, A.D. 681–742, a remarkable feat for a man whose life expectancy was under 40. His primary wife was his first cousin, Lady Xoc, and Yaxchilán's **Temple 23** is covered with reliefs in her honor—a unique homage for a Mayan noblewoman. Anthropologists believe that Shield Jaguar built Lady Xoc's temple to appease local lineages, because his actual heir-apparent was born to a wife of foreign birth. Shield Jaguar was succeeded by Bird Jaguar, who marked the stages of his 10-year-long accession to the throne (there were other pretenders) in a series of stelae and reliefs. According to engravings, his achievements included participating in the ball game, bloodletting, sacrificing captives, and fathering an heir with a wife from a politically powerful lineage. The Jaguar dynasty lasted until about A.D. 800, when the last ruler, Ta-Skull, constructed a small, badly built temple that celebrated his accession with one lintel relief. Thereafter Yaxchilán gradually returned to the jungle.

Practicalities

The archaeological zone is open 8 A.M.–5 P.M.; entrance US$3. Just past the ticket booth, the main road leads to the Main Plaza, with the Great Acropolis a long steep flight of stairs above. Instead of following the main road, however, consider taking the small path to your right up to the Little Acropolis and then across to the Great Acropolis from the back side. It's a nice walk, and less strenuous somehow. You also may see howler monkeys in the trees between the two temples and behind the Great Acropolis.

Yaxchilán is an hour down the Río Usumacinta on long canoelike boats with sun covers and powerful outboard motors. Along the way, you will probably see huge river crocodiles sunning themselves on the banks, their mouths standing open. Tours from Palenque should always include the boat fare, one of the main advantages of taking a tour. (See the *Getting There and Away* in the *Frontera Corozal* section for information on getting here independently.)

FRONTERA COROZAL

This small riverside border town is the jumping-off point for Yaxchilán ruins, which are an hour's boat ride downriver. Otherwise the town's main sight is the **Museo Comunitario Frontera Corozal** (main street, tel. 555/329-0995, free), an interesting and informative museum with three exhibition rooms. Displays include information on the area's history and culture, archaeological digs, and local flora and fauna. A good cheap restaurant is on-site. Spanish only.

Accommodations and Food

On the riverfront at the end of the main road in Frontera Corozal near the pier, **Escudo Jaguar** (tel. 555/329-0995, escudojaguar_hotel@yahoo.com.mx, www.chiapastours.com.mx/escudojaguar, US$13 s/d with shared bath, US$30–44 s/d with private bath) is a fine choice if you are looking to stay the night. In bright pink palapa-roofed buildings, rooms are simple, clean, and tranquil. All come with fans and screened windows and most buildings have nice porches with hammocks. If you want to camp, the rate is US$5.50 per tent; if you need to rent a tent, it'll set you back an additional US$4.50. The hotel restaurant, which overlooks the river, also is a plus.

© LIZA PRADO CHANDLER

one of the magnificent—and well-preserved— lintels at Yaxchilán

The State of Chiapas

Guided Tours

Tour operators in Palenque offer one- and two-day tours to Bonampak and Yaxchilán. Day trips typically begin at 6 A.M. and include one hour at Bonampak, two hours at Yaxchilán, and lunch in Frontera Corozal before driving back to Palenque, arriving shortly after dark. Two-day trips include visits to both ruins plus a four-hour hike through the Lancandón forests with a local guide and overnighting in rustic cabanas. (See *Tour Operators* in the *Palenque* section for prices and a list of reputable operators.)

Escudo Jaguar (tel. 555/329-0995, escudojaguar_hotel@yahoo.com.mx, www.chiapastours.com.mx/escudojaguar) also offers tours and transport, which you can organize right from the hotel. Prices are a bit steep and there are no bank, ATM, or credit-card services in Frontera Corozal, so if you're interested in a trip, either bring plenty of cash or deposit money in Escudo's bank account (Escudo Jaguar SSS; Banamex, Suc. 343, acct. 1116749) beforehand and bring the receipt. Besides transporting day-trippers back and forth to Yaxchilán, Escudo Jaguar offers excursions to Planchón de las Figuras (one-day US$243, two-day US$261, 1–10 people), Altar de los Sacrificios (two days US$355, 1–10 people), and Piedras Negras (7 A.M.–3 P.M., US$350, 1–10 people). Prices do not include camping gear or food; the former you should bring with you and the latter you can buy in town.

Getting There and Away

At the time of research, robberies along the road between Palenque and Yaxchilán were just common enough to convince us it was still best to take a tour. The situation may well improve in the next few years, and is something worth asking a few locals and other travelers about. That said, it is certainly possible to visit Bonampak and Yaxchilán independently. Plan to visit only one site as a day trip or to stay the night in Frontera Corozal if you want to see both—even the tours leave at 6 A.M. and don't return until after dark. Driving a rental car here is fast and convenient, of course, though

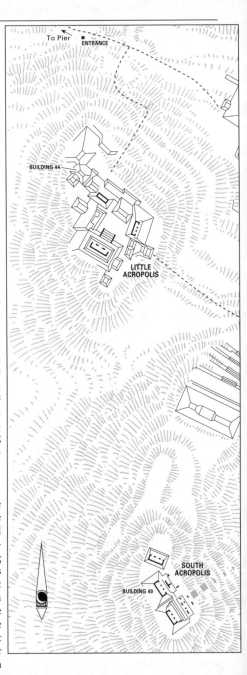

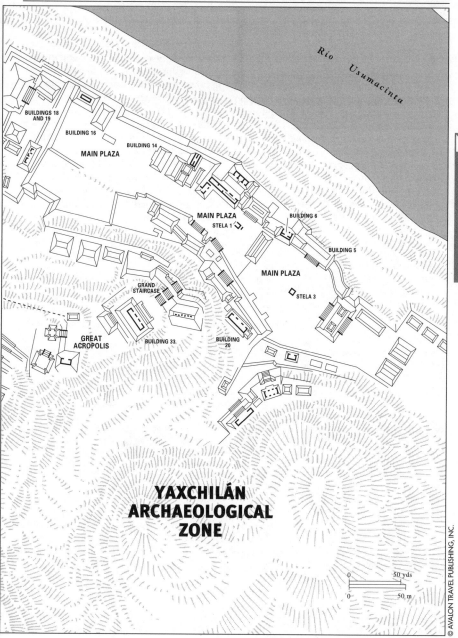

Río Usumacinta

BUILDINGS 18 AND 19

BUILDING 16

BUILDING 14

MAIN PLAZA

MAIN PLAZA

STELA 1

BUILDING 6

BUILDING 5

MAIN PLAZA

GRAND STAIRCASE

STELA 3

GREAT ACROPOLIS

BUILDING 33

BUILDING 20

YAXCHILÁN ARCHAEOLOGICAL ZONE

0   50 yds
0   50 m

The State of Chiapas

TROPICAL MONKEYS

The jungles of Mexico are home to three species of monkeys: spider, howler, and black howler. Intelligent and endearing, these creatures are prime targets for the pet trade. The have been so hunted, in fact, that today all three are in danger of extinction. Experts estimate that for every monkey sold, three die during transportation and distribution. In an effort to protect these creatures, the Mexican government has prohibited their capture or trade. As you wander through the ruins of Cobá or Yaxchilán, keep your ears perked and your eyes peeled. You're sure to see (or hear!) a few tropical monkeys if you're patient. A tip: Spider and howler monkeys alike are most active at sunrise and sundown; if possible, consider waking early or staying late to increase your chances of spotting a few. Other places to see these monkeys are the Punta Laguna reserve and the Calakmul ruins and reserve.

again it's not really recommendable due to roadside robberies.

Transporte Chamoan (Av. Miguel Hidalgo between Calles Allende and 1 Poniente) and **Transporte Río Chancala** (Av. 5 de Mayo between Calles Allende and 1 Poniente) both have *combi* service to Frontera Coro-

zal (US$4.50, 2.5 hours, every 60–90 minutes 5 A.M.–4 P.M.), where you can walk to the river for boats to Yaxchilán. Two boatmen cooperatives provide boat service to Yaxchilán from the pier at the end of the main road. Round-trip prices are scaled according to the number of people (US$50 for 1–3 people to US$100 for 8–10 people) and are pretty much non-negotiable. Getting there early gives you the best chance of being able to share a boat with other travelers or an arriving tour group.

Getting to Bonampak is a little trickier: The stop on the highway is San Javier (US$3.50, two hours) but ask the driver to take you to the entrance, which is another four kilometers (2.5 miles) down. If he doesn't go for it—most don't—someone should be waiting at the turnoff to drive you in and out (US$3.50 round-trip, with an hour at the site). Return to the highway to catch a *combi* on to Frontera Corozal (US$1.50, 20 minutes) or back to Palenque.

The last bus leaves Frontera Corozal at around 3 P.M. and passes San Javier about 20 minutes later.

Getting to Guatemala: The boat cooperatives at Frontera Corozal provide one-way transport to Bethel, Guatemala (from US$30 for 1–3 people to US$55 for 7–10 people) where buses to Flores depart daily at around noon.

Ocosingo

This small agricultural town is famous for three things. One, the impressive and oft-overlooked Mayan ruins of Toniná, about 12 kilometers (7.5 miles) from town and believed to be one of the last true Mayan capitals. Two, as the site of the heaviest fighting in the Zapatista uprising in 1994 and more recently where numerous ranches (including a former eco-hotel) have been occupied by Zapatista soldiers. And three, the cheese. Yes, Ocosingo makes a mean cheese, from the tasty *doble crema* to the spicy spreadable *queso botanero*.

Surrounded by low hills and lush green vegetation, Ocosingo has an attractive plaza, a few decent (though not deluxe) places to stay and

eat, Internet and other services—and almost no tourists. While not a place to spend your whole vacation, it is worth stop. You could even stop on your way to San Cristóbal, store your bags at the bus terminal, spend a few hours at the ruins and museum, and be back in time to catch an afternoon bus. Better yet, get a hotel and enjoy this pleasant town for a night.

SIGHTS

Toniná

Toniná (9 A.M.–4 P.M. daily, museum closed Mon., US$2.50) is one of the best Mayan ar-

LIZA PRADO CHANDLER

view from the top of Toniná's main structure

chaeology sites that no one seems to know about. Easy to reach from both Palenque and San Cristóbal, Toniná (House of Stone) sees only a trickle of tourists. Toniná's massive main structure rises 80 meters (262 feet) above the main grassy plaza, bustling with interweaving staircases, secondary temples, and well-preserved roof combs. Built on seven artificial terraces, it is not a true pyramid, but it is the highest pyramid-like structure known to have been built by the Classic Mayans. On the way up (or down if you just can't wait to get to the top) check out the labyrinthine palace, with winding passages and hidden doors and tunnels, and an excellent stucco mural depicting the end of the world. Archaeologists believe Toniná was the last Classic Mayan site, outlasting other cities by a century before finally being abandoned around A.D. 909. With the Mayan world collapsing around them, it's not surprising that Toniná's rulers were obsessed with death and sacrifice, which is depicted in many of the inscriptions and carvings here. Unfortunately, there are no plaques (and only a few hand-written signs in Spanish) explaining the structures at the site.

Definitely leave time to visit the **museum** which is one of the best at any Mayan site. Opened in September 2002, it contains fantastic artifacts and carvings, including figures that were deliberately decapitated (which was probably done when the personage depicted was himself decapitated) and distinctive round obelisks marking important dates.

Aerial Tours

Servicios Aéreos San Cristóbal (Aeródromo particular, Carretera Ocosingo-Altamirabo Km. 2.5, tel. 919/673-0188) offers scenic flights and aerial tours, including a 10–15-minute flyover over Agua Azul (US$175 for 1–4 people). Ask, also, about day trips to Yaxchilán and Bonampak ruins, or San Quintín and Miramar.

ACCOMMODATIONS

On the main plaza, **Hotel Central** (Av. Central No. 5, tel. 919/673-0024, US$14 s with fan, US$18 d with fan) offers small, simple, and very clean rooms. All have fans, cable TV, and private bathrooms with hot water. Half of the rooms on the second floor open onto a wide veranda overlooking the main square, which is noisy in the mornings but great for people-watching in the afternoons.

Just around the corner, **M Hospedaje y Restaurant Esmeralda** (Calle Central Norte No. 14, tel. 919/673-0014, info@ranchoesmeralda .net, US$10.50 s with shared bath, US$18 d with shared bath, US$13 s with private bath, US$21 d with private bath) is another good option. A reincarnation of Rancho Esmeralda—a popular hotel near Toniná that was taken over and shut down by the Zapatistas in 2003—the Hospedaje Esmeralda offers five large rooms in a remodeled historic home. Accommodations are simple and a little run-down but make up for it with homey touches such as Chiapanecan bedspreads, posters, and plants. The heart of the hotel is clearly in its restaurant and common areas, which are particularly inviting, with wood furniture, loads of tourist information in various languages, and shelves of books

ZAPATISTAS

On January 1, 1994, masked soldiers stormed government buildings in four cities in Chiapas, including San Cristóbal and Ocosingo. The soldiers were mostly indigenous peasants belonging to the **Ejército Zapatista de Liberación Nacional** (EZLN, Zapatista National Liberation Army). The Mexican army quickly responded and within a few days the Zapatistas, as they were known, had retreated back to the hills. About 150 people, mostly Zapatistas, died in the uprising. The rebellion was launched on the day the North American Free Trade Agreement (NAFTA) took effect, which opponents (correctly) believed would lead many peasants to lose livelihoods. The timing was not accidental—the seeds of the rebellion were planted much earlier.

The Zapatistas rose from eastern Chiapas, an area that has long tacked toward non-establishment leaders. Since the 1930s, the PRI, Mexico's long-time ruling party, nourished deep ties with indigenous leaders in western and northern Chiapas, mostly by rewarding loyalty with land and development programs. (Many indigenous communities did not support the Zapatista action, in part because of their historic ties to the PRI.) But these ties weren't formed in eastern Chiapas at first because the area was ignored and later because rural colonization programs of the 1970s made it more diverse and left fewer ethnic bonds for the PRI to exploit. The east also has many Protestants, which further alienated it from the mostly Catholic political elite.

By the 1980s, eastern Chiapas was an important base for anti-PRI peasant organizations. In 1982, facing a foreign debt of nearly US$100 billion, Mexico underwent an economic restructuring program that, among other things, cut vital agricultural subsidies to peasant farmers. President Salinas de Gotari gutted even more programs, and in 1992 a constitutional amendment all but ended more than a half century of land-reform policies in Mexico. More and more farmers lost their land, and those who could, moved to squatter camps outside San Cristóbal and other cities. "But in eastern Chiapas, which has no major commercial centers and is largely inaccessible to road transport, the impoverished ha[d] no place to turn and little to lose by joining in the rebellion." (George A. Collier, *Cultural Survival Quarterly,* Spring 1994)

Zapatista attacks and raids continued intermittently. But the ruggedness of the region made a military campaign unappealing (and probably unwinnable) for the Mexican Army. The two parties finally negotiated a settlement in 1996—known as the San Andrés Accords—but the government failed to fully implement the agreement and the situation remained tense, with more than 50,000 Mexican troops patrolling the remote Chiapas forests. There were sporadic raids and assassinations, and a major offensive by the army in 1999 uprooted thousands of ordinary Chiapanecans. President Fox, elected in 2000, has had little success implementing real reforms that can break the impasse.

More than 10 years since launching the first salvo and little to show for it, the Zapatista movement struggles to maintain the world's focus and attention. In 2003, Zapatistas took over an eco-lodge operated by two Americans outside the city of Ocosingo. It was just one of scores of private ranches—several hundred by some counts—that rebels have occupied. However, most of the occupied land is going unused, and even Zapatista sympathizers wonder what the campaign is really achieving. In December 2004 the EZLN's charismatic spokesperson, known as Sub-Comandante Marcos (since identified as Rafael Sebastián Guillén, a mestizo philosophy professor and now believed to be hiding in France), announced he was cowriting a mystery novel with Mexican writer Pablo Ignacio Taibo II. The novel, serialized in Mexico's main left-leaning newspaper, is about the wife of an indigenous rebel and seems to urge fellow Zapatistas to keep the faith.

(including a fascinating binder with newspaper clippings reporting on the Zapatista takeover of Rancho Esmeralda).

Next door, **Hotel Margarita** (Calle Central Norte No. 9, tel. 919/673-0280, hotel margarita@prodigy.net.mx, US$16 s, US$18.50 d) offers ample rooms with two queen beds, fans, and cable TV. The affordable junior suites (US$22.50), with king-sized beds and huge bathrooms, are worth the extra US$4. Some rooms have nice views of the surrounding hills—take a look at a couple before deciding.

FOOD

Hospedaje Rancho Esmeralda (Calle Central Oriente, US$4–10) has perhaps the best restaurant in town. A simple but varied menu— the chicken fajitas were quite good—is served on large wooden tables in the hotel's homey common area. There's an honor bar with soda, beer, and liquor.

Restaurante El Desvan (tel. 919/673-0117, 9 A.M.–10 P.M. daily, US$4–10) is one of many simple restaurants around the main plaza. Most serve standard Mexican fare; here you can also get pizza.

Ocosingo is famous for its cheeses, which are produced locally in a half dozen or more varieties, including a very tasty *doble crema* (double cream). **Quesos Santa Rosa** (1a Calle Oriente Norte s/n, tel. 919/673-0009, 7 A.M.–2 P.M., 4–8 P.M. daily) is a recommended shop just a block north of the plaza.

INFORMATION AND SERVICES

Tourist services were adequate although incomplete in Ocosingo when we passed through. By the time you read this, though, there may be a few more.

Pharmacies

Farmacias Similares (2a Calle Oriente Sur at 1a Sur Oriente, tel. 919/673-1515, 8 A.M.– 8 P.M. Mon.–Sat., 8 A.M.–2 P.M. Sun.) is around the corner from the main plaza, directly behind the church.

Money

Banamex (9 A.M.–4 P.M. Mon.–Fri.) has an office and a 24-hour ATM on the main plaza, a few doors up from the Hotel Central.

Post Office

The post office (8 A.M.–4:30 P.M. Mon.–Fri.) is on 2a Calle Oriente Norte at 2a Avenida Norte Oriente.

Internet

You can't throw a Frisbee in Ocosingo without hitting an Internet café. There are two across the plaza and a half dozen on Calle Central Norte alone. All charge around US$.70/hour for Internet and are open roughly 8 A.M.– 10 P.M. daily.

Laundry

Just around the corner from Hospedaje Esmeralda, you can get your threads cleaned at **Lavandería Espuma** (Av. 2 Norte s/n, no phone, 8 A.M.–9 P.M. Mon.–Sat. and 8 A.M.–2 P.M. Sun., US$.90/kilo—2.2 pounds). Next-day service unless otherwise requested.

Storage

The bus terminal has luggage storage for US$.50 per day.

GETTING THERE AND AROUND

Ocosingo's bus terminal (tel. 919/673-0431) is about seven blocks northwest from the center of town on the Carretera Internacional. Note that many of Ocosingo's bus departures are *de paso* (in passing), in other words, a brief scheduled stop along a longer route. If the bus you want is *de paso*—most of the morning routes to San Cristóbal, for example—be sure to arrive a half hour early as the bus may come and go ahead of schedule. You can't buy tickets until the bus arrives, either, so it's a good idea to be first in line in case the bus is full (not too common, but possible in high season). One asterisk denotes deluxe ADO-GL service; prices are 10–30 percent higher. Two asterisks denote second-class TRF service; prices are 30 percent lower but travel time significantly longer. Routes include:

Campeche, US$22, 10 hours, take any Mérida bus.

Cancún, US$43, 16 hours, 3 P.M., 5:15 P.M., 5:30 P.M., and 7 P.M.*

Chetumal, US$28, 10 hours, take any Cancún bus.

Mérida, US$30, 12 hours, 7:30 P.M.* and 9:30 P.M.

Mexico City, US$58, 16 hours, 3:45 P.M.; stops at TAPO, then Norte.

Palenque, US$5, 2.5 hours, 4 A.M., 9:35 A.M., 11:20 A.M.**, 1:15 P.M., 3 P.M., 5:15 P.M., 5:30 P.M., 7 P.M.*, 7:30 P.M.*, and 9:30 P.M.

Playa del Carmen, US$41, 15 hours, take any Cancún bus.

San Cristóbal, US$4, two hours, take any Tuxtla Gutiérrez bus.

Tulum, US$38, 14 hours, 3 P.M., 5:15 P.M., and 7 P.M.*

Tuxtla Gutiérrez, US$7.50, 4.25 hours, 1 A.M., 6 A.M., 7:30 A.M., 8:30 A.M.*, 9 A.M.*, noon, 1:55 A.M., 3:45 A.M., and 4:25 P.M.

Villahermosa, US$12, five hours, 1:15 P.M.

Taxis between the bus terminal and town cost US$1.25. To the Toniná ruins, a cab runs about US$4.50–6 each way; if you want a ride back, be sure to arrange it with the driver when he drops you off. You can also take a *combi* (van, US$.90 each way). They are marked "Predio-Ruins" and leave from 3a Avenida Sur Oriente in the market—ask as you go for the exact location. *Combis* leave whenever they are full, usually every 15–45 minutes. You can catch the same *combi* back.

San Cristóbal de las Casas

San Cristóbal is a wonderful old colonial city, definitely one of our favorite towns in this book. High in pine-covered mountains, San Cristóbal is refreshingly cool and crisp after the sticky Yucatán Peninsula—in the winter, you may even need to bring or buy a sweater or knit hat. Low colorful buildings with tile roofs and wrought-iron details line the narrow streets; inside some you'll find courtyards filled with plants and flowers and framed by stone archways and thick stone or adobe walls. Many of these old buildings are abandoned and in a charming state of disrepair; others are occupied by art galleries, restaurants, and small shops. Chiapas is famous for its amber, jade, textiles, and handmade clothing and crafts—it is a place where the genius and beauty of Mexican art is on full display.

In addition to its colonial charm, San Cristóbal has a strong, visible indigenous presence, more so than any other large city in Mexico. Dozens of indigenous villages surround San Cristóbal, and residents come into the city to sell goods, go to banks, and visit government and non-governmental organization (NGO) offices. In addition, thousands of disenfranchised Indians—those who have lost their land or have had to leave their villages because of political, religious, or other conflicts—live in makeshift slums on the outskirts of San Cristóbal; the women and children of those families make up the bulk of people selling bracelets, belts, and other crafts in the main plaza. With a little practice, you can easily identify villagers (at least the women) by the clothes they wear, since each village has a particular color and style. As in the outlying villages, and in parts of Guatemala, you should generally refrain from taking photographs of indigenous people, especially children, and never do so without permission.

SIGHTS

City Tour

Get your bearings on a short city tour operated by **Tranvía Turística** (Av. Insurgentes at Calle Hermanos Domínguez, tel. 967/678-0525). A motorized trolley makes a one-hour loop passing by (but not stopping at) most of San Cristóbal's sights and important spots. There is a recorded explanation, but in Spanish or French only.

Tours leave the Tranvía office daily at 10 A.M., 11 A.M., noon, 1 P.M., 4 P.M., 5 P.M., 6 P.M., and 7 P.M. and cost US$2.50 per person.

☒ Parque Central

The official name of San Cristóbal's leafy main plaza is Plaza de 31 de Marzo, but most people refer to it as the *parque central* (central plaza). Green iron benches are scattered along the wide walkways under tall shade trees. In the center, a two-story kiosk has a café that serves coffee, cold drinks, and snacks under pleasant umbrellas. During the colonial era, the square served several functions; a large fountain supplied water for the village, it was the gathering spot for the public market, and it was the scene of punishment during the years of the conquest. In 1994, Zapatista rebels stormed the plaza and adjoining Palacio Municipal (City Hall), which was significantly damaged. Today the square has resumed its tranquil ambience, though demonstrations by indigenous people and their supporters over poor living and working conditions (some of the same issues the Zapatistas were drawing attention to) occasionally spill out onto the square.

In the main plaza and in the one in front of the cathedral, expect to be approached by Chamulan women and children (some incredibly young) selling pretty handwoven bracelets, belts, and shawls. Their prices are unbelievably low, and even a small purchase seems greatly appreciated. A local nonprofit organization offers support and services to children of street vendors, who otherwise receive little or no formal education or medical attention.

Casa Sirena

Across from the square sits the oldest house in town. Constructed around 1555, it is quite a lovely old building, and you can still see a stylized version of what looks likes two serpent women, and over the corner of the building, a carving of a sea nymph that gives the house its name. Look for the carved lions, an indigenous craftsman's interpretation from some medieval representation. The insignia on the coat of arms over the door has been destroyed, so although the house is most often ascribed to be the original home of Diego de Mazariegos (the conqueror of Chiapas), some believed it might have been built by another, Andrés de la Tobilla.

Palacio Municipal

On the west side of the main square, the *Palacio Municipal* (City Hall) has been rebuilt many times since the first stone was laid in 1863. Rebel troops led by Juan Ortega burned the original building to the ground during a skirmish between royalists and republicans. When construction of the present, newer building began, the city was still the capital of the state and the plan included a much larger edifice. But the capital was moved to Tuxtla Gutiérrez, and the planned capitalesque construction was never completed. That said, the final product is still attractive, with neoclassical columns, arches, and a large plaza in the rear where civic ceremonies are held. Demonstrations take place here occasionally, and this building bore the major damage during the Zapatista uprising in 1994.

☒ Templo Santo Domingo

The first Santo Domingo Church, built in 1547, was a simple adobe structure. The present church is probably the most impressive of the many churches in the city. Santo Domingo has a gorgeous baroque facade covered with ornamented mortar with intricate carvings, Solomonic columns, and statues tucked into ornate niches. The interior is equally impressive, with a sensational pulpit with gold carvings everywhere. You'll see many nostalgic *retablos* (religious paintings) that are offered in place of money donations, or in thanks for favors or answered prayers. It's not unusual to find an Indian *curandera* (female healer) performing discreet rituals right inside the church: touching patients with flowers, surrounding him with smoking copal, murmuring incantations, passing burning candles over and around his head and body, all in front of the church altars.

To the left of the main church door is **Sna Jolobil,** a co-op of traditional weavers (mostly

The State of Chiapas

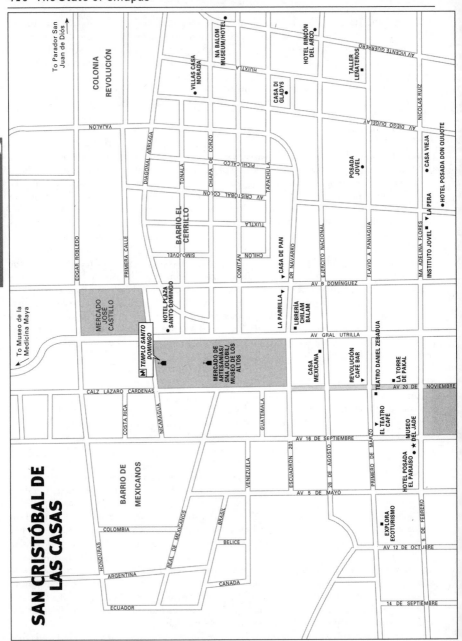

SAN CRISTÓBAL DE LAS CASAS

The State of Chiapas

To Templo de Guadalupe

REAL DE GUADALUPE

LIBRERÍA LA ISLA

BARRIO DE GUADALUPE

FRANCISCO I MADERO

LA ALMOLHONGA

HOSPITAL LA CARIDAD

CENTRO EL PUENTE

LAVANDERÍA SPLASH

DR. JOSÉ F. FLORES

BARRIO DE SANTA LUCÍA

SCALE NOT AVAILABLE

AV. JM SANTIAGO

CASA FELIPE FLORES

AV. JOSEFA ORTIZ DE DOMÍNGUEZ

POSADA MÉXICO

FRANCISCO LEÓN

JULIO M. CORZO

RAMÓN CORONA

SÓSTENES ESPONDA

HOTEL CASA MARGARITA/ AGENCIA CHINCULTIK

EL GATO GORDO

RESTAURANTE NORMITA

HOTEL VILLA REAL I

PALACIO MOCTEZUMA

CATHEDRAL

HOTEL REAL DEL VALLE

HOTEL SAN MARTIN

PARQUE CENTRAL

Plaza de 31 de Marzo

TICKET BUS

TODO NATURAL

HOTEL POSADA LOS ÁNGELES

POSADA SAN CRISTÓBAL

LAVANDERÍA LA RAPIDITA

TEMPLO DE SAN FRANCISCO

MERCADO DE DULCES/TRANVÍA TURÍSTICA

AV BENITO JUÁREZ

HOSPITAL GENERAL

AV INSURGENTES

FIRST-CLASS BUS TERMINAL

To Amatenango and Comitán

PALACIO MUNICIPAL

HOTEL CIUDAD REAL

HOTEL SANTA CLARA

TOURIST OFFICE

TULUC

POSADA FRAY BARTOLOMÉ DE LAS CASAS

MADRE TIERRA/ ZAPATA TOURS

FARMACIA SIMILARES

LA PARED

LA PALOMA

AV MIGUEL HIDALGO

CASA DE LAS ARTESANÍAS

TEMPLO Y ARCO DEL CARMEN

AV MIGUEL HIDALGO

GUADALUPE VICTORIA

EMILIANO'S MOUSTACHE

LA SELVA CAFÉ

AV CRESCENCIO ROSAS

BARRIO SAN ANTONIO

BARRIO DE LA MERCED

DIEGO DE MAZARIEGOS

POST OFFICE

NIÑOS HÉROES

IGNACIO ALLENDE

OBREGÓN

ÓPTIMA CAR RENTAL

MATAMOROS

Parque La Merced

LA PALMA

CUAUHTÉMOC

POSADA LOS MORALES

ALVARO

To Chamula and Huitepec Eco-Reserve

MUSEO DEL ÁMBAR

TEMPLO SAN CRISTÓBAL (EL CERRITO)

To Chiapa de Corzo and Tuxtla Gutiérrez

BLVD JUAN SABINES GUTIÉRREZ (CARRETERA PANAMERICANA)

© AVALON TRAVEL PUBLISHING, INC.

women) from various villages in the highlands. Some of San Cristóbal's finest weavings are found here; prices are a bit higher than at the market just outside (although still very reasonable), and you can be assured you are getting a quality product and that the profit is going directly to the artisan. In the church courtyard and adjoining park, indigenous and San Cristóbal artisans (and even a few foreigners) sell great handmade crafts in a large market.

La Catedral

San Cristóbal's cathedral was constructed in 1528 on the north side of the main square. The facade is a standout, its bright yellow-ochre contrasting with 17th-century white mortared niches and geometric designs painted white, rust, and black. The best photo-ops are in the mid- to late afternoon, when the sun ignites the west-facing church front in brilliant display. The nave and altar are decorated with fine religious art—don't miss the elaborately carved wooden pulpit. The cathedral and the plaza in front of it come to life during festivals and religious holidays, especially leading

© LIZA PRADO CHANDLER

the intricate columns of Templo Santo Domingo

up to Easter and December 12 (saint's day for the Virgen of Guadalupe).

Templo San Cristóbal (El Cerrito)

On July 17, the Catholic faithful stream up and down the path to this 17th-century church to give honor to St. Cristóbal. And that's no easy task—the church is on a *cerrito* (small hilltop) and is reached by a steep (and not very small) set of about 240 steps. It's a nice place to visit at any time of the year, affording a panoramic view of the entire town. If you're not up to the climb, there is a road up the backside; a cab to the top costs US$1.25. Do not visit here at night, as assaults have been reported.

Museo de Trajes Regionales

Anyone who is entranced with Chiapas's indigenous culture will enjoy a visit to the Museum of Regional Dress (Calle Guadalupe Victoria s/n, tel. 967/678-4289). Actually the private collection of local collector Sergio García, the "museum" has changed location a few times through the years and is liable to do so again during the life of this book. In any case, you must call ahead to make an appointment, at which point you'll be told when and where to go. Visitors are most often received in the afternoon, and García seems to prefer a minimum of three or four people to open up. Well versed in the cultural history of Chiapas, García gives tours/lectures in Spanish, English, or French, with explanations of the clothes that play such an important cohesive role in each village, and a few anecdotes and legends as well. There's no set admission fee, but a US$2–3 donation is customary.

Museo del Ámbar de Chiapas

Chiapas is the amber capital of Mexico and the world's third most important source of the ancient iridescent material, after the Baltics and the Dominican Republic. Amber is fossilized tree sap, 30–40 million years in the making, and is usually yellow but sometimes is found in red, green, blue, or pink. Anyone who has read or seen *Jurassic Park* knows that insects (and other things) are sometimes preserved in amber; while no one has managed to extract DNA from

AMBER

Amber comes from the resin of pine trees that covered various regions of the earth 40 million to 50 million years ago. Through time, natural catastrophes altered the earth's crust and buried forests of now-extinct conifers. Many of these vanished trees—among them, the *succinifer* pine—could secrete great quantities of resin. Eventually, through an almost eternal process of petrification, this resin transformed into amber.

Hard and brittle in form, amber is golden, although it can have many different tones such as white, pink, red, wine, brown, or black. It can be opaque, transparent, or marbled, depending on its degree of purity. It also emits a unique aroma when burned.

Insects sometimes are found trapped in the amber—an occurrence that dramatically raises its value. Samples found have enabled entomologists to classify almost 75 insect species from the Tertiary and Cretaceous periods. The advantage of studying an insect specimen preserved in amber is that the insect's molecular structure has remained intact—excellent conditions under which to study the creature.

Primitive civilizations attributed magical properties to amber and throughout history, numerous references have been made to its importance. Amber also has had many names. The Greeks called it *electron* because of its capacity to accumulate electricity; the Romans referred to it as *succo* (juice) because of its resinous origins; and because of its similarity to water bubbles, the Aztecs called it *apozonalli* (water foam).

In Chiapas, there is evidence of amber as early as 250 B.C. Its distribution has helped determine the commercial routes of ancient Mayan traders across Central America. It was principally used by Mayans as an adornment—nose and lip rings, earrings, and necklaces. Certain Mayan groups even placed amber bracelets on their children to protect them from the "evil eye." With the passage of time, the mestizo population adopted this custom and added to it attributes of good luck.

Amber was first mined near Simojovel, a small town in northern Chiapas. Throughout the years new veins have been discovered. Unfortunately for the amber miners, however, the resin has always been found in hard-to-reach places where landslides are a constant danger. To find amber deposits, miners begin by searching for layers of coal, a highly risky job because of the condition of the loose, shaky terrain. Once coal is found, a tunnel is drilled and large blocks of it are cut away until the amber is found.

Generally raw amber is sold to artisans, who with the help of sandpaper and files polish the pieces to give them a beautiful finish. Once the amber has been polished, the artisans shape pieces into a great variety of forms: Vine leaves, crosses, feathers, raindrops, triangles, and flowers are among the most popular. Amber also is used in jewelry—earrings, rings, bracelets, necklaces—you name it, it has probably been done.

amber, it does provide researchers with important insights on dinosaur-era insects, plants, and even atmospheric conditions, through analysis of trapped air bubbles. The worthwhile Museo del Ámbar de Chiapas (Ex-Convento de la Merced, tel. 967/678-9716, 10 A.M.–2 P.M. and 4–7 P.M. Tues.–Sun., US$1.75) has a large collection of raw and sculpted amber, of various colors and qualities, much of it quite beautiful. There are displays on how amber is mined, how it was used in Mayan society, and how to distinguish real amber from the glass and plastic imitations sold on the streets here (genuine amber is lightweight, never cold to the touch, has slightly irregular color and shape, and pieces with insects are rare and very expensive). While you're there, peek into the restored Merced convent, dating from the 16th century.

Museo Mesoamericano del Jade

The overglorified Mesoamerican Museum of Jade (Av. 16 de Septiembre at Calle 5 de Febrero, tel. 967/678-2557, www.eljade.com, noon–9 P.M. Mon.–Sat., 10 A.M.–6 P.M. Sun., US$2.50) is a small display in the Casa del Jade store. It is made up of jade reproductions of Mayan masks and artifacts, including ones from Tikal, Copán, and the famous funerary mask of K'inich Janaab Pakal found in the Temple of the Inscriptions at Palenque. At the end is a large, rather underwhelming reproduction of Pakal's tomb.

Museo del Café

Coffee was introduced to Mexico in the late 17th century and first grown in Chiapas around 1820–1850. But it wasn't until the Porfiriato (the 1877–1911 dictatorship of President Porfirio Díaz), and a coinciding worldwide coffee boom, that Mexican coffee really took off. Díaz was a fanatic of all things foreign, especially French, and he threw the Mexican economy open to European and American investment. Chiapas had fewer than 50 coffee plantations in 1900 but more than 180 just a decade later, with more in neighboring Oaxaca and Veracruz. Most were owned by German, British, and American planters. The one-room Museum of Coffee (Calle Mariá Adelina Flores between Avs. Belisario Domínguez and General Utrilla, tel. 967/678-7876, 9 A.M.–9 P.M. Mon.–Sat., 4–9 P.M. Sun., donations accepted) tells these and other stories of Chiapanecan coffee while gently prodding you into the much more spacious café in the back. To its credit, the café does serve excellent coffee. The museum and café are affiliated with Tuxtla-based COOPCAFE, a Spanish acronym for Organization of Small Coffee Producers (tel. 961/611-0563, coopcafe@prodigy.net.mx).

Museo Centro Cultural de los Altos

Los Altos (the highlands) refers to the Chiapanecan high country, where most of the state's indigenous people live. The fine Museo Centro Cultural de los Altos (Templo Domingo, 10 A.M.–5 P.M. Mon.–Sat., 10 A.M.–3 P.M. Sun., US$3, free on Sun.) includes displays in Spanish on pre-Hispanic customs and culture, the arrival of the Spanish, and ancient and contemporary Mayan art. Upstairs is a large gallery

space—when we visited, there was a spectacular collection of handwoven textiles from various highland regions. The building itself, part of Templo Santo Domingo, is quite impressive, with high archways, wood floors, and thick stone and adobe walls painted a rich yellow.

Taller Leñateros

Taller Leñateros (Calle Flavio A. Paniagua 54 at Calle Huixtla, tel. 967/678-5174, 9 A.M.–8 P.M. Mon.–Fri., 8 A.M.–1:30 P.M. Sat.) is an award-winning collective of more than 20 Mayan men and women who create beautiful handmade paper products using materials such as flower petals, grass, vines, moss, recycled paper, and rags. Along with unique art cards, notebooks, photo albums, and so on, you'll find woodblock prints representing both ancient and current Mayan artistic themes. The *taller* (workshop) also produces a good guide to natural dyes, and when we stopped in was putting final touches on an English version of a book of Mayan women's incantations and spells. It all began in 1974 as the private workshop of artist and naturalized-Mexican citizen Ámbar Past. After taking on a number of apprentices, Past (who speaks Tzotzil) converted the workshop into a cooperative, which operates collectively and accepts no outside funding. Some of the artists here have gone on to participate in international expositions. Free tours are offered anytime, or you can sign up for workshops (US$22, two hours) in papermaking, bookbinding, screen printing, making natural dyes, and more. There is a gift shop on-site.

Museo de la Medicina Maya

A long way from the center but worth the trip, the Mayan Medicine Museum (Av. Salomón González Blanco 10, Col. Morelos, tel. 967/678-5438, omiech@laneta.apc.org, 10 A.M.–6 P.M. Mon.–Fri., 10 A.M.–5 P.M. Sat.–Sun., US$1.75) has creative and interesting displays on ancient and contemporary Mayan medical practices, including a fascinating section on childbirth. A garden displays medicinal plants, while a small shop sells products made from them. The museum is a project of OMIECH, an association of indigenous doctors in Chiapas, and at the museum you can request a consultation for ailments of any sort (Mon.–Fri. only); remedies include ritual cleanings, prayers, and herbal products. The museum is a half-hour walk (or more) from town, straight north on Avenida General Utrilla. A cab there will cost US$1.25.

Na Bolom

Once the home of the late Swiss-Danish couple Gertrude (Trudy) Duby Blom and the archaeologist Frans Blom, Na Bolom (Av. Vicente Guerrero No. 33, tel. 967/678-1418, www .nabolom.org, 10 A.M.–6 P.M. daily) today is a museum/research center/guesthouse that is definitely worth a stop. Arriving in San Cristóbal in the 1920s to work on a dig at Moxviquil, the Bloms spent their lifetimes here—Frans involved in archaeological excavations throughout the Yucatán Peninsula (including Bonampak) and Trudy becoming one of the first (and most renowned) photographers of the reclusive Lacandón Indians. Both became very committed to the preservation of the Lacandóns and the Chiapanecan rainforest. The museum (10 A.M.–6 P.M. daily, US$3) is a natural extension of the Bloms' interests and has an excellent exhibit on life in the jungle (Na Balom means Jaguar House in Tzeltal); the rambling home itself, however, holds room upon room of Mayan artifacts, memoirs, and innumerable black and white photographs taken by Trudy. A lush and large garden also holds regional vegetables, trees, flowers, and plants—visitors are welcome to wander through it. Scholars and social scientists from around the world often can be found in the inviting library, which holds an impressive collection of books and articles relating to the indigenous peoples of Mexico and Central America. Guided tours of the museum and home are offered daily at 11:30 A.M. and 4:30 P.M. (English and Spanish, US$4) and include a film on the Bloms' work with the Lacandóns. There is also an excellent gift shop (see *Shopping;* for information on guestrooms, see *Accommodations*).

ENTERTAINMENT AND EVENTS

Fiestas

This is a very colorful city all year-round, but it comes to life on Catholic holidays, which indigenous people and communities celebrate with vigor. **Semana Santa** (Holy Week, leading up to Easter) is not only an important religious holiday but a big travel and vacation week for all Mexicans; San Cristóbal gets packed with indigenous faithful, local merchants, and visitors from Mexico City, Veracruz, and elsewhere. December 12th is saint's day for the Virgin of Guadalupe, and it is celebrated with *peregrinaciones* (pilgrimages)— groups of churchgoers who run or walk for several days from surrounding cities to San Cristóbal's hilltop Church of Guadalupe. No matter what the holiday, expect firecrackers, paper streamers, marimba music, and lots of street food.

Cinema

The large number of backpackers, researchers, and NGO workers in San Cristóbal has spawned several alternative cinema clubs, mostly showing art films, progressive documentaries, and a handful of Hollywood favorites here and there. **Cine Club La Ventana** (Av. Insurgentes 19 by Madre Tierra restaurant, cinelaventana@yahoo .com.mx) shows two movies every weeknight at 6:15 P.M. and 8:30 P.M., and three from Friday to Sunday at 5 P.M., 7 P.M., and 9 P.M. Admission is US$1.75, or US$3 for two movies and a bag of popcorn. You can find its monthly schedule at the tourist office and posted at many restaurants, shops, and hotels around town.

Other film clubs with a similar lineup include **Kinoki** (Calle Real de Guadalupe 20 between Avs. Utrilla and Belisario Domínguez, two films Sun.–Thurs. at 6 P.M. and 8 P.M., three films Fri.–Sat. at 6 P.M., 8 P.M., and 10 P.M., US$1.75) and **Centro El Puente** (Calle Real de Guadalupe 55 at Av. Josefa Ortiz de Domínguez, tel. 967/678-3723, two films nightly at 6:15 P.M. and 8:30 P.M., US$1.50).

Theater

The imposing, green-painted **Teatro Daniel Zebadua** (Av. 20 de Noviembre and Calle 5 de Febrero) regularly presents live theater and cultural expositions. When we visited, the theater was showing *Señor de la Tierra,* an innovative show inspired by the murals at Bonampak ruins and featuring fantastic costumes and dialogue entirely in Tzotzil Mayan. Tickets vary depending on the performance but are typically US$10–20 and are sold at the theater's box office or a small booth right on the pedestrian walkway.

Bars and Live Music Venues

San Cristóbal has a vibrant night life. Befitting the city's artsy progressive atmosphere, expect mostly small bars featuring live acoustic and rock music as opposed to loud glitzy nightclubs. Only a couple stay open past midnight, so don't wait too long to get your groove going.

Revolución Café (Av. 20 de Noviembre at 1 de Marzo, 11:30 A.M.–midnight Mon.–Sat.) is a popular corner bar with a small bandstand in the window. Come for two-for-one drink specials 5–8 P.M. and decent rock music starting around 9 P.M.

After Revolución Café closes, stagger a half block to **El Circo Bar** (Av. 20 de Noviembre Nat 1 de Marzo) where live music, drum and dance show, and general late-night revelry don't pick up until 11 P.M. and continue well into the wee hours. Thursdays are two-for-one drinks all night.

Other popular options include the more swanky **Blue Café Bar and Theatre** (tel. 967/678-2200), where a US$5 cover is sometimes collected and the fun starts around 11 P.M., and **Zapata** (Av. 5 de Mayo No. 2 at Diego de Mazariegos, tel. 967/678-3355) which has more of a local scene.

SHOPPING

If you like *artesanías,* you'll love San Cristóbal. Teeming with shops and markets, this town is a mecca for indigenous-made art—clothing, toys, linens, amber jewelry—you'll be hard-pressed to leave without buying something. Bargaining is accepted, but be fair. Many artisans simply charge for the cost of the materials; their time is given for free.

Markets

Every day the plaza surrounding Templo Santo Domingo is filled with artisans selling their work: colorful *huipiles,* thick wool sweaters, embroidered placemats, woven belts, Zapatista dolls. The list of handmade items is seemingly endless. That said, be sure to take a walk around the market before you buy—you're sure to be able to tell a machine-made knock-off from the real thing within a few minutes. The market is open 8 A.M.–sunset daily.

Art and Handicrafts

The excellent, state-run **Casa de las Artesanías** (Av. Miguel Hidalgo at Niños Héroes, tel. 967/678-1180, 9 A.M.–9 P.M. Mon.–Sat., 10 A.M.–3 P.M. Sun.) sells first-rate items at reasonable prices. Here you're sure to find something from every corner of Chiapas—from amber jewelry to hand-painted toys. Salespeople are particularly helpful and often will share their knowledge about an item—the region it comes from, the process of creating it, and in some cases, even about the artist herself.

Though specializing in Cuban books, **Librería Cultura Cubana** (Calle Real de Guadalupe No. 61 between Diego Dugelay and Cristóbal Colón, no phone 9 A.M.–2 P.M. and 4–6 P.M. daily) has a great Zapatista section (see the sidebar *Zapatistas*). In a town where Sub-Comandante Marcos's image is seen on almost every block, this store stands apart: You'll find beautifully hand-stitched T-shirts, colorful handkerchiefs, and one-of-a-kind wall hangings—all with messages in support of the EZLN cause.

Next door, **El Encuentro** (Calle Real de Guadalupe 63-A, tel. 967/678-3698, 9 A.M.–8 P.M. Mon.–Sat., 5–8 P.M. Sun.) sells beautiful regional art, including embroidered *huipiles,* ceremonial hats, and shawls. Beautiful bolts of woven cloth are also for sale.

For high-end Lacondón *artesanía* as well as artsy postcards and books, head to **Na Bolom** (Av. Vicente Guerrero No. 33, tel. 967/678-1418, 10 A.M.–2 P.M. and 4–7 P.M. Mon.–Sat.). A bit off the beaten track, it's well worth your every step. Consider stopping into its museum/

The State of Chiapas

Chiapanecan handicrafts are known for their brilliant colors, creative flair, and high quality.

research center across the street—it's a treat in itself. (See *Sights*.)

For some of the finest textiles around, visit **Sna Jolobil** (Templo Santo Domingo, Lázaro Cárdenas No. 42, tel. 967/678-2646, snajolobil@prodigy.net.mx, 9 A.M.–2 P.M. and 4–6 P.M. Mon.–Sat.). This profit-sharing co-op (whose name means House of Weaving in Tzotzil) is made up of 700 weavers from 20 Tzotzil- and Tzeltal-speaking villages in the highlands of Chiapas. In fact, the creation of Sna Jolobil has encouraged a revitalization of Mayan art—especially among the younger generation—and has confirmed the importance of preserving ancient designs as well as the creation of new ones. Definitely worth a visit, these outstanding works of textile art are hard to resist. Displayed with set prices. Credit cards accepted.

Another great co-op to check out is **Najel** (Belisario Domínguez No. 8-A between María Adelina Flores and Real de Guadalupe, tel. 967/674-0347, 9 A.M.–8 P.M. daily). Run by indigenous women, this is a small boutique selling handcrafted fabrics from neighboring villages. The artists themselves are often on

hand to tell you about their work; you're certain to leave in awe of their talent (and probably with an item or two). Credit cards accepted.

Bookstores

La Pared (Av. Miguel Hidalgo 2, tel. 967/678-6367, lapared9@yahoo.com, 10 A.M.–2 P.M., 4–8 P.M. Tues.–Sun.) is San Cristóbal's best source of English-language books, offering an excellent selection of new and used novels and classics, Mexican and Mayan history and art books, textbooks for learning Spanish, and current travel guides and maps. You can exchange books (two-for-one), and the shop usually has a small stock of high-quality *artesanía* as well. American expat/owner Dana Gay Burton has lived in San Cristóbal since 1994 and has plenty of no-nonsense information about the city and region. Open on Mondays during high season.

Just below the market at Templo Santo Domingo, **Librería Chilam Balam** (Casa Utrilla, Av. General Utrilla and Calle Dr. Navarro, tel. 967/678-0486, 9:30 A.M.–7:30 P.M. daily) has a decent selection of guidebooks, maps, Mayan and Mexican history books, and CDs. A number of titles are available in

English, French, Italian, and German. The bookstore is part of Casa Utrilla, a large building and courtyard with a restaurant, *artesanía* shop, and more. The French owner, Gerard, also speaks Spanish and English and has been in San Cristóbal since 1989.

La Isla (Calle Real de Guadalupe 4 at Av. Josefa Ortíz de Domínguez, no phone, 10 A.M.–2 P.M., 5–8 P.M. Mon.–Sat.) also carries English-language guidebooks and has a varied collection of CDs and new and used books, mostly in Spanish.

SPORTS AND RECREATION

Huitepec Reserve

Just a few kilometers from San Cristóbal, Huitepec is a cloud-forest reserve on the side of an extinct volcano, where several kilometers of well-marked trails make for a pleasant, safe outdoor excursion. Basic admission is US$1.25 per person, or you can hire one of three on-site guides for a two-hour tour (US$3.50 pp). At least one of the guides speaks English. With a day's notice, you can also arrange a 7 A.M. bird-watching tour (US$9 pp); more than 80 species of birds have been spotted in the park. To reserve a bird-watching tour, or for any additional information, visit or call **Pronatura** (Av. Miguel Hidalgo 9, tel. 967/678-5000, www.pronatura-chiapas.org, 9 A.M.–4 P.M. Mon.–Fri.). Otherwise, you can go straight there—take a *colectivo* toward San Juan Chamula from the market on Avenida General Utrilla (ask around as there are several bus stops). Tell the driver you are going to Huitepec (3.5 km/2.2 miles, US$.35); from the dropoff, it's about 200 meters (656 feet) to the reserve entrance. To return, walk to the road and catch a *colectivo* headed back to town. Camping is not allowed in the reserve.

Horseback Riding

The listed tour operators (see *Information and Services*) all offer half-day horseback-riding tours. The most popular is a 75-minute ride through the hills to the indigenous village of San Juan Chamula, which you can visit for

an hour or so before riding back. The cost is usually US$9–11 per person. Ideally, your riding guide would double as a guide to San Juan Chamula, but this is rarely the case. Be sure to confirm how much actual riding you'll get and that you won't be riding along the roadside.

Massage

Rakshita (also known as Elke Leiste, a German expat, Prol. Yajalón 59, Col. Revolución Méxicana, tel. 967/631-3249, www.rakshita .com) offers highly recommended two-hour full-body massages for the unbelievable price of US$18. Call ahead for an appointment.

ACCOMMODATIONS

San Cristóbal has plenty of lodging options in all price ranges, from great hostels to luxurious hacienda-type hotels. However, there are surprisingly few small bed-and-breakfasts—we have only one listed here—despite the number of beautiful colonial homes around town. Such hotels are very popular and successful in Mérida, and it seems only a matter of time before they begin popping up in San Cristóbal. When they do, they will surely make leaving here that much harder.

Under US$25

Without a doubt, **Posada México** (Dr. Felipe Flores No. 16, tel. 967/678-0014, posada mexico@hotmail.com, www.hostellingmexico .com, US$2.65 pp camping (tent not included), US$3.50 pp camping (tent included), US$3.50 pp hammock (BYO hammock), US$5.25 pp dorm, US$13 s/d with shared bath, US$16 s/d with private bath) is one of the best hostels in southeastern Mexico. Affiliated with Hostelling International, it is set in a converted colonial home with nice garden areas and courtyards. A charming reading room, two TV areas (with DVD players and VCRs), and a pleasant kitchen (with three refrigerators to boot) also are available to all guests. And the rooms? Three single-sex dorms, one mixed dorm, and 14 private rooms (eight of which are in independent *casitas* in the garden) are very well kept —when we passed through, all of the mattresses were being replaced and new, custom-made bunk beds were being installed. Breakfast (continental for tent/hammock/dorm guests, continental plus eggs for private room guests) is included in the rate. Area excursions, Internet access (US$.70/hour), and bike rentals (US$5/day with helmet) also are offered. English, French, and Italian spoken. An excellent choice.

A 10-minute walk from the main plaza brings you to **Casa Di Gladys** (Calle Cintalapa No. 6 between Av. Diego Dugelay and Calle Huixtla, tel. 967/678-5775, casagladys@hotmail.com, US$3.50 pp dorm, US$9/10.50–16 s/d private room with shared bath), a hip hostel on a quiet street. Psychedelic murals, a great kitchen with two stoves, comfy lounge areas, and a rooftop hammock/barbecue area are some of the nicer features here. Although needing a fresh coat of paint, the rooms are comfortable—dorms hold just 3–5 twin beds (no bunks here!) and some private rooms, while tiny, have king-sized beds. A free ride from the bus station is included, as is Internet access. Especially popular with younger 20-somethings.

The well-situated **Hotel San Martín** (Calle Real de Guadalupe No. 16, tel. 967/678-0533, hotelsanmartin@prodigy.net.mx, US$13 s, US$19 d) is a very simple but clean hotel. Rooms have twin beds, tile floors, and private bathrooms—and that's about it. Friendly service.

A fantastic value, **Posada Jovel** (Flavio Paniagua No. 28, tel. 967/678-1734, hotel jovel@hotmail.com, www.mundochiapas .com/hotelposadajovel, US$9 s with shared bath, US$11.50 d with shared bath, US$18 s with private bath, US$22 d with private bath, US$31 s/d deluxe) is a great place to stay if you don't mind being a little off the beaten track. Rooms here are sunny, attractive, and very clean. Even the lower-end ones! Internet access is available on-site (US$.90/hour) and a huge buffet breakfast is offered to guests every morning (US$3.50). The newer and more ample deluxe rooms are across the street in a renovated colonial building and are often filled with tour groups—be sure to call in advance if you'd like one of these. Also take a peek at the solarium—the views of the city are breathtaking. English and French spoken.

US$25–50

Totally renovated in 2004, the **Ⅶ Hotel Casa Margarita** (Calle Real de Guadalupe 34, tel. 967/678-0957, US$22 s, US$26 d) has transformed from a dingy posada into one of the best budget deals in town. Its 25 cozy rooms—all with private bath, hot water, cable TV, and parking—now grace the stone hallways of this colonial hotel. Just a couple of blocks from the main plaza, it is a serious find.

A pleasing, rambling place, the **Hotel Palacio de Moctezuma** (Av. Juárez No. 16 at Francisco Léon, tel. 967/678-0352, www.palaciodemoctezuma.com.mx, US$26 s, US$31 d) has 43 rooms, small courtyards, three gardens, a fountain, one solarium, and a quiet sitting room. Rooms are equally diverse—different sizes, ages, views, and decor—but all are modern, clean, and incredibly quiet—a rare commodity in this popular town. If your room doesn't have a view, be sure to check out the spectacular vista from the solarium—it is truly breathtaking.

Smack-dab in the middle of the action is the **Hotel Posada San Cristóbal** (Av. Insurgentes No. 3, tel. 967/678-6881, hotelsancristobal@ hotmail.com, US$37 s, US$42 d). Once a beautiful colonial home, it is now a charming 18-room hotel with heavy wood furnishings. Rooms here are an excellent value—spacious with brick or wood floors, *talavera*-tiled bathrooms and colorful Chiapanecan bedspreads. Some even have balconies overlooking the bustling street below. Be sure to set aside some time to enjoy a book or a glass of wine in the second-floor sitting area—with its rocking chairs and views of the piñata-filled courtyard, it's truly relaxing.

Just across the street from the Templo Santo Domingo is the cozy **Hotel Plaza Santo Domingo** (Av. Utrilla No. 35, tel. 967/678-6514, cielo3@prodigy.net.mx, www.hotelplaza santodomingo.com, US$35 s, US$44 d). Set throughout a remodeled colonial home, the 38 rooms are quiet, clean, and have comfortable beds. All have cable TV and telephones. Some rooms on the top floor also have great views of the neighboring temple. In the low season, ask for a discount—rates can drop up to 50 percent.

Once the childhood home of one of the co-owners, **Hotel Posada El Paraíso** (Calle 5 de Febrero No. 19 at Av. 16 de Septiembre, tel. 967/678-0085, hparaiso@prodigy.net .mx, www.hotelposadaparaiso.com, US$33 s, US$44 d) is a delightful hotel just steps from the main plaza. Completely renovated, the cozy rooms have textured ocher and blue walls, heavy wood beam ceilings, and Guatemalan bedspreads. Some also have handmade ladders that take guests to a loft with a twin bed—great if you're traveling with kids. Paraíso's restaurant also is considered one of the best in town—Swiss chef and co-owner Daniel Suter prepares excellent cheese and beef fondues, mushrooms sautéed in garlic, and the best steak in town (see *Food*).

Probably the best value in town is the  **Villas Casa Morada** (Av. Diego Dugelay No. 45 at Chiapa de Corzo, tel. 967/706-3996, lacasamorada@yahoo.com, www.geocities .com/lacasamorada). Set in a completely remodeled home, here you'll find five charming studios (US$39/night, US$210/week) and three two-bedroom condos (US$80/night, US$418/week) with views of the surrounding mountains. Each comes complete with ironworked furniture, fully equipped *talavera*-tiled kitchen, telephone (local calls included in the rate), free in-room Internet connection (BYO laptop and network cable), and wood-burning fireplace. The only downside is finding someone to rent you a room when the owner is away; there was no full-time attendant when we were in town and it took several phone calls and three visits to finally get in.

US$50–100

One of the places you'll wish you could call home is **Casa Felipe Flores** (Calle Dr. Felipe Flores No. 36, tel. 967/678-3998, www

.felipeflores.com, US$80–95 s/d), a bed-and-breakfast just a few blocks from the main plaza. A colonial-era gem, this home shines in every way; architectural nuances and beautiful folk art combine perfectly with lush courtyards and mountain views. Open the door to one of the five cozy guest rooms and you'll find fireplaces, high wood-beamed ceilings, and *talavera*-tiled bathrooms. The living room, with its rich fabrics, striking artwork, comfy couches, and—on cold nights—raging fire, will make you feel even more at home. In the evening, be sure to have a glass of wine with the charming owners—Nancy and David Orr—or, at the very least, make use of the honor bar tucked inside an antique chest. A true bed-and-breakfast, here a hearty and healthy breakfast is included in the rate.

About a 10-minute walk from the center of town is the **Hotel Rincón del Arco** (Ejercito Nacional No. 66 at Av. Vicente Guerrero, tel. 967/678-1313, www.rincondelarco.com, US$52 single, US$70–78 double). Originally built in 1650, this colonial complex has undergone several renovations since then. Today,

one of the gardens at Na Bolom

it is a beautiful architectural work: tile floors, brick-arched doorways, white stucco walls, heavy wood-beam ceilings, and flower-filled inner patios. Inside this complex, the 50 rooms are divided into two sections: some in the original dwelling with antique furnishings and fireplaces, the rest in newer sections with modern furniture and carpeting. The most charming are in the original building overlooking the expansive garden—rose bushes and all—that takes up almost an entire city block. Modern rooms on the top floor also have glorious views of the city and its churches.

A popular spot and with good reason is the museum/research center **Na Bolom** (Av. Vicente Guerrero No. 33, tel. 967/678-1418, www.nabolom.org, US$50 s, US$60–80 d; see *Sights*). Set in the lovely colonial-style home of the late Trudy and Frans Blom, the 16 rooms are colorful and earthy, each beautifully appointed with the artwork of different indigenous villages, and most with fireplaces that keep the rooms warm on chilly nights. The recently renovated junior suites are stunning—with king-sized beds, whirlpool bathtubs, and glorious views of the lush gardens, you'll never want to leave. An inviting library is a great place to relax as is the dining room, where guests—often visiting scholars, social scientists, and travelers with a keen interest in the Mayan culture—join for family-style dinners (US$10).

Hotel Casa Mexicana (28 de Agosto No. 1 at Av. Utrilla, tel. 967/678-0698, hcasamex@ prodigy.net.mx, www.hotelcasamexicana.com, US$65–72) is an upscale hotel in the heart of downtown. Set in a renovated colonial building with burnished terra-cotta colored walls and skylight-covered courtyards, it also has a lush atrium replete with tropical plants, palm trees, and a stone-edged pond. Original artwork on the walls leads to smallish modern rooms that are nicely appointed with carved wood headboards and bright Chiapanecan bedspreads. Some rooms on the second floor boast angled wood-beam ceilings. For a splurge, book one of the spacious junior suites, which have a living room and whirlpool tub. The annex across the street has similar rooms. A once-good, now-mediocre restaurant is on the premises.

The welcoming lobby of the **Hotel Casa Vieja** (Calle María Adelina Flores No. 27, tel. 967/678-6868, www.casavieja.com.mx, US$65–74 s/d) is a good indication of what you'll find inside: colonial-style rooms with wood-beam ceilings, hand-carved furniture, and *talavera*-tiled bathrooms. Although somewhat small, they are a lovely place to spend the night. The restaurant here is well recommended, especially for Sunday brunch (see *Food*).

Over US$100

Set on a green stretch of land on the edge of town, the 17th- and 18th-century buildings of **Parador San Juan de Díos** (Calzada Roberta No. 16, tel. 967/678-1167, www. sanjuandedios.com, US$145–270 s/d) are now home to one of the finest hotels in San Cristóbal. The 13 good-sized rooms have an eclectic art collector's feel to them: antique Mexican furnishings, original oil paintings, oriental rugs, and the finest in amenities. Think high society meets bohemian artist in colonial Mexico. Each different from the other, no room disappoints—they are breathtaking. Excellent service. An elegant Mediterranean restaurant on-site serves creative dishes (barbecued rabbit among them) but has received mixed reviews.

FOOD
Mexican

Emiliano's Moustache (Crescencio Rosas 7, tel. 967/678-7246, 8 A.M.–1 A.M. daily) has one of the best *comida corrida* deals in town: just US$3 for an appetizer, soup, entrée, dessert, beverage, and coffee. (1–6 P.M. only). But just as many people come for the *tacos al pastor,* the tasty red meat sliced off a rotating spit and served with corn tortillas made fresh on the spot. The very hungry should try Emiliano's Special, an artery-hardening delicacy composed of several meats, melted cheese, green peppers, mushrooms, and whatever else the cook has on hand at the moment, served with tortillas and big enough for two. Several vegetarian options are available as well.

Restaurante Tuluc (Insurgentes 5 at Calle Cuauhtemoc, tel. 967/678-2090, 6:30 A.M.– 10 P.M. daily, US$2–9) has a dim, narrow dining area with indigenous crafts displayed at the entrance. It's another good spot to go for lunch—the *comida corrida* includes a small mixed drink to start, followed by bread and soup, an entrée (fish, chicken, or meat, usually served with rice) and dessert and coffee. A couple of different *parrillada* specials include up to five different grilled meats, onions, and guacamole, and feed two.

For good cheap eats, **Restaurante Normita** (Av. Benito Juárez 6 at Calle José Felipe Flores, tel. 967/674-5317, 7 A.M.–11 P.M. daily, US$2.50–5) serves local specialties at a half dozen tables with Chiapanecan coverings. It's low-key and friendly, and locals and tourists alike stop in for *pozole,* squash flower quesadillas, platefuls of cheese enchiladas, and more.

Hotel Casa Vieja (7 A.M.–11 P.M. daily, US$6–15) has a great Sunday buffet and a fine selection of contemporary and classic Mexican dishes.

International

⋈ La Paloma (Av. Hidalgo 3 at Calle Cuauhtemoc, tel. 967/678-1547, 8 A.M.–midnight daily, US$3–9) is one of our favorite restaurants in San Cristóbal. The airy front dining area has exposed beams and windows facing the streets, while thick, green plants fill the garden area in back. Try the homemade raviolis, salmon fillet with wild mushroom, or the delicious squash flowers filled with cheese mousse and served with *cuitlacoche* (also written *huitlacoche,* it's a black corn fungus and a Mexican delicacy, though somewhat of an acquired taste).

El Gato Gordo (Calle Francisco Madero 28 at Av. Josefa Ortíz Domínguez, 1 P.M.– 10:30 P.M. daily except Tues., US$1.50–5) advertises as "the backpackers' restaurant" and boasts the cheapest lunch special in town: soup and main dish for US$2. The menu also includes crepes, standard Mexican dishes, and

lots of vegetarian options. It has a full bar and great eclectic decor, with murals, posters, and drawings hanging from the walls and ceiling.

La Parrilla (Av. Belisario Domínguez at Calle Escuadron 201, tel. 967/674-6214, 2– 11 P.M. Tues.–Sun., US$5–12) specializes, naturally, in *parrilla,* large plates of grilled meats served sizzling on metal plates atop wooden boards and usually accompanied by a baked potato or grilled onions. Gnaw on steaks, smoked chicken, pork chops, and sausages, plus a half-dozen variations of *queso fundido* (melted cheese served with tortillas) and *chiles rellenos.*

El Teatro Café (Calle 1 de Marzo 8 at Av. 16 de Septiembre, tel. 967/678-3149, noon– 10:30 P.M. Tues.–Sun., US$4–10) is a comfy, second-floor restaurant around the corner from the theater. The menu has a mix of French, Italian, and Mexican options, including crepes, lasagna, and seasoned grilled meats. The daily menus run US$6–7 and include a fresh salad, soup, main dish, and coffee.

The restaurant at **⋈ Hotel Posada El Paraíso** (Calle 5 de Febrero No. 19 at Av. 16 de Septiembre, tel. 967/678-0085, 7 A.M.–11 P.M. daily, US$6–18) is one of San Cristóbal's best. Swiss chef and co-owner Daniel Suter's cheese and beef fondue is great, Caesar salads are mixed right at your table, and the steak is the best in town. Simple but elegant wood tables occupy two small pleasant dining areas.

Vegetarian

Madre Tierra (Av. Insurgentes 19 at Calle Hnos. Domínguez, tel. 967/678-4297, restaurant 8 A.M.–10 P.M. daily, bar 8 P.M.–3 A.M. Mon.–Sat., US$5–9) is a San Cristóbal institution, serving quality food in a hip, progressive setting since 1987. The menu is mostly but not entirely vegetarian, varying from gnocchi to spinach crepes, and includes fresh breads (which you can also buy at the attached bakery) and a US$6 lunch special. The dining area is in a colonial house with heavy beams, high ceilings, and archways that lead to a lovely patio. At night, enjoy one, two, or more live bands (*trova,* world beat, reggae, and so on), always followed by a couple of hours of salsa. We found service to be a little uneven, but it's still a place worth visiting, day or night.

N Casa de Pan (Calle Dr. Navarro No. 10, tel. 967/678-5895, lacasadelpan@yahoo.com .mx, 8 A.M.–10 P.M. Tues.–Sun., US$3–6) has a bakery in front worth visiting all by itself for its chocolate chip cookies, brownies, croissants— even bagels—and homemade jams. The back dining room, **Papalote,** is a bohemian affair with art on the walls, bougainvillea climbing one wall, and a peaked glass-and-wood ceiling. Breakfast includes homemade granola, whole wheat muffins, and yogurt; lunch and dinner feature steamed rice and veggies, curried vegetable-filled *empanadas,* homemade soups, and quesadillas. A welcome stop for any veggie lover. Live music also is featured 8–10 P.M. Tuesday– Saturday, 2–4 P.M. and 8–10 P.M. Sunday.

Sandwiches and Coffeehouses

You'd be forgiven for thinking **N La Pera** (Calle María Adelina Flores 23 at Av. Cristóbal Colón, tel. 967/678-1209, 11 A.M.–11 P.M. Tues.–Sun., US$2–6) is named for the *pera* fruit (pear), but the name actually comes from the slang way of saying things are all right: *'ta pera* (it's cool). It's an apt name for this hip, friendly bar-restaurant-music venue, newly opened in November 2004. Stop in for an afternoon baguette or pasta dish, served in various small rooms or in the interior courtyard. Or come at night, when you can enjoy beer specials and live music (usually 8–9 P.M.), from *trova* to funk to reggae.

Literally a hole-in-the-wall, **Banabanana** (Av. Miguel Hidalgo between Calles Niños Héroes and Hnos. Domínguez, 9 A.M.–6 P.M. Mon.–Sat., US$1.50–5) has just five tables but the *tortas* and *liquados* are always freshly made and very tasty. Hamburgers, including soy burgers, go for US$2.50, or a bit more if you want fries (worth it). The walls are packed with posters, from Frida Kahlo and Che Guevara to Mayan ruins and random travel shots.

San Cristóbal has a number of homey cafés serving excellent locally grown coffee, plus soups, sandwiches, and pastries. One is **Casa Raíz**

(Calle Niños Héroes 8 at Av. Miguel Hidalgo, tel. 967/674-6577, 1:30 P.M.–midnight Tues.– Sun.) just off the pedestrian walkway, with a bright spacious dining area and attractive stainless steel tables and chairs. Besides a wide selection of coffees, the café has a good four-course lunch special for US$3.50 and live jazz Fridays and Saturdays starting at 9:30 P.M. **Aroma** (Av. 20 de Noviembre at 1 de Marzo, tel. 967/674-5783, 7 A.M.–11 P.M. daily) is smaller and at the other end of the pedestrian walkway, serving good coffee and cakes—try the raspberry cheesecake—at rustic wood tables and wrought-iron chairs. There's a small but good amber and jewelry shop there, too. **La Selva Café** (Av. Crescencio Rosas at Calle Cuauhtemoc, tel. 967/678-7244, 8 A.M.–11 P.M. daily) has 13 different types of coffee and a breakfast special with yogurt, fruit, biscuit, and coffee for US$4.50.

Groceries

Many locals derive no small pride from the fact that their modest little city now has a **Chedraui** megastore (8 A.M.–10 P.M. daily). On the highway west of the bus terminal, the store is fully stocked and even has a McDonald's next door.

Mercado José Castillo (7 A.M.–6 P.M. daily) is a huge sprawling public market with just about anything you could want, from great fresh fruit and vegetables to bootleg CDs and live turkeys. Worth a visit, even just to look.

INFORMATION AND SERVICES

Tourist Information Centers

Just off the main plaza, the **state tourist office** (Av. Hidalgo 1-B, tel. 967/678-6570, www.turismochiapas.gob.mx, 8 A.M.–9 P.M. Mon.–Sat., 9 A.M.–2 P.M. Sun.) has informative, English-speaking staff, and myriad fliers and brochures for area hotels, restaurants, tour operators, and sights. This office is considerably more helpful than the city tourist office, which keeps the same hours and is in the Palacio Municipal.

Medical Services

The best hospital in town is the private Catholic **Hospital la Caridad** (Calle Francisco I.

Madero 61 at Av. J. M. Santiago, tel. 967/678-0733) with 24-hour service, a small chapel, and at least one doctor (Dr. Luís José Sevilla) who speaks English. The public **Hospital General** (Av. Insurgentes 24 at Calle Julio M. Corzo, tel. 967/678-0770) has free 24-hour treatment and pharmacy, but the quality and speed of attention can be uneven. Recommended private doctors include **Dr. Roberto Lobato García** (Especialidades Médicas, Av. Belisario Domínguez 17 at Calle F. Paniagua, tel. 967/678-7777) and the English-speaking **Dr. Renato Zarate** (Clínica Dr. Bonilla, Av. Juárez 60, tel. 967/678-0783).

Pharmacies

Just off the central plaza, **Farmacia Similares** (Calle Diego de Mazariegos at Av. Miguel Hidalgo, tel. 967/678-5960) is open 24 hours.

Police

You can dial 066 from any public phone in Chiapas for emergency services.

Money

Banamex (9 A.M.–4 P.M. Mon.–Fri., 10 A.M.–2 P.M. Sat.) and **Bancomer** (same hours) have offices and 24-hour ATMs on the south and east sides of the central plaza, respectively. Bancomer also has less-busy ATMs at its office on Avenida 16 de Septiembre at Calle 5 de Febrero.

Post Office

The post office (8:30 A.M.–7 P.M. Mon.–Fri., 9 A.M.–1 P.M. Sat.) is at Avenida Ignacio Allende 3, between Calles Cuauhtemoc and Diego de Mazariegos.

Internet

San Cristóbal suffers no shortage of Internet cafés. Among many others are **La Torre de Pakal** (10:30 A.M.–9 P.M. daily) and **PCS** (9 A.M.–9 P.M. daily) across the street from each other on Avenida 20 de Noviembre and Calle 5 de Febrero, both charging US$.90/hour. **Infinitum** (Av. Josefa Ortiz de Domínguez between Calles Madero and Flores, 8 A.M.–10 P.M. daily) charges US$.50/hour for Internet and US$1.25 to burn a CD.

Telephone

El Locutorio (Av. Belisario Domínguez at Calle Real de Guadalupe, tel. 967/674-0529, 8 A.M.–10 P.M. daily) has good web-based phone service for rock-bottom prices: US$.17/minute to the United States and Canada, US$.25/minute to most of Europe. Otherwise, public phones charge US$.45/minute for calls to the United States and Canada. You'll need to buy a Ladatel phone card (the ones with a small gold chip) from any small market.

Immigration Office

The immigration office (tel. 967/678-0292) offers somewhat surly service at its office west of the center at Diagonal Hermanos Paniagua 2, Colonia San Ramón.

Laundry

The tendency of travelers to keep extending their time in San Cristóbal has created a healthy market for laundry shops. You'll find one around almost every corner, including **Lavandería La Rapidita** (Av. Insurgentes between Calles Cuauhtemoc and Niñoes Héroes, tel. 967/678-8059, 8:30 A.M.–8 P.M. Mon.–Sat., US$4 for three kilos, US$4.50 for up to five kilos self-service, 2–4 hour service) and **Lavandería Splash** (Av. Josefa Ortiz de Domínguez between Calles Real de Guadalupe and Madero, no phone, 9 A.M.–8 P.M. Mon.–Sat., 9 A.M.–2 P.M. Sun., US$.90/kilo, same-day service).

Storage

Store your bags at the **ADO bus terminal** (Av. Insurgentes at the highway, tel. 967/0291, open 24 hours) for US$.90 every 12 hours.

Spanish Schools

By far the most recommended Spanish school in town is **Instituto Jovel** (Calle Maria Adelina Flores 21 at Av. Cristóbal Colón, tel. 967/678-4069, www.institutojovel.com). The school offers private and group courses, all taught by professionally trained, native Spanish-speaking instructors. Private classes with homestay are US$240/week, including 15 hours of instruction and seven nights' lodging with three meals per day with a local family. Group classes (15 hours; 2–6 students) are US$185 with homestay. Without homestay, prices are US$165/week for private classes, US$115 for group lessons. The school also offers specialized classes for professionals, such as doctors, teachers, and social workers, which include an extra five hours/week of class (US$11/hour) and visits to local hospitals, and schools. Prices include all books and materials. The school arranges occasional guest lectures and workshops in salsa, cooking, and so on, and can plan excursions to area sights.

Another option is **Centro El Puente** (Calle Real de Guadalupe 55 at Av. Josefa Ortiz de Domínguez, tel. 967/678-3723, centroelpuente@prodigy.net.mex). The center offers one-on-one and group lessons by the hour, day, and week and can arrange homestays. A week package, including 15 hours of instruction, family homestay, and three meals a day, runs US$200/187 for private/group classes. A 10 percent discount applies when you reserve three weeks or more. The center also has a small restaurant, salsa and merengue classes, Internet service (US$.50/hour), nightly movies (US$1.50 pp), massage (approximately US$13/hour), and a small art and textile gallery (free), all open to students and nonstudents alike.

Tour Operators and Travel Agencies

Alex y Raul (tel. 967/678-3741 or tel. 967/678-9141, alexyraul@yahoo.com) has long offered the most highly recommended tours of San Juan Chamula, Zinacantán, and other indigenous villages. What started as a two-man operation has since grown to nearly a dozen guides, but it has not lost the balanced, insightful, and personalized quality that makes the tours so good. Day trips to San Juan Chamula and Zinacantán (US$8.75 pp) meet every day at 9:30 A.M. at the large wooden cross in front of the cathedral (corner of Av. 20 de Noviembre

and Calle Guadalupe Victoria). Alex and Raul are loosely affiliated with the agency **Usetur** (Av. Insurgentes 17 at Calle Niños Héroes, tel. 967/674-5789, usetur@hotmail.com, 9 A.M.–2 P.M., 2–9 P.M. daily), where you can go for additional information.

Zapata Tours (upstairs from Madre Tierra restaurant, Av. Insurgentes 19 at Calle Hnos. Domínguez, tel. 967/674-5152, www.zapata-tours.com, 8:30 A.M.–8 P.M. daily, open later in high season) is run by a young Czech/Mexican couple and offers a huge variety of good tours and transport options. The most popular day trips are to San Juan Chamula and Zinacantán (US$8.75 pp, 9:30 A.M.–1 P.M. and 3–6 P.M. daily), Lagunas de Montebello (US$18–22, 9 A.M.–6 P.M. daily), and Cañon de Sumidero (US$16–20, 9 A.M.–3 P.M.), but the agency also arranges multiday trips with stopovers in Agua Azul, Palenque, the Lacandón forest, Yaxchilán, and Bonampak, with the option to continue to Flores (Guatemala), Chetumal, or even Belize City. The agency is very flexible—with a few days' notice, you can essentially create your own trip from the different elements.

Agencia Chincultik (Calle Real de Guadalupe 34, tel. 967/678-0957, agchincultik@prodigy.net.com, 8 A.M.–10 P.M. daily) is another recommended tour agency, offering many of the same one-day and multiday trips for essentially the same prices. Chincultik also offers tours to Toniná ruins. Tours (US$31 per person, including entrance fees, minimum of three people) leave San Cristóbal at 9 A.M. and return 7 at P.M., and include three hours at the ruins and one hour at nearby Río Japaté.

Explora Ecoturismo y Viajes (Calle 1 de Marzo 30 between Avs. 5 de Mayo and 12 de Octubre, tel. 967/674-6660, www.ecochiapas.com) offers one- and multiday eco-tours to the area in and around the Lacandón rainforest (near Yaxchilán and Bonampak ruins), including hiking, river rafting, and archaeological excursions.

For plane tickets, try **Viajes Pakal** (Calle Cuauhtemoc 6-A, tel. 967/678-2818, www.pakal.com.mx, 9 A.M.–2 P.M., 4–8 P.M. Mon.–Sat.).

SAN CRISTÓBAL BUS SCHEDULES

Departures from the **first-class bus terminal** (Av. Insurgentes s/n, tel. 967/678-0291) include:

Destination	Price	Duration	Schedule
Campeche	US$24	11 hrs	take Mérida bus
Cancún	US$47	17 hrs	12:15 P.M., 2:30 P.M., and 4:30 P.M.*
Chetumal	US$32	11 hrs	take Cancún bus
Ciudad Cuauhtémoc (Guatemalan border)	US$8	3 hrs	7 A.M., 7:30 A.M., 9 A.M., 12:05 P.M., and 5:15 P.M.
Comitán	US$2.50	1.5 hrs	12:05 A.M., 6:45 A.M., 7 A.M., 7:30 A.M., 9 A.M., 10 A.M., 12:05 P.M., 1 P.M., 4:30 P.M., 5:15 P.M., and 9:30 P.M.
Huatulco	US$24	10 hrs	take Puerto Escondido bus
Mérida	US$35	14 hrs	5 P.M.* and 7 P.M.
Mexico City	US$58	13 hrs	4:05 P.M., 5 P.M.*, 5:45 P.M., 6 P.M., 6:30 P.M., 7 P.M.*, and 10:05 P.M.
Oaxaca	US$27	12 hrs	5 P.M. and 10 P.M.
Ocosingo	US$3	2 hrs	take Palenque bus
Palenque	US$9	5 hrs	7:15 A.M., 9 A.M.**, 11 A.M., 12:15 P.M., 2:30 P.M., 4:30 P.M.*, 5 P.M.*, and 7 P.M.

GETTING THERE

Air

San Cristóbal has a nice little airport, but at the time of research there were no commercial planes landing there. Until that changes, the closest major airport is in Tuxtla Gutiérrez, which is served by Mexicana/Aerocaribe and Aviacsa. **Mexicana/AeroCaribe** (tel. 967/678-9309 or toll-free Mex. tel. 800/623-4518, www.mexicana-inter.com.mx, 9 A.M.–10 P.M. daily) has an office in San Cristóbal at Avenida Belisario Domínguez 2-B, between Calles Real de Guadalupe and Madero.

Bus

The **first-class bus terminal** (tel. 967/678-0291) is about seven blocks south of the *parque central* on Avenida Insurgentes, and it has 24-hour luggage storage and an HSBC ATM machine. You can buy bus tickets in town at **Ticket Bus** (Calle Real de Guadalupe 5, half block from the plaza, tel. 967/678-8503, 9 A.M.–2 P.M., 4–8 P.M. Mon.–Sat., 9 A.M.–5 P.M. Sun.).

Getting to Guatemala

If you're headed to Guatemala, it's easy to take a bus to Tapachula or Ciudad Cuauhtémoc and cross from there. **Agencia Chincultik** offers private van service to Antigua (US$60 pp, eight hours), Quetzaltenango/Xela (US$40, five hours), and Panajachel (US$50, seven hours), with a minimum of four people (see *Tour Operators and Travel Agencies*). **Posada México** (Dr. Felipe Flores No. 16, tel. 967/678-0014) also has service, for guests and nonguests, at lower rates if enough people are going.

Destination	Price	Duration	Schedule
Playa del Carmen	US$45	16 hrs	take Cancún bus
Puebla	US$51	11 hrs	take any Mexico City bus except 5:45 and 6 P.M.
Puerto Escondido	US$29	14 hrs	6:15 P.M. and 9 P.M.
Tapachula	US$15	7 hrs	12:05 A.M., 7:30 A.M., 9 A.M., 12:05 P.M., 5:15 P.M., and 9:30 P.M.
Tulum	US$42	15 hrs	12:15 P.M. and 4:30 P.M.*
Tuxtla Gutiérrez	US$3.50	2 hrs	9 A.M., 9:35 A.M., 10:35 A.M., 11:35 A.M., 12:35 A.M., 3:30 P.M.*, 4:05 P.M., 5 P.M., 6:15 P.M., 7:15 P.M.*, 8 P.M.*, 9 P.M., 10 P.M., and 10:05 P.M.
Veracruz	US$38	9 hrs	7:45 P.M., 8:15 P.M.*, and 9:55 P.M.
Villahermosa	US$15	7 hrs	11 A.M., 7:30 P.M., and 9:45 P.M.*

*Denotes deluxe service.
**Denotes second-class service.

First-class buses from San Cristóbal do not enter (or even stop at) Chiapa de Corzo. To get there, catch a Tuxtla-bound *colectivo* on the Carretera Panamericana, the main highway south of the center. There is a stop just east of the bus terminal, or just flag one down along the road. To Chiapa de Corzo, the fare is US$2.50 and the trip takes about 1.5 hours.

Car

Only 50 years ago you could figure a trip up the mountain from Tuxtla Gutiérrez to San Cristóbal was 12 hours by mule. Today it's a 1.5-hour drive on a good but steep and windy road. The state has long promised it will build a modern highway between the two cities, which if/when completed will cut the drive time almost in half. A portion of the new highway has been completed (near Tuxtla) but a combination of bad politics and trouble spanning several ravines has left the rest of the project in limbo.

From Palenque to San Cristóbal, figure 4–5 hours on another winding road. You should never drive this road at night, as many people have been robbed. Groups of men place logs across the road to force cars to stop and then rob the passengers, sometimes at gunpoint. Driving during the day is safe and beautiful, however.

Car Rental

A car can be handy for visiting outlying areas, but bear in mind that tour agencies offer reasonably priced, guided tours to most of the places you're likely to visit with a car. Also, driving the narrow, crowded streets of San Cristóbal can be an adventure, and parking is a real problem; ideally your hotel will have its own parking lot. If you do rent a car, get hold of a good map (try La Pared bookstore) and be extra cautious of pedestrians, bicycles, and animals along the roadside. Again, never drive at night.

Óptima Car Rental (Calle Diego de Mazariegos 39 across from Parque La Merced, tel. 967/674-5409, 9 A.M.–2 P.M., 4–7 P.M. Mon.–Sat.) was the only car rental agency in town when we were here; prices start at around US$50/day for a basic VW bug, but there are occasional specials and you can bargain somewhat.

GETTING AROUND

San Cristóbal is a very walkable city, and all but a couple of sights are easily reached on foot. For those places (or if you're just tuckered out) a taxi is your best option. Scores of cabs ply the streets and you can always find one parked at the *parque central;* a ride costs just US$1.25 anywhere in the city. If you need one early in the morning or late at night, give the reliable **Taxis de San Cristóbal** a ring (tel. 967/678-0067). San Cristóbal also has a number of public buses, but they mainly serve local workers and those coming from surrounding villages, and they are not typically convenient for getting from one tourist sight to the next.

Villages Beyond San Cristóbal

Chamulan women are noted for their beautiful weavings and are easily distinguished by their traditional dress—white *huipiles* with simple flowers embroidered around the necklines and thick black wool skirts cinched with red belts. Many women also wear sky-blue wool *rebozos* (shawls) that sometimes hide a baby tucked into its folds. These garments are handwoven on a waist loom and generally are made of wool that has been carded by the women from animals raised on the family plot.

Chamulan men wear machine-made hats, Western-style pants and shirts, leather boots, and long, woolen tunics; most men wear white tunics and the village leaders wear black tunics. Generally there are three outfits in an Indian's adult life: wedding, fiesta, and everyday. A man also wears a special official dress of authority during the time he serves on the town council.

Women and little girls are often barefooted—it is partly a question of money, but it also stems from a traditional belief that the earth makes women fertile through their feet. Tourists are often tempted to give indigenous people or children shoes, but some recipients experience such unsolicited charity as offensive; it's better to donate shoes (or simply money) to organizations with established relationships with indigenous communities.

Ask at the tourist office, the Spanish schools, or Taller Leñateros for recommended groups.

SAN JUAN CHAMULA

This is the area's largest indigenous town (with more than 10,000 people in the main center area alone, it's really a small city) and most of the indigenous people you see in San Cristóbal are from here. It is also the most visited by outsiders, typically by tour from San Cristóbal. If you feel strange taking a tour—and we certainly did—bear in mind that this allows the town to reap some benefits of tourism while re-

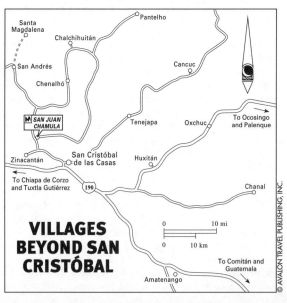

VILLAGES BEYOND SAN CRISTÓBAL

© LIZA PRADO CHANDLER

the cemetery in Chamula

taining control over the number of visitors who come and the things they do. The guides have to be approved by the town, and (as you see on the tour) are well regarded by most people there. You also learn immeasurably more with a guide than you can on your own.

At some point in his or her lifetime, each villager is expected to assume a religious *cargo*—literally burden, but in this case it means a position of responsibility. The primary role is to care for the statue of one of many saints honored by Chamulans. The term is typically one year, and it is no easy task. The statue has its own small home, which the caretaker and his or her family live in for the duration of the term. They must regularly cut or buy fresh pine boughs, flowers, and other offerings. On saints' days and special occasions, the caretakers must organize and host celebrations, including providing food, soda, and alcohol for the entire village at the caretaker's expense. Certain saints are more highly revered than others—caretakers earn greater honor but at greater expense.

A *cargo* can cost its caretaker the equivalent of thousands, even tens of thou-

sands, of dollars, which villagers can spend years or even a lifetime paying off. When asked how he managed it, one *cargo* holder shrugged and said, "Better to carry a burden for a year than for the rest of eternity."

As in most indigenous towns, cameras are viewed with considerable suspicion and you should be very discreet in taking photos. You can take "scenery" shots, such as of the church, but not of individual people or even larger crowd shots. Taking pictures inside the church is strictly prohibited—your camera should not even be visible when you visit, lest it be confiscated by local officials.

Saint John the Baptist Church

Along with the market in the main plaza, this colorful blue and white flowered church is the main attraction in San Juan Chamula and a deeply important place for villagers. Though it appears like any other church, it is obvious from the moment you enter that it is no ordinary Catholic space. There are no clergy here and the only standard Catholic ceremonies conducted here are baptisms, for which a priest is brought in specially. (It has not, however, been officially abandoned by the Church, which must recognize the futility of imposing strict Catholic mores here.)

A rich aroma greets you as you walk in the door: a mixture of pine, flowers, incense, and candles. The floor is covered with pine needles, cut fresh from the forest and carried here every Saturday. The statues of the saints are dressed in many layers of brilliantly flowered clothes with mirrors hung around their necks. Most of the statues are now kept in glass boxes because villagers occasionally sought revenge when a request to the saint was not fulfilled. It wasn't unusual for an angry churchgoer to break a statue's finger off, turn the statue backward to face the wall, or even to take the statue outside and stick its head in the ground.

Hundreds of candles placed on the floor glow reverently in the dim light—red candles burn for someone who is ill, black candles announce death, but most are white and are part of detailed private ceremonies performed

A CEREMONY FOR CHAC

Mayan rituals are still practiced for many occasions, but usually within the confines of a village or a home—and seldom when outsiders are present. These rituals are oftentimes a fascinating marriage of Catholic and Mayan mysticism.

One such rite is the **Chachaac,** in which a Mayan priest and his people beseech the rain god—Chac—for help. The altar, which is often set in a jungle clearing, is made of poles and branches and has a tall candle at each of its four corners; this is representative of the cardinal points—sacred in Mayan religions. In the center is a crucifix with a figure of Christ dressed not in a loincloth, but in a white skirt embroidered with bright red flowers—similar to a *huipil.*

The priest is always a revered village elder; he is brought offerings of cigarettes, soft drinks, and sometimes even raw chicken. Onlookers—typically only men—find large stones and sit in front of the priest for the ceremony.

The cigarette offerings are placed on one end of the altar next to small gourds. Nearby lies a plastic-covered trough made from a hollowed log. At the beginning of the ceremony, the priest lifts the plastic sheet and drops something into the log. Kneeling on an old burlap sack with a young helper beside him, he pours water into a bucket, adds ground corn, and mixes it with a small bundle of leaves. The two pray quietly to Chac. At an unseen signal, one of the seated men throws incense on a shovel of hot coals. As the exotic aroma spreads, the priest begins praying in Spanish. Everyone stands up and chants Hail Marys and Our Fathers. The priest dips his sheaf of leaves in the gourd and scatters holy water in all directions—the ceremony gains momentum.

Young boys sit under the altar and make repetitive frog sounds (a sign of coming rain) while gourds of the sacred corn drink *zaca* are passed to each person. Christian prayers continue, and more *zaca* is passed around. The ceremony continues for hours with only occasional rests. Bubbling liquid sounds come from the log trough—a mixture of honey, water, and bark from a *balché* tree.

As the evening passes the priest takes intermittent naps between rounds of prayers. The men occasionally stop and drink beer or smoke cigarettes from the altar. A young man gently nudges the napping priest. The praying begins anew. Each round of prayers lasts about 45 minutes; nine sessions are offered throughout the night. No one leaves and the fervor of the prayers does not diminish.

At dawn, after a long round of prayers, the priest spreads sacred divination stones on a burlap sack and studies them. Everyone watches him intently and after a long silence, the priest shakes his head. The verdict is in: Chac has decided. There will be no rain for the village this planting season.

The sun comes up and the men prepare a feast. Chac must not be insulted despite his decision. Thick corn-dough cakes layered with ground squash seeds and marked with a cross are placed in a large pit lined with hot stones. The cakes are covered with palm leaves and then buried with dirt. While the bread bakes and the gift chicken stews in broth, blood, and spices, gourds of *balché,* Coca-Cola, or a mixture of both are passed around. The mixture is not fermented enough to be as hallucinogenic as it is proclaimed to be but it makes a strong person ill. The rest of the morning is spent feasting and drinking. Chac has spoken.

Saint John the Baptist Church is one of the most sacred places in Chamula.

by people with the help of shamans for various daily or family matters. In addition to candles, ceremonies are conducted using chickens, eggs, a traditional homemade liquor called *posh* and—amazingly—Coca-Cola and Pepsi. An important means of ridding the body of bad spirits and energy is belching—*posh* once was used, but of course nothing is a better burp-inducer than Coke, which was quickly adopted by Chamulan shamans. Some may view this as corrupting, but it is one of innumerable instances in which indigenous people have of their own volition integrated the trappings of "modern" life into traditional practices. They are not, after all, blind to the world around them.

Festivals

The Chamula church is a scene to be experienced, especially during a holiday. Carnaval is one of the biggest celebrations and goes on for a week. Shrove (or fat) Tuesday, the day before Ash Wednesday, is especially colorful. December 12th, saint's day for the Virgin of Guadalupe, is also a major event. During festivals, *cargo* holders, town leaders, shamans, and ordinary villagers all wear special cer-

emonial clothing, all different depending on the wearer's position but none without bright colors and exquisite woven and embroidered designs. Solemn marches and special ceremonies are set against a backdrop of music, fireworks, and plenty of food and drink. A rich compelling scene—and you can't take even one picture!

ZINACANTÁN

In nearby Zinacantán, life moves at a different pace. The town's main industry is growing and exporting flowers, and driving there you'll see large hothouses dispersed in hills and valleys. A growing tourism business also helps explain the town's relative prosperity.

The traditional clothing worn by men here is the most colorful in the area, and includes straw hats, short white pants, and pinkish tunics decorated with bright embroidered flowers and fuchsia tassels. The women, on the other hand, wear dark skirts and white blouses trimmed with a minimum of color, topped with a beautiful blue *rebozo* (shawl). The Zinacantecans have been merchants since the early 1600s and still travel around the region selling their homegrown vegetables, fruit, and flowers.

A tour here will definitely include a visit to a weaver's home (in fact, some tours go *only* there, which is something of a disappointment). Zinacantecan textiles are noted for their colorful embroidery in flamboyant reds, pinks, purples, and blues. The work is done outdoors in a family yard with most of the women attached to a waist loom. They create tablecloths, bedspreads, placemats, and of course the men's tunics.

SAN ANDRÉS LARRAINZAR

This Tzotzil-speaking municipality consists of about 54 villages with 17,000 inhabitants scattered across the highlands. A few of the more well-known villages are Santa Marta, Santa Magdalena, and San Santiago. It is an extremely poor region with little economic activity, and although Larrainzars voted to outlaw bars in certain towns, alcoholism remains a problem here. San Andrés was and remains

© LIZA PRADO CHANDLER

The State of Chiapas

© LIZA PRADO CHANDLER

Tours of indigenous villages often include a stop at a typical Mayan home.

an important Zapatista stronghold and was the location of peace talks after the 1994 uprising. (This subject is not the focus of tours here, however, as guides are reluctant to appear to support one side or the other.)

Textiles

As elsewhere, weaving is an important part of life and a source of additional income. Larrainzar women do all the weaving and are well known for threading colored bits of yarn into the warp and weft of their backstrap looms to create special designs. One product is the brocade, an ancient design that incorporates traditional symbols such as the snake, diamond, flower, and monkey. The background color is usually bright red with many colors woven in.

GETTING THERE AND AROUND

You'll benefit most from your visit by going on a guided tour. (See the *Tour Operators and Travel Agencies* listings in the *San Cristóbal de las Casas* section for agencies offering guided tours to San Juan Chamula, Zinacantán, and San Andres Larrainzar.) You can visit these town independently, in a car or even by bus. Independent travelers are less common here, so you may have to explain yourself to curious town leaders. Do not plan to stay the night and know that towns beyond the most-visited ones tend to be very suspicious of strangers who just show up. Hiring a private guide is a good option, and something most tour operators can arrange.

South of San Cristóbal

AMATENANGO DEL VALLE

Highway 190, the Carretera Panamericana (Pan-American Highway), takes you past the small pottery-making village of Amatenango del Valle. A number of San Cristóbal–based tour operators stop in here on the way to or from the Lagunas de Montebello, but if you are driving it is easy enough to visit on your own. Here you'll find classic Tzeltal Mayan craftsmanship—most notable are immense jars up to four feet tall and 20–30 inches in diameter, and rustic clay doves, some tiny, some almost as big as the jars. All of these are made without a wheel. Pieces made from natural gray clay are sun-dried and then fired in an aboveground open fire rather than in a kiln. The pottery is not as durable as some, but the pieces are a wonderful souvenir if you can get them home.

Driving past town, you'll see jars, doves, and other pieces set up right on the highway's shoulder. If you stop, the owner of the particular collection of pieces you pull up to should come running out. You can try asking to see the artist's workshop—not all artisans are open to this (or are working at the moment you pull up) but it makes for an interesting few minutes. As elsewhere, refrain from taking pictures.

There are no services in Amatenango del Valle and no hotels or restaurants of any particular note. You're not far from San Cristóbal at this point, and you are better off spending the night there.

COMITÁN

A great base for exploring the nearby Lagos de Montebello, Comitán itself is a pleasant place to spend a day. Built on a hill, Comitán has steep inclines leading to the shady main plaza. Colonial buildings make up the center of town and services—hotels, restaurants, Internet, banks, and so on—are all just footsteps from one another.

Sights

The small **Museo Arqueológico de Comi-** tán (Calle 1 Sur Oriente between Av. Rosario Castellanos and Av. 2 Oriente Sur, tel. 963/632-5760, macomitan.chis@inah.gob.mx, 10 A.M.–5 P.M. Tues.–Sun., free) is a good museum that traces the history of the Mayans in the state of Chiapas. With excellent artifacts, especially those found in tombs, it is definitely worth a stop. Explanations are in Spanish only.

Accommodations

The lighthearted **⋈ Hotel San Francisco** (Av. 1 Oriente Norte No. 13 between Calles 1 and 2 Norte Oriente, tel. 963/632-0194, samuel22f@prodigy.net.mx, US$6.25 pp), is an eclectic hotel with brightly painted walls, tons of plants (real and fake), and lots of sunshine. Rooms are situated around two courtyards—one is part of a remodeled colonial home, and the other is part of the modern-style annex that has been added in the back. Rooms here are an incredible value for solo travelers—for about US$7, you get a spotless room with private bath (and hot water too).

Right on the *zócalo* (main plaza), the basic **Hotel Delfín** (Av. Central Sur No. 21, tel. 963/632-0013, US$18 s, US$21 d) is another good option. With private bathroom, cable TV, 24-hour hot water, and the park right outside you can't go wrong. Rooms on the second floor have exposed wood-beam ceilings.

For something nicer, head to the colonial **⋈ Posada el Castellano** (Calle 3 Norte Poniente No. 12 between Avs. Central and 1 Sur Poniente, tel. 963/632-0117, posadaelcastellano@comitan.com, US$26 s, US$30 d). This charming hotel has 22 rooms with tile floors, sparkling bathrooms, cable TV, and phones. All units surround a sunny courtyard with a gurgling fountain. Exceptional service.

Food

With soft lighting and nice windows that overlook the plaza, **Helen's Enrique** (Av. Central

ESCRITORÍO PÚBLICO

Not long after the conquest of the New World, there grew a need for the general populace to communicate through letters; loved ones moved away in search of work, business opportunities arose, officialdom required paperwork—the age of letter writing had arrived. Most people, however, were illiterate. As a result, a job was born: the *escritor público* (the public writer). This person could be found in the main plaza, tucked under an archway of a main building. He sat at a table with ink, paper, and a sign Escritorío Público (public desk) and, perhaps, a drawing of a quill and scroll (since his customers couldn't read). For a coin or two, townspeople could have a letter written—for business or pleasure.

Today, this job is still very much in existence. Look around the main plazas. In small villages and large cities alike, you'll see men—now with typewriters—waiting at the ready for their next customer.

No. 19, tel. 963/632-1730, 8 A.M.–midnight daily, US$2.25–6) is a popular spot for locals and travelers alike. The food is nothing special but the variety on the menu makes it easy to choose from. Especially good if you're tiring of tacos.

For mouthwatering pizza, head to **La Alpujarra** (on the *zócalo,* Av. Central No. 3 between Calles 1 Norte Poniente and 1 Sur Poniente, tel. 963/632-2000, 8 A.M.–midnight daily, US$5–13). Pies here come loaded with all the fixin's. Not sure which one to order? Served piping hot, the Rebollon Chiapaneco, which comes with oozing mozzarella, olives, capers, and green peppers, is a particularly tasty pie. Other dishes—sandwiches, pastas, and tacos—also are offered.

As soon as you step into **Matisse** (Av. 1 Poniente Norte No. 14, tel. 963/632-5172, noon–11 P.M., US$7–16) you'll feel as if you've walked into an upscale Manhattan restaurant. With streamlined furnishings, sparse decor, billowing fabrics, and skylights, it is the epitome of ultrachic. The classiness extends to the food—Italian gourmet—with a number of pasta and meat dishes to choose from. Excellent choice for a night out on the town.

Mercado Primero de Mayo (Av. 2 Oriente Norte at Calle Central Oriente, 6 A.M.–5 P.M. daily) sells the freshest produce, dairy, and meat in town. A good place to stock up on food if you're planning to head to the lake region for a few hours (or days).

Information and Services

Easy to miss but just a few doors north of the Palacio Municipal is the **tourist office** (Calle Central Oriente No. 6, tel. 963/632-4047, securcomitan@hotmail.com, 8 A.M.–7 P.M. Mon.–Fri., 9 A.M.–2 P.M. and 4 A.M.–7 P.M. Sat., 9 A.M.–1 P.M. Sun.). Here, along with a fistful of area maps and brochures, you'll also get lots of personalized attention. English spoken.

Farmacia del Ahorro (Calle 1 Sur Oriente at Av. Central Sur, tel. 963/632-7777, 7 A.M.–10:30 P.M. daily) is on the *zócalo.*

Just off the *zócalo* is **Bancomer** (Av. Rosario Castellanos at Calle 1 Sur Poniente, 8:30 A.M.–4 P.M. Mon.–Fri.), which has two ATMs. Nearby, you'll also find **Banorte** (Calle 1 Sur Poniente between Avs. Central and 1 Poniente Sur, 9 A.M.–4 P.M. Mon.–Fri., 10 A.M.–2 P.M. Sat., 1 ATM).

A block and a half from the *zócalo,* the **post office** (Av. Central Sur No. 45 between Calles 2 and 3 Sur Poniente) is open 9 A.M.–3 P.M. Monday–Friday.

In Pasaje Morales, **Cyber@dictos Internet** (Calle 1 Norte Poniente between Avs. Central and Rosario Castellano, 9 A.M.–9 P.M. daily) has reliable Internet. It charges US$.45 per hour and US$1.75 to burn CDs.

For making calls or sending faxes, a convenient option is **Caseta Maguis** (Calle 1 Sur Poniente between Avs. Central and 1 Poniente Sur, tel. 963/632-6713, 9 A.M.–9 P.M. Mon.–Sat., 9 A.M.–8 P.M. Sun.). Calls within Mexico cost US$.26 per minute and to the United States/Canada US$.70 per minute. Faxing is just a little more at US$.45 per page within Mexico and US$.90 per page to the United States/Canada.

If you are heading to Guatemala and have any questions, the **Guatemalan Consulate** (Calle 1 Sur Poniente No. 26 at Av. 2 Poniente Sur, tel. 963/632-2669, 9 A.M.–5 P.M. Mon.–Fri.) is in the center of town. At the time of research, citizens from the United States, Canada, and the European Union did not need visas to enter the country. Be sure to double-check this, however, as Guatemala's visa requirements may have changed by the time you read this.

Lavandería Express (Av. 1 Sur Poniente at Calle 3 Norte Poniente, no phone, 9 A.M.–2 P.M. and 4:30–8 P.M. Mon.–Fri., 9 A.M.–5 P.M. Sun., US$.90/kilo—2.2 pounds) offers next-day service only.

If you need **luggage storage,** head to the bus terminal. The rate is an incredible US$.45 per day.

Getting There

Comitán's modern bus terminal (tel. 963/632-0980) is on Avenida Belisario Domínguez several blocks from the city center. An asterisk denotes deluxe ADO-GL service; prices are 10–30 percent higher. First-class departures include:

Chetumal, US$36.50, 13.5 hours, 1:30 A.M.

Ciudad Cuauhtémoc, US$4, 1.5 hours, 8:15 A.M., 9:30 A.M., 10:50 A.M., 2:05 P.M., and 7:15 P.M.

Mexico City-Norte, US$62, 16–19 hours, 3 P.M.* and 4 P.M.

Mexico City-TAPO, US$62, 16–19 hours, 2:05 P.M., 3 P.M.*, 4 P.M., 4:30 P.M., and 8:20 P.M.

Ocosingo, US$8, 2.5 hours, 1:30 P.M.

Palenque, US$13.50, 4.5 hours, 1:30 P.M.

Playa del Carmen, US$51, 17.5 hours, 1:30 P.M.

Puebla, US$59, 14.5 hours, take any Mexico City bus except 4 P.M.

San Cristóbal, US$2, 1.5 hours, take any Tuxtla Gutiérrez bus.

Tapachula, US$11, four hours, 1:55 A.M., 9:30 A.M., 10:50 A.M., 2:05 P.M., 3:25 P.M., 7:15 P.M., and 11:30 P.M.

Tuxtla Gutiérrez, US$5, 2.5 hours, 3:40 A.M., 4:55 A.M., 8 A.M., 9 A.M., 10 A.M., 11 A.M., 1:45 P.M.*, 2:05 P.M., 2:45 P.M., 3:30 P.M., 4 P.M., 4:30 P.M., 6 P.M., 8:15 P.M., 8:20 P.M., and 11:15 P.M.

Veracruz, US$40, 12.5 hours, 8:15 P.M.

Transportes Montebello (2 Av. Sur Poniente between 2 and 3 Calle Sur Poniente) has *combis* every 10–15 minutes to the Lagos de Montebello region (US$2, 1 hour, 5 A.M.–6 P.M. daily).

Just 76 kilometers (47.2 miles) from San Cristóbal, Comitán is an easy drive away. Simply travel south on Highway 190 and you'll come straight to town. Once here, be sure to fill your gas tank before you leave town—gas stations are far and few between in this part of the state.

Servicios Aéreos San Cristóbal (Base Aeropuerto, tel. 963/632-4662) offers scenic flights and aerial tours, including flights over the Lagos de Montebello and Agua Azul. Be sure to ask about flights to the Yaxchilán and Bonampak ruins—while pricey, they make an unforgettable day trip.

Getting Around

The easiest way to get around town is by foot—it's a small enough place that if you get in a cab or bus, you'll just have to jump out a block or two later. If you're just arrived at the bus terminal, though, it's easy (and cheap) to take public transportation: You can stop city buses on most corners (US$.30) and hailing a cab is a cinch—they pass often (around US$1.35 into town).

BETWEEN COMITÁN AND LAGUNAS DE MONTEBELLO

Tenam Puente Archaeological Zone

Fifteen kilometers (9.3 miles) south on Highway 190 will bring you to **Tenam Puente** (9 A.M.–5 P.M. Tues.–Sun.), a site that reached its height around A.D. 1000—after the Mayans

© LIZA PRADO CHANDLER

Twenty-two lakes are easily accessible in the Lagunas de Montebello National Park.

abandoned the Petén region. While not particularly glorious, the site, with its large numbers of buildings, is popular among tour groups from San Cristóbal (one local hypothesized that the popularity of the site was in direct correlation to its price—free).

Chinkultíc Archaeological Zone

Just off the road to the Lagos de Montebello, you'll see a sign to Chinkultíc (10 A.M.–5 P.M. Tues.–Sun., US$3). A little-visited site, it dates to A.D. 600 and was abandoned by A.D. 1200. Partially excavated, this site's principal structures (Structures A, B, C, and D) afford spectacular views of a cenote and the region beyond. The ball court once held a unique bas-relief of a ballplayer; this artifact now rests in the National Museum of Anthropology in Mexico City.

Hotel Parador Santa Mariá

Hotel Parador Santa Maria (Carr. Trinitaria-Lagos de Montebello Km. 22, tel. 963/632-5116, paradorsantamaria@prodigy.net.mx, www.paradorsantamaria.com.mx, US$105 s/d) is a remodeled hacienda with a small religious art museum (US$1.50), a pleasant outdoor restaurant (8 A.M.–11 P.M. daily,

US$6–15), and eight rooms. Although appointed with admittedly beautiful colonial antiques and oil paintings, accommodations and living areas are somewhat sparse and have a cold feel to them. That said, this is by far the nicest place to stay in the Lakes region. Leave the door open to your room—the green fields and mountain view give the place a little life.

LAGUNAS DE MONTEBELLO NATIONAL PARK

About a 60-minute drive from Comitán (51 kilometers/31.7 miles), you'll hit the beautiful Lagunas de Montebello National Park (8 A.M.–sunset daily, US$2 pp). Set in the middle of the Lacandón Forest, the lakes cover more than 13,000 square miles and reflect myriad colors from pale blue to lavender, deep purple, and reddish black—a lush and stunning place. Twenty-two lakes are easily accessible to visitors and while you can see a few of them from your car, the best way to see the region is by boat, horseback, or foot. A visitors center at Lake Pojoj is the place to get something to eat, use the restrooms, and book a boat ride (US$15–35), horseback tour (US$13), or hire a guide.

Lake Tziscao

One of the largest and most accessible lakes in the region is Lake Tziscao. Just a few kilometers off the main highway, a dirt road leads to it and the village of Tziscao, where you'll find a handful of rustic places to stay the night. By far, the best place to stay around here is the lakeside cabanas at **Hotel Tziscao** (tel. 963/633-5244, US$8.75 pp with private bath). These plywood rooms are simple but clean and have terraces and electricity. Avoid the hotel rooms in the main building—they're sketchy at best. If this place is full, the cabanas next door at **Playa Escondida** (no phone, US$1.75 pp camping, US$5.25 pp with shared bath) are tolerable.

Getting There and Around

The easiest way to explore the lake region is by car—you'll have the freedom to stop where you want and you'll never have to wait by the side of the road for a *combi* to stop. To head to the area, take Highway 190 south out of Comitán and take a left at the sign "Lagos de Montebello"—you'll be sure to see it.

Without a car, take a bus operated by **Transportes Montebello** (2 Av. Sur Poniente between 2 and 3 Calle Sur Poniente) from Comitán. Departures are every 10–15 minutes 5 A.M.–6 P.M. daily (US$2, one hour). The bus drops you at the main tourist area, where you can see a few lakes, take horseback rides, or hire a cab to see lakes farther afield.

You can also hire a **taxi** in Comitán to take you to the lakes. One-way trips cost around US$20. For a day of sightseeing, ask the taxi driver to name his price and then bargain hard.

Tuxtla Gutiérrez

Although Chiapas is one of the most picturesque states in Mexico with rich colonial and indigenous influences, its capital is a busy modern city with more than a half-million residents. Tuxtla Gutiérrez is at the center of a thriving coffee-growing zone and has been the state's commercial and political center since it replaced San Cristóbal de las Casas as capital of Chiapas in 1892. But little evidence of Tuxtla's colonial past remains—government buildings, museums, theaters, and parks are of mostly contemporary design. Even the San Marcos cathedral on the Plaza Cívica is a modern interpretation of what once was a colonial church. Most travelers move through Tuxtla as quickly as possible, usually on the way to or from San Cristóbal de las Casas or Palenque. But Tuxtla does have a very good zoo, a decent museum, and easier access than San Cristóbal to Cañon Sumidero and the colonial village of Chiapa de Corzo.

SIGHTS

Plaza Cívica and Catedral San Marcos

The Plaza Cívica stretches across Avenida Central and includes the main square and government buildings. It's a shady, tree-lined place, surrounded by streamlined government buildings and anchored by Catedral San Marcos. The cathedral, a brilliant white building with modern lines, has a stark beauty. Its German-made clockwork mechanism (a carillon with 48 bells) sends 12 carved apostles in and out of the tower every hour to the chimes of a medley of international music. The church was originally built in the second half of the 16th century as a Dominican convent. Today the central part of the front arch is the only piece that remains from the colonial era. The church has been redesigned many times through the centuries—even the main altarpiece is new.

The plaza sometimes serves as a gathering place for protests and sit-ins by indigenous people and their supporters. Physical conflict or altercations are extremely rare, even as the demonstrations have become more frequent since the 1994 Zapatista uprising. At all other times, the plaza is placid and relaxing, both day and night.

Parque Marimba

This popular gathering place is a 15-minute walk west of the plaza, and it's a great place

The State of Chiapas

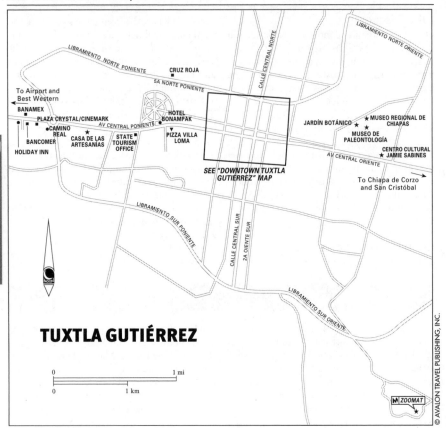

TUXTLA GUTIÉRREZ

To Airport and
Best Western

BANAMEX
PLAZA CRYSTAL/CINEMARK
CAMINO REAL
BANCOMER
CASA DE LAS ARTESANÍAS
STATE TOURISM OFFICE
HOLIDAY INN
AV CENTRAL PONIENTE
HOTEL BONAMPAK
PIZZA VILLA LOMA

LIBRAMIENTO NORTE PONIENTE
CRUZ ROJA
5A NORTE PONIENTE
CALLE CENTRAL NORTE
LIBRAMIENTO NORTE ORIENTE

JARDÍN BOTÁNICO
MUSEO REGIONAL DE CHIAPAS
MUSEO DE PALEONTOLOGÍA
CENTRO CULTURAL JAIME SABINES
AV CENTRAL ORIENTE

SEE "DOWNTOWN TUXTLA GUTIÉRREZ" MAP

To Chiapa de Corzo and San Cristóbal

LIBRAMIENTO SUR PONIENTE
CALLE CENTRAL SUR
2A ORIENTE SUR
LIBRAMIENTO SUR ORIENTE

0   1 mi
0   1 km

ZOOMAT

© AVALON TRAVEL PUBLISHING, INC.

to people-watch and enjoy live traditional music. Shade trees and walkways encircle a large attractive kiosk where musicians play a variety of styles, usually involving a marimba in one way or the other. The musical group varies among marimba bands, the police orchestra, a woodwind band, and visiting groups and musicians. The common denominator is the dancing: No matter what the beat, the whole family, young and old, gets up and dances. You definitely don't have to be an expert dancer, and visitors and foreigners are warmly welcomed. You'll find the park at Avenida Central Poniente between 8 and 9 Calle Poniente (shows 7–9 P.M. Mon.–Fri., 7–10 P.M. Sat.–Sun.; free).

San Pascualito Church

In 1892, a group of people from Tuxtla's San Roque and Calvario neighborhoods built a hermitage where they venerated a wooden skeleton they said represented San Pasqual. The faithful were purportedly the descendents of a religious sect that had been in hiding for almost 300 years, having drawn the ire of early Spanish priests for worshipping a human skeleton they said was the remains of San Pasqual. In 1934, a group of anti-Catholic fanatics burned all the statues and images of saints they could find. However, San Pasqual devotees protected their wooden skeleton by moving it from house to house.

A proper church was erected for the sect's

many (and ever-increasing) followers in the 1950s. The parish was and is especially popular among non-traditional healers and spiritualists, and the story of the sect's beginnings is told in many versions. Some believers are convinced the wooden skeleton you see today is the original, but others have doubts. In either case, the skeleton is kept in a coffin-cart in the church and is displayed once a year on May 14th, when a grand festival is held at the church (5 Calle Poniente Sur at 3 Av. Sur Poniente). A popular legend tells how the coffin-cart passes through the city and San Pascualito picks up the dead amid a wail of agony.

Museo Regional de Chiapas

The Museo Regional de Chiapas (Regional Museum of Chiapas, 9 A.M.–4 P.M. Tues.–Sun., US$3) is a spacious, detailed museum with displays covering Chiapanecan history from the Protoclassic era to the 20th century, a span of more than 10,000 years. Excellent exhibits and artifacts—and slightly less-impressive explanations—illustrate the Olmec florescence, the development of Chiapa de Corzo, the terrific Classic-period artwork, and effects of the widespread collapse of the great Mayan centers around A.D. 900. The upper floor has a very good exhibit of the colonial and republican era from the 16th century, including a fine collection of Chiapanecan colonial art. The museum building itself is notable. Architect Juan Miramontes Najera won first prize for his design at the Third Biennial of Architecture held in Europe in 1985, a year after the museum was built.

The museum is at the end of a broad, block-long walkway known as **Calzada de Los Hombres Ilustres** (Avenue of Illustrious Men), which is lined with busts of Francisco Madero, Pancho Villa, and other historical figures. Also along the *calzada* are the **Jardín Botánico** (Botanical Garden), a cool relaxing place to wander among examples of the state's flora, and the disappointing **Museo de Paleontología** (Museum of Paleontology, 10 A.M.–5 P.M. Tues.–Fri., 11 A.M.–5 P.M. Sat.–Sun., US$1), which has good general displays on fossils and the

geologic periods, but little specific information on the paleontology of Chiapas itself.

Centro Cultural Jaime Sabines

Just south, you'll find the Centro Cultural Jaime Sabines (12 Oriente Norte at Av. Central, 10 A.M.–9 P.M. Mon.–Sat.), where cultural exhibits are often mounted. You'll also find a park with lush grounds and a café (7 A.M.–11 P.M. Mon.–Sat.).

◪ ZOOMAT

A visit to the zoo (tel. 961/614-4765) is a highlight of a visit to Tuxtla, and for many the main reason to stop here at all. **Zoológico Regional Miguel Álvarez del Toro,** or ZOOMAT as it is known, occupies a 100-hectare (247-acre) swath of forest in the southeast part of the city and is open 8:30 A.M.–4 P.M. Tuesday–Sunday. After being free for decades, the zoo now charges a mandatory "donation" of US$1.75, except Tuesday and before 10 A.M., when the fee is waived. Founded in 1942, the zoo was named the best in Latin America in 1979 and is still considered by many to be one of the top zoos around. A 2.5-kilometer (1.6-mile) trail meanders up and down the side of a hill under tall trees with hanging vines. The animals—purportedly all the species found in Chiapas—are housed in large enclosures (mostly), with a minimum of cages and fences. You'll see jaguars, pumas, and little *tigrillos;* beautiful parrots, macaws, birds of prey, and the elusive, much-revered quetzal; and unusual creatures such as tapirs, otters, and anteaters. An interesting innovation of the zoo is the Casa Nocturna (Nighttime House), where artificial lighting has led various nocturnal creatures to think day is night and night is day. Once your eyes adjust, you can watch them going about their business—far more interesting than seeing the little guys curled up asleep. There is a tourist information booth (9 A.M.–3 P.M. Tues.–Sun.) at the zoo's entrance, and some small eateries and snack shops inside. To get to ZOOMAT, take the R-60 minibus (US$.45, 30 minutes) from the corner of 7 Avenida Sur Oriente and 1 Calle Oriente Sur or grab a cab (US$4).

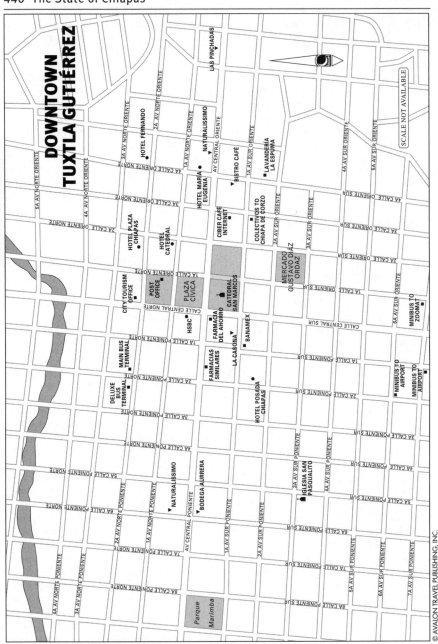

DOWNTOWN
TUXTLA GUTIÉRREZ

SCALE NOT AVAILABLE

© AVALON TRAVEL PUBLISHING, INC.

ENTERTAINMENT AND EVENTS

Auto Races

Tuxtla Gutiérrez is the starting point for an annual **road rally** that continues for seven days and covers 3,000 kilometers (1864 miles) along the Carretera Panamericana (Pan-American Highway). Professional drivers bring modern, high-tech automobiles from all over the world for the event, which usually takes place in the third week of October. If you happen to be in Tuxtla then, you can join locals in admiring scores of racing cars lined up on Avenida Central Poniente awaiting the big start.

Traditional Music and Dance

Parque Marimba (Av. Central Poniente between 8 and 9 Calle Poniente) is the best place to go for live, traditional music and a bit of low-key dancing and people-watching. (See *Sights.*) Restaurants **Las Pichanchas** (Av. Central Oriente 837 at 7 Calle Oriente) and **La Casona** (1 Av. Sur Poniente 134 at Calle Central Sur) also have nightly music and dance shows.

Discos

Tuxtla's nightclub scene is definitely a locals one; you're sure to get a good read of it, then, if you head out on a weekend and after midnight. When we were in town, the hottest clubs were: **Piña's and Charlies** (Blvd. Belisario Domínguez No. 871, tel. 961/602-5388, 9 P.M.–3 A.M. Tues.–Sat., cover US$3) where reggae is king; **Zhio** (Blvd. Belisario Domínguez No. 2820, tel. 961/615-7533, 9 P.M.–3 A.M. Thurs.–Sat., cover US$4.50) where techno rules; and **Sky** (Blvd. Las Fuentes s/n, no phone, 9 P.M.–3 A.M. Thurs.–Sat., cover US$3) where the DJ mixed it up.

Cinema

If you're in the mood for a Hollywood flick, head to **Cinemark** (Plaza Crystal, 2nd floor, Blvd. Belisario Domínguez at Oro Ferraro, tel. 961/615-2969, US$3.65, US$2.25 before 3 P.M. and on Wed.). Be sure to ask if the movie is *con subtítulos* (subtitled) if you don't want to hear Kevin Bacon dubbed over.

SHOPPING

Tuxtla is an excellent place to shop if you are looking for car parts, a washing machine, or tight disco clothes. It definitely is not a mecca of Chiapanecan handicrafts but rather a place to get last-minute T-shirts, machine-made knockoffs of indigenous products, and Guatemalan goods. The one exception is the fantastic **Casa de las Artesanías** (Blvd. Belisario Domínguez No. 2035, tel. 961/614-1833, 10 A.M.–8 P.M. Mon.–Sat. and 10 A.M.–3 P.M. Sun.). Six blocks north of the state tourist office, here you'll find a little of everything made from around the state: fine embroidery, wooden carvings, pottery, leather products, jewelry, and coffee. A must if you want to take home a few mementos.

If mall shopping is more your style, head to **Plaza Crystal** (Blvd. Belisario Domínguez at Oro Ferraro, 11 A.M.–9 P.M. daily). Inside you'll find department stores, upscale clothing boutiques, and a food court. There also is a Cinemark movie theater on the second floor (see *Entertainment and Events*).

ACCOMMODATIONS

Tuxtla has plenty of lodging options in the budget and high-end ranges, but not many for midrange travelers.

Under US$50

The bright red **Hotel Plaza Chiapas** (2 Calle Norte Oriente No. 299 at 2 Calle Oriente Norte, tel. 961/613-8365, US$10.50 s, US$13 d, US$15 s with cable TV, US$18 d with cable TV) offers no-frills accommodations just four blocks from the bus station. The rooms are a little run-down but they are relatively clean and have decent beds and private bathrooms. A good place to crash if you are on a tight budget.

In the thick of the action downtown, **Hotel Posada Chiapas** (2 Calle Poniente Sur No. 243 between 1 and 2 Calles Sur Poniente, tel. 961/612-3354, US$13 s with fan, US$18 d with fan) offers boxy but spotless rooms with cable

TV. While all face into a sunny courtyard, few get much sunlight from their one window. If you don't mind that, it's a good choice.

Just a block from the main plaza, the popular **Hotel Catedral** (1 Calle Norte Oriente No. 367, tel. 961/613-0824, US$19 s with fan, US$23 d with fan) is often full. The 31 rooms are ample, very clean, and come with cable TV. Be sure to ask for a room in back as the busy street in front makes for a short night's rest.

Another decent option is **M Hotel Fernando** (2 Calle Norte Oriente No. 515 at 4 Calle Oriente Norte, tel. 961/613-1740, US$19 s with fan, US$23 d with fan). With good-sized rooms, cable TV, and great views of the city from the top floor, you get some bang for your buck. Check out a couple of rooms before signing in—some have saggy beds and others smell a little off.

US$50–100

The aging **Hotel María Eugenia** (Av. Central Oriente No. 507, tel. 961/613-3767, US$60 s with a/c, US$68 d with a/c) is the only official four-star hotel in the center of town. The stars, however, are hanging on by a thread. The rooms are out of date, the pool is neglected, and the hallways—though gleaming—have no decor. What it does have is a great location, nice views of the city from the fifth floor, and a decent restaurant (see *Food*). The hotels near the airport are far better but if you want to be near the action, this is your best bet.

Walking distance to Parque Marimba, **Hotel Bonampak** (Blvd. Belisario Domínguez No. 180 at 14 Calle Poniente Norte, tel. 961/602-5916, hotbonam@prodigy.net.mx, US$57–65 s/d with a/c) offers 70 rooms that are oppressed by white furniture and persecuted by flower-print chairs and bedspreads. Somewhat basic for the price tag, these rooms do offer cable TV and in-room phones. A pool and a popular coffee shop on-site are pluses.

Five minutes from the airport is the **M Best Western Hotel Arecas** (Blvd. Belisario Domínguez Km. 1080, tel. 961/615-1121, www.hotelarecas.com.mx, US$60–70 s/d with

a/c). Set back from the road, rooms surround a manicured garden and a nice lap pool; all are ample and nicely appointed and have cable TV, phones, and minibars. An all-around pleasant place to stay. Check the website before you book—it often has killer specials.

Across the street from the Plaza Crystal mall, the gleaming **Holiday Inn** (Blvd. Belisario Domínguez Km. 1081, tel. 961/617-1000, www.holiday-inn.com/tuxtla, US$92–104 s/d with a/c) is worth a look. Most with Arabian-style windows, rooms are comfortable and have the modern amenities you would expect: cable TV, phones, and air conditioning. A large and inviting pool is in the center of the complex and an excellent restaurant faces it. Also on-site are a travel and car rental agency as well as a business center for guests. While a ways from the center of town, this makes a restful base from which to visit the city.

Over US$100

Hands down the best place to stay in this town is the **M Camino Real** (Blvd. Belisario Domínguez No. 1195, tel. 961/617-7777, toll-free U.S./ Can. tel. 800/7-CAMINO (800/722-6466), www.caminoreal.com/tuxtla, US$160–250 s/d with a/c). This modern architectural beauty sits on a hill overlooking Tuxtla and beyond the breathtaking views has some of the best breezes around. The 210 rooms are luxurious and have the finest in amenities and services, including a spa, fitness room, illuminated tennis courts, and a business center. A rock-inlaid pool with a waterfall is the centerpiece and an excellent restaurant (open 24 hours) overlooks it. It's only 15 minutes to the airport.

FOOD
Mexican

Tuxtla's best-known restaurant is **M Las Pichanchas** (Av. Central Oriente 837 at 7 Calle Oriente, tel. 961/612-5351, noon–midnight daily, US$5–15). The lively courtyard dining area is decorated with local pottery and *papel picado* (long streamers made from colorful tissue paper with designs cut into it). The menu has a good sampling of dishes from the countryside; try an assortment of tamales and the appetizer plate of local cheeses and sausages. For the complete experience, come when there is a performance: marimba 2:30–5:30 P.M. and 8:30–11:30 P.M. daily, *ballet folklórico* 9–10 P.M. daily.

Closer to the main plaza, **La Casona** (1 Av. Sur Poniente 134 at Calle Central Sur, tel. 961/612-7534, 7 A.M.–11 P.M. daily, US$3–8) has a similar concept, with colorful Mexican tablecloths and wrought-iron chairs. Mexican fare is mixed with some international options, so you can order either chicken mole or chicken cordon bleu. The lunch special is a good deal, with three courses for under US$4. Enjoy live marimba music 2–6 P.M. Monday–Saturday and 10 A.M.–6 Sunday.

International

The restaurant at the **Hotel María Eugenia** (Av. Central Oriente No. 507, tel. 961/613-3767, 7 A.M.–11 P.M. daily, US$4–9) isn't exactly scintillating, but it has good service and serves a variety of reliable meals, from pasta and quesadillas to grilled meat and fish fillets. The breakfast buffet is a bit pricey (US$7.50) but includes made-to-order eggs, pancakes, sausage, yogurt and cereal, and more.

Pizza Villa Loma (Av. Central Poniente 1357 at 13 Calle Poniente, tel. 961/618-1705, noon–midnight daily, US$4–13) is a half block from the Hotel Bonampak and the state tourism office and is considered the best pizza in town. Pizza connoisseurs will be underwhelmed, but it's still a decent pie (plus salads and pastas) and the service is excellent. A guitarist/singer plays mellow live music most weekend evenings. The restaurant is also a short walk from Parque Marimba, which makes for a pleasant after-dinner stop.

Vegetarian

Naturalissimo (tel. 916/613-9648) is a rare, but emerging, thing in Mexico: a natural food store and good vegetarian restaurant. There are two locations: Avenida Central Oriente at 4 Calle Oriente, and 6 Calle Poniente Norte at Avenida Central Poniente. The menu is identical at both and includes mostly soy-based faux-meat dishes, such as *tortas,* hamburgers, and *tacos al pastor.* The lunch special (US$4.50) includes soup, salad bar, main dish, and a drink. You can also order large deluxe shakes (US$2) made with various fruit and veggie juices, from papayas to beets. The setting is a bit sterile, but it's a nice alternative to standard Mexican eateries. And it delivers!

Sweets

Opened in December 2004, **M Bistro Café** (4 Calle Oriente Sur 138 between Av. Central and 1 Av. Sur, tel. 961/600-0745, 1–10 P.M. Mon.–Sat.) is a very welcome addition to Tuxtla's restaurant scene: a small San Francisco–style café with great coffee, pastries, and (by the time you read this) crepes, *tortas,* and other light fare. The setting is modern and comfy and the service excellent. A great place for an end-of-the-day cappuccino and piece of chocolate cake.

Groceries

Bodega Aurrera (Av. Central Poniente at 6 Calle Poniente, 8 A.M.–10 P.M. daily) is a huge supermarket with produce, canned food, and much more.

In the center of town, the **Mercado Gustavo Díaz Ordaz** (1 Calle Oriente Sur at 3 Calle Sur Oriente, 6 A.M.–6 P.M. Mon.–Sat. and 6 A.M.–3:30 P.M. Sun.) is always bustling. Here you'll see mountains of bright fruits and vegetables, rows of live chickens, tortillas being made, flower peddlers, shoe makers, bicycle repair shops—you name it, you'll probably find it here. Be sure to try a cold glass of *tazcalate,* a sweet drink made from local chocolate, cinnamon, and *pinole* (roasted corn) before you leave.

INFORMATION AND SERVICES

Tourist Information Centers

The **city tourism office** (Calle Central Norte at 2 Av. Norte, tel. 961/612-5511, ext. 214, 9 A.M.–8 P.M. Mon.–Fri., 8 A.M.–1 P.M. Sat.) has friendly, helpful staff. The **state tourism office** (Secretaría de Desarrollo Económico, Av. Belisario Domínguez 950 at 15 Calle Poniente Norte, 1st floor, tel. 961/602-5269, ext.147, toll-free

The State of Chiapas

TUXTLA GUTIÉRREZ BUS SCHEDULES

Departures from the **main first-class bus terminal** (2 Av. Norte and 2 Calle Poniente, tel. 961/613-5995, ext. 2431) and the **deluxe service terminal** (tel. 961/612-1639, ext. 2421) include:

Destination	Price	Duration	Schedule
Campeche	US$31	12 hrs	take Mérida bus
Cancún	US$50.50	18 hrs	10:15 A.M., 12:30 P.M., and 2:30 P.M.*
Chetumal	US$35	11 hrs	take Cancún bus
Comitán	US$6.50	3.5 hrs	4 A.M.*, 5:15 A.M.*, 5:30 A.M., 7 A.M., 8 A.M., 10 A.M., 11 A.M., noon, 2:30 P.M., 3:15 P.M., 7:30 P.M., and 10 P.M.
Huatulco	US$20	8 hrs	take Puerto Escondido bus
Mérida	US$38	15 hrs	5 P.M.
Mexico City-Norte	US$54	12.5 hrs	take almost any Mexico City-TAPO bus
Mexico City-TAPO	US$54	12.5 hrs	4:30 P.M., 5:25 P.M., 6 P.M., 6:30 P.M.*, 6:45 P.M., 7 P.M.*, 7:15 P.M., 7:45 P.M., 8 P.M.*, 8:15 P.M., 8:30 P.M., 9:15 P.M.*, 9:30 P.M.*, 11 P.M.*, and midnight
Oaxaca	US$23.50	11 hrs	11:30 A.M., 7:15 P.M., 10:15 P.M.*, and midnight
Ocosingo	US$7.50	3–4 hrs	5 A.M., 10:15 A.M., 11 A.M., 12:30 P.M., 2:30 P.M.*, 3 P.M.*, 5 P.M., 5:30 P.M., and midnight
Palenque	US$11.50	7 hrs	5 A.M., 9 A.M., 10:15 A.M., 12:30 P.M., 2:30 P.M.*, 3 P.M.*, 5 P.M., 5:30 P.M., and midnight

Mex. tel. 800/280-3500, 8 A.M.–9 P.M. Mon.–Fri., 9 A.M.–3 P.M. Sat.) also has a knowledgeable staff but is a bit far from the center. There is also a tourist information booth (9 A.M.–3 P.M. Tues.–Sun.) at the entrance to the zoo.

Medical Services
Cruz Roja Méxicana (Red Cross, 5 Av. Norte 1480 at 15 Calle Poniente, tel. 961/612-0096 or tel. 961/611-9514) and **Hospital Sanatorio Rojas** (2 Av. Sur Poniente 1487, tel. 961/602-5138 or tel. 961/602-5004) both have 24-hour emergency services.

Pharmacies
Farmacias del Ahorro (corner of Av. Central and Calle Central, no phone) is right across from the *catedral* and open 24 hours. **Farmacias Similares** (Av. Central between 1 and 2 Calle Poniente, no phone) is down the street and also has 24-hour service.

Police
There is no police station near the center area, but officers usually patrol the area on foot. You can also dial 060 or 066 from any public telephone for emergency assistance.

Destination	Price	Duration	Schedule
Playa del Carmen	US$49	18 hrs	take Cancún bus
Puebla	US$47.50	10 hrs	6 P.M., 6:45 P.M., 7:15 P.M.*, 8:30 P.M., 9:15 P.M.*, 9:30 P.M.*, 10:15 P.M., 10:45 P.M.*, and midnight
San Cristóbal de las Casas	US$3.50	2 hrs	3:15 A.M.*, 4 A.M.*, 5 A.M., 5:15 A.M.*, 5:30 A.M., 6:15 A.M.*, 8 A.M., 9 A.M., 10 A.M., 10:15 A.M., 11 A.M., noon, 12:30 P.M., 2:30 P.M., 3 P.M.*, 3:15 P.M., 5 P.M., 5:30 P.M.*, 6:30 P.M., 7 P.M.*, 7:30 P.M., 10 P.M., and midnight
Tapachula	US$17	6.5 hrs	6 A.M., 7:30 A.M.*, 8 A.M., 10 A.M., 11 A.M., noon, 1 P.M., 1:30 P.M.*, 3 P.M., 3:45 P.M.*, 4:30 P.M., 10 P.M., 10:45 P.M.*, 11:30 P.M., 11:45 P.M.*, 11:55 P.M.*, and midnight*
Tulum	US$46	17 hrs	10:15 A.M. and 12:30 P.M.
Veracruz	US$37	9 hrs	9:45 P.M., 10:30 P.M.*, and 11:45 P.M.
Villahermosa	US$15.50	6 hrs	3 P.M., 7:30 P.M.*, 11 P.M., 11:30 P.M., and midnight*
Villahermosa (via *puente*)	US$15.50	5 hrs	6 A.M., 11:15 A.M., 4 P.M., and 11:45 P.M.

*Denotes deluxe ADO-GL or UNO service; prices are 10–30 percent higher.

Money

Banamex (1 Av. Sur Poniente between 1 Calle Poniente and Calle Central Sur, 9 A.M.–4 P.M. Mon.–Fri.) and **HSBC** (Calle Central Norte between Av. Central and 1 Av. Norte, 8 A.M.–7 P.M. Mon.–Sat.) are both near the plaza. A few blocks west, **Bancomer** (Av. Central at 2 Calle Poniente, 8:30 A.M.–4 P.M. Mon.–Fri.) also has reliable ATMs.

Near the outlying hotels, try **Banamex** (Blvd. Belisario Domínguez at Oro Ferraro, 8:30 A.M.–4 P.M. Mon.–Fri.), which has three ATMs, or **Bancomer** (10 A.M.–5 P.M. Mon.–Fri. and 10 A.M.–2 P.M. Sat.), which is across the street. Both are in front of Plaza Crystal.

Post Office

The post office (9 A.M.–5 P.M. Mon.–Fri., 9 A.M.–1 P.M. Sun.) is on the east side of the Plaza Cívica.

Internet

Tuxtla's center area has a plethora of small Internet cafés, especially along Avenida Central and 2 Avenida Norte Oriente. **Ciber Café Internet** (3 Calle Oriente Sur between Calle

Central Oriente and 1 Av. Sur, 8:30 A.M.–9 P.M. Sun.–Thurs., until 6 P.M. Fri., US$.45/hour) is one of three cafés literally on top of each other; **Cyber Filharmónica** (2 Av. Norte Oriente at 2 Calle Oriente, no phone, 9:30 A.M.–10 P.M. daily, Internet US$.70/hour) is a few blocks away. **Enl@ce Sistemas** (2 Calle Poniente between 1 and 2 Av. Norte, tel. 961/600-0421, 9 A.M.–midnight Mon.–Fri., 8 A.M.–midnight Sat., 11 A.M.–2 P.M. Sun., Internet US$.70/hour) is a half block from the bus terminal.

Telephone

Tel Centro (2 Av. Norte at 2 Calle Oriente, tel. 961/612-7187, 9:30 A.M.–10 P.M. daily) places national and international calls for slightly less than the price you pay at public phones.

Immigration Office

The immigration office (tel. 961/614-3288) is on Libramiento Norte Oriente s/n near Paso Limón.

Laundry

The center has relatively few laundry shops. Try **Lavandería La Espuma** (4 Calle Oriente Sur between 1 and 2 Av. Sur Oriente, 8 A.M.–8 P.M. Mon.–Fri., 8 A.M.–5 P.M. Sat.) or **Magic Wash** (4 Calle Oriente Norte 201 at 2 Av. Norte, tel. 961/615-2480) a few blocks away. Both charge around US$1.25/kilo (2.2 pounds) to wash, dry, and fold.

Storage

Rápidos del Sur (2 Calle Oriente at 2 Av. Norte) is a second-class bus line right next to the first-class OCC/ADO terminal; luggage storage is US$.45 every 12 hours.

Travel Agencies

For plane tickets and local tours, try **Monarca** (4 Calle Poniente Norte 145-B at 1 Av. Norte Poniente, tel. 961/600-0236); **Viajes Kali** (Hotel María Eugenia, Av. Central Oriente 507, tel. 961/611-3175); or **Viajes Miramar** (1 Calle Oriente Norte 320, tel. 961/612-3983, www.viajesmiramar.com.mx).

GETTING THERE

Air

Aeropuerto Terán (tel. 961/671-5311 or tel. 961/671-5312) is Tuxtla's surprisingly small main airport at the southwestern edge of the city. Another airport (Aeropuerto Llano San Juan) is used when Terán is fogged in, and a new modern airport was planned for the east side of town. Like the new highway, the new airport will significantly reduce travel time to or from San Cristóbal, but (also like the highway) we'll believe it when we see it. Airlines serving Tuxtla include: **Mexicana/Aerocaribe** (Blvd. Belisario Domínguez No. 1748, tel. 961/612-5771, at airport tel. 961/671-5218 or toll-free Mex. tel. 800/502-2000) and **Aviacsa** (Av. Central Poniente 160 between Calle Central and 1 Calle, tel. 961/611-2000, at airport tel. 961/671-5246 or toll-free Mex. tel. 800/006-2200).

A cab (US$5) is the easiest way to get to the airport, especially if you have much luggage. Otherwise, the R-71 and R-81 minibuses (US$.30, 30 minutes) leave from their stops south of the market on the corners of 1 Calle Poniente Sur and 7 Avenida Sur Poniente, and 2 Calle Poniente Sur and 6 Calle Poniente Sur, respectively. The route can vary, so confirm with the driver that he is going to the airport (the windshield should say Aeropuerto) and ask to be let off when you pass the airport—it is easy to miss.

Bus

Colectivos to Chiapa de Corzo (US$.75, 30 minutes) leave every 10–15 minutes 5 A.M.–10 P.M. daily from the corner of 3 Calle Oriente Sur and 1 Avenida Sur Poniente.

The **main first-class bus terminal** (2 Av. Norte and 2 Calle Poniente, tel. 961/613-5995, ext. 2431) has ADO and OCC service, plus an ATM, mini-mart and Telmex Internet terminal. The **deluxe-service terminal** (tel. 961/612-1639, ext. 2421) has ADO-GL and UNO service and is just across 2 Calle Poniente from the main terminal.

Car

Rental cars start at around US$45–55/day for

a compact VW or Chevy. Some agencies in town include **Alamo** (5 Calle Norte Poniente No. 2260, tel. 961/602-1600, **Budget** (Blvd. Belisario Domínguez No. 2510, tel. 961/615-1382), and **Hertz** (Blvd. Belisario Domínguez No. 1195, tel. 961/615-5348).

GETTING AROUND

Tuxtla's numbered street grid can be confusing at first, but you'll quickly figure it out. The main thing to remember is that *avenidas* (avenues) run east-west (*oriente-poniente*), while *calles* (streets) run north-south (*norte-sur*).

On Foot

Tuxtla's downtown area is a decent size but not so big that you can't get around by foot. Hotels listed in this area are all a short distance to the main plaza. A walk from the Plaza Cívica to Parque Marimba will take about 15–20 minutes—taking a *colectivo* there and back is always an option too.

Bus

Colectivos (also called *combis*, public minibuses) are a good way to get to and from some of the outlying destinations, especially the zoo, the malls, and some of the higher-end hotels. For those sights served by buses, we have included fare and schedule information in the listing itself. Buses/*colectivos* are typically VW minibuses outfitted with seats in the back. If you're sitting on the bench nearest the driver, you will likely be asked by other passengers to pass up their fare, and then return their change. Buses use marked bus stops (unlike in some other cities) and generally cost US$.40. Route 1 is the most popular among tourists as it runs the length of Avenida Central, where most of the sights and hotels are.

Taxis

Taxi fares range US$2–5, depending on how far you are going. Drivers do not use meters, so agree on a price beforehand. To call a cab, try **Jaguar** (tel. 961/611-2678) or **Premier** (tel. 961/612-9869).

Around Tuxtla Gutiérrez

CHIAPA DE CORZO

For many generations before the Spanish conquest, the area of present-day Chiapa de Corzo was inhabited by indigenous people who immigrated from what is now Nicaragua. The settlement was on the Río Kandelumini, known today as the Río Grijalva. Those early Chiapanecos were fierce and courageous warriors, and it took the better-armed Spanish two brutal invasions—the first in 1524 led by Luís Marin and the second in 1528 by Diego Mazariegos—to conquer them. On April 3, 1528, the conquered Chiapaneco village was named Villa Real and dedicated under a large ceiba tree. Like most Spanish settlements in those early years, it was given as an *encomienda* to the conqueror, in this case Mazariegos. This arrangement made vassals of the Chiapanecos, who built the city under Spanish control and amid terrible living and working conditions.

Fortunately, the indigenous people had a hero in Bishop Bartolomé de las Casas, who began agitating for changes from the time of his arrival. By 1552 the *encomienda* was dismantled, and the city was renamed Villa Real Corona. It would change names another half dozen times through the succeeding years. In 1888, after being called Chiapa Español and Chiapa de los Indios the city adopted the present name in honor of the revered president of the municipality, Ángel Albino Corzo.

La Pila

The centerpiece of Chiapa de Corzo is La Pila (the well or fountain), the subject of countless photos and unmistakable in the middle of the large grassy plaza. Built in 1562, La Pila is the largest colonial fountain in the state and certainly among the most impressive. The fountain is an elegant Moorish-style structure, built of red bricks cut in unusual

© LIZA PRADO CHANDLER

La Pila is the largest colonial fountain in Chiapas.

three-dimensional diamond shapes and constructed in the form of the Spanish crown. The fountain was the village water supply, where women collected water in *calabasas* (containers made from large dried gourds), but also a place to do laundry, let the animals drink, and come together for important social events. Take time to read the informational plaques around the fountain for a thumbnail history of the city and the fountain. Unfortunately, today the actual fountain isn't well-maintained and was filled with algae and bits of trash when we passed through.

Catedral and Ex-Convento Santo Domingo

Santo Domingo Cathedral is a huge, though simple, white building that stands just up the hill from the Embarcadero. Its massive 10,000-pound bell was cast in gold, silver, and copper in 1576, and when it tolls it can be heard for miles around the countryside. The convent, which now serves as a cultural center, was built in 1554 in the usual design of the friars, with tile floors, thick walls, and broad archways edging once-lovely patios. Today a few of the

rooms on the second floor house an excellent gallery and museum, the Museo de Laca.

Museo de Laca

Inside the Ex-Convento Santo Domingo, the excellent Museum of Lacquerware (10 A.M.–5 P.M. Tues.–Sun., free) exhibits Chiapa de Corzo's stand-out lacquerware, another craft brought from Europe by the Spanish and mastered (and improved) by native Chapanecans. You'll see fantastic examples of this precision art form—from tiny, delicate jewelry boxes to enormous wooden chests, each covered with bright colors and intricate, hand-painted designs. In the same space are galleries with excellent exhibitions by local painters and craftspeople, plus an extensive collection of ceremonial masks produced and used in various regions of Mexico.

Casa-Museo de la Marimba

Mexican poet Oscar Oliva once said, "In all religious and sacred ceremonies, the marimba is there. With music from the marimba, we bury our friends, our parents, our brothers." And it is not just for sad occasions: Anyone who has spent much time in San Cristóbal or Tuxtla, or at any an outdoor festival or event in the state, will likely be familiar with the sound of the marimba. It is truly the sound and soul of Chiapanecan daily life.

Chiapa de Corzo is the purported birthplace of the marimba, at least in its present form. It is believed that an early version of the instrument was brought to the Americas on Spanish ships by enslaved Angolans. The instrument was adopted, and adapted, by local residents, and today it is highly revered in Chiapas, Guatemala, and beyond. (There is a statue of a marimba player prominently displayed in Quetzaltenango, one of Guatemala's largest cities.) Chiapas produces some of the world's finest marimbas; in the Chiapa de Corzo area, they are constructed from *hormiguillo,* known as the "singing wood," which gives the marimba a rash, brilliant sound. Sticks made from the strong but flexible *guisisil* wood are wrapped at one end with natural rubber to make mallets that fly across the keys. The marimba is no longer the stepsister of concert instruments—it lacks only two octaves to equal the range of a concert piano, and more and more fine music is being written for the marimba by classical and popular musicians worldwide.

The Casa-Museo de la Marimba (Av. Independencia 36, tel. 961/616-0012, tour and concert at noon Fri.–Sun., donations accepted) is run out of the home of the Nandayapas, an extended family of extraordinary marimba craftsmen and musicians. The Nandayapas are creators (and players) of perhaps the country's finest marimbas, still patterned from the 100-year-old templates of the first generations of the Nandayapa family. The keys function like the parts of a string quartet, says the elder Zeferino Nandayapa, and in them you can hear a violin, second violin (contralto voice), the viola, and the cello. The Nandayapas play Bach, Mozart, sambas, *sones,* and lively Mexican music. Their marimbas come in all sizes, but their concert-size instrument can be up to eight feet long and can range 6.5 octaves. A tour and concert at the Nandayapa home is well worth the time, and a highlight of any visit to Chiapa de Corzo.

Templo y Mirador de San Gregorio

This 17th-century church was obviously a grand building in its day. Built on the hill in the middle of town, it still evokes the history of Chiapa de Corzo's one-time wealth and importance. The church had three naves, and the remaining walls echo the influence of the Muhadin, Renaissance, and baroque architecture that Spain brought to the New World. Not a great deal is left today, just a few walls and fine arches, but the view remains, as impressive as ever.

Entertainment and Events

Chiapa de Corzo's biggest celebration—the **Festival de San Sebastián**—takes place every year January 8–22 in the park around La Pila. The main characters are the *parachicos:* boys and men dressed as colonial-era Spaniards, wearing pink-skinned, blue-eyed, mustachioed masks made from wood and topped with bright bushy yellow hair. They carry rattles and wear dressy pants and shirt, a belt of richly embroidered satin, and a brightly colored *zerape* from the city of Saltillo. Women and girls wear the typical dress of embroidered tulle. All decked out, the *parachicos* join in dances and parades in the city center.

Various legends relate how this party began. One is of a wealthy Spanish woman, Doña María de Ángulo, living in Central America with her crippled son. She prayed to San Sebastián and searched for a doctor who would cure the boy. After many false leads, she was told of a powerful herbalist in Namandiyugua near Chiapa de Corzo; she came to the village as soon as possible, praying that her son would be cured. The herbalist instructed her to bathe the boy in a small lagoon called Jaguey (where the wild pig swims). She did so, and she also continued praying to San Sebastián, just in case. When the boy was miraculously cured, Doña Ángulo gave credit to both the herbalist and San Sebastián. The herbalist suggested the boy needed time to recuperate and proposed a small fiesta to distract him. Doña Ángulo organized a party for her son and in honor of the saint who saved him, outfitting her servants with costumes of wooden masks, *zerapes,* and whips. Thus the first Parachico (*para* for, *chico* small boy) celebration was born.

Not everyone agrees with this version, of course. Some say the festival comes from war dances of the pre-Hispanic era; others say the origin lies in a dance performed by Arabs and Christians that was brought from Spain during the colonial period. Whatever the origin, it is a special time to be in Chiapa de Corzo. Reserve your hotel well in advance if you can. For those who don't get a hotel room (most don't), the buses to and from Tuxtla run late into the night.

Accommodations

Overnighters are few to Chiapa de Corzo, but with the growing attraction of Chiapas and the natural beauties it holds, this small town is trying to keep up with the pace. When we passed through, there were a limited number of hotels; most are simple, but almost all are decent.

A long way from California, but right on the plaza, **Hotel Los Ángeles** (Av. Julian Grajáles No. 2, tel. 961/616-0048, www.losangeles chiapas.com, US$18 s with fan, US$20 d with fan, US$4.50 extra for a/c) is a good value. Rooms are very clean and have private bathrooms with hot water and cable TV. Bright bedspreads make them feel that much more inviting.

Down the block, the **Hotel Posada Real** (Av. Julian Grajáles No. 192, tel. 961/616-1015, hotelposadareal@hotmail.com.mx, US$26–31 s/d with a/c) is slightly more upscale. Rooms are large and have new tile floors, air-conditioning, and cable TV. Near the plaza, it's also well situated.

The nicest place in town is **◤ La Ceiba** (Av. Domingo Ruiz No. 300, tel. 961/616-0389, US$51 s with a/c, US$56 d with a/c), three blocks west of the plaza. In a colonial construction, it has an Old World look but New World amenities. Each of the 42 rooms has a private bathroom and cable TV. There also is a welcoming pool in the middle of a lush garden and a good restaurant on-site.

Food

Across the street from the Hotel Los Ángeles, **Centro-Nutricional** (Calle Mexicanidad, southeast corner of plaza, no phone, 7 A.M.– 9 P.M. daily, US$1.50–5) whips up great *liquados* (fruit shakes with milk or water base) and good basic meals, such as quesadillas, empanadas, and scrambled eggs, mostly served on styrofoam dishes. Outdoor tables are in a pretty covered corridor facing the plaza.

Information and Services

Just a door down from the main plaza, the **state tourism office** (Av. Domingo Ruiz at 5 de Febrero, no phone, 8 A.M.–4 P.M. Mon.– Fri.) gives helpful information. You should get equally friendly service at the tourist office's **information desk** (Calle 5 de Febrero 1, 9 A.M.– 3 P.M. Tues.–Fri.), located in an *artesanía* store just off the southwest corner of the plaza.

Farmacia Esperanza (Calle 21 de Octubre between Calles Mexicanidad and Tomás Cuesta, tel. 961/616-0454, 7 A.M.–11 P.M. daily) is one of several pharmacies near the plaza.

You'll find reliable ATMs at **Bancomer** (Calle Mexicanidad, east side of plaza, 8:30 A.M.–4 P.M. Mon.–Fri.) and at **Banamex** (Calle 5 de Febrero, west side of the plaza, 9 A.M.–4 P.M. Mon.–Fri.).

A block north of the plaza, **Turbonet Xtreme** (Calle Mexicanidad 11-A, tel. 961/616-0004, 8 A.M.–10 P.M. daily, Internet US$.45/hour) has late-model computers and a good connection, and it is a much mellower place than its name suggests.

Getting There

From Tuxtla Gutiérrez, *colectivos* leave for Chiapa de Corzo (US$.75, 30 minutes) every 10–15 minutes 5 A.M.–10 P.M. daily from the corner of 3 Calle Oriente Sur and 1 Avenida Sur Poniente. They drop passengers in Chiapa de Corzo on Calle 21 de Octubre on the north side of the plaza. To return to Tuxtla, catch the bus headed the other direction on Calle 21 de Octubre. For San Cristóbal de las Casas, the majority of buses don't enter town, so you have to walk to the highway turnoff.

CAÑON DEL SUMIDERO

Chiapa de Corzo is the main starting point for trips down through the Cañon del Sumidero (Sumidero Canyon). This section of the Río Grijalva was formerly a roaring series of mighty rapids that literally cut their way through the stone to form a narrow canyon. In 1981 the water was harnessed with construction of the **Chicoasén Dam,** one of Mexico's largest, and the tranquil waterway that resulted now serves as a favorite recreational area for locals and visitors alike.

A two-hour boat ride (US$8 pp) starts at the Embarcadero in Chiapa de Corzo, downhill from main plaza at the end of Calle 5 de Febrero. Boats leave when they are full (12–16 people); although there is service until 4 P.M.—and afternoon trips are especially beautiful—you'll be more assured of a trip and have less waiting time if you arrive 9 A.M.–noon, especially in low season.

The boat motors an hour downriver to the dam and an hour back. Along the way, you'll pass below towering stone walls—your driver/guide should point out the highest spot, a sheer drop of more than one kilometer (0.6 mile). In the walls and along the water's edge, you'll see interesting rock formations, caves, waterfalls (during the rainy season), and an ever-changing vista of plants and trees. In one area, a wispy waterfall has created a beautiful formation of moss and plants that looks like a huge Christmas tree.

At a spot farther down you can see a restaurant and vista point high on top of the cliff. Indeed, an alternative way to see the canyon is by car. A road follows the 14-kilometer (8.7-mile) gorge and has five lookout points—**La Ceiba, La Coyota, Las Tepehuajes, El Roblar,** and **Los Chiapas**—all offering spectacular views. From above, you can't help recall the account (portrayed in a painting in the ex-Convento Santo Domingo in Chiapa de Corzo) of an indigenous community that fiercely fought off Spanish invaders, ultimately in vain. Facing defeat, men and women, some holding their children, jumped from the canyon walls to their deaths rather than be captured.

Another option is the newish **Cañon del**

The State of Chiapas

Visitors often take boat trips through the breathtaking Sumidero Canyon.

Sumidero Parque Ecoturístico, along the river just before you reach the dam. Operated by the same people who run Xcaret and Xel-Há near Cancún, the park includes a number of moderate- to low-impact outdoor activities, including kayaking, rappelling, zip lines, mountain biking, and hiking on interpretive trails. There are also a restaurant and small zoo to keep the whole family happy and entertained all day. Admission (including the boat trip through the canyon) is US$18/25 children/adults, and you pay an additional fee for most of the activities inside.

CAVE AND COUNTRY LOOP

A number of caves can be visited (along with some small roadside towns) near Tuxtla Gutiérrez. You will need a car and a guide to visit them, however, as none are set up for regular tourism. This is not a common trip, so tour operators don't typically offer it, but they may be able to provide you (or recommend to you) a private guide. Ask at the tourist office, too. Without a guide, the loop is still a pleasant drive, passing pretty little towns and exploring the countryside.

Headed south, state Highway 195 (a small road) crosses a broad agricultural region known as La Frailesca. After about 18 kilometers (11.2 miles), you'll reach the pleasant little town of **Suchiapa**—a former stronghold of Chiapa indigenous people, the town has a pleasant plaza overlooked by its 16th-century church, Iglesia San Esteban.

Another 30 kilometers (18.6 miles) down Highway 195 is a small sign and turnoff to **Grutas de Guaymas** (Guaymas Caves), which are another 14 kilometers (8.7 miles) down an unpaved single-track road. These caverns are still in their native state, the entrance hidden by coffee trees and containing beautiful stalactites and stalagmites. The area surrounding the caverns is quite pretty too—chestnut trees, orchids, bromeliads, delicate ferns, and numerous and vociferous birds.

Other caves in the area include Belén, El Nilar, La Calavera, El Jaragual, El Encanto,

and Grutas de Cristal—again, do not enter any of these caves without a guide.

Farther along the highway are a series of small- to medium-sized Chiapanecan towns that grew out of worker settlements around former haciendas. **Villaflores** was where workers on Santa Catalina hacienda lived—the hacienda is long gone, but the town is now the area's agricultural hub, producing mainly corn and cattle. Beyond Villaflores are more hacienda-born towns, including **Villa Corzo** and **San Pablo Buenavista,** which has remains of the old hacienda buildings.

From San Pablo Buenavista, take Highway 230 to Revolucíon Méxicana, where you can catch Highway 157 north to Chiapa de Corzo—a cutoff before Chiapa de Corzo crosses the Santo Domingo river and reconnects with Highway 195 back to Tuxtla.

SOUTHERN COAST

Parallel to the ocean, federal Highway 200 runs southeast from the Oaxaca border all the way to Tapachula at Mexico's border with Guatemala. To get there from Tuxtla, you first have to cross the imposing Sierra Madre range, an arid area with pretty views. Along the way, the road passes small towns, abandoned archaeological sites, and the remains of former haciendas.

From Tuxtla west to Cintalapa, Highway 190 passes through the Valley of Cintala, an area of sprawling ex-haciendas. Some of the shells of these old estates stand here and there: Las Cruces, with a beautiful old chapel and La Valdiviana with its tall chimney. Crossing the Sierra Madre Sur, the road winds through the dramatic pass of La Sepultura and eventually reaches Tonalá and Highway 200.

At Tonalá, small roads lead to the coast and to Puerto Arista. Though a popular getaway for Chiapanecans from Tonalá, Tuxtla, and even San Cristóbal, the beaches and facilities at Puerto Arista aren't exactly glorious. The surf can be quite heavy, but a small, protected inlet known as Boca de Cielo offers easy pleasant swimming (and is accordingly packed on summer weekends and holidays). Laguna La Joya is another popular spot.

Hotel Bugambilia (US$50 s/d) is a fine place to spend the night and has an adequate restaurant. Back in Tonalá, **Hotel Del Rey** (Av. Joaquin Miguel Gutiérrez, tel. 966/663-1969, US$25–35) has air-conditioning and is one of several okay but unremarkable places to crash.

From Tonalá east toward Tapachula, the town of **Pijijiapan** (pee-hee-hee-ah-PAN) has houses with tile roofs and crayon-colored facades and tile roofs, giving the streets a whimsical look. On the outskirts of town look for archaeological remnants on large granite stones with carvings from ancient Olmecs. The largest is called **Los Soldados,** which shows a group of indigenous warriors. It is easy to miss them—ask as you go.

Beyond Pijijiapan is **Mapastepec** and the entrance to **El Triunfo Biosphere Reserve.** This mountainous cloud-forest reserve straddles the international border with Guatemala and contains myriad streams, waterfalls, and lush tropical flora. Among the many bird species here are hummingbirds, forest falcons, tanager, trogon, and even quetzal. With its brilliant color and superlative tail feathers (up to 24 inches), the quetzal was revered by ancient Mayans but is nearly extinct now. It lives only in misty cloud forests such as this one, as well as in Guatemala, Honduras, and elsewhere in Central America.

This is a trip for hardy hikers, as you will be climbing the side of the (dormant) volcano, there are no roads, and depending which entry you take, it's at least an eight-mile hike, often on muddy trails in misty conditions. Ask in Tuxtla about guided trips.

Tapachula is the busy international border town and has plenty of hotels, restaurants, and services.

The State of Chiapas

Know the Yucatán Peninsula

An ancient Mayan homeland flanked by the Gulf of Mexico and the dazzling Caribbean Sea, the Yucatán Peninsula is a magical place. White beaches on the eastern shores and wetlands teeming with birds to the north and west surround a rugged interior with both tropical rainforest and arid scrubland. Rising out of the jungles and above the beaches, many grand stone ruins of the Mayans have been uncovered, renovated, and made tourist-friendly. These ancient relics harbor clues to the rise and fall of the great Mayan civilization, while scattered around the ruins and across the peninsula are villages where modern-day Mayans eke out difficult lives as subsistence farmers and, increasingly, wage laborers. For many, Spanish is a second language, and travelers in the Yucatán will hear various Mayan languages, still alive and very much in use today.

Set somewhat uneasily against this ancient history is the very modern story of mass tourism here. Although Cancún is today one of the most visited and well-known vacation destinations in the world, just 35 years ago it was no more than a deserted strip of sand, strewn with seaweed and covered in think mangroves. The effect of this explosive growth on the

San Cristóbal de las Casas

© LIZA PRADO CHANDLER

peninsula's ecology and culture may never be fully understood or agreed upon—to some it is development at its worst, while others see it as a vital source of economic activity in a long-isolated part of the country.

The Land

In the southeastern part of Mexico, the Yucatán Peninsula occupies approximately 113,000 square kilometers (70,215 square miles) and has a shoreline of more than 1,600 kilometers (994 miles). It is made up of three states: Yucatán, Campeche, and Quintana Roo. It is bordered by water on three sides: the Gulf of Mexico to the north and west and the Caribbean to the east. To the southwest are the Mexican states of Tabasco and Chiapas, and directly south are the countries of Belize and Guatemala.

Geologically, this flat shelf of limestone and coral composition is like a stone sponge; rain is absorbed into the ground and delivered to natural stone-lined sinks and underground rivers. It was this abundant limestone that provided the Mayans with sturdy material to create the glori-

ous structures that are now one of the region's chief tourist attractions. Unfortunately, while the soft rock was readily cut with hand-hewn implements, this porous rock allowed few surface rivers and lakes to form in the region. That said, in the extreme south, a sizeable river—the Río Hondo—cuts a natural boundary between Belize and Quintana Roo at the city of Chetumal. Four shallow lakes at Cobá also are scattered between ancient ruins, and here and there, short rivers are open to visitors.

THE COAST

The north and west coasts are bordered by the emerald waters of the Gulf of Mexico. Just inland, the land is dotted with lagoons, sandbars, and swamps. The east coast is edged by the turquoise Caribbean and just a boat ride away are the glorious islands of Isla Cozumel, Isla Mujeres, and Isla Contoy. The second-longest reef in the world, the Belize Reef—sometimes called the Mesoamerican Reef—is found off the eastern shores. Beginning at the tip of Isla Mujeres and extending a vast 250 kilometers (155 miles) to the Bay of Honduras, the reef is an impressive natural phenomena; its health, beauty, and great variety is the reason why thousands of sport divers from around the world come to explore it.

CENOTES

The limestone shelf is the primary reason why so many cenotes (natural wells) are formed throughout the region—it cannot collect water. Instead, it allows rain to seep through the ground, forming rivers and lakes below. During the dry season, however, these hidden waters aren't fed, causing the water level to fall. It is this ebb and flow that erodes the limestone container, creating steep wells. When the surface crust wears thin, it eventually caves in, exposing the water below—cenotes. Some of them are shallow, seven meters (23 feet) below the jungle floor; some are treacherously deep, with the surface of the water as much as 90 me-

ters (295 feet) below. It was around these water sources that Mayan villages grew. In times of drought, the Mayans gathered water by carving stairs into the slick limestone walls or by hanging long ladders into abysmal hollows that lead to underground lakes. Water was precious and continues to be today.

CLIMATE

The weather in the Yucatán falls into the rainy season (May–October) and a dry season (November–April). Though most travelers prefer the milder conditions of the dry season, you can enjoy the area any time of year. Travelers to the Yucatán Peninsula in the dry season will experience warm days, occasional brief cold storms called *nortes,* and plenty of tourists. In the rainy season, expect spectacular storms and hot, muggy days. The region is infamous for its heat and humidity in May and June, which hovers around 90°F *and* 90 percent.

Hurricane season runs July–November with most activity occurring mid-August–mid-October. Though tropical storms are common this time of year, full-fledged hurricanes are relatively rare. If one happens to hit—or even threaten to hit—don't try to tough it out. Head as deep inland as you can go... and quickly!

Flora

Quintana Roo's forests are home to mangroves, bamboo, and swamp cypresses. Ferns, vines, and flowers creep from tree to tree and create a dense growth. The southern part of the Yucatán Peninsula, with its classic tropical rainforest, hosts tall mahoganies, *campeche zapote,* and *kapok*—all covered with wild jungle vines. On topmost limbs, orchids and air ferns reach for the sun.

TREES
Palms

A wide variety of palm trees and their relatives grow on the peninsula—tall, short, fruited, and

even oil-producing varieties. Though similar, various palms have distinct characteristics:
• Royal palms are tall with smooth trunks.
• Queen palms are often used for landscaping and bear a sweet fruit.
• Thatch palms are called *chit* by Mayans, who use the fronds extensively for roof thatch.
• Coconut palms—the ones often seen on the beach—produce oil, food, drink, and shelter and are valued by locals as a nutritious food source and cash crop.
• Henequen is a cousin to the palm tree; from its fiber come twine, rope, matting, and other products. Because of its abundance, new uses for it are constantly sought.

Fruit Trees

Quintana Roo grows sweet and sour oranges, limes, and grapefruit. Avocado is abundant and the papaya tree is practically a weed. The mamey tree grows tall (15–20 meters/49–65 feet) and full, providing not only welcome shade but also an avocado-shaped fruit, brown on the outside with a vivid, salmon-pink flesh that tastes like a sweet yam. The *guaya* is another unusual fruit tree and a member of the litchi nut family. This rangy evergreen thrives on sea air and is commonly seen along the coast. Its small, green, leathery pods grow in clumps like grapes and contain a sweet, yellowish, jellylike flesh—tasty! The calabash tree provides gourds used for containers by Mayans.

Other Trees

The ceiba (also called *kapok*) is a sacred tree for the Mayans. Considered the link between the underworld, the material world, and the heavens, this huge tree is revered and left undisturbed—even if it sprouts in the middle of a fertile milpa (cornfield).

When visiting in the summer, you can't miss the beautiful *framboyanes* (royal poinciana). When in bloom, its wide-spreading branches become covered in clusters of brilliant orange-red flowers. These trees often line sidewalks and plazas and when clustered together present a dazzling show.

FLOWERS

While wandering through jungle landscapes, you'll see a gamut of plants that are so carefully nurtured and coaxed to survive on windowsills at home. Here in their natural environment, these plants simply thrive: Crotons exhibit wild colors, *pothos* grow 30-centimeter (11.8-inch) leaves, the philodendron splits every leaf in gargantuan glory, and common morning glory creeps and climbs for miles over bushes and trees. You'll also be introduced to many delicate strangers in this tropical world: the exotic white and red ginger, plumeria (sometimes called frangipani) with its wonderful fragrance and myriad colors, and hibiscus and bougainvillea, which bloom in

HENEQUEN

Henequen grows easily in the northern section of the Yucatán Peninsula, especially in the area surrounding Mérida. At one time hundreds of sprawling haciendas grew the thorny crop in this sparse, rocky soil—precisely what this type of agave needs. Henequen requires seven years of growth before its first harvest. Each man—barefoot and wearing shorts and kerchiefs—works close to the land, using a scythe to cut one selected tough leaf at a time. The leaves are brought into a field factory in bundles and then shredded and allowed to dry into pale yellow, straw-like sheaves of individual fibers. The sheaves are then processed, dyed, woven, braided, reshaped, and reworked into a multitude of forms by sophisticated machinery. The end product may be rope, twine, floor mats, interior car cushions, wall coverings, or burlap bags. A by-product is animal food. Adding blood meal (from packing houses) and protein (from soybeans) to plant residue produces a nourishing pellet for dogs, chickens, and other domesticated animals.

an array of bright hues. In fact, keeping jungle growth away from the roads, utility poles, and wires is a constant job for local authorities because the warm, humid air and ample rainfall encourage a lush green wonderland.

Orchids

In remote areas of Quintana Roo one of the more exotic blooms—the orchid—is often found on the highest limbs of tall trees. Of the 71 species reported on the Yucatán Peninsula, 20 percent are terrestrial and 80 percent are epiphytic, attached to host trees and deriving moisture and nutrients from the air and rain. Both types grow in many sizes and shapes: tiny buttons spanning the length of a two-foot-long branch, large-petaled blossoms with ruffled edges, or intense, tiger-striped miniatures. These beautiful flowers come in a wide variety of colors, some subtle, some brilliant.

© LIZA PRADO CHANDLER

Seventy-one species of orchids are found on the Yucatán Peninsula.

Fauna

Many animals—most found nowhere else in Mexico—inhabit the region's flatlands and thick jungles. With patience it's possible to observe animals not normally seen in the wild. Just be sure to bring a pair of binoculars, a camera, and plenty of bug repellent. And if you're really serious, consider bringing a small folding stool as well—it might take awhile.

LAND MAMMALS

Nine-Banded Armadillos

The size of a small dog, this strange creature looks like a miniature prehistoric monster. Its most unusual feature is the tough coat of plate armor that encases it. Even the tail has its own armor! Flexibility comes from nine bands (or external "joints") that circle the midsection. Living on a diet of insects, the armadillo's keen sense of smell can sense grubs 15 centimeters (5.9 inches) underground. Its front paws are sharp, enabling it to dig easily into the earth and build underground burrows. After digging

the hole, the animal carries down as much as a bushel of grass to make its nest. Here it bears and rears its young and sleeps during the day. Unlike some armadillos that roll up into a tight ball when threatened, this species will race for the burrow, stiffly arch its back, and wedge in so that it cannot be pulled out. The tip of the Yucatán Peninsula is a favored habitat because of its scant rainfall and warm temperatures since too much rain floods the burrow and can drown young armadillos.

Giant Anteaters

This extraordinary cousin of the armadillo measures two meters (6.6 feet) from the tip of its tubular snout to the end of its bushy tail. Its coarse coat is colored shades of brown-gray; the hindquarters are darker in tone, while a contrasting wedge-shaped pattern of black and white decorates the throat and shoulders. Characterized by an elongated head, long tubular mouth, and extended tongue (but no teeth), it can weigh up to 39 kilograms (86 pounds).

The anteater walks on the knuckles of its paws, allowing its claws to remain tucked under while it looks for food.

The cumbersome creature is found in forests and swampy areas in Mexico and through Central and South America. It is mainly diurnal in areas where there are few people but nocturnal in densely populated places. Its razor-sharp claws allow it to rip open the leathery mud walls of termite or ant nests, the contents of which are a main food source. After opening the nest, the anteater rapidly flicks its viscous tongue in and out of its small mouth opening. Few ants escape.

Tapirs

South American tapirs are found from the southern part of Mexico to southern Brazil. A stout-bodied animal, it has short legs and tail, small eyes, and rounded ears. The nose and upper lip extend into a short but very mobile proboscis. Totally herbivorous, tapirs usually live near streams or rivers in the forest. They bathe daily and also use the water as an escape when hunted either by humans or by their prime predator, the jaguar. Shy and placid, these nocturnal animals have a definite home range, wearing a path between the jungle and their feeding area. If attacked, the tapir lowers its head and blindly crashes off through the forest; they've been known to collide with trees and knock themselves out in their chaotic attempt to flee!

Peccaries

Next to deer, peccaries are the most widely hunted game on the Yucatán Peninsula. Often called a musk hog, peccaries often are compared to the wild pigs found in Europe. In fact, they're part of an entirely different family.

Two species of peccaries are found on the peninsula: the collared javelina and the white-lipped peccaries. The feisty collared javelina peccary stands 50 centimeters (19.7 inches) at the shoulder and can be one meter (3.3 feet) long, weighing as much as 30 kilograms (66 pounds). It is black and white with a narrow, semicircular collar of white hair on the shoulders. In Spanish Javelina (which means spear in Spanish) is descriptive of the two tusks that

You can see jaguars, the Yucatán's largest cats, at zoos in Villahermosa and Tuxtla Gutiérrez.

© LIZA PRADO CHANDLER

protrude from its mouth. This more familiar peccary is found in the desert, woodlands, and rainforests, and it travels in groups of 5–15. Also with tusks, the white-lipped peccary is reddish brown to black and has an area of white around its mouth. This larger animal, which can grow to 105 centimeters (41 inches) long, is found deep in tropical rainforests and lives in herds of 100 or more.

Felines

Seven species of cats are found in North America, four in the tropics. One of them—the jaguar—is heavy chested with sturdy, muscled forelegs. It has small, rounded ears and its tail is relatively short. Its color varies from tan and white to pure black. The male can weigh 65–115 kilograms (143–254 pounds), females 45–85 kilograms (99–187 pounds). The largest of the cats on the peninsula, the jaguar is about the same size as a leopard. Other cats found here are the ocelot and puma. In tropical forests of the past the large cats were the only predators capable of controlling the populations of hoofed game such as deer, peccaries, and tapirs. If hunting is poor and times are tough, the jaguar will go into rivers and scoop up fish with its large paws. The river also is one of the jaguar's favorite spots for hunting tapirs when it comes to drink.

SEA LIFE
Coral Reefs

The spectacular coral reefs that grace the peninsula's east coast are made up of millions of tiny carnivorous organisms called polyps. Coral grows in innumerable shapes: delicate lace, trees with reaching branches, pleated mushrooms, stovepipes, petaled flowers, fans, domes, heads of cabbage, and stalks of broccoli. The polyps can be less than a centimeter (.4 inch) long or as big as 15 centimeters (5.9 inches) in diameter. Related to the jellyfish and sea anemone, polyps attached to a hard surface (the bottom of the ocean, the rim of a submerged volcano, or the reef itself) can capture its minute prey with tiny tentacles that deliver a deadly sting. Polyps need sunlight and clear salt water no colder than 20°C (68°F) to survive.

Coral reefs are formed when polyps attach themselves to each other. Stony coral, for example, makes the connection with a flat sheet of tissue between the middle of both bodies. They develop their limestone skeletons by extracting calcium out of the seawater and depositing calcium carbonate around the lower half of the body. They reproduce from buds or eggs. Occasionally small buds appear on the adult polyp; when they mature, they separate from the adult and add to the growth of existing colonies. Eggs, on the other hand, grow into tiny forms that swim away and settle on the ocean floor. When developed, the egg begins a new colony.

As these small creatures continue to reproduce and die, their sturdy skeletons accumulate. Over eons, broken bits of coral, animal waste, and granules of soil all contribute to the strong foundation for a reef, which slowly rises toward the surface. To grow, a reef must have a base no more than 25 meters (82 feet) below the water's surface, and in a healthy environment it can grow 4–5 centimeters (1.6–nearly 2 inches) a year. One small piece of coral represents millions of polyps and many years of construction.

Reefs are divided into three types: atoll, fringing, and barrier. An atoll can be formed around the crater of a submerged volcano. The polyps begin building their colonies on the round edge of the crater, forming a circular coral island with a lagoon in the center. Thousands of atolls occupy tropical waters of the world. A fringing reef is coral living on a shallow shelf that extends outward from shore into the sea. A barrier reef runs parallel to the coast. Water separates it from the land, and it can be a series of reefs with channels of water in between. This is the case with some of the largest barrier reefs in the Pacific and Indian Oceans.

The Yucatán Peninsula's Belize Reef (sometimes called the Mesoamerican Reef) extends from the tip of Isla Mujeres to Sapodilla Caye in the Gulf of Honduras. This reef is 250 kilometers (155 miles) long, the second-longest in

© LIZA PRADO CHANDLER

The Mesoamerican Reef, the second-longest reef in the world, teems with fish and sea fans.

the world. The beauty of the reef attracts divers and snorkelers from distant parts of the world to explore its unspoiled marine life. The Mexican government has strict laws governing the reef to preserve this natural treasure; stiff fines await those who remove anything from the reef, and spearfishing is strictly prohibited.

Fish

The barrier reef that runs the length of the peninsula from Isla Mujeres to Belize is home to myriad fish species, including parrot fish, candy bass, moray eels, spotted scorpion fish, turquoise angelfish, fairy basslets, flame fish, and gargantuan manta rays. Several species of shark also thrive in the waters off Quintana Roo, though they're not considered a serious threat to swimmers and divers. Some divers even try to get a close look at sharks just off Isla Mujeres, where they "sleep" in caves (the low water salinity is thought to be the reason for their mellowness). Some brave divers boast of petting these sluggish predators, but most choose not to disturb them. Sportfish—sailfish, marlin, and bluefin tuna—also inhabit the outer Caribbean waters.

Inland, fishermen will find hard-fighting bonefish and pompano in the area's lagoons, and those snorkelers and divers looking to float through caves will find several species of blind fish in the crystal-clear waters of cenotes. These fish live out their existence in dark underground rivers and lakes and have no use for eyes.

Sea Turtles

At one time many species of giant turtles inhabited the coastal regions of Quintana Roo, laying their eggs in the warm Caribbean sands. Though many hatchlings didn't survive the appetites of birds, crabs, and sharks, thousands of turtles managed to return each year to their birthplace. The Sea Turtle Rescue Organization claims that during one day in 1947, more than 40,000 nesting Kemp's Ridley sea turtles were counted. By the mid-1990s, the numbers had dropped to approximately 500—a dramatic decline. The reason for the near-extinction is manyfold: the blackmarket sale of turtle eggs for food, the senseless slaughter for shells for fashion, the smuggling of meat—by the ton—into various countries to be canned or frozen (processors often claim the turtle meat in their

© LIZA PRADO CHANDLER

Four of the world's eight sea turtle species nest on the shores of the Yucatán Peninsula.

products is from the legal freshwater variety). Despite huge fines for anyone possessing turtle eggs, nesting grounds along the Yucatán Peninsula are raided. There is no hunting season for these threatened creatures and the sale of the meat is illegal (although some restaurants ignore the law and offer it anyway).

The Mexican government and various ecological organizations are trying hard to save the dwindling turtle population. Turtle eggs are dug up and reburied into the sand on safe beaches; when the hatchlings break through their shells, they are brought to a beach and allowed to rush toward the sea in hopes of imprinting a sense of belonging there so that they will later return to the spot. In some cases the hatchlings are scooped up and placed in tanks to grow larger before being released into the open sea. All of these efforts are in the experimental stage; the results will not be known for years. The government also is enforcing tough penalties for people who take turtle eggs or capture, kill, sell, or imprison these animals.

Manatees

The manatee—or the sea cow, as it is often called—is a creature of immense proportions

with gentle manners and the curiosity of a kitten. Thriving in shallow, warm water, large numbers of this enormous animal at one time roamed the shallow inlets, bays, and estuaries of the Caribbean. Images of them are frequently seen in the art of the ancient Mayans, who hunted it for its flesh. In modern times, the population has been reduced by the encroachment of people in the manatees' habitats along the riverways and shorelines. Ever-growing numbers of motorboats also inflict deadly gashes on the inquisitive creatures. It is a rare gift to see one, although they are sometimes sighted in the shallow bays between Playa del Carmen and Punta Allen.

At birth the manatee weighs 30–35 kilograms (66–77 pounds); it can grow up to four meters (13.1 feet) long and weigh more than a ton. Gray with a pinkish cast and shaped like an Idaho potato, it has a spatulate tail, two forelimbs with toenails, pebbled coarse skin, tiny sunken eyes, and numerous fine-bristled hairs scattered sparsely over its body. The head of the mammal seems small for its gargantuan body, and its preproboscidean lineage includes dugongs (in Australia), hyrax, and elephants. The manatee's

Once prevalent, manatees are now a rare sight on Mexico's Caribbean coast.

truncated snout and prehensile lips help push food into its mouth. The only aquatic mammal that exists on vegetation, the manatee grazes on bottom-growing grasses and other aquatic plant life. It ingests as much as 225 kilograms (496 pounds) per day, cleaning rivers of oxygen-choking growth. It also is unique among mammals in that it constantly grows new teeth—to replace worn ones, which fall out regularly. Posing no threat to any other living thing, it has been hunted for its oil, skin, and flesh.

BIRDS

Since a major part of the Yucatán Peninsula is still undeveloped and covered with trees and brush, it isn't surprising to find exotic, rarely seen birds all across the landscape. The Mexican government is beginning to realize the great value in this treasure of nature and is making efforts to protect nesting grounds. While a few reserves exist in the region, some of the best—and most accessible—bird-watching locales are the archaeological zones. At dawn and dusk, when most of the visitors are absent, the trees that surround the ancient structures come alive with birdsong. Of all the ruins, Cobá—with its marshy-rimmed lakes, nearby cornfields, and relatively tall, humid forest—is a particularly good site for birders. One of the more impressive birds to look for here is the keel-billed toucan, often seen perched high on a bare limb in the early hours of the morning. Others include *chachalacas* (held in reverence by the Mayans), screeching parrots, and, occasionally, the ocellated turkey.

Flamingos

At the northern end of the peninsula, the reserve at Río Lagartos plays host to thousands of long-necked, long-legged flamingos during the nesting season (June–August). They begin arriving around the end of May, when the rains begin. This homecoming is a breathtaking sight: a profusion of pink/salmon colors clustered together on the white sand, or sailing across a blue sky, long, curved necks straight in flight, the flapping movement exposing contrasting black and pink on the undersides of their wings. The estimated flamingo population on the Yucatán Peninsula is 30,000. This wildlife refuge, called El Cuyo, protects the largest colony of nesting American flamingos in the world.

Many of these flamingos winter in Celestún, a small fishing village on the northwest coast a few kilometers north of the Campeche-Yucatán state border. Celestún lies between the Gulf of Mexico and a long tidal estuary known as La Cienega. Since the disruption of Hurricane Gilbert, a flock of flamingos has found a new feeding ground near Chicxulub. If you're visiting Mérida and want to see flamingos during the winter season, it's a closer drive to Celestún or Chicxulub (about one hour) than to Río Lagartos (about three hours). Don't forget your camera and color film!

Sooty Terns

In Cancún, on a coral island just north of Playa Caracol, a breeding colony of sooty terns has been discovered. The sooty tern is one of several seabirds that lack waterproof feathers. Feeding on tiny fish and squid that swim near the ocean surface, the bird hovers close to the water, snatching unsuspecting prey. The sooty tern nests April–September; guests in the Zona Hotelera are urged to stay away from the rocky island during that time since approaching humans often frightened the parent birds, who panic and leave eggs exposed to the hot tropical sun or knock their young into the sea, where they drown immediately.

Estuary Havens

Estuaries play host to hundreds of bird species. A boat ride into one of them will give you an opportunity to see a variety of wintering ducks from North America, blue-winged teals, northern shovelers, and lesser scaups. You'll also see a variety of wading birds feeding in the shallow waters, including numerous types of heron, snowy egret, and, in the summer, white ibis. Seven species of birds are endemic to the Yucatán Peninsula: ocellated turkey, Yucatán whippoorwill, Yucatán flycatcher, orange oriole, black catbird, and the yellow-lored parrot.

Quetzals

Though the ancient Mayans made abundant use of the dazzling quetzal feathers for ceremonial costumes and headdresses, they hunted other fowl for food; nonetheless, the quetzal is the only known bird from the pre-Cortesian era and is now almost extinct. Today they are still found (though rarely) in the high cloud forests of Chiapas and Central America, where they thrive on the constant moisture.

REPTILES

Although reptiles thrive in Yucatán's warm, sunny environment, humans are their worst enemy. In the past some species were greatly reduced in number because they were hunted for their unusual skin. Though hunting them is now illegal in most countries, a few black marketers still take their toll on the species.

Caymans

Similar in appearance to the crocodile, the cayman is a part of the crocodilian order. Its habits and appearance are similar to those of crocodiles with the main difference being in its underskin. The cayman's skin is reinforced with bony plates on the belly, making it useless for the leather market. (Alligators and crocodiles, with smooth belly skin and sides, have been hunted almost to extinction in some parts of the world.)

Several species of cayman frequent the brackish inlet waters near the estuaries of Río Lagartos (River of Lizards). They are broad-snouted and often look as though they sport a pair of spectacles. A large cayman can be 2.5 meters (8.2 feet) long and very dark gray-green with eyelids that look swollen and wrinkled. Some species have eyelids that look like a pair of blunt horns. They are quicker than alligators and have longer, sharper teeth. Their disposition is vicious and treacherous; don't be fooled by the old myth that on land they're cumbersome and slow. When cornered they move swiftly and will ferociously attack a person. The best advice you can heed is to give the cayman a wide berth when you spot one.

Iguanas

This group of American lizards—family Iguanidae—includes various large plant-eaters seen

Know the Yucatán Peninsula

© GARY PRADO CHANDLER

Lizards can often be spotted sunning themselves at archaeological sites.

frequently in Quintana Roo. Iguanas grow to be one meter (3.3 feet) long and have a blunt head and long flat tail. Bands of black and gray circle its body, and a serrated column reaches down the middle of its back almost to the tail. The young iguana is bright emerald green and often supplements its diet by eating insects and larvae.

The lizard's forelimbs hold the front half of its body up off the ground while its two back limbs are kept relaxed and splayed alongside its hindquarters. When the iguana is frightened, however, its hind legs do everything they're supposed to, and the iguana crashes quickly (though clumsily) into the brush searching for its burrow and safety. This reptile is not aggressive—it mostly enjoys basking in the bright sunshine along the Caribbean—but if cornered it will bite and use its tail in self-defense.

From centuries past, recorded references attest to the iguana's medicinal value, which partly explains the active trade of live iguana in the marketplaces. Iguana stew is believed to cure or relieve various human ailments such as impotence. It also tastes pretty good—a lot like chicken.

Other Lizards

You'll see a great variety of other lizards in the peninsula; some are brightly striped in various shades of green and yellow, others are earth-toned and blend in with the gray and beige limestone that dots the landscape. Skinny as wisps of thread running on hind legs, or chunky and waddling with armorlike skin, the range is endless and fascinating!

Be sure to look for the black anole, which changes colors to match its environment, either when danger is imminent or as subterfuge to fool the insects that it preys on. At mating time, the male anole puffs out its bright-red throat-fan so that all female lizards will see it.

Coral Snakes

Several species of coral snakes, which are close relatives of cobras, are found in North America. The coral snakes found in the southern part of the Yucatán Peninsula grow to 1–1.5 meters (3.3–4.9 feet). Their bodies are slender, with no pronounced distinction between the head and neck.

The two North American coral snakes that are found in this region have prominent rings around their bodies in the same sequence of red, black, yellow or white. Nocturnal creatures, coral snakes spend the day in mossy clumps under rocks or logs. They don't look for trouble and seldom strike but will bite if stepped on; their short fangs, however, can be stopped by shoes or clothing. Even though Mexicans call this the "20-minute snake" (i.e., if you're bitten and don't get antivenin within 20 minutes, you die), it actually takes approximately 24 hours for the poison to kill you. According to Mexico's Instituto Nacional de Higiene (National Hygiene Institute), an average of 135 snakebite deaths per year are reported in the country. That number is declining as more villages receive antivenin.

Chances of the average tourist's being bitten by a coral (or any other) snake are slim. However, if you plan on extensive jungle exploration, check with your doctor before you leave home. Antivenin is available in Mexico, but it's wise to be prepared for an allergic reaction to the antivenin by bringing antihistamine and Adrenalin. The most important thing to remember if bitten: *Don't panic and don't run.* Physical exertion and panic cause the venom to travel through your body much faster. Lie down and stay calm and have someone carry you to a doctor.

Tropical Rattlesnakes

The tropical rattlesnake (*cascabel* in Spanish) is the deadliest and most treacherous species of the rattler. It differs slightly from other species by having vividly contrasting neckbands. It grows 2–2.5 meters (6.6–8.2 feet) long and is found mainly in the higher and drier areas of the tropics. Contrary to popular myth, this serpent doesn't always rattle a warning of its impending strike.

INSECTS AND ARACHNIDS

Air-breathing invertebrates are unavoidable in any tropical locale. Some are annoying (mosquitoes and gnats), some are dangerous (black widows, bird spiders, and scorpions), and others can cause pain when they bite (red ants), but many are beautiful (butterflies and moths), and *all* are fascinating. Note: Cockroaches also live in the jungle, so don't be surprised if you run into one.

Butterflies and Moths

The Yucatán has an abundance of beautiful moths and butterflies. Of the 90,000 types of butterflies in the world, a large percentage is seen in Quintana Roo. You'll see, among others, the magnificent blue morpho, orange-barred sulphur, copperhead, cloudless sulphur, malachite, admiral, calico, ruddy dagger-wing, tropical buckeye, and emperor. The famous monarch also is a visitor during its annual migration from Florida. It usually makes a stopover on Quintana Roo's east coast on its way south to the Central American mountains where it spends the winter.

Environmental Issues

RESERVA DE LA BIOSFERA SIAN KA'AN

With the growing number of visitors to Quintana Roo and the continual development of its natural wonders, there's a real danger of decimating the wildlife and destroying the resources that are vital to the Mayan inhabitants. In 1981, authorities and scientists collaborated on a plan to stem that threat. The plan, which takes into account land titles, logging, hunting, agriculture, cattle ranching, and tourist development—and which local people feel comfortable with—culminated in the October 1986 establishment of the Reserva de la Biosfera Sian Ka'an, part of UNESCO's World Network of Biosphere Reserves. Inside, visitors will find hundreds of species of birds including the ocellated turkey, great currasow, parrots, toucans, roseate spoonbill, jabiru stork, and 15 species of herons, egrets, and bitterns. Land mammals also are in abundance: jaguars, pumas, ocelots, margays, jaguarundis, spider and howler monkeys, tapirs, as well as white-lipped and collared peccaries. In the lagoons and ocean, you're also sure to see crocodiles, a myriad of turtles (green, loggerhead, hawksbill, and leatherbacks) and maybe even a manatee or two. Needless to say, this is an environmentally rich part of the region and one worth visiting.

CONSERVATION

Among the top concerns of environmentalists in Mexico is deforestation, which has accelerated with Mexico's burgeoning population. Slash-and-burn farming is still widely practiced in remote areas, with or without regulation. In an effort to protect the land, environmentalists are searching for alternative sources of income for locals. One is to train them to become guides by teaching them about the flora and fauna of the region as well as English. While not solving the problem, it does place an economic value on the forest itself and provides an incentive for preserving it.

Another focus is the plight of the palm tree. The palm is an important part of the cultural and practical lifestyle of the indigenous people of Quintana Roo—it is used for thatch roofing and to construct lobster traps. However, the palms used—*Thrinax radiata* and *Coccothrinax readii*—are becoming increasingly rare. Amigos de Sian Ka'an together with the World Wildlife Fund are studying the palms' growth patterns and rates; they are anticipating a management plan that will encourage future growth. Other environmental projects include limiting commercial fishing, halting tourist development where it endangers the ecology, and studying the lobster industry and its future. A number of other worthwhile projects are still waiting in line.

History

ACROSS THE BERING LAND BRIDGE

People and animals from Asia crossed the Bering land bridge into North America in the Pleistocene Epoch about 50,000 years ago, when sea levels were much lower. As early as 10,000 B.C., Ice Age humans hunted woolly mammoth and other large animals roaming the cool, moist landscape of Central Mexico. The earliest traces of humans in the Yucatán Peninsula are obsidian spear points and stone tools dating to 9000 B.C. The Loltún caves in the state of Yucatán contained a cache of extinct mammoth bones, which were probably dragged there by a roving band of hunters. As the region dried out and large game disappeared in the next millennia, tools of a more settled way of life appeared, such as grinding stones for preparing seeds and plant fibers. The epic human trek south continued until only 3,000 years ago, however, when, anthropologists say, people first reached Tierra del Fuego, at the tip of South America.

ANCIENT CIVILIZATIONS

Between 7000 and 2000 B.C., society evolved from hunting and gathering to farming; corn, squash, and beans were independently cultivated in widely separated areas in Mexico. Archaeologists believe that the earliest people we can call Mayans, or proto-Mayans, lived on the Pacific coast of Chiapas and Guatemala. These tribes lived in villages that might have held more than 1,000 inhabitants and made beautiful painted and incised ceramic jars for food storage. After 1000 B.C. this way of life spread south to the highlands site of Kaminaljuyú (now part of Guatemala City) and, through the next millennium, to the rest of the Mayan world. Meanwhile, in what are now the Mexican states of Veracruz and Tabasco, another culture, the Olmecs, was developing what is now considered Mesoamerica's first civiliza-

tion. Its influence was felt throughout Mexico and Central America. Archaeologists believe that before the Olmecs disappeared around 300 B.C., they contributed two crucial cultural advances to the Mayans: the long-count calendar and the hieroglyphic writing system.

LATE PRECLASSIC PERIOD

During the Late Preclassic era (300 B.C.–A.D. 250), the Pacific coastal plain saw the rise of a Mayan culture in Izapa near Tapachula, Chiapas. The Izapans worshipped gods that were precursors of the Classic Mayan pantheon and commemorated religious and historical events in bas-relief carvings that emphasized costume and finery.

During the same period, the northern Guatemalan highlands were booming with construction; this was the heyday of Kaminaljuyú, which grew to enormous size, with more than 120 temple-mounds and numerous stelae. The earliest calendar inscription that researchers are able to read comes from a monument found at El Baúl to the southwest of Kaminaljuyú; it has been translated as A.D. 36.

In the Petén jungle region just north of the highlands, the dominant culture was the Chicanel, whose hallmarks are elaborate temple-pyramids lined with enormous stucco god-masks (as in Kohunlich). The recently excavated Petén sites of Nakbé and El Mirador are the most spectacular Chicanel cities yet found. El Mirador contains a 70-meter/229.7-foot-tall temple-pyramid complex that might be the most massive structure in Mesoamerica. Despite the obvious prosperity of this region, there is almost no evidence of long-count dates or writing systems in either the Petén jungle or the Yucatán Peninsula just to the north.

EARLY CLASSIC PERIOD

The great efflorescense of the southern Mayan world stops at the end of the Early Classic period (A.D. 250–600). Kaminaljuyú and other cities

CORN: A MAYAN MAINSTAY

Corn was much more than food to the ancient Mayans—it was intertwined in Mayan legend with the notion of the beginning of life. It's depicted in many of the remaining ancient Mayan carvings and drawings; a fresco at the ruins of Tulum, for example, shows human feet as corn.

The crop was so significant to the Mayans that everything else would stop when signs implied it was time to plant the fields. It was Mayan priests who calculated—by means of astronomical observation—the perfect time to fire the fields before the rains. While some Mayan farmers still refer to the calendar keeper of their village for the proper planting date, today most base their planting date on observation of natural phenomena, such as the swarming of flying ants or the rhythm and frequency of croaking frogs—a Mayan version of a *Farmer's Almanac*. Corn is no longer the critical staple it was before the days of stores and supermarkets, but many modern Mayans still rely on it as a steady source of nourishment.

were abandoned; researchers believe that the area was invaded by Teotihuacano warriors extending the reach of their Valley of Mexico–based empire. On the Yucatán Peninsula, there is evidence of Teotihuacano occupation at the Río Bec site of Becán and at Acanceh near Mérida. You can see Teotihuacano-style costumes and gods in carvings at the great Petén city of Tikal and at Copán in Honduras. By A.D. 600, the Teotihuacano empire had collapsed, and the stage was set for the Classic Mayan eras.

LATE CLASSIC PERIOD

The Mayan heartland of the Late Classic period (A.D. 600–900) extended from Copán in Honduras through Tikal in Guatemala and ended at Palenque in Chiapas. The development of these city-states, which also included Yaxchilán and Bonampak, almost always followed the same pattern. Early in this era, a new and vigorous breed of rulers founded a series of dynasties bent on deifying themselves and their ancestors. All the arts and sciences of the Mayan world, from architecture to astronomy, were focused on this goal. The long-count calendar and the hieroglyphic writing system were the most crucial tools in this effort, as the rulers needed to recount the stories of their dynasties and of their own glorious careers.

During the Late Classic era, painting, sculpture, and carving reached their climax; objects such as Lord Pakal's sarcophagus lid from Palenque are now recognized as among the finest pieces of world art. Royal monuments stood at the center of large and bustling cities. Cobá and Dzibilchaltún each probably contained 50,000 inhabitants, and there was vigorous intercity trade. Each Classic city-state reached its apogee at a different time; the southern cities peaked first, with the northern Puuc region cities following close behind.

By A.D. 925 nearly all of the city states had collapsed and were left in a state of near-abandonment. The Classic Mayan decline is one of the great enigmas of Mesoamerican archaeology. There are a myriad of theories—disease, invasion, peasant revolt—but many researchers now believe the collapse was caused by starvation brought on by overpopulation and destruction of the environment. With the abandonment of the cities, the cultural advances disappeared as well. The last long-count date was recorded in A.D. 909 and many religious customs and beliefs were never seen again.

EARLY POSTCLASSIC PERIOD

After the Puuc region was abandoned—almost certainly because of a foreign invasion—the center of Mayan power moved east to Chichén. During this Early Postclassic era (A.D. 925–1200), the Toltec influence took hold, marking the end of the most artistic era and the birth of a new militaristic society built around a blend of ceremonialism, civic and social organization, and conquest. Chichén was the great power of northern Yucatán. Competing city-states either bowed before its warriors or, like the Puuc cities and Cobá, were destroyed.

LATE POSTCLASSIC PERIOD

After Chichén's fall in 1224—probably due to an invasion—a heretofore lowly tribe calling themselves the Itzá became the Late Postclassic (A.D. 1200–1530) masters of Yucatecan power politics. Kukulcán II of Chichén founded Mayapán A.D. 1263–1283. After his death and the abandonment of Chichén, an aggressive Itzá lineage named the Cocom seized power and used Mayapán as a base to subjugate northern Yucatán. They succeeded through wars using Tabascan mercenaries and intermarrying with other powerful lineages. Foreign lineage heads were forced to live in Mayapán where they could easily be controlled. At its height, the city covered 6.5 square kilometers (four square miles) within a defensive wall that contained more than 15,000 inhabitants. Architecturally, Mayapán leaves much to be desired; the city plan was haphazard, and its greatest monument was a sloppy, smaller copy of Chichén's Pyramid of Kukulcán.

The Cocom ruled for 250 years until A.D. 1441–1461, when an upstart Uxmal-based lineage named the Xiu rebelled and slaughtered the Cocom. Mayapán was abandoned and Yucatán's city-states weakened themselves in a series of bloody intramural wars that left them hopelessly divided when it came time to face the conquistadors. By the time of that conquest, culture was once again being imported from outside the Mayan world. Putún Mayan seafaring traders brought new styles of art and religious beliefs back from their trips to Central Mexico. Their influence can be seen in the Mixtec-style frescoes at Tulum on the Quintana Roo coast.

SPANISH ARRIVAL AND CONQUEST

After Columbus's arrival in the New World, other adventurers traveling the same seas soon found the Yucatán Peninsula. In 1519, 34-year-old Hernán Cortés sailed from Cuba against the wishes of the Spanish governor. With 11 ships, 120 sailors, and 550 soldiers he set out to search for slaves, a lucrative business with or without the government's blessing. His search began on the Yucatán coast and would eventually encompass most of Mexico. However, he hadn't counted on the ferocious resistance and cunning of the Mayan Indians. The fighting was destined to continue for many years—a time of bloodshed and death for many of his men. (This "war" didn't really end on the peninsula until the Chan Santa Cruz Indians finally signed a peace treaty with the Mexican federal government in 1935, more than 400 years later.) By the time Cortés died in 1547 (while exiled in Spain), the Spanish military and Franciscan friars were well entrenched in the Yucatán Peninsula.

Fray Diego de Landa

The Franciscan priests were shocked by Mayan idols and religious customs, such as body mutilation and human sacrifice, which they believed to be influences of the devil. The Franciscans believed it their holy duty to eliminate the Mayan religion and convert the Indians to Christianity.

The most notorious of Franciscan missionaries was Diego de Landa, who arrived in Mexico in 1547 as a 25-year-old friar and in 1549 became the assistant minister at the great cathedral in Izamal. In 1562, he oversaw the destruction of at least 27 Mayan codices, filled with characters and symbols that he could not understand, but which he believed contained "superstitions and the devil's lies." Since then, only four codices have come to light, and only parts of them have been completely deciphered. He also destroyed untold number of artifacts and other religious items.

Landa's *auto da fe* shocked many people and he was sent back to Spain in 1563 after colonial civil and religious leaders accused him of "despotic mismanagement." He spent a year in prison, and while his fate was being decided, he wrote his now-famous *Relaciones de las Cosas de Yucatán*. Both defensive and vaguely regretful, the book describes Mayan daily life in great

MAYAN TIMELINES

Period	Year
Paleoindian	before 7000 B.C.
Archaic	7000–2500 B.C.
Early Preclassic	2500–1000 B.C.
Middle Preclassic	1000–400 B.C.
Late Preclassic	400 B.C.–A.D. 250
Early Classic	A.D. 250–600
Late Classic	A.D. 600–800
Terminal Classic	A.D. 800–1000
Early Postclassic	A.D. 1000–1250
Late Postclassic	A.D. 1250–1519

detail, including the growth and preparation of food, the structure of society, the priesthood, and the sciences. Landa did not understand the Mayans' sophisticated "count of ages," but they left a one-line formula which, when used as a mathematical and chronological key by later researchers, helped illuminate Mayan mathematics and astronomy. Landa also included a rough alphabet of Mayan glyphs that turned out to be essential in the decipherment of Mayan inscriptions and texts. Landa was ultimately cleared and was allowed to return to the New World in 1573, where he became a bishop and resumed his previous methods of proselytizing. He lived in the Yucatán until his death in 1579.

The Caste War

By the 1840s, the brutalized and subjugated Mayans organized a revolt against Euro-Mexican colonizers. Called the Caste War, this savage war saw Mayans taking revenge on every white man, woman, and child by means of murder and rape. European survivors made their way to the last Spanish strongholds of Mérida and Campeche. The governments of the two cities appealed for help to Spain, France, and the United States. No one answered the call. It was soon apparent that the remaining two cities would be wiped out. But just as the governor of Mérida was about to begin evacuating the city, the Mayans picked up their weapons and walked away.

Attuned to the signals of the land, the Mayans knew that the appearance of the flying ant was the first sign of rain and signaled the time to plant corn. When, on the brink of the Mayans' destroying the enemy, the winged ant made an unusually early appearance, the Indians turned their backs on certain victory and returned to their villages to plant corn.

Help came immediately from Cuba, Mexico City, and 1,000 U.S. mercenary troops. Vengeance was merciless. Mayans were killed indiscriminately. Some were taken prisoner and sold to Cuba as slaves; others left their villages and hid in the jungles—in some cases, for decades. Between 1846 and 1850, the population of the Yucatán Peninsula was reduced from 500,000 to 300,000. Quintana Roo along the Caribbean coast was considered a dangerous no-man's-land for almost another 100 years.

Growing Mayan Power

Many Mayan Indians escaped slaughter during the Caste War by fleeing to the isolated coastal forests of present-day Quintana Roo. A large number regrouped under the cult of the "Talking Cross"—an actual wooden cross that, with the help of a priest and a ventriloquist, spoke to the beleaguered indigenous fighters, urging them to continue fighting. Followers called themselves Cruzob (People of the Cross) and made a stronghold in the town of Chan Santa Cruz, today Felipe Carrillo Puerto. Research (and common sense) suggest the Mayans knew full well that a human voice was responsible for the "talking," but that many believed it was inspired by God.

Close to the border with British Honduras (now Belize), the leaders of Chan Santa Cruz began selling timber to the British and were given arms in return. At the same time (roughly 1855–1857), internal strife weakened the relations between Campeche and Mérida, and their mutual defense as well. Mayan leaders took advantage of the conflict and attacked Fort Bacalar, eventually gaining control of the entire southern Caribbean coast.

Up until that time, indigenous soldiers simply killed the people they captured, but starting in 1858 they took lessons from the colonials and began to keep whites for slave labor. Women were put to work doing household chores and some became concubines, men were forced to work the fields and even build churches. (The church in Felipe Carillo Puerto was built largely by white slaves.)

For the next 40 years, the Mayan people and soldiers based in and around Chan Santa Cruz kept the east coast of the Yucatán for themselves, and a shaky truce with the Mexican government endured. The native people were economically independent, self-governing, and, with no roads in or out of the region, almost totally isolated. They were not at war as long as everyone left them alone.

The Last Stand

Only when President Porfirio Díaz took power in 1877 did the Mexican federal government began to think seriously about the Yucatán Peninsula. Through the years, Quintana Roo's isolation and the strength of the Mayans in their treacherous jungle had foiled repeated efforts by Mexican soldiers to capture the Indians. The army's expeditions were infrequent, but it rankled Díaz that a relatively small and

modestly armed Mayan force had been able to keep the Mexican federal army at bay for so long. An assault in 1901, under the command of General Ignacio Bravo, broke the government's losing streak. The general captured a village, laid railroad tracks, and built a walled fort. Supplies arriving by rail kept the fort stocked, but the indigenous defenders responded by holding the fort under siege for an entire year. Reinforcements finally came from the capital, the Mayans were forced to retreat, first from the fort and then from many of their villages and strongholds. A period of brutal Mexican occupation followed, lasting until 1915, yet Mayan partisans still didn't give up. They conducted guerrilla raids from the tangled coastal forest until the Mexican army, frustrated and demoralized, pulled out and returned Quintana Roo to the Mayans.

But beginning in 1917 and lasting to 1920, influenza and smallpox swept through the Mayan-held territories, killing hundreds of thousands of Indians. In 1920, with the last of their army severely diminished and foreign gum-tappers creeping into former Mayan territories, indigenous leaders entered into a negotiated settlement with the Mexican federal government. The final treaties were signed in 1935, erasing the last vestiges of Mayan national sovereignty.

LAND REFORMS

Beginning in 1875, international demand for twine and rope made from henequen, a type of agave cactus that thrives in northern Yucatán, brought prosperity to Mérida, the state capital. Beautiful mansions were built by entrepreneurs who led the gracious life, sending their children to school in Europe, cruising with their wives to New Orleans in search of new luxuries and entertainment. Port towns were developed on the gulf coast, and a two-kilometer (1.25-mile) wharf named Progreso was built to accommodate the large ships that came for sisal (hemp from the henequen plant).

The only thing that didn't change was the lifestyle of indigenous people, who provided most of the labor on colonial haciendas. Henequen plants have incredibly hard, sharp spines and at certain times emit a horrendous stench. Mayan workers labored long, hard hours, living in constant debt to the hacienda store.

Prosperity helped bring the Yucatán to the attention of the world. But in 1908, an American journalist named John Kenneth Turner stirred things up when he documented the difficult lives of the Indian plantation workers and the accompanying opulence enjoyed by the owners. The report set a series of reforms into motion. Felipe Carrillo Puerto, the first socialist governor of Mérida, helped native workers set up a labor union, educational center, and political club that served to organize and focus resistance to the powerful hacienda system. Carrillo made numerous agrarian reforms, including decreeing that abandoned haciendas could be appropriated by the government. With his

power and popularity growing, conservatives saw only one way to stop him. In 1923, Felipe Carrillo Puerto was assassinated.

By then, though, the Mexican Revolution had been won and reforms were being made throughout the country, including redistribution of land and mandatory education. In the late 1930s, President Lázaro Cárdenas usurped large parts of hacienda lands—as much as half of the Yucatan's total arable land, by some accounts—and redistributed it to poor farmers. Unfortunately, many indigenous villages that had grown up around the large haciendas were broken up in the process, and indigenous people were (as usual) given less than their fair or rightful shares. Conditions improved—and have improved further since—but discrimination against and exploitation of indigenous people remain deeply entrenched in the Yucatán and throughout Mexico.

Government and Economy

GOVERNMENT

Mexico enjoys a constitutional democracy modeled after that of the United States, including a president (who serves one six-year term), a two-house legislature, and a judiciary branch. For 66 years (until the year 2000) Mexico was controlled by one party, the so-called moderate PRI (Partido Revoluciónario Institutional, or Institutional Revolution Party). A few cities and states elected candidates from the main opposition parties—the conservative PAN (Partido de Acción Nacional) and leftist PRD (Partido de la Revolución Democrática)—but the presidency and most of the important government positions were passed from one hand-picked PRI candidate to the next, amid rampant electoral fraud.

Indeed, fraud and corruption have been ugly mainstays of Mexican government for generations. In the 1988 presidential election, PRI candidate Carlos Salinas Gortari officially garnered 51 percent of the vote, a dubious result judging from polls leading up to the election and rendered laughable after a mysterious "breakdown" in the election tallying system delayed the results for several days.

Salinas Gortari ended his term under the same heavy clouds of corruption and fraud that ushered him in—he is in hiding somewhere in Europe, accused of having stolen millions of dollars from the federal government during his term. That said, Salinas pushed through changes such as increasing the number of Senate seats and reorganizing the federal electoral commission that helped usher in freer and fairer elections. He also oversaw the adoption of NAFTA in 1993, which has sped up Mexico's manufacturing industry but seriously damaged other sectors, especially small farmers, many of whom are indigenous.

The 1994 presidential election was marred by the assassination in Tijuana of the PRI candidate Luis Donaldo Colosio, the country's first major political assassination since 1928. Colosio's campaign manager, technocrat Ernesto Zedillo, was nominated to fill the candidacy and eventually elected. Zedillo continued with reforms, and in 2000, for the first time in almost seven decades, the opposition candidate officially won. PAN candidate Vicente Fox, a businessman and former Coca-Cola executive from Guanajuato, took the reigns promising continued electoral reforms, a stronger private sector, and closer relations with the United States. He knew U.S. President-elect George W. Bush personally, having worked with him on border issues during Bush's term as governor of Texas. Progress was being made until the terrorist attacks of September 11, 2001, pushed Mexico far down the U.S. administration's priority list. With Mexico serving a term on the U.N. Security Council, Fox came under intense pressure from the United States to support an invasion of Iraq. He ultimately refused—Mexican people were overwhelming opposed to the idea—but it cost Fox dearly in his relationship with Bush. With Bush's reelection in 2004, Fox had less than two years to pursue the reforms he once seemed so ideally poised to achieve.

ECONOMY
Oil
The leading industry on the Yucatán Peninsula is oil. Produced by the nationally owned Pemex, the oil industry is booming along the gulf coast from Campeche south into the state of Tabasco. Most of the oil is shipped at OPEC prices to Canada, Israel, France, Japan, and the United States. Rich in natural gas, Mexico sends the United States 10 percent of its total output. Two-thirds of Mexico's export revenue comes from fossil fuels. As a result, peninsula cities are beginning to show signs of financial health.

Fishing
Yucatecan fisheries also are abundant along the gulf coast. At one time fishing was not much more than a family business, but today fleets of large purse seiners with their adjacent processing plants can be seen on the Gulf of Mexico. With the renewed interest in preserving fishing grounds for the future, the industry could continue to thrive for many years.

Tourism
Until the 1970s, Quintana Roo's economy amounted to very little. For a few years the chicle boom brought a flurry of activity up and down the state—it was shipped from the harbor of Isla Cozumel. Native and hardwood trees have always been in demand; coconuts and fishing were the only other natural resources that added to the economy—but neither on a large scale.

With the development of an offshore sandbar—Cancún—into a multimillion-dollar resort, tourism became the region's number-one moneymaker. The development of the Riviera Maya (extending from Cancún to Tulum)—and now, the Costa Maya (south of Sian Ka'an)—only guaranteed the continued success of the economy. New roads now give access to previously unknown beaches and Mayan structures. Extra attention is going to archaeological zones ignored for hundreds of years. All but the smallest have restrooms, ticket offices, gift shops, and food shops.

The People

Today, 75–80 percent of the Mexican population is estimated to be mestizo (a combination of the indigenous and Spanish-Caucasian races). Only 10–15 percent are considered to be indigenous peoples. For comparison, as recently as 1870, the indigenous made up more than 50 percent of the population. While there are important native communities throughout Mexico, the majority of the country's indigenous peoples live in the Yucatán Peninsula, Oaxaca, and Chiapas.

LANGUAGE

The farther you go from a city, the less Spanish you'll hear and the more dialects of indigenous languages you'll encounter. The government estimates that of the 10 million indigenous people in the country, about 25 percent do not speak Spanish. Of the original 125 native languages, 70 are still spoken, 20 of which are classified as Mayan languages, including Tzeltal, Tzotzil, Chol, and Yucatec.

Although education was made compulsory for children in 1917, this law was not enforced in the Yucatán Peninsula until recently. Today, schools throughout the peninsula use Spanish-language books, even though many children do not speak the language. In some of the rural schools, bilingual teachers are recruited to help children make the transition.

ART

Mexico has an incredibly rich colonial and folk-art tradition. In the region covered by this book, Chiapas is the artistic hub, especially for its handwoven textiles. While not art for the people who make and use it, traditional indigenous clothing is beautiful and travelers and collectors are increasingly able to buy it in local shops and markets. Prices for these items can be high, for the simple fact that they are handwoven and can literally take months to complete. Mérida has shops filled with pottery, carving, and textiles from around Yucatán state.

HOLIDAYS AND FESTIVALS

People in Mexico take their holidays seriously—of their country, their saints, and their families. You'll be hard-pressed to find a two-week period when something or someone isn't being celebrated. On major holidays—Christmas, New Year's Day, and Easter—be prepared for crowds on the beaches and ruins. Be sure to

PAPEL PICADO

Mexicans are famous for the numbers of celebrations that they have—whether it's in honor of a saint or to celebrate a neighbor's birthday, partying is part of the culture. Typically, fiestas feature great music, loads of food, fireworks, and brightly colored decorations, often including *papel picado*—row upon row of paper hung from above, dancing in the slightest breeze.

Papel picado (literally, paper cut into small pieces) is cut or stamped with a certain design that is apropos to the occasion: at Christmas you'll see a manger scene, for a wedding you'll see church bells and doves, for Day of the Dead you'll see skeletons in large swooping hats. Once cut, *papel picado* is strung across the streets high above the traffic or hung on wires in front of a church or in someone's backyard.

After the celebration, few are inclined to take down the decorations. Eventually, all that's left is bits of colored paper blowing in the wind, the cord that it was hung on, and the memories of the fine fiesta had.

REGIONAL HOLIDAYS AND CELEBRATIONS

Jan. 1: **New Year's Day**

Jan. 6: **Día de los Reyes Magos** (Three Kings Day—Christmas gifts are exchanged)

Feb. 2: **Virgen de la Candelaria** (religious celebration in which candlelight processions light up the streets in several towns)

Feb. 5: **Flag Day**

Feb./March: **Carnaval** (seven-day celebration before Ash Wednesday/Lent)

March 21: **Birthday of Benito Juárez** (born in 1806)

March 21: **Vernal Equinox in Chichén Itzá** (a phenomenon of light and shadow displays the pattern of a serpent slithering down the steps of the Pyramid of Kukulcán)

May 1: **Labor Day**

May 3: **Day of the Holy Cross** (Dance of the Pig's Head performed during fiestas in Celestún, Felipe Carrillo Puerto, and Hopelchén)

May 5: **Battle of Puebla,** also known as **Cinco de Mayo** (in remembrance of the 1862 defeat of the French)

May 20–30: **Jipi Festival in Becal** (in honor of the plant jipijapa, used in making *jipi* hats)

Early July: **Founding of Ticul** (weeklong celebration)

Sept. 16: **Independence Day** (celebrated on the night of the 15th)

Sept. 27–Oct. 14: **El Señor de las Ampollas** (religious celebration in Mérida)

Oct. 4: **Feast Day of San Francisco de Asisi** (a weeklong religious celebration in Conkal and Telchac Puerto)

Oct. 12: **Columbus Day**

Oct. 18–28: **El Cristo de Sitilpech** (religious celebration in Izamal—the height of the celebration is on the 25th)

Nov. 1–2: **All Souls' Day and Day of the Dead** (graveside and church ceremonies in honor of loved ones—a partylike atmosphere in all the cemeteries)

Nov. 20: **Día de la Revolución** (beginning of the Mexican Revolution in 1910)

Dec. 8: **Feast of the Immaculate Conception** (religious celebrations in Izamal and Celestún)

Dec. 12: **Virgen de Guadalupe** (religious celebration in honor of Mexico's patron saint)

Dec. 25: **Christmas** (celebrated on the night of the 24th)

book your hotel and buy your bus tickets well in advance; during holidays, the travel industry is saturated with Mexican travelers. (For a detailed—but by no means exhaustive—list of the major national holidays, see the *Regional Holidays and Celebrations* sidebar.)

In addition to officially recognized holidays, villages and cities alike often have festivals to celebrate... well, just about anything: patron saints, birthdays of officials, a good crop, a birth of a child. You name it, and it's probably been

celebrated. Festivals typically take place in and around the main plaza of a town with dancing, live music, colorful decorations, and fireworks. Temporary food booths are set up around the plaza and typically sell tamales (both sweet and meat), *buñuelos* (sweet rolls), tacos, *churros* (fried dough dusted with sugar), *carne asada* (barbecued meat), and plenty of beer.

If you're lucky enough to encounter one, a religious celebration is especially interesting (and fun!). You'll see a unique combination of religious fervor and ancient beliefs mixed with people's living it up. In the church plaza, you'll see dancers wearing symbolic costumes with bright colors, feathers, and bells, reminding local onlookers about their Mayan past. Inside the church, a human river of candle-carrying worshippers—some traveling long distances—enter on their knees, repaying a promise made to a saint for bestowing a personal favor or a healing.

Some towns often offer *corridas* (bullfights) as part of the festivities. Even a village will have a simple bullring made of bamboo (no nails are used—only henequen twine holds together two-tiered bullrings!). Rural *corridas* have a special charm. If celebrating a religious holiday, a procession carrying the image of the honored deity might lead off the proceedings. The bull has it good here; it is never harmed—only a tight rope around its middle provokes sufficient anger for the fight. Local men perform in the ring with as much heart and grace as professionals in Mexico City. The crowd shows its admiration with shouts, cheers, and of course—music—even if the band is com-

a Virgen de Guadalupe celebration in San Cristóbal de las Casas

© GARY PRADO CHANDLER

posed only of a drum and a trumpet. In the end, someone unties the bull—*very carefully!*

Getting There

For centuries, getting to the Yucatán Peninsula required a major sea voyage to one of the few ports on the Gulf of Mexico, only to be followed by harrowing and uncertain land treks limited to mule trains and narrow paths through the tangled jungle. Today, the peninsula is easily accessible. Visitors arrive every day via modern airports, a network of new highways, excellent bus service, or by ferry. From just about anywhere in the world, the Yucatán is only hours away.

PLANE

Two international airports are on the Yucatán Peninsula: Cancún and Mérida. Add those in Villahermosa, Tabasco state, and Tuxtla Gutiérrez, Chiapas state, and the total is four. Wherever you are coming from, or wherever

you are going, one of these airports surely will prove convenient.

CRUISE SHIP

Increasing numbers of cruise ships stop along Mexico's Caribbean coast every year, some carrying as many as 5,000 people. Many sail out of Miami and Fort Lauderdale, stopping at Key West before continuing to Punta Venado (servicing the Riviera Maya), Isla Cozumel, and Mahahual (servicing the Costa Maya). Many lines also will take you one-way and drop you off at any of these ports of call.

Prices are competitive and ships vary in services, amenities, activities, and entertainment. Dress is typically casual and pools, restaurants, nightclubs, and cinemas are commonplace. Fitness centers and shops also make ship life convenient. To figure out what type of cruise you'd like to go on, ask your travel agent about options, flip through the travel section of your local newspaper, and surf the net.

If your budget is tight, there are a few cost-cutting tactics you can take. Ships want to sail full and are willing to cut the price to do so—going standby can sometimes save up to 50 percent. Note: Once you're on the list, you'll have no choice of cabin location or size, and airfare is usually not included. Another cost-cutting measure is to join a last-minute travel club. These clubs charge a yearly membership fee (around US$50) and members receive information about upcoming trips and good values. Those able to leave at a drop of a hat can save a bundle. Finally, another good way to save a bit is to book early; some cruise lines will give a substantial discount to travelers who reserve between six months and a year in advance.

BUS

The Yucatán's main interstate bus hubs are Mérida and Cancún, with service to and from Mexico City, Veracruz, Oaxaca and other major destinations in the country. There are also buses between Chetumal and various cities in Belize, plus Flores, Guatemala. Travel agencies and tour operators in San Cristóbal

offer van service to Guatemala, including Quetzaltenango, Panajachel, Antigua and Guatemala City. Agencies in Palenque offer transport to Flores, Guatemala that includes taking a van, boat and bus.

FERRY

Yucatan Express (toll-free Mex. tel. 800/514-5832 or U.S. tel. 866/670-3939, www.yucatan express.com) offers seasonal ferry service between Tampa, Florida and the port town of Progreso, north of Mérida in Yucatán state. The ferry, which carries passengers, cargo, vehicles, and even fishing boats, usually sails twice weekly from October to April. However, service has occasionally been suspended in recent years—call ahead for up-to-date information.

GROUP TRAVEL

Travel agents offer a vast range of organized tours. You pay extra, of course, but all arrangements and reservations are made for you: from guided tours to plane tickets. Special-interest trips are also common—archaeological tours, hacienda and convent routes, and dive trips. Ask around, surf the Internet, and you'll soon find a world of (organized) adventure.

Getting Around

BUS

Mexico's bus and public transportation system is one of the best in Latin America, if not the Western Hemisphere, and the Yucatán Peninsula bus system is no exception. ADO and its affiliate bus lines practically have a monopoly, but that has not made bus travel any less efficient or less affordable. Dozens of buses cover every major route many times per day, and even smaller towns have frequent and reliable service. Wherever bus service is thin, you can count on there being frequent *colectivos* or *combis*—vans or minibuses that typically cover

local routes and can be flagged down anywhere along the road.

Buses come in three main categories or "classes." First-class—known as *primera close* or sometimes *ejecutivo*—is the most common and the one you will probably use most often. Buses have reclining seats and most have televisions, and you usually get a movie on long trips. First-class buses make some intermediate stops but only in large towns. The main first-class lines in the Yucatán are ADO and OCC (primarily serving Chiapas).

Deluxe class—usually called *lujo* or luxury—are a step up. The main deluxe line is

ADO-GL, whose buses typically have nicer seats and televisions (even better movies!) and sometimes have free bottles of water in a cooler at the back. Even nicer are UNO buses, which have fantastic, extra-wide seats (only three across instead of four), headphones, and usually a free sandwich and soda. ADO-GL doesn't cost too much more than regular ADO—typically 10–25 percent—but UNO can be close to double, although prices are still lower than in the United States. Deluxe buses may be slightly faster since they make fewer stops along the way.

Second-class buses—*segunda clase*—are significantly slower and less comfortable than first-class buses, and they're not all that much cheaper. Whenever possible, pay the dollar or two extra for first class. Second-class buses are handy in that you can flag them down anywhere on the roadside, but that is also precisely the reason they take so long to get anywhere. The main second-class lines in the Yucatán are Mayab, Oriente, Noreste, and ATS. In smaller towns, second-class may be the only service available, and it's fine for shorter trips.

For overnight trips, definitely take first-class or deluxe. Not only will you be much more comfortable, second-class buses are sometimes targeted by roadside thieves since they drive on secondary roads and stop frequently. In Chiapas, it is best to take first class at all times.

CAR

As great as Mexico's bus system is, a car is really the best way to tour the Yucatán Peninsula. That is because most of the things you are here to see—ruins, haciendas, caves, deserted beaches, and so on—are rarely right in the cities or along the highway. Rather they are outside of town several kilometers, or down long access roads, or on the way from one city to the next. Having a car saves you the time and effort of walking or cabbing all those "missing links" and frees you to enjoy the sights for as long or as little as you choose. If you're here for a short time—a week or less—definitely get a car for the simple reason that you'll see and do twice as much.

If renting a car for the whole time you are here isn't feasible moneywise, consider renting one for a few days at a time in choice locations: a couple of days in Mérida to see the Puuc Route, a few in Campeche to see the Río Bec archaeological zones, and a couple of days to explore the less-accessible parts of Quintana Roo. You probably don't need a car while you are visiting Cancún, Isla Mujeres, Mérida, or San Cristóbal de las Casas. You may want a car for a day in Cozumel, but perhaps not the whole time you are there.

Car Rental

International rental chains such as Hertz, Budget, and Avis sometimes have good online promotions but otherwise tend to be much more expensive than local shops, the large majority of which are perfectly fair, reliable, and honest. You may get a somewhat older car, but it is rare that travelers are tricked or ill treated. Be sure to ask about the insurance policy: Is it partial or full? How much is the deductible? Do it offer a zero-deductible plan? Before renting, the attendant will review the car for existing damage—definitely accompany him on this part and don't be shy about pointing out every nick, scratch, and ding. Other things to confirm before driving off:

Make sure there are a spare tire and working jack.

All doors lock and unlock, including trunk.

All windows roll up and down properly.

The proper legal papers are in the car, plus a 24-hour telephone number.

The amount of gas—you'll have to return it with the same amount.

You will be asked to leave a blank credit card imprint, ostensibly to cover the deductible if there is any damage. This should definitely be returned to you when you bring back the car—if it isn't, ask for it.

Driving Tips

Driving in Mexico isn't as nerve-wracking as you might think. Most travelers have heard horror stories about Mexican police and worry about

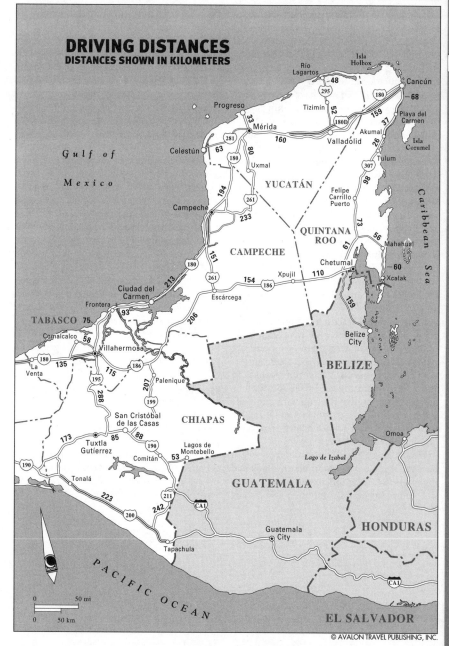

DRIVING DISTANCES
DISTANCES SHOWN IN KILOMETERS

Gulf of

Mexico

Isla Holbox

Río Lagartos — 48

295

Cancún

Progreso

180 — 68

Tizimín

52

Playa del Carmen

33

Mérida

180D

159

37

Akumal

281

63

Valladolid

26

Isla Cozumel

Celestún

80

160

Tulum

180

Uxmal

YUCATÁN

307

Felipe Carrillo Puerto

98

194

261

Campeche

233

QUINTANA ROO

73

Caribbean Sea

180

151

CAMPECHE

61

56

Mahahual

261

Chetumal

Xpujil

110

213

154

186

— 60

Ciudad del Carmen

Escárcega

Xcalak

Frontera

93

TABASCO 75

206

Comalcalco

58

Villahermosa

159

BELIZE

180

135

186

115

Belize City

La Venta

195

207

Palenque

288

199

San Cristóbal de las Casas

CHIAPAS

Omoa

173

85

88

Tuxtla Gutiérrez

190

Lagos de Montebello

Comitán

53

Lago de Izabal

190

223

211

GUATEMALA

HONDURAS

Tonalá

200

242

CA1

Guatemala City

0   50 mi

0   50 km

Tapachula

EL SALVADOR

P A C I F I C   O C E A N

CA1

© AVALON TRAVEL PUBLISHING, INC.

being taken for all their money or trundled off to jail for no reason. The *federales,* who drive black cars, are notorious for being corrupt and unforgiving. While it is true that corruption is rampant among the police, they do not as a rule seek out tourists to harass or swindle. Most people who get pulled over have actually done something wrong—speeding, running a stop sign, turning on red. In those situations, remain calm and polite. If you have an excuse, definitely give it. Unlike in the United States and elsewhere, it is not uncommon to discuss a given situation with an officer. (Obviously, your tone and demeanor should be respectful at all times.) Who knows, you may even convince him you weren't in the wrong—that's what happened to us the one and only time we were pulled over. As long as you are a careful and defensive driver, it is very unlikely you'll have any interaction with the police at all. In some areas, the police are actually quite pleasant—in Izamal, we were flagged down by an officer who just wanted to know if we needed directions.

More of a concern than the police are the young men and women who fill up your tank. Full service is the norm here—you pull up, tell the person how much you want, and he or she does the rest. A common scam is to start the pump at 50 or 100 pesos, while a fellow attendant distracts you with questions about wiper fluid, gas additive, or what have you. Always be sure the attendant "zeroes" the pump before starting.

Finally, be alert at all times for *topes*—speed bumps. They are common on all roads and highways, save the toll roads. They vary in size, but many are big and burly and hitting them at even a slow speed can do a number on you, your passengers, and your car. As soon as you see a sign announcing an upcoming town or village, be ready to slow down. By the same token, few roads have bike lanes or even much of a shoulder—watch for people and animals on the roads, especially around villages but even in places you don't expect.

If you break down or run out of gas on a main road during daylight hours, stay with your car. The Green Angels, a government-sponsored tow truck service, cruise most roads several times a day on the lookout for drivers in trouble. They carry a CB radio, gas, and small parts and are prepared to fix tires. If you are on a remote road, you may be better off hitching a ride to the nearest phone and calling your rental company.

Hitchhiking

Hitchhiking is not recommended for either men or women. That said, it can sometimes be hard to know what is a private vehicle and what is a *colectivo* (shared van or bus). If there's no bus terminal nearby, your best bet is to look for locals who are also waiting for a van or bus to come by and wait with them.

PLANE

Air travel is expensive in Mexico, even for short flights. And although the Yucatán is a big place, there are few flights within the region that make sense travelwise, unless your time is incredibly tight. And if that is the case, you may as well see what you can by car or bus and start planning a return trip.

Visas and Officialdom

PASSPORTS AND VISAS

Citizens of most countries, including the United States, Canada, E.U. members, New Zealand, and Australia, do not need to obtain a visa before showing up at the airport or border. You will be issued a white tourist card when you enter, with the number of days for which it is valid written on the bottom. If you plan to stay for more than two weeks, it is a good idea to mention this to the official and politely ask for the amount of time you need. (The maximum is 180 days, though some officials won't allow more than 90.)

Although it is not recommended, U.S. and Canadian citizens can enter Mexico without a passport. You will need an official photo I.D. and proof of citizenship, such as an original birth certificate. Most airports have a notary office where you can get a notarized letter attesting to your citizenship. These offices cater to people who have a flight in an hour and who left their passport at home, and thus they have no incentive to be affordable—expect to pay US$25 or more. All other nationalities must have a valid passport.

Anyone under 18 traveling without *both* parents or legal guardians must present a signed, notarized letter from the parent(s) staying at home granting permission to leave the country. This is a U.S. requirement aimed at preventing international abductions, but it causes frequent and major disruptions for vacationers, as you can imagine. Ask for details when you book your ticket.

If you plan on driving into Mexico, you will be required to show your driver's license, title, registration, and proof of insurance. Mexican authorities do not recognize foreign-issued insurance; Mexican vehicle insurance is available at most border towns 24 hours a day, and several companies also sell policies over the Internet. Do not cross the border with your car until you have obtained the proper papers. If you do, it will cause headaches (or worse) when

you exit the country, not to mention if you have a problem along the way.

Returning home, you will be required to declare all items you bought in Mexico. Citizens of the United States are allowed to carry through customs US$800 worth of purchases duty-free; the figure varies for other countries. Plants and fresh foods are not allowed into the United States and Mexico, and there are special limits on alcohol and tobacco products. Authentic archaeological finds, certain antiques and colonial art, and other original artifacts cannot be exported from Mexico, or only with special permission. And, of course, trying to bring marijuana or any other narcotic into or out of Mexico or the United States is plain stupid. Jail is one place in Mexico your trusty guidebook won't come in handy.

TRAVELING WITH DOCUMENTS

Make several copies of your passport, tourist card, and airline tickets. Store one copy in a separate bag and give another copy to your travel companion (and you take a copy of his). Carry another copy in your purse or wallet instead of carrying around your actual passport, which you can leave in the hotel safe or locked in your bag. You're a lot more likely to lose it or have it stolen on the street than to have a housekeeper steal it. When you move from place to place, carry your passport and important documents in a travel pouch—they typically hang around your neck or clip around your waist, always under your clothing.

Write down your credit card and ATM numbers and the 24-hour service numbers and keep those with the copies of your passport as well.

CONSULATES

The U.S. consulates in Mérida and Cancun handle passport issues (replacing a lost one, adding pages, and so on) and can help

American citizens involved in serious situations, including hospitalization, assault, arrest, legal suits, or death. They usually do not help resolve common disputes—with tour operators or hotels, for example—as the stern messages on their voicemail and office doors attest. The Mérida office tends to be less standoffish, probably because the staff handles many fewer people than the one in Cancún does.

Conduct and Customs

THE BEACH

The main issue with foreigners on Mexican beaches is topless bathing—while common and accepted in many places in Europe and elsewhere, it is definitely not the custom in Mexico.

BARGAINING

Bargaining is common and expected in street and artisans' markets, but try not to be too aggressive about it. Some tourists derive immense and almost irrational pride from haggling for the every last cent, and then turn around and spend three times that amount on beer and cigarettes. The fact is, most bargaining comes down to the difference of a few dollars or even less, and earning those two dollars is a much bigger deal for the artisan than spending them is to you. And the interaction is a more gracious and pleasant one for everyone involved.

PHOTOGRAPHING LOCALS

No one enjoys having a stranger take his or her picture for no good reason. Indigenous people in Mexico are especially opposed to having their pictures taken. The best policy is to simply not take these pictures—if you must, definitely ask permission in a way that allows the person to say no if that is what he or she chooses.

TIPPING

While tipping is always a choice, it is a key supplement to many workers' paychecks. In fact, for some, the tip is the *only* pay they receive. And while dollars and euros are appreciated, pesos are preferred. (Note: Foreign coins are useless in Mexico since moneychangers—whether banks or exchange houses—will not accept them.) Average gratuities in the region include:

Archaeological zone guides: 10–15 percent if you're satisfied with the service; for informal guides (typically boys who show you around the site) US$.50–1 is customary.

Gas station attendants: around US$.50 if your windshield has been cleaned, tires have been filled, or the oil and water have been checked; no tip is expected for simply pumping gas.

Grocery store baggers: US$.30–.50.

Housekeepers: US$1–2 per day; left at the end of your stay.

Porters: about US$1 per bag.

Taxi drivers: Tipping is not customary.

Tour guides: 10–15 percent if they do a good job, of course; and don't forget the driver—US$1–2 is typical.

Waiters: 10–15 percent; make sure the gratuity is not included in the bill.

Tips for Travelers

TRAVELERS WITH DISABILITIES

Mexico has made many improvements for the blind and people in wheelchairs—many large stores and tourist centers have ramps and/or elevators. A growing number of hotels have rooms designed for guests with disabilities, and we saw two museums—the stelae museum in Campeche City and the anthropology museum in Villahermosa—that had high-quality replicas of Mayan artifacts that visually impaired travelers could hold and touch. That said, Mexico is still a hard place to navigate if you have a disability. The smaller towns are the most problematic, as their sidewalks can be narrow and even some main streets may not be paved. Definitely ask for help—for what it lacks in infrastructure, Mexico makes up for in graciousness and charity.

WOMEN TRAVELERS

Mexico is a modern, enlightened, and yet still deeply paternalistic place. It is rare to see Mexican women traveling alone (or Mexican men for that matter) and there is something clearly titillating about the idea of an unattached woman. Solo women should expect a certain amount of unwanted attention, mostly in the form of whistles and catcalls. It typically happens as you walk down the street and sometimes comes from the most unlikely sources—we saw a man dressed as Bozo the clown turn mid–balloon animal to whistle at a woman walking by. Two or more women walking together attract much less unwanted attention, and a woman and man walking together will get none at all (at least of this sort—street vendors are a different story). While annoying and often unnerving, this sort of attention is almost always completely benign, and ignoring it is definitely the best response.

Making eye contact or snapping a smart retort will only get you more attention. Occasionally men will hustle alongside you trying to strike up a conversation—if you don't want to engage, a brief *hasta luego* or *no gracias* should make that clear. If it really gets on your nerves, we found that carrying a notebook—and appearing to be working—reduced the amount of unwanted attention greatly.

GAY AND LESBIAN TRAVELERS

While openly gay women are still rare in Mexico, gay men are increasingly visible in large cities and certain tourist areas. Mérida has a fairly large gay community, of which a number of expat hotel and guesthouse owners are a prominent part. Cancún and Playa del Carmen both have a visible gay presence and a number of gay-friendly venues. That said, this is still Mexico and most locals—even in large cities and especially the small villages—are not accustomed to open displays of homosexuality. Many hotel attendants simply don't grasp the idea that two men traveling together would want one king-sized bed—in some cases they will outright refuse to grant the request. Some couples find it easier to have one person go up to the counter instead of both.

STUDYING SPANISH

While it may never approach neighboring Guatemala for the sheer number of Spanish schools, Mexico and the Yucatán Peninsula in particular have a number of options for people who want to learn the language. San Cristóbal, Mérida, Playa del Carmen, Cancún, and Tulum all have schools or private instruction available, and all are well-situated to enjoy the area's richness, whether its beaches, Mayan ruins, or indigenous villages.

Health

SUNBURN

Snorkeling may be the most common way travelers get sunburned. Your back, neck, and the backs of your legs and arms, which probably don't see the sun much in the first place, suddenly get prolonged direct exposure, even worse than the oblique exposure they get when you are standing or sitting upright. And unlike during sunbathing, you don't get hot while you're snorkeling. Many dedicated snorkelers wear full or short wetsuits, but even a dark T-shirt and extra-long shorts will help. For the parts that remain exposed, use waterproof sunscreen.

In all situations, common sense is the most important factor in avoiding sunburn. Use waterproof and sweatproof sunscreen with a high SPF. Reapply regularly—even the most heavy-duty waterproof sunscreen washes off faster than it claims to on the bottle (or gets rubbed off when you use your towel to dry off). Be extra careful to protect parts of your body that aren't normally exposed to the sun, and give your skin a break from direct sun every few hours, especially if you are out in the middle of the day. Remember that redness from a sunburn takes several hours to appear on your skin—that is, you can be sunburned long before you *look* sunburned.

If you get a bad burn, treat it like any other burn by running cool water over it as long as often as you can. Do not expose it to more sun—if you can't stay in the shade, definitely cover the burned parts up. Reburning the skin can result in painful blisters that easily become infected. There are a number of products designed to relieve sunburns, most with aloe extracts in them. Drink plenty of water to keep your skin hydrated.

HEAT EXHAUSTION

The symptoms of heat exhaustion are cool moist skin, profuse sweating, headache, fatigue, and drowsiness. It is associated with (and complicated by) dehydration and commonly hits during or after a long strenuous day in the sun, such as visiting ruins or sightseeing in Mérida. You should get out of the sun, remove any tight or restrictive clothing, and sip a sports drink such as Gatorade, available in many supermarkets and minimarts. Cool compresses and raising your feet and legs may help too.

Heat exhaustion is not the same as heat stroke, which is when the victim's body temperature is high, the pulse rapid, possibly accompanied by delirium or even unconsciousness. It is an extremely serious, potentially fatal condition and victims should be taken to the hospital immediately. In the meantime, wrap the victim in wet sheets, but do not overchill. Massage arms and legs to increase circulation. Do not give large amounts of liquids. Do not give liquids if the victim is unconscious.

DIARRHEA

The most common tourist ailment has a lot of names: turista, Montezuma's Revenge, the trots, the runs, traveler's illness, or just plain diarrhea. Diarrhea is not an illness itself, but your body's attempt to get rid of something bad in a hurry; that something can be any one of a number of strains of bacteria, parasites, or amoebae that you likely got from contaminated water. No fun, it is usually accompanied by cramping, dehydration, fever, and of course frequent trips to the bathroom. Some travelers to Mexico worry about getting so-called Montezuma's Revenge the moment they cross the border. But with a few simple precautions, you should be able to avoid having any stomach problems at all.

The biggie, of course, is the water. Never ever drink tap water, and avoid using it even for brushing your teeth. Most hotels provide a bottle for this very purpose. Bottled water is available just about everywhere.

Avoid any raw fruits or vegetables that you haven't washed and cut up yourself, especially in budget and midrange eateries. While high-end restaurants typically use disinfectant to wash all produce—and say so on their menus—that is still not the norm at smaller places. Unless fruit and vegetables are dried thoroughly, they may have contaminated water still on them. Lettuce is especially worrisome, as water is easily trapped in the leaves. As tasty as they look, the bags of sliced fruit sold from street carts are better avoided.

Meat is the other big culprit in making tourists sick. If you've been to a market, you'll see that meat is handled very differently here. Any dish you order should be cooked well done, or at least medium if you are at a restaurant that specializes in fine meats.

If you do get sick, it should pass in a day or two. Anti-diarrheals such as Lomotil and Imodium A-D will plug you up but don't cure you—use them only if you can't be near a bathroom. That said, you have to be very con-scientious about drinking plenty of fluids—a sports drink such as Gatorade is best. This is extremely important—much of the malaise you feel from diarrhea is from dehydration, not the diarrhea or stomach infection itself. If it is especially bad, ask at your hotel for the nearest *laborotorio* (laboratory or clinic) where the staff can analyze a stool sample for around US$5 and tell you what you have. Assuming it's a common infection, they will even tell you what medicine to take, which you can buy at any pharmacy. Be aware that medicines for stomach infection are seriously potent, killing not only the bad stuff but the good stuff as well. They cure you but leave you even more vulnerable to another infection than you were when you started out. Avoid alcohol and spicy foods for several days afterward.

Information and Services

MONEY

ATMs

Almost very town of any size in the Yucatán Peninsula has an ATM and they are without question the easiest, fastest, and best way to manage your money. The ATM may charge a small trans-action fee (less than US$1 typically) and your home bank may as well, but you don't lose any more than you would by buying travelers checks and then exchanging them at a crummy rate.

Credit Cards

Visa and MasterCard are accepted at all large hotels and many medium and small ones, up-scale restaurants, travel agencies, and many shops throughout Mexico, and at main ADO bus terminals. American Express is accepted much less frequently. Some merchants tack on a 5–10 percent surcharge—ask before you pay.

Travelers Checks

With the spread of ATMs, travelers checks have stopped being useful for most travel, especially in a country as developed as Mexico. In fact, we don't carry them and haven't for several years. If you do bring them, you will have to exchange them at banks or a *casa de cambio* (exchange booth).

Cash

It's a good idea to bring a small amount of U.S. cash, on the off-chance your ATM an credit cards suddenly stop working; US$100 is more than enough. Stow it away with your other important documents, to be used only if necessary.

Taxes

A 12 percent value-added tax (IVA in Span-ish) applies to room rates, restaurant and bar tabs, and gift purchases. When checking in or making reservations at a hotel, ask if tax has already been added. In some cases it will be 17 percent.

COMMUNICATIONS AND MEDIA

Mail

Mailing and shipping from Mexico is easy within certain limitations. Items of less than

US$25 in value can be sent to the United States. The package must be marked "Unsolicited Gift—Under $25" and addressed to someone other than the traveler. Only one package per day may be sent to the same addressee.

Postcards to the United States and Canada cost US$.60, letters US$.80. Delivery times vary greatly, and letters get "lost" somewhat more than postcards.

Fax and Internet

Internet cafés can be found in virtually every town in the Yucatán Peninsula. (The last holdout we know of was Punta Allen in the Sian Ka'an biosphere reserve.) Prices vary—the cheapest we saw was US$.45/hour and the most expensive was US$7/hour. The vast majority charge US$.80–1.25/hour. Most places will also burn digital photos onto a CD—they typically have the blank CD, but you should bring your own USB cable. Expect to pay US$2–3/burn, plus the computer time. Many Internet shops also offer fax service, as do telephone stations.

Telephone Calls

Ladatel—Mexico's national phone company—maintains good public phones all over the peninsula and country. Plastic phone cards with little chips in them are sold at most minimarts and supermarkets in 30-, 50-, 100-, and 200-peso denominations. Ask for a *tarjeta Ladatel*—they are the size and stiffness of a credit card, as opposed to the thin cards used for cell phones. You insert the card into the phone, and the amount you have on the card is displayed on the screen. Rates are US$.09/minute for local calls, US$.34/minute for national calls, US$.44/minute for calls to the United States and Canada.

To dial a cellular phone, you must dial 044 and the area code, then the number. Note that calling a cell phone, even a local one, costs the same as a domestic long-distance telephone call (US$0.34/min.).

A number of Internet cafés offer inexpensive web-based phone service, especially in the larger cities where broadband connections make this sort of calling possible. Rates tend to be slightly lower than those of Ladatel, and

USEFUL TELEPHONE NUMBERS

Traveler Assistance
Emergencies: 060 or 066 (depends on the city)
Directory Assistance: 044

Long-Distance Direct Dialing
Domestic long-distance: 01 + area code + number
International long-distance (United States only): 001 + area code + number
International long-distance (rest of the world): 001 + country code + area code + number

Long Distance Collect Calls
Domestic long-distance operator: 02
International long-distance operator (English-speaking): 09

Long Distance Calls via U.S. Carriers
AT&T: 001-800/462-4240
MCI: 001-800/674-7000
Sprint: 001-800/877-8000

you don't have to worry about your card running out.

Newspapers

The main daily newspapers in the Yucatán Peninsula are *El Diario de Yucatán*, *Novedades Quintana Roo*, and *Voz del Caribe*. The main national newspapers are also readily available, including *Reforma*, *La Prensa*, and *La Jornada*. For news in English, you'll find the *Miami Herald Cancún Edition* in Cancún and occasionally in Playa del Carmen, Isla Cozumel, and Mérida.

Radio and Television

Most large hotels and a number of midsized and small ones have cable or satellite TV, which usually includes CNN (though sometimes in Spanish only), MTV, and other American channels. AM and FM radio options are surprisingly bland—you're more likely to find a good *rock en español* station in California than you are in the Yucatán.

Photography and Video

It's easy to find 35mm film in Mexico, but you can probably buy it much more cheaply at home. If you do bring your own film, do not send it through the X-ray machine at the airport or in your checked luggage (most of which is also X-rayed). Instead, ask the security officers to hand-inspect your film, both exposed and unexposed rolls. The modern machines are not supposed to hurt even 800-plus-speed film, but it's better to be safe than to risk coming home with 10 rolls of faded or grainy shots.

Digital cameras are as popular in Mexico as they are everywhere else, but memory sticks and other paraphernalia are still prohibitively expensive. Bring what you think you'll need, including a few blank CDs and the USB cable you use to download pictures—most Internet cafés allow you to download and burn photos, but may not have the CD or cable.

Video is another great way to capture the color and movement of the Yucatán. Be aware that all archaeological sites charge an additional US$2.50 to bring in a video, and tripods are prohibited.

MAPS AND TOURIST INFORMATION

Tourist Offices

Most cities in the Yucatán have a tourist office, and some have more. When there is more than one, one is probably state-run and the other city-run, and the two will have nothing to do with each other. Some tourist offices are staffed with friendly and knowledgeable people and have a good sense of what tourists are looking for—the city tourism office in Mérida is one of the best. At others you will seriously wonder how the people there got hired. It is certainly worth stopping in if you have a question—you may well get it answered, but don't be surprised if you don't.

Maps

A great source of maps of Cancún, Isla Mujeres,

Cozumel, and other places on the Riviera Maya is www.cancunmap.com. An American couple uses aerial photographs, GIS software, and a lot of old-fashioned legwork to create incredibly detailed city and area maps. Virtually every building and business is identified, most with a short review, plus useful info such as taxi rates, driving distances, ferry schedules, and more. It is amazing how much information they manage to cram on the map, yet still make it easy to use. Maps cost around US$8.

Otherwise, maps can be hard to come by in the Yucatán Peninsula. The tourist office is always a good place to start—in Chiapas, for example, the state has created a large set of city maps and brochures that are distributed to tourists free of charge. Car-rental agencies often have maps they may let you have if you ask nicely, and many hotels create maps for their guests of nearby restaurants and sights.

WEIGHTS AND MEASURES

Measurements

Mexico uses the metric system, so distances are in kilometers, weights are in kilograms, gasoline is sold by the liter, and temperatures are given on the Celsius scale. A chart at the back of this book will help you make conversions. In short, a kilogram is just over two pounds, a kilometer is 0.6 mile and a mile is 1.6 kilometers, and if temperatures get above 40°C (104°F) it is *hot!*

Time

After a brief and ill-advised attempt on the part of Quintana Roo's former governor to eschew daylight saving time, the entire Yucatán Peninsula is on the same hour—U.S. Central Standard Time Zone—and switches to Central Daylight Time April–October.

Electricity

Mexico uses the same 60-cycle, 110-volt AC current common in the United States, and all travel appliances, chargers, and other devices can be used. Bring a surge protector if you plan to plug in a laptop.

Mayan Glossary

MAYAN GODS AND CEREMONIES

Acanum—protective deity of hunters
Ahau Can—serpent lord and highest priest
Ahau Chamehes—deity of medicine
Ah Cantzicnal—aquatic deity
Ah Chhuy Kak—god of violent death and sacrifice
Ahcit Dzamalcum—protective god of fishermen
Ah Cup Cacap—god of the underworld who denies air
Ah Itzám—the water witch
Ah kines—priests, lords who consult the oracles, celebrate ceremonies, and preside over sacrifices
Ahpua—god of fishing
Ah Puch—god of death
Ak'Al—sacred marsh where water abounds
Bacaboob—supporters of the sky and guardians of the cardinal points, who form a single god, Ah Cantzicnal Becabs
Bolontiku—the nine lords of the night
Chac—god of rain and agriculture
Chac Bolay Can—the butcher serpent living in the underworld
Chaces—priest's assistants in agricultural and other ceremonies
Cihuateteo—women who become goddesses through death in childbirth (Nahuatl word)
Cit Chac Coh—god of war
Hetzmek—ceremony when the child is first carried astride the hip
Hobnil Bacab—the bee god, protector of beekeepers
Holcanes—the brave warriors charged with obtaining slaves for sacrifice. (This word was unknown until the Postclassic era.)
Hunab Ku—giver of life, builder of the universe, and father of Itzámna
Ik—god of the wind
Itzámna—lord of the skies, creator of the beginning, god of time

Ix Chel—goddess of birth, fertility, medicine; credited with inventing spinning
Ixtab—goddess of the cord and of suicide by hanging
Kinich—face of the sun
Kukulcán—quetzal-serpent, plumed serpent
Metnal—the underworld, place of the dead
Nacom—warrior chief
Noh Ek—Venus
Pakat—god of violent death
Zec—spirit lords of beehives

FOOD AND DRINK

alche—inebriating drink, sweetened with honey and used for ceremonies and offerings
ic—chili
itz—sweet potato
kabaxbuul—the heaviest meal of the day, eaten at dusk and containing cooked black beans
kah—pinole flour
kayem—ground maize
macal—a type of root
muxubbak—tamale
on—avocado
op—plum
p'ac—tomatoes
put—papaya
tzamna—black bean
uah—tortillas
za—maize drink

ANIMALS

acehpek—dog used for deer hunting
ah maax cal—the prattling monkey
ah maycuy—the chestnut deer
ah sac dziu—the white thrush
ah xixteel ul—the rugged land conch
bil—hairless dog reared for food
cutz—wild turkey
cutzha—duck
hoh—crow

icim—owl
jaleb—hairless dog
keh—deer
kitam—wild boar
muan—evil bird related to death
que—parrot
thul—rabbit
tzo—domestic turkey
utiu—coyote

MUSIC AND FESTIVALS

ah paxboob—musicians
bexelac—turtle shell used as percussion instrument
chohom—dance performed in ceremonies during the month of Zip, related to fishing
chul—flute
hom—trumpet
kayab—percussion instrument fashioned from turtle shell
Oc na—festival of the month of Yax; old idols of the temple are broken and replaced with new
okot uil—dance performed during the Pocan ceremony
Pacum chac—festival in honor of the war gods
tunkul—drum
zacatan—a drum made from a hollowed tree trunk, with one opening covered with hide

ELEMENTS OF TIME

baktun—144,000-day Mayan calendar
chumuc akab—midnight
chumuc kin—midday
chunkin—midday
haab—solar calendar of 360 days made up with five extra days of misfortune, which complete the final month
emelkin—sunset
kaz akab—dusk
kin—the sun, the day, the unity of time
potakab—time before dawn
yalhalcab—dawn

NUMBERS

hun—one
ca—two
ox—three
can—four
ho—five
uac—six
uuc—seven
uacax—eight
bolon—nine
iahun—10
buluc—11
iahca—12
oxlahum—13
canlahum—14
holahun—15
uaclahun—16
uuclahun—17
uacaclahun—18
bolontahun—19
hunkal—20

PLANTS AND TREES

ha—cacao seed
kan ak—plant that produces a yellow dye
ki—sisal
kiixpaxhkum—chayote
kikche—tree the trunk of which is used to make canoes
kuche—red cedar tree
k'uxub—annatto tree
piim—fiber of the cotton tree
taman—cotton plant
tauch—black zapote tree
tazon te—moss

MISCELLANEOUS WORDS

ah kay kin bak—meat-seller
chaltun—water cistern
cha te—black vegetable dye
chi te—eugenia, plant for dyeing
ch'oh—indigo
ek—dye
hadzab—wooden swords
halach uinic—leader

mayacimil—smallpox epidemic, "easy death"

palapa—traditional Mayan structure constructed without nails or tools

pic—underskirt

ploms—rich people

suyen—square blanket

xanab—sandals

xicul—sleeveless jacket decorated with feathers

xul—stake with a pointed, fire-hardened tip

yuntun—slings

Spanish Phrasebook

Your Mexico adventure will be more fun if you use a little Spanish. Mexican folks, although they may smile at your funny accent, will appreciate your halting efforts to break the ice and transform yourself from a foreigner to a potential friend.

Spanish commonly uses 30 letters—the familiar English 26, plus four straightforward additions: ch, ll, ñ, and rr, which are explained in "Consonants," below.

PRONUNCIATION

Once you learn them, Spanish pronunciation rules—in contrast to English—don't change. Spanish vowels generally sound softer than in English. (Note: The capitalized syllables below receive stronger accents.)

Vowels

a — like ah, as in "hah": *agua* AH-gooah (water), *pan* PAHN (bread), and *casa* CAH-sah (house)

e — like ay, as in "may:" *mesa* MAY-sah (table), *tela* TAY-lah (cloth), and *de* DAY (of, from)

i — like ee, as in "need": *diez* dee-AYZ (ten), *comida* ko-MEE-dah (meal), and *fin* FEEN (end)

o — like oh, as in "go": *peso* PAY-soh (weight), *ocho* OH-choh (eight), and *poco* POH-koh (a bit)

u — like oo, as in "cool": *uno* OO-noh (one), *cuarto* KOOAHR-toh (room), and *usted* oos-TAYD (you); when it follows a "q" the **u** is silent; when it follows an "h" or has an umlaut, it's pronounced like "w"

Consonants

b, d, f, k, l, m, n, p, q, s, t, v, w, x, y, z, and **ch** — pronounced almost as in English; **h** occurs, but is silent—not pronounced at all.

c — like k as in "keep": *cuarto* KOOAR-toh (room), Tepic tay-PEEK (capital of Nayarit state); when it precedes "e" or "i," pronounce **c** like s, as in "sit": *cerveza* sayr-VAY-sah (beer), *encima* ayn-SEE-mah (atop).

g — like g as in "gift" when it precedes "a," "o," "u," or a consonant: *gato* GAH-toh (cat), *hago* AH-goh (I do, make); otherwise, pronounce **g** like h as in "hat": *giro* HEE-roh (money order), *gente* HAYN-tay (people)

j — like h, as in "has": *Jueves* HOOAY-vays (Thursday), *mejor* may-HOR (better)

ll — like y, as in "yes": *toalla* toh-AH-yah (towel), *ellos* AY-yohs (they, them)

ñ — like ny, as in "canyon": *año* AH-nyo (year), *señor* SAY-nyor (Mr., sir)

r — is lightly trilled, with tongue at the roof of your mouth like a very light English d, as in "ready": *pero* PAY-doh (but), *tres* TDAYS (three), *cuatro* KOOAH-tdoh (four).

rr — like a Spanish r, but with much more emphasis and trill. Let your tongue flap. Practice with *burro* (donkey), *carretera* (highway), and Carrillo (proper name), then really let go with *ferrocarril* (railroad).

Note: The single small but common exception to all of the above is the pronunciation of Spanish **y** when it's being used as the Spanish word for "and," as in "Ron y Kathy." In such case, pronounce it like the English ee, as in "keep": Ron "ee" Kathy (Ron and Kathy).

Accent

The rule for accent, the relative stress given to

syllables within a given word, is straightforward. If a word ends in a vowel, an n, or an s, accent the next-to-last syllable; if not, accent the last syllable.

Pronounce *gracias* GRAH-seeahs (thank you), *orden* OHR-dayn (order), and *carretera* kah-ray-TAY-rah (highway) with stress on the next-to-last syllable.

Otherwise, accent the last syllable: *venir* vay-NEER (to come), *ferrocarril* fay-roh-cah-REEL (railroad), and *edad* ay-DAHD (age).

Exceptions to the accent rule are always marked with an accent sign: (á, é, í, ó, or ú), such as *teléfono* tay-LAY-foh-noh (telephone), *jabón* hah-BON (soap), and *rápido* RAH-pee-doh (rapid).

BASIC AND COURTEOUS EXPRESSIONS

Most Spanish-speaking people consider formalities important. Whenever approaching anyone for information or some other reason, do not forget the appropriate salutation—good morning, good evening, etc. Standing alone, the greeting *hola* (hello) can sound brusque.

Hello. — *Hola.*
Good morning. — *Buenos días.*
Good afternoon. — *Buenas tardes.*
Good evening. — *Buenas noches.*
How are you? — *¿Cómo está usted?*
Very well, thank you. — *Muy bien, gracias.*
Okay; good. — *Bien.*
Not okay; bad. — *No muy bien*; *mal.*
So-so. — *Más o menos.*
And you? — *¿Y usted?*
Thank you. — *Gracias.*
Thank you very much. — *Muchas gracias.*
You're very kind. — *Muy amable.*
You're welcome. — *De nada.*
Goodbye. — *Adios.*
See you later. — *Hasta luego.*
please — *por favor*
yes — *sí*
no — *no*
I don't know. — *No sé.*
Just a moment, please. — *Momentito, por favor.*

Excuse me, please (when you're trying to get attention). — *Disculpe* or *Con permiso.*
Excuse me (when you've made a mistake). — *Lo siento.*
Pleased to meet you. — *Mucho gusto.*
How do you say … in Spanish? — *¿Cómo se dice … en español?*
What is your name? — *¿Cómo se llama usted?*
Do you speak English? — *¿Habla usted inglés?*
Is English spoken here? (Does anyone here speak English?) — *¿Se habla inglés?*
I don't speak Spanish well. — *No hablo bien el español.*
I don't understand. — *No entiendo.*
My name is … — *Me llamo …*
Would you like … — *¿Quisiera usted …*
Let's go to … — *Vamos a …*

TERMS OF ADDRESS

When in doubt, use the formal *usted* (you) as a form of address.

I — *yo*
you (formal) — *usted*
you (familiar) — *tu*
he/him — *él*
she/her — *ella*
we/us — *nosotros*
you (plural) — *ustedes*
they/them — *ellos* (all males or mixed gender); *ellas* (all females)
Mr., sir — *señor*
Mrs., madam — *señora*
miss, young lady — *señorita*
wife — *esposa*
husband — *esposo*
friend — *amigo* (male); *amiga* (female)
sweetheart — *novio* (male); *novia* (female)
son; daughter — *hijo; hija*
brother; sister — *hermano; hermana*
father; mother — *padre; madre*
grandfather; grandmother — *abuelo; abuela*

TRANSPORTATION

Where is … ? — *¿Dónde está … ?*
How far is it to … ? — *¿A cuánto está … ?*

from … to … — *de … a …*

How many blocks? — *¿Cuántas cuadras?*

Where (Which) is the way to … ? — *¿Dónde está el camino a … ?*

the bus station — *la terminal de autobuses*

the bus stop — *la parada de autobuses*

Where is this bus going? — *¿Adónde va este autobús?*

the taxi stand — *la parada de taxis*

the train station — *la estación de ferrocarril*

the boat — *el barco* or *la lancha*

the airport — *el aeropuerto*

I'd like a ticket to … — *Quisiera un boleto a …*

first (second) class — *primera (segunda) clase*

round-trip — *ida y vuelta*

reservation — *reservación*

baggage — *equipaje*

Stop here, please. — *Pare aquí, por favor.*

the entrance — *la entrada*

the exit — *la salida*

the ticket office — *la boletería* or *la taquilla*

(very) near; far — *(muy) cerca; lejos*

to; toward — *a*

by; through — *por*

from — *de*

the right — *la derecha*

the left — *la izquierda*

straight ahead — *derecho; directo*

in front — *en frente*

beside — *al lado*

behind — *atrás*

the corner — *la esquina*

the stoplight — *el semáforo*

a turn — *una vuelta*

right here — *aquí*

somewhere around here — *por acá*

right there — *allí*

somewhere around there — *por allá*

street; boulevard — *calle; bulevar*

highway — *carretera*

bridge; toll — *puente; cuota*

address — *dirección*

north; south — *norte; sur*

east; west — *oriente (este); poniente (oeste)*

ACCOMMODATIONS

hotel — *hotel*

Is there a room? — *¿Hay cuarto?*

May I (may we) see it? — *¿Puedo (podemos) verlo?*

What is the rate? — *¿Cuál es el precio?*

Is that your best rate? — *¿Es su mejor precio?*

Is there something cheaper? — *¿Hay algo más económico?*

a single room — *un cuarto sencillo*

a double room — *un cuarto doble*

double bed — *cama matrimonial*

twin beds — *camas gemelas*

with private bath — *con baño*

hot water — *agua caliente*

shower — *ducha*

towels — *toallas*

soap — *jabón*

toilet paper — *papel higiénico*

blanket — *cobija*

sheets — *sábanas*

air-conditioned—*aire acondicionado*

fan — *abanico; ventilador*

key — *llave*

manager — *gerente*

FOOD

I'm hungry — *Tengo hambre.*

I'm thirsty. — *Tengo sed.*

menu — *carta; menú*

order — *orden*

glass — *vaso*

fork — *tenedor*

knife — *cuchillo*

spoon — *cuchara*

napkin — *servilleta*

soft drink — *refresco*

coffee — *café*

tea — *té*

drinking water — *agua pura; agua potable*

bottled carbonated water — *agua mineral*

bottled uncarbonated water — *agua sin gas*

beer — *cerveza*

wine — *vino*

milk — *leche*

juice — *jugo*

cream — *crema*

sugar — *azúcar*
cheese — *queso*
snack — *antojito; botana*
breakfast — *desayuno*
lunch — *almuerzo* or *comida*
daily lunch special — *comida corrida* (or *el menú del día* depending on region)
dinner — *cena*
the check — *la cuenta*
eggs — *huevos*
bread — *pan*
salad — *ensalada*
fruit — *fruta*
mango — *mango*
watermelon — *sandía*
papaya — *papaya*
banana — *plátano*
apple — *manzana*
orange — *naranja*
lime — *limón*
fish — *pescado*
shellfish — *mariscos*
shrimp — *camarones*
meat (without) — *(sin) carne*
chicken — *pollo*
pork — *puerco*
beef; steak — *res; bistec*
bacon; ham — *tocino; jamón*
fried — *frito*
roasted — *asada*
barbecue; barbecued — *barbacoa; al carbón*

SHOPPING

money — *dinero*
money-exchange bureau — *casa de cambio*
I would like to exchange traveler's checks. — *Quisiera cambiar cheques de viajero.*
What is the exchange rate? — *¿Cuál es el tipo de cambio?*
How much is the commission? — *¿Cuánto cuesta la comisión?*
Do you accept credit cards? — *¿Aceptan tarjetas de crédito?*
money order — *giro*
How much does it cost? — *¿Cuánto cuesta?*
What is your final price? — *¿Cuál es su último precio?*

expensive — *caro*
cheap — *barato; económico*
more — *más*
less — *menos*
a little — *un poco*
too much — *demasiado*

HEALTH

Help me please. — *Ayúdeme por favor.*
I am ill. — *Estoy enfermo.*
Call a doctor. — *Llame un doctor.*
Take me to . . . — *Lléveme a . . .*
hospital — *hospital; sanatorio*
drugstore — *farmacia*
pain — *dolor*
fever — *fiebre*
headache — *dolor de cabeza*
stomach ache — *dolor de estómago*
burn — *quemadura*
cramp — *calambre*
nausea — *náusea*
vomiting — *vomitar*
medicine — *medicina*
antibiotic — *antibiótico*
pill; tablet — *pastilla*
aspirin — *aspirina*
ointment; cream — *pomada; crema*
bandage — *venda*
cotton — *algodón*
sanitary napkins — use brand name, e.g., Kotex
birth control pills — *pastillas anticonceptivas*
contraceptive foam — *espuma anticonceptiva*
condoms — *preservativos; condones*
toothbrush — *cepilla de dientes*
dental floss — *hilo dental*
toothpaste — *pasta de dientes*
dentist — *dentista*
toothache — *dolor de dientes*

POST OFFICE AND COMMUNICATIONS

long-distance telephone — *teléfono de larga distancia*
I would like to call . . . — *Quisiera llamar a . . .*
collect — *por cobrar*

station to station — *a quien contesta*
person to person — *persona a persona*
credit card — *tarjeta de crédito*
post office — *correo*
general delivery — *lista de correo*
letter — *carta*
stamp — *estampilla, timbre*
postcard — *tarjeta*
air mail — *correo aereo*
registered — *registrado*
money order — *giro*
package; box — *paquete; caja*
string; tape — *cuerda; cinta*

AT THE BORDER

border — *frontera*
customs — *aduana*
immigration — *migración*
tourist card — *tarjeta de turista*
inspection — *inspección; revisión*
passport — *pasaporte*
profession — *profesión*
marital status — *estado civil*
single — *soltero*
married; divorced — *casado; divorciado*
widowed — *viudado*
insurance — *seguros*
title — *título*
driver's license — *licencia de manejar*

AT THE GAS STATION

gas station — *gasolinera*
gasoline — *gasolina*
unleaded — *sin plomo*
full, please — *lleno, por favor*
tire — *llanta*
tire repair shop — *vulcanizadora*
air — *aire*
water — *agua*
oil (change) — *aceite (cambio)*
grease — *grasa*
My . . . doesn't work. — *Mi . . . no sirve.*
battery — *batería*
radiator — *radiador*
alternator — *alternador*
generator — *generador*

tow truck — *grúa*
repair shop — *taller mecánico*
tune-up — *afinación*
auto parts store — *refaccionería*

VERBS

Verbs are the key to getting along in Spanish. They employ mostly predictable forms and come in three classes, which end in *ar, er,* and *ir,* respectively:

to buy — *comprar*
I buy, you (he, she, it) buys — *compro, compra*
we buy, you (they) buy — *compramos, compran*

to eat — *comer*
I eat, you (he, she, it) eats — *como, come*
we eat, you (they) eat — *comemos, comen*

to climb — *subir*
I climb, you (he, she, it) climbs — *subo, sube*
we climb, you (they) climb — *subimos, suben*

Got the idea? Here are more (with irregularities marked in **bold**).

to do or make — *hacer*
I do or make, you (he she, it) does or makes — **hago,** *hace*
we do or make, you (they) do or make — *hacemos, hacen*

to go — *ir*
I go, you (he, she, it) goes — ***voy, va***
we go, you (they) go — ***vamos, van***

to go (walk) — *andar*
to love — *amar*
to work — *trabajar*
to want — *desear, querer*
to need — *necesitar*
to read — *leer*
to write — *escribir*
to repair — *reparar*
to stop — *parar*
to get off (the bus) — *bajar*
to arrive — *llegar*

to stay (remain) — *quedar*
to stay (lodge) — *hospedar*
to leave — *salir* (regular except for **salgo,** I leave)
to look at — *mirar*
to look for — *buscar*
to give — *dar* (regular except for **doy,** I give)
to carry — *llevar*
to have — *tener* (irregular but important: **tengo, tiene,** tenemos, **tienen**)
to come — *venir* (similarly irregular: **vengo, viene,** venimos, **vienen**)

Spanish has two forms of "to be." Use *estar* when speaking of location or a temporary state of being: "I am at home." *"**Estoy** en casa."* "I'm sick." *"**Estoy** enfermo."* Use *ser* for a permanent state of being: "I am a doctor." *"**Soy** doctora."*

Estar is regular except for **estoy,** I am. *Ser* is very irregular:

to be — *ser*
I am, you (he, she, it) is — **soy, es**
we are, you (they) are — **somos, son**

NUMBERS

zero — *cero*
one — *uno*
two — *dos*
three — *tres*
four — *cuatro*
five — *cinco*
six — *seis*
seven — *siete*
eight — *ocho*
nine — *nueve*
10 — *diez*
11 — *once*
12 — *doce*
13 — *trece*
14 — *catorce*
15 — *quince*
16 — *dieciseis*
17 — *diecisiete*
18 — *dieciocho*
19 — *diecinueve*
20 — *veinte*
21 — *veinte y uno* or *veintiuno*
30 — *treinta*
40 — *cuarenta*
50 — *cincuenta*
60 — *sesenta*
70 — *setenta*
80 — *ochenta*
90 — *noventa*
100 — *ciento*
101 — *ciento y uno* or *cientiuno*
200 — *doscientos*
500 — *quinientos*
1,000 — *mil*
10,000 — *diez mil*
100,000 — *cien mil*
1,000,000 — *millón*
one half — *medio*
one third — *un tercio*
one fourth — *un cuarto*

TIME

What time is it? — *¿Qué hora es?*
It's one o'clock. — *Es la una.*
It's three in the afternoon. — *Son las tres de la tarde.*
It's 4 A.M. — *Son las cuatro de la mañana.*
six-thirty — *seis y media*
a quarter till eleven — *un cuarto para las once*
a quarter past five — *las cinco y cuarto*
an hour — *una hora*

DAYS AND MONTHS

Monday — *lunes*
Tuesday — *martes*
Wednesday — *miércoles*
Thursday — *jueves*
Friday — *viernes*
Saturday — *sábado*
Sunday — *domingo*
today — *hoy*
tomorrow — *mañana*
yesterday — *ayer*
January — *enero*
February — *febrero*
March — *marzo*

April — *abril*
May — *mayo*
June — *junio*
July — *julio*
August — *agosto*
September — *septiembre*
October — *octubre*
November — *noviembre*

December — *diciembre*
a week — *una semana*
a month — *un mes*
after — *después*
before — *antes*

Courtesy of Bruce Whipperman, author of *Moon Handbooks Pacific Mexico.*

Suggested Reading

The following titles provide insight into the Yucatán Peninsula and the Mayan people. A few of these books are more easily obtained in Mexico, but all of them will cost less in the United States. Most are nonfiction, though several are fiction and great to pop into your carry-on for a good read on the plane, or for any time you want to get into the Yucatecan mood. Happy reading.

Coe, Andrew. *Archaeological Mexico: A Traveler's Guide to Ancient Cities and Sacred Sites.* Emeryville: Avalon Travel Publishing, 2001.

Coe, Michael D. *The Maya.* New York: Thames and Hudson, 1980. A well-illustrated, easy-to-read volume on the Mayan people.

Coe, Michael D. *Breaking the Maya Code.* New York: Thames and Hudson, 1992, 1999. A fascinating well-explained account of how epigraphers, linguists, and archaeologists succeeded in deciphering Mayan hieroglyphics.

Cortés, Hernán. *Five Letters.* Gordon Press, 1977. Cortés wrote long letters to the king of Spain telling of his accomplishments and trying to justify his actions in the New World.

Davies, Nigel. *The Ancient Kingdoms of Mexico.* New York: Penguin Books. Excellent study of preconquest (1519) indigenous peoples of Mexico.

De Landa, Bishop Diego. *Yucatán Before and After the Conquest.* New York: Dover Publications, 1978. This book, translated by William Gates from the original 1566 volume, has served as the base for all research that has taken place since. De Landa (though the man destroyed countless books of the Mayan people) has given the world insight into their culture before the conquest.

Díaz del Castillo, Bernal. *The Conquest of New Spain.* New York: Penguin Books, 1963. History straight from the adventurer's reminiscences, translated by J. M. Cohen.

Fehrenbach, T. R. *Fire and Blood: A History of Mexico.* New York: Collier Books, 1973. Mexico's history through 3,500 years, told in a way to keep you reading.

Ferguson, William M. *Maya Ruins of Mexico in Color.* Norman: University of Oklahoma Press, 1977. Good reading before you go, but too bulky to carry along. Oversized with excellent drawings and illustrations of the archaeological structures of the Mayan Indians.

Franz, Carl. *The People's Guide to Mexico.* Emeryville: Avalon Travel Publishing, 2002. A humorous guide filled with witty anecdotes and helpful general information for visitors to Mexico. Don't expect any specific city information, just nuts-and-bolts hints for traveling south of the border.

Greene, Graham. *The Power and the Glory.* New York: Penguin Books, 1977. A novel that takes place in the '20s about a priest and the anti-church movement that gripped the country.

Heffern, Richard. *Secrets of the Mind-Altering Plants of Mexico.* New York: Pyramid Books. A fascinating study of many substances, from ancient ritual hallucinogens to today's medicines.

Laughlin, Robert M. *The People of the Bat.* Smithsonian Institution Press, 1988. Mayan tales and dreams as told by the Zinacantán Indians in Chiapas.

Mallan, Chicki, and Oz Mallan. *Colonial Mexico: A Traveler's Guide to Historic Districts and Towns.* Emeryville: Avalon Travel Publishing, 2001.

Meyer, Michael, and William Sherman. *The Course of Mexican History.* Oxford University Press. A concise, one-volume history of Mexico.

Nelson, Ralph. *Popul Vuh: The Great Mythological Book of the Ancient Maya.* Boston: Houghton Mifflin, 1974. An easy-to-read translation of myths handed down orally by the Quiché Mayan, family to family, until written down after the Spanish conquest.

Riding, Alan. *Distant Neighbors.* Vintage Books. A modern look at today's Mexico.

The Rise and Fall of the Maya Civilization. Norman: University of Oklahoma Press, 1954. One man's story of the Mayan Indian. Excellent reading.

Sodi, Demetrio M. (in collaboration with Adela Fernández). *The Mayas.* Mexico: Panama Editorial S.A. This small pocket-book presents a fictionalized account of life among the Mayans before the conquest. Easy reading for anyone who enjoys fantasizing about what life *might* have been like before recorded history in the Yucatán. This book is available in the Yucatecan states of Mexico.

Stephens, John L. *Incidents of Travel in Central America, Chiapas, and Yucatán.* 2 vols. New York: Dover Publications, 1969. Good companions to refer to when traveling in the area. Stephens and illustrator Frederick Catherwood rediscovered many of the Mayan ruins on their treks that took place in the mid-1800s. Easy reading.

Thompson, J. Eric. *Maya Archaeologist.* Norman: University of Oklahoma Press, 1963. Thompson, a noted Mayan scholar, traveled and worked at most of the Mayan ruins in the 1930s.

Webster, David. *The Fall of the Ancient Maya.* New York: Thames and Hudson, 2002. A careful and thorough examination of the possible causes of one of archaeology's great unsolved mysteries—the collapse of the Classic Mayans in the 8th century.

Werner, David. *Where There Is No Doctor.* Palo Alto, California: The Hesperian Foundation, 1992. This is an invaluable medical aid to anyone traveling not only to isolated parts of Mexico, but to any place in the world where there's not a doctor.

Wolf, Eric. *Sons of the Shaking Earth.* University of Chicago Press, 1962. An anthropological study of Indian and mestizo people of Mexico and Guatemala.

Wright, Ronald. *Time Among the Maya.* New York: Weidenfeld and Nicolson, 1989. A narrative that takes the reader through the Mayan country of today with historical comments that help put the puzzle together.

Internet Resources

www.MayaYucatan.com
Official website of the Yucatán state tourism authority.

www.YucatanToday.com
Website of the helpful monthly tourist magazine of the same name. Based in Mérida but contains coverage for all of Yucatán state and parts of Campeche.

www.QR.gob.mx
Official website of the Quintana Roo state tourism authority.

www.CancunTips.com.mx
The online version of Cancún's main tourist magazine, with tons of listings, travel tips, and tourist resourses.

www.CancunMap.com
An excellent source of detailed maps of the Riviera Maya.

www.LogoGringo.com
Privately operated website with extensive business listings for Playa del Carmen and other areas on the Riviera Maya.

www.La5ta.com
The online version of a hip Playa del Carmen magazine, with nightlife, restaurants, art, and culture listings.

www.InTulum.com
The best site on Tulum, though listings are a bit a sparse.

www.VisiteTabasco.com
Official website of the Tabasco state tourism authority.

www.TurismoChiapas.com
Official website of the Chiapas state tourism authority.

www.Campeche.gob.mx
Official website of the Campeche state tourism authority.

www.RutasDeChiapas.com
A handy paper and online publication of the Chiapas state tourism authority.

Index

Archaeological Sites and Collections

Ecological Reserves and Parks

Snorkeling and Diving

Acknowledgments

To our grandmothers—Trinidad Corral, Agustina Alcalá, Beatrice Kerr, and Mary Chandler—whose courage to see the world in a different light gave us the inspiration to explore it.

Para nuestras abuelitas—Trinidad Corral, Agustina Alcalá, Beatrice Kerr, y Mary Chandler—cuya valentía de ver el mundo de otra manera nos inspiró a explorarlo.

This guidebook could not have been written without the varied and voluminous help of hundreds of everyday Mexicans, most of whose names we never learned. From friendly bus drivers to helpful shop owners to patient hotel receptionists, they made this project possible and have our sincere gratitude. We also received a great deal of help from expatriates and fellow travelers, whose advice and insight were invaluable to our work.

In Mérida, we are indebted to Armando at the city tourism office, David and Keith at Los Dos, and Roger at Casa Mexilio. Thank you as well to Lee at Genesis Retreat in Ek' Balam, Diane at Hacienda San Antonio Chalanté in Izamal, and Christine and Santiago at Flycatcher Inn in Santa Elena.

In Quintana Roo, we are grateful to the friendly staff at the Casa de Cultura in Cancún, Carlos at Salads Internet café in Playa del Carmen, Diane at Mama's Bakery in Puerto Morelos, Eliane and Jorge at Tamarindo Bed & Breakfast in Cozumel, John at Weary Traveler in Tulum, Margo and Robert at Sin Duda in Xcalak, Eva and Bruce at Villa La Guacamaya in Xcalak, and Onny and Carmelo at Posada Mawimbi in Isla Holbox.

In Campeche, thank you to Rick and Diane at Río Bec Dreams in Xpujil, and Felix at the state tourist office in Campeche city. In San Cristóbal, we received invaluable help from David and Nancy at Casa Felipe Flores and Dana at La Pared bookstore. Thanks also to the friendly folks at the Comitán tourist office.

We'd also like to thank our editor, Ellie Behrstock, whose professionalism, support, and constant good cheer made this book, and our experience working on it, immeasurably better. Thank you to Marisa Solís who brought us to Moon in the first place (and visited us midtrip!), and to Amy Scott, who got us started. We're grateful to everyone in the cartography department for their excellent work on the maps, and to the folks in the graphics and marketing departments for making this book look so great.

A special acknowledgment goes to Chicki Mallan, who, with husband and photographer Oz Mallan, wrote the first seven editions of this book—a remarkable achievement. Chicki is one of the pioneers of modern-day travel in the Yucatán Peninsula and her dedication, experience, and enduring love for the area are a model for any would-be travel writer.

Finally, and above all, thank you to our families and friends for their unwavering love and support—Mom and Dad Chandler, Ellen, Elyse, Joey, Sue, Katy, Kyle, Dave, Jav, Debbie, Owen, Sammy, Kelly, Dan, Kaitlyn, TJ, Kathy, Lita, Brian, Becky, Rukaiyah, David C., Lalo, Carlos, and especially to Mom and Dad Prado, who have lent their support, patience, and dining room table to six different guidebooks, making each that much better.

U.S.~Metric Conversion

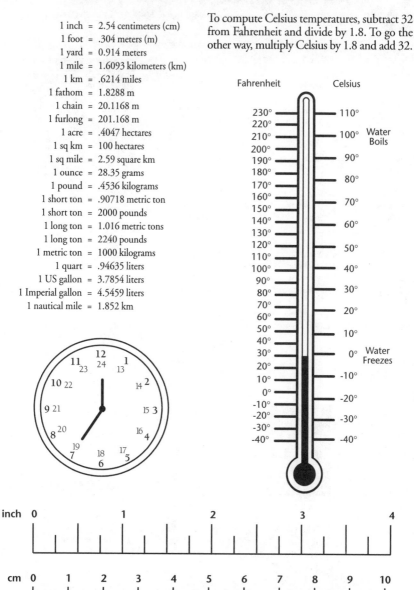

1 inch	=	2.54 centimeters (cm)
1 foot	=	.304 meters (m)
1 yard	=	0.914 meters
1 mile	=	1.6093 kilometers (km)
1 km	=	.6214 miles
1 fathom	=	1.8288 m
1 chain	=	20.1168 m
1 furlong	=	201.168 m
1 acre	=	.4047 hectares
1 sq km	=	100 hectares
1 sq mile	=	2.59 square km
1 ounce	=	28.35 grams
1 pound	=	.4536 kilograms
1 short ton	=	.90718 metric ton
1 short ton	=	2000 pounds
1 long ton	=	1.016 metric tons
1 long ton	=	2240 pounds
1 metric ton	=	1000 kilograms
1 quart	=	.94635 liters
1 US gallon	=	3.7854 liters
1 Imperial gallon	=	4.5459 liters
1 nautical mile	=	1.852 km

To compute Celsius temperatures, subtract 32 from Fahrenheit and divide by 1.8. To go the other way, multiply Celsius by 1.8 and add 32.

Keeping Current

Although we strive to produce the most up-to-date guidebook humanly possible, change is unavoidable. Between the time this book goes to print and the moment you read it, a handful of the businesses noted in these pages will undoubtedly change prices, move, or even close their doors forever. Other worthy attractions will open for the first time. If you have a favorite gem you'd like to see included in the next edition, or see anything that needs updating, clarification, or correction, please drop us a line. Send your comments via email to atpfeedback@avalonpub.com, or use the address below.

Moon Handbooks Yucatán Peninsula
Avalon Travel Publishing
1400 65th Street, Suite 250
Emeryville, CA 94608, USA
www.moon.com

Editors: Ellie Behrstock, Amy Scott
Series Manager: Kevin McLain
Acquisitions Manager: Rebecca K. Browning
Copy Editor: Karen Gaynor Bleske
Graphics Coordinator: Gerilyn Attebery
Production Coordinator: Darren Alessi
Cover Designer: Kari Gim
Interior Designer: Amber Pirker
Map Editor: Kat Smith
Cartographic Manager: Mike Morgenfeld
Cartographers: Kat Kalamaras, Suzanne Service
Indexer: Rachel Kuhn

ISBN-10: 1-56691-576-7
ISBN-13: 978-1-56691-576-2
ISSN: 1098-6707

Printing History
1st Edition—1986
8th Edition—November 2005
5 4 3 2 1

Text © 2005 by Chicki Mallan.
Maps © 2005 by Avalon Travel Publishing, Inc.
All rights reserved.

Avalon Travel Publishing
An Imprint of
Avalon Publishing Group, Inc.

AVALON
publishing group incorporated

Some photos and illustrations are used by permission and are the property of the original copyright owners.

Front cover photo: © John Elk III

Printed in the USA by Malloy, Inc.

About the Author

Liza Prado Chandler

Liza Prado Chandler spent almost every summer from preschool to high school in Mexico, visiting her grandparents and extended family in Monterrey and Mazatlán. Born in Buffalo, NY to a travel-loving family, Liza visited 10 countries by the time she was 15 years old and 20 (including six months in Italy) by the time she graduated from Brown University in 1994 with a degree in international relations. By that time, she was fluent in four languages.

After a stint in New York City, Liza moved to California for better weather, better parking, and three years at Stanford Law School. Then it was 50 miles north to San Francisco, where she worked in a corporate law firm (and met future husband Gary Chandler).

Following two and a half years of fascinating and intense work, Liza left the Bay Area and moved to Guadalajara, Mexico, where she and Gary were married. Over the next two years, they traveled to the Yucatán Peninsula, Belize, Honduras, Guatemala, El Salvador and (for their honeymoon) Brazil. A mutual love of Latin America and travel made writing *Moon Handbooks Yucatán Peninsula* a natural next step. Liza plans to continue working as a travel writer, but (just in case) remains an active member of the California Bar Association.